# PHILOSOPHICAL THOUGHT IN RUSSIA IN THE SECOND HALF OF THE TWENTIETH CENTURY

Also available from Bloomsbury

Knowledge in Ancient Philosophy
*Edited by Nicholas D. Smith*

Knowledge in Medieval Philosophy
*Edited by Henrik Lagerlund*

Knowledge in Modern Philosophy
*Edited by Stephen Gaukroger*

Knowledge in Contemporary Philosophy
*Edited by Stephen Hetherington and Markos Valaris*

Skepticism: From Antiquity to the Present
*Edited by Diego Machuca and Baron Reed*

# PHILOSOPHICAL THOUGHT IN RUSSIA IN THE SECOND HALF OF THE TWENTIETH CENTURY

## A CONTEMPORARY VIEW FROM RUSSIA AND ABROAD

*Edited by Vladislav A. Lektorsky and Marina F. Bykova*

BLOOMSBURY ACADEMIC
NEW YORK • LONDON • OXFORD • NEW DELHI • SYDNEY

BLOOMSBURY ACADEMIC
Bloomsbury Publishing Plc
50 Bedford Square, London, WC1B 3DP, UK
1385 Broadway, New York, NY 10018, USA

BLOOMSBURY, BLOOMSBURY ACADEMIC and the Diana logo are trademarks of Bloomsbury Publishing Plc

First published in Great Britain 2019



Cover design: Toby Way



A catalogue record for this book is available from the British Library.

A catalog record for this book is available from the Library of Congress.

ISBN: HB: 978-1-3500-4058-8
ePDF: 978-1-3500-4060-1
eBook: 978-1-3500-4059-5

Typeset by RefineCatch Limited, Bungay, Suffolk
Printed and bound in Great Britain

To find out more about our authors and books visit www.bloomsbury.com and sign up for our newsletters.

# CONTENTS

# NOTES ON CONTRIBUTORS

**Natalia S. Avtonomova** is Principal Research Associate at the Institute of Philosophy, Russian Academy of Sciences (RAS) in Moscow (Russia). She also serves as Senior Researcher at both the Russian State University for the Humanities and the Russian Presidential Academy of Economy and Public Administration. Her main interests include philosophy of science, history of contemporary French philosophy, translation as a philosophical problem, and translation and reception from a cross-cultural perspective. She is the author of numerous books and articles including *The Philosophical Language of Jacques Derrida* (Moscow, 2011) *and Cognition and Translation: Experiences of the Philosophy of Language* (Moscow, 2008, 2016 [2nd expanded ed.]).

**David Bakhurst** is Charlton Professor of Philosophy at Queen's University, Kingston (Canada). His research interests include Russian philosophy and psychology, metaphysics, ethics, and philosophy of education. He is the author of *Consciousness and Revolution in Soviet Philosophy: from Bolsheviks to Evald Ilyenkov* (Cambridge, 1991), *The Formation of Reason* (Wiley-Blackwell, 2011), and numerous articles in books and journals. In 2016, he was elected a Fellow of the Royal Society of Canada.

**Marina F. Bykova** is Professor of Philosophy at North Carolina State University (USA), and the editor of the journal *Russian Studies in Philosophy*. Her area of specialization is the history of nineteenth century continental philosophy, with a special focus on German idealism. She is the author of four books and more than 200 articles on classic German philosophy. She has edited *Hegel's Philosophy of Spirit: A Critical Guide* (Cambridge, 2019) and *The German Idealism Reader* (Bloomsbury, forthcoming).

**Maryse Dennes** is Professor in the Department of Slavic Studies at the Université Bordeaux Montaigne (France). She is an international expert for the East European research programs. Her area of expertise is Russian philosophy and intellectual history. She has authored 177 publications and translated into French Shpet's *Iavlenie i smysl* [Appearance and Sense] (2013). She is the founder and editor of a special book series *Russie Traditions Perspectives* (RTP) that focuses on Russian philosophy.

**Mikhail N. Epstein** is Samuel Candler Dobbs Professor of Cultural Theory and Russian Literature at Emory University (USA). Between 2012–2015, he was Professor of Russian and Cultural Theory and Founding Director of the Centre for Humanities Innovation at Durham University (UK). His research interests include new directions in the humanities and methods of intellectual creativity, contemporary philosophy, postmodernism, Russian literature, philosophy and religion of the twentieth and twenty-first centuries, and language evolution and neologisms. He has authored 32 books and more than 700 articles and essays. His work has been translated into 23 languages.

**Abdusalam A. Guseynov** is Academician of the Russian Academy of Sciences in Moscow (Russia). He is Principal Adviser for Academic Affairs at the Institute of Philosophy, RAS. His area of specialization is history and theory of ethics. He is the author of 27 books, and numerous articles and encyclopedia entries. His most recent books are *Great Prophets and Thinkers. The Moral Theories from Moses to Our Days* (Moscow, 2009) and *Philosophy–Thought and Deed* (St. Petersburg, 2012).

**Alexander A. Khamidov** is Principal Research Associate at the Institute of Philosophy, Political Sciences, and Religious Studies in Almaty (Kazakhstan). His research interests include ontology, anthropology, the history and theory of dialectics, philosophy of culture, philosophy of history, social philosophy, and philosophy of science. He is the author of more than 200 publications. His recent books include *Humanism as Discourse* (Almaty, 2012) and *Karl Marx's Philosophy of History* (Almaty, 2014).

**Vladislav A. Lektorsky** is Academician of both the Russian Academy of Sciences and the Russian Academy of Education in Moscow (Russia). He is Principal Research Associate at the Institute of Philosophy, RAS, Head of the Department of Philosophy of the Russian State University for the Humanities, and editor-in-chief of the journal *Philosophy of Science and Technology*. He works on topics relevant to epistemology, philosophy of mind, and philosophy of cognitive science. He has authored more than 500 research publications. His books include *Philosophy, Cognition, Culture* (Moscow, 2012) and *The Perspectives of Realism in the Contemporary Philosophy* (ed., Moscow 2017).

**Vitaly L. Makhlin** is Professor at Moscow State Pedagogical University (Russia). His area of expertise is history of Western and Russian philosophy and methodology of cognition. He is a leading Bakhtin scholar and a translator of some of the thinker's works originally published in English. His recent book is the collection of essays, *M. M. Bakhtin* (Moscow, 2010), that he edited for the series *Russian Philosophy of the Second Half of the 20th Century*.

**Viktor A. Malakhov** is an independent scholar who lives in Naharia (Israel). Until 2015, he served as Principal Research Associate at the Skovorada Institute of Philosophy, the Ukrainian Academy of Sciences in Kiev (Ukraine). His research interests include topics in ethics, philosophy of dialogue, and the history of the Soviet philosophy of the 1960s–1980s.

**Vadim M. Mezhuyev** is Principal Research Associate at the Institute of Philosophy, RAS in Moscow (Russia). His area of expertise includes philosophy of history, philosophy of culture, and social philosophy. He has published more than 300 works. His recent books include *The Idea of Culture. Essays in Philosophy of Culture* (Moscow, 2006) and *Marx contra Marxism* (Moscow, 2007).

**Alexander P. Ogurtsov** (1936–2014) was Head of the Research Center for Methodology and Ethics of Science at the Institute of Philosophy, RAS, in Moscow (Russia). He worked on topics central to philosophy, methodology and history of science as well as philosophy of culture. He was co-founder and editor-in-chief of the online journal *Vox*. He published seven books and more than 250 articles and book chapters.

**Vesa Oittinen** is Professor of Philosophy at the Aleksanteri Institute, University of Helsinki (Finland). He has widely published on Spinoza, the history of German and Scandinavian philosophy, Marxism, and Soviet philosophy. His recent publications include *Dialectics of the Ideal* (Brill, 2014; co-edited with Alex Levant), and *The Practical Essence of Man* (Brill, 2016; co-edited with Andrey Maidansky).

**Boris I. Pruzhinin** is Professor at the School of Philosophy of the National Research University—Higher School of Economics (Moscow, Russia) and editor-in-chief of the Russian principal philosophical journal *Voprosy filosofii*. He is the author of six books and more than 200 articles and essays on epistemology and philosophy of science.

**Yuri V. Pushchaev** is Senior Research Associate at the Institute of Scientific Information for Social Sciences, RAS, in Moscow (Russia). His research interests include the history of Russian and Soviet philosophy, epistemology, philosophy of religion, and ethics.

**Tom Rockmore** is Chair Professor of Humanities, Professor of Philosophy, and Member of the Institute of Foreign Philosophy at Peking University (China). He has held regular or visiting appointments at Yale, Nice, Laval, Vanderbilt, Fordham, Duquesne, Temple, and Peking. He is the author of numerous research articles and books; the most recent of them is *German Idealism as Constructivism* (University of Chicago, 2016).

**Vadim M. Rozin** is Principal Research Associate at the Institute of Philosophy, RAS, in Moscow (Russia). His area of expertise is methodology and philosophy of science. He has published 76 monographs and textbooks and more than 400 journal articles and book chapters. His most recent books include *Renewal of the Methodology. The Open Letters to the Members of the Moscow Methodological Circle* (Moscow, 2017) and *Nature. The Concept and Stages of the Development in European Culture* (Moscow, 2017).

**Petr G. Shchedrovitsky** has a PhD in philosophy. He is President of the Russian non-profit research foundation: The Georgy Shchedrovitsky Institute for Development in Moscow (Russia). His research focuses on the methodological problems of philosophy.

**Maja E. Soboleva** is Privatdocent at the Philipps-University of Marburg (Germany). Her areas of specialization are epistemology, philosophy of language, and history of philosophy, including Kant and Russian philosophical thought. Her recent book is an anthology, *Culture as Organization in Early Soviet Thought. Bogdanov, Eisenstein, and the Proletkult* (Aalto University, 2016, co-edited with Pia Tikka, John Biggart, Vesa Oittinen, Giulia Rispoli).

**Daniela Steila** is Professor at the Department of the History of Russian Philosophy at the University of Turin (Italy). She works on such topics as Russian culture in the nineteenth and twentieth centuries, early Russian Marxism, empiriocriticism in Russia, Russian philosophical historiography, Lev Vygotsky's thought, and philosophy in the Soviet era. Among her books is *Science and Revolution: the Reception of Empiriocriticism in Russian Cultur*e (Moscow, 2013), which is a translation of her earlier book *Scienza e revoluzione* (Ferenze, 1996).

**Vyacheslav S. Stepin** is Academician of the Russian Academy of Sciences in Moscow (Russia). He is the Honorary Director of the Institute of Philosophy, RAS, Head of the RAS Section of Philosophy, Sociology, Political Science, Psychology, and Law of the Division for Social Sciences, and the President of the Russian Philosophical Society. His research areas include the philosophy and history of science as well as philosophy of culture. He has published more than 30 books and 400 articles. Among his books are *Theoretical Knowledge* (Springer, 2005) and *Man's Cognition and Culture* (Moscow, 2013).

**Karen A. Swassjan** is Senior Lecturer at the Forum für Geisteswissenschaft in Basel (Switzerland). Before moving to Basel, he held a regular Professor appointment at the University of Yerevan (Armenia). He has translated and edited the first post-revolutionary edition of Nietzsche's *Works* (in 2 vols., Moscow, 1990). In his research, he focuses on topics in the history of philosophy and philosophical anthropology. His recent books are *Geschichte der Philosophie in Karmischer Perspektive: Ein Nachruf auf das Denken von Plato bis Stirner* (Dornach, 2016) and *Rudolf Steiner: Eine Einführung*. EM Edition (Dornach 2017).

# ACKNOWLEDGMENTS

In large part, the present collection is an English translation of the Russian volume *Problemy i diskussii v filosofii Rossii vtoroi poloviny 20-go veka: sovremennyi vzgliad* [Topics and Discussions in Philosophy of Russia in the Second Half of the Twentieth Century: A Contemporary View] edited by Vladislav Lektorsky and published by ROSSPEN Publishers (Moscow, 2014). The publication of this volume was preceded by an international research conference on Soviet philosophical thought in the post-Stalin epoch held at the Institute of Philosophy, Russian Academy of Sciences in Moscow. The book publication was carried out under the auspices (series editors) and with financial support from the Institute of Philosophy and the non-profit research foundation: the Georgy Shchedrovitsky Institute for Development (Moscow, Russia). The editors are grateful to both organizations as well as to the ROSSPEN Publishers for permission to translate and publish essays which appeared in the Russian volume.

We would also like to thank the daughter of Evald Ilyenkov, Elena Illesh, for her permission to translate and publish both full and abbreviated versions of the "Theses on the Question of the Interrelation of Philosophy and Knowledge of Nature and Society in the Process of their Historical Development" authored by Evald Ilyenkov and Valentin Korovikov. Translated and printed by permission of the copyright holder and the publishers.

Additionally, we gratefully acknowledge Koninklijke Brill Publishing House for permission to reprint in our volume Vladislav Lektorsky's essay "The Activity Approach in Soviet Philosophy and Contemporary Cognitive Studies" which originally appeared in *The Practical Essence of Man* (2016), edited by Vesa Oittinen and Andrey Maidansky. Reprinted by permission of the publishers.

We are grateful to Colleen Coalter of Bloomsbury Publishing for her interest in commissioning this volume. The publication project would never have materialized without Colleen's encouragement and support. We also appreciate valuable suggestions and comments that we received from the anonymous reviewers recruited by Colleen. These suggestions proved to be very helpful and led to many important improvements made throughout our work on the volume.

We wish to thank numerous translators—both anonymous and named—for their valuable contributions to the project at different stages of its realization. Thanks also go to Joshua Waters and Victor Eduardo, philosophy majors at North Carolina State University. Joshua helped with proofreading and editing bibliographies for most of the essays, and Victor provided valuable assistance in the compilation of this book's indexes.

The editors are truly grateful for the honor of working with the distinguished group of scholars whose essays constitute this volume.

# Introduction

## *Philosophy in Soviet Russia: A Brief Overview*

MARINA F. BYKOVA AND VLADISLAV A. LEKTORSKY

The Russian political upheaval of 1917 and the subsequent consolidation of Marxism—and later Marxism-Leninism—as the ruling ideology have long served to obscure the logic of the progression of Russian intellectual history, most notably of the development of philosophical thought. When it comes to philosophy in Russia, its Soviet period is usually treated with disdain and contempt and is viewed as entirely dogmatic. This attitude, which is based on a false assumption about the work of philosophers in Soviet Russia, is largely a product of Western Sovietology that dominated the field of Russian and Soviet study until recently. The most prominent among the Sovietologists, Józef Bocheński and Gustav Wetter, have openly denied any value of Soviet philosophical thought and expressed disbelief that it has any relevance to philosophical inquiry at all, claiming that its sole purpose was to justify the dictates of the Communist Party (Sarlemijn 1985, 317; cf. Bocheński 1950; 1973; Wetter 1985). On this view, official philosophy in Soviet Russia was nothing more than dogma, and it was rather detrimental to Russian cultural and intellectual life.

Certainly, there were those who openly disagreed with this assessment and who continued doing solid work on Russian philosophy of both the pre-revolutionary and Soviet periods. It is worth mentioning such scholars of Russian thought as George L. Kline, James P. Scanlan, Thomas J. Blakeley, Philip T. Grier, Helmut Dahm, David Bakhurst, Evert van der Zweerde, and others (see Kline 1968; Grier 1978; Scanlan 1985; Dahm 1988; Van der Zweerde 1998; Bakhurst 1991).[1] These intellectuals greatly contributed to the study of Russian thought through their original publications, translations, and editorial work. Their studies have not lost their relevance and philosophical significance. They, however, were a small minority, and the Russian studies field was largely dominated by Sovietologists who cultivated a negative and inimical view of Soviet Russia. Swayed by numerous prejudices, they undermined any form of thought that emerged in the Soviet Union, claiming it to be inherently dogmatic and doctrinaire. While this kind of hostility to Soviet intellectual life has recently lost traction within the Western academic community, misconceptions about the real status quo in philosophy under the Soviet regime persist.

To be sure, official aspects of philosophical life in Soviet Russia, especially under the Stalin regime, had been far from propitious. The dominant intellectual paradigm of the period was Marxism in its most dogmatic (orthodox) form, and the social setting in which philosophy operated under the Soviet regime was oppressive. It was not simply unaccommodating, but malicious to any appearance of free and non-Marxist thought. However, during the roughly seven-decade-long Soviet period that began soon after the Russian Revolution of 1917, intellectual life in Russia was not homogeneous. Rather, it had been marked by a variety of philosophical and political struggles producing many intellectual milestones that could serve as evidence of the rise and fall of thought. This calls into question the appropriateness of the often-used designation "Soviet philosophy," as well as of any monolithic reading of the philosophy of the Soviet period at all.

The purpose of this volume is to show that, contrary to the widely spread view, not all Soviet philosophical thought was dominated by dogmatic orthodox Marxism and Marxism-Leninism. Not only did some independent thinkers endure through the immediate aftermath of the political rupture of 1917, but the second half of the twentieth century also brought to light numerous highly original and creative thinkers. Indeed, rigid censorship and severe state control suppressed almost all but a select number of authors and ideas. Yet although much of the philosophical production during this period was coarse and counterfeit, there remained some corners of the philosophical realm that brimmed with life. Under difficult conditions and in dwindling numbers, thinkers emerged who not only preserved but also successfully advanced the high standards of criticism and creativity achieved by pre-revolutionary Russian philosophy and culture.

Unfortunately, the genuine philosophical thought of the Soviet period remains largely unknown to Anglophone readers who continue to harbor suspicions and doubts about its real value and relevance to contemporary intellectual debates. Our goal with this book is to offer a more complex account of the multifaceted terrain of Soviet philosophy by introducing Western readers to the genuine philosophical ideas produced by Soviet thinkers. This volume addresses a highly understudied period in the development of Russian thought, focusing on the work of philosophers in Soviet Russia in the post-Stalin epoch (roughly from the mid-1950s to the early 1990s). In order to explain the reason for our decision to focus on this particular period, it is necessary to provide some details about the progression of philosophical thought in Soviet Russia and to discuss specific historical and political features that greatly influenced its development.

## THE POLITICAL TIMELINE AND PERIODIZATION OF SOVIET PHILOSOPHICAL THOUGHT

The peculiar characteristic of Russian philosophy, emphasized by many commentators, is that the politics and political happenings in Russia's history have played important roles in shaping its development. The seventy-year long Soviet epoch left perhaps the most severe imprints on the state of Russian intellectual life and philosophical thought, and major periods in Russian philosophy at the time were closely tied to political happenings. Roughly, we can divide the development of philosophy in the

Soviet epoch into three main stages. The first one began immediately after the October Revolution of 1917 and lasted until 1930. This phase had the most continuity with pre-revolutionary Russian philosophy and still bore resemblance to the tradition associated with a free dialogue of thought. The second stage, perhaps the most disastrous in Russian philosophical history, coincided with the rise of Stalin and Stalinism in politics. Lasting for about a quarter-century, this phase was marked by dogmatism and a rejection of everything that contradicted Marxist-Leninist ideology. Khrushchev's "thaw" is associated with the de-Stalinization of the entire Soviet society, and it created favorable conditions for genuine philosophical inquiry which re-emerged in the early 1950s, thus marking the beginning of the third phase in the progression of philosophy in the Soviet Union.

The development of philosophy in Soviet Russia was tightly linked to the evolution of Soviet Marxism. The latter became a decisive and dominant force in Russian philosophy at the end of the nineteenth century. Many Russian thinkers, including Nikolai Berdyaev, Sergei Bulgakov, and Semyon Frank, had actually started their intellectual careers as sympathizers of Marxism and the socialist idea. Initially, Marxism was embraced as a progressive social theory, and Russian "pro and contra" discussions about Marxism created a productive dialogue concerning Western thought. Even after Marxism was adopted and gained momentum in Russia (largely through the work of Georgi Plekhanov, traditionally considered "the father of Russian Marxism"), for a while it did not occupy a central place in debates of pre-revolutionary Russian philosophy and existed within intellectual discourse as one among multiple theories and concepts to be discussed. The situation began to change after the 1909 publication of Lenin's *Materialism and Empiriocritism*,[2] where he confronted Ernst Mach and his philosophical views (Machism), which had gained popularity among a large segment of Russian intelligentsia, including such diverse thinkers as Anatoly Lunacharsky, Viktor Chernov, Vladimir Basarov, Nikolai Valentinov, and others. Foremost among them was Alexander Bogdanov, who represented a younger generation (as opposed to Plekhanov[3]) of Marxist writers in Russia. Equating Machism with idealism and fideism, Lenin rejected it as incompatible with the scientific and political character of Marxism. He also argued that the mechanistic (vulgar) materialism that arose from positivism was equally unable to deliver the sought-after result. Instead, he endorsed dialectical materialism (initially expounded by Marx and Engels), which thereafter was deemed the philosophical worldview of the Bolsheviks. He claimed that dialectical materialism was the only suitable position for Marxist philosophers. Lenin's philosophical views can ultimately be explained by his political agenda, specifically by his attempt to promote the Bolshevik faction within the Russian Social-Democratic Workers' Party. The political ramifications for those involved in the debate followed almost immediately. However, an even bigger blow was felt on the philosophical front: Lenin's phraseology had damaging effects, not only on Russian Marxism, but also on the subsequent character of philosophy in the Soviet period. The evolution of philosophical thought was thereafter marked by a need to constantly demonstrate its commitment to materialist dialectics and dialectical materialism. However, despite this already forced requirement, Russia's philosophical life in the first decades of the century was uncommonly rich in both achievements and events.

## 1. *First Phase: Post-Revolutionary Decade*

After the 1917 Revolution and ensuing Civil War, philosophical discussion flourished, producing original thinkers and theories. Well into the 1920s, Soviet Marxism still maintained relatively open debates in a tradition of thought that originated at the crossroads between Russian "legal Marxism" and "Christian socialism," now mixed with different attempts to reconcile Marxism with positivism and the philosophy of Mach. Additionally, until about 1930, philosophizing in a non-Marxist manner and even publishing the obtained results still continued to be a legitimate business. During this time, the thinker Alexei Losev emerged whose studies of ancient philosophy, illuminated by the Orthodox faith, crossed the boundaries of many disciplines: from classical mythology and classical aesthetics, to the theory and morphology of classical culture, and to the philosophical theory of myth and symbol. The philosophical thought of that period proved to be productive in generating ideas and theories far ahead of their time. Alexander Bogdanov, for example, formulated an original philosophy, which he named *tectology* and is now regarded as a forerunner of systems theory. In 1929, Mikhail Bakhtin published his first major work, *Problems of Dostoevsky's Art*,[4] where he introduced the concept of *dialogism*, which brought to attention the dialogical nature of man and human culture. This influenced a variety of Western intellectual schools, including social constructivism, structuralism, and semiotics. Lev Vygotsky, a Russian psychologist who was active in philosophical discussions of the 1920s, produced theories that stress the fundamental role of social interaction in the development of cognition. His work provided the foundation for much of the future research—both psychological and philosophical—in cognitive development.

With a wide range of topics under debate, in the late 1910s through the 1920s, philosophy successfully maintained its disciplinary focus. Yet this time was also marked by the increasing politicization of philosophical debates. By the mid-1920s, two primary camps were formed in philosophy: the mechanists and the dialecticians (also known as Deborinists).[5] In the beginning of the twentieth century there was a growing concern about the role of the natural sciences in philosophical inquiry. This concern was fueled by positivism that, despite its defeat in the West, still remained popular in Russia. The mechanists, most of whom had backgrounds in science, believed that Marxist philosophy must confine itself to the data of experience and the examination of simple mechanisms in nature. Endorsing positivism, they argued that the natural sciences would resolve all philosophical problems. To the contrary, the Hegelian dialecticians defended the existence of philosophy as a separate discipline needed in order to explain the very possibility of scientific knowledge. They criticized the mechanists' conception of nature as narrow and restricted, arguing that the laws of dialectics should not be seen simply as a property of philosophical thinking, but rather that they could be found in nature itself. True to their Hegelian roots, they also emphasized the dynamic (dialectical) nature of the world and insisted that dialectics could not be reduced to a simple mechanical procedure. They maintained that only dialectical materialism would be able to deliver an accurate picture of the external world and to provide adequate solutions to philosophical problems.

The debate that initially offered a relatively open forum for the exchange of ideas on many complex issues was soon deadlocked; and in 1929, at the Meeting of the Second All-Union Conference of Marxist-Leninist Scientific Institutions, the mechanicism was condemned and discredited in the name of Marxism as the one that undermined dialectical materialism. However, even following this event and despite rising political and ideological tensions, philosophical thought was not yet fully suppressed and some genuine activity within the discipline was still tolerated, although not for long.

### 2. *Second Phase: Stalin Epoch*

Stalin's intervention in December 1930 put an end to this relatively productive phase in the development of Russian philosophy by issuing a decree that proclaimed the beginning of the Leninist stage in Marxist philosophy and declared dialectical materialism as the philosophical foundation of Marxism–Leninism. This completed the victory of the Stalin regime. In 1938, the main ideas of Marxism-Leninism became codified in the so-called *Short Course*[6] that depicted—in a highly primitive and simplistic form—the principles of dialectical materialism. Henceforth, every academic, but especially professional philosophers, had to espouse the *Short Course* in their work. It was treated like a sacred text that could not be challenged or transcended.

The political control over philosophy, along with the imprisonment and execution of many genuine Marxists during the political repressions of 1936–1938 known as the Great Purge, had a devastating impact on Russian philosophical thought. Marxism was converted into a dogma that acquired supremacy in Russia. Spiritual terror was fully unleashed and gaining in strength, and free thought had been banished and forbidden. The development of an independent and politically free philosophy became virtually impossible. Philosophy was turned into a weapon in the class war. Lenin's idea of the partisanship (*partiinost'*) of philosophy, now conceived as a purely political concept, was employed as a powerful ideological tool to warrant the criticism of theories on entirely political grounds.

In its ongoing contest for political and ideological supremacy, the victorious Stalin establishment openly deployed dogmatic Marxism in its attacks on scientific theories and every creative thought that did not fit into the narrowly understood (and largely artificial) criteria of Marxist-Leninist materialism. In the 1940s–1950s, many theories in cosmology and physics, as well as such disciplines as cybernetics, were criticized on ideological grounds as being at odds with Marxism. But perhaps the most appalling example of the interference of dogmatic philosophy in the natural sciences came to be Lysenkoism (from the name of the crusade leader, Trofim Lysenko), an ideologically driven political campaign against genetics, which was declared a "bourgeois pseudoscience." The underlying argument was that genetics and other similar attempts based upon Darwinian/Mendelian biology render life unacceptably deterministic, which supposedly could not be consistent with the view of human nature presented by Marxist-Leninist dogma. The Lysenkoists used this argument to advance their own theoretical position (they argued for a slightly modified Lamarckian evolutionary theory), but they also had more insidious motives.

In their fight with Darwinian biologists, they employed Stalinist terror that sent many prolific scientists to their deaths or costed them arrest and loss of employment.

The situation in the philosophical field itself was not much better. Political repressions and a ban on teaching and publication that was imposed on many open-minded scholars had devastating effects on philosophical life during that period. Although there remained a few thinkers who tried to resist the dogma, mainstream philosophy became exceedingly dogmatic. The single philosophical theory that was accepted and preached from university lecterns and through powerful state propaganda was orthodox Marxism. The official philosophy saw its only goal as guarding the purity of Marxist-Leninist dogma. The possibilities for philosophical research independent of the official dogma virtually vanished. Perhaps the direst time for philosophy in the Soviet Union was the last decade of Stalin's rule, when the Communist Party's exercise of power and control over philosophy were at its peak. It began in the early 1940s with the official condemnation of the multi-voluminous anthology, *History of Western Philosophy*, widely known as "the grey horse"—a nickname that points to the color of the book's binding but also hints at its intellectual power. The publication project had been overseen by Georgy Alexandrov, a high-ranking party functionary[7] and a philosopher by training. Initially, the project enjoyed great success far beyond expectations, and for the first two volumes, the editors of the work (including Alexandrov himself) received the Stalin Prize in the category of "philosophical research." Yet, the third volume of the *History* included a long chapter on Hegel, where the German philosopher was praised as a "genius thinker" central to understanding of the pre-history of Marxism and where Hegelian dialectics received appraisal as the "pinnacle of all bourgeois thought" (Alexandrov 1943, 210). Apparently, such admiration of the German philosopher did not fit well into the ideological rhetoric of the war years, and in 1944, the Party, on Stalin's personal order, denounced the volume for allegedly failing to expose the limitations of Hegel's idealism and to criticize Hegel's pro-German sentiments. This verdict decided the fate of "the grey horse," which was originally conceived as a seven-volume work. The entire publication was suspended, and the editors banished from academia.

After the victory in the Second World War (the Great Patriotic War in Russia), the climate in Russia became even more suffocating. The political campaign led by Andrey Zhdanov used allegiance to Marxism-Leninism to promote a dangerous agenda of Russian nationalism. The most conspicuous example that illustrates this chauvinistic attitude is another ideologically driven philosophical controversy, which, ironically, also involved Alexandrov. In 1947, Zhdanov (acting on behalf of the Communist Party) rebuked Alexandrov's entirely orthodox (in both spirit and letter) textbook *A History of Western European Philosophy* (1946) as "abstract" and "lacking *partiinost'*," and this was essentially for its failure to demonstrate the intellectual power of Russian (Soviet) philosophical thought and emphasize "the undeniable supremacy" of Soviet philosophy over its Western counterpart. Those who opposed this view came to be criticized and persecuted for cosmopolitanism and for kowtowing to the West and Western values. This controversy cost Alexandrov his job at the Communist Party Central Committee. However, fired from this highly-ranked position, he was made Director of the Institute of Philosophy at the Soviet Academy of Sciences, the principal philosophical institution in the country. His installation to "watchdog" philosophy, at the very epicenter of its activities, was one of the most obvious demonstrations of the Communist Party's political power and its ideological control over philosophical thought.

This is not a place to discuss the severe damage philosophy suffered in this period in the Soviet history. It is remarkable that at least some components of philosophical culture survived the Stalin epoch and were able to recover, despite it being a very long and painful process.

### 3. *Third Phase: Post-Stalin Era*

The next phase in the unfolding of Soviet philosophy is associated with Khrushchev's "thaw." It was a period in Soviet history in which the intellectual, cultural, and social atmospheres were again in flux after the death of Stalin.

The main political event that triggered important changes was the Twentieth Congress of the Communist Party of the Soviet Union in February 1956, which declared the course of the de-Stalinization of the country. Nikita Khrushchev's Secret Speech to the Congress ushered a decade of relative liberalization into most spheres of Soviet life. The initiated political transitions led to positive changes such as economic reforms, a softening of the political regime, openness to educational and cultural contacts, relaxed censorship, and the nascent atmosphere of "new thinking." These important transformations shaped conditions for creative philosophical work. Khrushchev certainly did not attempt to reverse the communist regime or reject Marxist ideology, and the initial relaxation was tempered that same year by a harsh military crackdown on protests in Hungary and Poland. However, the years between 1956 and 1964, which encompassed the period of Khrushchev's "thaw," allowed some space for dogmatic ideas to be challenged by a new generation of philosophers who began to emerge at this time.

The first wave included Evald Ilyenkov and Alexander Zinoviev, soon joined by Merab Mamardashvili, Georgy Shchedrovitsky, Boris Grushin, and others. Despite the stifling atmosphere in most academic institutions—involved in both research and teaching—the new generation saw its very purpose as renewing philosophy in Soviet Russia. Their point of departure was Marx—not a Marx turned into dogma, but rather a Marx that stimulated free thought and independent-mindedness. Returning to the authentic Marx, they re-energized Soviet Marxism, demonstrating the creative potential of a genuine philosophical enterprise. In their efforts, they had been joined by a handful of participants in the debates of the 1920s who had survived and continued to engage in academic life (such as influential philosophers Mikhail Bakhtin, Alexei Losev, Valentin Asmus, Mikhail Dynnik, Mikhail Lifshitz, and Bonifaty Kedrov as well as prominent psychologists Alexander Luria, Alexei Leontiev, Sergei Rubinshtein, and a few others).

This was the period of a renaissance of philosophy (as well as a rejuvenation of culture in general) in the Soviet Union, and it involved not merely a return to a genuine philosophy or its awakening from its forced "dogmatic slumber;" but most importantly, it was marked by the emergence of new, original philosophical thoughts and results which have effectively advanced philosophical knowledge, and which remain of significance even today.

It would be a mistake to view the years of Khrushchev's rule as a stable and flourishing period in Soviet history. It was a tumultuous time fraught with many political tensions, as well as ideological and cultural confrontations. However, despite Khrushchev's ineptitude in his attempts at de-Stalinization, the political and cultural contexts of the Khrushchev-era "thaw" were largely favorable to innovative work in philosophy, and allowed for a relatively open exchange of ideas and less severe censorship.

In 1964, when Khrushchev was ousted from power by a coalition led by Leonid Brezhnev, Stalinism did not return. But there was much less freedom allowed for individual expression, independent thought, and creative work. Dogmatic Marxism, which largely preserved its central position through the Khrushchev era, had essentially stagnated during the following period, becoming an even bigger obstacle for new ideas and novel methods in philosophy. Not only did many of the Stalinist "old guard" maintain their presence in academia, they also regained power under a new, more conservative ruling. The Communist Party never lost its grip on philosophy, and it tightened its control over philosophical discussions, restricting choices of topics and themes and placing ideological pressure on scholarly work.

The "thaw" phase was short-lived, and the following era restored an authoritarian ideology, heightened repressions, and put a clampdown on freedom of thought. However, the philosophical renaissance initiated in the decade from the mid-1950s to the mid-1960s was not wasted. Despite fading optimism and intensified ideological clashes in the post-"thaw" period, there emerged a philosophical discourse of sustained debates that generated stimulating results in a variety of philosophical disciplines, such as from more-or-less traditional Marxist fields as epistemology and ontology to revived areas such as logic and ethics. Even more important is that, for the first time, Soviet Marxism attempted to critically evaluate its own nature and roots. This is when the need to have an internal dialogue concerning Marxism and its relations to the traditions of Western thought was acutely felt, and when engagement with the non-Marxist philosophical tradition in Russia and abroad came to the forefront. While a direct dialogue with Western philosophy was still difficult and often forbidden, and works discussing Soviet Marxism in critical conversation with the Western tradition were rare, Russian philosophers began to reject the concept of Marxism as a Russian cultural and social project. The openness toward Western thought also revitalized an interest in pre-revolutionary Russian philosophy. Indeed, contrary to the widespread belief that the re-discovery of the original Russian philosophical thought would be an event of the later *perestroika* years, the pre-revolutionary thought was first revived and studied in the late 1970s to early 1980s, albeit in politically conditioned waves of appropriation.

Mikhail Gorbachev, who came to power in 1985, initiated reforms supposed to restructure (*perestroika*) the Soviet economic and political system. Coupled with the policy of openness (*glasnost'*), the *perestroika* of the 1980s brought substantial liberalization to the intellectual and cultural life of Soviet society. Significant changes came to philosophy, which finally acquired genuine freedom and the ability to express views divergent from the doctrinal Marxism-Leninism. The term "Marxism-

Leninism" itself was soon abandoned and dogmatic Marxism ceased to be a mandatory discipline in institutions of higher education. This epoch of great inspiration and optimism proved to be fruitful for philosophy and independent thought. Scholars brought attention to previously banned and never-before-permitted topics of debate, such as the Western roots of Marxism and the connection between Soviet Marxism and pre-revolutionary Russian philosophical thought, which encouraged a massive publication of works by Russian philosophers, whose ideas had still largely remained unknown to a wider audience. The new climate prompted debates about the fate of Soviet Marxism and some participants began questioning the appropriateness of Marx's ideas for the analysis of contemporary reality. However, a look at the general trend might rather suggest a continuity of the Marxist discourse. While in letter the "official" Soviet philosophical thought of that time broke with Marxism in its most dogmatic form, in spirit, the loyalty to Marxism per se was still largely preserved and defended. The situation began to change only after the dissolution of the Soviet Union in 1991, which led to the collapse of the ideals fostered throughout the seventy-year history of the Soviet regime. The intellectual attractiveness of Marxism had faded, and eventually Russia's commitment to Marxism was abandoned entirely. This topic, however, goes beyond the scope of the present volume, and it would require a special consideration in another philosophical discussion. Now it is time to say a few words about the project of our volume and its composition.

## ON THE TIMELINE AND COMPOSITION OF THE VOLUME

Our book is a collection of essays that focus on the development of philosophy in Russia in the third period of the Soviet epoch, namely from the beginning of Khrushchev's "thaw" era in the mid-1950s to the dismantling of the Soviet Union in 1991. This period roughly encompasses the second half of the twentieth century, which for Russia is both notorious and intellectually rich. Not everything that happened in the field of philosophy in the Soviet Union and Russia in those decades could be the subject of our attention here. We do not cover the official aspects of ideological, educational, and academic lives, which were prevalently dogmatic. Also of little interest nowadays are the multi-volume tracts on dialectics and other similar "compendiums." Our concern is not with every minute detail of what occurred in philosophy in Soviet Russia during that time, but rather with original results produced by Soviet scholars, which did not only appear new then, but also retain their originality and philosophical value today. We focus on this period precisely because we believe it bears scholarly and philosophical importance.

Like other periods in the history of Russian philosophy, intellectual discourse during the second part of the twentieth century was dramatically affected by the ever-changing political situation, and the philosophical dynamic of the period came to be determined by the actual evolution of Soviet Marxism. However, what makes the targeted period so unique is that, in addition to supporting the then "traditional" dogmatic Marxism, it created an illicit hybrid. While still committed to the ethos of Marxism, this new thought undermined Marxist orthodoxy from within, thus preparing its inevitable collapse. Furthermore, some scholars began to deviate from Marxism and launched searches for new ideas and forms of philosophical expression.

Indeed, the Soviet philosophical landscape of the second part of the twentieth century was both more complex and more interesting than it is usually considered. Alongside dogmatists and conformists worked remarkable thinkers, who managed to come up with new ideas and major breakthroughs in research in a number of philosophical disciplines, including epistemology and philosophy of science, ethics and anthropology, logic, and the history of philosophy. Only recently did we begin to appreciate their efforts and recognize the relevance and value of their ideas to the central issues of contemporary philosophy. The work of these thinkers, their key ideas, and the results they produced are our main interests in this volume. Our task is not to simply review these ideas, but also to assess them from our current vantage point.

The aim of the volume is not to provide a comprehensive survey of Soviet philosophical thought in the post-Stalin period, but rather to focus on those areas of philosophy which produced the most ingenious results, and on those thinkers who offered the most original contributions to the discipline. Thus, instead of focusing on the well-known official aspects of philosophical life, the essays included in this collection shift their attention toward largely unknown and often ignored original ideas and theories produced during those decades. The volume introduces the readers to important figures of this period who are not widely known in the West (including the already mentioned Zinoviev and Shchedrovitsky, as well as Genrikh Batishchev, Vladimir Bibler, Vyacheslav Stepin, and Sergei Rubinshtein) and their contributions to philosophy. There is also a detailed analysis of central notions and concepts of internationally celebrated Russian/Soviet philosophers, such as Bakhtin, Lotman, Losev, Ilyenkov, and Mamardashvili, whose ideas are further elucidated and examined from the perspective of central philosophical discussions that took place in Soviet Russia and that have been largely unknown to Western readers. Those discussions produced outstanding philosophical results which remain of interest to numerous disciplines within philosophy. Among these results are the development of the so-called general theory of activity originally introduced to analyze cognition but which is also applicable to different organizational structures (Shchedrovitsky), a new interpretation of Bakhtin's idea about a dialogical nature of culture and consciousness, as well as a transformation of dialectics into a dialogue of theoretical and cultural systems (Bibler), the introduction of a new model of scientific theory understood as a multi-layered open system containing a number of partly independent non-linear sub-systems (Stepin), the development of some central anthropological conceptions, particularly a phenomenon of individual consciousness (Mamardashvili), etc. The discussion of these and other original ideas and theories comprises a core of the book.

In part, the present book is an English translation of the Russian volume published in 2014 in Moscow (Lektorsky 2014). In addition to the essays originally printed in the Russian collection, two new chapters have been introduced: "Punks versus Zombies: Evald Ilyenkov and the Battle for Soviet Philosophy" by David Bakhurst; and "Alexander Zinoviev's Teaching on Life" by Abdusalam A. Guseynov. They further clarify topics central to Russian philosophical development in the post-Stalin period contributing to the realization of the book's goals.

Before considering the structure and content of this volume, it might be useful to address a question about its genre. This book is a scholarly collection, which includes contributions by Russian and Western researchers working on different topics in Russian philosophy during the Soviet period. While this valuable approach has some obvious advantages and allows for a more objective analysis of Soviet philosophical thought, it also presents serious challenges, especially in terms of the writing style and composition of material. As it is well known, the genre of Russian academic publications differs from what is customary for this kind of publications in English. And since many of the chapters in the volume are translations from Russian, the question of genre becomes very important. We would like to emphasize that our concern is not with the standards for scholarly publications, which are equally high in Russia and in the West, but rather with the form of how arguments are presented, the level of engagement with supplementary material, and the writing model itself. The existing disparity between the Russian and English conventional styles of academic literature creates difficulties when one attempts to translate one tradition into another. It is also worth noting that the Russian cultural and academic context is distinct from that of the West and largely unfamiliar to the English-speaking readers.

In order to avoid misunderstanding and to minimize unnecessary confusion, chapters included in our collection have been revised to provide the appropriate context needed for non-Russian readers and to meet the norms of the English edition. When possible, we have tried to reduce difficulties by introducing some contextual remarks and adding appropriate clarifications and references. However, we quite deliberately avoided adjusting all the chapters to a single genre of traditional scholarship. While we certainly hoped that the volume would present a scholarly account of Russian philosophy in the post-Stalin era, we were also keen to introduce another well-respected genre, especially common to Russian research on philosophy of Soviet period: a genre of so-called "philosophical reflection." This is a firsthand account of a particular period or thinker produced by an esteemed scholar who has first-person knowledge or experience of the event or figure under consideration. In most cases, the authors of the reflection pieces took part in the events or had direct access to thinkers they discuss, which make their narrations truly invaluable, both as personal recollections and as philosophical reflections.

Thus, rather than imposing the uniformity of a genre, we included chapters written both in a more traditional academic style (traditional scholarship) and others as reflection or opinion pieces. The former should be familiar to our English readers, whereas the latter might be new to a non-Russian audience. The philosophical reflection pieces have been clearly noted in the table of contents and also marked in the titles of the appropriate chapters. It should also be mentioned that the chapters that fall into a standard genre of traditional scholarship vary considerably in their structure and approach. Some of the essays in the volume are historical explorations of their subjects. Others adopt a "case study" approach. Several chapters take the form of conceptual philosophical discussions. A few use comparative research as their main methodological tool. We believe that this diversity is a considerable asset and hope that the readers will appreciate it.

The book consists of twenty-five chapters written by distinguished scholars from Russia and abroad. These chapters have been thematically organized into six parts.

Part I, "Russian Philosophy of the Second Half of the Twentieth Century in the Context of Culture and Science," begins with an analysis of the broad social and cultural contexts of the renaissance in philosophy that occurred in the 1950s–1960s. It shows that, during Khrushchev's "thaw" and the associated process of de-Stalinization, there emerged a number of original thinkers opposed to the official dogma who in their writings' rigorously defended human rights and the basic freedoms of individuals. However, their philosophical ideas became largely suppressed and thus many of their thoughts went unnoticed to the reading public. Committed to fighting for their ideas and values, they had to endure significant political and professional struggles. One of the chapters in this section carefully restructures and reviews a fateful controversy of 1954 which was sparked by the famous "Theses on philosophy"[8] authored by Evald Ilyenkov and Valentin Korovikov, then young faculty members at Moscow State University (MGU). The debates that were initiated by these "Theses," and which cost both authors their teaching jobs, marked the beginning of a revival in Russian philosophy dated back to the 1950s. Our volume includes the first English translation (by David Bakhurst) of the "Theses" reproduced here in two (abbreviated and full) versions. The present translation gives the readers the opportunity to have access to this important text and gain first-hand accounts of the controversy associated with it.

The non-dogmatic philosophical thought that emerged in the second half of the 1950s was largely focused on the philosophical analysis of knowledge and science. Thinkers such as Ilyenkov, Zinoviev, and others who worked on these topics demonstrated a highly critical attitude toward the prevailing social situation and existing social and political conditions. At the same time, they believed that positive changes of this social reality could be brought about only through the development of scientific knowledge and advancement of theoretical thinking, the single reliable methodology of which they saw in philosophy. Only in the 1970s, when some of the representatives of this movement (such as Mamardashvili, Bibler, and Batishchev) became disappointed with the naïve scientism and shifted their interests toward anthropological and value theory issues did there occur some essential transformation in their views. The final chapters in the first section of the book closely follow this development, showing that some thinkers of anthropological orientation departed from Marxism and appropriated phenomenological and existential insights of Western and pre-revolutionary Russian philosophy. Several of them even went on to give existential interpretations of Marx's ideas.

It is worth noting that not all authors in this section shared this optimistic assessment of the situation in Russian philosophy during the 1950s–1990s. For example, Karen Swassjan remains skeptical about the actual value of Soviet philosophical thought, stressing the emptiness of philosophical ideas developed during this period. He argues that during the Soviet regime, philosophy lost its own subject, thus making it impossible to do genuine work within this discipline. While the view Swassjan advances is rather atypical for scholars of Russian philosophy and not necessarily shared by the majority of those who study its Soviet period, we found it important to include his essay in this volume, first, because despite being unpopular this position deserves attention, and, second, in order to acquaint the readers with different approaches to Soviet philosophical thought. We believe that by introducing

Swassjan's chapter we offer a more objective and balanced discussion of philosophical accomplishments in the Soviet period.

Part II, "Philosophy of Science," addresses topics and themes that are relevant to Russian philosophical studies of science and how they were formulated and advanced in the 1950s–1990s. The analysis of scientific knowledge at that time was largely focused on studying the origins and historical development of scientific theory (Kedrov and others). Thinkers such as Ivan Kuznetzov and Vyacheslav Stepin came up with a new understanding of the model of a scientific theory. They proposed to construe it as a multi-level open system that would include several relatively independent sub-systems, related to each other in a non-linear manner. Novel in its nature, this interpretation stood in contrast to the standard hypothetico-deductive model of a scientific theory, which was dominant in Western philosophy of science at that time. Drawing from the suggestion of a non-linear relation, Stepin formulated the idea of historically changing foundations of a scientific theory. He was joined by other scholars who attempted to understand what exactly could form such foundations. They demonstrated that one of those foundations is a scientific world picture which provides important links between science and culture. This approach allowed them to account for changes occurring in scientific rationality and to differentiate among its three historical types: classical, non-classical, and post-non-classical rationality. The chapters in this section successfully reconstruct this development and examine each of these three types of rationality, pointing to specific criteria that allow for their distinction.

Part III, "Philosophy as the History of Philosophy," surveys notable achievements in the field of the history of philosophy. It shows that despite prevailing dogmatism, there emerged significant studies that not only enriched philosophical understanding of the tradition but also formulated new approaches to important issues of the day. The most illustrative examples came to be a new interpretation of Spinoza (particularly, the philosopher's understanding of substance) as well as very advanced studies of such idealist thinkers as Kant and Hegel, who were now seen as progressive figures able to teach us important ideas about ethics, morality, and philosophy of law (*die Rechtsphilosophie*), in addition to already familiar concepts of dialectics and alienation inherited by Marx. A special chapter is devoted to Losev's phenomenological conception of myth and its reception by contemporary Western thought.

The so-called "activity approach," which was developed in philosophy during the Soviet period, has become a subject of Part IV titled "The Problem of Activity in Philosophy, Methodology, and Human Sciences." Chapters included in this section introduce and thoroughly discuss some of the most important ideas which evolved in this approach. Among those is the idea of the significant role of activity in the formation of human consciousness, advanced by Rubinshtein, the original conception of the ideal, proposed by Ilyenkov, and other valuable insights. The section also examines the claim about the complex interrelations between activity and contemplation as well as between activity and communication formulated in Batishchev's works, as well as a general theory of activity as a generation of different types of organization introduced by Shchedrovitsky. Chapters in this section discuss different versions of the activity approach. They also highlight many correlations that exist between the activity approach in philosophy and similar studies in both traditional and contemporary psychology, sociology, theory of education, and the history of science, putting this problematic into a broader context of social and cognitive sciences. A special chapter analyzes the activity approach developed by Soviet scholars from the perspective of current discussions in analytic philosophy.

Part V, "Dialogue and Communication," commences with a chapter that examines some key ideas as well as the Soviet reception of the philosophy of dialogue, elaborated by Bakhtin. His discussions with another original thinker, Yuri Lotman, who around the same time introduced his semiotic theory of communication, are also carefully analyzed in this section. One of the chapters thoroughly surveys Bibler's theory of "the dialogue of logics" and its promising applications to the study of such differing phenomena as the history of philosophy, science, and culture. Special attention is given to the highly original conception of "deep communication" pioneered by Batishchev.

Discussions in Part VI, "Philosophical Anthropology," deal with questions of the ontology of the human person, interpersonal relationships, and how they are governed by ethics and morality. A central topic under consideration is an original concept of human being that emerged in Russian philosophy in the post-Stalin epoch. In this view, a human is understood as an autonomous being, endowed with a creative nature and the ability to become self-transcendent. The actualization of both is possible only through man's practical agency in the world and his participation in communal and social life. This interpretation of human motivated a number of advanced studies that would examine such questions as man's relations to Others (Batishchev) and man's place in the structure of Being (Rubinshtein). Additionally, this section includes two chapters that discuss questions of morality, which have acquired a prominent place in Russian intellectual and philosophical discourses. One of the chapters turns to Oleg Drobnitsky's studies on the nature of morality, while another takes a closer look at the treatment of the conception of moral responsibility and ethical behavior from the perspective of the Soviet lifestyle in the works of Zinoviev and Mamardashvili.

Each of the volume's six parts not only introduces specific concepts and ideas developed by Russian thinkers of the Soviet period but also puts these ideas into the context of contemporary philosophical discussions in relevant fields.

The volume concludes with "A Chronology of Key Events in the Russian Philosophy (1953–1991)" and "Selected Bibliography" that encompasses key publications of that period.

* * *

There are many original Russian thinkers, including those who happened to work during the Soviet period, who merit attention and scholarly consideration yet remain virtually unknown to the West. Our publication was motivated by a desire to introduce Western readers to the genuine philosophical ideas that evolved during the Soviet period and thus contribute to a better understanding of Russian thought. We hope that this volume will meet the needs of all who seek accurate, specific, current, and in-depth knowledge of the main aspects of the development of philosophy in post-Stalin Soviet Russia, whether they be established or younger scholars, students of philosophy or other humanities disciplines, or broadly educated readers interested in the Russo-Soviet intellectual tradition.

## NOTES

1. In addition to monographs and collective volumes devoted to the analysis of the philosophical thought in Russia, since 1962 there has been a published professional journal—*Soviet Studies in Philosophy* (since 1992—*Russian Studies in Philosophy*)—which allows Western readers access to selected Russian language writings by translating and printing them in English. See Scanlan 1987, 3.
2. The full title of Lenin's book is *Materialism and Empiriocriticism. Critical Comments on a Reactionary Philosophy*. It was published in May 1909 in Moscow by the Zveno Publishers under the pseudonym Vladimir Ilyin.
3. By that time, Plekhanov had already established himself as the leading Russian Marxist theoretician.
4. The original Russian title of the book is *Problemy Tvorchestva Dostoevskogo*. It was published in Leningrad (nowadays, St. Petersburg) by Priboj Publishers.
5. The leading dialectician was Abram Deborin, the disciple of Plekhanov who was the first to introduce the term "dialectical materialism."
6. The full title of the document read: *Istorija Vsesoiuznoi kommunisticheskoi partii (bol'shevikov). Kratkii kurs* [History of the Communist Party of the Soviet Union (Bolsheviks). Short Course]. (Moscow: Pravda, 1938). See History 1943.
7. Between 1939 and 1947, Alexandrov served as Head of the Central Committee's Department of Propaganda and Agitation, which controlled philosophy and all ideological activities in the country.
8. The full title of the work is "Theses on the Question of the Interrelation of Philosophy and Knowledge of Nature and Society in the Process of their Historical Development." The translation of the text has been provided as the Appendix to Ch. 3 of the present volume.

## BIBLIOGRAPHY

Alexandrov, Georgy F., *et al.* (eds.). 1943. *Istorija filosofii* [History of Philosophy], vol. III, *Filosofija pervoi poloviny XIX veka* [Philosophy of the First Half of the Nineteenth Century]. Moscow: Ogiz; Gospolitizdat.

Bakhurst, David. 1991. *Consciousness and Revolution in Soviet Philosophy: From the Bolsheviks to Evald Ilyenkov.* Cambridge: Cambridge University Press.

Bocheński, Józef M. 1950. *Der sowjetrussische Dialektische Materialismus*, Bern: Francke.

Bocheński, Józef M. 1973. *Marxismus-Leninismus. Wissenschaft oder Glaube?* München: Olzog.

Dahm, Helmut, Thomas J. Blakeley, and George L. Kline (eds.). 1988. *Philosophical Sovietology: The Pursuit of a Science*, Dordrecht and Boston: Reidel.

Grier, Philip T. 1978. *Marxist Ethical Theory in the Soviet Union.* Dordrecht: D. Reidel Publishing Company.

*History of the Communist Party of the Soviet Union (Bolsheviks). Short Course*. 1943. Edited by a Commission of the Central Committee of CPSU(B). Moscow: Foreign Languages Publishing House.

Kline, George L. 1968. *Religious and Anti-Religious Thought in Russia*, Chicago: University of Chicago Press.

Lektorsky, Vladislav A. 2014. *Problemy i diskussii v filosofii Rossii vtoroi poloviny 20-go veka: sovremennyi vzgljad* [Problems and Discussions in Philosophy of Russia in the Second Half of the Twentieth Century: A Contemporary View]. Moscow: ROSSPEN.

Sarlemijn, Andries. 1985. "Convergence in the Philosophy of Science? A Contribution on the Possibility of East-West Discussions in the Field of the Philosophy of Science." *Studies in Soviet Thought* 30 (4): 305–36.

Scanlan, James P. 1985. *Marxism in the USSR: A Critical Survey of Current Soviet Thought*, Ithaca, N.Y.: Cornell University Press.

Scanlan, James P. 1987. "Editor's Introduction," *Soviet Studies in Philosophy*, 26 (1): 3–6.

Van der Zweerde, Evert. 1998. *Soviet Historiography of Philosophy: Istoriko-Filosofskaja Nauka*. Dodrecht: Kluwer/Springer.

Wetter, Gustav A. 1985. "Philosophie, Dialektik und Einzelwissenschaften bei Engels." *Studies in Soviet Thought* 30 (3): 269–89.

PART I

# Russian Philosophy of the Second Half of the Twentieth Century in the Context of Culture and Science

CHAPTER ONE

# The Russian Philosophy of the Second Half of the Twentieth Century as a Sociocultural Phenomenon

VLADISLAV A. LEKTORSKY

Soviet philosophers were either simpletons, or in the service of an impious regime, or both. That is the opinion of many whose idea of Soviet philosophy was drawn from the officially sanctioned manuals they had to read in their student years. Those textbooks left an impression that Marxism-Leninism had easy and simple solutions to the most complex problems of human existence that had puzzled the greatest minds for centuries. Should the above opinion be correct, in the years of the Soviet regime, Russia could not have any philosophy worthy of mentioning. And if contemporary Russia might be in need of philosophy, it would be argued, it has to start anew from the point zero. Two options are usually being considered. One is to revive the tradition of religious idealism broken in 1922 when a group of distinguished Russian thinkers was sent into exile on the "philosophers' ship."[1] The other is to join one of the popular schools of contemporary Western philosophy.

In fact, "Soviet philosophy" is a term that stands for a variety of things.[2] Western sovietologists that dealt with Soviet philosophy proceeded from the assumption that it was not philosophy at all. Philosophy implies a critical attitude and is, indeed, a critical examination of whatever is taken for granted, be it in life or in science. Soviet philosophy, they argued, was in fact an ideology, an attempt at a presumed theoretical justification of the Communist policies and a means of indoctrination. Philosophy of that sort discouraged independent thinking and was duly loathed. It has become customary for some contemporary columnists, including a number of professional philosophers, to disparage the entire Russian philosophy of the Soviet time in this manner. Examples are easily found to justify this attitude. Most textbooks on philosophy and numerous philosophical writings, especially those that dealt with problems of historical materialism and "scientific communism," deserved no better, as did the official figures of that philosophy: Mark Mitin, Pavel Yudin, Fyodor

Konstantinov and the like. In short, the phenomenon that fits the above description of "Soviet philosophy" was certainly present.

However, there was also something else, something that could not, it seemed, exist in the highly ideological Soviet society—it could not, but it did. The Soviet philosophical landscape was both more complex and more interesting than described. Working alongside dogmatists and conformists were remarkable thinkers, brilliant minds, people that felt at home in both Russian and world culture, as well as in human and natural sciences. It is only recently that we have learned to duly understand and value what they did in those years and what has emerged as relevant and topical today.

There are two points I would like to emphasize from the outset. Firstly, the innovative minds of Soviet philosophers belonged to the society in which they lived. Employed by Soviet academic institutions, they wrote for Soviet philosophical journals and sent their books to state publishing houses. Most of them shared Marx's ideas, even if they interpreted them in their own ways, and endorsed the ideals of humane socialism. This is not to say they formed a team with dogmatists and official ideologues. In fact, both personal and ideological antagonisms between the two parties were sharp, and both were well aware of these opposition and antipathy.

Secondly, the ideas proposed in those years were no prisoners of their time. It would be wrong to view those ideas as inalienable parts of a self-contained system. Some of them are easily taken out of their philosophical and cultural contexts to be included in different contexts and interpreted in a variety of ways. This is what has happened to the activity approaches developed in Soviet philosophy and psychology, to Evald Ilyenkov's theory of the ideal, not to mention the ideas of Mikhail Bakhtin and Lev Vygotsky.

Trends set in Russian philosophy at that time proved to be promising and productive for both the country's philosophical development and the cooperation with the world philosophy today. Two periods stand out as particularly important: the 1920s and the second half of the twentieth century, separated, as they were, by decades of an almost unrestrained dogmatism promoted by the Stalinist regime.

* * *

In the 1920s the Russian philosophy and philosophy-based human sciences originated ideas that allowed for new approaches to knowledge, particularly to the study of man. They were, by no means, late echoes of the Russian pre-revolutionary philosophy. On the contrary, some of the most original thinkers of the time conscientiously challenged the pre-revolutionary tradition. Perhaps, Alexei Losev was the only true heir to that tradition. In the 1920s Losev published a number of books in which a novel interpretation of Ancient philosophy was coupled with original philosophy of myth, language, music and mathematics. Such a global approach to the study of symbolic forms was unprecedented in the Russian philosophy.

Alexander Bogdanov, an unorthodox Marxist, developed *Tectology*, a "universal organization science," as a methodology of systems understanding alternative to the elementarism and atomism of classical science. Bogdanov's tectological ideas went unacknowledged during his lifetime and were only appreciated and developed, both in Russia and in the West, in the second half of the twentieth century when the systems approach became a trend in a variety of sciences (Biggart, Glovelli, Jassour 1998). Parallel developments included the structural method in linguistics (Roman Jakobson et al.) and the formal method in literature studies (Boris Eikhenbaum, Viktor Shklovsky, Vladimir Propp and others), both to prove sources of world structuralism in philosophy and human sciences in the second half of the twentieth century.

The 1920s witnessed a philosophical trend characterized by two features (I would not call it a school or even a movement because thinkers associated with it were too different for that). One of the features has to do with the opposition both to religious philosophy predominant in pre-revolutionary Russia and to dogmatized Marxism. The opposition took the form of focusing on spheres peripheral to both religious philosophy and the simplified interpretations of Marxist materialism. These were spheres of culture, language, art, semiotic and symbolic systems. To philosophers exemplifying that trend, culture was a key to problems of anthropology and ontology. The other feature of this philosophical trend was the close connection that existed between philosophical studies and the new ideas in human sciences. Philosophers often came up with innovative ideas in the humanities; on the other hand, students of humanities did not simply adopt new philosophical ideas, but actively used them to substantiate novel approaches.

Worth mentioning here is, first and foremost, Mikhail Bakhtin, who went beyond the simple application of his philosophical ideas to the analysis of literature and language (novels of Dostoevsky, for instance) and substantially elaborated on them in the course of that work. Bakhtin's ideas concerning the interrelation of the Self and the Other in the process of dialogue, the complex dialectic of the "consciousness for the Self" and "the consciousness for the Other," the dialogical and polyphonic structure of consciousness and culture, the methodology of humanities were far ahead of his time and would be properly appreciated, studied and understood in our country only in the 1970s and in the West even later. Bakhtin's legacy is not just a new methodology of humanities, but also and primarily a new philosophical anthropology that synthesizes the traditional Russian anti-individualism with the substantiation of the uniqueness and importance of personality. In the West the Bakhtin studies now amount to a trade of their own (Spektor, Denischenko, et al. 2017).

I should then mention Lev Vygotsky whose ideas, according to some contemporary Western scholars, have marked a turning point in the development of world psychology (some do even speak of "the Vygotsky Boom.") Vygotsky used a number of Marx's ideas to develop an original understanding of consciousness as a communicative process and an outcome of the evolution of inter-subject relations, as a social construct included in a cultural historical context. These philosophical ideas formed the basis of a psychological theory that, to a large degree, defined the course of theoretical and experimental psychology in this country and became influential throughout the world (Daniels, Wertsh, Cole 2007).

I must, finally, mention Gustav Shpet, who studied phenomenology under Edmund Husserl and then developed his own theory that was the first attempt to synthesize phenomenology and hermeneutics. Shpet, who was highly critical of the

Russian pre-revolutionary religious philosophy (this attitude is evident, for example, in his *Outline of the Development of Russian Philosophy*) and clearly looked to the West, was, simultaneously, fully aware of his own originality. His ideas influenced Russian psychology (it was Shpet who came up with a project of ethnic psychology), linguistics (for instance, linguistic structuralism), and literature studies. He was one of the pioneers of semiotics as the general science of signs and sign systems.

* * *

In the mid-1950s the Soviet philosophy reached a turning point which proved to be an important part of the complex process of de-Stalinization of the Soviet society. It was the beginning of a new stage in the development of Russian philosophy, the essence of which can be summarized as follows: philosophy turned back to its own problems and resumed its creative work. It was, in short, a revival of philosophical thinking.[3]

Some may find this assertion too strong. After all, ideological censorship still existed. Many questions, including those of philosophy, might not be debated. University textbooks of philosophy were so dogmatic that they could not help spreading strong distaste for what they taught—and not just for Marxist philosophy, but for philosophy in general. Western scholars of Soviet philosophy often base their conclusions on the analysis of manuals and other such ideologically sanctioned texts. In reality there was a great difference between those dogmatic texts and the real philosophical thought that was alive, and the activists of the new philosophical movement were keenly aware of the difference.

The leaders of the movement were Evald Ilyenkov and Alexander Zinoviev, young graduates of the Faculty of Philosophy at Moscow State University. Within the scopes of their influence were other thinkers, a number of whom would later found their own schools and distance themselves (sometimes significantly) from their onetime teachers.[4]

Some of the thinkers of the 1920s were active again. Alexei Losev published more in those years than in all his previous life. He elaborated, often in an innovative manner, on his ideas of the 1920s. Those years witnessed the new discovery of Alexander Bogdanov, Mikhail Bakhtin, and Lev Vygotsky. Their books were republished and their ideas discussed. Some of their previously unpublished writings became available. One may say that in the 1960s and the 1970s these ideas acquired lives of their own, influencing new conceptions, finding supporters and opponents, etc. Bakhtin continued his creative work, coming up with a number of new ideas.

Bonifaty Kedrov published original works, being one of the first in the world to bring philosophy and history of science together. Sergei Rubinshtein returned to activity elaborating on his old philosophical ideas to develop an interesting version of philosophical anthropology. Valentin Asmus was at his prime. Teodor Oizerman published significant works on methodology of the history of philosophy. Mikhail Lifshitz developed his original concept of onto-epistemology (Lifshitz himself called it "ontognoseology").

The Russian philosophy of the second half of the twentieth century saw what it had missed for decades, namely a variety of philosophical schools that stood on different conceptual platforms, schools that endured, developed, and engaged in debate. Moscow was the seat of some such schools. In addition, there appeared several philosophical schools and movements in Kiev, Minsk, and other intellectual centers.[5] Their members could have their writings published, though not without difficulties.

The peculiar feature of the Russian philosophical Renaissance of the 1960s–1980s was its initial orientation to the philosophical analysis of knowledge, thinking and science. It was not a chance feature. These fields of philosophical inquiry, namely epistemology, logic, philosophical problems of natural sciences, were less closely related to ideology and politics than, for example, social philosophy, and afforded greater opportunities for independent research. By the late 1950s party authorities became aware of the impossibility or, at least, the harmful consequences of ideological interference with science. If not with all scientific discipline, then at least, with natural science. In the 1960s, moreover, further progress of socialism was generally believed to depend on the success of the scientific and technological revolution.

The leaders of the new philosophical movement were, by no means, indifferent to human problems. They were quite critical of the social reality around them, not of socialism, but of the bureaucratic version of it that prevailed in the Soviet Union. (As a person close at the time to Ilyenkov, Zinoviev and other leaders of the movement, I have every right to assert this with full responsibility.) They believed that emphasis on scientific knowledge, theoretical inquiry and philosophical reflection as the methodological basis of that inquiry was the key to changing social reality. The function of philosophy is not to sanction attitudes or rationalize emotional responses. Nor is it to serve as the handmaiden of the prevalent ideology; but to understand and explain the reality and the ways to change it. Philosophy is essentially criticism of reality rooted in its understanding. This critical reflection is the defining feature of philosophy that distinguishes it from all other forms of knowledge and all other attitudes toward the world; and this means that development of a theory of knowledge is the vital task of philosophy and a specific means of social criticism and humanization of reality.

The analysis of the logic and methodology of science began with the study of the logical structure of *The Capital*. The findings of this inquiry were, after significant modifications, applied to explore the structure of theoretical knowledge in other fields. It is sometimes claimed that this escape into logic and epistemology left philosophers in the ivory tower of pure philosophizing unrelated to whatever went on outside of it. This is absolutely wrong. The new philosophical movement was aware of the developments outside philosophy as such: in the natural and human sciences, in a number of cultural spheres, and interacted intensively and fruitfully with them.

The "cognitive turn" of the new philosophy coincided with the rigorous study of cognitive processes in psychology (studies of thought process by Rubinshtein and Leontiev schools), symbolic logic (Vladimir Smirnov), mathematic models of thought processes and cognitive linguistics (Vyacheslav Ivanov), semiotics (works of Yuri Lotman and his school, directly relevant to philosophy), cybernetics (Andrey Kolmogorov), methodology of systems analysis (Igor Blauberg, Erik Yudin, Vadim Sadovsky), and history of natural science (Bonifaty Kedrov, among others). All these works satisfied the highest world standards and won international recognition. Leading mathematicians and natural scientists, such as Andrey Markov (mathematician), Pyotr Kapitsa (physicist), Ivan Schmalhausen and Vladimir

Engelgardt (biologists) and others showed interest in philosophy and joined philosophical discussions relevant to their research. Philosophers, natural scientists, and some representatives of human sciences established and maintained intensive interaction. Conferences on the methodology of science became regular events.

Significant changes began in the 1970s. Politically, they were influenced by the military interference in Czechoslovakia in 1968 that put an end not only to the Prague Spring, but to hopes for the renovation of socialism in Russia. Many members of the philosophical movement felt disappointed with the naïve scientism that had inspired them in the late 1950s and 1960s. They gradually began to put forward anthropology as an independent field of inquiry, not as a derivative of epistemology and methodology. Some philosophical anthropologists turned away from Marxism, espoused phenomenological and existentialist ideas of the Western and Russian philosophy and, in some cases, attempted to reinterpret Marxism along the existentialist and anthropological lines. Whereas at the initial stage of the new philosophical movement humanitarian and social agenda loomed ahead as the ultimate goal of critical philosophical reflection, the second stage of the Soviet philosophical development in the second half of the twentieth century saw problems of man, human values and philosophy of culture shift into the foreground and form the focus of philosophical inquiry. As a result, close links were established with a number of leading students of literature, linguistics and history (Sergey Averintsev, Vyacheslav Ivanov, Yuri Lotman, Aron Gurevich and others).[6]

The original ideas proposed by the new Russian philosophical movement of the second half of the twentieth century can be summarized as follows:

1. Problems of logic and methodology of science were subjects of rigorous research. The analysis of the logical structure of *The Capital* by Karl Marx allowed the formulation of the general principles of the ascension from the abstract to the concrete as that method was applied by Marx himself—considerably earlier than the respective studies were undertaken by Western philosophers, e.g. Louis Althusser. Ilyenkov analyzed Marx's method departing from of the classical philosophical tradition, Hegel in the first place (see Ilyenkov 1960). Zinoviev sought to identify the various logical tools and techniques of thought used in *The Capital* (Zinoviev 2002). It is noteworthy that both Ilyenkov and Zinoviev interpreted their inquiries as falling within the domain of dialectical logic. The same was true about the early works of Georgy Shchedrovitsky, Mamardashvili and Grushin. Since dialectical logic was discredited by dogmatic interpretation, however, the term soon fell into disuse among Zinoviev and his disciples. Shchedrovitsky, for example, renamed his theory "content genetic logic" (Shchedrovitsky 1995). The relevance of Marx's methodological ideas concerning the use of an initial idealized model as the nucleus of theory development to theoretical knowledge in other fields of scientific inquiry was corroborated, particularly in contemporary physics (Kuznetsov 1975). The main feature of the logical and methodological studies of scientific knowledge undertaken by Russian philosophers at that time was their accent on the genesis of scientific theories and the logic of their subsequent development. As a result, scientific theories

came to be seen as multilayered open systems that comprised a number of relatively independent subsystems, the relations between which could not be properly described in terms of linear dependence. That understanding presented a sharp contrast to the standard hypothetico-deductive model of scientific theory dominant in the Western philosophy of science at the time, and it was ahead of the Western efforts in that field. In that context, a concept of historically changing foundations of scientific theories was developed, prominent among which was the scientific world picture instrumental in linking the theories in question to the wider realm of culture (Stepin 1992).

2. The philosophy of natural science is studied in a variety of ways: the problem of causality in contemporary science, the correspondence principle, the complementarity principle, the observationality principle, the reduction principle, the global evolutionism problem, etc.[7]
3. The study of dialectic acquired a new character. It was no longer understood as merely an ontological scheme, but as the logic of development of theoretical thought, as a method of analysis and resolution of contradictions of thinking in the traditions of Hegel and Marx. Losev proposed a kind of synthesis of Neoplatonism and Hegel as a new interpretation of dialectic. In the course of his study of creative thinking, Vladimir Bibler transformed the concept of dialectic into that of dialogic, i.e. dialogical communication of different theoretical and even cultural systems; this concept was substantiated by analysis of the materials provided by the history of science and culture. He thus attempted to offer a new interpretation of Bakhtin's ideas about the dialogical nature of culture and consciousness (Bibler 1975).
4. Ilyenkov developed an original interpretation of the ideal as residing in the forms of human activity, initially in the forms of collective activity, i.e. as a kind of objective reality contrasted with and related to individual psyche (Ilyenkov 2004, Bakhurst 1991, Oittinen 2000). This new interpretation went against the philosophical tradition that habitually linked the ideal to individual consciousness. It was also heretical from the standpoint of the official Soviet interpretation of philosophical materialism. Ilyenkov's concept resembled (somewhat) the concept of the ideal akin to the "World 3" proposed later by Karl Popper, with the important difference that, according to Ilyenkov, the ideal can only exist in the framework of human collective activity and disappears when this activity stops.

This concept influenced strongly both philosophy and human sciences, particularly psychology and, more specifically, the followers of Vygotsky's cultural-historical school: Alexei Leontiev and Vasily Davydov. On the other hand, it came under criticism, and not only from the side of the official Marxism. Some members of the new philosophical movement argued against it, too. Lifshitz, for example, offered an alternative interpretation of the ideal as having objective existence in nature itself. David Dubrovsky criticized Ilyenkov's concept from the standpoint of his philosophical analysis of the findings of neurophysiology, information theory, and cybernetics. Ilyenkov's concept of the ideal is currently a subject of active debate among the followers of the rapidly developing cultural-historical psychology (see Engeström 2005).

5. The activity approach was intensively elaborated in two ways. Firstly, it is a way of understanding man, his creative nature and his ability to transcend any given situation. Secondly, it is an important methodological principle of human sciences that made it possible to overcome the seemingly impenetrable barrier between the external and the internal subjective reality. When working on these problems, philosophers invoked Marx's early writings as well as the German philosophical tradition from Fichte to Hegel and some philosophical ideas of the twentieth century (Batishchev 1969;[8] Lektorsky 1990; Shvyrev 1970; Oittinen and Maidansky 2016). On the basis of this philosophical approach, Leontiev developed his psychological theory of activity, related to the Vygotsky tradition, into a program of theoretical and experimental research. G. Shchedrovitsky developed a "general theory of activity" he and his followers used to analyze not only the mind's cognizing activity, but the methodology of project planning and organization design (Shchedrovitsky 1995). Philosophers, methodologists, psychologists, systems technologists and other specialists who espoused that theory engaged in both theoretical debate and practical problem solving. They constituted a movement that has continued successfully until the present day. The problems of activity and the activity approach developed by Soviet philosophers and psychologists have drawn attention of some cognitive scientists who believe that this approach is the key to the further advancement of their discipline (see Clark 1997, 45).
6. Since the 1970s, as already mentioned, special attention was given to problems of philosophical anthropology and philosophy of culture. Ilyenkov concentrated on the issues of personality, imagination, ideals, freedom of will, and social alienation.[9] While initially the majority of philosophers involved in the new movement saw the principle of activity as the key to understanding man, some would later accentuate communication as the core feature of human existence, emphasizing that communication was not reducible to activity (Batishchev 1997). Existential states such as faith, hope and love came under scrutiny (Vladimir Shinkaruk). The interrelation of philosophy and natural science was the context of Frolov's analysis of the meaning of life and death (Frolov 1990). Mamardashvili proposed an anthropological theory that centered on the phenomenon of individual consciousness. He drew upon some ideas of phenomenology and existentialism in an attempt to link them to the idea of objectified ideal patterns and Marx's concept of transmuted forms of activity (Mamardashvili, Solovyov, Shvyrev 1970). Rubinshtein developed an original ontological anthropology that saw consciousness not as the opposite of being, but as an integral feature of human existence and hence part of the being which it augmented and restructured by its very presence (Rubinshtein 1997). Needless to say, that interpretation went against the form of philosophical

materialism prevailing at the time. Bibler devised a unique philosophy of culture as a means of understanding both cognition and man (Bibler 1988). That context of revived interest in the problems of man proved conducive to serious theoretical work in the field of ethics (Oleg Drobnitsky and Abdusalam Guseynov).

Zinoviev's work in social philosophy was also unique. Its uniqueness lay not only in the originality of his ideas, but also in the fact that his findings stood absolutely no chance of being published in any form under the circumstances. Zinoviev's "logical sociology" was a philosophic-scientific framework for the analysis of sociocultural and anthropological problems, including the two systems of "Communism" and "Westernism" (Zinoviev 1981). Zinoviev was exiled in 1978. His works were published in the West and banned in our country. They were not to be discussed, not to be even read. Nevertheless, they were read, albeit behind closed doors, were vehemently discussed and greatly influenced our philosophy, as well as our culture in general.

An important philosophical event proved to be the publication of Losev's eight-volume *History of Ancient Aesthetics* (Losev 1963–1994). The author, guided by his conviction that the ancient Greek, as well as the Hellenistic/Roman culture, had been essentially aesthetically and cosmologically oriented, presented an original and comprehensive panorama of Ancient philosophy that could be appropriately considered as the Russian version thereof.

The revival of philosophical activity in Russia in the 1960s and the 1970s involved also fields of philosophy other than theory of knowledge, logic and methodology of science, although to a far lesser degree. Worth mentioning here is, first of all, the upsurge in the study of the history of philosophy. The methodological aspects of these studies were elaborated by Teodor Oizerman and Aleksei Bogomolov. A series of new major works on the history of Ancient, Medieval, Renaissance, Modern and contemporary philosophy were added to the Russian historical-philosophical library (Vasily Sokolov). The various trends and schools of contemporary Western philosophy, such as Phenomenology, Existentialism, Neothomism, Philosophical Anthropology, Critical Rationalism, Pragmatism, Neopositivism, Hermeneutics, Structuralism and others, were also subject of elaborate research.[10]

An exceptional role in the philosophical life of that time was played by *Voprosy filosofii* [Questions of Philosophy], especially in the 1960s and the 1970s, when the journal, edited by Frolov with Mamardashvili as his deputy, became the center of gravity for many Soviet intellectuals, not only philosophers. The journal served as the platform for discussion of the relationship between philosophy and natural science, as well as the problems of ecology, culture, education, and history (in short all the controversial issues of the time). Another salient event that transcended the professional boundaries and had a wider cultural effect was the publication of the 5-volume *Encyclopedia of Philosophy* in the 1960s and the 1970s. It was an attempt, uncharacteristic of the time, to give a comprehensive and more or less objective account not only of the Marxist understanding of the philosophical problems, but also of their non-Marxist interpretations. The *Encyclopedia* made available an enormous amount of historical-philosophical data. It offered information, indeed for the first time in decades, about Russian religious philosophers, whose ideas were not open for academic discussion. The *Encyclopedia* entries were resonant theoretical articles written by Ilyenkov, Zinoviev, Mamardashvili, Batishchev, Averintsev, Levada and others. Several hundred entries were authored by Losev. Granted the time was more liberal and more favorable than before, a project of that scale and character was still a challenge. And this challenge was successfully met. Though officially headed by the dogmatic editor-in-chief Fyodor Konstantinov, the team of enthusiasts that included the deputy editor-in-chief Alexander Spirkin, editors Renata Galtseva, Zakhar Kamensky, Yuri Popov and others succeeded in doing the seemingly impossible.

A number of prominent Russian philosophers of the time were initially against Marxism. It was the case with Losev and Bakhtin. Zinoviev broke with Marxism at an early stage and developed into a vehement critic of the Soviet regime. However, for all their repugnance for the official Marxism-Leninism, the majority of the philosophers active in the Renaissance movement of the second half of the twentieth century still believed that Marx had proposed a number of ideas worth considering and developing. It was not before the 1970s or the 1980s that some of them went beyond Marxism. Consider, for example, Batishchev, originally one of the most promising interpreters of Marx's early humanist ideas, or Mamardashvili, whose concept of "transmuted forms" was easily traced to *The Capital*. Rubinshtein, Bibler, and Petrov followed suit, but Ilyenkov, Lifshitz, Kedrov, Frolov, and Kopnin remained convinced Marxists, even though the authorities viewed their Marxism with deep suspicion.

It is worth mentioning, though, that practically all notable Russian philosophers of the time, whether they saw themselves as Marxists or not, were subjected to harsh ideological criticism bordering on persecution. For any original philosophical concept or theory was in danger of being accused of heretical "revisionism." The ideological bosses suspected disguised criticism of the leadership and the regime—not without reason. Losev served several years in a labor camp and was denied the right to publish his philosophical writings for decades. In the 1970s he saw his major work on the philosophy of Vladimir Solovyov banned. Bakhtin was in exile for a long time and only started to gain recognition in the 1970s. Rubinshtein suffered persecution. Kedrov would be regularly dismissed from his posts and receive party reprimands. Zinoviev was expelled from the party, sacked from his job, deprived of all his titles and decorations and finally exiled from the USSR. Kopnin, Director of the Institute of Philosophy, died at the age of 49 in consequence of a disease aggravated by unbridled ideological bullying. Frolov had to withstand squalls of criticism both as the author of "heretical" texts and the editor-in-chief of the "revisionist" journal *Voprosy filosofii*. Ilyenkov paid all sorts of party penalties and was fired from the Moscow State University. His premature death was partly due to ideological harassment. Mamardashvili first lost his job as deputy editor-in-chief of *Voprosy filosofii*, then was sacked from the Institute of History of Natural Science and Technology, after which he moved to Tbilisi. Shchedrovitsky and Petrov were expelled from the party and had employment problems. Erik Yudin spent several years in a labor camp. Bibler, always under suspicion, had to change jobs many times. Lifshitz was harassed throughout his life. Batishchev was often on the brink of being expelled from the Institute of Philosophy. Asmus was suspected of all sorts of ideological sins, both on the account of his own writings and because of his friendship with the disfavored poet Boris Pasternak. Vladimir Smirnov lived a difficult life. The official attitude toward the Tartu-Moscow semiotic school headed by Lotman had always been that of apprehension.

Practically all philosophers of the new movement had problems publishing their works. Many left numerous manuscripts to be published posthumously and usually after times had changed. Some of the unpublished writings would be available to friends and disciples, distributed privately, discussed at seminars. Some materials would circulate in the form of tape-recorded lectures.

It is worthwhile to emphasize, however, that genuine (non-official) philosophical life was quite intensive despite the gruesome ideological situation. In my recollection those were the years of new ideas, of debates, of reading, both interested and critical, of each other's writings, of common seminars and conferences, intensive contacts with men of science and culture. Philosophy was, by no means, an exoteric sphere, as some people nowadays wrongly believe it to have been. The philosophy I write about here interacted in a lively manner with leading representatives of natural and human sciences, of culture in general. The former have already been mentioned; the latter included such notable figures as Ernst Neizvestny, Yuri Lyubimov, Nazim Hikmet, etc.

One important feature of the Russian philosophical life of that time is worth mentioning. The philosophers this paper is about were keenly aware of having belonged to a common movement that was in opposition to the official philosophy of the Soviet era (as represented by people like Mark Mitin, Pavel Yudin, Fyodor Konstantinov and others). On the other hand, those above became themselves engaged in sharp polemics with each other: Ilyenkov with Zinoviev; Shchedrovitsky with them both; Batishchev with Bibler; Mamardashvili with Ilyenkov and Batishchev; Lifshitz with Mamardashvili and Ilyenkov, etc. It is sometimes questioned whether it is appropriate to view thinkers so different and in a seemingly perpetual opposition to each other, as belonging to a common movement. But what is the history of philosophy if not an unending debate, an eternal polemic about the most important problems of human existence? Philosophy has never had and will never have just one true theory, one correct solution to any of its problems. Throughout its history philosophy has asked the same questions and discussed the same problems for which different cultures and different times suggested their specific interpretations and developed their specific approaches. The Aristotle versus Plato controversy was, in a sense, won by them both, because the entire Western philosophy was born out of that controversy. The matter is not whether this or that approach is right or wrong, the matter is whether it is capable of influencing the existing cognitive and cultural practices, whether it meets the intellectual challenges of its time and can be incorporated into this or that research or activity program. True, not every philosophical theory is that lucky. But as far as the activists of the new Soviet philosophical movement of the second half of the twentieth century are concerned, every one of them can be said to have had a notable impact on various fields of science and culture, including theory of natural science, psychology, cultural studies, history of science, and theory and practice of education. Their followers were not limited to the professional field of philosophy. They founded philosophical schools, many of which continue into the present. Their ideas have been operational in contemporary philosophical debates.

Three names are prominent in the history of Russian literature: Leo Tolstoy, Fyodor Dostoevsky and Ivan Turgenev. The three writers were not fond of and did not particularly cherish each other. But each one of them is a classic without whom Russian culture would not have become what it is. The same can be said about the notable Russian philosophers of the second half of the twentieth century.[11]

I would like to emphasize once more that the ideas proposed by our philosophers in those years, the theories elaborated by them did not die with their time, as is sometimes asserted by people not properly acquainted with the genuine history of our philosophy. I am fully convinced that many of them are truly topical and quite capable of counteracting with the approaches proposed by the world philosophy nowadays.

## NOTES

1. The "philosophers' ship" (or "philosophers' steamer") is a neologism used by historians to dub the ships carrying more than 160 Russian intellectuals expelled from Russia at Lenin's decree. Transported from Petrograd (modern-day St. Petersburg) to the seaport of Stettin in Germany in the fall of 1922, most of them never came back spending the rest of their lives in exile. The list of the deported individuals included such thinkers as Nikolai Berdyaev, Semyon Frank, Ivan Ilyin, Nikolai Lossky, Fyodor Stepun, and other great Russian philosophers whom Lenin considered the dangerous ideological opponents of the new Soviet state. For more details about the 1922–1923 deportation of Russian intellectuals, see Chamberlain 2007.—Ed.
2. It is very important to take this fact into account. Otherwise, one cannot understand what really took place in Russian philosophy in the Soviet time.
3. The proper study of this period has just started. See Lektorsky 1998; Lektorsky and Stepin 2007–2015.
4. Among Ilyenkov's initial disciples, the most prominent were Genrikh Batishchev, Vladislav Lektorsky, Lev Naumenko, Vadim Mezhuyev, and Yuri Davydov. Georgy Shchedrovitsky, Merab Mamardashvili, Boris Grushin, and some others belonged to those of immediate Zinoviev's disciples.
5. Ilyenkov, Zinoviev, Bibler, Batishchev, and Shchedrovitsky represented Moscow schools. Additionally, also in Moscow, there was the systems movement with such key figures as Igor Blauberg, Erik Yudin, Vadim Sadovsky and others. Kiev was the seat of Kopnin school; Minsk—of Stepin school, etc.
6. I refer to professional philosophers and professional students of humanities here, not to philosophizing authors of literary and other such texts, whether published or unpublished.
7. For details on these and other central ideas developed in the Russian philosophy of science of this period see Vyacheslav Stepin's essay (Ch. 7) in the present volume. Among those Russian thinkers who represented this specific branch of philosophical inquiry in the period of interest are Bonifaty Kedrov, Mikhail Omelyanovsky, Nikolai Ovchinnikov, Ivan Frolov, and others (see Kedrov 1963, Omelyanovsky 1973, Ovchinnikov 1966, Frolov 1965).

8. Batishchev's article on the activist essence of man in which the author argued that creative critical inquiry allowed of no external authority evoked a furious response of none other than Mikhail Suslov, the Secretary of the CPSU Central Committee and the official party ideologue. The consequences were grave: it was only with great difficulty that Batishchev escaped being ousted from the Institute of Philosophy.
9. An English translation of Ilyenkov's article was included in a collection of papers edited by Nikolaus Lobkowicz and published in the USA in 1967 (Ilyenkov 1967). In that article Ilyenkov argued that alienation was not a feature of capitalism alone, but existed under socialism, too, which made Ilyenkov the object of ideological persecution.
10. See, for example works by Piama Gaidenko, Erikh Solovyov, and Nelli Motroshilova.
11. I remember that in 1954 when A. Zinoviev's candidate (PhD) dissertation was discussed at the department of logic of the Moscow State University Faculty of Philosophy, Ilyenkov who had recently defended his dissertation on a similar topic (by that time Ilyenkov's defense had not been yet approved by the National Higher Attestation Commission, responsible for awarding of advanced academic degrees; as far as I remember, it took the Commission some two years to come with its approval) attended the discussion and supported Zinoviev, even though Ilyenkov's and Zinoviev's approaches to the interpretation of the logical structure of *The Capital* were radically different. Furthermore, Ilyenkov commended Zinoviev for "scholarly audacity." Zinoviev, on his part, defended Ilyenkov when half a year later the Faculty's Academic Council discussed Ilyenkov's and Korovikov's heretical theses on the subject of philosophy (for details see David Bakhurst's essay (Ch. 15) in the present volume). Being at that time a PhD student in the Sector of Dialectical Materialism of which the two philosophers were members, I also recall numerous occasions on which Ilyenkov and Zinoviev would have a pleasant conversation in a café immediately after sharp panel discussions at the Institute of Philosophy at RAS.

## BIBLIOGRAPHY

Bakhurst, David. 1991. *Consciousness and Revolution in Soviet Philosophy: From the Bolsheviks to Evald Ilyenkov*. Cambridge: Cambridge University Press.

Batishchev, Genrikh S. 1969. "Deyatel'naya suchost' cheloveka kak filosofsky printsip" [Activity Essence of the Human Being as a Philosophical Principle], *Problema cheloveka v sovremennoy filosofii* [The Problem of the Human Being in Contemporary Philosophy]. Moscow. Mysl'.

Batishchev, Genrikh S. 1997. *Vvedenie v dialektiku tvorchestva*. [Introduction to the Dialectic of Creativity]. Sankt-Peterburg: RHSK.

Bibler, Vladimir S. 1975. *Myshlenie kak tvorchestvo (Vvedenie v logiku myslennogo dialoga)*. [Thinking as Creativity (Introduction to the Logic of a Mental Dialogue)]. Moscow: Izdatel'stvo politicheskoi literatury.

Bibler, Vladimir S. 1988. *Nravstvennost'. Kul'tura. Sovremennost'*. [Morality. Culture. Contemporaneity]. Moscow: Politizdat.

Biggart, John, Gloveli, Georgii, Jassour, Avraham (eds). 1998. *Bogdanov and His Work: A Guide to the Published and unpublished Works of Alexander A. Bogdanov (Malinovski). 1873–1928*. Aldershot: Ashgate.

Chamberlain, Lesley. 2007. *Lenin's Private War: The Voyage of the Philosophy Steamer and the Exile of the Intelligentsia*, New York: St Martin's Press.

Clark, Andy. 1997. *Being There: Putting Brain, Body and World Together Again*. Cambridge, MA: MIT Press.

Engeström, Yrjö. 2005. *Developmental Work Research: Expanding Activity Theory in Practice*. Berlin: Lehmanns Media.

Frolov, Ivan T. 1965. *Ocherki metodologii biologicheskogo issledovanija. (Sistema metodov biologii)*. [Sketches on Methodology of a Biological Research. (The System of the Biological Methods)]. Moscow: Mysl'.

Frolov, Ivan T. 1990. *Man, Science, Humanism: A New Synthesis*. Buffalo, N-Y. Prometheus Books.

Ilyenkov, Evald V. 1960. *Dialektika abstraktnogo i konkretnogo v "Kapitale" K. Marksa*. [Dialectics of the Abstract and the Concrete in Marx's *Capital*]. Moscow, Nauka.

Ilyenkov, Evald V. 1967. "From the Marxist Point of View." In *Marx and the Western World*, edited by N. Lobkovich. Notre Dame: University of Notre Dame Press.

Ilyenkov, Evald V. 2014. "Dialectics of the Ideal." In *Dialectics of the Ideal: Evald Ilyenkov and Creative Soviet Marxism*, translated by A. Levant, edited by A. Levant and V. Oittinen, 25–78. Leiden: Brill.

Kedrov, Bonifaty M. 1963. *Edinstvo dialektiki, logiki i teorii poznanija*. [The Unity of Dialectics, Logic and Theory of Knowledge]. Moscow: Gospolitizdat.

Kuznetsov, Ivan V. 1975. *Izbrannye trudy po metodologii fiziki* [Selected Works on Methodology of Physics]. Moscow: Mysl'.Lektorsky, Vladislav A. (ed.). 1998. *Filosofiia ne konchaetsia* [Philosophy Does Not End], vol. 1–2. Moscow: ROSSPEN.

Lektorsky, Vladislav A. 1980. *Sub"ekt, ob"ekt, poznanie*. [Subject, Object, Cognition]. Moscow: Nauka. [Translation: Lektorsky Vladislav A. 1984. *Subject, Object, Cognition*. Moscow: Progress publishers.]

Lektorsky, Vladislav A. (ed.). 1990. *Activity: Theories, Methodology, and Problems*. Orlando: Paul Deutsch.

Lektorsky, Vladislav A. (ed.). 1998. *Filosofiya ne konchaetsya* [Philosophy Does Not End], vol. 1–2. Moscow: ROSSPEN.

Lektorsky, Vladislav A. and Stepin, Vyacheslav S. (eds.). 2007–2015. *Filosofiia Rossii vtoroi poloviny XX veka* [Russian Philosophy in the Second Half of the Twentieth Century]. 22 vols. Moscow: ROSSPEN.

Losev, Alexei F. 1963–1988. *Istoriia Antichnoy Estetiki*. In 8 vols. [History of Antique Aesthetics]. Moscow: Vysshaja shkola, Mysl.

Mamardashvili, Merab K. 1968. *Formy i soderzhanie myshlenija* [Forms and Content of Thinking]. Moscow: Vyschaja Shkola.

Mamardashvili, Merab K., Solovyov, Erikh Yu., Shvyrev, Vladimir S. 1970. "Klassicheskaya i sovremennaya burzuaznaya filosofiya: opyt epistemologicheskogo sopostovleniya. Chast' 1" [Classic and Contemporary Bourgeois Philosophy: An Attempt of Epistemological Comparison. Part 1]. *Voprosy filosofii*, (12): 23–28.

Oittinen, Vesa (ed). 2000. *Evald Ilyenkov's Philosophy Revisited. Proceedings of the Symposium in Helsinki, 7th–8th September 1999*. Helsinki: Kikimora Publishers.

Oittinen, Vesa, Maidansky, Andrey (eds.). 2016. *The Practical Essence of Man. The "Activity Approach" in Late Soviet Philosophy*. Leiden, The Netherlands: Brill.

Omelyanovky, Mikhail E. 1973. *Dialectica v sovremennoi fizike* [Dialectics in Contemporary Physics]. Moscow: Nauka.
Ovchinnikov, Nikolai F. 1966. *Printsipy sokhranenija*. [Principles of Conservation]. Moscow: Nauka.
Rubinshtein, Sergei L. 1997. *Izbranny filosofsko-psihologicheskie trudy. Osnovy ontologii, logiki i psikhologii.* [Selected Philosophical and Psychological Works. Fundamentals of Ontology, Logic and Psychology]. Moscow: Nauka.
Shchedrovitsky, Georgy P. 1996. *Filosofiya. Nauka. Metodologija* [Philosophy. Science. Methodology]. Moscow: School of Cultural Policy.
Spektor, Alexander, Denischenko, Irina M., et al. 2017. "Bakhtin Forum: The Dark and Radiant Bakhtin. Wartime Notes," *Slavic and East European Journal*, 21 (2): 233–298.
Stepin, Vyacheslav S. 1996. "Genetically-Constructive Ways of Theory Building." In *Philosophical Logic and Logical Philosophy. Essays in Honor of Vladimir A. Smirnov*, edited by Peter I. Bystrov and Vadim N. Sadovsky, 17–31. Dordrecht: Springer.
Zinoviev, Alexander A. 1981. *Kommunizm kak real'nost'*. [Communism as Reality]. Lausanne: l'Age D'Homme.
Zinoviev Alexander A. 2002. *Voskhozhdenie ot abstraktnogo k konkretnomu (na materiale "Kapitala" K. Marksa* [Ascension from the Abstract to the Concrete (On the Material of "Kapital" by K. Marx)]. Moscow: Institut filosofii Rossiskoi Akademii Nauk.

CHAPTER TWO

# Main Configurations of Russian Thought in the Post-Stalin Epoch

MIKHAIL N. EPSTEIN

The fact that one can annihilate a philosophy . . . or that one can prove that a philosophy annihilates itself is of little consequence. If it's really philosophy, then, like the phoenix, it will always rise again from its own ashes.

— Friedrich Schlegel. *Athenaeum. Fragments*, trans. Peter Firchow, 103.

The more total society becomes, the greater the reification of the mind and the more paradoxical its effort to escape reification on its own.

— Theodor Adorno. *Prisms*, trans. Samuel and Shierry Weber, 34

SOCRATES: The ideal society we have described can never grow into a reality or see the light of day, and there will be no end to the troubles of states, or indeed of humanity itself, till philosophers become kings in this world, or till those we now call kings and rulers really and truly become philosophers.

— Plato, *The Republic*, trans. H. D. P. Lee, 473 C10

That kings should become philosophers, or philosophers kings, is not likely to happen; nor would it be desirable, since the possession of power invariably debases the free judgment of reason. It is, however, indispensable that a king—or a kingly, i.e. self-ruling, people—should not suppress philosophers but leave them the right of public utterance.

— I. Kant. *On Eternal Peace*. Second Supplement, trans. Karl Popper

It's a property of the Russian people to indulge in philosophy. . . . The fate of the philosopher in Russia is painful and tragic.

— Nikolai Berdyaev. *The Russian Idea*

## IDEAS AGAINST IDEOCRACY. PLATO–MARXISM

The academic community in the West tends to be suspicious of the very phenomenon of Russian philosophy. At best, it is categorized as "ideology" or "social thought." But what is philosophy?

There is no simple and universal definition, and many thinkers consider it impossible to formulate one. The most credible attempt seems to be a nominalistic reference: philosophy is that with which Plato and Aristotle, Kant and Hegel were occupied. Perhaps, the best-known and most widely cited—if slightly eccentric—definition belongs to A. N. Whitehead:

> The safest general characterization of the European philosophical tradition is that it consists of a series of footnotes to Plato. I do not mean the systematic scheme of thought, which scholars have doubtfully extracted from his writings. I allude to the wealth of general ideas scattered through them . . . European philosophy is a series of footnotes to Plato. (Whitehead 1979, 39)

If this is true, Russian philosophy must be viewed as an integral part of the Western intellectual heritage, since it provides perhaps the most elaborate footnotes to Plato's most mature and comprehensive dialogues: the *Republic* and the *Laws*. Questions of social ethics and political philosophy, of an individual's relationship to the State, of adequate knowledge and virtuous behavior, of wisdom and power, of religious and aesthetic values, of ideas and ideals as guidelines for human life—all of these are central to Russian philosophy and exemplify its continuing relevance to the Western tradition. Moreover, the very status of ideas in Russian philosophy mirrors Plato's vision of them as ontological entities, "laws," or ideal principles—in distinction from mere epistemological units, the tools of cognition. In discussing Russian philosophy, especially that of its Soviet period, we will inevitably consider the practical fate of various Platonic conceptions as we explore the final outcome of an ideocratic utopia, wherein philosophy was designated to rule the republic.

Accordingly, Russian philosophy deserves an honored place in the Western intellectual history. Nowhere have Plato's teachings on the relationship of ideas to the foundation of a State been incarnated so vigorously and on such a grandiose scale as in communist Russia. To *philosophize reality*, to transform it into a transparent kingdom of ideas was considered the goal of thinking. This is why thought itself, in the very moment of its triumph, became a prisoner in the Crystal Palace that Soviet ideocracy erected on a philosophical foundation. In the Soviet State more than anywhere else in history, philosophy became a supreme legal and political institution, acquiring the power of a transpersonal, universal reason, which in its unrestricted dominion was equivalent to madness—since, being a State philosophy, it ruthlessly victimized individual thinkers. Russia has suffered not from a lack, but from an excess of philosophy. In other countries the supreme value and highest level of authority is assigned to religious beliefs, or to economic profits, but in communist Russia, it was philosophy that served as the ultimate criterion of truth and the foundation of all political and economic transformations. Loyalty to the teachings of dialectical and historical materialism was the prerequisite of civil loyalty and professional success. Neither worker nor peasant, scientist nor politician, writer nor artist, could succeed in their respective fields without a specific philosophical preparation in "the dialectical forms of matter's motion" or "the ABC of historical materialism."

If we try to isolate the central trend of Russian philosophy that can be compared with that of "rationalism" in French philosophy or "empiricism" in English philosophy, this would be "totalism." Such diverse Russian thinkers as Pyotr Chaadaev and Vissarion Belinsky, Ivan Kireevsky and Alexander Herzen, Vladimir Solovyov and Vasily Rozanov all put forward the category of "integrity," "wholeness," "totality" (*tsel'nost'*, *tselostnost'*) or "total-unity" (*vseedinstvo*), which presupposes, first of all, the unity of knowledge and existence, of reason and faith, intellectual and social life. Gregory Skovoroda (1722–1794) who is often dubbed "the first original Russian-Ukrainian thinker," expressed the following credo in his prayer to God on sending a new Socrates to Russia:

> I believe that knowledge should not be limited to the high-priests of science and scholarship, who stuff themselves to overflowing with it, but should enter into the life of the whole people. (Skovoroda 1987, 17–18)

Ivan Kireevsky (1806–1856), a founder of Russian Slavophilism, sought to inaugurate "an independent philosophy corresponding to the basic principles of ancient Russian culture and capable of subjecting the divided culture of the West to the integrated consciousness of believing reason" (Kireevsky 1987, 213). Characteristically, Kireevsky derived this tendency of Russian philosophy from Plato's heritage, as opposed to "the mind of Western man [which] seems to have a special kinship with Aristotle," that is, with "one-sided abstract rationalism" (ibid, 182). Invoking the legacy of Eastern Christian thought, Kireevsky asserts that:

> in Greek thinkers we do not notice a special predilection for Aristotle, but, on the contrary, the majority of them overtly prefer Plato . . . probably because Plato's very mode of thinking presents more integrity *(tsel'nost')* in the exercises of mind, more warmth and harmony in the speculative activity of reason. That is why virtually the same relationship that we notice between the two philosophers of antiquity [Aristotle and Plato] existed between the philosophy of the Latin world as it was elaborated in scholasticism, and the spiritual philosophy that we find in the writers of the Eastern Church, the philosophy that was especially clearly expressed by the Holy Fathers who lived after the defection of [Catholic] Rome. (Ibid., 272)

This inclination to relate Russian thought to Plato in contrast to Aristotle became a hallmark of the Russian intellectual tradition, which assumed that "in Plato's teaching, religion and philosophy are in the closest contact, but already in Aristotle's system philosophy breaks off with religion definitively" (Abramov 1979, 222).

This Platonic tendency to integrate philosophical and religious teachings and to implement them politically culminated in twentieth century Russia. In discussing Russian philosophy, especially the Soviet period, we have inevitably to consider the practical fate of "integrative" Platonic conceptions as we explore the final outcome of an ideocratic utopia, in which philosophy was designated to rule the republic as the supreme religious and political authority.

One might even say that the philosophy of the Soviet epoch is the final stage of the development and embodiment of Plato's ideas in the Western world. During this stage, the project of ideocracy came to a complete realization and exhausted itself. In a certain sense, Russian philosophy of the past two hundred years both summarizes and creates a gloss on more than two thousand years of the Platonic tradition and points the way for a return to foundations that are not susceptible to idealistic and ideological perversions.

From the 1920s through the 1940s, the tsardom of communist ideas succeeded in equating itself with social reality, but beginning with the mid 1950s, stimulated by Khrushchev's denunciations of Stalin in 1956, this "ideal republic" increasingly revealed its illusory quality and its sharp discrepancy with reality. Religious and personalist philosophy, structuralism and culturology, the philosophy of national spirit—all of these were attempts to de-ideologize social life and let it take root in some authentic reality. Ultimately, Russian philosophy, in the transition to its post-Soviet stage, came to be characterized by conceptualism, a style of thought that ironically reproduces and exaggerates the world of abstract ideas in order to demonstrate their artificial and chimerical nature. All that remained of the principle of ideocracy by the late 1980s was a museum of obsolete ideas, a carnival side-show of ideological oddities. A relatively short period of seventy years sums up a two-millennial adventure of Western thought that followed Plato's search for the world of pure ideas. Among these footnotes to Plato, Soviet philosophy appears to the attentive eye as the final entry, signifying "The End."

What was the role of Marxism in the Platonic drama of Russian philosophy? Marxism, which deduces all ideas from the economic base of society, would seem to be diametrically opposed to Platonism. But let us remember that Marxism is nothing else but a reversal of Hegelian idealism, the final moment in the self-development of the Absolute Idea. What is principally new in Hegel, as compared with Plato, is the progressive historical development of the Idea, but the end of this process is postulated as the universal State, presumably conceived on the model of the Prussian monarchy, which embraces the totality of the self-cognizant mind. Both Platonic and Hegelian idealism culminate with the concept of the ideal State. Although Marx removed this ideal from the causality of the historical process, it remains in his system as a teleological motive and grows into a vision of a future communist society.[1]

Plato, Hegel, and Marx represent three stages in the development of idealism in its progressive symbiosis with social engineering: (1) the supernatural world of ideas, (2) the manifestation of the Absolute Idea in history, and (3) the transformation of history by the force of ideas. For Plato, ideas are abstracted to a transcendental realm. For Hegel, the Idea is already ingrained as the alpha and omega of the historical process: it generates, and at the same time consummates, history in the course of its progressive self-awareness. Marx abolishes the idea as the alpha of history in order to emphasize the omega-point: the prospect of a historical culmination of unified humanity in the transparent kingdom of ideas, the self-government of collective reason.

Moreover, Marxism potentially proves more staunchly idealistic than even Platonism. According to the Greek philosopher, the world of ideas exists in and of itself, without necessarily demanding historical embodiment. For Marx, ideas are inseparable from the material process and are greedy for realization and implementation. In his own words, "theory itself becomes a material force when it has seized the masses" (Marx 1972, 18). The message of "militant materialism" (Lenin's term), as realized in Russia by Lenin and his disciples, was that the power of "progressive" ideas should not be *abstracted from* but rather *attracted to* material life, even subordinating and transforming the economic base: hence, the institution of five-year plans that subordinated the entire development of the country to ideal projections. Whereas ideas in Plato and Hegel still soared above the earth, constituting a separate sphere of Supreme Mind or Absolute Spirit, in Soviet Marxism they were grounded in the foundation of material life, from heavy industry to everyday reality, and from the rituals of party purges to ceremonial cleansings of neighborhoods. The ruling ideology would not forgive the slightest flaw or deviation from the purity of ideas. Because ideas had descended into the substance of Being, they demanded the complete submission of every person at every moment of his or her life. Soviet materialism proved to be an instrument of militant idealism, craving ever newer sacrifices for the altar of sacred ideas.

For these reasons, the dominant intellectual movement of the Soviet epoch should be identified not just as Marxism, but as Marxist Platonism, an idealism that asserts itself as the regulative principle of material life. If Plato, proceeding from idealist assumptions, deduced the system of the communist State, then Marx, proceeding from communist assumptions, deduced a system of severe ideocracy that was realized through the efforts of his most consistent and determined Russian followers. Materialism became an ideology, and the very phrase "materialist ideology" came to sound perfectly natural to Soviet citizens. No less natural is the term "Marxist Platonism." Platonism is the underside of Marxism, and the eventual collapse of the Soviet ideocratic State can be viewed as a death sentence of both these *-isms*.

## THREE PHILOSOPHICAL AWAKENINGS

Further we will focus on the period from the apex of the Soviet ideocratic empire, which by the middle of the twentieth century had included one third of the world's population and established itself as "the global socialist system," to its downfall in 1991. These dates are not just political signposts, but demarcate an important stage of Russian philosophical development that remains uncharted in the West.

Russian philosophy of the first half of the twentieth century has been explored more or less systematically in the extensive historical surveys of Nikolai Lossky, Vasily Zenkovsky, Sergei Levitsky, and Frederick Copleston.[2] Regardless of the time of their completion, these narratives end abruptly in the middle of the twentieth century, as if to imply that nothing significant occurred thereafter. The last names mentioned in these four most comprehensive surveys are those of Sergei Bulgakov (1871–1944), Vladimir Lossky (1903–1958), Lev Shestov (1866–1938), and Boris Vysheslavtsev (1877–1954), respectively.

Typically, the discussions of post-revolutionary Russian philosophy focus on two elements: (1) the religious and idealistic thought of emigre authors, and (2) dialectical materialism in the Soviet Union. The third major constituent—non-Marxist thought within the Soviet Union—remains mostly ignored. It is true that official Marxism strived to subsume all independent philosophical thought in the domestic arena. Nevertheless, even in the 1920s–1940s, in the period of the hardest ideological pressure, many brilliant thinkers managed to write and occasionally to publish substantial portions of their work. Besides professional philosophers, this list includes scientists, writers, literary scholars, some of whom are celebrated in their respective fields.[3] A coherent history of Russian *non-Marxist and non-emigre* thought of this epoch has yet to be written.

This deficiency becomes even more striking with regard to the second half of the twentieth century. The cohort of Russian "philosophers in exile" almost disintegrated with the deaths of the last survivors of the pre-revolutionary Silver Age (Nikolai Berdyaev, Dmitry Merezhkovsky, Semyon Frank and others). Consequently, almost all existing histories of Russian philosophy after the mid-twentieth century are restricted to "Sovietology," exploring the official ideology and doctrine of dialectical materialism and its various thematic divisions and internal debates.[4] Non-Marxist philosophy, with rare exceptions,[5] is simply ignored or relegated to adjacent, narrow fields, such as aesthetics or poetics, where Marxism had not established well defined views. The universal recognition of Mikhail Bakhtin, whose works represent a small but significant part of the Russian philosophical scene, has failed to bring attention to the coherent development of Soviet non-Marxist thought.

Even the most recent investigations of certain trends, such as Cosmism, Eurasianism, or Orthodox thought, concentrate their historical narratives on preceding periods, especially the nineteenth and first half of the twentieth centuries. For example, George Young (Young 2012) focuses mainly on Nikolai Fyodorov (1828–1903). In her book, Marlène Larue concentrates on the first generation of Eurasianist thinkers of the 1920s (see Laruelle 2012). In his book on modern orthodox thinkers, the prominent scholar Andrew Louth only briefly surveys late twentieth-century authors Aleksandr Men' and Sergei Averintsev (see Louth 2015).

Only in the past few years has late Soviet philosophy begun to attract scholarly attention in Russia. This new interest has so far not produced any comprehensive systematic research and is limited to collections of articles on individual thinkers, issues, and trends (Lektorsky 1998, 2014; Motroshilova 2012).

Paradoxically, even the newest investigations of Russian contemporary philosophy tend to ignore the late Soviet period. Thus, Alyssa DeBlasio provides a persuasive analysis of Russian thought of the 1990s–2000s (DeBlasio 2014). Meanwhile, the preceding period of the 1950s–1980s remains mostly on the margins of contemporary research. This circumstance underscores the need to restore the meaning of this period as the crucial historical and intellectual link between Russian philosophy of the first half of the twentieth century (mostly idealist or Marxist) and its latest post-Soviet development (mostly pluralistic-liberal or archaic-nationalist).

The last period of the Soviet ideocracy, approximately from the early 1960s through the late 1980s, can be characterized as a period of "philosophical awakening," to use the felicitous expression of the theologian Georgy Florovsky (1893–1979):

> Such awakening is usually preceded by a more or less complicated historical fate, the abundant and long historical experience and ordeal, which now becomes the

object of interpretation and discussion. Philosophical life begins as a new mode or a new stage of national existence . . . One can feel in the generation of that epoch some irresistible attraction to philosophy, a philosophical passion and thirst, a kind of magical gravitation toward philosophical themes and issues. (Florovsky, 1988, 234, 235)

Florovsky refers here to the *first* "philosophical awakening" which happened in the 1830s and 1840s and affected the generation of Chaadaev as well as the early Westernizers and Slavophiles, such as Belinsky, Herzen, Bakunin, Khomiakov, the brothers Aksakov, and the brothers Kireevsky.

Russia's *second* philosophical awakening occurred in the first two decades of the twentieth century, in particular, following the unsuccessful revolution of 1905 and the disenchantment of the intellectual elite with populism, Marxism and other socialist theories, marked by primitive materialism. This intellectual renaissance is associated with the philosophical collection *Signposts* (1909) and the writings of Merezhkovsky, Rozanov, Berdyaev, Bulgakov, Frank, Florensky, Shestov, and other outstanding figures of the so-called Silver Age.

Finally, after the soporific years of Soviet materialist scholasticism, the *third* philosophical awakening fell on the 1970s–1980s. The new renaissance took its origins in the period of Khrushchev's "thaw" (the mid-1950s through the early 1960s), which engendered, mostly unintentionally, new trends of thought implicitly independent of, or even opposed to official Marxism, leading to the latter's radical transformation. In this period, forbidden philosophical works were circulated in various forms of "samizdat" ("self-publishing"), "tamizdat" ("there-publishing," i.e. in the West) and "togdaizdat" ("then-publishing," i.e. in prerevolutionary Russia). They conveyed a profound charm that could not be explained in terms of "truth or falsity," "persuasiveness or dubiousness." The very touch of these books, by Berdyaev, Shestov, and others, instilled in the readers the joy and mystery of self-reflexive existence. According to Florovsky, before the first philosophical awakening, in the 1810s–1820s, it was poetry—that of Zhukovsky, Batyushkov, Pushkin, and Griboedov—that was on the top of cultural priorities and played the role of spiritual magnet for the educated society. The same became applicable to Soviet intelligentsia who in the late 1950s–early 1960s was obsessed with the poetry of Evtushenko, Voznesensky, Akhmadulina, and Okudzhava. By the 1970s, however, poets lost their influence to thinkers and scholars, such as Mikhail Bakhtin, Alexei Losev, Yury Lotman, Sergei Averintsev, and Merab Mamardashvili. Florovsky has coined a formula for this process of maturation: "From the *poetical* stage Russian cultural-creative consciousness passes into the *philosophical* stage" (Florovsky 1988, 236).

In the Soviet Union, the term "philosophy" was reserved for orthodox Marxism-Leninism. Officially the philosophy was regarded as a "party discipline": only members of Communist party and highly ranked Komsomol leaders were eligible for enrollment at philosophical departments of Soviet universities. Therefore, many original Russian thinkers emerged from or retreated into different fields of the humanities that were relatively more free from ideological pressure: literary studies, aesthetics, linguistics, ethnology, and psychology. As Gary Morson and Caryl Emerson remark in their study of Bakhtin, it often happens that, "in Russia, criticism and theory become the practice of philosophy by other means" (Morson and Emerson 1990, 37). Even in reference to pre-revolutionary Russia, the term "philosophy" usually covered a broad range of social, religious, ethical, and literary thought and cannot be reduced to a narrow academic discipline. The greatest Russian thinkers of the nineteenth century, including Petr Chaadaev, Alexander Herzen, Mikhail Bakunin, Fyodor Dostoevsky, Leo Tolstoy, Nikolai Fyodorov, Konstantin Leontiev, and Vladimir Solovyev, were writers, journalists, critics, politicians, and librarians, but not university professors or academic scholars.[6] This is also true of the twentieth-century thinkers, which explains my preference for the broader term "philosophical thought," or even the transliteration of the Russian word "*filosofia,*" to designate the broad conceptual scope of these intellectual practices, as distinct from the more specialized field of academic *philosophy*. "Filosofia," an outcome of the Russian spiritual tradition, encompasses various fields of the humanities and cultural theories insofar as they contribute to universal intellectual systems and respond to the most general and "absolute" demands of the human mind and spirit.

## MAJOR TRENDS OF SOVIET THOUGHT IN THE POST-STALIN EPOCH

Over the period of forty years, since Stalin's death to the death of the Soviet Union (1953–1991), several "philosophical" schools have emerged to challenge the ideocratic principles of Soviet Marxism, which itself has undergone considerable changes. Below, I will briefly outline eight major trends in Russian thought of the 1950s–1980s.

### 1. *Humanized and Nationalized Marxism*

One vector of transformation was the infusion of nationalism into Marxism, initiated by Stalin himself in his long article "Marxism and the Questions of Linguistics" (1950). Stalin abolished the class categories of traditional Marxism in favor of a notion of national unity, as exemplified in the integrity of the national language. This tendency resurfaced in the 1980s, with the increasing rapprochement of official Marxism and grassroots, nationalist ideology, which later grew into a political alliance of communists and neo-fascists. Another revisionist tendency, toward the humanization of Marxism, emerged in the mid-1950s, with the first publication of K. Marx's early *Economic and Philosophic Manuscripts* (1844), and found expression in the writings of Evald Ilyenkov, Genrikh Batishchev, and Yakov Mil'ner-Irinin. This tendency suffered a severe political blow: the attempt to build "socialism with a human face" in Czechoslovakia was crushed by Soviet tanks in 1968, revealing the incompatibility of humanism and Marxism.

The 1980s witnessed three new revisionist approaches to Marxism. The first was an attempt to revitalize and modify Marxism in the wake of the failure of the Soviet communist project. This version of *post-communist Marxism*, exemplified in the work of S. Platonov[7] claimed the purification of Marxism from its Leninist and especially Stalinist contaminations and the incorporation of new realities, such as the persistent success of market economy. The second approach suggested that Leninism and

Stalinism had been consistent with the premises of Marxism, which must therefore be held responsible for all of communism's crimes against humanity. This version was developed by Alexander Yakovlev, the chief official ideologist of *perestroika*, and involved the radical criticism of Marxism as a non-scientific and anti-humanist theory, which, with its all-inclusive determinism, underestimated the sovereignty of consciousness, reducing personality to a function of a social system. The third approach, which can be called *post-Marxist communism* (as distinct from *post-communist Marxism*), glorified the religious aspects of communism, which were abandoned by classical Marxism in favor of a quasi-scientific materialism. This position, articulated by Sergei Kurginian and, to a lesser extent, by Alexander Zinoviev, proclaimed the rebirth of communism as a moralist and salvationist doctrine, encompassing the deepest insights of many Eastern and Western religions and challenging the soulless hedonism and consumerism of capitalist civilization. Thus Marxism was presented as the latest form of "humanist religion" destined to save humanity from the pitfalls of bourgeois individualism through high spiritual ideals and collectivist aspirations.

In the 1960s, new directions of thought began to replace Marxism which, despite many attempts of its renovation, continued to lose intellectual ground in the socialist countries, especially after the violent suppression of "Prague Spring" in 1968.

## 2. *Neo-Rationalism and Structuralism*

A number of new methodological approaches starting from the early 1960s may be united under the title of *neo-rationalism*. Soviet structuralism came to the fore almost simultaneously with analogous movements in France and the USA. Structuralism revived interest in the forgotten and almost forbidden legacy of Russian formalism and at the same time brought it closer to the new disciplines and theories developed in the postwar period, such as cybernetics, semiotics, and general systems theory. Yuri Lotman (1922–1993), the founder of the Tartu school of Soviet structuralism, initiated a comprehensive research on what he called the "semiosphere," the universe of signs. He offered numerous methodological insights on the role of sign systems throughout history and culture. This project of rapprochement between the sciences and humanities was also developed by the Moscow school of structuralism (Vladimir Toporov, Vyacheslav Ivanov and others). Merab Mamardashvili (1930–1990) and Alexander Piatigorsky (1929–2009) (some of their works were written in collaboration) undertook a phenomenological analysis of consciousness, with a special interest in non-classical, post-rationalist and Oriental types of logic. The theory of systems and general methodology, as related to the philosophical problems of social organization, artificial intelligence and cybernetics, mathematical models and probabilistic approaches to language and the biosphere, have been elaborated by Georgy Shchedrovitsky (with his influential "methodological seminars" and "organizational games"), Vasily Nalimov and Yuly Shreider. The principle shared by all these schools was the systematic analysis of consciousness and search of those properties of human activity and cultural models, which are adequately cognized or organized by reason (logical and mathematical models, binary oppositions, methodological algorithms and reflexive procedures, etc.) Neo-rationalism, and especially structuralism, achieved its greatest impact in the late

1960s to early 1980s when it boldly challenged the social mysticism of the orthodox Soviet Marxism. However later in the 1980s, the role of the primary philosophical alternative passed from structuralism to nationalist and religious thought, which increasingly opposed itself to old-fashioned Marxist rationalism.

## 3. *The Philosophy of National Spirit*

The grassroots ideology (*pochvennichestvo*), which emerged in the early 1970s and escalated rapidly in post-communist Russia, has produced its own intellectual elite: writers, critics, historians, who attempted to create a philosophy of national spirit (which is routinely, though not necessarily, linked to rightist views). Its major intellectual predecessors include the Russian Slavophiles of the nineteenth century and the Eurasianists of the 1920s. Twentieth century German, French and Italian sources, such as René Guénon and Giulio Evola, are also abundantly used. The influential socio–political, moralist and journalistic writings by Alexander Solzhenitsyn and the historic-ethnographic treatises by Lev Gumilev (1912–1990) are characteristic of this trend insofar as they concern general philosophical issues, such as the relation between culture and nation, collective responsibility and guilt, biological energy and the moral patterns of ethnic groups. For example, L. Gumilev advanced an original theory of "ethnogenesis" (echoing Oswald Spengler's "morphology of culture") that explained the rise and decline of ethnic formations by biological rather than social factors, namely by disproportionate infusions of cosmic energies into the biological mass of humankind. Gumilev's key concept is "drive," or "passionality," that allegedly is accumulated in the "heroic personalities," representative of certain nations and epochs and accounting for their historical accomplishments. Even more radicalist figures of the same conservative trend were the critic Vadim Kozhinov and mathematician Igor Shafarevich, who have developed a pessimistic view on Russian and Soviet history as permanently threatened and undermined from within by non-Russian ethnic groups, particularly Jews. The philosophy of national spirit absorbs many underground keys of the Russian culture, including the extremely archaic, pagan beliefs. It produces both quasi–empirical doctrines about biological and geographical factors of ethnogenesis and neo-fascist fantastic geopolitical utopias inspired by the myths of "Great Tradition" (Alexander Dugin, the main ideologist of militant Eurasianism).

## 4. *Personalism and Liberalism*

Between the poles of rationalism and nationalism, many thinkers represent various trends of personalist philosophy whose supreme values are freedom and individuality. Russian personalism, related to the heritage of Nikolai Berdyaev and Lev Shestov, is skeptical of any generalizing statements. No comprehensive systematic treatises have been produced in this field, but there are numerous essays, articles and philosophical diaries by Mikhail Prishvin (1873–1954), Yakov Druskin (1902–1980), Lidiia Ginzburg (1902–1990), Grigory Pomerants (1918–2013), and Boris Khazanov (born 1928). The formation and self-awareness of personality, its attitudes toward nature and society, love and death, and time and fate are the central motifs of personalist thought. Personalism is inherently connected with pluralism, with neo-

Leibnizean views on the individuality of multiple monads in their dissonant chorus. Closer sources include F. Dostoevsky, V. Rozanov, M. Bakhtin and European existentialism from Kierkegaard to Camus. More politicized versions of the same intellectual trend is liberalism as expressed by Andrei Sakharov, Arkady Belinkov, Andrey Amalrik, Mikhailo Mikhailov, and Alexander Esenin-Vol'pin. This tradition of philosophical liberalism has attracted influential supporters from the field of the humanities, such as historians Natan Eidel'man (1930–1989), Leonid Batkin and Yury Afanasiev, as well as outstanding proponents in poetry and fiction, including Joseph Brodsky and Andrei Bitov, who express personalist views in their essays and philosophical prose. Thus the range of this trend stretches from Ya. Druskin and G. Pomerants's religious personalism to A. Sakharov and A. Esenin-Vol'pin's secular liberalism; from the focus on the irrational and mysterious core of the personality to the defense of human rights as the basis of social and scientific progress.

### 5. *Orthodox Christian Thought*

Among the most influential trends in the 1970s–1980s were varieties of religious thought, including orthodox Christianity as well as synthetic, occult, non-traditional teachings. Such major writers as Boris Pasternak and Alexander Solzhenitsyn powerfully expressed Christian visions of history and contemporary society. The Orthodox thought, as represented by Anthony Bloom, Alexander Schmeman, and Sergei Averintsev, dates back to the heritage of the Eastern Fathers of the Church and merges with theology, while at the same time opens a dialogue with the traditions of others' religions and with the world of contemporary European culture. The priest Aleksandr Men' (1935–1990) was by far the most influential Russian theologian and Orthodox spiritual leader of the 1970s and 1980s. In his seven-volume treatise, *In Search of the Way, Truth, and Life* and in his other books, he elaborates a philosophy of spiritual ascension that leads humanity from paganism to the Christian revelation of Godmanhood. A younger generation of religious thinkers is represented by Sergei Horujy, Evgenii Barabanov, Tatiana Goricheva, Vladislav Zelinsky, and Oleg Genisaretsky, who focus on the problems of the interaction of Christianity with secular culture, science, feminism, communication networks, and contemporary philosophical and theological movements.

### 6. *Cosmism and Esoterics*

Syncretistic, or universalistic, thought incorporates various gnostic, occult, Hindu, Buddhist, theosophical, neopaganist sources and often attempts their synthesis with the "crazy" ideas of modern science and technology. The legacy of Nikolai Fyodorov, Konstantin Tsiolkovsky, Vladimir Vernadsky, Velimir Khlebnikov, Nicholas Roerich is crucial for this trend. Daniil Andreev (1906–1959) in his treatise *The Rose of the World* (1950–1958) developed an original "meta-historic" and "trans-physical" vision that strived to absorb the religious wisdom of both West and East and to pave the way for a future "inter-religion" and harmonious world order based on a universal theocracy. Nicholas Roerich version of Oriental mysticism and many other para-philosophical and esoteric teachings were intensely promoted and publicized by numerous contemporary intellectual groups. Another influential trend included "the philosophy of the common cause," originating in Nikolai Fyodorov's ideas about the universal resurrection of the dead, physical immortality and the technological transformation of the cosmos. Often identifying itself as "cosmism" or "anthropocosmism," this philosophy employs the broad categories of "universal reason," "noosphere," "immortality," "general resurrection," "transformation and spiritualization of nature," "the conquest of the universe," etc. In the late Soviet period this philosophy was presented by the works of Georgy Gachev (1929–2008) and Svetlana Semyonova (1941–2014).[8]

## 7. *Philosophy of Culture, or Culturology*

Culturology is the philosophy of cultural dialogue and self-determination of culture through "otherness." It received a powerful impetus from Mikhail Bakhtin (1895–1975), who asserted in his later works that a culture exists only on its borders with other cultures. Another strong impulse came from Aleksei Losev (1893–1988), who developed his philosophy of "dialectical idealism" and "absolute mythology" primarily on the material of classical antiquity (*History of Classical Aesthetics*, in 8 volumes, 1963–1988). P. Florensky, O. Spengler, T. Mann and H. Hesse's cultural metaphysics had decisive impact on the formation of Russian culturology. One of its major representatives was Vladimir Bibler (1918–2000) who managed to create his own methodological school of "dialogical logic" and "the dialogue of cultures," investigating the history of sciences and humanities under this angle. Sergei Averintsev (1937–2004), an outstanding scholar in the field of antiquity and Byzantine civilization, had elaborated the philosophical approaches to cultural heritage, giving special emphasis to the problems of symbol and wisdom, the specifics of the humanities, and the interaction between religious and secular types of culture. Other representatives of this movement include Olga Freidenberg, Dmitry Likhachev, Nikolai Konrad, Aron Gurevich, Leonid Batkin, and Vadim Rabinovich. Each scholar focused on a specific historical domain—antiquity and Byzantium, Japan, ancient Russia, medieval France and the Italian Renaissance—showing a peculiar integrity of each cultural type and at the same time, in distinction from the Spengler's theory of the closed cultural worlds, their openness, mutual permeability. This intellectual wandering across the boundaries of cultures responded to the ripened public need for overcoming loneliness and self-isolation of the Soviet society behind the "iron curtain" (both in space and in history). Key concepts of this movement emerged in opposition to both Marxism and structuralism: "dialogue," "symbol," "otherness," "outsideness," "polyphony," "carnival," and they characterized the specific methodology of the humanities in their distinction from natural and social sciences. Sharing a structuralist tendency to rational objectivity, culturology at the same time objected to the introduction of mathematical and cybernetic methods, attempting to develop special criteria of humanistic precision and adopting some methods of hermeneutics and spiritual–historical school (Dilthey, Rickert).

By the 1980s, religious-mystical and nationalist trends began to dominate in the mentality of late Soviet society. Sometimes religiosity and nationalism sharply diverged, as, for example, in ecumenical and liberal Christian philosophy of

Aleksandr Men', Aleksandr and sometimes converged, as in the thinking of Nicholas Roerich's or Ivan Ilyin's followers. The destiny of other directions was indicative of the growing irrationalism. Marxism and structuralism were increasingly perceived as obsolete paradigms rooted in the ideas of progress and revolution (socio–political or scientific–technical). Culturology, with its inclination for distant intellectual itineraries, kept, but did not strengthen its positions as the accent was more and more transferred to dramatic contradictions within the country. Personalism and pluralism, while winning victories in public consciousness and defining political process during the era of *glasnost'* and *perestroika*, at the same time lost their philosophical depth and existential intensity in liberal journalism. As paradoxical as it may seem, the public success of personalism and pluralism increasingly undermined their intellectual value.

## 8. *Conceptualism and Post-Structuralism*

The latest trend worthy of mention corresponds to what was called poststructuralism in the West; one of its original Russian varieties was conceptualism. This name usually refers to a well-known movement in Russian arts and literature of the 1970s and 1980s, but it can also be aptly applied to a broad spectrum of critical and philosophical ideas that complement and illuminate this movement. Conceptualism assumes that certain conceptual schemes underlie the ideological construction of reality and determine its artificial, conventional character. Conceptualist thinking is imbued with irony, parody, and a sense of relativity, since "truth" and "reality" are regarded as empty categories. The relationship between conceptualism and Marxism is somewhat reminiscent of the dispute between nominalists/conceptualists and realists in the epoch of the medieval scholastics: whereas Marxists assert the historical reality of such concepts as "collectivism," "equality," "progress," and "the people," for conceptualists these notions are purely mental or linguistic structures. Every cultural form is conceived as a combination of pre-established codes, such as the Soviet ideological language or the code of the Russian psychological novel. Conceptualism operates with mental universals in various genres of writing and artistic performance: textual–visual installations by Ilya Kabakov, the collective actions of Andrei Monastyrsky's group, poetic and novelistic "kontsepty" of Dmitry Prigov and Vladimir Sorokin, the "inspection" practice of the "Medical Hermeneutics" (Pavel Peppershtein and Sergei Anufriev). The metaphysically loaded play with pure concepts can be found also in theoretical and artistic works of Andrei Siniavsky, Vitaly Komar, Alexander Melamid, and Boris Groys. In conceptualism, everything, a gesture, an act, a work of art becomes a "concept," i.e. an act of thinking, ironically contemplating its object (a fly, a piece of trash, an old notebook, etc.), and thus the field of philosophical reflection is extended infinitely. It is essential to point out the proximity of conceptualism both to the postmodernist philosophy of pan-textuality (Jacques Derrida) and hyperreality (Jean Baudrillard) and to the Buddhist meditation that reveals meaningless spaces and voids in the texture of objective world.[9]

Another, more academic version of philosophical post-structuralism is represented by Valery Podoroga, Mikhail Yampolsky, Mikhail Ryklin, Elena (Helen) Petrovsky and the Laboratory of Non-Classical Philosophy at the Institute of Philosophy RAS in Moscow. In the 1990s, this group published a philosophical collection *Ad Marginem*, which was methodologically inspired by contemporary French thinkers (Derrida, Deleuze and Guattari et al.). Podoroga's works originally combine phenomenological, hermeneutical and deconstructionist readings of German philosophers and Russian writers, with a special emphasis on "visual anthropology" and the corporeal and spatial quality of texts as "landscapes."

Of course, the eight philosophical movements, as briefly outlined above, do not exhaust the entire complexity of intellectual life in this period, nor do they even account for the "hybrid" work of some individual authors. For example, Mikhail Bakhtin can be regarded both as a representative of personalist–pluralist thought and a founder of culturology. Andrei Sinyavsky's work demonstrates soft, smooth transitions between personalist and poststructuralist paradigms. Georgy Gachev has created an original holistic system including such components as "living-thinking" (*zhiznemyslie*), "national images of the world," and a "humanistic approach to natural sciences." His thinking bridges such disparate trends as culturology, personalism, and the philosophy of national spirit. Contemporary Russian thought is polyphonic, not just pluralistic, in the sense that different positions and voices interact in the consciousness of the most creative thinkers. It would be productive to investigate the philosophy of this period at the intersection of two axes: 1) "Movement," embracing the works of many authors; 2) "Author," embracing various aspects of several movements.

The philosophical thought of the second half of the twentieth century in Russia and in the Russian diaspora is a single process and needs an integrated approach. In contrast to the first post-revolutionary period 1920s–1950s, when the Soviet and emigre thought had two separate, divergent histories, in the post-Stalin epoch they gradually come together and finally merge in the *perestroika* period. Such administrative and ideological supervisors of Soviet philosophy of the 1930s–1940s, as Mark B. Mitin and Pavel F. Yudin, can hardly be regarded as members of the same discipline as N. Berdyaev and L. Shestov. But Grigory Pomerants, Andrei Sinyavsky and Mihajlo Mihajlov, working respectively in Moscow, near Paris, and in Zadar (Yugoslavia), belong to the same intellectual formation (personalism, pluralism, liberalism).

Rarely in the history of thought has philosophy been such a liberating force as it was in Russia from the 1960s through the 1980s. The Soviet State had generated a rigid system of "proven" and "irrefutable" ideas that aimed to perpetuate its mastery over individual minds. For this reason, philosophical thinking, which by its nature transcends the limits of the existing order and questions sanctioned practices, was under permanent suspicion as a potentially anti-State activity. To philosophize was an act of self-liberation via an awareness of the relativity of the dominant ideological discourse. Philosophical ideas in the Soviet Union rarely matured into well-balanced, self-sufficient systems, because the State arrogated to itself the privilege of elaborating and consummating ideas in a systematic way. The fate of non-Marxist thinkers was to dissolve this ideocratic rigidity in a stream of critical, spontaneous thinking that attempted to go beyond all possible systems, in order to undermine rather than consolidate them. Since the official philosophy functioned as a tool of power, it was the task and merit of non-official philosophy to advance anti-totalitarian modes of thinking, thus decentralizing the structure of discourse. Thought tried to free itself from ideocracy by putting down roots in authentic, concrete forms of being, such as faith in a living God, the existential uniqueness of personality, the organic soul of the nation, the empirical credibility of science, the symbolic meanings of culture, or by challenging the master-discourse of Soviet ideology through parodic imitation and exaggeration. All of these trends: religious, personalistic, national, rationalist, culturological, post-structuralist—were initially and intentionally forms of intellectual self-liberation. The internal logic of development, however, has led some of these schools of thought, especially the philosophy of national spirit, to renovated and "improved" projects of post-communist fundamentalism and ideocracy.

Russian intellectual history is a history of thought that fights desperately to escape the prison of an ideocratic system created by the strenuous and sacrificial efforts of thought itself. What makes Russian thought so unique is its internal tension, its struggle against itself, against its own ideational constructions and political extensions.

In the West, the field of philosophy is more or less clearly divided into ontology, the philosophy of being, and epistemology, the philosophy of knowledge. In Russia, such a division is almost irrelevant since philosophy addresses a conception of being that is itself constructed by thinking. Beginning with Chaadaev, and the Westernizers and Slavophiles, Russian philosophy focused on the second-order reality, the one created by ideas. It may have been "derivative" and "secondary," but not so much in respect to Western thought, as in relation to the properly Russian, utterly artificial, ideologically fabricated, and fantastic reality. In Russia, thought tried to confront the triumph of thought. One speculative capacity, the "intelligentsia," opposed itself to another speculative capacity, the "ideocracy,"—but the former also created the latter. This self-contradictory movement of thought, shattering its own foundations, gives an unprecedented, sometimes "suicidal" quality to Russian philosophy.

## NOTES

1. On the totalitarian implications of Platonism and its connection with Marxist philosophy, see Popper 1966. Comparisons of Marx and Plato are scattered throughout the book and can be followed in the Index of Names. In particular, Popper remarks: "The whole idea—which was not Marx's invention—that there is something behind the prices, an objective or real or true value of which prices are only a 'form of appearance,' shows clearly enough the influence of Platonic Idealism with its distinction between a hidden essential or true reality, and an accidental or delusive appearance" (ibid., vol. 2, 165).
2. See Lossky 1951; Zenkovsky 1953; Levitsky 1968, 1981; Copleston 1986. The same applies to all existing anthologies and collections of Russian philosophy. To cite a few examples: Edie, Scanlan and Zeldin 1964, ends with a section on Russian and Soviet Marxism; Schmemann 1977 ends with Sergei Bulgakov; Frank 1965 ends with Semyon Frank (1877–1950).
3. Among those thinkers were Andrei Bely, Mikhail Prishvin, Vladimir Vernadsky, Konstantin Tsiolkovsky, Pavel Florensky, Aleksei Losev, Gustav Shpet, Aleksandr Meier, Mikhail Bakhtin and his circle, Lev Vygotsky, Viktor Shklovsky, Iakov Druskin, Iakov Golosovker, Olga Freidenberg.

4. See Bochenski 1963; Blakeley 1964; Laszlo 1967; Jeu 1969; Callinicos 1983; Scanlan 1985; Dahm, Blakeley, and Kline 1987. There is an obsolete if consistent tendency in the West to take seriously the claims of Soviet Marxism for philosophical leadership and to equate all post-revolutionary and non-emigrant Russian thought with dialectical materialism.
5. See, for example, Seyffert 1985. Kline 1975 is devoted to three Russian "non-official" thinkers. Several chapters on non-Marxist currents in Soviet philosophy are found in Graham 1987; Goerdt 1984; Jeu 1969.
6. In his younger years, 1875–1881, V. Solovyev lectured at Moscow University but, symptomatically, was forced to retire after he concluded his public lecture with a political statement: he condemned revolutionary activities and simultaneously called the Tsar to forgive the terrorists who recently murdered his father, Alexander II.
7. "S. Platonov" was a collective pseudonym of the three authors: Viktor Aksyonov, Vasily Krivorotov, Sergei Chernyshev. See: Platonov 1989.
8. Svetlana Semyonova was among very few women engaged in philosophical debates in this epoch. Characteristically, Nikolai Fyodorov's system which she advocated was based on extremely patriarchal views and denigrated the role of women as "seducers" of men preventing them from fulfilling their duties of resurrection toward the "fathers." There are many historic-cultural factors accounting for a lesser role of women in Russian philosophy than in Russian literature. This unexplored field is covered in Vanchungov 1996.
9. In more detail, conceptualism is discussed in my article: Epstein 2010.

## BIBLIOGRAPHY


Abramov, Aleksandr I. "Otsenka filosofii Platona v russkoi idealisticheskoi filosofii" [Evoluation of Plato's Philosophy in Russian Idealistic Philosophy]. In: *Sbornik statei v pamiat' stoletiia Imperatorskoi Moskovskoi Dukhovnoi Akademii*, Sergiev Posad, 1915, part 1, p.153. [Cited in the article: published in the collection *Platon i ego epokha* (*Plato and his Epoch*), Moscow: Nauka, 1979, p. 222.]

Bochenski, Józef M. 1963. *Soviet Russian Dialectical Materialism [Diamat]*. Dordrecht-Holland: D. Reidel Publishing Company.

Blakeley, T.J. 1964. *Soviet Philosophy: A General Introduction to Contemporary Soviet Thought*. Kluwer Academic Publishers.

Callinicos, Alex. 1983. *Marxism and Philosophy*. New York: Oxford University Press.

Copleston, Frederick C. 1986. *Philosophy in Russia From Herzen to Lenin and Berdyaev* Search Press, University of Notre Dame.

Dahm, Helmut, Blakeley, Thomas, and Kline, George L. (eds.). 1987. *Philosophical Sovietology. The Pursuit of a Science*. Dordrecht et al.: D. Reidel Publishing Company.

DeBlasio, Allyssa. 2014. *The End of Russian Philosophy: Tradition and Transition at the Turn of the 21st Century*. New York: Palgrave Macmillan.

Edie, James M., Scanlan, James P. and Zeldin Mary-Barbara. (eds.). 1964. *Russian Philosophy*, 3 vols, with the collaboration of George L. Kline. Chicago: Quadrangle Books.

Epstein, Mikhail N. 2010. "The Philosophical Implications of Russian Conceptualism," *Journal of Eurasian Studies* 1, (1): 64–71.

Florovsky, Georgy. 1988. *Puti russkogo bogosloviia* (1937). 4th ed. Paris: YMCA-PRESS.

Frank, Semyon L. 1965. *Iz istorii russkoi filosofskoi mysli kontsa X1X i nachala XX veka. Antologiia* [From the History of the Russian Philosophical Thought]. Washington-New York: Inter-Language Literary Associates.

Goerdt, Wilhelm. 1984. *Russische Philosophie. Zugänge und Durchblicke*. München: Verlag Karl Alber Freiburg, 94–112.

Graham, Loren R. 1987. *Science, Philosophy, and Human Behavior in the Soviet Union*. New York Guildford: Columbia University Press, 1987.

Jeu, Bernard. 1969. *La philosophie soviétique et l'Occident. Essai sur tendances et sur la signification de la philosophy soviétique contemporaine (1959–1969)*. Paris: Mercure de France.

Kireevsky, Ivan. 1979. "O kharaktere prosveshcheniia Evropy" [On the Character of European Enlightenment], in *Kritika i estetika* [Critic and Aesthetics], Moscow: Iskusstvo.

Kireevsky, Ivan. 1987. "On the Necessity and Possibility of New Principles in Philosophy." In *Russian Philosophy*, edited by James M. Edie, James P. Scanlan, Mary-Barabara Zeldin with the collaboration of George L. Kline, vol. 1. Knoxville: The University of Tennessee Press.

Kline, George L. 1975. "Recent Uncensored Soviet Philosophical Writings." In *Dissent in the USSR. Politics, Ideology, and People*, edited by Rudolf L. Tokes. Baltimore and London: The Johns Hopkins University Press, 158–190.

Laruelle, Marlène. 2012. *Russian Eurasianism: An Ideology of Empire*. Baltimore: Johns Hopkins University Press.

Laszlo, Ervin (ed.). 1967. *Philosophy in the Soviet Union. A Survey of the Mid-Sixties*. Dordrecht, Holland: D. Reidel Publishing Company.

Lektorsky, Vladislav A. (ed.). 1998. *Filosofiia ne konchaetsia . . . Iz istorii otechestvennoi filosofii. XX vek. 1960–e—1980–e gg.* [Philosophy does not End . . . From the History of the Russian Philosophy. The Twentieth Century. 1960s–1980s], vol. 2. Moscow: ROSSPEN.

Lektorsky, Vladislav A. 2014. *Problemy i diskussii v filosofii Rossii vtoroi poloviny 20-go veka: sovremennyi vzglyad* [Problems and Discussions in Philosophy of Russia in the Second Half of the Twentieth Century: A Contemporary View]. Moscow: ROSSPEN.

Levitsky S.A. 1968. 1981. *Ocherky po istorii russkoi filosofskoi i obshchestvennoi mysli*, 2 vols. Frankfurt/Main: Posev.

Lossky, Nikolas O. 1951. *History of Russian Philosophy*. New York: International Universities Press, Inc.

Louth, Andrew. 2015. *Modern Orthodox Thinkers: From the Philokalia to the Present*. Westmont, IL: InterVarsity Academic.

Marx, Karl. 1972. "Contribution to the Critique of Hegel's *Philosophy of Right*: Introduction." In *The Marx-Engels Reader*, edited by Robert C. Tucker, New York: W.W. Norton & Co.

Morson, Gary S., Emerson, Caryl. 1990. *Mikhail Bakhtin. Creation of a Prosaics*. Stanford (California): Stanford University Press.

Motroshilova, Nelli V. 2012. *Otechestvennaia filosofia 50–80–kh godov XX v. i zapadnaia mysl'*. [The Russian Philosophy of the 1950s–1980s and the Western Thought]. Moscow: Akademicheskii proekt.

Platonov, Sergei. 1989. *Posle kommunizma. Kniga, ne prednaznachennaia dlia pechati.* [After Communism. A Book Not Intended for Publication]. Moscow: Molodaia gvardia.

Popper, Karl R. 1966. *The Open Society and Its Enemies*, 2 vols. London and Henley: Routledge and Kegan Paul.

Seyffert, Peter. 1985. *Soviet Literary Structuralism. Background. Debate. Issues.* Columbus, Ohio: Slavica Publishers, Inc.

Scanlan, James P. 1985. *Marxism in the USSR. A Critical Survey of Current Soviet Thought.* Ithaca and London: Cornell University Press.

Schmemann, Alexander (ed.). 1977. *Ultimate Questions: An Anthology of Modern Russian Religious Thought.* Crestwood, N.Y.: Saint Vladimir's Seminary Press.

Skovoroda, Gregory. 1987. "Socrates in Russia." In *Russian Philosophy*, edited by James M. Edie, James P. Scanlan, Mary-Barabara Zeldin with the collaboration of George L. Kline, vol. 1. Knoxville: The University of Tennessee Press, 17–18.

Vanchugov, Vasily. 1996. *Zhenshchiny v filosofii: Iz istorii filosofii v Rossii kontsa XIX—nach. XX vv.* [Women in Philosophy: From the History of Philosophy in Russia in the Late Nineteenth and Early Twentieth Centuries]. Moscow: Rits–Pilgrim.

Whitehead, Alfred N. 1979. *Process and Reality*. Sherburne: Free Press.

Young, George. 2012. *The Russian Cosmists: The Esoteric Futurism of Nikolai Fedorov and His Followers.* Oxford: Oxford University Press.

Zenkovsky, Vasily V. 1953. *A History of Russian Philosophy.* Translated by G. L. Kline. 2 vols. London and New York: Routledge and Kegan PLC.

CHAPTER THREE

# Punks versus Zombies: Evald Ilyenkov and the Battle for Soviet Philosophy

DAVID BAKHURST

This chapter is devoted to Evald Vasilevich Ilyenkov, one of the most—perhaps *the* most—significant philosopher of the Soviet era. Ilyenkov, who lived from 1924 to 1979, is known for his writings on Marx's method, for highly influential essays on "the problem of the ideal," for his resolute defense of a broadly humanistic vision in the face of Soviet optimism about the scientific-technological revolution, and for his work on education, especially his collaboration with Alexander Meshcheryakov on the upbringing of blind-deaf children, which Ilyenkov took to exemplify his conception of the social nature of the human mind.

It has been acknowledged in the West that there is interesting work by Soviet thinkers on the relation of culture and cognition since the early 1960s, when Vygotsky's masterpiece, *Thought and Language*, appeared in a much-abridged English translation with the enthusiastic endorsement of Jerome Bruner. Since then, it has become clear that Vygotsky was no isolated figure, but a representative of a broad movement that included his students Alexander Luria and Alexei Leontiev, as well as a number of other prominent thinkers, among whom Ilyenkov is the most important philosophical voice.

Now is a good time to revisit these thinkers and explore their legacy and its contemporary relevance. Where their work has been examined in the West, it is often reconstructed, simplified, and deployed in ways distant from its original context. In Western social science, cultural-historical research (inspired by Vygotsky) and activity theory (inspired by Leontiev), sometimes united under the acronym "CHAT," may be descendants of their Russian originators, but they are not animated by the same spirit or philosophical ethos, which we are at risk of forgetting. Second, although this is a time when new research materials are becoming available—as Soviet archives are opened—we are fast losing touch with the oral culture, immersion within which was a precondition of understanding much that was written. So we are approaching a turning point. If we are going to explore this Soviet tradition (if it is correct to speak of it as *one*), we should not delay.[1]

* * *

My focus is an incident that occurred at the very beginning of Ilyenkov's career, about which relatively little was known until recently. In April 1954, Ilyenkov and his friend Valentin Korovikov, both junior lecturers at Moscow State University (MGU), wrote a set of "theses on philosophy."[2] The following month, the theses were the subject of an open discussion, attended by some 200 people, at a meeting of their department, the *Kafedra* of the History of Foreign Philosophy. The subsequent furor pitched Ilyenkov and Korovikov against the Soviet philosophical establishment, controlled by philosophers who had come to prominence at the height of Stalinism and whose conception of philosophy was defined, to a greater or lesser extent, by the rigid form of Marxism-Leninism that had been codified during that period. That form found its most definitive, and most primitive, expression in 1938 in the notorious fourth chapter of *The History of the Communist Party of the Soviet Union (Bolshevik): Short Course*. The establishment cast Ilyenkov and Korovikov as "punks," or in the Russian idiom of the day, *stilyagi*, disrespectful of authority, contemptuous of orthodoxy and indifferent to the "class character" of philosophy.[3] In turn, Ilyenkov, Korovikov and the students they inspired, saw the old guard as brain-dead automata, empty shells moved around by ideological dictates rather than the deliverances of free thought—the zombies of my title. The controversy—the ensuing confrontation between Punks and Zombies—was a formative moment in Ilyenkov's own philosophical development. Moreover, it influenced an entire generation and through them the subsequent course of Soviet philosophy, or so it has been claimed.[4]

Though the incident was known to have occurred, the theses themselves were lost and no record of events was available until the publication in 2016 of a book, edited by Ilyenkov's daughter, Elena Illesh, which contains fascinating archival material, including transcripts of Faculty and Party meetings and various unpublished writings by Ilyenkov (Ilyenkov and Korovikov 2016, hereafter *IK*).[5] This material helps us understand exactly what happened and why, and gives unprecedented insight into Ilyenkov's mind and character at the time.

In what follows, I recount the story of the theses and evaluate its significance. The story is a tortuous one, and before we begin, I must note a further twist that occurred only recently. In her book, Illesh attempts a partial reconstruction of the theses, a translation of which is given in Appendix I at the end of the present chapter. After the book's completion, however, Illesh discovered a complete text of the theses in the Archives of the Russian Academy of Sciences in materials pertaining to the Institute of Philosophy (АРАН. Ф. 1922. Оп. 1. Д. 767. Л. 109–119). The manuscript is translated as Appendix II.[6] If Illesh had had the complete text available to her earlier, she might have composed her book differently. Nevertheless, the need to scour the archives for clues about the content of the theses forced her to take an interest in the detail of discussions that might otherwise have been overlooked. It may be that the almost Gogolian elusiveness of the manuscript, turning up only after its story had been told, enriched rather than hindered scholarship into the circumstances of its reception. Time will tell. Now to the story itself.

* * *

Let us begin with the furor. It was intense and protracted. On March 29, 1955, eleven months after the theses were first presented, the Scientific Council of the Philosophy Faculty of Moscow University passed six resolutions after two days of impassioned discussion before a large audience (*IK*, 61). The first resolution is an act of self-criticism, admitting that the Council had not acted soon enough to prevent the propagation of Ilyenkov and Korovikov's supposedly "anti-Marxist" views. Thereafter the Council chastises Ilyenkov and Korovikov. The second resolution castigates their stance as a pernicious idealist deviation. The third reproaches Ilyenkov and Korovikov for "insincerity," for hypocritically pretending to acknowledge their mistakes in public while continuing privately to hold fast to their heretical views. The fourth instructs faculty members to set students right about the philosophy of Marxism, particularly on those matters wrongly interpreted by Ilyenkov and Korovikov. The fifth enjoins the Dean to take decisive measures to prevent the further dissemination within the Faculty of anti-Marxist ideas connected with the theses. Finally, the sixth resolution charges the Presidium of the Faculty Council with reevaluating Ilyenkov's Candidate's dissertation, which he had defended, apparently successfully, in 1953.

To contemporary Western eyes, such resolutions appear almost comic, so remote do they seem from the realities of academic life as we tend to know it. But it is important to remember that in Moscow in 1955, such charges put one's livelihood, and possibly one's liberty, at risk. And the criticism was to become even more intense over the next several months. What, then, had Ilyenkov and Korovikov done to provoke this response?

* * *

The central issue posed in the theses is "What is philosophy?" or rather, "What ought philosophy to be?" and the principal contention is the rejection of the orthodox Soviet view, usually attributed to Engels, that philosophy is the science of "the world as a whole" or of the most general laws of nature, society and thought. This orthodox view was very widely embraced in the USSR, even among philosophers who had not been entirely zombified. In Ilyenkov's *Philosophical Notebook*, included in *IK*, he quotes his supervisor Teodor I. Oizerman, who, writing with V.I. Svetlov, says that "[t]he world as a whole, the world in its material unity, in its movement, change and development—such is the subject of Marxist philosophy." Ilyenkov comments that on the next page Oizerman and Svetlov add that philosophy studies the most general laws of nature, society and consciousness (*IK*, 182; Oizerman and Svetlov 1948). Ilyenkov and Korovikov propose to overturn this view.

Anyone who teaches first year philosophy classes knows it can be difficult to define philosophy. It is not uncommon to suggest that philosophy operates at a higher level of generality than natural science, that in studying being qua being philosophy has pretensions to understanding "things as a whole." In Wilfrid Sellars's famous phrase: "The aim of philosophy, abstractly formulated, is to understand how things in the broadest possible sense of the term hang together in the broadest possible sense of the term" (Sellars 1963, 1). Not so contentious a definition. So why do Ilyenkov and Korovikov protest so vigorously about the standard Soviet characterization?

I think there are three principal reasons. Note that, in articulating them, I draw on the archival materials in Illesh's volume as well as the theses. This is essential, since the accusations made against Ilyenkov and Korovikov go far beyond the claims made in the theses themselves—this is very clear now that we have the complete text—to engage with views that Ilyenkov and Korovikov defended in discussion, taught in seminars, and so on.

(1) The first reason is that the orthodox view makes for bad philosophy. Part of the problem resides in the notion of *law*. What are these "most general laws" that philosophy is supposed to study? Leaving aside the problem of how one evaluates degrees of generality (*IK*, 206), Soviet philosophers appeared to mean either basic laws of particular fundamental sciences (cosmology, physics, political economy, etc.), or they had in mind broad philosophical claims of the kind that appeared in textbooks of dialectical materialism, such as the principle of the primacy of matter over spirit, the dialectical law of the unity of opposites, and so on. Ilyenkov argues that natural-scientific laws are not the province of philosophy, but of the sciences in question, and that philosophical claims dressed up as universal laws become empty slogans without explanatory power. In his *Notebook*, Ilyenkov scorns the law of the transformation of quantity into quality, and back again, as "philosophical twaddle" (*pustozvonstvo*) (ibid., 195). He complains that the orthodox view of philosophy "opens up infinite possibilities for dialectical games—for exploring the interpenetrations of the general and the particular and such like—but all that is about as far as you can get from a well-formed question" (ibid., 206). It thus:

> directs the powers of philosophy toward fruitless reflection of a foolish kind, discrediting the philosophy of dialectical materialism in the eyes of practitioners of other sciences, and inevitably reducing philosophy itself to a parade of examples illustrating things long known. That this is so is incontrovertibly borne out by the way we have practiced philosophy in recent years. (ibid., 230)

Ilyenkov argues that all positive knowledge about nature, society, and thought, however particular or general in kind, is to be established by natural science, and there is no further "more general" knowledge for philosophy to lay claim to.[7] Nor can philosophy play a synthesizing role, reconciling the approaches of particular sciences and integrating them into a vision of reality as a whole. No philosophy (not even Marxism-Leninism) is equipped to do this (ibid., 183). It is for the sciences themselves to represent the world as a materially developing whole (see Theses 12 and 13, and ibid., 187). There is no place for a "science of sciences," subsuming scientific laws under somehow yet more universal laws (ibid., 213–214).[8]

So, if the orthodox view is wrong, what is the alternative? Ilyenkov and Korovikov argue that the subject-matter of philosophy is *thought*, or the apprehension of reality in or by thought. Philosophy elucidates the forms in which we think the world, the character of the movement of scientific thought (see Theses 13 and 14), or the logic of theoretical thought (ibid., 193). This is consistent, they argue, with Lenin's famous identification of dialectics, logic and the theory of knowledge. Only by embracing this task does philosophy itself become a science (ibid., 180) with a well-defined subject matter: "the order (*zakonomernost'*) of cognizing thought" (ibid., 185, 202–203).[9]

(2) The second reason to challenge the orthodox view is that it is in fact wrongly attributed to Engels. Ilyenkov and Korovikov argue in a short paper[10] that Engels, in *Anti-Dühring*, "Ludwig Feuerbach and the End of German Classical Philosophy," and *Dialectics of Nature*, explicitly claims that, with the emergence of dialectical materialism, philosophy loses its status as the science of sciences (*IK*, 229–230; see also 202–203). Engels makes it clear that what natural science leaves to philosophy is thought ("the study of the laws of the process of thought itself, logic and dialectics") (Engels 1968, 621; cf. Thesis 13).

Of course, Ilyenkov and Korovikov continue, there is a sense in which that view can be reconciled with the idea that philosophy's business is the most general laws of nature, society and thought, properly understood. A philosophical exploration of our modes of thought will disclose the most fundamental forms in which we think reality. And if we hold that those forms of thought capture the nature of things (if we endorse what Ilyenkov calls the identity of thinking and being, which he thinks a materialist conception of logic demands[11]), then philosophy does disclose the general form of reality, and so a version of the Engelsian claim stands. As Ilyenkov puts it:

> Thought itself, if it correctly apprehends/cognizes the world, realizes in its development objective laws—and in that sense, of course, philosophy discloses the objective laws of reality, the so-called most general relations . . . of nature, society and thought. (Ibid., 222, Ilyenkov's ellipses; see also Thesis 14[12])

Many subjects study thought (psychology, cognitive science, neurophysiology, linguistics) but philosophy studies thought in its relation to being, as truth, as knowledge (in this sense, the basic question of philosophy *is* the relation of thinking and being). And thus, it falls to philosophy to study how thought brings reality into view, and that includes exploring the nature of theoretical thinking and scientific method in a way that answers the question of how rigorous scientific understanding of the world is possible. This is the real province of philosophy.

(3) Finally, the orthodox view distorts the revolutionary character of Marxist philosophy. Soviet Marxism-Leninism declared Marxist philosophy a *worldview*, indeed, the first truly scientific worldview. This idea embodied two different senses of "worldview." The first was the idea of a complete conception of the nature of reality (from which it seemed to follow that philosophy had to embody the most general laws of reality). The second was the idea of a political or ideological identity. Marxist philosophy, it was argued, was the worldview of the revolutionary proletariat engaged in class struggle against the bourgeoisie, which embraced a contrary

worldview, idealist in character and politically reactionary. Philosophy is therefore essentially partisan (*partiinyi*).

Ilyenkov allows that Marxist philosophy embodies a worldview, but not in the sense that it has a monopoly on the question "What is the world?" (*IK*, 205). Philosophy cannot answer empirical questions or disclose facts. Its worldview significance lies in its status as *method*.[13] Philosophy "is first a method, and thereby, penetrating all the other sciences, directing their development, enriching them, it represents a worldview" (ibid., 207). There *is* a close relation between philosophy and politics, in that philosophy can establish methodological insights of value in political inquiry, but we should not politicize the problems of epistemology—seeing them as expressions of the class war (ibid., 218–219). Political issues cannot be addressed by throwing around philosophical phrases, but demand the application of concrete political methods, albeit informed by philosophical frameworks (which themselves are deepened and refined in the process).

The revolutionary character of Marxist philosophy lies, not in its interest in class war, the dictatorship of the proletariat, etc., but in its invocation of the concept of practice, *activity*, in its understanding of the relation of thinking and being, mind and world. It may be true that the emergence of the proletariat is a precondition of this philosophical insight, but that does not mean the struggle of the revolutionary proletariat is a genuine subject of philosophy.[14]

It is important that, when he speaks of philosophy as method, Ilyenkov does not see method as a set of a priori principles to be applied to any concrete subject matter. Method must change and adapt in relation to the material under consideration (*IK*, 197) and thus can be understood only in application to concrete material (ibid., 216). We need to understand the movement of thought in grasping the object, the objectuality (*predmetnost'*) of thought (ibid., 196). So the deep question is how to characterize method if it must be understood in its concrete particularity (ibid., 198–199). We need to adjust our conception of the appropriate modes of inquiry in light of our emerging conception of the object, just as we adjust our conception of the object itself in light of the deliverances of our methods of inquiry. The picture he offers seems broadly Neurathian.[15] And, of course, we gain insight into such methodological issues by carefully studying successful cases of scientific inquiry in order to disclose just how, in those particular cases, thought captures the logic of the object under scrutiny.

Needless to say that this picture is a long way from orthodox Soviet views of Marxist philosophy as a weapon in the class war.

* * *

Although these three reasons probe deep into Soviet philosophy's conception of itself, and although the third has clear political resonance, one may yet wonder why the controversy gained such momentum. And indeed, when it first broke, there was little to suggest that things might get out of hand. We have the minutes of the Party Organization of the MGU Philosophy Faculty from October 16, 1954, five months after the theses were first presented (*IK*, 24–27). At this meeting some colleagues complain that Ilyenkov and Korovikov are creating a clique of students interested in their unconventional views and that this is dampening students' interest in other parts of the curriculum (especially History of Russian Philosophy). But others recognize the importance of the questions Ilyenkov and Korovikov are addressing, and treat the enthusiasm generated among the students as a positive thing. Oizerman even suggests that Korovikov should publish a paper on the subject of philosophy. Admittedly, Kosichev, deputy dean of the faculty, pronounces that Korovikov "practically rejects Marxist Philosophy" (ibid., 26).[16] But at that time, this does not ruffle Korovikov, and over the next several months he is bold, confident and defiant. He resists those who would cast things as an intergenerational battle between young upstarts and established professors, arguing that the debate concerns serious questions about the nature of philosophy that obviously warrant discussion, and he complains it is deplorable if some of his colleagues are too ignorant even to see this, let alone to contribute to the discussion.

Ilyenkov does not appear in these minutes because his primary position was at Moscow's Institute of Philosophy, which was, as it is today, a research institute under the auspices of the Soviet (now Russian) Academy of Sciences and independent of the University. He taught at MGU on secondment, so his party affiliation was at the Institute. But he became very much involved as the controversy heated up. And by the end of March 1955, when the Scientific Council of MGU's Philosophy Faculty passed the resolutions described above, the temperature had risen considerably. The atmosphere at that meeting was one of a trial, and in true Russian fashion, a trial in which the outcome is a foregone conclusion. In his opening statement, Dean Molodtsov reads the charges, or rather, the verdict: Ilyenkov and Korovikov

(i) reject the Bolshevik principle of the party-character of philosophy,
(ii) deny that dialectical materialism is a worldview,
(iii) deny that Marxist-Leninist dialectics are the science of the most general laws of nature, society and thought, and reduce Marxist-Leninist dialectics to the science of thought, and
(iv) deny that historical materialism is an inextricable part of Marxist-Leninist philosophy (ibid., 29–30).

Korovikov and Ilyenkov are then permitted lengthy statements. Now Korovikov's attitude has changed. He is conciliatory, admitting that the theses contain significant mistakes and "any number of unclear, slipshod and incorrect formulations" (ibid., 32). He pledges to heed his colleagues' wise criticisms in future. He denies that anything in the theses was meant to be inconsistent with Marxist philosophy's status as a worldview or with its class character. He apologies for discussing the theses with students—this, he now sees, was inappropriate. Throughout his speech, however, Korovikov tries to maintain that the issue is primarily a scholarly one—What is Philosophy?—and accordingly, he volunteers to run a seminar among young faculty members to clarify the issues (a proposal that suggests he did not quite appreciate the seriousness of his situation).

Ilyenkov, for his part, remains composed (ibid., 39–44). He immediately concedes he is in complete agreement with Korovikov, and he plays down the significance of the whole affair. The theses are a working document, written to stimulate discussion. They have no definite form, having evolved in various ways over the course of many debates, so much so that he cannot remember exactly what is in them. No doubt they are full of mistakes, so he has no problem with people challenging whatever version of the theses they care to address. But anyway, what *he* thinks on the subject ought not to be the issue. All that is important is that the nature of Marxist philosophy is seriously discussed. The one thing he cannot accept is the accusation that he has behaved "insincerely" or "duplicitously." That is unfair. Otherwise, Ilyenkov avers, let the Council pass whatever resolutions it likes.

Ilyenkov's strategy was to defuse the debate over orthodoxy while defending his academic integrity. But he was only prepared to compromise so far. When asked by Molodstov, "Do you deny that philosophy has developed during the Soviet period?", he replies, "My view is that Marx, Engels, Lenin and Stalin did a service to philosophy, but there's no way that's true of our philosophy" (ibid., 41).[17] This remark caused a stir in the room, and was met by applause from the groundlings.[18]

On day two, Korovikov and Ilyenkov are not permitted to speak and the case for the prosecution becomes increasingly hysterical, in both senses of the word. Prof. Gagarin (no relation to the astronaut) announces that the nature of philosophy is no longer in dispute, having been settled by Stalin in Ch.4 of the *Short Course* (ibid., 47). Prof. Kosichev responds to Ilyenkov's skepticism about the achievements of Soviet philosophy by asking: "Could the successes of Michurinist biology really have been gained without the application of dialectical materialism? Could the battle against Morganism-Weismannism really have been successful without dialectical materialism?" (ibid., 57). This was, of course, the time when the USSR was committed to the pseudo-scientific biology of Trofim Lysenko. And Molodstov causes laughter in the auditorium when he rebukes Comrades Korovikov and Ilyenkov for "dragging us into the realm of thinking" (ibid., 59). Ilyenkov and Korovikov are variously accused of positivism, Trotskyism, deborinismism, and menshevizing idealism. They are said to be self-appointed innovators, evangelizing their heretical views, and portrayed as hypocritical and duplicitous, philosophically dissolute, depraved, and debauched.

Many of these terms of abuse recall Soviet controversies in the 1920s between the positivist "mechanists" and the Hegelian "dialecticians," led by Abram Deborin, a controversy in which the deborinites were briefly victorious, before both camps were swept aside by a young generation of Party-activists which Stalin himself established on the "philosophical front" (see Bakhurst 1991, Ch.2). Many of the old guard in Ilyenkov's time owed their careers to the rout of the debornites, and so in defending themselves against Ilyenkov they reached for the old insults, though by the 1950s, these terms had lost any content at all and were used entirely indiscriminately.

* * *

So why the growing hysteria? There is no doubt that the old guard felt threatened by Ilyenkov and Korovikov. The orthodox Soviet interpretation of philosophy made it possible for the majority of Soviet philosophers to do philosophy without knowing anything about its history (except as the history of previous error terminating in Marxism-Leninism) or about science (insofar as the project of establishing the most general laws operated at an entirely abstract and vacuous level). The conception of philosophy recommended by the theses, in contrast, required real knowledge of the history of philosophy, knowledge of natural science, and a willingness to engage critically with the classics of Marxism, thought to contain methodological insights not yet fully understood. This was therefore extremely intimidating, since the old guard could not do philosophy as Ilyenkov and Korovikov understood it. And it was no surprise the punks' position was attractive to students, some of whom were well versed in the content of Ilyenkov's dissertation, a circumstance that was potentially humiliating to the senior faculty, who could not cope with the questions the students were now putting to them.

So even seen as a merely scholarly issue, as Ilyenkov and Korovikov tried to cast it, this was not just an arcane debate about orthodoxy, but a battle for hearts and minds, and one that threatened to leave the philosophical establishment in the doldrums while Soviet philosophy took a new course. That is one reason for the severity of the reaction.

But the controversy had also acquired a new political dimension that contributed to the rising temperature. On March 15, 1955 (beware the Ides of March), at a party meeting in the Philosophy Faculty that was supposed unanimously to affirm the resolutions of the January Plenary of the CP USSR, a number of students had made critical objections, arguing that the resolutions should be merely "taken under advisement," and calling for electoral reform, greater transparency, and moves against corruption in the Party. This was a scandal. One philosopher, I. Ya. Shchipanov, head of the *Kafedra* of the History of Russian Philosophy, immediately tried to lay the blame for this at Ilyenkov and Korovikov's door. We know this because there is a statement in Ilyenkov's archive, dated March 22, in which he defends himself from the charge, arguing that he had never had anything to do with the students in question. But it is clear that the stakes had now been raised, for the implicit suggestion is that Ilyenkov and Korovikov, by cultivating a group of like-minded students, were involved in sedition. That was a very dangerous accusation indeed.

Moreover, the Central Committee had become aware of the student discontent and had accordingly initiated a review of the Faculty. The old guard was therefore anxious to find a scapegoat for student unrest, and Ilyenkov and Korovikov were the perfect targets. After all, whether or not the students in question had in any way been influenced by them directly, there was no doubt that Ilyenkov and Korovikov stood for a climate of independent thought. Few among the old guard would go as far as Shchipanov and all but accuse Ilyenkov and Korovikov of sedition, but most were happy to offer them to the Central Committee in sacrifice. A few figures dissented, but no-one would now dare openly defend the philosophical integrity of the theses, so those friendly to Ilyenkov, such as Oizerman, were reduced to endorsing the charge of heresy, but suggesting that blame lay with the Faculty's Scientific Council for failing expeditiously to prevent such revisionist views from gaining momentum.[19] The strategy was to give the University an incentive to downplay or bury the controversy, for fear of being burnt along with the heretics.

Unfortunately, the strategy did not work. At the end of April 1955, the Central Committee concluded that, while it was true that the quality of teaching in the Faculty had been lamentable for years, and hence had caused students to lose interest in orthodox Marxism-Leninism, Ilyenkov, Korovikov, and a number of other young faculty, were to blame for irresponsibly teaching revisionist doctrines. Accordingly, the review recommended that they should be relieved of their duties.[20] Korovikov was suspended from teaching. He received a strong rebuke and warning from the Faculty's Party organization, and he was fired from MGU on June 28. This was not as bad as it could have been. In May, the Faculty's Party organization apparently voted for his exclusion from the Communist Party, but for some reason this did not proceed. Moreover, though fired from MGU, he was given a reference and offered a position at the Stalingrad Pedagogical Institute (*IK*, 90). Korovikov chose instead to quit academia altogether and eventually became a journalist, serving as a foreign correspondent for *Pravda* for many years, principally in Africa. The British and Americans apparently thought he was a Soviet spy and had him under surveillance. In any case, he seems to have lived a happy life, and died in 2010 (ibid., 141–142).

Ilyenkov was also suspended from teaching at MGU, but since his primary appointment was at the Institute of Philosophy, he was not in danger of losing his job and the Faculty's Party organization had no power over him. The only real danger was that he would be stripped of his Candidate's dissertation, but Oizerman contrived that the committee established to reassess the work included Mark M. Rozenthal, a philosopher, not of the old guard, but of the old school—one of the few figures at MGU who was genuinely respected for his intellectual contribution. Oizerman was sure Rozenthal could be trusted to affirm the merits of Ilyenkov's dissertation and stare down know-nothing opposition, and that, it seems, is what happened.

I had previously thought that the Institute of Philosophy was a calmer, more scholarly institution than the University, where Ilyenkov was protected by figures with integrity, such as Bonifaty M. Kedrov (see Bakhurst 2013, 272). But Illesh's book reveals that this view is quite wrong. The Institute was in just as a big a mess as the University. In fact, it was a worse mess. For one thing, figures who had enjoyed a distinguished career in some or other avenue of Soviet life—be it engineering, agriculture, state security, or whatever (the more hands-on the better)—would sometimes be put out to pasture at the Institute. So, the faculty complement included people, now expected to write books on philosophy, who had no qualifications, let alone expertise. Some, such as ex-KGB operative Elena Modrzhinskaya, relished the chance to put their previous expertise to work in this new area, but most were simply at sea and lingered as "*bezdel'niki*" (loafers). Moreover, in Spring–Summer 1955, the former director of the Institute, Georgy F. Aleksandrov, who had stepped down in 1954, was under a storm of criticism and embroiled in a scandal of some kind, which led to his being exiled to Belarus to head the sector of dialectical and historical materialism at the Institute of Philosophy and Law in Minsk (see *IK*, 258).

From Illesh's narrative, one might surmise that the general shenanigans at the Institute distracted people's attention from the controversy going on over at the University, but this is not so. On April 6 and 7, 1955, on the heels of the trial-like proceedings at MGU, similar meetings were held at the Institute's Sector of Dialectical Materialism.[21] Eighty-one people were present at meetings where the principal agenda item was "The Theoretical Mistakes of Comrade Ilyenkov, E.V." And once again the outcome was resolutions condemning Ilyenkov for his antiscientific, revisionist reading of Marxism—which, so it was stated, amounts to an idealist form of neopositivism—and removing him from the role of leader of the graduate special seminar. Ilyenkov was also much criticized for his hubris and arrogance.

And that was by no means the end of the matter. By the fall of 1955 the situation had worsened still. Now the Institute was under scrutiny from above: questions were being asked about its role, and about the quality of work coming out of it. And, as at MGU, members of the establishment sought a scapegoat in Ilyenkov. Throughout the fall, the Institute hosted a (protracted) conference on the nature of philosophy, at which many figures, including Ilyenkov, gave presentations. Since Ilyenkov was continuing to develop the ideas first expressed in the theses 18 months previously (notwithstanding his public retractions of his errors), he became the target of familiar accusations of revisionism. These accusations were now supplemented, however, by charges pertaining to Ilyenkov's behavior, which is variously described as politically "tactless," "disgraceful," and "criminal."

What had he done now? First, Ilyenkov had asked that Korovikov be permitted to address the conference, which many considered inappropriate. But second, Ilyenkov had requested that a letter from Todor Pavlov be read out at the conference. Pavlov was a Bulgarian philosopher, President of the Bulgarian Academy of Sciences. The Ilyenkov-Korovikov theses had found their way to him, conveyed by Bulgarian students studying in Moscow, and Pavlov had written a letter to the Directorship of the Institute. It seems that Ilyenkov did not know what was in the letter, but he wanted its contents made public. The Directorship did not want that to happen. Pavlov was no free thinker, but he was interested in epistemology, and so one might surmise that he would at least have endorsed Ilyenkov's efforts to get Marxist philosophy to take epistemological issues seriously. In addition, Ilyenkov and Korovikov had also written to Palmiro Togliatti, leader of the Italian Communist Party, whose article, "From Hegel to Marx," had appeared in the April 1955 issue of *Voprosy filosofii*. In the letter, Ilyenkov and Korovikov pointed out that they had been accused of revisionism for advancing a reading of Engels not dissimilar to Togliatti's own (*IK*, 95–96).

In the disputes at MGU, Ilyenkov and Korovikov were often criticized for involving students in the debate, and they drew special criticism for involving foreign students. Corrupting the youth was bad, but corrupting foreign youth was especially malevolent. Now Ilyenkov was under fire for attempting to draw foreign Marxists into the discussion. This was considered outrageous. Ilyenkov, it was argued, was either amazingly naïve or incredibly arrogant (or both) to think that he could do this, and at a time when Khrushchev was counselling all to avoid confrontation with their foreign friends in the socialist brotherhood. On November 2, a motion was passed at the Party organization giving Ilyenkov a severe warning and reprimand for his behavior (*IK*, 121).

This almost hysterical concern over the involvement of foreigners was prompted by fear on the part of the establishment—fear of losing control of the debate, fear of being seen to wash dirty linen in public, fear of making tactical errors, which would draw the ire of the Central Committee, fear of appearing to be no longer the vanguard of Marxist thought, and fear of being exposed as ignorant of the issues. No one in the academic establishment took an interest in the *ideas* of thinkers like Pavlov or Togliatti. If their work was published in Russia, the reason was intellectual diplomacy, not debate. The last thing anyone wanted was to address the question of the plausibility or otherwise of the philosophical content of what was said (unless it proved expedient to criticize it as heretical). By trying to force that, Ilyenkov was playing with fire.

The seemingly inevitable conflagration, however, never happened. For although the controversy continued till the end of December, when a closed Party meeting at the Institute of Philosophy condemned the "rejection of Marxist philosophy in the articles and speeches of E. V. Ilyenkov," it was eventually overtaken by the Twentieth Party Congress in February 1956, where Khrushchev gave his "secret speech," denouncing Stalin's crimes and the cult of personality (ibid., 141). Thereafter, the Ilyenkov-Korovikov theses were no longer the subject of discussion.

* * *

The abstract of Illesh's book describes it as a "*filosofskii detektiv*" (*IK*, 2), a crime thriller or "whodunnit." It certainly took detective work on her part to collect and interpret the archival material on which the story is based, but one might question whether "*detektiv*" is an apt description. In a whodunnit, there is always at least one body, but so far we don't have one. True, we have witnessed an internecine struggle between, on the one hand, the zombies of the Soviet philosophical establishment, and on the other, the critical Marxists or philosophical *stilyagi*, exemplified by the young Ilyenkov. But this is not so much a tale of murder, but of survival, even rebirth. For the message of Illesh's book is that a new generation of Soviet philosophers drew inspiration from Ilyenkov, from the range of philosophical issues his thinking opened up to them. This is what philosopher Vladimir S. Bibler meant when he said that "we all came out from under Ilyenkov's overcoat" (alluding to Dostoevsky's remark about Gogol).[22] Moreover, Ilyenkov was an inspiration for his independence of mind. Few were prepared to stand up for him during the original controversy, but it is interesting to read the words of one who did, Elena Basova of the Institute of Philosophy, who came to his defense at a party meeting. She said:

> We all know that Ilyenkov is a young philosopher. He has passion, but he is also very observant. He has a lot of life-experience, erudition in philosophy, and importantly, he has a love of science. He works incredibly hard. He has what is most important of all, independence (*samostoyatel'nost'*), inner independence (*nezavisimost'*); he learns from everyone, but follows no one. He listens hard to all the advice he is given, but does things his way, as his scientific conscience dictates.
>
> —*IK*, 124

It must have taken great courage to say these words—indeed Basova's speech breaks off as she is shouted down. They give us insight into Ilyenkov's status as an inspirational figure.

It is worth noting that Ilyenkov has sometimes been portrayed as a rather weak, beleaguered, even cowardly figure. But the transcripts published in Illesh's book show otherwise. He always behaves with poise and is resolute in his insistence that what is at issue is a theoretical matter of great importance—the nature of philosophy—and that all eyes should be on that and that alone. He is never cowed by the institutional power of his adversaries, and he never concedes that the sword is mightier than the pen, telling V. I. Chertkov, head of the Institute's Party organization, that Chertkov was in no position to comment on the philosophical quality of the work produced by those in Ilyenkov's department, since he took no interest in it. You had to be very brave in Soviet Russia to stand up to authority in that way.[23]

The story is also one of the birth of Ilyenkov's own philosophical career. It may have been a long and painful labor, but Ilyenkov went on to do important work, and all of it can be seen as originating in the ideas sketched in his *Notebook* and propounded in the theses. His study of Marx's method, begun in his Candidate's dissertation, was developed into an influential book, *The Dialectics of the Abstract and the Concrete in Marx's* Capital (1960). He took up the nature of thought in his seminal 1962 paper on "The Ideal," written for the five-volume *Philosophical Encyclopedia*, a work symbolic of Khrushchev's "thaw." Here, he argues that our most fundamental forms of thought should be seen, not as pure a priori categories, but as essentially embodied in forms of collective human activity (a kind of "cultural a priori"). Accordingly, he argues that human beings become thinking things, acquire powers of reason, as they are initiated into collectively-instantiated modes of activity, objectified both in the practices of the community and in the form of the humanized environment. It is precisely in this, he maintains, that the revolutionary philosophical significance of the concept of activity resides, a theme signaled in his earliest writings but substantiated only later. The idea of the social formation of mind brought Ilyenkov into dialogue with the Vygotskian tradition and also inspired his writings on education, in which he at once stressed the social (i.e. state) responsibility to create the conditions in which human minds can flourish and extolled the importance of intellectual creativity and independence of mind. These and other prominent themes in his work—such as the nature of dialectical logic, the identity of thinking and being, and the defense of humanism against technocracy—all have their seeds in his writings from the time of the theses.

So is not this a story of renaissance, rather than a whodunnit? Well, in fact this is one of those zombie stories when, just when you think the world restored to order and the hero safe, he turns a corner and . . .

Sadly, there is a corpse in the story. Ilyenkov's own. Although the Twentieth Party Congress put a stop to the controversy over the theses, and the subsequent "thaw" made it possible for Ilyenkov to proceed with his work, the Zombies that almost got him in 1955 were not vanquished. Far from it. They all maintained their positions of power and influence within the Soviet academic world[24] and many continued in their animosity to Ilyenkov, whose career lurched from one controversy to the next. For example, although he finished his manuscript on Marx's method in 1956, it was published only in truncated form in 1960 and after intense opposition from the directorship of the Institute of Philosophy. The complete version appeared only in 1997. Eventually the stress of such controversies wore him down, the last straw coming when a substantial paper he had written on the problem of the ideal was refused publication. That event reputedly led to his suicide (see Bakhurst 2013). The story of the end of his life is tortuous and much detail remains unknown. But it is very much the conclusion, perhaps the natural conclusion, of the tale I have told: the story of one young punk, Ilyenkov, in a strange and surreal land, who unlike his friend Korovikov, chose to be a Zombie fighter till the end, and who, despite many noble victories, was eventually torn apart.

# APPENDICES

The two appendices present, first, a translation of the theses as reconstructed by Ilesh in Ilyenkov and Korovikov 2016, 143–147, and, second, a translation of the complete text of the theses, discovered only after Ilesh's book was completed. I am very grateful to Alex Levant for advice on the translations.

## *Appendix I*

*Theses on the Question of the Interconnection of Philosophy and Knowledge of Nature and Society in the Process of their Historical Development*

*E.V. Ilyenkov and V. I. Korovikov*

*Translated by David Bakhurst*

**1.** "The necessity of the emergence of philosophy coincides totally and completely with the necessity of scientific knowledge in general."[25]

**2.** ". . . It is essential to understand the internal necessity (*zakonomernost'*), the fundamental historical tendency, which has produced historical change in the subject of philosophy, notwithstanding numerous contingencies and digressions, and despite the intentions of particular philosophers."

**3.** "Philosophy in its origin comes forth immediately as theoretical thought." ". . . [it is inevitable (*zakonomerno*) that philosophy arises out of a demand for the general, from the demands of the concept of the general."[26]

[4–6]

**7.** "In what does the necessity of the rise of philosophy consist? On the one hand, in the fact that the subject of philosophical research since the time of Aristotle is that which carries the name 'primary substance' (*sushchnost'*), 'substance as such,' in distinction from, and even in opposition to, those 'substances' that can be directly disclosed in the very phenomena of nature and society by means of their theoretical analysis, and on the other hand, in [the question of] the kind of reality those objects (*predmet*) have that are studied in a form mystified in light of conceptions of 'primary substance.' The answer to this question can be given only if we understand the necessity of philosophy growing out of the development of scientific-theoretical knowledge."

". . . the need for a relatively independent, specifically philosophical mode of investigation emerges from the nature of 'concrete,' that is, to use a more exact term—scientific-theoretical knowledge."

[8–10]

**11.** "Before the emergence of Marxism, philosophy spoke as the science with a monopoly on the interpretation of the laws of the universe precisely because positive knowledge had not given a constructive understanding of these connections, did not view its subject in its necessary connection with the subject of cognate sciences, did not reveal in it movement, development and, consequently, did not give an understanding of the world as a materially developing whole. Therefore, for example, alongside empirical history there arose the distinct field of philosophy of history, alongside empirical natural science there arose the philosophy of nature, and so on."

**12.** "Marx and Engels showed that the basic task of natural science, and science as such, studying the socio-historical order confronting them in the nineteenth century, was the task of collecting the totality of the finest results achieved in the 2000-year development of philosophy, which amounted to a paraphrase of the demand to think correctly, grammatically, in the theoretical analysis of phenomena. Marx provides an exemplar of the constructive application of philosophy to particular branches of concrete knowledge, in particular political economy.

And this is the best proof of the proposition that positive knowledge is itself able to reach, and is obliged to reach, that very final essence of the object of research, beneath, above and beyond which there is nothing to find for the reason that there is nothing more."

**13.** "But insofar as the sciences arrive at a constructive dialectico-materialist method of thinking, insofar as they nourish themselves on all the achievements of philosophy, they will inevitably be led to an explication of their mutual relations, connections (*perekhodov*), and moreover to give in its totality the only possible picture of the world as a unity in all its interconnections, in comparison with which a purely philosophical system of representations of the world as a unified whole would be thoroughly redundant, and the aspiration to create such a thing would be an antiquated and reactionary aspiration."

**13, 14 or 15.** "Dialectical laws, in their purity and abstractness, can be studied and clarified by philosophy only as logical categories, as laws of dialectical thought. Only by making theoretical thinking, the process of cognition, its object does philosophy include in itself the study of the most general characteristics of being, and not the reverse, as it is so often maintained. Philosophy is the science of scientific thinking, its laws and forms."[27]

[14–15]

**On p. 6 of the Theses:** "Notice, by the way, that one will never completely rid oneself from this, so long as one interprets philosophy as the science of the world, of its most general laws."[28]

**Not known which thesis:** "The dialectic is not the monopoly of philosophy, it is present in any scientific knowledge, the laws of the dialectic are disclosed by any science, in any object; philosophy is the science of scientific thought and its laws."[29]

**Not known which thesis:** "The propositions formulated by philosophy, though they are abstracted from reality, in the form they are given by philosophy, have value and significance only for thought and for nothing else. Accordingly, they are not laws of reality, but laws of thought."[30]

**Quotation from the Theses (p. 5):** "Theoretical thought is the real subject of philosophy."[31]

**Quotation from the Theses (p. 7):** "It is impossible to free oneself completely from this [from Hegelianism] if one interprets philosophy as the science of the world."[32]

## *Appendix II*

*Theses on the Question of the Interconnection of Philosophy and Knowledge of Nature and Society in the Process of their Historical Development*

*(Complete)*

*E.V. Ilyenkov and V. I. Korovikov*

*Translated by David Bakhurst*

**1.** To examine the given problem on a historico-philosophical plane is one of the most important forms of research into the interrelation of the philosophy of dialectical materialism and the sciences of nature and society. This question is unarguably topical, and on its resolution depends the further development of philosophy as a science, the direction in which philosophy's content will be developed.

**2.** That there is the closest internal interconnection between the development of philosophy and the development of knowledge of nature and society is a fact, and the entire question is to understand the historical forms of this interconnection and their evolution. For the historian of philosophy, it is above all necessary to understand the history of the interrelation between philosophy, on the one hand, and knowledge of natural and socio-historical phenomena, on the other, at the level of the evolution of the historical forms of philosophy, in the changing of its subject matter. In other words, it is essential to understand the internal necessity (*zakonomernost'*), the fundamental historical tendency, that has *produced historical change in the subject of philosophy*, and moreover, in the forms of philosophy's interrelation with knowledge of nature and society, notwithstanding numerous contingencies and digressions, and despite the intentions of particular philosophers.

**3.** Above all, the question is to understand the social necessity of the emergence of philosophy as a particular form of knowledge, as a particular sphere in the division of intellectual labor. We must understand the nature of the social needs that can only be satisfied by philosophy and not by other forms of social knowledge—not by religion, art, legal or political ideas.

Therefore, the question is *not only, and not so much*, to research the causes of philosophy's emergence in the same general terms we use for understanding the emergence of ideology, the superstructure as such, as to understand the specific grounds of the historical necessity of its emergence, the grounds on which philosophy emerged and developed as a science, acquiring a specific subject-matter and methods for the solution of its problems.

In science, there are many different points of view on this score. The opinion is familiar that philosophy arises from the need for a general, synthesizing representation of the world as a whole, out of our dissatisfaction with "finite," particular, detailed knowledge.

In its blatant form, this point of view was developed by representatives of positivism in the history of philosophy (see, e.g., Lewes's *History of Philosophy*[33]). This point of view does not withstand scrutiny however, because at the beginning of philosophy's development, the distinction between philosophy and the concrete sciences has no place, it being a product of a much later time. In Ancient Greece, we are confronted by an undifferentiated, unified science.

Philosophy in its origin comes forth immediately as theoretical thought, perfecting itself in the course of understanding the phenomena of nature and society. In this, logical knowledge as a whole stands against religious forms of awareness, the spiritual exploration of phenomena that have immediate significance for social man.

*The necessity of the emergence of philosophy coincides totally and completely with the necessity of the emergence of scientific knowledge in general*,—in opposition to religious forms of consciousness. In this sense, it becomes completely clear that philosophy at its birth could be nothing other than naïve materialism with elements of just as naïve dialectics.

**4.** It is characteristic of ancient philosophy to differentiate scientific-theoretical knowledge, which on account of its lack of development, appears as something whole and unified, directly connected to one scientific-philosophical system.

But even in antiquity there is (in Aristotle) the attempt to distinguish the subject of *genuine philosophy*.

**5.** Thereafter begins the process of the differentiation of the sciences, including the process of the dissociation of philosophy from other branches of knowledge. In this movement of knowledge, philosophy acts as *the science of sciences*, and keeps this quality as its characteristic attribute in the system of sciences right up to the emergence of dialectical materialism. Countenancing this specific situation of pre-Marxist philosophy represents one of the central points in understanding the history of philosophy as a science.

**6.** What are the causes of the separation of philosophy as "the science of sciences," as a specific domain of research, relatively independent in relation to theoretical knowledge as a whole?

We can answer this question only if we give full consideration to: (a) the undeveloped state of knowledge of the world, the hypothetical and speculative character in many of its parts, and (b) the battle, which begins inside philosophy itself,—the battle that manifests itself above all in the appearance of idealism, as a transformed form of religion, adopting a theoretical form of posing questions and thereby expressing itself as a tension within philosophy.

The whole meaning of the idealist tendency in philosophy consists in the fact that it, in one or other form, in one or other style of argumentation, proceeds from a conception of the inadequacy of scientific-theoretical research into the phenomena of nature and society—from the thesis of science's in principle inability to reach the final, deepest universal and the necessary essence of things. Parasitizing on the historical immaturity and limitedness of knowledge of nature and society, idealism insists on the necessity of *paths to knowledge of truth* that are different in principle from the scientific-theoretical analysis of the phenomena of nature and society, namely religious or speculative-logical conceptions of the "essential," of the "universal."

The necessity of fighting idealism, and also religion (the battle against which is never off the agenda for a single moment in the course of the development of theoretical knowledge of natural and socio-historical phenomena), creates for materialism an issue, which does not coincide entirely with the immediate knowledge of nature and society in the course of their theoretical analysis.

One aspect of this consists above all in the need to *defend* (stand up for) the worldview significance of knowledge, acquired in the course of the theoretical analysis of the phenomena of nature and society, and in the battle against the worldview conception of religion and idealism. This defense of knowledge takes the form of an absolutization, the construction of the essence of the world.

7. As is well known, the battle of materialism and idealism in Ancient Greece gave us the philosophy of Aristotle, whose philosophical system already clearly expresses and crystallizes the tendency to transform philosophy into the science of "primary substance."

On the one hand, by what *necessity* does the subject of philosophical research since the time of Aristotle become that which carries the name "primary substance" (*sushchnost'*), "substance as such"—in distinction from, and even in opposition to, those "substances" that can be directly disclosed in the very phenomena of nature and society by means of their theoretical analysis, and, on the other hand, *what kind of reality* has that object (*predmet*), which is studied in a form mystified by conceptions of "primary substance"?

The answer to such questions can be given only if we understand *the necessity of philosophy* growing out of the very development of scientific-theoretical knowledge.

This necessity absolutely does not consist in the fact that scientific-theoretical knowledge of "finite," particular phenomena "fails to satisfy the need for a conception of the world as a whole." That kind of need can be satisfied completely and with a vengeance by a simple summary of the most important judgements about these phenomena.

The need for a relatively independent, specifically philosophical mode of investigation emerges from the nature of "concrete," that is, to use a more exact term—theoretical knowledge.

Scientific-theoretical thinking emerges and develops, as Engels showed, together with research into "the nature of its very concepts," without which it is in general impossible. Scientific-theoretical knowledge presupposes that we carefully address the very forms in which, and by means of which, we reflect the world, the phenomena of nature and society, scientific-theoretically.

*Research into logical categories*—as the form, in and by means of which scientific-theoretical knowledge of nature and society perfects itself, taking place in philosophy in parallel with, and on the basis of, the formation and development of those very categories themselves, which occurs always and everywhere in the course of human beings' concrete scientific-theoretical knowledge of the world—*acts in the history of philosophy as its objective content, as its genuine subject.*

Careful understanding of this circumstance is possible only by philosophical thought, which has reached a very high level *of its development, precisely self-conscious dialectical materialism.* The necessity with which this occurs makes a road for itself spontaneously, and is historically connected precisely with the conception of philosophy as the science of sciences, researching the deepest, most fundamental, definitive, universal and necessary forms of being.

**8.** Historically, philosophical research into this real subject took the form of directly researching "the deepest and most elemental features and forms of the universe," of directly aspiring to apprehend some kind of *essence of the world*, lying supposedly "beyond," "above" and "below" those substances, knowledge of which is attained, or may in principle be attained, in the course of concrete scientific-theoretical research into the phenomena of nature and society.

The understanding of philosophy as the "science of sciences," as a system of categories, reflecting, in its totality, the final, most profound essence of all things and phenomena, as the science of the universal and the infinite, in contrast with and addition to "finite knowledge," is characteristic, as already noted, of all pre-Marxist philosophy, including pre-Marxist materialism.

Nevertheless, of course, even here there exists a profound, principled difference between materialism and idealism. For materialism, it is characteristic to recognize that all the categories that philosophy (or the philosophical sciences) expresses as universal forms of knowledge of real phenomena of nature and society, existing outside and independently of human beings, are given to us in sensation, contemplation and representation, and therefore, and only therefore, are *universal forms of these phenomena themselves.*

Idealism characteristically has the opposite understanding. For it, the categories of philosophy are not universal forms of the cognition of phenomena, given to man in sensation, but forms enabling us to grasp "the infinite, universal essence of the world," which is not the subject of "finite knowledge." Let us take a concrete example of such an understanding.

Hegel very clearly gives philosophy this role in relation to concrete (finite) knowledge when he writes:

> The Philosophy of Nature takes up the material which physics has prepared for it empirically, at the point to which physics has brought it, and reconstitutes it, so that experience is not its final warrant and base. Physics must therefore work into the hands of philosophy, in order that the latter may translate into the Notion the abstract universal transmitted to it, by showing how the universal, as an intrinsically necessary whole, proceeds from the Notion. The philosophical way of putting the facts is no mere whim, once in a way to walk on one's head for a change, after having walked for a long while on one's legs, or once in a way to see our everyday face bedaubed with paint: no, it is because the method of physics does not satisfy the Notion, that we have to go further. (Hegel 1970, 10)

Notice, by the way, that one will never completely rid oneself of this [view], so long as one interprets philosophy as the science of the world, of its most general laws.

There can be no doubt of course that in reality both materialism and idealism in their philosophical systems, revealing the essence of the world, expressed nothing other than universal forms of one and the same "finite" knowledge, nothing other than universal forms of the theoretical thought of their epoch, expressed as universal spirit (Hegel), or nature (Holbach).

In reality, both *The System of Nature* and *The Encyclopedia of the Philosophical Sciences* are in their content identical results of the "generalization" of scientific-theoretical knowledge that had been attained by human beings at the time they were written. In this relation, the difference between Hegel and Holbach consists only in that the former, as an idealist, erroneously draws his conclusions from purely speculative thinking, while the latter consciously generalizes data that are given by science and consciously views *philosophical categories as universal* forms of the world, and therefore—of scientific-theoretical thought.

**9.** Philosophy was not turned into the science of sciences because philosophers apparently assumed that philosophy builds systems of categories independently of "finite knowledge," and attempted to construct general systems of belief about the world as a whole (worldviews) independently of the development of knowledge of nature and society. This was not attempted even by the idealists, as is shown by the quotation from Hegel. Philosophy was made the science of sciences by the fact that it evolved historically in the form of a system of concepts, reflecting "the world as a whole," the world in its most general relations.

This striving to create a picture or system of the world as a whole presupposes that the totality of positive scientific judgements about the phenomena of nature and society do not give, and in principle cannot give, a unified representation of the world, in all its connections. Therefore, the reflection of the world in the human head was doubled, appearing once in the form of the aggregate of "finite knowledge," and a second time, in the form of one or another philosophical or religious system. We will not discuss the social roots and causes of this phenomenon. They are sufficiently clear, particularly in relation to religion and idealism, which directly insist on the thesis that no matter how complete the sciences of nature and society become, they never give, and in principle can never give, an exhaustive understanding of the phenomena of nature and society. This is demonstrated most clearly of all, it would seem, by Kant, who limits knowledge in order to clear *space for faith*.

**10.** It is essential to examine the epistemic causes and grounds of this most important phenomenon in the history of the philosophy of science. Why did materialist philosophy up until Marx share with idealism the understanding of philosophy as the science of sciences, which is able to build such a conception of the world, of nature and society, which the sciences of nature and society cannot get near?

The fundamental cause of this phenomenon, it would seem, resides in the general lowering of the level of theoretical thought about research into nature and society at the emergence of modernity (in the sixteenth century), which is the *other side* of the rapid accumulation of factual, empirical material characteristic of this era, and which has its objective basis in the development of production, beginning its capitalist stage.

There can be no doubt that here the development of scientific judgements on the content, on the richness, of the facts under examination, is given by what Engels calls "the formal side" of scientific research, meaning theoretical thought at a level able to use already worked-out logical categories. But since "one cannot bring two natural facts into relation with one another, or understand the connection between them, without theoretical thought," and since the issue consists entirely in "whether one's thinking is correct or not" (Engels 1976, 60), then, insofar as theoretical thinking continued to develop, it was infinitely lower in its level than thought consciously assimilating to itself the higher exemplars of theoretical thinking developed by the ancient undivided science. Therefore, it was philosophy in the early modern period that was able to find a higher point of view on things, the ability deeper to penetrate theoretically those very same phenomena studied by non-philosophers.

This is exactly why the theoretical understanding of the phenomena of nature and society given in philosophy offers an incomparably higher model of theoretical understanding than the separate sciences, which are unable to cope with the theoretical analysis of facts precisely because too many facts are being discovered every day and must above all be regimented, classified, and subsumed under a fundamental order, and so on and so forth.

*From all this the illusion grows*, reflecting actual historical fact, that philosophy in its nature is called upon to make up for the inadequacy, the deficiency of "finite" knowledge. But this fact, the historically-conditioned and therefore transitory fact, that the sciences of nature and society were grounded in this period in a spontaneous, empirical, anti-dialectical conception of the aims and means of the methods of theoretical thinking, was perceived by philosophy—and this is absolutely natural in light of the total ahistoricism of the thought of this period—as a fact, expressing not the historically transient state of science, but its eternal, "finite" nature. This reading makes intelligible Marx's well-known saying about the *importation into philosophy* of the narrow empiricism of the natural science of the seventeenth century, which appears in philosophy as a powerful stream of metaphysical thinking, drowning out the dialectic of the ancients.

This state of the interrelation of philosophy and the science of nature and society continued right up to the emergence of Marxism.

**11.** The overcoming of the dualism of philosophy and positive knowledge is one of the principal achievements of dialectical materialism.

Before the emergence of Marxism, as we showed above, philosophy spoke as the science with a monopoly on the interpretation of the laws of the universe precisely because positive knowledge had not given a constructive understanding of these connections, did not view its subject in its necessary connection with the subject of cognate sciences, did not reveal in it movement, development and, consequently, did not provide an understanding of the world as a materially developing whole. Therefore, for example, alongside empirical history there arose the distinct field of the *philosophy of history*, and so on.

**12.** Marx and Engels showed that the basic task of natural science, and science as such, studying the socio-historical order confronting them in the nineteenth century, was the task of collecting the totality of the finest results achieved in the 2000-year development of philosophy, which amounted to a paraphrase of the demand to think correctly, grammatically, in the theoretical analysis of phenomena. Marx provides an exemplar of the constructive application of philosophy to particular branches of concrete knowledge, in particular political economy.

And this is the best proof of the proposition that "positive knowledge" is itself able to reach, and is obliged to reach, that very final essence of the object of research, beneath, above and beyond which there is nothing to find for the reason that there is nothing more.

But if that is how things are, then it would be extremely reactionary, from the point of view of the relation of philosophy and science, to place alongside Marx's political economy a further field, "the philosophy of political economy."

The latter would be nothing other than an abstract restatement of the first. There cannot be two sciences of exactly the same thing. But this pertains to the interrelations of philosophy and all the particular sciences. Insofar as any science approaches *Capital* in its theoretical literacy and completeness, then it renders unnecessary a special philosophical inquiry into the same subject.

And on the other hand, if some or other science stands at a low level of theoretical literacy, then the task of philosophy is not to make up for its ineptitude by its own means, leaving it as it is and raising next to it a "philosophical understanding" of the object of the given science, but to lead that same science to an appropriate level of theoretical development, to help it understand its object dialectico-materialistically, that is, in connection with development, in its internal, specific, order.

**13.** But insofar as the sciences arrive at a constructive dialectico-materialist method of thinking, insofar as they nourish themselves on all the achievements of philosophy, they will inevitably be led to an explication of their mutual relations, connections (*perekhodov*), and moreover in their totality to give the only possible picture of the world as a unity in all its interconnections, [in comparison] with which a purely philosophical system of representations of the world as a unified whole would be thoroughly redundant, and the aspiration to create such a thing would be an *antiquated and reactionary* aspiration.

Engels expresses this thought in all his major works. "That which still survives, independently, of all earlier philosophy is the science of thought and its laws—formal logic and dialectics" (Engels 1978, 36).

**14.** The dialectic is not the *monopoly of philosophy*, it is present in any scientific knowledge. Exactly for this reason, the laws of the dialectic are universal, and are studied (disclosed) by any science, whatever its object, and thereby the truth of the object is revealed.

Dialectical laws, in their purity and abstractness, can be studied and clarified by philosophy only as logical categories, as laws of dialectical thought. Only by making theoretical thinking, the process of cognition, its object does philosophy include in itself the study of the most general characteristics of being, and not the reverse, as it is so often maintained.

Philosophy is the science of scientific thinking, its laws and forms; moreover, of course, a materialist science, investigating the forms and laws of thought as an analogy to the corresponding objective universal forms of the development of objective reality.

**15.** The significance of philosophy for the science of nature and society consists in the fact that philosophy replaces the spontaneity of knowledge with considered, more perfect methods of approaching the object of research, it teaches the well-grounded all-sided use of thought, it arms scientific knowledge with self-consciousness. "One cannot bring two natural facts into relation with one another, or understand the connection existing between them, without theoretical thought. The only question is whether one's thinking is correct or not" (Engels 1976, 60). That is the *question* that *scientific* philosophy must answer, in that resides the meaning and necessity of its existence in the system of the sciences.[34]

## NOTES

1. Copious references to Ilyenkov's works and other relevant writings can be found in my other chapter in this volume, "Activity and the Formation of Reason."
2. The full title appears to have been "Theses on the Question of the Interrelation of Philosophy and Knowledge of Nature and Society in the Process of their Historical Development."
3. *Stilyagi*, in the words of novelist Francis Spufford (2010, 402n), were "quaffed, music-loving members of the Soviet Union's first distinctive teenage tribe. Associated with delinquency, and therefore conveniently blamable for all ills, and not just by the Russians: Anthony Burgess claimed that it was a violent encounter with *stilyagi* outside a Leningrad nightclub that inspired him to create Alex and his droogs in *A Clockwork Orange*."
4. For example, by Lektorsky, *IK*, 236n1.
5. The title of the book, *Strasti po tezisam o predmete filosofii*, is hard to translate. "*Strasti*" can mean "horrors," but I prefer "passion" because it preserves the religious connotations of the original ("*Strasti po Matfeiu*" for example, is the St. Matthew Passion). Thus, I propose *The Passion of the Theses on the History of Philosophy*.

   The archival material is supplemented by valuable commentary by Illesh herself, Ilya Raskin and one of the editors of this volume, Vladislav Lektorsky, who was an eyewitness to the events, and who later went on to a distinguished philosophical career, which included many years as editor of *Voprosy filosofii*.

   I should stress that I played no part whatsoever in the archival research. My role here is simply to make the history known to a wider audience than might be expected to become acquainted with the book.
6. There are some differences (significant ones are referenced in the notes to Appendix I) between the passages in the reconstruction and the original theses. For example, Illesh's extract from Thesis 1, appears in Thesis 3 in the original; part of Illesh's Thesis 3 does not appear at all in the original. The cause of these discrepancies may be human error, possibly by those who recorded the meetings where the theses were discussed (e.g. misinterpreting a paraphrase as a direct quotation). But it may also have been the case that different versions of the theses were in circulation. In what follows references to the theses are to the complete text as presented in Appendix II.

7. See Thesis 12, where Ilyenkov and Korovikov praise Marx for applying philosophical insights to concrete issues of political economy, and conclude: "This is the best proof of the proposition that positive knowledge is itself able to reach, and is obliged to reach, that very final essence of the object of research, beyond, above and below which there is nothing to find for the reason that there is nothing more."
8. The critique of the idea of philosophy as "the science of sciences" is a constant theme throughout the complete text of the theses.
9. The term *zakonomernost'*, akin to the German *Regelmäßigkeit*, is difficult to translate. "Regularity" does not capture the sense of necessitation implicit in the Russian term; "lawfulness" is too legal in connotation; "law-governedness" is barely English. In this context, I use "order," but this will not suffice for many uses of *zakonomernost'*.
10. The paper, "With Regard to the Question of the Subject of Philosophy as a Science," is either a preparatory study for the theses, or a subsequent attempt to defend them. It is included in *IK*, 229–234.
11. At this stage, Ilyenkov is not great at characterizing the nature of this identity: "The laws of thought are nothing other than the laws of objective reality itself transplanted into the human head and transformed therein" (echoing Marx on the ideal in the Afterword to the second edition of *Capital*). This is not a happy way of seeing things, and Ilyenkov continued to work on this theme, producing a notable paper in 1964.
12. Consider also: "Insofar as the historically-sedimented order (*zakonomernost'*) of theoretical thought is the analog of the objective order, it remains correct to give the most general definition of philosophy as the science of the most general order of nature, society and thought" (*IK*, 189). And: "the laws of cognizing thought cannot in principle contradict the laws of nature and society in so far as thought is objective, object-oriented" (ibid., 207).
13. This issue is not developed in the theses, but is prominent in Ilyenkov's *Notebook*.
14. As even Oizerman maintains (*IK*, 193). Ilyenkov writes that we need to create "a never-before-existing dialectico-materialist theory of knowledge, which incorporates *partiinost'* together with practice, and makes it not an external stimulus to thinking, but its internal essential character" (ibid., 195).
15. Consider: "these principles, these laws (*zakonomernosti*), characteristic of the present stage of theoretical thought, must not be turned into blinkers, into categorical limits to the further development of thought. No—if the material convinces the researcher that certain laws, till now considered the *sine qua non* of cognizing thought, need to be reconsidered, broadened, clarified, then that is a completely normal and justified phenomenon. Dialectic as a method changes and develops together with the development of theoretical thought, wh . . . [manuscript breaks off]." (*IK*, 199–200).
16. Though, as Illesh notes, Kosichev paints a rather different picture in his 2007 memoir (see *IK*, 26–27).
17. Lektorsky comments on how strange it is to see Ilyenkov referring to Stalin, and even Zhdanov, while making arguments that were utterly heretical (*IK*, 236n).
18. It is interesting that the protocol of these meetings contains notes on audience reactions.
19. To some extent Korovikov and Ilyenkov deployed the same tactic themselves; see Korovikov arguing that he was a child of the Faculty of Philosophy ("I didn't fall from

the sky" (*IK*, 75)) and that his views, whatever their (no doubt many) errors, are a product of the poor climate of research and teaching.

20. See the finding of A. Rumiantsev, Head of the Central Committee's Department for Science and Culture, dated April 29, 1955 (*IK*, 85–90).
21. These meetings are not mentioned in *IK*. They are documented in the archives of the Russian Academy of Sciences (АРАН. Ф.1922.Оп. 1.Д. 767.Л. 40–106). It was among these materials that a complete text of the theses was found. See P. E. Fokin's posting from 27.12.2016 at: http://russophile.ru/2016/12/27/тезисы-к-вопросу-о-взаимосвязи-филосо/#_ftnref2 (accessed March 20, 2017).
22. Lektorsky, personal communication. Lektorsky quotes this remark, but does not attribute it to Bibler, in Lektorsky 2012, 329.
23. Of course, the Illesh volume is selective in what it presents to us, and Illesh is Ilyenkov's daughter, so she might be expected to paint as rosy a picture as possible. However, she makes no attempt to edit out her father's favorable references to Stalin and Zhdanov, from which we can conclude that her editorial policy took fidelity to the truth very seriously.
24. Illesh's volume includes helpful biographical sketches of the *dramatis personae* (*IK*, 258–68). Not one was a "victim" of de-Stalinization.
25. From Thesis 3 in the complete text.
26. The second fragment does not appear in the complete text.
27. Part of Thesis 14 in the complete text.
28. Part of Thesis 8 in the complete text.
29. Condensed version of part of Thesis 14 in the complete text.
30. Not in the complete text.
31. Not in the complete text.
32. This seems to be a version of the passage from Thesis 8, cited above as on p. 6 of the manuscript.
33. Here Ilyenkov is likely referring to Liuc 1892.
34. The complete Russian text of the Theses appears in Ilyenkov 2017, 242–254, a sequel to *IK*, covering the period 1950–1960. A third volume of materials, relating to the period 1960–1979, was published as Ilyenkov 2018. The three books, all curated by Illesh, together provide remarkable insight into Ilyenkov's life and work.

## BIBLIOGRAPHY

Bakhurst, David. 1991. *Consciousness and Revolution in Soviet Philosophy: From the Bolsheviks to Evald Ilyenkov*. Cambridge: Cambridge University Press.

Bakhurst, David. 2013. "Ilyenkov's Hegel." *Studies in East European Thought* (65): 271–285.

Engels, Friedrich. 1968. "Ludwig Feuerbach and the End of German Classical Philosophy." In *Marx-Engels Selected Works in One Volume*, 584–622. London: Lawrence and Wishart.

Engels, Friedrich. 1976. *Dialectics of Nature*. Trans. C. Dutt. Moscow: Progress.

Engels, Friedrich. 1978. *Anti-Dühring*. Trans. E. Burns. Moscow: Progress.

*History of the Communist Party of the Soviet Union (Bolsheviks)*. 1943. *Short Course*. Edited by a Commission of the Central Committee of CPSU (B). Moscow: Foreign Languages Publishing House.

Hegel, Georg Wilhelm Friedrich. 1970. *The Philosophy of Nature. Being Part Two of the Encyclopedia of the Philosophical Sciences (1830)*. Trans. A. V. Miller. Foreword by J. N. Findlay. Oxford: Clarendon Press.

Ilyenkov, Evald V. 1960. *Dialektika abstraknogo i konkretnogo v "Kapitale"Marksa* [*The Dialectics of the Abstract and the Concrete in Marx's "Capital"*]. Moscow: Nauka.

Ilyenkov, Evald V. 1962. "Ideal'noe" ["The Ideal"]. In *Filosofskaya entsiklopedia*, vol. 2, 436–439. Moscow: Sovetskaya Entsiklopedia.

Ilyenkov, Evald V. 1964. "Vopros o tozhdestve myshleniya i bytiya v domarksistskoi filosofii" ["The Question of the Identity of Thinking and Being in Pre-Marxist Philosophy"]. In *Dialektika—teoriya poznaniya* [*Dialectics—The Theory of Knowledge*], 21–54. Moscow: Politizdat.

Ilyenkov, Evald V. 1997. *Dialektika abstraknogo i konkretnogo v nauchno-teoretichecskom myshlenii* [*The Dialectics of the Abstract and the Concrete in Scientific-Theoretical Thinking*]. Moscow: ROSSPEN.

Ilyenkov, Evald V. 2017. *Ot abstraknogo k konkretnomu. Krutoi marshrut. 1950–1960* [*From the Abstract to the Concrete: A Steep Route*]. Compiled and edited by E. Illesh. With contributions by V. Lektorsky, I. Raskin, and A. Maidanksy. Moscow: Kanon+.

Ilyenkov E. V. 2018. *Ideal'noe. I realnost'. 1960–1979* [*The Ideal. And Reality. 1960–1979*]. Compiled and edited by E. Illesh. With contributions by V. Lektorsky and A. Maidansky. Moscow: Kanon+.

Ilyenkov, Evald V. and Korovikov, Valentin I. 2016. *(IK) Strast' po tezisam o predmete filosofii* [*The Passion of the Theses on the History of Philosophy*]. Compiled and edited by E. Illesh. With contributions by V. Lektorsky and I. Raskin. Moscow: Kanon+.

Lektorsky, Vladislav A. 2012. *Filosofia, poznanie, kul'tura*. [Philosophy, Cognition, Culture]. Moscow: Kanon+.

Liuc, Georg G. 1882. *Istoriya filosofii ot nachala eya v Gretsii do nastoyashchago vremeni*. St. Petersburg: A.S. Semenova. [Translation of G. H. Lewes, *The History of Philosophy from Thales to Comte*, 2 vols., 5th edition. London: Longmans, Green, 1880.]

Oizerman, Teodor I. and Svetlov, V. I. 1948. *Vozniknovenie marksizma—revoliutsionnyi perevorot v filosofii* [*The Rise of Marxism—the Revolutionary Turn in Philosophy*]. Moscow: Gospolitizdat.

Sellars, Wilfrid. 1963. "Philosophy and the Scientific Image of Man." In *Science, Perception and Reality*, 1–40. London: Routledge and Kegan Paul.

Spufford, Francis. 2010. *Red Plenty*. London: Faber and Faber.

CHAPTER FOUR

# On Soviet Philosophy

## *A Philosophical Reflection*

KAREN A. SWASSJAN

Soviet philosophy becomes a matter of great interest and is probably second to none, when it comes to its special status within the synopsis of our generalized concept of philosophy. This is not simply because philosophy was given the status of the reigning discipline, but because here, in this part of the world, virtually everything was philosophy including the state and the power itself. The latter, known as the Soviet Union, turned out to be an incredible master-plan, which came to life as a *fulfilled philosophy*, i.e., a philosophy transposed from the realm of the mind of those few who had conceived it into the realm of everyday life inhabited by millions of individual destinies who had neither professional nor even amateur relation to philosophy. The reason why Lenin focuses on the names of Hegel (and Feuerbach) in his analysis of the three sources of Marxism, especially in the part concerning classical German philosophy, is understandable; yet after seizing power they should have been resorting to Fichte—the author of *The Closed Commercial State*—rather than to Hegel. There was some disconformity in the fact that, in theory, philosophy had been given (by philosophy itself) the role of the *superstructure*, and not the determinant role of the *base*. Yet every knowledgable insider, unlike superficial onlookers from without, would know that those were the rules to be understood not literally but dialectically. Perceived dialectically, Marxist-Leninist philosophy (or, technically, the *superstructure*) was actually neither the *base* nor the *superstructure*, but the unity of the two, let us underline it again—dialectics itself. Therefore, being the rule itself, it was an exception to that rule. In other words, it excluded itself from itself and, by means of this self-exclusion, established itself in itself. To understand this, one needs to make sure that this could be understood at all, and to be sure that it could be understood at all one needs to be a *Homo Sovieticus* (Latin for "Soviet man"[1]). The rest is easy. To be a *Homo Sovieticus*, one needs to understand Soviet philosophy. *Intelligo, quia absurdum*.[2]

The parody of Tertullian is not coincidental. Soviet philosophy was in fact nothing other than a *theology*, a very effective one, in fact—be it under the banner of militant atheism or of inverted theism—everything conformed with the good old pattern: To believe in God, one needs God; but to deny God's existence, one also needs God. These are two sides of the same coin. *God exists because He exists* is engraved on the one side, while, *God does not exist, because He does not exist*, is engraved on the other. The God of atheism bears the name *matter* and owes his existence to the God of theism, whose Golem he has become. Viewed like that, the history of philosophy is impaled on a pendulum oscillating between the two extremes: the bodiless spirit (idealism) and the spiritless body (materialism), with both extremes proving to be illusionary due to the trick with a glove turned inside out. When the time came for idealism to be turned inside out, *matter* replaced *God*, while theism was in its turn substituted by atheism. There is no essential difference between the two except when used for terminological camouflage. A priest would speak of *God* implying the same entity as an atheist speaking of *matter*. Thus, to make a smooth transition from a chair of scientific atheism to a chair of theological studies, it was sufficient to replace *matter* with *God* within the framework of a textbook definition of *matter* given by Engels and Lenin as objective reality existing outside and independent of our consciousness and perception.

The absolute paradox of Soviet philosophy is analogous or homologous with Kant's thing-in-itself and could be formulated following the pattern of Kant's critique by philosopher Jacobi: *it was impossible to become a Homo Sovieticus without philosophy, just as it was impossible to remain one with it*. It was *impossible to become*, because to be born here meant to be born into a kind of philosophical fiction, entering which without first taking a corresponding philosophical vaccination would have brought about an immediate "rejection of the transplant." It was *impossible to remain*, because *remaining* with philosophy meant to think and there was *nothing* to think about: The *Homo Sovieticus* had already been omniscient. Who would think about something he already knew?! No wonder that throughout the Soviet times *thought-crime* was ranked among the most serious outrages (as it was considered to be committed against state). A tiniest minimum of thought—were it even to pass under the righteous motto of a "creative approach to Marxism"—would bring about ferocious rejection. Should one happen to make a cautious comment that, for example, knowledge of the laws of nature were attained not in the realm of philosophy but in natural sciences, and that philosophy dealt not with knowledge, but with the theory of knowledge, the vigilant colleagues would start choking with indignation. When, in Spring 1954, Ilyenkov and Korovikov, young lecturers of the Moscow State University, tried to hold academic discussion around this thesis, the Dean of the Department of Philosophy, Professor V. S. Molodtsov made an unforgettable remark—a most substantive of all *sanctae simplicitatis*[3] of Soviet philosophy: "Where are they taking us, Ilyenkov and Korovikov? They are taking us into the stuffy realm of thought, but we shall not go there" (Baranets 2008, 108).

It is beyond doubt that, among all special inmates of the Soviet Demonium, Soviet philosophers were the most *Homo Sovieticus*. That they belonged to a privileged class would not catch the eye immediately as it happened, say, with the class of natural scientists, especially after the invention of the atomic bomb. Ordinary physicists would enjoy and share the glory of their world-famous colleagues—heroes and demiurges. Encouraged by the state-commissioned satirists they would parody the "lyricists" and philosophers. However, this only testified to their utter naïveté. The simple truth was that, at a certain point, the authorities would have to understand something, which France's powerful Minister of Finance, Colbert, had realized as far back as in the seventeenth century: gather all *weirdoes* at the Academy of Sciences and hand-feed them the view that a day would come when they would untie the Gordian knot and invent the atomic bomb as a side-dish. What they were naïve about and failed to notice was blatantly obvious: it was them, the laureates and lucky customers of special distribution stores, wooed and wedded by the authorities, who had to learn philosophy by heart, and time and again be deprecated for not knowing it well enough. They could make fun of the colleagues from philosophy chairs as much as they wished, and yet, in the long run it was them who had to take an exam in philosophy, and not the philosophers in physics. Philosophers (in strict conformity with tradition) had the knowledge of the knowledgeable and were, therefore, *at the top*. While physicists had to explain nature, philosophers would explain physics to physicists, after which not only physical theories and experiments were obediently adjusted to philosophical knowledge, but also to the laws of nature. Hegel, who once parried a reproach that his speculations were in discord with nature with his brilliant "so much the worse for Nature," set the tone for future guardians of philosophy. The latter took it as a license to act and started to adjust nature to the same speculations (now transferred from Hegel's mind to their own), although it was as impossible to generate such voluntary cosmogony without physicists as it was for physicists to practice physics without passing an exam in Marxism-Leninism. Once again, the main postulate of Soviet philosophy can be summarized in the following formula: *not to think, but to know*. It sounds in consonance with the theological postulate: *not to think, but to believe*. In fact, a Soviet philosopher knew the beliefs of a Christian theologian. The difference was that one believed in what he knew, while the other did not know what he believed.

This knowledge looked particularly impressive in the *Supplement to the History of Philosophy*. Centuries-old figures of thought were locked between two parallel lines of a driver's manual of sorts, with Plato and Democritus on opposite sides. The objective was to find the correct answer with the help of a multiple-choice exercise little different, if at all, from a driver's license test. With all this in place, the answers would still quite frequently turn out to be too outlandish, if not completely senseless. The task was to make Democritus's line appear to be an equivalent of Plato's, while pretending to be not a mere dummy, but a smart—even a creative—one. When I worked at the Institute of Philosophy in Yerevan (Armenia), there used to be an aging doctoral candidate at our Department of Dialectical Materialism and Natural History, who was writing his dissertation on Plato. In it, he was trying to prove that Plato was a materialist as well as an atheist, who had to pretend to be an idealist hiding his real views from the Athenian tyranny. During academic discussions, his arguments were met by outbursts of laughter, yet it never embarrassed him. (It was only once that I could recall him being confused, when someone suggested that he himself was an idealist hiding under the guise of materialist interpretation of Plato in the era of Brezhnev's humanism.) At that time it was funny, today it has become understandable. That doctoral candidate was simply defending Democritus's line in his own way, and even if, at times, he crossed the line, it was done in the spirit of what was then called "local overzealousness." The worst-case scenario was when that overzealousness was accompanied by personal feelings which were in discord with it. I recall a conversation I had with a philosopher from Leningrad in the late 1970s. He made a lengthy confession of his passionate love for Kierkegaard, who he had just happened to discover and read. Later he sent me a copy of his new book on something I cannot really remember. The only thing that stands out vividly in my mind was that it discussed Kierkegaard, who was labeled as a reactionary and obscurantist. I assume that it was not an easy task for him, but the Soviet *serum of truth* proved its worth as eventually he duly denounced the Danish misanthrope, because keeping silence would have been equal to covering up, and it would take only one step from covering up to national treason. Of course, those were the mistakes and miscalculations of the authorities, whose ban on bourgeois books would provoke a doubly increased interest in them. To say nothing of the fact that, among those banned, were not only prominent authors, but also unworthy ones. Who of the party bureaucrats would care whether the "bourgeois philosopher" Husserl was any better than another bourgeois, such as Jambet, or Lardreau, if you wish? As a result, not only the demand for Husserl would increase, but also for thinkers such as Glucksmann and others, about whom dissertations were being written, and who would be taken aback by that sudden avalanche of "international recognition" lavished upon them. The ban would only make sense if it were practiced within the boundaries of Fichte's "closed commercial state." However, since after Khrushchev times the iron curtain would be repeatedly breached, the ban appeared to be not only impossible, but also counterproductive. Forbidden fruit would only stir up more interest, after which the demand for Glucksmann, Lyotards, and others would increase, the way it happened with imported beer and cigarettes. If anything was to be banned, it should have been the books by Marx, just like the Roman Catholic Church forbade the unrighteous to read the Bible during the reign of the great Pope Innocent III. And truly, why would anyone read something that he already knew from a parish priest?! That it did not happen to Marx was probably because few would read his books even without the ban. The air was permeated with Marx (and, with him, the Death), and there was no other escape from this bearded Baphomet than to look at his four-fingered hand and see all five of them.

It might be interesting to take a quick look at several important stages in the history of Soviet philosophy. Pushing the limits of permissible generalization we could divide this history into three conventional stages, outlined as *fermentation*, *stagnation* and *decomposition* and being perceived as a partial replica of the Soviet history in general. The period of *fermentation* falls upon the 1920s and, partly, the 1930s. This was the time of a non-stop experiment without any solidified structures and institutions to reinforce it. We could have started the count from a slightly earlier point, from singling out a short-lived upbeat, when the outgoing Russian philosophy, caught in the wilderness of Russia's devastated space, dwindled into a ghostly feeling. Meanwhile, the incoming Marxism had not as yet realized that it had suddenly become a sole beneficiary of an absolute fortune. Between this initial stupor of unawareness and the gradual coming back to senses of the victorious Marxism, the last silver decade of Russian philosophy was stretched and strung. In 1918, Ilyin (I am just giving random examples that come in a flash) published his book *Hegel's Philosophy as a Study of God's and Man's Concreteness*. In the same year Blonsky's *Filosofiia Plotina* [The Philosophy of Plotinus] and Andrei Bely's

*Krizis Kul'tury* [The Crisis of Culture] were published. *Lichnost' I Uchenie Sant Avgustina* [The Personality and Teaching of St. Augustine]—a masterpiece by I. V. Popov had been released a year earlier. It was during that time that Gustav Shpet published his most important works starting with *An Outline of the Development of Russian Philosophy* (1922) and continuing with *Inner form of the Word*. In 1929, *Dialektika Kanta* [Kant's Dialectics] by Valentin F. Asmus was released, simultaneously, Alexei Losev began to be self-published. It was understandable that every minute mattered and that, sooner or later, one had to choose between international fame (with a prospect of immigrating to Europe under the label of a "Russian philosopher" in exile) and an oblivious death of a nameless outcast who stayed behind in the homeland—more often a death by a firing squad. Needless to say that it was those who had stayed behind that became the core of the never fully realized Russian philosophy! The last resort, through which they tried to destroy the overhanging web of spidery deafness, were literary translations. Denied the possibility to write their own works, they would re-write the works of others in Russian: Kubitsky *re-wrote* Aristotle's *Metaphysics*, Focht translated the *Analytics* of the same author and also Hegel's *Philosophy of the Spirit*, while Shpet translated the *Phenomenology of the Spirit*. Their gradual departure remained unnoticed against the background of the noisy emergence of the new and the young—the same old revolutionaries—sailors with legendary nicknames, who stormed into the space of cultural wilderness to do there what they had once been doing in the cultureless realm. It goes without saying that philosophy could not have been an exception here, although at that time it was no longer sought and found at university chairs and classrooms, but at random and in odd places.

Experiments and performances would virtually begin the next day, but, as a rule, they would end before they could even start. First it was the "Proletkult"[4]—an initial attempt to recruit red professoriate.[5] Then, in 1922, the so-called "mininshchina" ("Mininism") came to the fore. Minin, a former member of the Revvoensovet[6] and Frunze's aide, authored an article titled "Down with Philosophy," in which he called for a total abolition of philosophy that had no place in the country of the victorious proletariat. And then there emerged entire loads of projects and ideas replacing one another or existing simultaneously: rejection of ideology and psychologization of Marxism; an attempt to merge Marxism with Freudianism; the debate between "dialecticians" and "mechanists," "enchmenism" or Soviet behaviorism.[7] Stabilization would gradually transform into *stagnation*. It is difficult, if not altogether impossible, to chronologically follow and establish the exact moment of transition from the last "heartbeats" of thought to its full stop. In the mid-1930s, academic publications (Machiavelli, Guicciardini) were still possible, with gorgeous hundred-page introductory articles by Djivelegov and with unambiguous forewords by Kamenev. Even in the notoriously demonstrable 1937 publication, Asmus could write about Descartes's cosmogony and cosmology without compromising academic integrity, while Mordukhai-Boltovski was able to publish his work about Newton's mathematics. However, at some point, probably after the Second World War, this last semblance of freedom began dwindling away. Now the paradigmatic figures of Soviet philosophy were Mitin, Yudin and Konstantinov. Philosophy itself would always remain guided by an irrevocable motto: "from nonsense to more nonsense" (*ab absurdum ad absurdiorem*). One can assume that a text can be nonsense, while its interpretation could be even more nonsensical. Let us, for example, look at the following sentence:

> Only by immersing itself into the never-ending springs of life Marxism-Leninism would again and again emerge from them revitalized, reinvigorated, and capable of solving most arduous and complex questions of societal development on a genuinely scientific basis.

No doubt, this phrase is nonsense, yet it displays an interesting pattern, as any attempt to make it meaningful makes this statement even more nonsensical. If we read it, say, with a Southern accent typical of the Caucasus, it could sound like a toast, yet who would wish to have a drink after such a toast? Associative reading of this phrase drawing an analogy with Faustus is also possible: a feeble old man of Marxism-Leninism immerses himself into the never-ending spring of Satanism to come out of it revitalized, reinvigorated by Priapus himself, capable of having a drunken brawl in a wine cellar and of seducing young women.

Then came the period of *decomposition*. Curious as it may seem, it started with attempts to revive a corpse. A group of young philosophers, who felt they belonged to the paradigm of Khrushchev-Lutheran denomination, would cautiously begin to test ground for a possible revision under the auspices of a program to return to the Marxist-Leninist principles flagrantly trampled in the years of Stalin's personality cult. In a flash, everybody became passionately nostalgic about Marx and embarked upon a "back to Marx" pilgrimage. The analogy with Luther, who sought a direct contact with God and rose against Catholic "brokers" and "commissionaires," is self-evident: at long last, here also, the time had come to get rid of bureaucratic middlemen in search of the lost Marx. Unexpectedly, it turned out that Marx was not such a dogmatist and all that hopeless as he had been portrayed by overzealous functionaries. Suffice it to remember a remark he made to Engels, "I know that I am not a Marxist," which could make one lose his head savoring a prospect of drawing analogies with apophatic theology and gnosis. Marx, acting as a *Deus absconditus*[8] threatened to blur all the fixed boundaries and was dangerously open to any kind of transformation. The catchword and the pass giving access to the closed philosophical space would suddenly become *the discovery of Marx*—and not just Marx, but everything in Marx and Marx in everything. And if, within the exegesis of Stalin's synopsis, he used to be everything for *us*, after the Khrushchev time hangover he was put on a mission to become everything for *everybody*. It goes without saying he still remained a materialist, but in a weird, all-encompassing, even occult sense. Try to talk with such a mellow materialist about Jacob Boehme or, say, the Blessed John of Ruysbroeck, and he would persuade you that all they talked about could be found in Marx, and that the mystics mentioned above were Marxists. This sudden outbreak of a pandemic Marx-mania marked the beginning of the decomposition of Soviet philosophy. The mystical, discovered (or invented) Omni-Marx was proving to be a Joker, substituting or beating any playing card. Taking advantage of this de-Stalinized, de-Sovietized and, therefore, humanized and Europeanized Marx, a small number of Soviet philosophers laid the foundations of dissidence, after which the shop window of "Russian philosophy" in the West had to be enlarged to vacate a section for a "Soviet philosophy" which, due to the efforts of a few rebels, managed to break through into "*the stuffy realm of thought*."

The decomposition of Marxism became irreversible since the very moment when its Soviet and, simultaneously, anti-Soviet exponents came up with the idea to invent a "Marxism with a human face." The difference between them was that the former lived the *life* of their philosophy running a permanent risk. The Marxism of Ilyenkov, Bibler, Shchedrovitsky, Mamardashvili, both of Vasily Davydov and Yuri Davydov was a Marxism of the *frontoviks* (war veterans), a heroic Marxism, different from the non-combatant, at times even selfish, Marxism of Korsch, Reich, Lefebvre or Althusser. The *frontoviks* would live in Marx, fight for Marx and put everything at stake for him, which could hardly be said about the wheeler-dealers from Frankfurt,[9] Brecht, Bloch, and other adepts of Marxism, and even about Marx himself, who was quite sincere when he said he was not a Marxist, because he was really not one. It seems we are dealing here with the second (and the last) moment of truth in Soviet philosophy, with the first one having lasted briefly at its very birth: both moments revealed its true nature. With all the *truth* of these separate *moments*, they could not be integrated without becoming untrue. The ghost would continue experimenting, dialectically counterposing itself to its other self and fooling around with the exposition of its own pseudo-incompatibilities and pseudo-irreconcilabilities. A day would probably come, when it will become possible to think about the history of the twentieth century in terms of the history of metastasizing Marxism, the spread of which was often impossible to locate. Heidegger (in his 1944 lectures) noted that, viewed from the standpoint of history and metaphysics, Communism, Americanism and National Socialism were identical. To understand this, one has to ideate the above-mentioned ideologies, not merely skim through them as a journalist would do. Here also the commonalities promise to be much more fascinating than the differences: say, the commonalities between Hitler and Thälmann, or Thälmann and Roosevelt, or Roosevelt and Stalin within the framework of innovative strategies to reinvent the world. The exponents of this unified and universal Marxism would just need to aspire, each in his own right, to be the one and only truthful and genuine source of it. That Marxism, as the subject of the Soviet experiment, found itself in a limbo could be understood if one observes it in the light of purely Russian unpredictabilities. Yet this should never be viewed as an argument against an even higher degree of authenticity in the Soviet version of Marxism. No matter what, Lenin developed and realized the deepest potential of Marxism, just like Stalin did with Leninism. Is it not quite obvious that the Soviet experiment was also the most risky one? Here they did not just speak of class struggle, but fought to the death. Lenin's and later Stalin's fury against the opportunists and revisionists of Marxism is understandable and even legitimate from the Marxist standpoint. If Marxism is just a teaching and not also a license to act, one has to choose between inadequacy and provocation. Both choices could happen to be made either at a German University or at a Paris café.

Having lost power and credibility as the Avatar of Workers and Peasants, the shapeshifter surfaced again, trying to find a new home among Paris students. It was no longer riding on the back of Mitin and Livshits, but saddled Sartre and Foucault instead, enchanting everyone around not only with the wit and genius of interpretation, but also with the bold mix of ideas, from Nietzsche, Husserl and Heidegger to Genet and Artaud. Young Soviet Marxists of the first order were in fact weaving an identical ornament without decadent luxury but with the very same goal: strip Marxism of Catholic lunacy and endow it with the charm of secularism that would enchant rather than put off everyone around. They would, of course, stop short of approaching Nietzsche and Artaud, but instead, without even bothering to hide it, they would feed on existentialism, logical positivism, structuralism and general systems theory (GST). Once again, there was a need to set Marxism free from the Soviet, officially approved stereotypes, expanding it beyond recognition and covering the tracks by making an academic excursus to von Bertalanffy, Descartes, and—why not?—Marcel Proust. In fact, this was the very mission that the Sixtiers[10] were trying to accomplish, and, who knows, they might have proved to be more successful than their colleagues from Paris and Zagreb, had they been given more time, and, with it, more liberties. When Brezhnev came to replace Khrushchev and the old guard of Stalinism hurried to celebrate the *return* of the past, their expectations were at once fulfilled and confounded: while a *return* of sorts did happen, the past failed to return in its original form, manifesting itself—to use a Hegelian train of thought—as a farce, diagnosed with *dementia senilis*. The Sixtiers let themselves be bamboozled by the *Ottepel* (Khrushchev's "thaw") interpreting Khrushchev's reforms in the spirit of historical materialism. With their eyes *wide shut*, they would continue to believe even when at their work places they were berated by supervisors and reported by colleagues. In a flash, against their will, they turned out to be dissidents or joined the ranks of the suspicious, i.e., they became more than they had been. They had been the advocates of what they believed to be the genuine Marxism. After the *Ottepel*, they became labeled as *aesops* and *fabulists*. The time was quick to dot the i's and cross the t's, and, during the long, crawling years of stagnation, the majority of them had nothing left to do but master the useless homeopathy of risks and indulge in the reading of their luckier French contemporaries. Their tragedy is that of the subjunctive mood, into which Russian history, constantly failing in the indicative mood, is dreaming to transpose itself. "If only the lips of Nikanor Ivanovich could be matched with the nose of Ivan Kuzmich, and with the easy-going manners of Baltazar Baltazarovich and, on top of it, with, say, the corpulence of Ivan Pavlovich . . ."[11] Thus, if only they had been granted some degree of a real freedom of thought, and if only their life in 1968 had been no different from life in 1986, one should not rule out that it would not have been them who read Foucault and Althusser, but, vice versa—Foucault and Althusser would have been reading them.

The decomposition of Soviet philosophy was gaining momentum alongside with a momentary flash and subsequent gradual dwindling of the illusion of a humanized Marx. The general picture was drawn in accordance with the usual "above/below" pattern: the few chosen ones were above, the rest stayed below. The chosen ones, in their turn, were split by a tripartite distribution of roles. First came the echelon of philosophers—one can name them the generals. They were followed by a *limited contingent* of those who, by a wave of some "magic wand," were allowed to write and speak outside the mainstream. Lastly, a few lonely ghosts and relics of yesteryear brought up the rear. Should we begin with the last category, the names of Losev and Asmus would come to mind first. The former might have breathed the same air with

Plotinus and Proclus (which he virtually did), the latter, in secret, lived out the remaining part of Dr. Zhivago's unfinished life, who stopped writing poetry and became a philosopher . . . Yet the most influential, of course, was the second group, among those who chose the path of internal emigration and were the rays of light shining in the Kingdom of Darkness, should we borrow the metaphor often used in Soviet secondary school compositions. The glorious names of Averintsev, Lotman, Shchedrovitsky, Davydov, Gaidenko and others come to mind here. (The paradoxical personality of Alexander A. Zinoviev, a logician, a satirist and fictionalized town-planner should be mentioned separately. A day would come, when his imaginary town of Ibansk[12] should be put on the map as a sister town of Dostoevsky's Skotoprigonievsk, most probably somewhere in the vicinity of the Golden Ring.) Members of this second group were given the privilege to breathe shallowly, with the occasional luxury of taking a deeper breath. Not that this privilege was a philosophical analogue of Potyomkin's buildings[13] or a pass to the network of "Beryozka" state-run hard currency stores. Yet the publications and lectures by those who had been commissioned to belong to this elitist group were utterly different from ordinary Soviet books sold for "nickels and dimes." They served as a sort of philosophical window on Europe against the background of special repositories and prohibitions of all descriptions. This was a kind of a commissioned philosophical challenge to the West similar to how the state would encourage the privileged spheres of hockey, ballet and circus. What leapt to the eye here was, among other things, a risky handling of the texts of the classics of Marxism and even blatantly few citations from their works compared with abundant quotes from other authors, inaccessible to the public at large. Those were small oases amidst the monotonous sands of endless deserts. Where else could young Soviet philosophers feel the burning touch of Nietzsche, Spengler or Ortega y Gasset (he was thought to be two persons),[14] or Max Weber? Members of this second group were tragelaphus or goat-stags, whose every "bleat" would be relished and valued as high as any archeological find in the Red Sea. Citations would usually overshadow the rest of the subject matter; they were extracted from the text like raisins are from cookies. There also existed special translations of books for "*internal consumption*" aimed at the generals, the philosophical monoglots of the upper echelon. A number code was assigned to each and every of those books and a special receipt needed to be signed to borrow one. This fitted perfectly into the general norms and style of consumption, where texts by foreign authors were distributed in accordance with name lists analogous to those compiled for the chosen ones to obtain consumer goods. The only difference between the two was that books could be copied, while consumer goods could not.

In conclusion, it should be said that the fundamental fault of Soviet philosophy was found in its Hegelian hereditary pathology. It was blindly obsessed with the absolutization of matter, making it the basis of everything and failing to notice the underlying root-source, philosophy itself. This was probably Hegel's terrible revenge: to make matter primary and thought secondary, one needed to first conceive of the former and the latter as such, and consequently to understand that matter can only be primary in the form of thought about matter. In fact, this was nothing other than inverted idealism—Hegel's absolute idea, which had become full of itself, masqueraded as absolute matter and went forth among the people and into the revolution. A more panoramic view would reveal Platonism, or rather a kind of *levée en masse*[15] of Platonism (or Platonism as a *militia*), where each and everyone was ready to die in the struggle for the Idea. A few practitioners of such idealism could even leave a heartwarming impression. When John Henry Mackay, who discovered in the late nineteenth century Max Stirner and attempted to popularize him in Europe and who, because of a serious illness and hard living conditions, tried to pass Stirner's archive he had bit by bit put together into reliable hands, nobody in Europe bothered to respond. Instead, the response came from Moscow, where in 1925 the Marx and Engels Institute purchased the archive for four thousand dollars. Stirner, a young Hegelian, used to belong to the same circle and breathe the same air with Marx and Engels. A unique portrait of Stirner, his only extant image drawn from memory by Engels years later, has miraculously survived into our days. Of course, the whole thing was exclusively about a relic, the hallowed member of the "holy family." (Bernd A. Laska, a German researcher of Stirner, who visited the archive in 1989, found that it had not been touched for over 60 years.) Yet this was genuine idealism in action—not simply idealism, but a religious idealism. Here too, the Devil, as always, was in the details, finding dangerously much in common with the guardian angel of the religious-philosophical gatherings in St. Petersburg at the dawn of the bygone century. It would take a sufficiently strong and unprejudiced motivation to radicalize the outlined topic and find conciliatory elements in a domain, where all nomenclatorial signs of irreconcilability are blatantly present. It would have been easier to do it conceptually and in a more difficult manner, as far as the power of credibility is concerned, within the realm of the sentient. While, for example, in the unity of Merezhkovsky's two abysses (the Flesh and the Spirit), the law of the unity and struggle of opposites is easily recognizable, when it comes to Berdyaev's trepidations, one has to deal not as much with the logic of concepts as with pathetics of the states of mind, coming across a weird mixture of bolshevism and mysticism: not a mystical bolshevism, but one spiced with Jacob Boehme and storming the Old Testament the way it had stormed the Winter Palace of St. Petersburg in 1917. No wonder that many of those mystics had begun their path from Marxism, and some were even briefly sent into exile, just like it is no accident that they would end up in another exile, now named emigration, where they returned to the very roots from which they had started. One should remember the feeling of elation with which Berdyaev proclaimed a natural bond between the so-called Russian Idea and Communism. Yet there was nothing out of the ordinary and unexpected in it. He simply found his philosophical-religious dreams came true within the realm called the USSR. Henrik Ibsen's Hilda,[16] with a bigotry of a young member of the Komsomol, would come before the aging architect Solnes not with an intent "to claim the kingdom" she had been offered by the builder ten years before, but to embarrass him with "the best laws in the world," to which he eventually preferred the Satanic West that gave him wealth and high position in society (probably instead of bestowing upon him the grace of becoming, say, a cab driver).

It is utter nonsense to call them existentialists and even take pride in the fact that they had come to the fore before Camus and Sartre. One only needs to check on their proclaimed existentialism against the background of their own *existentias*. Let us, for instance, compare the fate of the philosopher Shpet executed by a firing squad with the destiny of heavily promoted philosopher Berdyaev. Reading Berdyaev's 1931 critique of Asmus's *An Outline of the History of Dialectics in New Philosophy* published in Moscow I cannot rid myself of the feeling that what I read is not a critique at all, but a dilation. The existentialist Berdyaev would expose hypocrisy and anti-Marxism in the Soviet philosopher Asmus . . . If it were a "must-use" name, it would not be them who should be called existentialists, but their compatriots who had stayed behind in the Soviet Union not to dwell upon the Apocalypse in emigration, but to live in it. This, not just some personal traits, probably explains the syndrome of stopping the heartbeat of thought: Soviet philosophy was designed and standardized for the soldiers, or if you wish, for the obedient novices of philosophy, but not for philosophers. You could either live and breathe it or not live it at all; those who could not live it had no other option than die a permanent death—not their own but this philosophy's death, final and irreversible, falling into the dark oblivion of the dead of night.

## NOTES

1. It was thought that the Soviet period had born a new kind of man, who was dubbed the *Homo Sovieticus*.—Trans.
2. The author makes play of words, using the famous line attributed to Tertullian: "*Credo, quia absurdum est*" or "I believe because it is absurd." The author replaces this line with the formulation, *Intelligo, quia absurdum*," or "I understand because it is absurd."—Ed.
3. A Latin phrase meaning "holly innocence" or "holy simplicity." In this context, it is used ironically.—Ed.
4. Proletkult is a portmanteau of the words *proletarian culture* in Russian transcription. It was a short-lived, experimental artistic institution, established immediately after the Revolution of 1917.—Trans.
5. "Red professoriate" are persons graduated from the Institute of Red Professors, which existed in Moscow in 1921–1938 and where philosophy and social sciences were taught in the spirit of dogmatic Marxism.—Ed.
6. "Revvoensovet" is another portmanteau word, which stands for Revolutionary Military Soviet.—Trans.
7. Emanuel Enchmen (1891–1966) was a Soviet behaviorist and biologist, who in the early 1920s proposed a psychological theory that he called the "theory of new biology." Instead of focusing on the conscious processes, the theory advocated the study of human behavior. Despite being popular among intellectuals, the theory was officially condemned in 1923 for its anti-Marxist tendencies.—Ed.
8. Hidden God.—Ed.
9. This is a reference to thinkers of the Frankfurt School.—Ed.
10. For a detailed discussion of main ideas and key representatives of the generation of the 1960s (the so-called Sixtiers), see the chapter by A. Guseynov (Ch. 5) in this volume.
11. A quote from Gogol's play *Svad'ba* [The Marriage] (see Gogol 1999), describing a wealthy but aging Russian maiden, who tries to choose between potential husbands. —Trans.

12. Ibansk is a fictionalized town from Zinoviev's novel *Yawning Heights* (Zinoviev 1979 [1976]); Skotoprigonievsk is a name Dostoevsky chose for a town described in *The Brothers Karamazov* (Dostoevsky 2002). A literal translation of the names of these towns would sound like *F-ville* for Ibansk and *Cattledriveborough* for Skotoprigonievsk. The Golden Ring is a chain of old cities northeast of Moscow, which played an important role in the history of the Russian Orthodox Church.—Trans.
13. Potyomkin's buildings or villages with gorgeous external decorations and makeshift stores was a controversial project by Prince Grigori Potyomkin, Governor General of Novorossiya, to attract Europeans during the reign of Catherine the Great.—Trans.
14. The Spanish conjunction *y* ("and") used in family names connects the father's name (*apellido paterno*) to that of the mother (*apellido materno*). Monolingual Soviet philosophers, whose native tongues had no linguistic equivalent of the aforementioned Spanish conjunction would often find themselves in embarrassing situations by mistaking one person for two.—Trans.
15. *Levée en Masse* was a mass conscription decreed on August 23, 1793 in response to the dangers of foreign war.—Ed.
16. A metaphoric allusion is made to Henrik Ibsen's play *The Master Builder* (Ibsen 2008).—Trans.

## BIBLIOGRAPHY

Baranets, Nataliia G. 2008. *Metamorfozy etosa rossijskogo filosofskogo soobshchestva v XX veke* [Metamorphoses of the Ethos of the Russian Philosophic Community in the Twentieth Century]. Uljanovsk: University Press.

Dostoevsky, Fyodor. 2002. *The Brothers Karamazov*. Translated from the Russian by Richard Pevear and Larissa Volokhonsky. New York: Farrar, Straus and Giroux.

Enchmen, Emmanuil S. 1923. *Teorija novoj biologii i marksizm* [The Theory of New Biology and Marxism]. Moscow: P. G. U. "Vulkan."

Gogol, Nikolai, 1999. "Zhenitba" [The Marriage]. In *Three Plays*. Translated from the Russian by Stephen Mulrine. London: Methuen Publishing.

Ibsen, Henrik. 2008. "The Master Builder" [Bygmester Solness]. In *Four Major Plays*. Translated from the Norwegian by Jens Arup. Oxford: Oxford University Press.

Zinoviev, Alexander A. 1979. *The Yawning Heights* [Zijajushchie vysoty]. Translated from the Russian by Gordon Clough. New York: Random House.

CHAPTER FIVE

# The Philosophy of the Russian Sixtiers in the Humanist Context

## *A Philosophical Reflection*

ABDUSALAM A. GUSEYNOV

Speaking of the Soviet (Russian) philosophy of the second half of the twentieth century, one must bear in mind that it was relatively uniform, much more uniform, indeed, than one can imagine these days and is generally expected under the more or less normal conditions of intellectual freedom. It was what it was because it invariably presented itself, albeit with varying degree of sincerity, as Marxist and was institutionally incorporated in the system of plan-governed state. When distinguishing between its innovative and dogmatic tenets, one should not forget that those were the trends and aspects of one and the same intellectual community that intertwined and influenced each other. Individuals exemplifying those trends worked on the same projects, co-authored the same texts, and that such podia of innovative philosophical thought as *The Philosophical Encyclopedia* and, for many years, the journal *Voprosy filosofii* [Questions of Philosophy] were under the most dogmatic of philosophical dogmatists.

The thinkers whose works and achievements justify the focusing on that period as a specific stage in Russian philosophical development have already been named. In the hitherto most comprehensive form it was done in a series of studies that were the joint effort of the Institute of Philosophy of the Russian Academy of Sciences, the Georgy P. Shchedrovitsky Institute of Development, and the ROSSPEN Publishers. Arguably, the project did not cover every philosopher of the time who deserved mentioning, and those who were covered were not of equal importance. However, the names mentioned are renowned enough.[1] Our joint present task is to identify the problem fields in which they worked, the challenges to which they responded, and to decide whether those original thinkers that lived at the same time in the same country do amount to a whole something or are best seen as walking by themselves. Were they like isolated trees or did those trees make up a wood? I would formulate the issue we are currently facing as follows: do we have a right to treat the Russian philosophy of the last half of the twentieth century as a specific stage in the history of contemporary philosophy? And if we do, what was its specific character? In order to respond to these questions, we must identify the place the period in question occupies in Russian philosophy and the role it played in the intellectual development of the nation. This is the aspect on which I intend to focus.

Writings that deal with the Russian philosophy of the second half of the twentieth century tend to assess its level and achievements by comparing it with the world philosophy. This approach was proposed as a methodological principle and realized in Nelli V. Motroshilova's recent book (Motroshilova 2012). As she writes, "the real and objective inclusion of philosophical research done at some time in some country in the process of world philosophy is the principal indicator of, as well as a stimulus to, its quality, trustworthiness, durability, and sometimes its universal significance" (ibid., 6). The approach is, in my opinion, correct. The author, it should be noted, refers to "the real and objective inclusion" in the world philosophy, doubtless aware of possible partiality, distortion, and ideological bias. Soviet official philosophers were rumored to boast about negative foreign reviews of their writings as a *bona fide* testimony of their ideological propriety; whereas positive appraisals or, worse still, translations into Western languages would bring the authors under suspicion. Nowadays it is all vice versa: recognition in the West is seen as an all but decisive criterion of scientific quality. Granted, the new situation is better, indeed much better, than the old one, but there is something detrimental about it, too. One more point seems important in Motroshilova's quoted passage: included in the process of world philosophy is research "done at some time in some country." The road to world philosophy leads through the national one. This is due to the fact that philosophy is linked to philology more closely than science, more closely even than religion: contemporary philosophical thought exists in the space of national languages. By considering the period in question in a national context, I advocate no new looking glass, nor do I challenge the validity of its analysis in a world context; I simply choose my focus.

The shift, or rather the major change that marked a new stage in the history of Soviet philosophy, began in the mid-1950s. The two names with which it is primarily associated are those of Alexander Zinoviev and Evald Ilyenkov, then students of the Faculty of Philosophy at the Moscow State University. They graduated with theses on Karl Marx: Ilyenkov with the work titled "Some Aspects of Materialist Dialectic in K. Marx's Contribution to the Critique of Political Economy," and Zinoviev wrote the dissertation under the title, "Ascending from the Abstract to the Concrete (on the Materials of K. Marx's *Capital*)."[2] Both dealt with logical issues, albeit in different ways. Ilyenkov's concern was with the problem of thought; he focused on the tradition leading from Spinoza to Hegel and developed the concept of dialectical logic. Zinoviev followed the path of the twentieth century analytic philosophy with its emphasis on clarity akin to one employed in logic. The two men became focal points for groups of followers, some of whom would later develop into foci of their own. Out of this movement a community of intellectuals emerged that retained, for all their internal diversities and contradictions, a degree of unity. Their major efforts and greatest achievements were in the field of logic, epistemology, methodology and philosophy of science. They focused on the problems of correct thought and method, with accent on the natural and technical sciences. Erikh Solovyov commented later that our philosophy had sought to escape the pressure of ideology by means of accentuated scientism, which accounted for a certain "deficiency of the humanist perspective" in our philosophical studies (Solovyov 1998, 114).

This is, of course, true inasmuch as the philosophers who set the standards of philosophical professionalism showed little interest in social philosophy, ethics, axiology, to say nothing about political philosophy or philosophy of religion. Even as late as in 1983 Ivan Frolov's article "On Life, Death and Immortality: Studies in New (Real) Humanism" published in two consecutive issues of *Voprosy filosofii* (see Frolov 1983) was seen as something unusual—precisely because it was unusual for problems of ethics and humanism to be addressed by a scholar previously known for his writings on the philosophy of natural science. The humanitarian poverty of the Soviet philosophy of the 1950s–1970s was indubitable, as indubitable as its ideological causes. However, there was an undeniable humanitarian aspect to our philosophers' concentration on the logical, epistemological and methodological problems and their accentuated scientism: they proved to be a singularly important, I would even say, a natural and necessary step toward personal emancipation. It is worthwhile to note that a nation's intellectual entry into European modernity acquired solidity and maturity only after critical consideration of the role of Reason and development of a new Method; suffice it to mention the names of Francis Bacon, René Descartes and Immanuel Kant. The era of democracy was sanctioned philosophically through substantiation of the scientific Method and the role of Reason as a universal road to Truth. It was, therefore, only natural to expect that our philosophical road to democracy will also begin with examination of thinking and method. However, the thematic priorities of the emerging philosophical movement did not simply reproduce the general logic of intellectual development of other European nations, they were also shaped by factors related to the philosophical and historical development of our country. I shall consider our philosophical development first.

Toward the end of the nineteenth century, philosophy in Russia was institutionalized as a professional academic vocation in the forms known in the Western countries: chairs, journals, academic associations. This did not make it a purely professorial, "cabinet desk" trade. For that matter, it still is not. The absence of a definitive line between the professional academic philosophy and the popular common-sense philosophizing, between philosophical inquiry and philosophical essayistic journalism, seems to be a characteristic feature of the Russian philosophical process. The same turn of the century saw the formation of the three principal schools, or traditions, that were to shape the Russian philosophical development throughout the twentieth century and on until our time: the Russian Silver Age religious philosophy, the Russian Cosmism and the Russian Marxism. This is not to say that other schools were out of fashion, one can speak of Russian Neo-Kantianism, Russian Positivism, or Russian Phenomenology; Western philosophers were both published and read widely, too. Nevertheless, if one were to name the schools and traditions that were peculiar to Russia, that gave it its specific philosophical profile, that guided its professional intellectual effort and determined its social impact, one would have to refer to the three mentioned above.

For all their obvious and essential differences, for all their mutual criticism and mutual rejection, those three traditions professed the same accentuated anti-individualism and shared a common collectivist, sobornost'-type ideal that saw individual good to be directly linked to and depend upon the good of the nation. The latter, in turn, was to depend on that of the mankind. The good of the mankind thus emerged as both the final goal and the foundation of all philosophy:

- the Russian religious philosophy emphasized religious unity and envisaged, in the writings of Vladimir Solovyov, restoration of the Godmanhood;
- the Russian Cosmism treated of the transformation of the Universe and the man's role in it as an answer to human aspirations, including, first and foremost, human striving for the eternal life (the attainment of immortality as the natural human state and the subsequent resurrection of all the dead as foreseen by Nikolai Fyodorov);
- the Russian Marxism professed the ideal of a universal fraternal association in which the development of each would be the condition for the development of all.

Three different possible approaches to transformation of society were suggested:

1. on the spiritual basis, by the Solovyov's school,
2. through transformation of human nature itself, by the Cosmists, and
3. through transformation of social relations, by the Marxists.

Philosophers of the first group focused on the spiritual; those of the second group, on the natural; those of the third group, on the social. The three aspects implied three projections, three philosophical images of happy future for the mankind.

Social functions of philosophy are usually interpreted in two ways. One of the interpretations was epitomized by Hegel: philosophy is time apprehended in thought. Its principal function, therefore, is to sanction the universal and to comprehend the foundations of collective life. An alternative approach was exemplified by Heidegger who saw in philosophy a unique chance for an autonomous creative existence. The function of philosophy is thus linked to personal autonomy. These two visions of philosophy are not, of course, mutually exclusive. All great philosophical systems have sought to combine them. History of philosophy, however, provides ample evidence that either one or the other tends to dominate. Russian philosophy developed mostly along the Hegelian line and was basically seen as the self-understanding of a culture (a society). Russian philosophy presumed to speak on behalf of the universal (history, mankind, society), not on behalf of a particular (a person, an individual). With rare, perhaps even with one, exception (that of Leo Tolstoy) it never asked *What am I to do*? Philosophers did not address their theories to themselves: they taught wisdom, they did not seek it. To give but one example, Russian philosophy is believed to have paid great attention to morals. Moralization is often seen as its specific feature. In this regard, is it not surprising that its analysis of morals has never resulted in concrete formulae of responsible individual behavior? It always speaks on behalf of *we*, never on behalf of *me*. Even Vladimir Solovyov's ultimate two-volume *The Validation of The Good* (see Solovyov 1988) offered no normative program of individual life.

The fate of Russia's twentieth century philosophy was a tragic one, as was its political history to which philosophy was intrinsically linked. Russian religious philosophy went into exile, Cosmism was marginalized, intellectual contacts with the West were lost, and Marxism, turned Soviet, became the official state ideology. That monopoly status only reinforced its initial anti-individualism.

For the Marxist philosophy to be elevated to the rank of state ideology, it had, first, to be presented as the only true one and, second, to be stripped of all its original complexities and simplified to a creed that could be learned, understood and accepted by broad masses. To do the latter it was necessary to develop an infrastructure of educational and ideological institutions that would permeate the whole society and secure the dissemination of that simplified and canonized philosophy. To do the former, i.e. substantiate the canon as the pinnacle of philosophical thought, the rest of philosophy had to be reduced to the level of an immature preparatory stage. Both tasks were fulfilled. A canonized text, compact and popular as an exemplary abstract, appeared in the form of Joseph Stalin's *On the Dialectical and Historical Materialism* (see Stalin 1939). It reduced philosophy to a set of generalized statements, unconditional mandatory truths, ready to be accepted as a matter of party discipline and easily translated into general premises of syllogisms of action for demagogic manipulations. On the other hand, academic institutes, chairs and journals were established and supplemented by a network of institutions of political education.

Soviet philosophy is sometimes referred to as a kind of secular religion. It may be true as far as the 1930s and the 1940s are concerned, when philosophy was demoted to the level of party-state ideology and all philosophical activities (education, as well as research) were directly controlled by party bureaucracy. Those who take a nihilistic attitude to the philosophy of the Soviet era and claim that it yielded nothing of value are grossly mistaken. They fail to take into account the diverse varieties of names and connotations and, first and foremost, the significant differences of stages. One has to distinguish between, at least, three stages, namely the 1920s, when pre-revolutionary philosophical vivaciousness was marginalized but not extinguished and the conquering Marxist philosophy still allowed for diversity of interpretation and debate; the 1930s and the 1940s, that were, indeed, a "dead season," when something of philosophical value (like the publication of the three-volume *Istoriia Filosofii* [The History of Philosophy] (Aleksandrov, Bykhovskii, Mitin and Yudin 1941–1943) was but a chance episode; and finally, the 1950s–1980s, that is my focus in the present chapter.

As to the above-mentioned unrestrained nihilism, it may be justified as long as we deal with the 1930s and the 1940s. Philosophy of those two decades, inasmuch as it functioned in the public space, was reduced to serving the party ideology and philosophical institutions were under direct party control. Its agenda was dictated by party bureaucracy, its judgments were peremptory, and its language was confrontational, even abusive. Philosophers did not do research, they warred (see the title of the work of then main official philosopher, Mark Mitin 1936), they did not speak on their own behalf, they spoke on the behalf of Marxism-Leninism's supreme truth (the phrase "the Marxism-Leninism teaches us that" was a typical cliché), they did not criticize, they "unmasked" (it did not suffice to condemn contemporary Western philosophy as "bourgeois," it had to be labeled as "pseudo-science," "adulteration," a form of "philosophical decay," etc.). It should be noted that the *Short Course* (1938), was, by resolution of the Communist Party of November 14, 1938, proclaimed "the encyclopedia of Marxist-Leninist philosophy" that allowed "no arbitrary interpretation" (*CPSU CC* 1954, 316). If one may speak of the Soviet philosophy as a specific ideological construct, to be distinguished from the philosophy of the Soviet period, it must be identified as the official philosophy of the 1930s and the 1940s. And if one was to point out its most characteristic feature, it was its specific holism stretched to exclude any form of personal individuality, its rejection of the very right of independent, responsible thought.[3]

What was not bent cannot be straightened, as the saying goes. The political pressure on philosophy went so far in the 1930s and the 1940s that its subsequent existence could be nothing else but the retroactive straightening movement. The philosophy of the 1950s–1980s, inasmuch as it concerns us here, was essentially the negation, moreover the conscientious and persistent negation, of the philosophy of the 1930s and the 1940s. There was no continuity there, only rupture. The ideological distancing from the philosophy of the 1930s and the 1940s that often took the form of personal confrontation became both the pathos and the criterion of philosophical work for the new generation of scholars.

The distancing was initially thematic: the younger philosophers tended to focus on the logical and methodological issues. This is usually explained away by reference to the fact that those areas of philosophical research happened to be far less ideologized than, for instance, social philosophy. The explanation is not wrong, of course, but there were other motives as well. This development signified a shift, indeed a radical shift, of the focus of philosophical inquiry. The new agenda testified to the reassessment of the very subject, role and mission of philosophy. Of even greater importance was, however, the younger philosophers' approach to their agenda and their research pathos.

The creative effort of scholars, young at the time and renowned by now, in the fields of epistemology, contemporary logic, methodology, cognitive science, philosophy of science, and philosophical problems of natural sciences that marked a new stage in the development of Russian philosophy served a purpose: it was meant to justify Reason's sovereign right to Truth and its role as the universal, i.e. democratic, way to it. To what degree those scholars adapted the findings of their European colleagues to the Russian reality, to what degree they expanded upon them, and what their individual contributions were, is another question and a matter of special inquiry. What I want to emphasize here is the Enlightenment character of that development. Its motto could be *One can and must live by one's mind*. It was an intellectual movement and a social stand for which one had to fight and sometimes pay. And this raises the question of the social context of the new stage of our philosophical development.

This new stage in the development of philosophy was but an aspect of a broader process of de-Stalinization of the Soviet society that was later called *Khrushchev's "thaw"* and that climaxed, as far as criticism of the cult of Stalin was concerned, at the Twentieth Congress of the CPSU. That was a multifaceted process, full of contradictions and driven by conflicting motivations, but, viewed from the humanitarian standpoint, it set the course of spiritual liberation, emancipation of life and, to some extent, of public behavior from the total control by the Party apparatus and the security forces. The Soviet social model that matured in the 1930s and the 1940s and was associated with Stalin rested on the ideology of unqualified priority of the interests of state and society as formulated by the top party and state leadership over personal and group interests. The members of the new intellectual movement did not share that belief. They sought to broaden criticism of Stalin's cult to include defense of personal dignity and personal status of everyone which implied, first and foremost, intellectual and moral maturity, independent thought and action. These students of scientific knowledge and scientific method proceeded from the belief that criticism of Stalin's cult was to be extended to criticism of any cult and rejection of all forms of intellectual paternalism. The criteria of reason, truth, scientism and scientific demonstration were of greater importance than criteria of class struggle, party principles, and political expediency. They substantiated the individual's right to independent and responsible judgment, including that concerning public good and state interests, and the right to be guided by one's own mind. And they realized that this right was in need of corroboration and defense.

This understanding of the new processes was not universal. It was welcomed, openly or tacitly, by the educated, especially in science and engineering (albeit less so in literary circles) but it was far from universal. And it was certainly not official. Here is a telling episode. In the early 1970s the party committee of the faculty of philosophy at the Moscow State University declined (not unanimously, to be fair) the membership application of a young student, a Komsomol activist, who said that, in the case that a party body resolution went against her conscience, she would abide by her conscience. It was declined because she said what she said and because she believed what she said.

The Sixtiers stood out against the general background of their colleagues, both teachers and researchers: they were distinguished by higher inquiry skills, higher professionalism and more responsible attitude toward their professional work. Moreover, they were aware of and, to some extent, cultivated their intellectual elitism. They brought in a new agenda and new, higher, standards of research work. They took philosophy with a seriousness and responsibility not shared by the trade in general. They knew they were different and cherished that difference. Moreover, they generated a very special environment and formed a kind of tacit community. Their professional connections were supported by and intertwined with friendly personal relations; they saw the very exercise of philosophy as a mission and a life stand. I might put it even stronger: the Sixtiers' lifestyle somewhat resembled that of a commune. Apart from the purely professional tasks, they were united by a common urge for mutual support and protection. It would be worthwhile to inquire into this solidarity.

Like all creative people, they were not above professional jealousy, of course. Their personal relations were, as is the case with all normal people, not unproblematic. Let me give you but two examples. Lektorsky, for instance, remarked, when talking of his sector of epistemology in the 1970s, that his colleagues had been people of different, sometimes contrary philosophical views, and that sharp debates and merciless criticisms had been common at the workplace. Yet this had not prevented the arguers from dining together and generally maintaining friendly relations. "Everyone realized, that for all our discord, we all had a common, worthy cause," he said (Lektorsky 2012, 569). And here is another remarkable testimony. Igor Kohn, our notable sociologist and philosopher, writes in his memoirs titled *80 let odinochestva* [The Eighty Years of Solitude]:

> I attended a banquet on the occasion of E. V. Ilyenkov's doctoral dissertation [it was toward the end of 1968] where, and in the course of a few days that followed, I met literally all members of the philosophical elite [he does not mean the official elite, of course, but the characters this article is about], personal contact with whom I had missed so much. They were all worthy respectable people I had been accustomed to look up at. And no one of them turned out to have a good word to say about any other—only something bad! (Kohn 2008, 141)

Kohn was a man to be trusted. So what was it that kept together the people (and they did, indeed, stick together) who were at odds professionally, ready for mutual criticism and unable to say a good word about each other confidentially? In my opinion, all facts indicate that the force behind their unity was their common critical attitude to the social order localized in their opposition to the dogmatized official philosophy, their struggle against it and, especially, against the administrative regime that set the framework for philosophical life. The mechanisms used to control mind in the previous period were, as a matter of fact, weakened, but not eliminated. Philosophy was still taught in accordance with officially sanctioned unitary programs and textbooks, and the educational process remained under vigilant control. Heads of philosophical institutions, even of their research sections, were either appointed or directly controlled by party authorities. Party bodies interfered in the research programs. The philosophical life was generally subject to party ideology and party control. The Sixtiers, with their concept of sovereign reason and their pronounced sense of professional dignity, were but a minority of the trade. They might have been superior in terms of quality, but they were obviously inferior in terms of quantity. The Sixtiers had to stick together, had to support each other, had to create and maintain a kind of new milieu, a new community that might serve as a center of gravity for all those who sought to do philosophy in good faith if they were to hold on, to safeguard their right to free intellectual activity, their right to do philosophical work according to philosophical standards and philosophical criteria, to rip philosophy from the paws of ideological administrators. The philosophical life of the 1950s–1980s was rich in episodes of collective resistance to party inquests, of mutual support, of creativity displayed not only in academic research, but in everyday life struggle. Much has already been said and written about all these.[4]

Philosophy was still under control of people from the 1930s and the 1940s, whose views had hardly changed since those years. They viewed the new thinkers with suspicion, although this is not to say hostility. Allow me a personal reminiscence. When I was working on my candidate dissertation my supervisor was Professor Spirkin. He was a man of free judgment and was quite outspoken.

He worked at the time under a big philosophical boss, Academician Konstantinov who was the editor-in-chief of the *Filosofskaya entsiklopediya* (see Konstantinov 1960–1970), Spirkin being his deputy. When in the course of a discussion the name of Oleg Drobnitsky was mentioned, a brilliant teacher from the Sixtiers' cohort, Spirkin remarked that, according to Konstantinov, people like Drobnitsky had to be treated like "bourgeois specialists" were treated after the revolution. That was the status of the Sixtiers in the opinion of the philosophy bosses: sound professionals who had to work under supervision of commissars. The Sixtiers were not, in fact, dissidents, even though they sympathized with them and were connected to them in various ways. And I do not think they were against Marxism or communism as a social ideal, even if the professed Marxism of their writings is viewed in retrospect as enforced disguise. Their ideal is better described as socialism with a human face. It should be remembered that they were all employees of official state institutions and party members; that no one was forced to join the party (I mean the CPSU); on the contrary, party membership was sought after, and the entry procedure provided for a personal application written and duly signed by one's own hand. The Sixtiers' ideal identified as socialism with a human face, it would be worthwhile to add, perhaps, that they cherished the human face more than socialism. Personality and individuality were doubtless their priorities.

To conclude, the Russian philosophy of the second half of the twentieth century was, in its greatest achievements as represented by the works of the Sixtiers, a new stage in the development of our philosophy. It proved able to play an important role in the process of democratization of the Russian society due to its humanism and its defense of the intellectual and moral sovereignty of man.

## NOTES

1. They are usually referred to as "the Sixtiers," implying the 1960s that witnessed the transition they represented. Philosophers were named in this manner by analogy, following the example of the men of letters of that decade, just like the early twentieth-century philosophy is more and more often referred to as that of the Silver Age, the term that initially designated the respective period in the history of Russian poetry.
2. Zinoviev's thesis was first published by the Institute of Philosophy in 2002 (Zinoviev 2002). Ilyenkov's thesis remains unpublished, however, it served as the basis of his book completed in a few years after the dissertation defense. See Ilyenkov 1960.
3. Speaking of that period of Soviet philosophy, it is worthwhile to observe that, for all its insignificance from the standpoint of research result, it is of considerable scholarly interest. For it demonstrates what happens to philosophy when it is reduced to the level of ideology and how philosophy itself, in its history and in its theoretical content, resists this deformation of its cultural role and its social function. The tragic life stories of philosophers alone, not only those who belonged to alternative, non-Marxist, traditions, such as Gustav Shpet, Pavel Florensky or Alexei Losev, but numerous representatives of the official Marxist philosophy, including members of the Institute of Philosophy at the Russian Academy of Sciences, who fell victim to red repressions, must keep us from passing superficial and peremptory judgments about the intellectual life of that epoch, and from assuming the very role of judge, spurious as it is on the onset, of old generations.
4. See Mamchur, Ovchinnikov, Ogurtsov 1997; Lektorsky 1998; Gulyga 2000; Mitrokhin 2005.

## BIBLIOGRAPHY

Abdildin, Jubaikhan M. (ed.). 1986–1987. *Dialekticheskaya logika.* [The Dialectical Logic]. Books 1–3. Alma-Ata: Nauka.

Aleksandrov, Georgi F., Bykhovskii, Bernard E., Mitin, Mark. B., and Yudin, Pavel F. (eds.). 1941–1943. *Istoriya filosofii. V 3-kh tt.* [History of Philosophy. In 3 vols.]. Moscow: Politizdat pri TsK VKP(b).

Gulyga, Arseny V. 2000. "Polveka na Volkhonke" [Half a Century on Volkhonka Street]. In *Estetika v svete aksiologii* [Aesthetics in the Light of Axiologys], edited by I. Andreeva and A. Gulyga. St. Petersburg: Aleteya.

Frolov, Ivan T. 1983. "O zhizni, smerti i bessmertii: etyudy novogo (real'nogo) gumanizma" [On Life, Death and Immortality: Studies on New (Real) Humanism]. Parts 1 and 2. *Voprosy filosofii* [*Questions of Philosophy*]. (1): 83–98; (2): 52–64.

Ilyenkov, Evald V. 1960. *Dialektika abstraktnogo i konkretnogo v "Kapitale" Marksa* [Dialectics of the Abstract and the Concrete in Marx's Capital]. Moscow: Publishing House of the Academy of Sciences of the USSR.

Ilyichev, Leonid F. (ed.). 1982–1987. *Materialisticheskaya dialektika kak obshchaya teoriya razvitiya.* [The Materialist Dialectic as a General Theory of Development]. Books 1–4. Moscow: Nauka.

Kohn, Igor S. 2008. *80 let odinochestva* [The Eighty Years of Solitude]. Moscow: Vremya.

Konstantinov, Fedor V. 1960–1970. *Filosofskaya entsiklopediya v 5-ti tt.* [The Encyclopedia of Philosophy in 5 vols.]. Moscow: Soviet Encyclopedia.

Lektorsky, Vladislav A. (ed.). 1998. *Filosofiya ne konchaetsya . . . Iz istorii otechestvennoy filosofii. XX v.* [Philosophy Never Ends . . . From the History of Russian Philosophy. The 20th c[entury]], Books 1–2. Moscow: Russian Political Encyclopedia.

Lektorsky, Vladislav A. 2012. "O zhizni i filosofii. Beseda B. I. Pruzhinina" [On Life and Philosophy: Conversation with B. I. Pruzhinin]. In *Chelovek v mire zhaniy* [Man in the World of Knowledge], edited by B. I. Pruzhinina, 551–595. Moscow: ROSSPEN.

Mamchur, Elena A., Ovchinnikov, Nikolai F., Ogurtsov, Alexandre P. 1997. *Otechestvennaya filosofiya nauki: predvaritel'nye itogi* [The Russian Philosophy of Science: Preliminary Results]. Moscow: ROSSPEN.

Mitin, Mark B. 1936. *Boevye voprosy materialisticheskoi dialektiki* [The Fighting Issues of Materialistic Dialectics]. Moscow: Partizdat TsK VKPb.

Mitin, Mark B. (ed.). 1981–1985. *Materialisticheskaya dialektika. V 5-ti tt.* [The Materialist Dialectics. In 5 vols.]. Moscow: Mysl'.

Mitrokhin, Lev N. 2005. *Moi filosofskie sobesedniki* [My Philosophical Interlocutors]. St. Petersburg: Russian Christian Academy of Humanities.

Motroshilova, Nelli V. 2012. *Otechestvennaya filosofiya 50–80-kh godov XX veka i zapadnaya mysl's* [The Russian Philosophy of the 1950s–1980s and the Western Thought]. Moscow: Akademicheskiy proyekt.

Solovyov, Erikh Yu. 1998. "Filosofskiy zhurnalism shestidesyatykh: zavoevaniya, obol'shcheniya, nedodelannye dela" [The Philosophical Journalism of the 1960s: Achievements, Delusions, Unfinished Work]. In *Filosofiya ne konchaetsya* [Philosophy Never Ends], Book 4. Moscow: Russian Political Encyclopedia.

Solovyov, Vladimir S. 1988. "Opravdanie dobra: nravstvennaya filosofiya" [The Validation of The Good: Moral Philosophy]. In *Sochineniya v dvukh tomakh*, [Works in 2 vols.]. Moscow: Mysl'. Vol. 1, 47–548.

Stalin, Joseph V. 1939. *O dialekticheskom i istoricheskom materializme* [On the Dialectical and Historical Materialism]. Moscow: Gosudarstvennoe izdatel'stvo politicheskoi literatury.

Zinoviev, Alexander A. 2002. *Voskhozhdenie ot abstraktnogo k konkretnomu (na materiale "Kapitala" K. Marksa)* [Ascending from the Abstract to the Concrete (on the Materials of K. Marx's *Capital*)]. Moscow: Institut filosofii RAN.

1938. *Kratkii kurs istorii VKP(b)* [History of the All-Union Communist Party (Bolsheviks): Short Course], Moscow: Gosudarstvennoe izdatel'stvo politicheskoi literatury.—Abbreviated as *Short Course*.

1954. *KPSS v rezulyutsiyakh i resheniyakh s'ezdov, konferentsiy i plenumov TsK.* [The CPSU in the Resolutions and Decisions of Its Congresses, Conferences and C[entral] C[ommittee] Meetings], Seventh ed., Part III. Moscow: Gospolitizdat.—Abbreviated as *CPSU CC*.

CHAPTER SIX

# Philosophy From the Period of "Thaw" to the Period of "Stagnation"

## *A Philosophical Reflection*

VADIM M. MEZHUYEV

Let me begin with some preliminary remarks. Firstly, there is a tendency—especially notable in contemporary scholarly Russian literature—to talk about the nowadays of Russia in terms of modernity. I find it very puzzling. I think Russia today is more remote from modernity than it was at the end of the last century. We constantly talk about modernization, but are moving in the opposite direction if we look at what is happening around us today. That already reveals a problem: why this backward movement?

One has to admit that so far Russia has failed to overcome the boundary that separates modernity from pre-modernity (in other words the civil society from traditional society). The buzz today is about a return happening before our eyes to some kind of Russian medievalism with its autocracy and clericalism. Nothing in history repeats itself exactly of course, but certain things can rhyme. I think some of the responsibility for this regression rests with Russian philosophers regardless of all their efforts to fight official Soviet ideology. I would like to address the topic of our (scholars') responsibility for what is happening in Russia today.

Secondly, the second half of the twentieth century is a fairly large stretch of time in Russia's history comprising different periods with occasionally conflicting results. We, Russians, are a nation focused on literature, and accordingly we often tend to designate these periods by resorting to literary metaphors: thaw (*ottepel'*), stagnation (*zastoj*),restructuring (*perestroika*), and the wild 1990s (*likhie devjanostye*). Each period is associated with a different key political figure: Khrushchev, Brezhnev, Gorbachev, and Yeltsin. These leaders cannot be bracketed together; not only because they all had very different personalities, but also on account of their policies. Suffice it to recall that the half century on which the present volume focuses began in the USSR and ended in the Russian Federation. And those periods had been followed by other historical phases leading to the current state of affairs. Can all these events pass unnoticed by philosophers without affecting their work and the direction of their thinking? Perhaps there are some such philosophers, but I am interested in those who respond to these events, and not just emotionally, like most people, but also intellectually, by changing something in their philosophical discourse.

The Russian philosophical community today tends to lump all these periods together as the period of gradually purging the "Marxist-Leninist philosophy" that was rammed down our throats in the Soviet times, not only in its Stalinist version but also in any other versions. This is roughly how that stage is usually assessed. It is fashionable today to portray that stage as an uncompromising fight against the dogmatism of that philosophy even though in the Soviet times by no means all had the courage to openly challenge it. The main philosophical outcome of that time is considered to be final liberation of Russia from the grip of Marxism, not only as a state ideology, but also as a doctrine that claims to be at least partially true. While the second half of the twentieth century began with the attempts of the philosophers of the 1960s (the so-called Sixtiers) to liberate Marxism from its Stalinist version, it ended during the Yeltsin period with the total banishment of Marxism not only from political and ideological spheres, but also from the education system. Before that, it was not compulsory but at least recommended for reading and studying. During the brief period when this country was run by liberal reformers, Marxism was declared a false and harmful ideology and the cause of all country's woes. In effect, it was thrown into the dustbin of history in the same arbitrary fashion as it was once imposed upon Russia. Who could have known that liberalism would share the same fate as Marxism? Today liberalism is just as much hated by the authorities and their supporters as Marxism was only a few decades ago. As a recent survey of famous Russian figures has shown, the most popular figure in Soviet history today is Stalin.[1] The demise of Marxism for some reason has revived in people's souls the worst things that existed under Soviet power. I have warned earlier about a possible repeat of another version of Stalinism here, only without Marxism, which attests that this phenomenon has not Marxist, but rather Russian roots.

But if this is the result of our history, in fighting for the liberation of Russia from the power of Marxism and Marxists, a serious miscalculation has been made, including by our philosophers. The miscalculation, in my opinion, was that this struggle failed to simultaneously be the struggle for the liberation of Marxism from Russia, or rather the distorted version that sprouted on Russian soil, the so-called "Russian Marxism" whose history, incidentally, has yet to be written. One may reject Marxism until one is blue in one's face, but without understanding the logic of its appearance and existence in Russia, it is impossible to understand and chart the path of the development of our philosophy beyond Marxism. Even Stalinism as an ideology is not as primitive as it may look at first glance. It is not by chance that it rules the minds of a large number of people to this day. I suspect that some of these people in many ways determine the situation in Russia even today. I would suggest that even some of the best country's philosophical minds of the last century who had simply cast Marxism aside without bothering to understand the "sources and meaning of Russian communism" have suffered a defeat in their own country, a defeat from which they still have not yet recovered. It is worth recalling that the main question in European philosophy has always been and remains the question of what does it mean to be a European, to be a person belonging to the European culture? Russian philosophy is still struggling to explain what Russia was in the past and what it is today, how it can continue and what distinguishes a Russian (both in the positive and negative sense) from any others. If this is the case, who needs such philosophy, and who can be interested in it?

Russian Marxism was born long before the October 1917 Revolution and even before the Bolshevik party emerged in Russia. The first Russian translators of Marx were not Marxists, but the anarchists and Populists (Narodniki), such as Bakunin, Tkachev, and Danielson. Once emerged, Russian Marxism instantly split into two branches. The first consisted of the so-called "legal Marxists" (Berdyayev, Bulgakov, Struve, Kistyakovsky, Frank, Tugan-Baranovsky and others). A few years later, many of them became the classics of Russian Silver Age religious philosophy. The evolution from atheist and materialistic doctrine to idealism and then to religious philosophy in a country where Orthodoxy is deeply rooted in popular consciousness is quite natural and logical.

The other branch, preaching "revolutionary Marxism," emerged directly from Populism and was initially represented by a small group of Marxists that called themselves "Emancipation of Labor" (Plekhanov, Martov, Zasulich, Akselrod, Deich). They contributed to the spread of Marxism in Russia, to attracting new and younger names, among whom Lenin was a most prominent figure from the very beginning. That trend led to the creation of the first Russian Social-Democratic Labor Party, or RSDLP. However, it faced another and equally acute Russian problem: how to be and remain a Marxist, i.e. a proletarian revolutionary in a predominantly peasant country, in the absence of sufficiently developed classes of the bourgeoisie and the proletariat on a national scale? The question was the main cause of the split of Russian revolutionary Marxists into Mensheviks and Bolsheviks. Lenin, who founded the Bolshevik Party, approached the issue in a way that was anything but Marxist: the absence of the proletariat as a class can be compensated for by creating a proletarian party of professional revolutionaries, which would undertake the task of preparing a proletarian revolution. Class was supplanted by party which, under the circumstances that emerged quite early on, enabled it to seize power but then led to its bureaucratic mutation that was eventually crowned with Stalinism. Such is the logic of any revolutionary movement in a peasant country, and Marxism is not to blame for this. Marxism in Russia was replaced with Leninism, i.e. was adapted to address a very different task (seizing power in a peasant country) than the task for the sake of which it was created.

Now a few words about Stalinism. Stalinism is not only about terror, GULAG and so on, but also a myth about the victory of socialism created by Stalin. Even Lenin believed that we do not have socialism and will not have it for quite some time because of the historical backwardness of our country compared with Western civilization (think of the Cultural Revolution, the New Economic Policy and all the rest of it). Twelve years after Lenin's death Stalin declared that socialism "has been built in the main" offering as socialism the system of semi-feudal coercion into work and state violence over the individual that he created. The essence of Stalin's myth about socialism is that it identified the socialist idea with reality. Reality was passed off for what it never was. It is another question how many came to believe that myth. Stalinism in fact is the belief that we lived under socialism and that socialism cannot be of any different kind. Many still hold this belief. I call these people Stalinists regardless of how they personally feel about Stalin. It does not matter whether or not they approve of the regime he created. The main thing is that they consider it to be socialism. Granted, some of them reject socialism on these grounds while others defend Stalinism, but in any case, they are Stalinists because they think in a Stalinist way, that is, they believe in what he believed or pretended to believe.

Not surprisingly, the myth survived even after Stalin was denounced. Stalin is gone, but the myth about the socialism he had built has survived. Even after Stalin, Soviet history has been dominated by the same myth. Even the most enlightened part of our intelligentsia during the periods of Khrushchev's "thaw" and Brezhnev's "stagnation," while differing in their assessment of socialism, did not put into question the fact that it existed. This brings me to the main question of my presentation, namely, why have our philosophers failed to eradicate Stalinism from people's consciousness? To identify the reason for that I propose to compare the philosophies of Evald Ilyenkov and Merab Mamardashvili, two of the most high-profile, although mutually exclusive, representatives of the periods of "thaw" and "stagnation."

First a quotation that explains the link between these two figures. The quotation belongs to Mamardashvili and deals with his attitude to Ilyenkov. In his conversation with Ukrainian philosopher Yu.D. Prilyuk he referred to Ilyenkov in this way:

> I can describe the general atmosphere at the Philosophical Department at Moscow University that prevailed in 1953–1956 . . . Of course, I remember the names, but it is impossible to isolate them from the general atmosphere of mutual induction of thought—no, that is impossible. And anyway, it is not the names that matter, but the very atmosphere of communication, the sparks of revelation and creativity . . . Many of us who were steeped in that atmosphere later evolved into very different kinds of philosophers. That is normal, what matters is that they have become philosophers and interesting personalities. I might mention, for example, Evald Ilyenkov, although not in connection with his philosophy which I actually repudiated. He was important for me because he generated the energy of repulsion: in repudiating his, undoubtedly, interesting thoughts that I found alien to me and of which I was intensely critical. Especially because of the element (more than an element) of Hegelianism. However, without this energy of repulsion some positive things would perhaps not have happened. (Mamardashvili 1990, 35)

That observation already shows that the more notable philosophers of the post-war generation, in spite of conformity with Marxism that was imposed from above, rather than being immanent in their philosophical views, were *different*. Only by understanding what the difference was can one find the key to the subsequent evolution of philosophical thought in our country. In the overall field of philosophical attractions and repulsions of the time Ilyenkov and, a little later Mamardashvili, were the towering figures for all their polarity with regard to each other. Side by side with them, there, of course, were other philosophers whose contribution to philosophy will perhaps be appreciated by future generations, but at the time none of them could match Ilyenkov and Mamardashvili in terms of the popularity of their ideas and their influence on young philosophers. And this despite (and probably because of) the fact that they opposed each other not just as philosophers preaching different views, but as people who reflected in their philosophies the mindsets and ideas of two different and in some ways very opposite periods of our post-war history which came to be known as the "thaw" and "stagnation." While I see Ilyenkov as the main philosophical star of the period of "thaw," Mamardashvili is the recognized philosophical leader of the period of "stagnation" when Ilyenkov's popularity among young philosophers was waning. Far be it from me to belittle the philosophical importance of either of them. I merely maintain that their difference from each other can best be understood only by comparing these two epochs.

The "thaw" was the period of liberation from the Stalinist cant in life and ideology, destalinization of the regime and consciousness without however breaking with socialism and Marxism, but on the contrary, seeking to tease out their genuine meaning and content. The stagnation that set in after the suppression of the Prague Spring was an era of disappointment of much of our intelligentsia in both. For the generation of the period of "thaw" Soviet reality was invested with reason. Even though it was temporarily distorted by Stalin's reprisals, it could be explained in rational terms by reinterpreting Marxism. With the collapse of the hope for the building of "socialism with a human face," the same reality came to be perceived as something totally irrational, devoid of any human content and meaning. All that was real, to use Hegel's language, ceased to be reasonable and all that was reasonable lost any connection with what was real.

The sense that reality was reasonable, even though it existed in an alienated form until a certain moment, permeates Ilyenkov's philosophy, which is Hegelian and Marxist in its origin and spirit. The method of understanding the reasonableness is provided by dialectical logic, which he considered to be the highest achievement of philosophical thought. It makes it possible to see behind all these alienated forms their human essence, to present as historically transient stages in the evolution of the human spirit in its societal wholeness and integrity. The overwhelming majority of people in the 1960s, shared a conviction that the social world, for all its frustrations and falls, is not hostile to man and is, at the end of the day, driven by humanistic goals. That conviction was expressed in the most consistent and complete form in the philosophy of Ilyenkov, which can be defined as the logic or theory of cognizing reality as reasonable. What is important is the very faith that the objective world is reasonable, faith that collapsed in the period of "stagnation." Those loyal to Ilyenkov probably did not notice the collapse, but those who had lost that faith found solace in the philosophy of Mamardashvili.

Mamardashvili, who emerged from the generation of the 1960s, expressed his attitude to his fellow compatriots and to Khrushchev's "thaw" in general in clear terms. In an interview to Spanish journalist Pilar Bonet, when asked about his perception of the spirit of the twentieth century, he replied that his life experience was different from that of his contemporaries, was "not typical" for that time. He describes "normal experience" for the time with which he never identified himself as:

> a life path in which the reference point was Marxism or socialism and faith in the ideals of Marxism and socialism. A faith that presupposed sincerity . . . Well, their further path, of course, was a path of disenchantment when confronted with reality which certainly did not correspond to their ideals. They embarked on a search of ideological positions with the aim of correcting the distortions and restoring the purity of Marxist-Leninist theory, etc. (Mamardashvili 2000, 385)

A very accurate description of the generation of the 1960s. Khrushchev's "thaw," according to Mamardashvili, was "of course . . . their time." He continues: "For them it was an era of intensive inner work, reflections on the foundations of socialism, an attempt to invent new concepts that would rectify its distortions, etc." (ibid., 386).

That position, Mamardashvili believes, was in many ways disingenuous and hypocritical. In challenging the dogmatism and conservatism of the Stalin times and posing as the champions of an idea, many 1960s philosophers were in reality concerned about their career growth and material well-being combining in an odd way their alleged asceticism with the wish to live well. "Such a 'martyr', without any logical inner contradiction, inevitably ends being concerned only with his own well-being" (ibid., 385). This opinion may be justified with regard to Mamardashvili's colleagues in the journal *World Marxist Review*, which he recalls in his interview, but can hardly be associated with the name of Ilyenkov. Those philosophers are mostly remembered as party ideologues and functionaries (though not without some liberal habits), Ilyenkov, who was more harassed by ideological bosses than others, cannot be accused of being a self-serving career seeker. His sincere and unselfish dedication to the spirit of Marxism has never been called into question.

It is this spirit that Mamardashvili rejects. He finds it very alien in practical and theoretical terms. "The Khrushchev era," he says, "was absolutely unacceptable for me" (ibid., 390). He attributes his rejection of the "thaw" and everything that accompanied it not to any adherence to Stalinism, but to his innate aversion to politics, his indifference to any projects and plans of social reform and restructuring inasmuch as they originated from the top. What distinguishes me from other 1960s people, he says, is:

> that I have never followed their path. I have always, from my youth, perceived power and politics as having no inner connection with me. I do not invest my attitude to power and what it does—be it Khrushchev's goals or someone else's—with any inner convictions . . . If you like, I have always been in a kind of inner exile. (Ibid., 388–389)

I am not a man of the "thaw," Mamardashvili says about himself, I am not a man of any period of Soviet history, I am outside history and outside politics which tries to introduce something—even if it is something progressive—into history. He explained the apolitical nature of his philosophy in a letter to Althusser (November 1968) by pointing out that the socio-political system, existing in the USSR lacked any policy of common sense:

> For us a good policy is depoliticization of philosophy because it is impossible (because of censorship, ideological pressure, totalitarianism) to create, present and publish good political critique, to act politically in the spirit of common sense, in general we avoid politics as such. For it can only be bad politics. So, down with politics. (Epelboin 2009, 357)

Depoliticizing philosophy on the grounds that there can be no good policy under Soviet power points to the Soviet origin of that philosophy. Many at the time, instead of participating in political life, withdrew into their own shells, became internal exiles, inhabiting the sphere of pure thought, i.e. thought about thought itself, which created an illusion of the thinker's freedom and independence. This illusion, I think, inspired the philosophy of Mamardashvili.

Of course, I am talking about my own perception of his philosophy without purporting to give a definitive assessment. As I see it, its core is total reduction of the objective—natural and social—world from philosophical knowledge. Philosophy has no direct bearing on this world, like religion, "it is not of this world," except that it constitutes its subject not through faith, but through reflexive acts of thought that have a symbolic nature. The subject matter of philosophy is not the world objectively given, but something that goes beyond it and presents itself not in an act of external observation, but in the process of transcending these limits.

What interested Mamardashvili above all could be formulated in the following way: how can one remain a philosopher in a world which has turned philosophy into party and state ideology, a pseudo-science justifying the existing order of things and passing off what is real for what is reasonable? Can philosophy regain its lost position of independent thought based solely on its own premises? To him the philosophy of Hegel, and later Marx, was the most vivid example of the mutation of philosophy into ideology. Both considered transforming reality to be the task of philosophy (Hegel spoke of spiritual transformation and Marx of practical transformation) and both fell victim of this reality. For Marx it resulted in what amounted to abdication from philosophy, an admission of its end and futility, its replacement with historical science, which he called materialist interpretation of history. According to Engels, if anything remained of classical philosophy, it was only logic. This position, first put forward in this country by Ilyenkov, generated the movement of so-called "epistemologists" who reduced philosophy to the theory of cognition. True, many of them soon veered toward Positivism, which adhered to a similar point of view, but was alien to Ilyenkov who was dedicated to dialectical thinking.

However, if philosophy is nothing but the logic and theory of cognition, what about historical materialism? For Mamardashvili all those who pursued this area of knowledge were not just the servants of power, but also veritable enemies of philosophy. In the aforementioned interview with Pilar Bonet he said:

> In my time at the philosophy department—from which I graduated in 1954—we despised anyone who did historical materialism because we accepted only those who did logic and epistemology. . . . The very sign that you are engaged in some kind of talk called historical materialism attested that you were a scoundrel. Whether this was good or bad was another question. But such was our history. (Mamardashvili 2000, 394)

In another place he wrote:

> Decent people, so to speak, chose certain themes of a theoretical and cognitive nature and thus set themselves apart from indecent people who identified themselves by engaging, for example, in historical materialism, the theory of Communism, etc. (Mamardashvili 1991, 48)

Such a choice "meant that a person wanted to serve as an ideological cogwheel (ibid., 45).

Mamardashvili's repudiation of Ilyenkov begins with the issue of defining philosophy, in particular the philosophy of Marxism. Mamardashvili did not consider himself a Marxist (certainly not at the end of his life), nor did he consider himself to be an anti-Marxist or deny Marx's influence on him. Like most 1960s people, he began with the study of the logic of *The Capital*, but his approach to it differed from that of Ilyenkov even then. This is how Mamardashvili himself described his attitude to Marx:

> Perhaps, unlike others, I was the only Marxist because in philosophy I was in some ways influenced by Marx while many had no idea of Marx. But I was not a Marxist in terms of social-political theory. In terms of the concept of socialism and the movement of history toward communism, I was never a Marxist in that sense. But I was not an anti-Marxist. Simply, I have always resented the surrounding life order and never felt inwardly dependent on the ideology and the ideals that could inform that order. (Mamardashvili 2000, 389)

What interested him was not the content of the Marxist theory or even its method, but his experience of thought activity, a certain experience of consciousness. He admitted: "For us the logical aspect of *The Capital* . . . was simply material for thought which we didn't need . . . to invent, we had it given to us as a specimen of intellectual work" (Mamardashvili, 1991, 48).

For all his differences with Ilyenkov, Mamardashvili shared with the latter his understanding of philosophy as *analysis of consciousness*. However, in interpreting consciousness he diverged not only from Ilyenkov but also from Marx himself, for whom, as is well known, consciousness is no more than "conscious being." Marx sought answers to the questions that engaged his mind not in consciousness, but in social being which the main subject of his socio-historical theory was. Nevertheless, the best of what has been written about Marx in this country has to do with his understanding of consciousness, and not of social being. The latter was censored by the authorities to such an extent that it deterred thinking people from dealing with it at all. Thereby, however, understanding of the true meaning of Marx's doctrine was blocked.

Interest in consciousness in fact is what Ilyenkov and Mamardashvili had in common. Beyond that, as I have said, there are deep differences in their interpretation both of consciousness and philosophy itself. While for Ilyenkov the main business of philosophy is developing dialectical logic as a theoretically understood unity of being and thought, for Mamardashvili, consciousness cannot be derived either from natural or social being and is "a special kind of entity" that is not captured by means of logic or psychology. Consciousness is the subject matter of philosophy; it is a type of reality that cannot be reduced to anything else. Not *the logic of cognition* but *the ontology of cognition*—this is what interests Mamardashvili above all. While Ilyenkov is predominantly a logician and epistemologist, Mamardashvili is an ontologist and metaphysician. For Ilyenkov, dialectics, being the logic and theory of cognition, is simultaneously the logic of being. For Mamardashvili no logic, including dialectical logic, can fathom consciousness in its own being. The nature of consciousness is not logical but symbolic, and it is not reduced to a sum of logical operations.

Consciousness as interpreted by Mamardashvili is an ultimate concept in any philosophy. It is present in philosophy not simply as knowledge of nature, society, law, science, religion, art, etc. but as an intellectual effort that makes any knowledge possible. Philosophy, basically, is the mode of Man's being in the form of thought (cogito), his self-consciousness as a thinking creature.

On the other hand, consciousness cannot be represented as a naturally existing thing and consequently, cannot be the subject of any theory. Consciousness does not lend itself to theorizing, objectivizing, it allows only of a mediated, indirect (symbolic) language to describe it. Therefore, the approach to philosophy understood not as knowledge about something but as consciousness in its own being calls for great caution. One can define science or law, but one cannot precisely define philosophy.

Mamardashvili tries to explain the difference of philosophizing from simple cognition by citing the phrase "sorry, that's not what I have in mind." He cites the example of the Kantian concept of beauty. One cannot judge duty (and a person) on the basis of what the individual wants for himself owing to his sensual nature, i.e. only on the basis of purely empirical arguments. Empirically speaking, man is no more than an animal. The philosophical idiom which has to do with what is beyond what is sensual and reasonable, deals not with empirical but with transcendental arguments pointing to something that cannot be directly experienced.

Unlike in science, there is no progress in philosophy, and there are no final solutions. In general, it is not a system of knowledge that can be transmitted in the process of education. Philosophy is given to us as an internal act, as individual presence of the thinker with whom you communicate directly. Not the transformation of the external—natural and social—world, but building oneself into a human being as a conscious (free-thinking) and moral individual capable of holding on to humanity in the changing world—this is the task of genuine philosophy as interpreted by Mamardashvili. It is less a cognitive than ethical task. It is driven not by the wish of social reforming but of individual self-creation. For man:

> is a creature that exists to the extent that it creates itself by certain means not given in nature. Or, in other words, the human part of man is not a natural creature and in that sense man does not originate from an ape. (Mamardashvili 1996, 15)

Man is not a natural but a cultural creature and to understand him means to become aware of the gulf, the abyss separating culture from nature.

As a self-creating creature man cannot rely on anything outside himself. All that Mamardashvili would later describe as means of self-generation, self-creation of man has to do not with natural but with supranatural world that is outside time (eternal) understood however not in a religious, but in a natural and moral sense, i.e. without any reference to God. Mamardashvili defines this other world not as a mythological or divine world and not as a world of nothing but as something understood as some kind of higher world order that we try to grasp through philosophy. He believes that philosophy begins with the question of what exactly this "something" is. One can access it through transcendence, but unlike religious faith, it is transcendence without the transcendent world. Something is given to us in our wonderment at what exists in the world, at the fact that it is dominated not by chaos but some order which we seek to understand through philosophy, obviously without ever reaching a final result. But it is this constant effort of thought aimed at identifying that in us which is supranatural and that takes us beyond purely natural existence that constitutes the work of consciousness.

From that point of view a philosopher is not just a person who knows something about the world or introduces some changes to it, but an individual who confronts the world and lives exclusively in accordance with the bidding of his own reason and conscience. It is not by chance that people like Mamardashvili were dubbed in our time as the last "cultured generation" sincerely believing that it was possible to preserve in the modern world (through intellectual or some other symbolic activity) the position of a subject freely defining the boundaries of its own existence in the world. For Mamardashvili, as I have always felt, engaging in philosophy free of any politics and social projections, could make an individual free, even in the world which is beyond freedom in all its manifestations. While Ilyenkov linked human freedom with changes of the social world hostile to culture, Mamardashvili saw culture itself as the rescue of human freedom from that world.

This, as I see it, was the typical mindset of people in the period of "stagnation" who tried to escape from the hated reality either into the "kingdom" of metaphysics, "pure reason," free of any sensual concerns, or into the world of abstract artistic innovations and experiments. An example of existence exclusively "in consciousness" unconnected with the social needs of people, were, for Mamardashvili, Descartes and Kant, although I very much doubt that their philosophy is all that remote from the social challenges of their time. Indeed, Mamardashvili's philosophy, for all its seeming remoteness from social and political life, was in a way a reaction to this life, its most audible echo.

Lack of social and political engagement, paradoxically, can morph either into conformism, reconciliation with reality, or lack of readiness to accept radical social change. I think this is what happened to Mamardashvili in the period of *perestroika*.

He is not among the most popular figures of the time although many of the so-called “stewards of perestroika” and its heralds and champions were clearly inferior to him intellectually. At the same time he developed a lively interest in Russia and the processes taking place in his native Georgia (this last short period of his life has even been called “the period of rallies”), but his philosophy in the period of *perestroika* moved from the center to the periphery of Russian spiritual life of the time. Earlier published works or recordings of his lectures are reissued, some short articles and interviews are printed, but he has ceased to be for his audience what he used to be during the years of “stagnation.” Other names and authorities have appeared in the press and on television who have not eclipsed Mamardashvili in terms of philosophical talent, but have turned out to be more consonant with the times and more appealing to the audience. Everyone wanted more politics and social commitment, something that was absent in Mamardashvili’s philosophy. It is only today, in the period that is witnessing a certain regression rollback from the course of democratization proclaimed by *perestroika* that he is regaining some of his former popularity. He is being reissued and read, conferences in his honor are being held, articles and books are being written about him and he is undoubtedly becoming a philosophical idol for many who feel uncomfortable in modern Russia. The question is, what are the implications of the new groundswell of interest in him: is it just a tribute to one of our outstanding philosophers of the past century or a sign of a new stagnation that has afflicted our country?

The fate of Mamardashvili’s philosophy in our time, with all due respect for his memory (can you name any one as his follower today?) convinces me that no form of philosophy has a future unless it seeks to understand man’s social and historical being. Neither logic in itself (even dialectical logic) nor any other analysis of language and consciousness can replace that connection. The fact that social, historical and cultural being of man (in other words, society, history and culture) are banished from the purview of philosophers, the preoccupation of the majority of post-Stalin generation of philosophers with the problems of logic and theory of cognition and later the philosophy of science (because they are relatively closed to Soviet censorship) explain the inability of our philosophy to put an end to the myth of Stalinism and the misunderstanding of socialism, as I have said earlier. The events and processes happening in “historical materialism,” despised by Mamardashvili and other philosophers, were vastly more important for our social and humanitarian thought than the events in so-called “dialectical materialism” which dealt primarily with the “philosophical problems of natural science” whose usefulness for natural sciences has always seemed dubious. Even one discussion of the “Asian mode of production” in the 1970s which overturned the idea about the historical theory of Marx and the whole of history, which discovered “later” Marx who was very different from the “early” Marx with his theory of activity, outweighs in my opinion all the logical and epistemological and methodological researches and theories of our philosophers. I would like to remind you that it is in the sphere of socio-philosophical knowledge that Russian sociology, political science and cultural studies have their origins. I think it should help to revive in this country the philosophy of history, culture, law, religion, political philosophy, etc. My own interest in culture was stimulated in its time by the wish to restore the lost link of our philosophy to social being as represented in the context of our history. I am not of course against logic and analysis, but I still believe that the main task of philosophy is to understand the human being in the conditions and circumstances of the history and culture that have generated it.

## NOTES

1. Administered by Russia's independent Levada Center in April 2017, the survey included a representative sample of 1,600 Russians from 48 regions of the country. Stalin had the largest share (38 percent) of the vote, followed by Russian President Vladimir Putin at 34 percent, in a tie with Alexander Pushkin, the great patron of Russian Romantic verse. The full ranking is published on the Levada Center website at http://www.levada.ru/2017/06/26/vydayushhiesya-lyudi/

   For an English report of the survey results, see Filipov 2017—Ed.

## BIBLIOGRAPHY

Epelboin, Annie. 2009. "Perepiska M.K. Mamardashvili s Lui Al'tyusserom" [Correspondence between M.K. Mamardashvili and Louis Althusser]. In *Merab Konstantinovich Mamardashvili*, edited by Nelli V. Motroshilova, 349–367. [Series: Filosofiya Rossii vtoroi poloviny XX veka [Russian Philosophy in the Second Half of the Twentieth Century]]. Moscow: ROSSPEN.

Filipov, David. 2017. "For Russians, Stalin is the 'most outstanding' figure in world history, followed by Putin," *The Washington Post*, June 26.

Mamardashvili, Merab K. 1989. "Interv'yu 'Byt' filosofom—eto sud'ba'" [Interview "Being a Philosopher is a Fate"]. *Filosofskaya i sotsiologicheskaya mysl'* [Philosophical and Sociological Thought], (2): 29–36. Kiev. [Printed in the book: Mamardashvili, Merab K. 1990. *Kak ya ponimayu filosofiyu*. [How I Understand Philosophy] Moscow: Progress.]

Mamardashvili, Merab K. 1991. "Nachalo vsego istorichno, to est' sluchaino" [The Origin of Everything is Historical, that Means Accidental']." *Voprosy Metodologii* [Questions of Methodology], (1): 45–53.

Mamardashvili, Merab K. 1996. *Neobkhodimost' sebya* [The Need for the Self]. Moscow: Labirint.

Mamardashvili, Merab K. 2000. *Moi opyt netipichen* [My Experience is Not Typical]. St. Petersburg: Azbuka.

PART II

# Philosophy of Science

CHAPTER SEVEN

# The Russian Philosophy of Science in the Second Half of the Twentieth Century

VYACHESLAV S. STEPIN

After the disintegration of the Soviet Union and the second coming of capitalism to Russia, the entire intellectual legacy of the previous more than seventy year period was placed under scrutiny. There were many attacks on Soviet philosophy especially. Many argued that being subject to harsh ideological control Soviet philosophy had produced no original works and no new ideas. Having been isolated from the world philosophy, it lagged behind and lost track of what it was doing now. Thus, in an attempt to join in the international philosophical process and catch up with the West, it had to start almost from scratch.

In the early 1990s such an assessment was very common and could be found not only in journal articles, but also in textbooks and philosophical dictionaries. Ironically, this belief itself was a product of an ideological attitude that worked by selectively highlighting some facts while ignoring others. The attitude was expressed in an overly simplified thesis that a lack of democracy and freedom led to cultural impotence. The logic behind that thesis, if duly followed, would render inexplicable the great music of Johann Sebastian Bach under the conditions of the eighteenth-century European absolutism, doubt the intellectual legitimacy of the poetry of Alexander Pushkin and Mikhail Lermontov during the reign of Nicholas I of Russia, and question the possibility of the classical German philosophy during the times notoriously deficient in democracy and freedom. In fact, there is no simple, straightforward relation between political order and cultural creativity. This relation is complex, multi-faceted, and sometimes ambivalent.

There is no doubt that the Stalinist totalitarian regime constrained the development of philosophical thought. However, even at the times of "ideological purges," an active intellectual life did not cease to exist: the notable philosophers, such as Mikhail Bakhtin and Alexei Losev continued their innovative studies, the great psychologist Lev Vygotsky developed his ingenious ideas about the social nature of consciousness, and Alexander Zinoviev and Evald Ilyenkov embarked on their philosophical inquiries.

The late 1950s and early 1960s marked the turning point in the history of Soviet philosophy. Under conditions of Khrushchev's "thaw," there emerged a new generation of thinkers that was to determine the course of our philosophy in the decades to come. Ideological control was by no means nonexistent throughout that and the subsequent periods of the Soviet era, but it was substantially softened allowing some creative work. Furthermore, the ideological pressure substantially varied in different spheres of philosophical research. Social philosophy was scrutinized much greater than, for instance, history of philosophy or, even more so, philosophy of science.

The period from the 1960s to 1980s came to be surprisingly quite favorable and highly fruitful for Russian philosophy of science, which during those years gradually developed into one of the most captivating fields of philosophical inquiry. Many scholars involved in research in this field had background in physics, biology, and other specific areas of the natural sciences. By the end of the 1960s there emerged a large and well-developed community of philosophers of science. The key factor in this development was a conceptual integration of philosophy of natural science, logic and epistemology and a joint effort of scholars working in these fields.

In the late 1950s and the first half of the 1960s, the impetus for these activities was the work of such thinkers as Bonifaty Kedrov (1903–1985), Pavel Kopnin (1922–1971) and Mikhail Omelyanovsky (1904–1979). All three of them held academic appointments and, at certain time periods, also influential administrative positions at research institutes of the Soviet Academy of Sciences. They produced numerous publications, which did not only play an instrumental role in overcoming the dogmatic Marxism of the Stalinist era, but also laid a foundation for the subsequent research in the field.

The 1950s highly politicized campaigns against genetics and cybernetics, attacks on the relativity theory and quantum mechanics were accompanied by gross distortions and caricaturing oversimplification of Marxist philosophy itself. Its vulgarized versions were used as a theoretical basis for destructive ideological crusades against science. Thus returning to authentic Marx and recovering genuine Marxism was thus a necessary prerequisite for the development of the national philosophy of science.

In his works, Kopnin emphasized the activity/praxis aspects of Marxist epistemology, the historicist approach to the analysis of knowledge, the interdependence of the subject and methods of cognition (Kopnin 1962; 1966). From that standpoint integration of sciences was viewed as the transfer of the conceptual means and methods of one science to another and the development of general scientific notions and ideas about the objects of research.

The problem of differentiation and integration of scientific knowledge was among the central to the works of Kedrov. He identified the principles of the dialectical materialist approach to philosophy of science:

1. the analysis of relations between objects of scientific research as specific states of matter in development and
2. the importance of the historical development of science, its methods, ideas, and concepts that determined this or that world outlook (Kedrov 1963; 1983).[1]

Proceeding from Friedrich Engels' concept of basic forms of motion and his respective classification of the sciences, Kedrov modified the notion of motion based on the twentieth-century discoveries. He argued that the idea of mechanical motion as one of the forms of developing matter was a vestige of the mechanistic world outlook. Mechanical motion would be more properly seen as an aspect of physical processes: it had no one material vehicle but was rather a common feature of physical processes in the macroworld. Physical processes in the microworld would be characterized as quantum mechanical motion that was also an aspect of physical processes related to a number of interactions—from the interaction of elementary particles to the formation of nuclei, atoms, and molecules. Therefore, the physical form of matter motion in the microworld was to be seen as two forms: the atomic physical and the molecular physical (Kedrov 1969). A special chemical form of motion studied by a variety of chemical disciplines lay in between. Quantum mechanical motion was related not only to the atomic physical, but to the chemical form of motion (considering the emergence of quantum chemistry). Kedrov recognized a geological form of motion instrumental in the formation of planets in the course of cosmic evolution. According to him, it was this form of matter motion that the Earth sciences studied. Kedrov's classification sparked a series of discussions concerning the development of forms of motion and the respective forms of matter. The fruitful aspect of those discussions was clarification of such categories as *matter*, *motion*, *space* and *time* in view of the achievements of the twentieth-century natural science (the works by Serafim Melyukhin, Nikolai Ovchinnikov, Rafail Aronov, Yakov Askin, and others).

Kedrov's research also included the process of scientific discovery, specifically the development of concepts and methods of scientific knowledge. By the mid-1960s, he succeeded in demonstrating the effectiveness of the close connection between philosophy and history of science.

Kedrov's analysis of scientific discovery invoked concrete examples from the history of chemistry that revealed and demonstrated the interdependence between the logico-methodological and the socio-psychological aspects of scientific work. His reconstruction of Dmitri Mendeleev's discovery of the periodic law was an early instance of a *case study* soon to become fashionable in the Western philosophy and history of science. This type of research would treat a particular event in the history of science as the interplay of logico-methodological, psychological, sociocultural and personal factors resulting in creation of new knowledge.

One of the topical problems of Russian philosophy of the 1960s was the interrelation of philosophy and science. With the overcoming of the dogmatic Marxism of the 1940s–1950s, the field lay open for the elaboration of fundamental philosophical categories in the light of recent achievements of science. Of special importance was the philosophical explication of the discoveries of relativistic quantum physics. Omelyanovsky put forward a research program that combined two interrelated tasks: the clarification of how contemporary physics contributed to the development of philosophical categories and the analysis of the methodological ideas and criteria elaborated by the philosophy that influenced the development of the twentieth-century physics. It was in this context that Omelyanovsky approached the category of *reality*. He emphasized the importance of distinguishing between *objective reality*, *empirical reality* and *abstract reality*. The first of these notions referred to the objective world which science was to study; the second to that aspect of reality that was revealed through phenomena and expressed in empirical knowledge (observation and facts); the third expressed the essential relations and the systemic structural conceptions about the studied objects as defined by theoretical laws and models (see Omelyanovsky 1956).

These distinctions defined Omelyanovsky's approach to the observationality principle of contemporary physics. He was among the first in our literature to draw attention to Albert Einstein's idea that distinguishing between observable and unobservable depended on the theoretical concept of reality that outlined the domain of knowledge. Hence the observationality principle should regulate not the development of hypotheses, but their empirical validation, the linking of theoretical entities to those of experience.

The rapid development of logical studies and application of logical tools to the analysis of scientific knowledge proved to be an important landmark in the development of Russian philosophy. Here an important role was played by Alexander Zinoviev. In the 1940s–1950s, Russian scholars shown certain skepticism toward mathematical logic, which was primarily considered as a branch of mathematics. Any attempt to apply it to the analysis of cognitive processes was viewed as a concession to positivism. Mathematical logic was seen as relevant only within the sphere of already established knowledge, but was declared inapplicable to the complex processes of its attainment. It was assumed that the appropriate tool to study cognitive processes was dialectical logic, with traditional formal logic serving exclusively as a supplementary means.

This approach was challenged by Zinoviev in the early 1950s. In his dissertation, Zinoviev argued that attributing development of concepts in *The Capital* to dialectical, rather than to formal logical contradictions did not agree with facts. Knowledge progressed through discovery of logical paradoxes and their sublation by redefinition of concepts. Hence refinement of logical means of discovering paradoxes was an important aspect of the methodology of science. Zinoviev's subsequent works in the field of logic and methodology stimulated both the logical studies as such (including such a new field as a many-valued logic) and the application of the newly developed logical tools to the analysis of scientific knowledge.

By the end of the 1960s the efforts in philosophy of science grew multi-aspect in character. Original schools and professional communities came into being. Some of them were active in Moscow. The Moscow Methodological Circle headed by Georgy Shchedrovitsky dealt with a wide range of problems related to the theory of activity. The activity approach to the analysis of science fit naturally with the analysis of reflection and the studies in the semiotics of culture. The works of Georgy Shchedrovitsky, Erik Yudin, and Vladimir Lefebvre played an important role in this process.

Recent discoveries in various fields of science and their philosophical import were actively analyzed at the Institute of Philosophy of the USSR Academy of Sciences.[2] These studies went hand in hand with the analysis of the epistemological and logico-methodological aspects of scientific research.[3] Logicians of the Institute of Philosophy established close cooperation with their colleagues from the Moscow University.[4]

The logical tools that they used for the analysis of scientific thinking was successfully applied to the solution of logical and methodological problems of mathematics as well as the natural and social sciences.

An important role in the development of these new approaches to the philosophy of science was played by a community of philosophers and historians of science centered at the Institute of History of Natural Science and Technology of the USSR Academy of Sciences in the 1960s–1970s.[5] The intellectual leader of community was Vladimir Bibler, who established an informal group of science savvy intellectuals, later joined by some of the members of the Institute of History of Natural Science and Technology. This group contributed substantially to the integration of the philosophical analysis and the historical studies of science.

Among the scholarly communities that promoted new approaches to philosophy of science, a special place belonged to a group of philosophers, logicians and scientists involved in the systems studies.[6] Moscow research communities of philosophers, logicians and methodologists of sciences interacted both with each other and with schools elsewhere in the country.[7] Moscow scientific schools and research communities were, by no means, the only scholarly collectives to practice philosophy and methodology of science; similar schools emerged and functioned successfully in other academic centers, including Leningrad (now St. Petersburg), Novosibirsk, Rostov-on-Don, Kiev, Minsk and others.[8]

The 1970s saw birth of informal exterritorial communities that would operate on the principle of "invisible college" and unite scholars specializing in particular fields of philosophy of science. First among them was the community of logicians that focused on methodology of mathematics; later, on methodology of computer sciences.[9] Studies in philosophy and methodology of social and human sciences developed into a special field of research.[10] In addition, studies of institutional forms of scientific research and their evolution grew into a special branch of philosophy and sociology of science.[11]

It was a time when philosophy of natural science was in the process of diversification. A broad informal community of scholars specializing in philosophical and methodological problems of physics included not only professional philosophers, but also a number of notable physics. Professional philosophers also cooperated with biologists and historians of biology, which played an important role in the consolidation of the community of students of methodological problems of biology.

The diversity of schools did not exclude integrative tendencies: common discussions of findings and intercommunication of scholars belonging to different research communities. A salient role in these processes belonged to the journals, *Voprosy filosofii* [*Questions of Philosophy*] and *Filosofskie nauki* [*Philosophical Sciences*] and the organizational effort of the Council for Philosophy and Social Problems of Science and Technology established in the USSR Academy of Sciences in the 1970s. Since the mid-1970s the Council was headed by Ivan Frolov, a notable philosopher himself. His own works helped broaden the scope of the philosophy of science. Frolov expanded the context of his renowned studies of philosophical problems of biology by adding to them his analysis of the ethics of science and of global problems of contemporary civilization. He was among the pioneering inquirers into global problems and the ways they affected the character of scientific and technological development. Thanks to Frolov, new research programs were developed to deal with the interdependence of science and high technology, the potential synthesis of natural and human sciences, the ethos of science and the novel ethical problems of scientific endeavor. The Council he headed proved to be a key factor in initiating and holding a number of national and international conferences and congresses—including the Nineteenth World Congress of Philosophy (Moscow, 1993)—that gave new life to research in philosophy of science.

A significant role in the expansion and consolidation of the community of philosophers of science was played by "schools of young scholars" regularly held in the 1970s–1980s. A number of their participants would later become renowned philosophers of science. In the 1980s to early 1990s a number of leading universities created special chairs in philosophy and methodology of science. The two most famous of them today—at the Moscow Lomonosov University and at the University of Saint Petersburg—serve as centers not only of education of young specialists, but of wide-range philosophical and methodological research.

The rise of the philosophy of science in Russia was a remarkable process, and even this sketchy overview of the institutional and communicative aspects of this undertaking can testify to the diversity and expanse of this movement. Loren R. Graham, a celebrated American historian of science and professor emeritus of the Massachusetts Institute of Technology, concluded his fundamental study of the history of philosophy of science in the USSR stating that this field of research was an "impressive intellectual achievement" and that the dialectical materialist interpretation of nature was "unequaled in universality and elaboration" among contemporary systems of thought (Graham 1991, 415).

Comparative analysis of Russian and Western studies demonstrates that Russian scholars working in the field have not only offered constructive criticism of the positivist and post-positivist philosophy of science while having learned their most important lessons, but produced new and important results. Below I will attempt to summarize those achievements that while discussed in some details in a variety of studies (Ventskovsky 1982, Mamchur, Ovchinnikov, Ogurtsov 1997, Stepin 2000, Mikeshina 2006, Chapters II, III, VII, Kurashov 2007, Motroshilova 2012, Section II, Chapter 3), have yet to be addressed systematically in their entirety.

## *(1)*

The Russian works of the 1960s to 1980s treated the problem of interaction between philosophy and science far more deeply than it was done in scholarly publications in the West. Due to predominance of positivist concepts in Western philosophy the subject long remained outside the scope of historical and methodological research. On the contrary, critical attitude to positivism in Russian philosophy encouraged detailed analysis of the matter. Drawing on concrete historical material, our scholars first established the heuristic role of philosophical ideas in the genesis of fundamental scientific theories. The next task was to explain this role, to substantiate the need for preliminarily developed conceptual frameworks as prerequisites to theorizing about hitherto unknown types of objects fundamental science encountered. Finally, philosophical pursuits were scrutinized in order to discern the means and procedures of developing such frameworks and elucidate the function of philosophy in scientific research. This function is dual:

1. the heuristic one, i.e. to assist in the process of emerging of novel scientific ideas, and
2. the substantiation function, i.e. to endorse the fundamental discoveries of science and help integrate them into the process of cultural transformation.

### *(2)*

The structure of scientific knowledge was analyzed with greater detail in our works of the 1970s than in the respective Western studies. It was demonstrated that the idea of a network of theoretical constructs in relation to which theoretical statements were made was but a first approximation to description of a theory's content structure. Levels of organization of theoretical constructs were identified, as well as their interrelations and their relations to empirical knowledge. Correlations between operational and objective meanings of empirical and theoretical statements were clarified. Special attention was given to scientific world picture as a specific form of theoretical knowledge. Western philosophical literature had long ignored this form of knowledge; post-positivist writings would have at best mentioned it. Russian works demonstrated considerable progress in this analytical endeavor: the problem of identifying the differentia that distinguished a scientific world picture from a theory was formulated and solved; the content structure of a scientific world picture was elucidated, as were its relations to theories and empirical facts. Typology of scientific world pictures was developed that discriminated between three major types:

(a) special scientific world pictures (disciplinary ontologies);
(b) natural scientific and socio-scientific world pictures;
(c) universal scientific world picture.

Among the first in the field, Russian scholars investigated the functions of an existing world picture in scientific research shown that it

(i) serves as a research program for both the empirical and the theoretical searches;
(ii) has a power to integrate scientific knowledge; and
(iii) plays a crucial role in the objectification of the research findings and their incorporation into the existing culture.

Ideals and norms of scientific research, as well as philosophical foundations of science were scrupulously analyzed and identified as components of the principles of science. Here again our scholars brought the subject to deeper scrutiny than did the Western philosophers of science. This pertains to the typology of ideals and norms, as well as to their contents and processes of their transformation in the historical development of science. Among the important results were the distinction drawn between philosophical foundations of science and the rest of philosophical knowledge and the analysis of changes in philosophical foundations in the course of historical advancement of scientific knowledge.

These inquiries into the structure of science revealed the inadequacy of the traditional approach to the analysis of scientific knowledge which took as its basic unit a single scientific theory in its relation to experience. This seemingly obvious approach implicitly pictured scientific knowledge as a simple system the character of which depended wholly on the character of its constituents (theories and facts). But theoretical knowledge belongs to a more complex type of historically developing systems. According to this systems approach, the appropriate unit of methodological analysis is to be not a single theory, but a scientific discipline as a system of developing theories to be viewed in their interaction both between themselves and with experience, as well as with other disciplines.

*(3)*

Logical analysis of theory elaboration procedures yielded new results, too. It was demonstrated that the hypothetical-deductive method was not the only one used for construction of scientific theories, another one was the genetic-constructive method that operated with abstract objects. The latter was the dominant method for theory elaboration in sciences based on experience. As Thomas Kuhn justly argued, a theory is elaborated by using patterns it incorporates for problem solving. This posed questions about the structure of patterns and their genesis. The genetic-constructive method allowed to answer both of them, and the priority of solution belonged to our philosophy of science.

*(4)*

These novel ideas about the structure of scientific knowledge proved instrumental in revealing new and vitally important aspects of its expansion. This relates, first of all, to the advancement of hypotheses and the logico-methodological principles of that process. Positivist and post-positivist writers approached this subject matter primarily from the standpoint of psychology, not the logic of discovery. Studies undertaken by Russian scholars clarified the logical procedures necessary for the process, the role of scientific world picture in formulating problems and choosing tools for the construction of hypotheses, the functions of analogical models and translations of abstract objects as the means of building hypothetical nuclei of future theories.

Positivism distinguished sharply between logic of discovery and logic of validation. The result was virtual exclusion of the former from the scope of analytical examination. In our studies the two aspects of theory development were analyzed in their interdependence. Russian scholars discovered a hitherto unknown procedure of constructive substantiation of hypothetical models that had never been described in foreign philosophical literature. They demonstrated how repeated application of that procedure helped shape empirical interpretation of mathematical apparatus of a theory, redefine its notions and perfect its conceptual framework.

*(5)*

Our analysis of scientific revolutions proved more profound than in the Western philosophical literature of the 1970s and the 1980s; it took into account interdisciplinary interaction and sociocultural factors and yielded a typology. A particular type of scientific revolution, the one not preceded by "anomalies" and "crises" and related to interdisciplinary "paradigm graft," was left practically unexamined in the West. It was thoroughly investigated by Russian researchers.

*(6)*

Our studies of scientific revolutions were linked to enquiries concerning types of scientific rationality and their historical development. Scientific rationality was studied in two aspects: firstly, as examination of changes in scientific activities related to encounters with different types of systemic objects; secondly, as examination of changes of broad sociocultural context and fundamental values of which scientific rationality was a constituent part. That approach allowed us to account for historical changes in scientific rationality and distinguish between its three major historical types, viz. the classical, the non-classical and the post-nonclassical. Their criteria were specified as

1. the type of systems organization of objects of research (simple systems, for the classical; complex self-organizing systems, for the non-classical; complex self-developing systems, for the post-nonclassical;
2. changes in the ideals and norms of research (explanations, descriptions, structures and constructions of knowledge);
3. the type of philosophic reflection effecting the absorption of knowledge by culture in transition.

It was found that no new type of rationality annulled the previous one, but it did set limits to the latter's applicability for solution of scientific problems.

The results outlined above referred to the general problems of philosophy of science. But the contribution of our scholars to the field was not limited to them. Of no less importance were studies of philosophical and methodological problems of particular sciences: physics, chemistry, biology, technical, social and human sciences. Recent years have witnessed marked progress in philosophical and methodological analysis of interdisciplinary studies. Nowadays this kind of research becomes ever more closely linked to studies of objects that turn out to be complex self-developing systems. Since such systems possess synergetic characteristics, methodological problems of the synergetic play an important role in their philosophical and methodological elucidation. They are an important aspect of methodology of post-nonclassical science. The mid-1990s saw emergence of an expanding community of philosophers, mathematicians and natural scientists focusing on these problems.[12]

With the advent of the post-nonclassical type of scientific rationality, the field of philosophy of science has broadened. Besides traditional epistemological and methodological issues it now includes and accentuates axiological problems.

Questions arise about the value of science in contemporary culture, the likely changes in modern civilization's values structure and the prospects of scientific rationality. Appreciated at the turn of the centuries, all these problems are now actively debated by Russian philosophers of science with reference to Western and Oriental cultural traditions and their potential transformations.

## NOTES

1. See a detailed list of these and other important works by Kedrov in the "Selected Bibliography" at the end of this volume.
2. Such scholars as Lev Bazhenov, Yuri Sachkov, Igor Akchurin, Yuri Molchanov, Regina Karpinskaya, Vadim Kazyutinsky, Igor Liseyev, and others specifically worked in the field of philosophy of science.
3. Such thinkers as Vladislav Lektorsky, Ivan Kuznetsov, Vladimir Shvyryov, Elena Mamchur, Evgenii Nikitin, Alexander Nikiforov, Dmitry Gorsky, Georgy Ruzavin, Viktor Tyukhtin, Igor Merkulov, Vladimir Porus, Ilya Kasavin, Natalia Avtonomova, and others focused on epistemological and logico-methodological issues of the time.
4. In this period, perhaps the most interesting work in logic was produced by Vladimir Smirnov, Evgenii Sidorenko, Elena Smirnova, Evgenii Voishvillo, Valery Meskov, later Alexander Karpenko, Vyacheslav Bocharov, Vladimir Markin, and others.
5. Here it is worth naming such scholars as Boris Kuznetsov, Semyon Mikulinsky, Naum Rodny, Mikhail Yaroshevsky, Piama Gaidenko, Lyudmila Kosareva, Vladimir Kurashov, Merab Mamardashvili, Nikolai Ovchinnikov, Anatoly Akhutin, Boris Yudin, Alexander Ogurtsov, Vladislav Kelle, Alexander Pechyonkin, Vadim Rabinovich, Ivan Kuznetsov, Yuri Solovyov, Georgy Bykov, Vladimir Vizgin, Grigory Idlis, Viktor Vizgin, Tatyana Romanovskaya, Alexei Postnikov, Eduard Mirzoyan, Eduard Kolchinsky, Elena Muzrukova, Vera Gutina, Sergei Khaitun, Lyudmila Markova, Ilya Tomofeyev, and Natalia Kuznetsova.
6. Among those were well- and less-known scholars, such as Igor Blauberg, Vadim Sadovsky, Erik Yudin, Alexander Malinovsky, Eduard Mirsky, Julius Schreider, Gelly Povarov, Yunir Urmantsev, and others.
7. Here it is worth mentioning for considerable personal contribution not only members of the Institute of Philosophy and the Institute of History of Natural Science and Technology, but also scholars from the Moscow State University and other Moscow educational and academic institutions: Vladimir Gott, Anatoly Zotov, Boris Gryaznov, Vladimir Kuptsov, Anatoly Rakitov, Engels Chudinov, Arkady Ursul, Lyudmila Kosareva, somewhat later Alexei Barabashev, Vladimir Mironov, and others.
8. There was an original Leningrad school, represented by scholars such Viktor Shtoff, Vladimir Bransky, Anatoly Karmin, Maria Kozlova, Mikhail Mostepanenko, Alexander Mostepanenko, Yuri Solonin, Eduard Karavayev, and Boris Markov. A prolific school was active in Kiev. It is worth mentioning here Miroslav Popovich, Sergei Krymsky, Anatoly Artyukh, Pyotr Dyshlevy, Nadezhda Depenchuk, Vyacheslav Naidysh, Vladimir Kuznetsov, Viktoria Khramova, Valentin Lukyanets, and Irina Dobronravova. The Novosibrsk school, represented by Mikhail Rozov, Igor Alekseev, Stalina Rozova, Lyudmila Sychova, distinguished itself in the late 1960s and early 1970s for its effort to bring together the study of the dynamics of science and

sociocultural studies. A special contribution to the philosophy of science was made by Tomsk philosophers Anatoly Sukhotin, Vladislav Cheshev, who was later joined by Irina Tchernikova. Original work in the field of science studies was done by Mikhail Petrov's school in Rostov-on-Don. The city was also a center of rigorous inquiries into philosophical problems of natural science, being represented by such figures as Yuri Zhdanov, Larisa Minasyan, and others. The Kazakhstan scholars Zhabaikhan Abdildin, Abdimalik Nysanbayev, Gerasim Yugay also contributed to the development of the philosophy of science in the Soviet period. In addition, in the late 1960s and early 1970s, there emerged the Minsk school of philosophy of science. While the author of this chapter is usually credited with being its leader, the scholars such as Lev Tomilchik, Anatoly Zelenkov, Albert Elsukov, Evgenia Petushkova, Lydia Kuznetsova, and Jadwiga Yaskevich, also played a significant role in its success. The Minsk school drew on concrete material from the history of science to offer detailed analysis of the structure and dynamics of scientific knowledge in the form of historical reconstructions of the genesis of key theories and concepts in physics, biology and social sciences.

9. In addition to the logicians of the Institute of Philosophy and the Moscow University listed above, the community also included Yuri Yershov, Viktor Finn, Evgenii Lednikov, Avenir Uyomov, Vitaly Tselishchev, and some others. Another community united philosophers of technology such as Vitaly Gorokhov, Vadim Rozin, Boris Ivanov, Vladislav Cheshev, Oksana Simonenko, to name only a few.
10. I would like to bring to the reader's attention the works by Anatoly Rakitov, Vladislav Kelle, Valentina Fedotova, Lyudmila Mikeshina, Moisey Kagan, Vadim Rozin; and in the late 1980s also by Nikolai Rozov, and Valery Kuznetsov.
11. Among those were Eduard Mirsky, Anatoly Kulkin, Nelli Motroshilova, Tamara Dlugach, Mikhail Yaroshevsky, Elena Mirskaya, and Alexander Ogurtsov.
12. It is worth mentioning Sergei Kurdyumov, Gennady Malinetsky, Dmitry Tchernavsky, Vladimir Arshinov, Vladimir Budanov, Elena Knyazeva, Vyacheslav Stepin, Irina Dobronravova, Moisey Kagan, Vladimir Bransky, who greatly contributed to this development.

## BIBLIOGRAPHY


Graham, Loren R. 1991. *Estestvoznanie, filosofiya i nauki o chelovecheskom povedenii v Sovetskom Soyuze*. Moscow: Politizdat. [Graham, Loren R. 1987. *Science, Philosophy, and Human Behavior in the Soviet Union*. Columbia University Press.]

Kedrov, Bonifaty M. 1969. *Tri aspekta atomistiki*. [Three Aspects of Atomistics]. Moscow: Nauka.

Kopnin, Pavel V. 1962. *Gipoteza i poznanie dejstvitel'nosti*. [Hypothesis and Knowledge of Reality]. Kiev: Gospolitizdat USSR.

Kopnin, Pavel V. 1966. *Vvedenie v marksistsuju gnoserologiju*. [Introduction to Marxist Epistemology]. Kiev: Naukova Dumka.

Kurashov, Vladimir I. 2007. *Nachala filosofii nauki* [The Basics of the Philosophy of Science]. Moscow: KDU.

Mamchur, Elena A., Ovchinnikov, Nikolai F., Ogurtsov, Alexander P. 1997. *Otechestvennaya filosofiya nauki: predvaritel'nye itogi* [The Russian Philosophy of Science: Preliminary Summing-up]. Moscow: ROSSPEN.

Mikeshina, Ludmila A. (ed.). 2006. *Filosofiya nauki. Epistemologiya. Metodologiya. Kul'tura: Khrestomatiya* [Philosophy of Science. Epistemology. Methodology. Culture: A Reader]. Moscow: Izdatel'skii dom Mezhdunarodnogo universiteta v Moskve.

Motroshilova, Nelli V. 2012. *Otechestvennaya filosofiya 50–80-kh godov XX veka i zapadnaya mysl* [The Russian Philosophy of the 1950s–1980s and the Western Thought]. Moscow: Akademicheskiy proyekt.

Omelyanovky, Mikhail E. 1956. *Filosofskie problemy kvantovoi mekhaniki* [Philosophical Problems of Quantum Mechanics]. Moscow: Nauka.

Stepin, Vyacheslav S. 2000. *Teoreticheskoe znanie*. Moscow: Progress-Tradizia. [Translated into English as: Stepin, Vyacheslav. 2005. *Theoretical Knowledge*. Synthese Library, Vol. 326. Dordrecht: Springer].

Ventskovsky, Lev E. 1982. *Filosofskie problemy razvitiya nauki (obzor literatury za 70-e gody)* [Philosophical Problems of the Development of Science (A Review of the Literature Published in the 1970s)]. Moscow: Nauka.

CHAPTER EIGHT

# Systemic Analysis of Science: Ideas of Equifinality and Anthropo-Measurement

ALEXANDER P. OGURTSOV

One of the most promising and profound research trends in the philosophy of science in the second half of the twentieth century was systemic analysis of science. Systemic analysis of science in the USSR dates back to the 1960s. The liberation of philosophy from rigid Manichean ideological attitudes and of philosophical consciousness from the juxtaposition of "bourgeois" and "Soviet" science, which extolled alleged successes of Soviet science, caused philosophical-methodological consciousness to take a long hard look at the realities of practical science—a turnaround that also happened in the 1960s. Systemic thinking developed in an atmosphere of hostility, ideological-philosophical and dogmatic criticism that reflected anti-science principles both in Russia and abroad. While in the development of scientific methodology the principles and methods of systemic thinking were progressively asserting themselves, the approach met with misunderstanding and with challenge posed by principles that were alien to science and philosophy. In the USSR, those were the principles of narrow-minded dogmatism which saw the world through the prism of dialectical materialism, and elsewhere in the world those principles were most clearly expressed, for example, in Martin Heidegger's "fundamental ontology."[1]

## SYSTEMIC APPROACH TO SCIENTIFIC KNOWLEDGE AND ITS FORMS

Systemic approach to scientific knowledge is represented, first, by the idea of the structure of scientific knowledge as a *system of concepts* (B. M. Kedrov, A. I. Uyemov). This version of systemic thinking was based on the history of the emergence and development of scientific concepts (atom, chemical element, etc.). Second, systemic thinking in the analysis of science is represented in the perception of scientific knowledge as *a system of propositions and logical analysis of the language of science.* At the first stage, it is represented by the syntactical approach to the language of science. It also involved the use of modern symbolic logic for the analysis of the structures representing scientific knowledge and the emergence of the logic of science (Alexander Zinoviev). This version of systemic thinking has elaborated the premises and principles of the standard concept of science and revealed the snags inherent in the one-sidedly syntactic approach to knowledge: the gaps between the levels of language—above all between the empirical and theoretical levels, the search for correspondences between them, etc. The exposure of the flaws of the syntactic approach led to the rise of the semantic approach in the logic of science (Vladimir Smirnov, Elena Smirnova). The attempt to bridge the gap between the syntactic and semantic approaches to science gave rise to the *semiotic* (Yuri Levin) and the *systemic-structural approach* to scientific knowledge (Igor Blauberg, Vadim Sadovsky, Erik Yudin).

The same period saw a broadening in the range of the study of science: examination of the procedures and acts of cognition through modeling (Evgenii Nikitin, Boris Gryaznov), an awareness of the specific nature of theoretical objects, i.e., ideal objects of theory and their role, reflection on the methods of science and the formation of a *logic of scientific research* and *methodology of science* (Regina Karpinskaya). A program of the logic of scientific research was unfolded in the works of Kiev philosophers and logicians (Pavel Kopnin, Miroslav Popovich, Sergei Krymsky). The program covered the distinction between a problem and a question, a fact and its interpretation, the features of scientific research, and methods of systematizing knowledge and the forms of its representation. The gap between the logic of science and the logic of scientific research was characteristic both of foreign scientists (for example, between the logic of science of the Vienna Circle and Karl Popper's logic of research) and authors in this country, and it has to be bridged yet. The same period saw Georgy Shchedrovitsky hit his stride in studying the *content-genetic logic* in which he sought to close the gap between logic and psychology, turning to the tradition of genetic psychology and epistemology of Jean Piaget and combining it with the mathematical theory of groups and the formation of operational intelligence. Shchedrovitsky developed new methods of analysis of science, namely, ontology and its schemes, conceptual schemes of consciousness, the specificities of systemic methodology, etc. An original, but, sadly, unrecognized concept of science as a *self-organizing information system* offering opportunities for the analysis of the language of science was proposed by Vasily Nalimov and Sergei Meyen.

Along with diverse versions of systemic thinking, there was an approach that interpreted science as *activity*. Mention should be made of the interpretation of science as "general work of the human spirit" which led to the differentiation of science universals and forms of cooperative scientific work (Bibler, Kelle, Zlobin, Mezhuyev) and the concept of *ideals and norms of scientific activity* developed largely by Stepanov and the Minsk research group.

### *From a Small Group to a Systemic Movement in the USSR (1970s–1990s)*

Systemic thinking is best exemplified by the groups of scholars led by Blauberg that included Sadovsky, Yudin, Yablonsky, Mirsky, Starostin and Kostyuk. Many attribute the systemic approach to science to this group because it started publishing the *Systemic Studies Yearbook* and sought to present the methodological specificity of systemic thinking in a generalized way. At the first stage, the group was part of the USSR Academy of Sciences' Institute of the History of Natural Science and Technology, and later of the Academy's Institute of Systemic Analysis. That research unit initially presented itself as a methodological enterprise that sought to identify the features of the systemic approach to various research objects and avoided putting forward any ontological premises or conclusions. It is worth mentioning that the group initiated and was an informal leader of the systems movement in the USSR which was taken up and recognized in several education and research centers in the USSR (in such towns as Pushchino, Kazan, Odessa, Kiev, Novosibirsk, etc.).[2] Among the members of the systemic movement outside that group, mention should be made of G. Shchedrovitsky, A. Uemov, Yu. Urmantsev, C. Tyukhtin, V. Kremyansky, Yu. Shreider and many other representatives of the natural sciences and the humanities. According to one member of the group that was formed at the USSR Academy of Sciences' Institute of the History of Natural Sciences and Technology, two paradigms in the interpretation of the systemic approach emerged in the early 1970s: one (Blauberg, Yudin) had largely to do with worldview and methodology, while the other, advocated by Sadovsky, was about building a systemic meta-theory (Sadovsky 1996, 72–73).[3] I think there were many more versions of systemic thinking than two. The systemic approach was diverse and was represented both in the natural sciences and the humanities and, in accordance with these differences, was given contrasting interpretations in terms of methodology: along with the two paradigms noted by Sadovsky, the USSR saw the development of research in the general theory of systems by Urmantsev, the parametric concept of Uyemov, the concept of system levels by V. Kremyansky, while in the socio-humanities field the best known approaches were structural-functional studies of various structures ranging from language to society (the works of Vyacheslav Ivanov, V. Toporov, Yu. Levada and others). Systemic thinking was also represented in the technical, architectural and urban development works. These too were marked by different methodological preferences. Generally speaking, the systemic movement both in terms of methodological preferences and its results correlated with the traditions of scientific thought both in Russia and abroad. The most frequently mentioned sources of systemic thinking are Alexander Bogdanov's tectology (also called "tektology") (Bogdanov, 1989) in this country and, among foreign sources, Ludwig von Bartalanffy's general systems theory and Tadeusz Kotarbinski's praxeology. I believe that the systems thinking was more widely represented in the scientific and methodological consciousness of twentieth-century scientists: it includes integrative levels concept of R. Gerard, A. Novikov and A. E. Emerson, A. Ukhtomsky's doctrine of the dominants, V. Sukhachev's theory of population systems in biology. The use of the systemic approach to science and its growth was based on the tradition of the science of science: Ivan Borichevsky (1925–1926) was the first to speak of the science of science as distinct from the philosophy of science, and Vasily Nalimov was the first to introduce the scientometric approach as distinct from the science of science (1969) in proposing an original probabilistic concept of language and thought. Systems analysis of disciplinary scientific knowledge as distinct from scientific research was pioneered by mathematician G. Gruzintsev in the late 1920s, while the first attempt to use quantitative methods in analyzing the history of scientific discoveries in physics was made by T. Rainov during the same period. Turning to these pioneering but forgotten studies, the group of the Institute of the History of Natural Sciences and Technology sought to combine the systems methods of analyzing scientific knowledge with the bibliometric methods developed at the American Institute for Scientific Information (citation index, quotation, impact-factor, etc.).

Of course, different versions of the systems approach drew on different sources: the interpretation of systemic thinking as a meta-theory was based on the works of Alexander Bogdanov and Ludwig von Bertalanffy, the view of systemic thought as the methodology of modern science originated with Bogdanov and O. Lange, the parametric concept of systemic thinking drew on the works of William Ross Ashby, A. Hall and R. Feigin, the concept of integrative levels on the works of A. Whitehead, R. Gerard and A. Novikov.

### *M. K. Petrov's Systems Thinking: Achievements and Problems*

Undoubtedly, the evolution of the systems approach in various spheres of scientific knowledge and in the development of the systems approach merit a more thorough study. In this article, I will pick the variant of systemic analysis of science proposed by Mikhail Petrov out of the whole array of variants of the systems movement in the USSR. His was a dramatic career path: for a long time, he was debarred from working in his field, and his works were either not printed at all or printed under other names. It was only after his death that his friends managed to get his seminal works published. Despite the fact that the originality of his articles on the systems approach to science and his science-study approach to systems thinking had not been properly appreciated, his pioneering works on the science of science, based on vast data on the history of science and on thorough analysis of contemporary world literature, were themselves a sample of systems approach. M. K. Petrov's systems thinking was essentially both the semiotic (note his distinction between the nominal and professional-universal codes) and the scientific and science-history approach (note his constant references to the evolution of the organization and disciplinary structure of science in European countries).[4] To get an idea of Petrov's contribution to systems thinking and of its origins, one has to study his posthumous publications in which they stand out much more prominently (see: Petrov 1991; Petrov 1992; Petrov 1997; Petrov 2004; Petrov 2006).[5] Petrov's systems analysis of the science of science and scientometric indicators of the integrity of scientific texts (for example, Zipf distributions) is based on certain ontological premises (or principles, as he called them), i.e., the principles of equifinality and anthropo-measurement. My retrospective study will focus on these two principles.

*1. Ontological Prerequisites of the Functioning of Science as a System.* Equifinality and anthropo-measurement are the two concepts underlying M. Petrov's sociological concept of science. Petrov uses the former in the systems analysis of science, putting forward the latter himself. In my opinion, they provide the philosophical-ontological and methodological foundations of his study of science. Systems thinking oriented toward methodology does not imply the identification of its ontological prerequisites. That applies even more to the interpretation of systems thinking as a meta-theory. Unlike these variants of systems thinking, Petrov sees equifinality and anthropo-measurement both as methodological and ontological characteristics of systemic scientific descriptions. He uses these characteristics as a reference system within which science is studied and, simultaneously, as the reality that science represents as a systemic entity. In other words, these two concepts determine not only the method of systemic vision of science, but the reality to which systemic features and dimensional characteristics are attributed. I would like to take a closer look at these two concepts, trace them to their sources, find various interconnections, and demonstrate their results.

2. *The Concept of Equifinality.* That concept was introduced by H. Driesch, a German biologist and philosopher in his book *Vitalism* (Leipzig, 1905, Russ. transl.: St. Petersburg, 1915). It is one of the results of experimental embryology and comparative morphology characterizing the process of development when its end state is preserved even if the ways of achieving that state change dramatically. A. Lyubishchev notes that the concept of equifinality restores the concept of ultimate causes, *causae finales* (Lyubishchev 1982, 239–240). Thus the final, target causes, which evolutionary biology had allegedly thrown overboard, were introduced into the structure of biological theory as one of its key principles. For *entelecheia*, understood as a target, determines the paths of evolution, and natural selection can be understood as the target inherent in evolving organisms. Biology has never renounced the concept of purposiveness (whether it was called "final causes," "entelechy" or "teleonomy") though it often concealed its use.

The concept of "equifinality" evolved into the idea of a "dynamically pre-existing morph" proposed by A. Gurvich, though he later gave it up in favor of the cell field theory. In his letters to Gurvich, Lyubishchev draws attention to this change of stance, describing it as replacement of the holistic vision of the field with an interference-based one and considering "the abrupt change of front" unjustified (Lyubishchev, Gurvich 1998, 158–159). However, as noted by L. Belousov, "the main thrust of the theory remained the same: it was always about a single factor that determined the direction and order of biological phenomena" (Belousov, Gurvich, Zalkind, Kanegiser 1970, 91).

At the same time, the concept of "equifinality" came to be used not only with regard to cell fields, cell exchange, cell renewal and to the organism as a whole, but also to populations. Thus, the American ecologist Whittaker used the concept of equifinality with reference to the development of plant communities starting from different initial conditions but reaching the highest point of evolution (Whittaker 1953, 536–544). As a result, not only has the use of this concept broadened (it came to be used in psychology, sociology, psychiatry and management), but it has also become universal, being one of the key concepts in the natural and social sciences and the humanities. Equifinality is transition, given different initial conditions, to the same final state, the existence of different paths and different starting conditions for reaching the same end state. The final state is the aim of formation, evolution and transition. Such processes turned out to be characteristic of the phenomena of life, the processes of embryogenesis, evolution, ecology, etc. The wide spread of the concept caused its universalization, that is, turned it into a methodological instrument of the general theory of systems, which is associated with the name of Ludwig von Bertalanffy.

In 1973, the idea of equifinality morphed into the idea of autopoiesis, a new term introduced by Humberto Maturana (the English translation of this work came out in 1980: *Autopoiesis and Cognition. The Realization of the Living*. Boston, 1980). He started analyzing living systems in terms of the processes that actualized them and turned them into bigger, integrated systems. In the 1980s to 1990s, the term "autopoiesis" was used by Niklas Luhmann to characterize not only forms of self-organization, but methods of self-description of communities.

Petrov refers to the works of Ludwig von Bertalanffy who juxtaposed open and closed systems, believing that an open system, upon reaching a state of mobile equilibrium, preserves its structure "in the process of continuous exchange and movement of the substance that constitutes it. The mobile equilibrium of open systems is marked by equifinality, i.e., unlike the state of equilibrium in closed systems fully determined by the initial conditions, an open system can achieve, independently of time, a state that does not depend on the starting conditions and is determined solely by the system's parameters" (Bertalanffy 1969, 42). It is to this property of open systems that he attributes their negentropy and increased order and complexity.

Petrov brings in urban development and the science of science to reveal the equifinal character of their development. Thus, citing the works of N. Mullins and T. Kuhn, he draws attention to the equifinality of the final stages in the restoration of the disciplinary norm, institutionalization of a scientific discipline which involves the founding of journals, establishment of chairs and staff positions for new specialties. The formation and evolution of scientific research is crowned with the same result, that is, institutionalization of a scientific discipline, the creation of a stable and universal set of identifiers of a scientific discipline, although the paths of its emergence and evolution may differ (revolutionary change of paradigm vs. normal science, according to T. Kuhn; four stages of development of scientific groups into disciplines—norm, network, swarm or cluster, specialty or discipline, according to Mullins). The science of science has started studying such "universal processes of integration of cognitive-social units, the processes of equifinality" (Petrov 2004, 26). In my opinion, the concept of equifinality can be safely applied to the processes of the formation and development of scientific disciplines. Petrov is right in this respect. Indeed, disciplinary knowledge is formed in various ways, in diverse starting conditions and is crowned with the recognition of a scientific discipline first by a micro-community of scientists and then by the macro-community comprising not only scientists but also managers of science, the education system, etc. Historical-scientific reconstruction of various ways in which new scientific specialties are formed and evolve into disciplines with specific norms is a challenge, but a challenge that needs to be met. Besides, the formation and development of scientific disciplinary activity involves the creation of departments, journals, a system of training and retraining scientists, etc. Moreover, the mechanisms of cognitive and social institutionalization of scientific disciplines turn out to be inseparably connected, warranting the conclusion that there is a single cognitive-social process of the formation of disciplinary structures in which disciplinary knowledge along with the disciplinary community form a "cognitive-social field" that, being an organism-like whole structure, causes their micro-changes and micro-processes.

However, I have doubts about the applicability of the concept of "equifinality" to urban development and the formation of cities. My doubts are based, above all, on the elements of chaos in urban development (notwithstanding the existence of various supervisory bureaucratic agencies), the insertion of one-off buildings in residential neighborhoods, structures with disparate architectural styles, etc. A city retains the old layout of streets, blocks and districts. Urban planning is in many ways spontaneous, even though today starting a new construction project requires sheaves of approvals by various agencies. Thus, Moscow has preserved its ring structure of a feudal city with the sacral and administrative center, the Kremlin, and radial streets converging on the Kremlin. The layout of the city remains the same no matter how hard the architects and developers try to change it. Indeed, new construction fits into the ring-radial logic, as exemplified by the building of the subway in accordance with this plan.

Can the stability of the ring-radial structure of Moscow and its subway (the "metro") be described as "equifinal"? In a certain sense, it can. But then the completed equifinal architectural structures are already a given. They are not designed anew, but are predetermined by the former urban development practices and survive in the new conditions that are very different from the old ones. Such "equifinality of urban development" is impossible to abolish. New generations have to live with it and face the discrepancy between the city structure and the new conditions. I have a feeling that the many-hour-long traffic jams in Moscow streets are due not to the large number of private cars, but above all to the sacral-bureaucratic equifinality of urban development. In other words, the present-day structure of the city is determined by the initial conditions and not solely by the parameters of the actual system. One may argue that urban development attests rather to *anti-equifinality*—the growth, within the city structure, of components that match not the parameters of the existing system but those of the initial conditions and that have remained significant over centuries. Petrov himself is aware of the fact, speaking of heteronomous syntheses of subjective and natural objective conditions of human existence in a city, of the "whole pictures of cities being slashed along the lines of heteronomous syntheses" (Petrov 2004, 23). But his recipe is to ignore the significance of such urban development specifiers and "throw into the trashcan" the inessential initial conditions and the specifiers of "open systems" (ibid.). The idea of equifinality has an element of pre-formism, i.e., predetermination of movement from various starting conditions toward the wholeness of an open system which unfolds according to its own foundations. Pre-formism is very much in evidence in biological theories of the eighteenth-nineteenth centuries, but it is just as strong in the theories of other sciences. Granted, an organically whole system forms its own parameters of movement and determines different paths of its evolution. However, the determinism of whole systems and its components and levels should grow into super-determinism that leaves no room for a probabilistic interpretation of the relationship between the whole and its components. The probabilistic view of the formation and unfolding of a whole structure rules out rigid determinism, stressing the significance of trends, points of bifurcation and possible choices between them.

3. *The Concept of "Anthropo-Measurement."* The concept was put forward by M. Petrov. He has thought it up and it has become central to his systems analysis of science. I had occasion to recall our conversation about this concept. In response to his explanation of the term (admittedly very brief), I remarked: "Isn't the concept an expression of Man-God idea? Does not it anthropomorphize that which doesn't lend itself to being measured in human parameters?" To which Petrov replied "No," and proceeded to argue that our activity (any kind of activity, be it cognitive, social or technical) objectifies structures commensurate with man. In a book published after his death, he maintains that the mechanisms of equifinality manifest human metrics (Petrov 2004, 246). Again, he tries to shoehorn the larger—and ontological—concept of equifinality into a kind of anthropology, Protagorean metrics.

I have not come across a definition of the concept by Petrov himself. He notes that anthropo-measurement is "the universal equivalent and universal integrator of all urban systems" (Petrov 2004, 23), that Protagorean metrics integrates and orders diverse phenomena and events: "Although cubes, square meters and other objective measures may have their uses even here, they are derivatives of a very different kind of metric, a translation from the metric language of Protagoras—'man is the measure of all things'—a translation from the language of anthropo-measurement" (Petrov 2004, 22). Behind equifinality stands "man with all his physical and mental capacities and limitations." (Petrov 2004, 26).

What is the relationship between scientific descriptions and the "man-is-the-measure-of-all-things" principle? Can one imagine the evolution of cognitive and social structures of science in terms of that principle which Petrov calls Protagorean metrics? There is no denying the fact that the genesis of geometry is connected with anthropomorphic measures of the Earth—the ancient and imperial foot, the historical units based on the length of the forearm (the Latin *cubitus*, both ell and cubit in the imperial system, the Russian *lokot'*, and so forth), etc. Over centuries, various countries tried to introduce uniform measures, such as "the king's foot" (*pied du roi*), compiled tables of correspondences of units of length, weight, etc. In other words, parts of the human body were initially used as units of measure. However, that was not geometry as science yet. It had to do with the measurement of plots of land, various measurement units that differed from region to region. But that was not the geometry that took shape at Plato's Academy.

Before it could appear several conditions were required—from the homogenization of space to the emergence of ideal objects (points, lines, planes and various geometric "Platonic" bodies). It was only centuries later, in the Enlightenment era, that what is now known as the new system of weights and measures was formed, to be adopted much later (in the nineteenth century in some European countries and the USA, and on September 14, 1918, in Russia). The early attempts (for example, by Dupont de Nemour) to introduce a uniform system of weights and measures stressed that the proposed weights and measures best met the nature of things, according to the universal and unchanged system based on a unit borrowed from nature (the words of Talleyrand, one of the authors of the new system of units). Thus, the reform was not just about unification of weights and measures that differed even from province to province in France, but about renouncing the former anthropomorphic units and constructing a system of weights and measures matching the nature of things, that is, de-anthropologizing the system, depriving it of any link with anthropology, and making it objective. It was also about securing their universal recognition by adopting government decrees. Ideal measurement standards were devised (kilogram, gram, meter, decimeter, centimeter, millimeter) that were adopted not only by the Revolutionary Convent, but by all France, becoming a key factor in unifying it into a single state.

The introduction of a new system of weights and measures was one of the more significant achievements of revolutionary France, unlike the attempts to introduce a revolutionary calendar. That new system has put an end to the man-centered measurements: from then on, metrics became uniform and objective. True, it called for enormous effort to change all the measuring instruments beginning with scales and devices measuring the Earth's diameter and ending with scientific equipment.

It is worth mentioning that Petrov considers the new system of weights and measures to be a derivative of the measurement system of Protagoras. I think that statement does not hold water. The standard of length is the arc of the meridian 9.5 degrees long between Dunkirk and Barcelona (one meter equals 1/10 of the line), and the standard of weight is the mass of 1 cubic centimeter of water at its densest. Platinum prototypes of length were created. In other words, the new system of weights and measures has nothing to do with the human body and there is no question of the metric system being derived from anthropometrics. This is my first objection to the idea of anthropo-measurement. Science is not anthropomorphic. It is free of any links with anthropological characteristics, creating its own world of objectively ideal entities which are "superimposed" on the real world through measuring procedures of approximation.

My second objection is that scientific knowledge has long been at home with the idea of infinity, both actual and potential. The fact that a finite creature has measurements poses formidable difficulties for introducing and grasping the notion of infinity. If anthropometrics are used as the basis for cognitive processes, then infinity will end up being something like the Kantian thing-in-itself in that it exists, but only its phenomena are cognized. Beginning from the period regarded by historians as "modern," science has been constructing devices that enabled it to grasp infinity, formed conceptual means in mathematics, astronomy and physics in order to understand infinity. Modern cosmology deals with distances of a billion light years, i.e., the distances light travels in a billion years.

Science has long been dealing with objects that go beyond anthropo-measurements, and scientific revolutions expand the use of non-anthropo-measurement and study the universe with the aid of new ideal objects and new constructed devices. These devices have not used anthropo-measurements—on the contrary, they show that man's cognitive capacity, aided by scientific-technical devices, has gone beyond anthropo-measurements and is objectively capable of grasping infinity. The expansion of human perceptive faculties—sight and hearing—through various technologies and high-precision instruments attests that the limits of anthropo-measurement have greatly widened and that the designers of the space probes that have been sent and will be sent to Mars stand to gain little from being reminded of the limited measurements geared to the human body. Infinity shines through the finite: this is one interpretation of the human essence, and insisting on anthropo-measurement of things implies confinement to what is finite and renunciation of self-awareness of man as an infinite creature.

Does not Petrov see the obvious fact that science is not geared to anthropo-measurement—it seeks to obtain abstract results free of any connection with the human being? In juxtaposing scientific and dynamic descriptions, he notes again and again that "scientific description gravitates toward non-human objective measurement of the surrounding world, derived, for example, from the rotation of the Earth, the length of the Earth meridian, etc., whereas dynamic description implies human measurements . . ." (Petrov 2004, 174). In other words, for Petrov, scientific description is "divorced from the subject, typically exists separately from the subject in graphic records," whereas a dynamic record "does not imply separateness from the subject . . ." (Petrov 2004, 174). Thus, science, according to Petrov, is not geared to anthropo-measurements and anthropo-measurements refer merely to dynamic records of scientific achievements. Thesaurus dynamics—which Petrov identifies with dynamic description of transitions from Tu to Ti—ranging from the thesaurus of a secondary school graduate to that of a specialist researcher in some field, is the model of the education process put forward by Petrov: "Anthropo-measurement is the essence of dynamic descriptions" (Petrov 2004, 175).

However, while distinguishing the non-anthropo-measurement of scientific knowledge from the anthropo-measurement of thesaurus dynamics represented in education, he spoke of the latter as part of the system of all theoretical-cognitive and organizational-technological creations of man (Petrov 2004, 156). It remains unclear whether a systemic record of scientific achievements is geared to anthropo-measurement or not. Or is it the case that the anthropo-measurement parameter refers only to the dynamics of education, to the transition from one thesaurus to another, more generalized and specialized one?

Petrov posits the principle of translatability of non-anthropo-measurement into the form of dynamic records and sequence of the subject's actions. Such translatability of these directly opposite forms of descriptions may identify certain requirements for the subject that underlie the thesaurus dynamic of the education process. He criticizes the anthropology of the "neo-Dyonisians" (T. Roszak and others) who argue that man is biologically and genetically wanting, shortcomings being compensated for, among other things, by systems of knowledge. It is worth recalling A. Gelen who considers human nature to be "incomplete" and limited, as well as G. Anders who declared man to be antiquated and man's nature—the soul and life—to be inadequate and unable to keep up with the requirements and pace of modern technology (see: Anders 1956; Anders 1980).

The foundations of philosophical anthropology advocated by A. Gelen, T. Roszak and G. Anders can be challenged by advancing other principles, stemming, for example, from the notion of the openness of man's nature, man's ability to overcome his identity, and his constant changeability and dynamism in his relations with other humans. Yet even in these endless transformations of his relations with other people, one needs to find certain invariants of changes beyond which human life and consciousness are impossible.

Petrov argues that "the amount of accumulation of new knowledge as it happens in disciplines and in science as a whole, imposes no visible limitations on anthropo-measurement" (Petrov 2004, 173). He draws an analogy between the loads of disciplinary publications in science and icebergs. However, if he refers to a scientific discipline as an "anthropo-measured fragment of activity" (Petrov 2004, 186), what about the submerged part of the iceberg which is obviously not included in the horizon of the human subject, being largely hidden from him? Many past and present thinkers have noted the fact that the growth of scientific knowledge that, according to Price, follows a logistical curve (Price 1963, 20–21)[6] which leads to the content of science not being commensurate with man. Thus, Pavel Florensky, recalling the biblical myth of the Tower of Babel wrote: "The content of a specialty other than one's own has long become inaccessible not only to an ordinary cultured person, but to a specialist in a related field. Moreover, individual disciplines are inaccessible even to a specialist in the same science. If a mathematical specialist takes a new issue of a specialized journal and does not find anything to read there because he does not understand a word in any of the articles, is it not *reductio ad absurdum* of the whole course of our civilization?" (Florensky 1999, 368). The alienation of science from the scientists who create it and from the people beginning to master it has reached an appalling degree.

The alienation of science from man can only be achieved by forming new, more capacious methods of representing knowledge. Petrov draws attention to the "mechanisms of compressing" (Petrov 2004, 227) scientific knowledge, but unfortunately he does not explain their essence, although disciplinary organization of scientific knowledge and the types of its publication (text-books, reviews, summaries, etc.) undoubtedly represent methods of compacting the achievements and the information obtained by science. Generalized theories from which preceding theories can be derived by applying certain operations can also be viewed as cognitive methods of compressing scientific information. Thus, within the theory of numbers, an abstract theory of complex numbers was built from which the German mathematician H. Hankel derived the other numbers theories using the principle of permanence (Ogurtsov 1979). The principle of correspondence put forward by Niels Bohr is another method of compressing scientific information. The development of forms of presenting knowledge, transition from paper to electronic data storage, major advances in computer technology—all this furnishes methods of compacting and compressing scientific data that minimize the efforts involved in searching and assimilating information.

The gap between the unlimited growth of scientific knowledge and the finite capacity of the human brain to "contain" it, noted by Petrov, can be overcome in several ways: by building a new philosophical anthropology or with the help of sociological imagination (Petrov 2004, 717). The first path, leading to the myth of the shaping of a new type of human being, is rejected by Petrov, although the idea of anthropo-measurement, which is the nucleus of equifinality and thesaurus dynamics, does imply an anthropological view of man. Petrov is wedded to the sociological approach to epistemology, the trend which is now called social epistemology. The social epistemologist focuses on the characteristics of scientific knowledge that differ from those that engaged classical epistemology: a scientific community is preferred to a creative individual; stereotypes and norms, to an author's innovations; codes, to an expression of individual vision of problems. I think the sociological approach leads Petrov to look for "mechanisms of integrating science into a totality of a supranational global phenomenon" (Petrov 2004, 731), uniform rigorous rules of the game accepted by the scientific community. The sneaking desire to see a common language of science led him to the utopia of Global Parliament of Science, an organizational form that would offer an intensive model of "scientification" of advanced societies (Petrov 2004, 765 ff.).

If one looks at the Soviet philosophy of science in terms of equifinality and anthropo-measurement, one has to admit that it was not equifinal, because its initial conditions and paths were different, resulting in different and even alternative interpretations of science. Besides, man was not "a measure of all things" for the Soviet government. It was not anthropo-measured—rather, it was hostile to man, a view that M. K. Petrov shared.

## NOTES

1. According to Heidegger, "one cannot expect any understanding of man and his world from modern system theories. They all essentially remain in thrall to the principle of causality and are engaged in reifying everything that exists. But thereby they give up forever the opportunity to see real human being-in-the-world" (Heidegger 2012, 315). This assessment, which I consider to be unfair, seems to be a sample of "little science" which, according to Heidegger, not only fails to think, but also reifies its methods. He overlooked the fact that systems thinking is based on new forms of determination—determination by the totality of its components and determination by the goal, or the future, as Russian physiologist M. A. Bernstein put it.
2. That research group published a series of monographs and collections of works on the systemic approach (Blauberg, Yudin 1973; Sadovsky 1974; Problemy metodologii sistemnogo issledovaniya, 1970 and others) and translations of books and articles by foreign authors (above all: Issledovaniya po obshchey teorii sistem. Sbornik perevodov 1989).
3. On the history of systemic research in the USSR, see (Blauberg 1991; Blauberg 1997).
4. M. K. Petrov's publications in the *Systemic Studies Yearbook* are limited, as far as I know, to his article (Petrov 1973, 30–46). I believe that some of his ideas were promoted by his daughter (Petrova 1975; Petrova 1976, 43–54).
5. The last two books will form the focus of this retrospective article.
6. On Logistical Growth, see (Petrov 2006, 126–128).

## BIBLIOGRAPHY

Anders, Günter. 1956. *Die Antiquartheit des Menschen. Bd. 1. Über die Seele im Zeitalter der zweiten industriellen Revolution.* Műnchen: Beck Verlag.

Anders, Günter. 1980. *Die Antiquartheit des Menschen. Bd. 2. Über die Zerstörung des Lebens im Zeitalter der dritten industriellen Revolution.* Műnchen: Beck Verlag.

Belousov, Lev V., Gurvich, Alexander A., Zalkind, Semyon Ya., Kanegiser, Nina. N. 1970. *Alexandr Gavrilovich Gurvich (1874–1954)* [*Alexander Gavrilovich Gurvich (1874–1954)*]. Moscow: Nauka.

Bertalanffy, Ludwig von. 1969. "Obshchaya teoriya system: kritichesky obzor." In *Issledovaniya po obshchey teorii system* [Studies in the General Theory of Systems]. Moscow: Progress.

Blauberg, Igor V., Yudin, Erik G. 1973. *Stanovlenie i sushchnost' sistemnogo podhoda* [The Emergence and Essence of the Systemic Approach]. Moscow: Nauka.

Blauberg, Igor V. 1991. "Iz istorii sistemnyh issledovaniy v SSSR" [From the History of Systemic Studies in the USSR]. In *Sistemnye issledovaniya. Metodologicheskie problemy: Ezhegodnik 1989–1990* [Systemic Research. Methodological Problems Yearbook. 1989–1990]. Moscow: URSS.

Blauberg, Igor V. 1997, *Problema tselostnosti i sistemnyi podhod* [The Problem of Wholeness and the Systemic Approach]. Moscow: URSS.

Bogdanov, Alexander A. 1989. *Tektologiya: (Vseobshchaya organizatsionnaya nauka)* [Tectology: (Universal Organizational Science)]. Moscow: Economica.

Driesch, Hans. 1905. *Geschichte des Vitalismus.* Leipzig: Johann Ambrosius Barth.

Florensky, Pavel A. 1999, "U vodorazdelov mysli" [At the Watersheds of Thought]. In Florensky, Pavel A. *Sochineniya v 4 tomakh.* Tom 3 (1) [Works in 4 vols. Vol. 3 (1)], 118–152. Moscow: Mysl'.

Heidegger, Martin. 2012. *Zollikonovskie Seminary* [Zollicon Seminars]. Vilnius: EHU.

*Issledovaniya po obshchey teorii sistem. Sbornik perevodov*, 1989 [Studies in the General Theory of Systems. Collection of Translations]. Moscow: Progress.

Lyubishchev, Alexandr A. 1982. "Reduktsionizm i razvitie morfologii i sistematiki" [Reductionism and the Development of Morphology and Systematics]. In Lyubishchev, Alexandr A. *Problemy formy, sistematiki i evolutsii organizmov* [Problems of the Form, Systematics and Evolution of Organisms], 103–110. Moscow: Nauka.

Lyubishchev, Alexandr A. and Gurvich, Alexandr G. 1998. *Dialog o biopole* [Dialog about Biofield]. Ulyanovsk: Izdatel'stvo Ulyanovskogo gosudarstvennogo pedagogicheskogo universiteta.

Ogurtsov, Alexander P. 1979, "Iz predystorii printsipa sootvetstviya." [Historical Background of the Correspondence Principle.] In *Printsip sootvetstviya* [Principle of Correspondence], edited by B. M. Kedrov and N. F. Ovchinnikov. Moscow: Nauka.

Petrov, Mikhail C. 1973. "Sistemnye harakteristiki nauchno-tehnitcheskoy deyatel'nosti." [Systemic Characteristics of Scientific-Technical Activities] In *Sistemnye issledovaniya. Yezhegodnik* [Systemic Studies. Yearbook 1972], 30–46. Moscow: URSS.

Petrov, Mikhail C. 1991. *Yazyk, Znak, Kultura* [Language, Sign, Culture]. Moscow: Izdatel'stvo vostochnoy literatury.

Petrov, Mikhail C. 1992. *Sotsio-kul'turnoye osnovanie razvitiya sovremennoy nauki* [Socio-Cultural Foundations of the Development of Modern Science]. Moscow: Nauka.

Petrov, Mikhail C. 1997. *Antichnaya kul'tura* [Antique Culture]. Moscow: ROSSPEN.

Petrov, Mikhail C. 2004. *Istoriya evropeyskoy kul'turnoy traditsii i eyo problemy* [A History of the European Cultural Tradition and Its Problems]. Moscow: Rossiyskaya politicheskaya entsiklopediya (ROSSPEN).

Petrov, Mikhail C. 2006. *Filosophskie problemy "nauki o nauke." Subyekt sotsiologii nauki* [Philosophical Problems of "the Science of Science." The Subject of the Sociology of Science]. Moscow: ROSSPEN.

Petrova, Tatiana M. 1975. "Matematicheskie modeli oblasti nauchnogo issledovaniya" [Mathematical Models of a Scientific Research Area]. In *Sistemnye issledovaniya. Yezhegodnik 1974* [Systemic Studies Yearbook. 1974], Moscow: URSS.

Petrova, Tatiana M. 1976. "Metodologicheskie osobennosti kolichestvennogo vydeleniya strukturnyh yedinits nauki." [Methodological Features of Quantitative Isolation of Structural Units in Science.] In *Sistemnye issledovaniya. Yezhegodnik 1975* [Systemic Studies Yearbook. 1975], 43–54. Moscow: URSS.

Price, Derek J. de S. 1963. *Little Science. Big Science*. N.Y.: Columbia University Press.

*Problemy metodologii sistemnogo issledovaniya* 1970 [Problems of Methodology of Systems Research]. Moscow: Mysl'.

Sadovsky, Vadim N. 1974. *Osnovaniya obshchey teorii sistem. Logiko-metodologicheskiy analiz* [Foundations of the General Theory of Systems. Logical and Methodological Analysis]. Moscow: Nauka.

Sadovsky, Vadim N. 1996. "Izmenenie Paradigm v sistemnoy mysli" [Change of Paradigms in Systemic Thinking]. In *Sistemnye issledovaniya. Metodologicheskie problemy. Yezhegodnik 1992–1994* [Systemic Research. Methodological Problems. Yearbook. 1992–1994], 70–79. Moscow: URSS, ISA.

[Collection]. 1969. *Studies of the General Theory of Systems. Collection of Translations*. Moscow: Progress.

Whittaker, Robert H. A. 1953. "Consideration of Climax Theory: The Climax as Population and Pattern." In *Ecological Monographs* 23: 530–549.

CHAPTER NINE

# Soviet Philosophy and the Methodology of Science in the 1960s–1980s: From Ideology to Science

## *A Philosophical Reflection*

BORIS I. PRUZHININ

In this essay, I will try to answer a very tricky question: who in the USSR needed a philosophy of science (and the related methodological programs) and for what purpose? In the context of this question, I propose to discuss the status and extent of the development of Soviet philosophy of science in the 1960s–1980s, its logical-methodological, epistemological and, to some extent, the relevant sociocultural studies.

As seen from the above remark, I use the term "philosophy of science" in a broader sense than it is used today. And yet, in the 1960s, the expression referred to neo-Positivist philosophy of science (above all, "logical empiricism") and was routinely described as being "bourgeois" or "Western." Later, partly under the influence of post-Positivist philosophy of science, the meaning of the term began to expand to include various sociocultural aspects of scientific-cognitive activity and corresponding philosophical meanings. True, its conceptual content was becoming more and more heterogeneous and vague, so that today the term denotes an area of very diverse philosophical interests rather than a specific philosophical area of study.

Yet another important preliminary remark is in order. In my view, it is only by taking into account the specific cultural-historical functions of philosophy with regard to various areas of human activity that we can meaningfully discuss the effectiveness of the philosophical approach in a certain period. Accordingly, I maintain that one can only discuss the destinies and status of the philosophy of science in the USSR in the 1960s–1980s in the context of its relationship with the science of the time, moreover, predominantly Soviet science. In reality, this is by no means always the case, and the discussion is not limited to Soviet philosophy of science. However, if a fragment of philosophy is extracted (I stress, *extracted*) from its concrete historical context and is examined as a "section" or a "specimen," we will end up with something very trivial. When associated exclusively with concrete historical functions of philosophy, the philosophical content of such a "specimen" is easily reduced to something commonly known, i.e., to that which the more advanced "contemporaries" derived from other contexts or "predecessors," or even to the ideas of antique philosophers. The cultural-historical meaning of ideas treated as "samples" is diluted in the flood of generalities. This leads to value judgments of various hues (more often negative): subjective, personal, corporate, ideological ones, etc.—anything but philosophical. What is important, however, is the historical role, the cultural function that makes a philosophical idea necessary at this or that period in history, under certain circumstances. It is in the context of this function that the inherent content and specificity of an idea is revealed—the thought processes and accents whose true relevance sometimes becomes apparent centuries later.

I am going to discuss the historical context of the 1960s–1980s in the USSR and the functions of the philosophy of science at the time as a contemporary, i.e., the way I experienced them. I would not restrict myself to merely stating: "This is how it was." Rather, I shall speak of how I saw it, i.e., as an eyewitness. I understand that the research and conceptual generalizations in the field have yet to be made.

So, let us go back to the 1960s. I was a student at the Philosophy Department at Moscow State University (MGU), in which I was enrolled in 1962. My attitude to science (notably natural science) at the time was determined by a number of intertwining ideological-existential principles (by and large shared by my peers).

First of all, the future—in the broadest sense, from my personal future to that of the whole humankind—was linked with the development of science. The main role in this future and this perspective was assigned not so much to science-driven technical achievements (that seemed trivial), as to hopes pinned on the social role of an institution that generates the truth, i.e., develops an ideal entity that banishes any manipulations and arbitrariness from our life. Perhaps today such an assessment of science seems naïve even for the 1960s. And indeed, even then we had heard (if only a rendering) of the general drift of the works of Michael Polanyi, Norwood Russell Hanson, and we knew about the ideas of Thomas Kuhn. We were well aware of the powerful anti-science movements associated with Existentialism. We perceived the arguments advanced by these movements as a problem. However, the surrounding reality fostered a positive image of the institution of science suggesting a certain angle from which to regard this range of problems. Even today, I consider the heuristic potential of our view of science at the time to be far more relevant than the post-Positivist interpretation of cognition that prevailed later (which, however, was equally situational).

The positive attitude to science as a sociocultural institution capable of renewing itself was projected onto the past, including the tragic fate of Soviet science and society in the 1930s–1950s and implying a sense that genuine science was bound to triumph (with everyone accorded recognition on merit because science has something objective about it, and offers a reference point for assessments). Before our very eyes, we saw Lysenko and all he stood for being dethroned, which was perceived in the 1960s as the continuation of the process of overcoming social and political tyranny. Sociocultural connotations, and not technological utopias, were paramount to us in our perception of and reflections on the phenomenon of science. As I saw it, our expectations were vindicated by the changes in the way the institution of science was functioning.

It is another matter that positive use of the results of science called for social control, social effort, and a socio-ideological stance that was justified, among other ways, philosophically. We philosophy students took it for granted at the time. Battles were fought between those who believed in science and anti-scientists, but it was basically clear to us that science, as a social institution, by virtue of the essence of what it was doing, rather than by its actual achievements, opened up a bright future to society, or rather a door of opportunity. I have to say that our interest in this topic was fueled, among other things, by science fiction. As for the application of the results of science, that was a widely discussed topic. However, we did not see a philosophical problem there, since in a healthy, rational society the use of scientific results would be controlled reasonably. The autonomy of science as a cognition institution was another matter.

On that point, the views of philosophy students, at least in my circle, were in a delicate relationship with the party and state ideology. The authorities also linked society's future with the development of science. The authorities were also mindful of the dire results of administrative meddling with science (genetics, cybernetics and much else, including the social and studies and the humanities). The authorities looked to scientific and technological progress, they needed the natural sciences and were forced to tolerate a measure of their autonomy. The state supported science (military and space research above all, but this attitude was extended to all positive science) offering it a certain degree of freedom. However, it was difficult to separate the cognitive processes proper from social and institutional ones. First, the state did not interfere with cognition proper only inasmuch as it had to do with natural sciences and not the social ones. Secondly, tensions arose over the subject of the use of knowledge. This could not but affect research activity because science was expected to deliver practical results. However, what worried the authorities most of all, and not without reason, was the social atmosphere that was generated by the autonomy of science, limited though it was.

As the institutions of science were self-governing, they eluded social control. The social environment that arose in science made at least some individuals independent of society's political subsystems. We students were keenly aware of it. While in a summer volunteer construction camp in 1967 we read Andrei Sakharov's texts—I do not remember how we had got hold of them, but we read them together and even tried to discuss them. We felt we were treading on dangerous ground there, but we were sure that, as philosophers, we were entitled to be doing it and indeed were duty-bound to read, understand and assess them.

Of course we understood the implications of the socio-political processes of the time (our country invaded Czechoslovakia in 1968, the year I graduated from university) and most of us were aware of the possible consequences as well as toward what processes this might be leading. We were far from being idealists and we did not think that scientific truths would gain recognition in social life by themselves. Most of us philosophy students had no particular illusions about "an ideal society" and the role of science in its emergence. But all these sober-minded considerations did not diminish the social role and cultural value of scientific cognition as such, with its history, its experience of resistance and adherence to its cultural attitudes and its place in modern society. For many of us turning to science, logic and epistemology was a way of escaping into areas where we could continue being philosophers. Incidentally, a similar choice was made by those who withdrew into the history of philosophy. This happened almost intuitively, as a rule it was not a conceptual, let alone a conscious ideological choice. I for one was just interested in the phenomenon of cognition. The rest was just a background to my choice, but a significant and largely conscious one.

The state and the party of course tried to control science in many ways, including through ideology—for example, through philosophy, by controlling philosophical research, including the philosophy of science and theory of knowledge. However, these attempts at control hardly affected me personally. Being an undergraduate and graduate student, and later a junior research associate at the Institute of Philosophy of the USSR Academy of Sciences, I was cushioned against the consequences of such control by my senior colleagues who, by the way, had taught me to regard scientific truth as a cultural value. I perceived attempts to impose ideology as external invasions prompted by expediency which had nothing to do with the essence of philosophical (or, broadly, scientific) cognition. It was up to science and philosophy to use its own means to tell truth from untruth. Paradoxically, that attitude, for all its upfront naivety, did not demand any particular ideological or existential efforts of us. That was probably because I had people by my side who assumed responsibility for solving the problems that inevitably arose. These people secured for themselves and for me islets of ideological independence where we could freely reflect and uphold our views. At least, that was the case in the field of epistemology and the philosophy of science.

We were introduced to the theme of philosophical problems of natural sciences by teachers who felt very much at home in the natural sciences. Philosophical problems of modern physics were taught to us by Vladimir Kuptsov, those of biology by Vincent Fyodorov. Boris Glinsky immersed us in the general theory of systems. My group attended lectures on biochemistry and genetics by professors from the biology and chemistry departments. We were kept up to date on all the details of the battle against the Lysenko school (a major role in that battle was played by Ivan Frolov who gave lectures at our department at the time). We attended the essentially Neo-Kantian lectures by Anatoly Zotov. Anatoly Korshunov laid out the ideas of "activity-based reflection" before us. Evgenii Voishvillo and Elena Smirnova told us about the potential of mathematical logic. In the philosophical-methodological field, lectures by Vladimir Shvyrev and Boris Griaznov are etched on our memory.

The themes connected with natural sciences dominated the philosophy of science at the time. But discussions were not confined to this. The atmosphere created during these discussions was conducive to the discussion of diverse areas of the philosophy of science. It may be an odd thing to say, but it was my orientation toward natural science that enabled me to identify with the ideas of Ilyenkov about the dialectics of "ascending from the abstract to the concrete," and by the same token revealed to me the hollowness of dialectical logic as presented to us by

V. I. Cherkesov and V. I. Maltsev. I cannot claim that my attitude was conceptually consistent, but it enabled me to pick my way through the ideological trends of the time (in this country and abroad). We undergraduates were of course aware of the discussions between dialecticians and formal logicians and even took sides. But we could tell what lay beyond philosophy. As to what was and what was not scientific, we focused on the existential dimension, the very possibility of rational philosophical thinking. That was probably the most important thing at the time.

We were able to distinguish between "science bosses" and "science authorities" and were aware of the real conflicts that broke out between them. We had no illusions on that score. But we were convinced that science had its essence and we sensed the intellectual and existential impulse generated by that "essence." That constituted the science orientation of my ideas of the role of philosophy of science: the task of philosophy of science was to formulate the conditions under which true knowledge of the world could be obtained. I am not ashamed to admit that I still adhere to this kind of "scientism." I believe that the possibility of true knowledge of the world is one of the mainstays of European culture. That attitude, incidentally, met the need of science in this country for autonomy. Science at the time badly needed philosophical support for its right to search for the truth independently of any external conditions, and such support was provided by the philosophy of science. Science returned the favor.

I would like to stress that I was clearly aware at the time that the conditions for true cognition were not limited to formal methodological standards, and I was critical of the "anti-metaphysical" programs of Neo-Positivist philosophy of science. This was reflected in my Candidate's (Ph.D.) dissertation I defended in 1974 when I worked at Vladislav Lektorsky's sector at the Institute of Philosophy in Moscow. As far as I remember, this was the opinion shared by all those who worked in that sector: scientific truth arises only through human activity, is inherently historical and only exists within culture. Apart from everything else, philosophers who actively worked in the field of epistemology and philosophy of science thus escaped from the clutches of the primitive theory of reflection. Moreover, I believe that the everlasting work to overcome this theory, probably prompted by external circumstances, oriented researchers toward the sociocultural aspects of cognition (which, incidentally, were far from being alien to Marxism).

Orientation toward the truth seen from the point of view of history and activity was characteristic of many of our philosophers with whom I found myself working at the Institute of Philosophy's sector of dialectical materialism.[1] My generation in that sector—Natalia Avtonomova, Igor' Merkulov and Sergei Mareev—thought along the same lines. We were all very different. But we all shared the idea that the truth is only revealed to man through activity, specifically cultural-historical activity.

Such orientation created its own conceptual basis for the critique of Positivist methodological programs and the development of alternative philosophical-methodological approaches. That is why, in the 1970s and 1980s, we did not only absorb the post-Positivist philosophy of science with ease, but also formed our own ideas of what determined the development of science, which did not rule out its sociocultural autonomy. We reinterpreted the ideas of the activity-based approach to epistemology (Lektorsky), developed original methodological patterns of theoretical cognition (Stepin); writers on the philosophy of science discussed Yury Sachkov's idea of styles of scientific thinking; Trubnikov was elaborating the idea of "the time of human being" and Nikitin the idea of the wholeness of man's spiritual world which has a direct bearing on the methodology of research in the humanities.

By the time I joined Lektorsky's sector (the "Dialectical Materialism" sector subsequently renamed the sector of "The Theory of Knowledge"), I had made up my mind concerning my area of interests: philosophical-methodological themes and the problem of rationality of scientific knowledge. It has to be said that, in those years, in spite of external pressures, the idea of autonomous philosophical study independent of official ideology and corresponding to the spirit of Russian/Soviet science, permeated every area of philosophy in the country. The work of the sector, which was taking place before my eyes, saw a concerted and active effort to *overcome the unidimensional teleological orientation of ideology* in the philosophy of science. Similar processes were going on in other areas of Soviet philosophy. Naturally, the closer our studies moved toward social problems the more problematical—and fraught with the risk of incurring victimization—liberation from ideological pressure became. A glaring example of this was the closure of the Historical Materialism Department then headed by Vladislav Kelle and his own fate following that event.

I recall the lectures of D. I. Chesnokov when he told his students that there was no need for concrete sociological studies because other sources of information about society were available: letters from whistle-blowers sending signals, newspapers and magazines and competent agencies . . . It is not my purport to assess the scientific potential of historical materialism (*istmat*), but it was in those years that Kelle attempted to prove that scientific analysis of society was possible within its framework. Administrative measures could not stop this train of thought from unfolding. (See: Pruzhinin and Kelle 2011.) The closure of the Kelle department had not brought about fatal consequences for scholarly work. Nelli Motroshilova, Erikh Solovyov and other former members of that department continued to work in the same field in other departments and on "newly gained ideological territory."

All (literally *all*) the members of the Theory of Knowledge sector worked in the same direction overcoming the ideological distortions of philosophy and attempts to make philosophy one-dimensional. This general thrust can be traced in Lektorsky's publications of the time. I witnessed how these people were overcoming the one-dimensional ideological hierarchy—Marx, Engels, Lenin—while the rest of philosophy's history and present day were to be positioned and assessed in relation to that pinnacle. Within such a "hierarchy" the contribution of any philosopher was determined based on the degree to which his/her ideas corresponded to the straight line leading to the "pinnacle." Everything that diverged from that line was qualified as deviations and errors. The article "of the three authors" played a huge role in overcoming that attitude (see: Mamardashvili, Solovyov and Shvyrev 1972). In general, I have to note that such "rectitude" is characteristic of any ideology. It inherently needs a rigid core, clear and unambiguous coordinates for assessment. And yet, before my very eyes, the "territory of free research" in the philosophy of science was expanding. Social and cultural issues were brought into philosophical-methodological analysis of science, including analysis of sociocultural factors involved in the dynamics of knowledge, analysis of the cognitive role of sociocultural subsystems of science, etc. And, looming on the periphery of this expanded territory, was critical analysis of the philosophical-methodological problems of social and humanities cognition.

I would like to highlight an important feature of "social" behavior of the leaders of Soviet philosophical community at the time—to be specific, their ability to spot among the motley assemblage of researchers those for whom the goals and values of philosophizing came before everything else. You could discuss with them the most acute and controversial problems without fear that the discussion would be reduced to certain ideological—or worse, pragmatic-political—matters that could lead to victimization. What caused resentment was not the ideology in itself, but the claim of the predominant ideology to be universal, to play the role of a philosophical worldview (with a total lack of a critical view of itself). That claim was opposed by the clear consciousness of a community of people sharing a common, albeit variously understood, idea of philosophy being a cultural value in its own right. To repeat, they had differing perceptions of scientific cognitive activity and proceeded from very different concepts and worldview principles. However, one thing that this community did not tolerate was invoking "administrative-ideological arguments" in philosophical discussions. The members of the unit with whom I worked, many members of the Institute community and, in general, many philosophers whom I had occasion to meet espoused very different worldviews and held very diverse opinions as to the goals of philosophy. However, there was a distinct sense of a community sharing a common goal, i.e., to preserve the intellectual territory for free philosophical discussion.[2]

The philosophical theme that consolidated this community, as I see it today (a theme around which meaningful discussions were conducted, and not some common generally accepted ideological principle), was, even at that early stage, the inherent multidirectionality of historical dynamics, the theme of multidimensional history (in our case, multidimensional history of philosophy). My retrospective formulation of the pivotal problem of the philosophy of science at the time may be somewhat crude—it rested on the possibility of history taking different directions and, accordingly, posited the existence of different perspectives in its course—but I still adhere to it. Such subjects have become highly relevant today, and I think that pursuing this theme further holds out a promise for the philosophy of science in this country (and not only philosophy of science, and not only in this country). But at this point I would like to stress a circumstance that is important for understanding and assessing the philosophy of science in the USSR: the opening up of this still relevant theme in the 1970s and 1980s was prompted by resistance and opposition to the idea that history moves along a one-dimensional, predetermined track. Overcoming the latter ideologeme at the time was similarly very important for the self-consciousness of our science and for the active scholars, because preservation of the autonomy of science, combined with that idea, enabled them to retain their right to independent quests, to stepping into the unknown, and to avoiding the dead-end goals set by the dominant paradigms.

This was the attitude of our philosophy of science in the 1960s–1980s prevailing over "bad unidirectional ideologism" that consolidated the community in which I worked in those years. This attitude made the philosophy of science meaningful and useful to science itself, because it marked out those areas of philosophical quests whose non-trivial methodological nature is only being fully revealed today. In my opinion, there is nothing unusual about philosophical work being meaningful. Philosophy is simply impossible in a cultural vacuum where everything is either permitted or forbidden. A philosopher cannot exist outside a cultural and social environment. He is immersed in it, reflects on it, assesses and criticizes it and looks for support in it. The real-life environment forms the philosophical Ego, position and concept. Faced with the resistance of a specific cultural-historical environment, the philosopher upholds the freedom of thought, concrete thought which is invested with specific content, or rather lends relevance to general philosophical truths only in this environment, through this environment and through the attitude toward it.

The cultural-historical environment may be aggressively totalitarian, or it may appear to be quite free, but for the philosopher it is reality whose resistance he overcomes, it is the object of his reflections. Philosophy always lives *contrary* to something, as a challenge to the state of affairs given once and for all, it exists as critique and demonstration of the historicity of everything that surrounds us, as a demonstration of our own historicity. Whether or not it is "needed" is decided only in a dynamic, constantly changing cultural environment. In the 1960s and 1980s, the battle waged by the philosophy of science was for the idea of autonomy of science and of the multidimensionality of thought within it. It was in search of the experience of confrontation, its preservation and its right to creative quests that the country's leading scientists turned to the philosophy of science. Academicians Aksel Berg (radio engineering, cybernetics), Nikita Moiseyev (general mechanics and applied mathematics), Boris Raushenbach (physicist, mechanic, one of the pioneers of Russian space exploration), Sergey Kurdyumov (computational mathematics, mathematical physics), and Pavel Simonov (psychophysiologist) all thought it important to be members of the editorial board of the journal *Voprosy filosofii*. There were a number of humanities scholars on the board, including Alexei Leontiev and Dmitry Likhachev.

I think it is important to understand today in what conditions philosophical thought existed at the time. Sometimes it took on very fanciful conceptual forms. But the most important thing for today's philosophy is to understand and assimilate the experience of overcoming, through thought, the pressure of an ideological environment whose criticism generated the content of the philosophy of science in the 1960s and 1980s. If that experience is lost, if we are not interested to know how Ilyenkov or Batishchev challenged dogmatic Marxism, how science was asserted by Lotman in Soviet literary studies, by Erik Yudin and other "Sixtiers" in Soviet methodology of science, there is no point in talking about restoring the philosophical tradition in Russia. Without that experience we would not be able to understand Russian philosophy of the nineteenth and twentieth centuries—both religious and secular—which resisted the ideological pressure of its environment. And, I should add, we shall not be able to assimilate Western philosophical thought which would remain something external and alien because it has its own experience of "asserting itself" and we cannot understand it without comparing it with our own historical-cultural experience. This is the work of understanding its own history (see Shchedrina 2011).

## NOTES

1. Those who worked in this tradition included Vladislav Lektorsky, Nikolai Trubnikov, Boris Dynin, Evgenii Nikitin, Vladimir Shvyrev, Nelli Mudragey, Evald Ilyenkov, Genrikh Batishchev, Ksenia Abulkhanova-Slavskaya.
2. I can attest that this was the attitude of Igor' Akchurin, Lev Bazhenov, Alexander Zinoviev, Bonifaty Kedrov, Vadim Sadovsky, Vladimir Smirnov, Petr Tavanets, Nina Yulina and many others.

## BIBLIOGRAPHY

Mamardashvili, Merab K., Solovyov, Erikh Yu., and Shvyrev, Vladimir S. 1972. "Klassika i sovremennost': dve epokhi v razvitii burzhuaznoy filosofii." [Classics and Modernity: Two Epochs in the Development of Bourgeois Philosophy]. In *Filosofiya v sovremennom mire. Filosofiya i nauka* [Philosophy in the Modern World. Philosophy and Science], 28–94. Moscow: Nauka.

Pruzhinin, Boris I. and Kelle, Vladislav Zh. 2011. "Beseda B. I. Pruzhinina s V. Zh. Kelle (11 maya 2010 g.)." ["Conversation between B. I. Pruzhinin and V. Zh. Kelle (May 11, 2010)"]. In *Voprosy filosofii* (1):60–66.

Shchedrina, Tatiana G. 2011 "Arkhiv epokhi: stranitsy istorii filosofii v Rossii vtoroy poloviny XX veka" ["Archive of an Era: Pages from the History of Philosophy in Russia in the Second Half of the Twentieth Century"]. In *Voprosy filosofii* (6):123–132.

## NOTES

1. [illegible]

2. [illegible]

## BIBLIOGRAPHY

[illegible]

# PART III

# Philosophy as the History of Philosophy

CHAPTER TEN

# Spinoza in Western and Soviet Philosophy: New Perspectives after Postmodernism

VESA OITTINEN

The reception of Spinoza is one of the points where the differences between Soviet and Western Marxism come to the fore in a poignant form. Indeed, when one reads the "leftist" Spinoza interpretations published in the West since the 1960s (Gilles Deleuze, Louis Althusser, Antonio Negri) on the one side, and then the Soviet philosophical literature discussing Spinoza, from Abram Deborin to Evald Ilyenkov, one wonders whether they are dealing with the same thinker at all. Of course, all the great classic philosophers are prone to different interpretations. But it seems that the case with Spinoza is a more serious one. There is some fundamental dissonance here, which is worth a closer examination.

Perry Anderson outlined the differences between the "critical," Western Marxism and what he saw as an ideological and dogmatic Soviet Marxism as early as 1976 in his influential book *Considerations on Western Marxism*. I am not trying to argue with Anderson here, especially as I agree with most of his conclusions, especially with his main insight that the rather heterogeneous vein of ideas called "Western Marxism" is characterized, above all, by attempts to combine Marx's thought with some other, non-Marxist, theories (Marx and Hegel; Marx and Existentialism; Marx and Structuralism, and so on). Anderson dated the origins of Western Marxism back to the 1920s, with the seminal event of Lukács's *Geschichte und Klassenbewusstsein* published in 1923. The young Lukács—he distanced himself later from his "juvenile sin"—laid the foundation for a tradition which has lasted until our times. Most non-orthodox forms of Marxist thought, seeking an alternative to Soviet Marxism-Leninism, in one way or another had recourse to young Lukács. One must say that Robert Steigerwald, the ideologist of the present-day German Communist Party (DKP) was, in a way, quite right when he described Lukács's early work as the "Pandora's Box of revisionism."

## SPINOZA AS SEEN BY SOVIET PHILOSOPHERS

Although the divide between Soviet and Western Marxism traces its origin to the 1920s, the difference in their interpretations of Spinoza is of a later date. For a long time, both currents relied on the picture of Spinoza formed in the debates of the Second International. This picture emerged from the struggle of the left current of Social-Democracy against the attempts of the Bernsteinian revisionists to depict Kant (actually, not Kant himself, but the Neo-Kantian interpretation of the Königsberg philosopher) as the most suitable philosopher for the workers' movement and the goal of a socialist society as a kind of "categorical imperative." Against such attempts, Franz Mehring hailed Spinoza as the vigorous materialist thinker much more worthy to be the precursor of the socialist movement than the "philistine" Kant.[1] Georgi Plekhanov, another influential thinker of the left wing of the Second International, had already preceded Mehring in declaring Marxism as a continuation of Spinozism. "I assert with full conviction," he wrote in *Die Neue Zeit* in 1898, "that, in the materialist period of their development, Marx and Engels never abandoned Spinoza's point of view" (Plekhanov 1976, 339).

Plekhanov's interpretation of the Amsterdam philosopher as a direct precursor of Marxism was restated in the 1920s by his pupil Abram Deborin. The well-known reproach against Deborin was that he treated Spinoza as a "Marx without the beard." Such criticisms notwithstanding, Deborin's interpretation formed the cornerstone of the later Soviet view of Spinoza. Although discussions arose about how consequential Spinoza's "materialism" should have been, no Soviet philosopher tried to question radically what Plekhanov had written. Even Evald Ilyenkov, one of the most unorthodox of the Soviet Marxists, frequently cited Plekhanov to support his own Spinoza lecture.

As I attempt to make only a general comparison of the Spinoza reception of Soviet and Western Marxism, a detailed exposition of Spinoza's role in Soviet philosophy is beyond the scope of this chapter. Here it suffices to give only a brief outline. Generally, one can say that in Soviet Marxism, Spinoza's significance was assessed from the viewpoint of his contribution to materialism in philosophy. Materialism, in turn, was understood in the "classical" sense in which Friedrich Engels described it in his *Ludwig Feuerbach and the End of Classic German Philosophy*, namely as one of the two currents in the history of philosophy, which differed from its antagonist, the current of idealism, in that it acknowledged the primacy of Being over Thought.

Deborin set the main tone in his essay "Spinozismus und Marxismus," which was published (as a Russian-German bilingual text) in the 1927 issue of the international yearbook of Spinoza researchers, *Chronicon Spinozanum*, dedicated to the 350th anniversary of Spinoza's death. Deborin repeated Plekhanov's thesis, according to which the "leading, most revolutionary and thoroughly *materialist* doctrine of the present days, the Marxism, derives its philosophical worldview from Spinozism" (Deborin 1927, 152). He then proceeded, noting that in contrast to the vulgar mechanistic materialism of thinkers like Vogt and Moleschott, Spinoza stays "on the viewpoint of *concrete monism*," by which Deborin meant that Spinoza was able to avoid the narrow mindedness of Cartesian dualism as well as of "abstract monism":

his substance was a "dialectical unity of opposites," being at the same time matter and thought (ibid., 153). On the other side, Spinoza's deficiency in comparison with Marxism consisted in the fact that his understanding of Man was characterized by an "abstract individualism" (ibid., 157). Man was primarily seen as product of nature, not of society.

During the 1920s, Deborin's school did not remain unchallenged. Along the "Hegelian" current of Deborin and his adherents, there existed a more heterogeneous trend in early Soviet philosophy, which was dubbed "Mechanicism." One of the most prominent representatives of this current, Liubov Akselrod (1868–1946) delivered a poignant critique of the Deborinist interpretation of Spinoza. She adhered to Feuerbach's assessment, according to which Spinoza's philosophy was a pantheistic doctrine, and pantheism in turn a kind of "theological materialism," a negation of theology which, however, remains built upon a theological foundation.[2] Akselrod wrote that this "theological element" in Spinoza's system should not be downplayed, as the Soviet philosophers generally did. Because of the ambivalence in Spinoza's materialism, Akselrod thought that Holbach and La Mettrie, as more consequent materialists, would be better suited for the title of the forefathers of Marxian materialism. Akselrod's Spinoza interpretation remained, however, solitary in its kind in Soviet literature.

Deborin was soon dethroned from his position as the "Pope" of early Soviet philosophy and branded a "Menshevizing Idealist." This ill-famed concept was coined by Stalin himself, as a part of his campaign to squeeze the ex-Mensheviks out from leading posts in Soviet science, culture and philosophy. But it was symptomatic, that the new generation of Soviet philosophers which replaced a substantial part of the "old guard" of the 1920s, never was able to specify the content of the "idealism" allegedly represented by the Deborinites.[3] So even in its now Stalinized version, the Soviet philosophy continued in viewing Spinoza, in like manner with Deborin, above all through his contribution to the "materialist solution of the main question of philosophy." For example, Vagan Vandek and Vladimir Timosko, in their introduction to the Russian translation of Spinoza's correspondence, published in 1932, reproached Deborin of presenting Spinoza's "bourgeois political ideals" as the socialist doctrine of the revolutionary proletariat and for bringing Spinozism too close to dialectical materialism. After that, however, they continued:

> To show the crucial difference of Spinoza's philosophy—as an ideology of the seventeenth century bourgeoisie—from the dialectical materialism does not in any way mean that Spinoza should be handed over to the idealists . . . In the person of Spinoza, we have one of the greatest metaphysical materialists with splendid elements of dialectics; he occupies an important place in the history of materialism. (Vandek, Timosko 1932, 7)

This interpretation of Spinoza as not quite being able to reach to the level of the Diamat doctrine, as a kind of St. John the Baptist paving way for the true Messiah to come, remained, of course with variations, the main tenor in Soviet literature. The focus was almost always on the question of materialism. In post-Stalin times, Vasily Sokolov was the most important exponent of Spinoza's philosophy. He wrote an extensive biography of Spinoza and published in 1957 a two-volume set of the selected works of the philosopher, which was of good editorial quality. In the foreword to this edition, Sokolov, quite expectedly, rebukes Spinoza for the metaphysical character of his materialism, although he at the same time acknowledged that there were some "elements of dialectics" in Spinoza, above all the idea of *causa sui* (Sokolov 1957, 21, 23–24). But Sokolov did not analyze further the dialectics he claimed to be found in Spinoza—even this was typical for most Soviet philosophers since Deborin.

In the history of Soviet philosophy, there were some deviations from this general line of Spinoza interpretation. Already in the 1930s the psychologist Lev Vygotsky tried to utilize Spinoza's doctrine of affects in order to overcome the crisis of contemporary psychology, which, according to Vygotsky, was mainly caused by the fact that it was stuck in the Cartesian dualism. But Vygotsky's planned "Spinoza book" was never completed, and its manuscript was published posthumously in 1984 as a part of his collected works.

Another important exception from the general picture of Soviet Spinozism was Evald Ilyenkov, who especially insisted on the importance of Spinoza's ideas concerning the role of activity in the process of human cognition (the famous thesis, according to which Man's *cogitandi potentia* equals to his *agendi potentia*, occurs in Spinoza in various formulations, for example in *Ethics* IV, prop. 24). Ilyenkov's interpretations of Spinoza were unique not only in the history of Soviet philosophy, but also in the existing scholarly world literature on Spinoza. He saw Spinoza as a precursor of not only Marxism in general, but especially as foreshadowing the ideas of the so-called cultural-historical school of Soviet psychology (e.g. Leontiev et al.). Ilyenkov is nowadays acknowledged as one of the most creative Soviet philosophers, and his ideas are worth a detailed specific study. Unfortunately, here I can only refer to further research literature on Ilyenkov.[4]

Ilyenkov's Spinoza interpretation was later challenged by another non-ordinary Soviet philosopher, Genrikh Batishchev. He, too, was an interesting, but at the same time somewhat extravagant, thinker, with a predilection for themes one might call "existentialistic." In the 1960s he was a near friend of Ilyenkov, although he soon grew more critical toward him. For Batishchev, the fault of Ilyenkov was that he had a too objectivistic view of Man's situation in the world. According to Batishchev, Ilyenkov drowned the individual subject in society, into the "social substance," thus depriving him of autonomy. According to Batishchev, Ilyenkov's predilection toward Spinoza was the source of this fault. Although the claim that Ilyenkov had an "objectivistic" tendency was not quite unfounded, Batishchev's own knowledge of Spinoza was rather superficial—he saw in him a merciless determinist and a thinker of totality.[5]

The prevalent picture of Spinoza in Soviet philosophy was thus that of a "metaphysical materialist" who had some "dialectical ideas" (which, however, were seldom specified). But there was yet another distinctive trait of the Soviet Spinoza interpretation(s). This was the trend toward ontology, where matter—or the "materialist solution of the main question of philosophy"—took priority over thinking, and thus over the subjective factor, too. This is a trait we might call "ontologism." As such, it was characteristic for pre-revolutionary Russian philosophy, too, and reflected the unwillingness of many Russian thinkers to accept the Copernican turn of modern philosophy, which placed the cognizing subject into the foreground of philosophical enquiry. Philosophy was for them rather a study of the Being than an analysis of human cognition.

As Sergei Mareev has stressed, the ontologism was reborn in Soviet Marxism and it was a constant feature of the whole Diamat tradition (Cf. Mareev 2009, 16). Spinoza himself should not be blamed for the ontologism of his Soviet interpreters. On the contrary, Spinoza begins his *Ethics* by defining the attributes of thought and extension as something, which the *intellect* "perceives in the substance as constituting its essence" (*Ethics* I, def. 4). If we take "extension" as a synonym of "matter" (which is a widespread interpretation), we must admit that Spinoza here seems to have accomplished a Copernican turn already a century before Kant, since matter is clearly dependent on how the human subject sees it—that is, epistemology has priority over ontology.

On the other hand, it is true that Spinoza's Copernican turn gets stuck halfway, since he had not yet developed a concept of human subjectivity. Actually, one can say that Spinoza's view of the human mind is rather crude, lacking an elaborated theory of the self-consciousness. He has nothing which could even remotely be compared with Kant's doctrine of the Transcendental Apperception.[6] So this "pre-Kantian" position which Spinoza held undoubtedly contributed to the trend toward ontologization which was so palpable in the Soviet Diamat.

## DELEUZE, ALTHUSSER, & CO.—SPINOZA AS "THE OTHER"

The earlier thinkers of the Western Marxist tradition, such as Lukács, Korsch, Gramsci or even Sartre (to mention the main exponents of the current as listed by Anderson) did not pay much attention to Spinoza. They were more interested in combining Marx with Hegel, or, as in the case of Sartre's existentialism, with their own philosophy. The picture of Spinoza created during the heyday of the Second International thus remained unchallenged at least until the 1950s. A turning point came in the 1960s, when both the "structuralist Marxist" Louis Althusser and the post-structuralist (or rather, postmodernist) Gilles Deleuze turned to Spinoza independently of each other. I have elsewhere given a more thorough and critical examination of Althusser's and Deleuze's Spinoza lecture (see Oittinen 1994), so it may suffice here to highlight some main points which are relevant for the scope of this paper.

Althusser's interest in Spinoza was linked to his much-debated and provocative thesis on Marxism as "theoretical anti-humanism." According to Althusser and his disciples, Marxism should be seen as a strictly objectivistic, even a scientistic doctrine. The human subject (subjectivity) was for them merely an illusionary (i.e. ideological) form of consciousness created by the circumstances of the bourgeois society and capitalist production. Because the core of humanism expressly lies in its view on Man as a subject, so it followed for the Althusserians that humanism, too, was but bourgeois ideology. Consequently, even dialectics, because it tries to thematize subject-object-relations, was nothing but a bourgeois ideological illusion. It had to be replaced with reflections on structural relations, purified of all "unscientific" humanism.

In carrying out this anti-humanistic programme of Marxism in his works of the 1960s, Althusser did not yet explicitly connect it with Spinoza, but a little later in the next decade, especially in the notorious booklet, *Éléments d'autocritique* (1974), he confessed that he and his disciples had been Spinozists. In fact, Spinoza's philosophy starts from strongly deterministic presuppositions and (so it at least seemed to the Althusser school) denied the idea of a free subject in criticising Descartes' conception of Man as "an empire within an empire."[7] Of the pupils of Althusser, Pierre Macherey in particular has systematized his master's interpretation of Spinoza. Macherey sketched in his *Hegel ou Spinoza* a rigidly deterministic picture of the Dutch thinker (see Macherey 1979). Macherey's Spinoza is an antipode not only to Descartes, but to the modern idea of a free subject in general: everything that takes place or happens in the world consists only of processes without a subject. This viewpoint implied a radical denial of dialectics and especially Hegel's philosophy, which were interpreted as illusory, "bourgeois" forms of thought. In the history of modern philosophy, Spinoza was the radical "Other," the anti-dialectician *par excellence*, whose full significance becomes clear only now, when the revolutions are sweeping the bourgeois society into the dustbin of history.

This Althusserian lecture on Spinoza was closely linked to the ultra-Leftism of the 1960s, which produced many other similar theories among the French intelligentsia and which from a present-day viewpoint already seem rather bizarre—for example, the strange predilection for Maoism.[8]

A yet more original kind of Spinoza *lecture* appeared in 1968, when Gilles Deleuze published his *Spinoza et la philosophie de l'expression*. The book which formed a part of Deleuze's habilitation (the other part was *Différence et répetition*, which came a year later) made him famous and laid the foundation for a new kind of Spinoza interpretation, which in many aspects conformed to that of the Althusserians despite the fact that Deleuze was not a Marxist. Deleuze, one of the important figures behind the breakthrough of postmodernism in the latter half of the twentieth century, is an elusive thinker and it is not easy to capture his thought in a few sentences.

The starting-point of Deleuze's interpretation, to which the title of his book refers, was his discovery that Spinoza uses the verb *exprimere* ("to express") in several central definitions of his *Ethics*. So, for example, in one of the initial definitions opening the first part of the book, Spinoza writes that he understands by God an absolutely infinite Being, consisting of infinite attributes, of which everyone *expresses* the eternal and infinite essence.[9] Deleuze's observation is of course, as such, correct, although one must at once add that the entries *sub verbo* "exprimere" in Emilia Giancotti Boscherini's well-known Spinoza dictionary listing the occurrences of the word in Spinoza's *oeuvre* are not especially numerous (cf. Giancotti Boscherini 1970, 410–411). One can thus question Deleuze's claim that this word delivers to us a key to Spinoza's system.

Be that as it may, the Deleuzian idea of an expressive substance contrasts at first sight favourably with the older idea of the Plekhanovian-Deborinite orthodoxy of substance as matter which in Soviet Marxism-Leninism, of course, was defined according to the form given by Lenin in 1908:

> Matter is a philosophical category denoting the objective reality which is given to man by his sensations, and which is copied, photographed and reflected by our sensations, while existing independently of them. (Lenin 1962, 130)

However, reading Deleuze's Spinoza book more carefully, it soon becomes evident that his interpretation contains some highly problematic assertions. Deleuze tries to make out of Spinoza a precursor to his own "philosophy of difference." He claims that Spinoza's doctrine is thoroughly affirmative. For Spinoza, Being is always affirmative; the negativity as such does not exist at all. Hence, according to Deleuze (and here he thinks quite in the same fashion as the Althusserians) Spinoza is not a dialectic thinker. The dialectician thinks in the concepts of Being and Other (Hegel's German terms are *Sein* and *Anderssein*), which always imply some kind of negativity, because the Other is constituted by its negative relation to that of which it is the Other. Deleuze was even more resolute than the Althusserians in his critique of dialectics. He said outright that dialectics is "the form of thinking I hate most."

Another central point in Deleuze's interpretation is that he connects Spinoza with Nietzsche. Whilst the Althusserians had a rather neutral attitude to Nietzscheanism, for Deleuze there exists a long historical line of "emancipatory thinking," starting from Epicurus, continuing in Spinoza and culminating in Nietzsche. According to Deleuze, Nietzsche is the most important "subversive" thinker, even more important than Marx. Both Spinoza and Nietzsche are philosophers of emancipation, but not in the political sense that Marx had thought the emancipative processes to be. On the contrary: Spinoza and Nietzsche seek for Man only a personal liberation from sorrow, resentment and negative effects. Spinoza does not only precede Nietzsche in the fact that he denounces the received morals and values of the society of his days; he preaches, in addition, a "philosophy of joy" which is almost identical to the Dionysic worldview so revered and recommended by Nietzsche. It is only consequent that Deleuze ends up with interpreting the Spinozistic "wise" *(vir sapiens)* as a kind of Nietzschean *Übermensch*.

How should one evaluate the Deleuzian interpretation of Spinoza? There exists already a vast literature on the subject, and here I cannot, of course, go into detail. There are, however, two points I would stress. First, I do not find the critique of dialectics by the Althusserians and Deleuze convincing, not to speak of their attempts to stylise Spinoza into a bailsman of their views. Contrary to what, for example, Deleuze claims, Spinoza operates expressly with the concepts of Being and Other. Moreover, these concepts are quite central in his metaphysics, as one can easily see already in the first definitions of the *Ethics*. Spinoza stresses here that in the created nature *(Natura naturata)*, the relations between entities (i.e. the *modi*) are defined by otherness: *"Per modum intelligo id, quod in alio est et per alio concipitur"* (*Ethics* I, def. 5). This is quite a "dialectical" figure and can well be compared to what Hegel writes in his *Wissenschaft der Logik* on the relations between *Sein, Anderssein* and *Sein-in-Anderem*. In my book *Spinozistische Dialektik* (1994), I have attempted to show that Spinoza's *Ethics* abounds with such dialectical figures and topoi, so I will not delve further into the matter here.[10] Suffice it to say, that Soviet historians of philosophy were right in claiming that there exist "elements of dialectics" in Spinoza, although they did not bother to discuss them, save occasional references to the concept of *causa sui*.

The second point is that it is rather problematic to connect the perspectives of emancipation with Nietzsche's teaching. True, Nietzsche is a polyvalent thinker and one would do him an injustice if one saw him only as a reactionary and a direct precursor of Nazi thought (as, for example, György Lukács did in his famous analysis *Die Zerstörung der Vernunft*. But it is, on the other hand, quite obvious that Nietzsche is not a thinker of emancipation in the same sense in which Spinoza, the eighteenth century Enlightenment philosophers, or Marx were. Actually, Deleuze defines Nietzsche's character very accurately when he writes that Nietzsche is a *subversive* thinker. That is the point! Subversion, i.e. a more or less anarchistic mutiny without clearly defined goals, is the *differentia specifica* of the radicalism inspired by Nietzscheanism—not emancipation.

Furthermore, it is just this "subversiveness" which is the hallmark of present-day Western radical Spinozism, often (but not always) in connection with Marxism. The Deleuzian interpretation has been in most of its main tenets continued by Antonio Negri, the former theoretician of the Italian "autonomous Left," in a very suggestive and ingenious manner. His seminal books *L'anomalia selvaggia* (1981), flanked a decade later by *Spinoza sovversivo* (sic!) in 1992, have laid the foundation for that which we can today call "Left Spinozism." It is a particularly influential current in Italy and France. In these countries, several books on Spinoza and Spinozism are published every year, and in most of them the basic presuppositions of the Deleuzian-Negrian interpretation have been accepted without question.

Western—or maybe better expressed as Franco-Italian—Left Spinozism seems to me to be a parallel phenomenon to the "Left Nietzscheanism" analyzed recently by the German-American scholar Jan Rehmann.[11] Rehmann, who belongs to the *Das Argument* group of German Marxists, insists that the manner in which Western Left intellectuals since the 1970s have embraced a postmodernist Nietzscheanism is actually highly problematic, since Nietzsche's thought contains, despite attempts at a "benevolent" lecture of his works, a strong anti-humanist and reactionary potential, which makes the social and cultural projects of the Left relying on Nietzschean ideas very ambivalent. I believe the same can *mutatis mutandis* be said of the Left Spinozism in the tradition of Althusser, Deleuze and Negri.

## THE TWO SPINOZISMS

Now, after the brief survey above, it might be worth returning to the dichotomy between the Spinoza *lectures* of the Soviet philosophers on the one side, and the postmodernist Spinozism on the other. A comparison between them is motivated by both currents presenting themselves as leftist and pro-Marxist readings of Spinoza. I said at the beginning of my paper that there seem to be some quite deep-running dissonances between these different Spinoza interpretations. If we compare Western Left Spinozism with the Soviet view, which continues the tradition of the Spinoza reception of the Second International, it soon becomes obvious that the differences are grounded in the diversities of their philosophical backgrounds. While the postmodernist Left Spinozism relies above all on the legacy of Nietzsche, which it tries to interpret as a kind of theory of subversion, the Soviet Spinoza is read in the light of a classical materialist tradition, stretching from eighteenth century Enlightenment thinkers (Holbach, Helvétius) via Feuerbach to Marx. The differences between these two traditions of Spinoza *lecture* are so great that it is difficult to reconcile them.

I believe it is not trivial to emphasize this difference in the philosophical background. For it seems to me that many people who favor Spinoza and think that he is a radical and democratic theoretician still useful in the actual social and political discourses easily overlook these fundamental differences in the ways in which his philosophy has been interpreted by the left and radical thinkers. To make my point clear, I think it is useful to make the following juxtaposition, even if I hereby risk making some over-simplifications.

One is now, of course, tempted to ask which of these lines of interpretation is more faithful to the "authentic" Spinoza, the philosopher who lived in the seventeenth century. But one must be cautious in posing such questions, since the actualization of a philosopher always means an interpretation, at least to some degree. It is an illusion to believe that we could reconstruct a "pure" Spinoza and apply his ideas to the realities of our life today.

Nevertheless, I would claim that the postmodernist "Left Spinozism" has created a picture of Spinoza which in some respects arrives at a caricature. I have already mentioned some of the rather doubtful assertions Deleuze has made as regards the doctrine of Spinoza, such as his attempts to stylize him into a "philosopher of expression" or an anti-dialectician. It is important to note, though, that this distorted picture of Spinoza is a result of the interpretative method which Deleuze has

**Comparison of Western Left Spinozism with the Soviet Interpretation of Spinoza**

| *Western "Left" Spinozism* | *Soviet Spinoza Interpretation* |
|---|---|
| Philosophical background: Nietzsche, sometimes even Heidegger | Philosophical background: Enlightenment materialism, Feuerbach; Marx in the Diamat interpretation |
| Influenced by postmodernism and its break with the "old" Left | Continues the traditions of the "old" Left |
| Subjectivistic, voluntaristic | Objectivistic, deterministic |
| Spinozism seen as a "philosophy of expression" | A more or less "ontological" Spinoza interpretation |
| The emancipatory perspective in Spinozism seen as a "subversive" action | Emancipation must be based on science (Spinoza's *libera necessitas* as a forerunner of "scientific socialism") |
| Against Hegel, against dialectics | Pro-Hegelian, dialectical (there is a contradiction between the "metaphysical crust" of Spinoza's system and its dialectical contents) |

consistently applied. In his own words, Deleuze wanted "to see the history of philosophy as a sort of buggery." As he himself describes his method:

> I saw myself as taking an author from behind and giving him a child that would be his own offspring, yet monstrous. It was really important for it to be his own child, because the author had to actually say all I had him saying. But the child was bound to be monstrous too, because it resulted from all sorts of shifting, slipping, dislocations, and hidden emissions that I really enjoyed. (Deleuze 1997, 6)

If the Spinoza of postmodernist subversive radicalism is thus a "monstrous child" with little resemblance to its original model, what could be said of the Spinoza of the Soviets? I would dare to say that the Soviet picture of Spinoza is in many respects more like the actual archetype—but here one must at once make some severe reservations. Spinozism has been interpreted in the Diamat tradition as a kind of materialist ontology, moreover, as a doctrine which has not been able to reach the level of the dialectical subtleties of Marxist philosophy.

Another important—and very revealing—trait of the Soviet Spinoza lecture, which I am not able in my limited space to analyze here in depth, is that it has with only a few exceptions focused on Spinoza's theoretical philosophy and his substance metaphysics. Spinoza's political philosophy, and especially his radical theory of democracy, has mostly been bypassed by Soviet philosophers. The reason for this is rather obvious. If one had seriously begun to deal with Spinoza's theory of democracy in the Soviet Union, it would surely have led to difficulties, insofar it might have come in conflict with the Party monopoly of how to interpret politics. Here is yet another great point of difference between the Soviet and Western Left Spinozisms, since Negri's *idée-maître* has always been to apply Spinoza's concept of multitude to actual politics. Of course, Negri's anarchic *multitudo* cannot, as such, serve as a starting-point for a realistic politics for the Left,[12] but it has, nevertheless, produced much secondary literature on the subject, which even contains many interesting works on the perspectives of a "Spinozistic democracy"—I believe it suffices to mention here the anthology edited by Yves Citton and Fréderic Lordon which summarizes some points of the recent discussion (Citton and Lordon. 2008).

So, what remains on the balance sheet after this comparison of the Soviet and Western Left interpretations of Spinoza? I think we should not hurry in making final assertions. However, in connection with the new renaissance of Marxist thought that we are witnessing today, I would make a prediction: new attempts to read Spinoza will emerge—attempts which are more able to give an adequate picture of Spinoza and the importance of his thought than the previous ones have been.

## NOTES

1. In a review of Jakob Stern's popular book on Spinoza, Mehring wrote: "Spinoza was a poor devil, much poorer than Kant, but in him there were no traces of an anxious philistine, and he would never have surrounded to a meek concession toward the authorities [like Kant's sentence] 'I had to cancel the knowledge in order to make room for faith'" (Mehring 1907/08, 673).

2. Akselrod (Ortodoks) 1925, 144–168, quoted here from Maidanskij 2012, 541. Maidanskij addresses Akselrod's interpretation saying that it "reminds of Neo-Kantian portraits of the philosopher" as a "God-intoxicated atheist" (Maidanskij 2012, 792).
3. That the concept of "Menshevizing Idealism" actually was but a political label intended to justify the Stalinist turn of 1929/30 and devoid of authentic philosophical content, is well documented, such as in the work of Yakhot 2012.
4. I have tried to lay first foundations of such an investigation in: Oittinen 2005, 319–338.
5. For a survey on the Ilyenkov–Batishchev controversy, see Oittinen 2011, 13–20.
6. For Spinoza, the mind *(mens)* is, basically, nothing but an idea of the body, as he formulates in *Ethics* II, prop. 13: *Objectum ideae, humanam Mentem constituentis, est Corpus, sive certus Extensionis modus actu existens, & nihil aliud.* True, Spinoza stresses, too, that the human mind is necessarily a part of the infinite intellect of God (*mentem humanam partem esse infiniti intellectus Dei—Ethics* II, prop. 11 coroll.), which is an original insight in the trans-individual determination of the mind and thinking, but even this assertion does not imply any idea of self-consciousness.
7. So Spinoza in the Preface of Part III of *Ethics*: "there are many [. . .] which seem to regard Man in Nature as an empire within an empire (*hominem in natura, veluti imperium in imperio, concipere videntur*)." The context makes it clear that Spinoza is hinting here at the Cartesian doctrine of the thinking I as a substance quite independent from the material nature.
8. An interesting analysis of these intellectual meanders is given, for example, in Richard Wolin 2010.
9. *Ethics* I, def. 6: *Per Deum intelligo ens abolute infinitum, hoc est, substantiam constantem infinitis attributis, quorum unumquodque aeternam, & infinitam essentiam exprimit.*
10. For further discussion, see in addition Oittinen 2008.
11. See Rehmann 2004. Despite its good argument, the book has passed almost unnoticed in the Anglophone world, but there is an Italian translation: Rehmann 2009.
12. For a well-founded critique of Negri's ideas around the *multitudo*, see for example Hindrichs 2006.

## BIBLIOGRAPHY


Akselrod (Ortodoks), Lubov' I. 1925. "Spinoza i materialism" [Spinoza and Materialism]. In: *Krasnaja Nov'* (7):144–168.

Althusser, Louis. 1974. *Éléments d'autocritique*, Paris: Hachette.

Citton, Yves, Lordon, Frédéric (eds.). 2008. *Spinoza et les sciences sociales. De la puissance de la multitude à l'économie des affects*, Paris: Éditions Amsterdam coll. "Amsterdam Poches."

Deborin, Abram M. 1927. "Spinozism i marksizm" [Spinozismus and Marxismus]. In *Chronicon Spinozanum*, Tomus VI, Hagae Comitus: Curis Societatis Spinozanae.

Deleuze, Gilles. 1968. *Spinoza et le problème de l'expression*. Paris: Minuit.

Deleuze, Gilles. 1968. *Logique du sens*. Paris: Minuit.

Deleuze, Gilles. 1997. *Negotiations 1972–1990*, New York: Columbia Univ. Press.

Giancotti Boscherini, Emilia. 1970. *Lexicon Spinozanum*, vol. I. La Haye: Martinus Nijhoff.

Hindrichs, Gunnar (ed.). 2006. *Die Macht der Menge. Über die Aktualität einer Denkfigur Spinozas*. Heidelberg: Universitätsverlag Winter.

Lenin, Vladimir I., 1962. *Materialism and Empirio-Criticism*. In Lenin, Vladimir I. *Collected Works*, vol. 14. Moscow: Progress.

Macherey, Pierre. 1979. *Hegel ou Spinoza*, Paris: Maspero..

Maidanskij, Andrej. 2012. *Benedikt Spinoza: pro et contra*, Sankt-Peterburg: IRKhGA.

Mareev, Sergei N. 2009. *Iz istorii sovetskoj filosofii. Lukács—Vygotskij—Ilyenkov* [From the History of the Soviet Philosophy. Lukács—Vygotskij—Ilyenkov] Moscow: Kul'turnaja revolucij.

Mehring, Franz. 1907/08. [Review of] J. Stern, *Die Philosophie Spinozas*, in *Die Neue Zeit*, 26. Jg., 673–675.

Negri, Antionio. 1981. *L'anomalia selvaggia*, Rome: Feltrinelli.

Negri, Antonio. 1992. *Spinoza sovversivo: variazioni (in) attuali*, Roma: A. Pellicani.

Oittinen, Vesa. 1994. *Spinozistische Dialektik. Die Spinoza-Lektüre des französischen Strukturalismus und Poststrukturalismus*, Frankfurt am Main/Bern etc.: Peter Lang.

Oittinen, Vesa. 2005. "Eval'd Il'enkov as An Interpreter of Spinoza," In: *Studies in East European Thought*, No. 3, 319–338.

Oittinen, Vesa. 2008. "Dialektik und die Moderne—von Spinoza zu Marx." In: *Das Argument* 274 (1): 49–63.

Oittinen, Vesa. 2011. "Svobodnaja sub'ektivnost' protiv substantsializma: kritika Ilyenkova i Spinozy Genrikhom Batishchevym" [The Free Subjectivity Contra Substantialism: Genrikh Batizhchev's Critique of Ilyenkov and Spinoza]. In *Vestnik slavjanskikh kul'tur*, No. 2, 13–20.

Plekhanov, Georgi V. 1976. "Bernstein and Materialism." In *Selected Philosophical Works in Five Volumes*, Vol. II, Moscow: Progress Publishers.

Rehmann, Jan. 2004. *Postmoderner Links-Nietzscheanismus. Deleuze & Foucault—Eine Dekonstruktion*, Berlin: Argument Verlag.

Rehmann, Jan. 2009. *I Nietzscheani di sinistra. Foucault, Deleuze e il postmodernismo: una decostruzione*. Odradek: Edizioni. [French translation of Rehmann 2004.]

Sokolov, Vasily V. 1957. "Mirovozzrenie Benedikta Spinozy" [The Worldview of Benedict Spinoza]. In: B. Spinoza, *Izbrannye proizvedeniya*, tom I [B. Spinoza. Selected Works, vol. I], Moscow: Gos. izd. politicheskoy literatury, 1957, 5–65.

Spinoza, Benedictus. 1985. *Ethics*. In: B. Spinoza, *The Collected Writings of Spinoza*, 2 vols. Translated by Edwin Curley. Vol. 1. Princeton: Princeton University Press.—Cited as *Ethics*.

Vandek, Vagan, Timosko, Vladimir. 1932. "Predislovie" [Preface]. In: B. Spinoza, *Perepiska* [Correspondence], Moscow: Partiinoe izdaltel'stvo, 3–44.

Wolin, Richard. 2010. *The Wind from the East: French Intellectuals, the Cultural Revolution, and the Legacy of the 1960s*. Princeton: Princeton University Press.

Yakhot, Yekhoshua. 2012. *The Suppression of Philosophy in the USSR (The 1920s and 1930s)*, Oak Park, Michigan: Mehring Books.

CHAPTER ELEVEN

# On the Reception of German Idealism

MARINA F. BYKOVA

In his *Lectures on the History of Philosophy*, Hegel argues that the history of philosophy stands apart from any traditional historical discipline because its "content and matter" are not "the individual, according to the peculiarity of his disposition, talents, affections, the strength or weakness of his character." In the history of philosophy "the productions are all the more excellent the less is their merit attributed to a particular individual, the more . . . do they belong to freedom of thinking" (Hegel 1985, 9). Hegel calls these "productions" the "deeds of thought." These *deeds of freethinking*, which are an integral part of spiritual reality, comprise the main subject of the history of philosophy.

## HEGEL AND HISTORICO-PHILOSOPHICAL SCIENCE

My reference to Hegel is not incidental. The fact that the history of philosophy became a relatively independent discipline in German university education in the first half of the nineteenth century is often associated with Hegel's influence. Indeed, Hegel was one of the first thinkers who made the history of philosophy essential to his philosophical system, and thus he brought attention to both the historicity of philosophy and the philosophical nature of history itself. Relying on the results of his predecessors—such as Johann Jakob Brucker, Wilhelm Gottlieb Tenneman, and Johann Gottlieb Buhle, the authors of the comprehensive historico-philosophical compendiums[1]—Hegel introduced the idea of the shared identity between philosophy as a system of rational cognition and the history of philosophy. While for Hegel the history of philosophy appeared as a succession of philosophical schools, attitudes and movements, he never intended to develop a descriptive chronicle of philosophy's historical progression. He associated the history of philosophy with free thought and how it penetrates nature and spirit. The study of the "deeds of thought" could be only a field of reflective knowledge, which Hegel conceived as a philosophy of the history of philosophy. Aimed at assessing the real history of the human spirit, it must be impartial and cannot serve any particular interest or end; its conception is "to be established in a scientific, and not in an arbitrary, way" (Hegel 1985, 7). Hegel thus presents the history of philosophy as a *science* of spirit.

It is this tradition that has been pursued in Russian philosophy since the early stages of the emergence of the historico-philosophical discipline. What is special about the Russian model of the history of philosophy is that the latter has a *scientific* status, which implies a systematic and holistic approach to the subject matter. A subject of its own discipline, the history of philosophy aims at tracing a progression of philosophy from its origin through a variety of historical epochs to explain how it is expressed in philosophical texts, theories, and concepts. Not only is its focus its own content, but it is also shaped by the spiritual aspirations of history, and this science of spirit is inherently reflective and naturally resistant to indoctrination and bigotry. For some commentators this explains why in contrast to many other philosophical disciplines that prevailed in the Soviet period—such as dialectical or historical materialism, which for ideological and political reasons were limited or completely devoid of independent thinking—the historico-philosophical science found itself, relatively speaking, in a more favorable situation. This, however, was not merely because the history of philosophy, focusing on the past, happened to be somewhat remote from the "pressing" ideological and political issues of the time. Neither a narrow specialization nor a high level of scholarship in the historical research of philosophy had been the determining factors either. Official philosophy, which regarded itself as a faithful adherent and direct successor of Marx's philosophical doctrine, needed a thorough theoretical justification for its unique position. Charged with this task, the history of philosophy turned out to be that very area of philosophical investigation where critical thinking and philosophical reflection came to be not just tolerated, but de facto imposed as important requirements. This relative immunity of the historico-philosophical discipline from restrictions on freedom of philosophical thought attracted a considerable number of original thinkers to it. Many brilliant scholars, including those who began their careers working in other philosophical areas and disciplines, eventually found their asylum in the history of philosophy as the field most attuned to freedom of thought.

However, it would be a mistake to think—and such a view is still common in both Russian and Western literature on the philosophy of the Soviet period—that the history of philosophy was a happy exception to the general rule and did not experience any ideological pressures. Those who support this view argue that freedom from ideological control by the state allegedly allowed the history of philosophy to "save face" and remain one of the last "strongholds" of philosophical culture in the Soviet period. In fact, Soviet historico-philosophical science did not escape ideological confusion and muzzling either, and it had its own share of humiliation. It was entrusted with two tasks: first, to give a new interpretation of the entire (or immediately preceding) history of philosophy as a pre-history of Marxist-Leninist theory (or the Soviet version of Marxism), and, second, to "deepen and develop in a comprehensive way" the Leninist criticism of the so-called bourgeois philosophy. A heavy ideological predicament, indeed! This makes it even more significant that in spite of damaging ideological and political influences, historico-philosophical studies produced during the Soviet period did not turn into an uncritical defense of some philosophical theories and indiscriminate criticism of others. Furthermore, for the most part, these studies remained best examples of well-justified critical philosophical analyses, both in their grasp and quality. And, in some respect, it was even superior to the foremost standards of world scholarship in the history of philosophy.[2]

Of course, not everything went smoothly. Like other areas of philosophical study, the history of philosophy also experienced setbacks and problems, some of them associated with an ideologically driven misconception of a number of topics and theories. The consequences of this are felt even today. One of such "troublesome issues" of the Russian historico-philosophical science came to be its treatment of classical German thought in general and of German idealism in particular. This topic is my focus in the present chapter. I shall discuss the peculiarities of the Russian reception of classic German philosophy and show how political and ideological changes in the country shaped the study of German idealism. I argue that despite political and philosophical struggles that marked the Russian history of philosophy scholarship of the Soviet period, the study of German idealism continued to advance. Yet, the most productive and largely innovative work emerged in the second half of the last century, a period associated with the fundamental changes in many areas of life in Soviet Russia. These changes have been reflected in the radical shift in values and norms, including those playing a decisive role in the history of philosophy. In this chapter, I shall explore some of the most interesting results of the Russian scholarship on German idealism produced in this period. An important contribution to the field, this work remains unfairly unknown and largely ignored in the West today.

However, before turning my attention to the second half of the twentieth century, I find it necessary to provide a historical context important for understanding the specific situation that has developed in Russia with regard to classical German philosophy by the middle of the twentieth century.

## ON THE INFLUENCE OF GERMAN IDEALISM IN RUSSIA AT THE END OF THE NINETEENTH CENTURY AND FIRST HALF OF THE TWENTIETH CENTURY

The reception of German idealism in Russia has a long and complex history. While the first works discussing Kant had been published in St. Petersburg as early as in 1805 (Lubkin 1805)—only one year after the philosopher's death—it was not until the late 1820s–early 1830s that Russian intellectuals became acquainted with German idealism through their encounter with the works of Hegel and Schelling, which they began, at first mostly uncritically, assimilating.

An event of a vital significance for Russian intellectual life in general, the exposure to German idealist theories was instrumental to the emerging in Russia of a genuine philosophy, which originally appeared as a mixture of religious, psychological, speculative-metaphysical, and cosmological thoughts and ideas. There was a short-lived period of pure admiration and uncritical enthusiasm for German idealism, but this quickly gave way to constructive analyses and reflection upon the legacy of classical German thought, whose central topics began increasingly entering into local philosophical discourse and came to occupy a prominent place in the second half of the nineteenth century.

One of Russia's earliest introductions to German idealism was Alexander Galich's two-volume *History of Philosophical Systems* from 1818–1819. Recently returned from his study in Germany, where he became exposed to the pioneering philosophical ideas of the time, Galich offered an extensive exposition of Schelling's philosophical views and perhaps the first Russian discussion of Hegel, particularly of his *Science of Logic*. Even in the troublesome atmosphere of imperial Russia—a gloomy period for Russian philosophy and intellectual life—a presence of German idealist thought, as well as of themes and topics central for German thinkers, have always been very evident in Russian intellectual discussions. In Moscow, there was an active group of young former university students who organized a philosophical circle led by the poet Nikolai Stankevich. This group took it upon itself to systematically study German idealist philosophy. While initially their study focused on Kant, they soon gradually progressed to Fichte, Schelling, and Hegel. One of the relentless representatives of the Circle was Mikhail Bakunin, who joined the group around 1835. A year later, Bakunin produced the first Russian translations of two works by Fichte: *Some Lectures Concerning the Scholar's Vocation* and *The Way to a Blessed Life*. The second one, as Bakunin famously claimed, remained his favorite book for the rest of his life.

In Moscow and St. Petersburg, Schelling's influence dominated philosophical debates about natural sciences and their true place within other academic disciplines. There emerged a fair number of original Schellingians, such as Daniil Vellansky, Mikhail Pavlov, and the aforementioned Alexander Galich. The early "Kiev School" with its focus on the history of Western philosophy, most notably on its insights into epistemology, has seen a strong influence of Fichte, especially evident in works by Josef Mikhnevich.

Kant's philosophy remained relatively unimportant for Russian thought until the end of the nineteenth century. For more than six decades, Russia was the land of Hegel and Schelling par excellence. The situation began to change only in the 1880s–1890s with the publication of the first Russian translations of Kant's major works, including all three of his *Critiques*.[3] By the end of the nineteenth century and beginning of the twentieth century, Kant's influence in Russia could be felt not only among philosophers, but also among broader groups of intellectuals which included social thinkers, writers, poets, and politicians. To some extent, this echoed the Neo-Kantianism movement in Germany, but had some uniquely Russian characteristics.[4] Unsurprisingly, however, the "turn" to Kant at the end of the nineteenth century was largely motivated by a deeper study of the philosophies of Hegel and Schelling, whose ideas dominated the local terrain at that time, and whose comprehensive study had required a re-examination of Kant's critical philosophy.

In the 1840s, most of philosophical discussions turned exclusively to Hegel and his philosophical system, which was mostly received with great enthusiasm yet with little appreciation for the actual meaning of Hegel's writings.[5] Some of Hegel's key works—such as the *Phenomenology of Spirit*—remained virtually unknown in Russia until the 1890s.[6] In spite of this, nineteenth-century Russian philosophy developed under a strong influence of Hegelian ideas, and much of the Russian religious philosophy of the time was a unique blend of Hegel and Slavophilism. Impressed by Hegel's metaphysics, Russian thinkers came to recognize its overly religious content and ostensibly Christian connotations. The Hegelian system was also viewed as instrumental in understanding Russia's history of violent cultural alternations.[7]

Yet, although the reception of German idealism in nineteenth-century Russia was very influential, and the ideas of Hegel (as well as Schelling, and perhaps to a lesser extent, Fichte) profoundly affected Russian religious philosophical thought, the latter was not a pure imitation or uncritical adaptation of Western philosophies of the time. Even those most receptive to foreign ideas adopted them with significant qualifications, which reflected specifically Russian concerns and interests. While at the end of the nineteenth century most of these concerns had a purely religious and theological character, largely determined by the Russian Orthodox Church's interest in Plato (so-called Christian Platonism), at the end of the nineteenth to the early twentieth century this interest had shifted more toward ontological and ethical issues. This, in turn, caused a renewed interest in Kant and his Critical philosophy. Most prominent figures in Russian philosophy of the time, such as Vladimir Solovyov, Sergei Trubetskoi, Semyon Frank, Nikolai Berdyaev, and Nikolai Lossky, did not only draw their inspiration from Kant, but also felt the need to address the issues central to Kant's critical philosophy, and even recast Kant's transcendental idealism into a new theory. Around this time, Russia saw a blossoming of Kantianism that eventually led to the significant development of Russian Kant scholarship.[8]

However, in the years immediately preceding and immediately following the October Revolution of 1917, Kant's philosophy in Russia was almost consigned to oblivion. Many consider it an inevitable consequence of a decline of philosophical activity in Bolshevik Russia after many original (non-Marxist) philosophers had fled or been banished from the country. Undoubtedly, a mass exodus of intelligentsia that included many brilliant thinkers, writers, and other *hommes de lettres* had a truly devastating and long-lasting impact on Russian philosophy, culture, and general intellectual discourse. However, the reason Kant had fallen out of favor with Russian intellectuals at that time was of a peculiar ideological nature, and it might be rather viewed as a result of an implementation of the infamous principle of partisanship in philosophy that Lenin championed in his book, *Materialism and Empiriocriticism* published in 1909 (Lenin 1977). In this work, viciously criticizing empiriocriticism as "a reactionary philosophy," Lenin warned that "behind the epistemological scholasticism of empiriocriticism one must not fail to see the struggle of parties in philosophy, a struggle which in the last analysis reflects the tendencies and ideologies of the antagonistic classes in modern society" (Lenin 1977, 358). The parties in philosophy to which Lenin referred are philosophical materialism and philosophical idealism, and the ideological struggle between the two concerns the question of the independently existing material world and, most important, of the primacy of matter. Defending philosophical materialism over philosophical idealism, or the supremacy of matter over consciousness, Lenin declared the primacy question as the basic question of philosophy and, simultaneously, made it the main evaluation criterion to use in assessing various philosophical movements, schools, and developments.

Approached through such a narrow evaluative lens, all philosophical schools, trends, theories, as well as the classical thinkers themselves became divided into two warring camps: those who recognized the primacy of matter (materialists) and those who insisted on the primacy of ideas or consciousness (idealists). For Lenin and his associates, the contradiction between materialism and idealism was far from being a purely theoretical question of ontology. It was rather a practical question of great importance. It was an irreconcilable struggle between the two opposing worldviews, introduced by the two "warring parties." This grew into a crucial ideological issue.

Officially confined to Marxist-Leninist thinking, philosophy had to embrace this division as an inescapable predicament, and, essentially, the entire history of philosophy in Soviet Russia was viewed as the arena of the struggle between materialism and idealism. Materialism was declared the single "true" view and was associated with the progressive development of philosophical thought, while idealism was accused of distorting the truth and linked to decline and regress. Therefore, everything labeled as idealistic—be this philosophical theories, trends, or even individual thinkers—awaited a tragic fate: it had to be inescapably exposed, overthrown and eradicated as erroneous and harmful. Kant was not spared the fate of many other giants of philosophical thought. In the same *Materialism and Empiriocriticism*, Lenin criticized him for being "insufficiently materialistic," portraying him as a reactionary philosopher, who would undermine cognition and promote an idealistic "thing-in-itself." In a political regime with a set ideology, this accusation unequivocally meant a ban on any official Kant scholarship.

However, while severely censuring Kant, Lenin simultaneously praised classical German philosophy as one of the main sources and components of Marxism.[9] This praise was taken as an approval, thus creating some opportunities for scholarship in German idealism. This was certainly not an easy task under a narrowly construed and uncompromised commitment to materialism. Yet, ironically, the scholarly interest essentially shifted toward Hegel, with whom the zenith of idealist philosophy is usually associated. Two factors contributed to this development.

First concerned methodology. In the Soviet period, the development of philosophy through history was traditionally described as a linear successive process, where each previous philosophical school or theory has been surpassed by those that follow it. Historical philosophy appeared then as a single vector process, and it was described as a ladder-like path that presented philosophical thought as ascending from uncomplicated and plain to radically advanced philosophical forms. Such an interpretation created a contorted and substantially impoverished picture of the real development of the world's historical and philosophical thought by not taking into account the vast variety and multidimensionality of philosophical development and by essentially ignoring the complexity of its intertwined trends and movement's vectors. Furthermore, according to this interpretation, each subsequent school, movement, or thinker was viewed as essentially transcending the historically preceding forms of philosophical thought, thus largely undermining the value and independent significance of each of these forms.

Applied to classical German philosophy, this interpretation led to a distorted picture where Hegel and his philosophical system appeared as the crown of the development of German idealism, while the systems of his immediate predecessors, such as Kant, Fichte, and Schelling, were considered only intermediate stages, inevitably leading to Hegel. It is worth mentioning that Friedrich Engels greatly contributed to shaping this fundamentally incorrect view of the progression of classical German thought. In his *Ludwig Feuerbach and the End of Classical German*

*Philosophy* (1886), he offered a linear, ladder-like interpretation of the development of the nineteenth century German philosophy. It is also worth mentioning that it was Engels who first rendered the term "classical German philosophy," which was later adopted by Lenin and used in the manuals of Soviet Marxism and has been in use ever since. This continues to mislead a wide audience of students of German philosophical thought.[10]

The second factor that produced a renewed interest in Hegel was of an ideological nature. Hegel's dialectics had long been regarded as the highest achievement in the development of German thought because it allegedly led to Marx. Thus, there was no surprise when, after the victory of Marxist-Leninist ideology in Bolshevik Russia, the scholarly interest greatly shifted toward Hegel, and the emphasis in the study of his philosophy was placed on his dialectics. While in the short run, it has appeared as a very significant development, which allowed the undertaking of a number of successful translation and publication projects—such as the fourteen-volumes academic edition of Hegel's *Collected Works* (Hegel 1929–1959)—in the long run, the restricted approach had rather negative result. Attempting to demonstrate loyalty to the regime, official Soviet philosophy began to downplay Hegel's idealism in order to venerate his dialectics, wrongly presenting it as the only living core of a decayed philosophical system. This project could not be successful simply because, in Hegel, both his dialectics and system are intrinsically interrelated and inseparably bound together, so that one cannot grasp the specific nature of his dialectics without understanding the profound content of his system.

Khrushchev's "thaw" had a significant impact on the revival of genuine interest in German idealism. The ease of ideological pressure created certain opportunities for the scholarly exchange of ideas and literature, both inside and outside of the country, and allowed for research and publication about new philosophical figures and topics that had previously suffered heavy ideological and political censorship. These notable changes undoubtedly greatly contributed to revitalizing scholarship in the history of philosophy and other other philosophical disciplines. However, I suggest that the resurgence of interest in German idealism was rather a consequence of internal processes that took place within Russian philosophy at that time. The most notable among those was a far-reaching revitalization of Marx studies that came into sight. For the first time since the 1917 Russian Revolution, Soviet scholars turned to the philosophical analysis of known and unknown writings by Marx, attempting to achieve an authentic reading of his theoretical legacy. That, in turn, required not only a good grasp of the philosophical origins of Marx's theory, but also a discussion of its content in the context of the world (and, primarily, German) historical and philosophical traditions.

## MARXIST HEGELIANISM AND HEGELIAN MARXISM

Russian appreciation of Marx and his intellectual legacy has a troublesome history, which is inseparable from and directly influenced by the development of Soviet Marxism. In just one generation, the Russian attitude toward Marx has transformed from an officially imposed admiration and a nearly obligatory reverence of his works in scholarly and essayistic publications and talks, to the present, near-total neglect.

Having lived for much of the last century under official Marxism, Russia has viewed Marx through its distorted prism. And while the Russian philosophical discourse has substantially changed over the past few decades, and dogmatic Marxism has been discredited and subjected to severe criticism, contemporary Russian philosophy might need more time to completely heal from the residual dogmatic thinking. Still associated with orthodox Marxism, Marx is not only out of fashion, but he is also denied philosophical significance in today's Russia.

To be sure, equating Marx with Marxism is not a uniquely Russian problem. Beginning with Engels, who pioneered a variety of ideas later adopted into official Marxist manuals, Marx has been consistently identified with Marxism. This gave rise to numerous misconceptions and misrepresentations of Marx's philosophical view, while his essential insights were obscured and rejected. Such an unfortunate situation has continued to persist even after the decline of official Marxism.

Thus, as I have argued elsewhere (Bykova 2014), recovering Marx from Marxism is one of the most pressing philosophical tasks, both in Russia and worldwide. Such a recovery involves freeing Marx not only from dogmatism but also from all versions of Marxism, including its classical kind emanating from Engels and his—highly accessible yet inaccurate—presentation of Marx's philosophical ideas in a series of works, both jointly and individually authored. It is crucial to distinguish between the thoughts and ideas formulated by Marx and those developed by Engels. For in dogmatic Marxism these two names have always been used together based on a faulty assumption of a supposedly shared view between the two thinkers. Ironically, Marx is often introduced merely as a social scientist, historian, and revolutionary, while Engels is considered a philosopher. Although I am not able to delve into details here, I would like only to say that this is clearly an erroneous judgment. Marx is an original and dynamic thinker, and his views do not always coincide with those of Engels; he is able to penetrate the very depths of many important phenomena that often remain unnoticed by his lifelong associate and collaborator. Even if Marx's professional training in philosophy might be contested, the philosophical dimension is central to his economic and political works. In this sense, his philosophical writings are not limited, as many believe, only to his "Economic and Philosophical Manuscripts of 1844"; his main work—the *Capital*—is also a significant contribution to philosophical thought and should be treated accordingly.

In spite of appearing to be off-topic, the above thoughts have a direct relevance to our discussion. As I already mentioned, in the late 1950s and early 1960s—partially under the influence of Khrushchev's "thaw"—Marx scholarship in Russia underwent significant changes. In addition to the already existing (and dominating) ideologically driven dogmatic Marxism, there emerged a fundamentally new type of Marxism, which was later dubbed creative. In its design and actual content, this was not Marxism *per se*. It was rather an effort to return to the genuine Marx, largely buried by prevailing official Marxism. It focused on a careful analysis of Marx's writings, including his *Capital* and later also his early texts.[11] In essence, this was a departure from dogmatic Marxism and a turn toward sound philosophical Marx studies, a process which largely coincided with a renewed interest in Marx in the Western philosophy. Up to the 1950s–1960s, Russia had been enforcing the obligatory citations from the "founding fathers" of Marxism to Leninism, especially from

Marx's writings, but the real content of those writings remained virtually unknown. Marx's ideas, while widely circulated and endorsed as true, suffered from a primitive understanding and misconception. The historical significance of Marx came to be seen mainly as Marx's materialist reinterpretation of Hegel, where this reinterpretation was perceived as a pure mechanistic process of "turning Hegel, who was standing on his head back on his feet again." There was a lack of deep comprehension of Hegel and German idealism. Similarly, a grasp of Marx's writings, especially of his *Capital*, was insufficient for any serious philosophical work.

A competent analysis of the logic of the *Capital* had been launched only in the late 1950s, and one of the first works on this topic was the book *The Dialectics of the Abstract and the Concrete in Marx's "Capital"* by Evald Ilyenkov, which first appeared in an abbreviated version in 1960. Marx's *Capital* also served as a source for Alexander Zinoviev's doctoral dissertation, which was a work in logic rather than the history of philosophy (Zinoviev 2002). Around the same time, other scholars began publishing their works on Marx. Merab Mamardashvili's first essays on "transformed forms of consciousness" in Marx, the books by Yuri Davydov and Nikolai Lapin, as well as the articles by Mark Turovsky and Genrikh Batishchev were released. In the next few years, Pavel Kopnin, Evgenii Sitkovski, Mark Rosental, Vladislav Lektorsky, Victor Vazyulin and some others authored works that also attempted to rethink Marx's philosophical legacy.

However, the significance of the radical shift in philosophy in the Soviet Union in the 1960s was not limited only to a formation of a creative Marxism and the development of genuine Marx scholarship.[12] It became clear that a serious study of Marx required a change in attitude to German idealism. It was necessary to understand the logic of Marx's thought, and therefore, to rethink that on which it is based—Hegel's philosophical system and his dialectics. Therefore, the theme of dialectical logic has become the focus of creative philosophical discussions of the time. Philosophical works on Marx somehow turned to Hegel and his analysis of contradictions, his dialectics of the logical and the historical, the universal and the individual, etc. Essentially groundbreaking philosophical studies—which remained virtually unnoticed by Western scholars—they convincingly demonstrated the Hegelianism of Marx and his *Capital*.[13] Such studies were by no means a safe exercise in Soviet Russia, since in official circles this was perceived as a threat to the very foundation of Soviet ideology and was openly persecuted. Nevertheless, this development gave a great impulse to advancing historico-philosophical studies in general, and most notably, scholarly work on German idealism. It did not only stimulate a renewed interest in Hegel and other German thinkers, but it also charted the way forward to the insightful study of classical German philosophy free from any ideological posture and motivation.

This period of the vital intellectual revival was characterized by a rapid increase in scholarly activity on German idealism, especially on Kant and Hegel, which marked the beginning of genuine Kant and Hegel scholarship in Soviet Russia. Research on Fichte and Schelling also intensified, allowing for a deeper analysis of the thinkers' philosophical systems, concepts, and ideas. Scholarly works by Valentin Asmus, Arsenij Gulyga, Konstantin Bakradze, and Aleksei Bogomolov made significant contributions to the study of the philosophical systems of German idealists, and thus laid the groundwork for a broader and deeper Russian reception of their ideas.[14]

Perhaps one of the major achievements of that time was the 1963 launching of a series called *Filosofskoe nasledie* [Philosophical Heritage], which had published an impressive body of classical philosophical literature, including key texts of German idealists.[15] Not all translations that appeared in this series were of equally good quality, and some of them, including reprints of early translations, could have benefited from thorough editing, but the very fact that many earlier inaccessible texts became available contributed to a growing interest in German idealists, giving vitality to the study of their thoughts.

Interestingly, in the 1960s, Hegel and his dialectics remained a high research priority. The "ladder" approach still prevailed in the history of philosophy in general and in the study of classic German idealism in particular. Considered from this viewpoint, German idealism appeared as a progression toward Hegel and his philosophical system, whereas theories developed by Kant, Fichte, and Schelling did not have any independent significance. Instead, they were considered a sort of "stepping stone," inevitably leading to the system of Hegel. It is therefore no coincidence that many prominent Russian thinkers, such as Merab Mamardashvili, Vladislav Kelle, Yury Davydov, and some others began their journey into philosophy through an intensive study of Hegel's thought, and many of them advocated for ideas of Hegelian Marxism even at the latter stages of their careers.

Obviously, this "ladder" approach essentially misconstrued both the narrative of the development of classic German idealism and the real content of the philosophical systems introduced by thinkers representing this tradition. The problem was not only that thoughts of such German philosophers as Kant, Fichte and Schelling came to be evaluated only through the "prism" of Hegel's; the entire traditions and schools of thought appeared beyond the scope of the Russian historico-philosophical research interest. This, for example, happened to the German Enlightenment, whose importance for Kant and nineteenth century German philosophy was recognized only recently. A significance of Early German Romanticism has also been largely overlooked, leading to an inadequate picture of the history of ideas central to German thinkers. In addition to existing gaps in the scope of scholarly work, the Marxist interpretation of classical German philosophy still suffered from ideological "residue" left in place by Leninism, which required one to view the entire historico-philosophical development through the prism of the fundamental question in philosophy, that of the primacy of matter.

However, instead of merely rejecting German idealism as erroneous, which would be more characteristic of earlier stages of dogmatic Marxism, there now was an attempt to find some hidden materialism in German idealist thought. This unachievable goal largely remained a wishful desire, but in some cases, it led to very artificial interpretations of German idealism and even the oversimplification of some of its key concepts, including dialectics (especially with regard to Kant and Fichte).

## GERMAN IDEALISM IN RUSSIAN HISTORICO-PHILOSOPHICAL STUDIES AFTER THE KHRUSHCHEV "THAW"

By the end of the 1970s, the situation with the study of nineteenth century German thought began to change, manifesting first of all, in a new fascination with Kant's philosophy. This shift was triggered by both ideological and practical concerns. First, institutions of higher education began offering courses on classical German philosophy. In these courses, Hegel was included along with other thinkers belonging to the tradition. And since Kant in the Russian model of the history of philosophy had always been regarded as the founder of the entire tradition, the study of his philosophical system became an urgent task. Second, from the 1970s onwards, ethical and moral topics and issues moved to the foreground of philosophical research, becoming the subjects of monographs and articles in their own right. This explains the growing interest in Kant's moral philosophy. Third, Khrushchev's "thaw" opened some opportunities for—still limited—contacts with philosophers abroad and allowed some access to Western philosophical literature. At that time, Western (especially Continental) philosophy was experiencing a kind of Kantian "booming" as a direct consequence of new publications of Kant's works, including newly discovered notes of his lectures. This could not escape the attention of Russian scholars, especially those fluent in German, who by that time became well-versed in the particularities of Kant's thought. All these processes significantly contributed to a notable intensification of research on Kant, and the number of publications on his philosophy began to grow. To be sure, not everything written on Kant in this period was of equal quality, and some of the publications that appeared around this time still remained confined to dogmatic (orthodox) Marxism. Nevertheless, this period produced groundbreaking studies exploring the conceptual difference between Kant's notions of "thing-in-itself" and the phenomenon (Piama Gaidenko, Teodor Oizerman), as well as analyzing Kant's central conceptions of time, space, intuition, understanding, and antinomies of reason (Arsenij Gulyga, Igor' Narsky).

Influenced by the results of Kant scholarship and in response to the growing interest within Marxist philosophy in such topics as freedom and autonomy and the problematic nature of moral agency and practical activity, there began emerging works on Fichte's philosophy, particularly on its key topic: activity as a means of the realization of freedom.[16]

Although the research devoted solely to Hegel's philosophy did not prevail during this period, Soviet Hegel studies continued to flourish beyond the 1960s, experiencing a kind of "renaissance" in the 1970s–1980s as a result of the extensive and productive translational and editorial work.[17] In the summer of 1974, Moscow welcomed the International Hegel Congress—one of the first international philosophical conferences held in Russia after Khrushchev's "thaw"—organized by the Internationale Hegel-Vereinigung and hosted by the Academy's Institute of Philosophy. Along with prominent Western Hegel scholars, many Soviet scholars working on topics in classical German philosophy attended the Congress, presenting papers and participating in numerous discussions.[18] This further motivated research on Hegel and German idealism.

However, the rigid ideological control of the mid-1970s, which effectively replaced Khrushchev's "thaw," and the subsequent situation of political stagnation had a damaging effect on research in the history of philosophy. Opportunities for dialogue with colleagues abroad became extremely rare and officially discouraged. Despite having already gained awareness of a variety of Western historico-philosophical traditional and schools, it was not always possible to escape political prejudices and to adequately express one's position in a manner free from Marxist clichés under heavy ideological pressure. Like many other historico-philosophical studies of this period, scholarly work on classical German philosophy was primarily Marxist, and often still with some ideological coloring. The following anecdote may illustrate this idea more clearly.

Back in 1974, Gulyga, in conversation with writer and mathematician Elena Venttsel (known by her pen name as Irina Grekova), pondering the then-contemporary situation in Russian philosophy, noted that Russia has been able to produce genuine philosophers. Among those, he continued, are a few Kantians (he considered himself one of them), Hegelians (such as Ilyenkov and some others), existentialists (here he pointed to Erikh Solovyov and Gaidenko), quite a few positivists, and one Platonist (referring to Alexei Losev). Puzzled, Venttsel asked, "and what is it about Marxists?"—"But they are all Marxists," answered disappointed Gulyga.[19] Thus, Gulyga's assessment accurately reflected the then-current status quo in historico-philosophical science.

The cardinal changes and unprecedented flourishing of Russian German idealism studies began in the mid-1980s. It could be seen as a scholarly reaction to a new "renaissance" of Kant and Hegel studies in Western Europe, most notably in Germany, which manifested primarily in the substantial development of textual studies based on the recently discovered and published original texts and other sources. Through restored contacts with intellectuals abroad and new access to Western professional literature, Russian scholars received an opportunity to participate in world discussions on the subject for the first time in several decades. This materialized into a series of foreign publications by Russian authors on a variety of topics in Kant's and Hegel's philosophy.[20] The Russian publications also grew in numbers. These high-quality works discussed specific concepts and issues central to German thinkers' philosophical systems, drawing material from their recently published writings. At about the same time, there was also considerably intensified research on Schelling and Fichte, whose major texts became available, including those previously unknown. Fundamentally new studies, both in nature and in quality, began to penetrate into an array of complex questions attempting to explicate some of the most difficult problems of German idealist thought. Instead of relying on Russian translations of classical works—which was a common practice in the earlier decades—new studies employed a method of close textual analysis of original philosophical texts. Such an approach proved to be very successful and prompted very intensive discussions of the merits, defects, and contemporary significance of classical German philosophy and some of the insights formulated by German thinkers.[21]

Without going into the specific philosophical details, I would like to stress that the changes that took place in this period were indeed paradigmatic. They concerned not only an introduction and inclusion in research of new topics and new texts, originally located beyond those traditionally discussed by Russian historians of philosophy. In addition to establishing novel research focuses and launching scholarly work on German thinkers' writings (previously unknown to the Russian audience), scholars began rethinking traditional themes and concepts and reinterpreting already known texts.

But perhaps the most important shift occurred in an attitude to philosophical research itself, which manifested in a total liberating from bias against classical German philosophy and idealism associated with this tradition. This led to a number of philosophically positive results. For example, on the basis of the textual analysis of Hegel's works, along with already well-known reading of his philosophical paradigm as inherently logical, theosophical and theological interpretations of his system were introduced and argued,[22] which would have been impossible a few years earlier under the dictate of militant materialism and atheism. Furthermore, famously, in the period of the absolute domination of dogmatic (orthodox) Marxism, if one was allowed to discuss classic German thinkers in an affirmative way, then they could only in the context of their contributions to the development of materialism and dialectics; all their other insights had to be subjected to criticism. By the end of the 1980s, this trend was certainly eradicated.

This, however, was soon replaced by another trend. As I mentioned earlier, after the collapse of the Soviet Union and the renunciation of Marxist ideology, not only the entire Marxist doctrine but also Marx himself fell out of favor in Russia. It was fashionable to reject everything that had even remote relation to Marx and Marxism, and this had a devastating effect on the attitude to Hegel too. A hostility to Hegel and his philosophy in post-communist Russia became so strong, that some tried not merely to break him, but destroy him entirely. In the 1990s, he was criticized not only for abstract thoughts and speculative constructions: based on misinterpretation of the socio-political and socio-ethical models of his philosophy, he was accused of being a theoretician of absolute power and even of a totalitarian regime.[23] Hegel's metaphysics was condemned for creating a cult of the universal, for "absolutizing" the universal and suppressing the individual, singular, and personal. Thus, it is no accident that serious Hegel studies were virtually absent in Russia until the early 2010s. The resulted gap has still been felt in contemporary Russian studies on Hegel, which are not so plenty in number.

In this regard, a recently published collection of essays written by an international group of authors and devoted to the 200th anniversary of Hegel's *Phenomenology of the Spirit* has been an important event (Motroshilova 2010). What makes this publication so valuable is that it succeeded in demonstrating the contemporary significance and relevance of Hegel's ideas not only for philosophy, but also for such disciplines as pedagogy, law theory, psychology, and other cognitive and social sciences. In this sense, a decisive step has been made in the direction of the complete overcoming of the hostility toward Hegel that still exists in Russian philosophical discourse.

This is not a place to discuss a status quo in the contemporary study of classical German philosophy in Russia. However, I would like to mention some growing research activity in the area of Fichte and Schelling studies. A series of new and improved translations of Fichte's and Schelling's texts has been published, as well as a number of specialized scholarly works discussing their philosophical systems. However, I should admit that currently the most impressive and productive research has been undertaken on Kant's philosophy.

Perhaps one of the most significant achievements in Russian Kant scholarship is a bilingual German-Russian edition of Kant's *Works* that now comprises five volumes (with three sub-volumes) and includes Kant's three *Critiques*, his main works on moral philosophy, and other short essays on practical philosophy (Motroshilova and Tuschling 1994–2014). This ongoing project is unique in both its conception and execution. This edition is a collective effort of leading Russian Kant scholars and their German colleagues from the University of Marburg. The general editors of the *Works* are Nelli Motroshilova and the late Burkhard Tuschling. The edition that began in 1994 provides new translations of Kant's works, which are the most accurate and informative Russian translations of these epochal philosophical texts. While clear and direct in style, these translations exhibit a philosophical and textual sophistication and recreate Kant's texts with the same interpretative nuances and richness as the originals. This is an outstanding edition because of the easy access to original texts, the quality of both translations and supplementary materials, and as such is of a great historico-philosophical value.

An important result of those positive changes in attitude to German idealism (and especially to Kant) that Russian history of philosophy has witnessed over the last 10–15 years, this impressive edition would not be possible without the serious work done in this field back in the 1990s that laid down a foundation for productive scholarly activity.

## CONCLUSION

If we try to summarize the achievements of Russian historians of philosophy—most specifically experts on classic German thought—we should first recognize and appreciate the originality and independence of their judgments. Indigenous and creative thinkers, Russian scholars never attempted to repeat or imitate classic German philosophers or the way in which they were interpreted in the West. The Russian history of philosophy always viewed a simple imitation and reproduction as ineffective and non-productive. This attitude persisted through the perception of German idealism both in pre-revolutionary Russian philosophy and in Marxist philosophy of the Soviet period. The Russian reception of German idealism has always been original, and in any situation, even the most difficult, it has reflected the specific cultural and intellectual needs of a particular historical period and philosophical aims associated with it.

Over the Soviet period, Russian studies in classical German philosophy—and especially in German idealism—suffered numerous ups and downs. However, despite all these difficulties, scholarship in German idealism never ceased, and Russian scholars succeeded in their complex undertakings. Furthermore, these studies and their results always appeared specifically Russian, addressing topics and issues that manifest the Russian spirit.

Russia's interest in classical German philosophy has traditionally focused on issues central to philosophy of right, moral philosophy, and philosophical anthropology. This applies not only to Kant, but also to Fichte and Hegel. Topics of human freedom and autonomy, the significance of human subjectivity, and the role of moral self-consciousness in shaping personality, i.e., topics of chief concerns for German idealists, have not only resonated with Russian scholars, but these issues became the subject of their own studies. This created opportunities for a deep philosophical reflection on ethical and moral issues, especially those relevant to Russian contemporary problems. Thus, the best works on moral and anthropological issues in German idealism (by such authors as E. Solovyov, Guseynov, Motroshilova,

Karimsky, and Gaidenko) go beyond traditional studies on Kant, Fichte, or Hegel, also making significant contributions to the development of special philosophical disciplines such as ethics, the philosophy of law, moral philosophy, as well as social and political theory.

Additionally, an ongoing interest in dialectics, especially in Hegelian dialectics, led to formulating the fundamental ideas of dialectical logic, which made it possible to explain such key dialectical notions and concepts as contradiction, negation, alienation, a unity of the opposites, the ascent from the abstract to the concrete, etc. Despite the increasingly growing body of philosophical work, the topic of dialectics is not addressed frequently. There is also not much literature that discusses Hegel's dialectics in a systematic and comprehensive way. In this sense, Russian scholarly work is a rare exception to this rather common situation. Hegelian dialectics received serious attention from Russian philosophers, and not only those steeped in the Marxist tradition. It would be no exaggeration to say that Russian scholars, such as Ilyenkov, Motroshilova, Oizerman, Karimsky, and Nersesyants produced some of the most insightful and compelling studies showing the centrality of dialectics for Hegel's philosophy. An in-depth analysis of a systematically developed exposition of dialectics led to an expansion of this topic to include complex epistemological questions. This allowed scholars to address a variety of issues associated with the logic and dialectics of cognition, including questions about the structure and content of thinking, as well as its nature. This is where works by German idealists provided an invaluable study material.

It is worth noting that discussions about Hegel's understanding of the social nature of thinking began in Russian historico-philosophical literature long before it became an important topic in Western Hegel studies. Similarly, Russian Fichte scholars began to appreciate the social character of Fichte's conception of freedom much earlier than their counterpart in the West did. Such examples are abound, and not only those that deal with German idealism and classic German thought.

I hope that the current policies of openness and collaboration and a philosophical dialogue free from any ideological or political prejudices will allow Russian scholars and their ideas to be heard and appreciated on a global scale.

## NOTES

1. Brucker was the author of *Historia Critica Philosophiae* [Critical History of Philosophy], originally published in five volumes that came out in 1742–1744; Tenneman is known for his twelve-volume *History of Philosophy* (1789–1819). Buhle wrote a massive *Manual (Lehrbuch) of the History of Philosophy and the Critical Literature on the Subject*, that appeared in 1796–1804 and included nine volumes.
2. There is much evidence in support of this claim, including international publications of Russian scholars, which were rather rare at that time. One example is a collection of articles written by Russian philosophers that appeared in Germany and was received with a great interest by the European readership (Motroshilova 1986). For the discussion of the philosophical value of the collection, as well as its reception in Europe, see the Book Review written by Evert van der Zweerde (1989). See also note 12 in this chapter.

3. The first translation of Kant's *Critique of Pure Reason*, prepared by Mikhail Vladislavlev, was published in St. Petersburg in 1867. Another substantially improved edition of the work, translated by Nikolai Sokolov, appeared in 1896–1897.
4. For more details about the Russian reception of Kant and his philosophy, see editor's Preface to the first volume of the bilingual German-Russian edition of Kant's *Works* (Motroshilova and Tuschling 1994–2014, 1:42–56). For a systematic analysis of the nineteenth century's studies on Kant in Russia, see Krouglov 2006.
5. The appropriation of Hegel in Russia was not an easy process. It was a path associated with the continuous struggle between the two warring camps: those who severely criticized Hegel and his philosophical system, and those who passionately supported the ideas of the philosopher and were ready to accept all of them without exception. An attitude toward the theoretical and practical consequences of Hegel's philosophy was similarly complicated.
6. Even then, only a few Russian intellectuals knew and understood the actual meaning and key ideas of Hegel's *Phenomenology of Spirit*. The broad Russian audience received access to the complete text only after publication of the first Russian translation of Hegel's work in 1913. Despite the immense significance of the event, the first translation prepared by Ernest Radlov could not serve as a reliable source for serious scholarly research due to numerous terminological mistakes and inaccuracies concerning the articulation of Hegel's ideas. It was not until 1937 that Gustav Shpet, known for his work in phenomenology, produced a substantially improved Russian translation of Hegel's *Phenomenology of Spirit*, which is still in use today.
7. About a far-reaching Russian engagement with Hegel's philosophy see Kliger, Bakhurst 2013, esp. 159–241.
8. For a comprehensive study of this period see: Kalinnikov 2005; Krouglov 2009.
9. In 1913, Lenin wrote an article titled "The Three Sources and Three Component Parts of Marxism" (Lenin 1977, 19:21–28). In this article (dedicated to the thirtieth anniversary of Marx's death) Lenin identified the three theoretical sources of Marxism: classical German philosophy, classical English political economy, and French utopian socialism. Here he also claimed that in the line of philosophical ancestry, Hegel and Feuerbach were the direct predecessors of Marxism, and that they made the greatest impact on the philosophical views of Marx and Engels.
10. According to this interpretation, classical German philosophy includes not only the idealist systems of Kant, Fichte, Schelling and Hegel, but also the materialist doctrine of Feuerbach, who allegedly managed to substantially transcend Hegel. As Engels argued, Feuerbach, "in many respects forms an intermediate link between Hegelian philosophy and our [his and Marx's] conception" (Engels 2016, 7).
11. Marx's early writings came into the focus of Russian scholars only in the early 1970s. First published in the early 1930s, they were suppressed under Stalin as the texts which did not entirely break with German idealism. They were released and began attracting scholarly attention only in the wake of Khrushchev's "thaw." See, for example, Lapin 1976.
12. For details on some specific features of Marx studies in Russian philosophy of the 1950s–1970s and the influence of these studies on the development of philosophical thought in Russia, see Motroshilova 2012, 52–64.
13. One of such examples is work by Victor Vazyulin, who, in his 1968 book on the logic of Marx's *Capital*, convincingly showed that Marx's thought in the *Capital* follows a

triple spiral path, thus reproducing the movement of Hegel's *Science of Logic* (Vazyulin 1968). Ten years later, Michael Theunissen, not familiar with Vazyulin's publication, proposed the same reading of Marx's *Capital* in his celebrated book, *Sein und Schein* [Being and Appearance] (Theunissen 1978, 142).

14. For details about this period's major publications on German idealism of these and other authors see *Selected Bibliography* included in this volume.

15. The series initiated by the Institute of Philosophy at the (then) Soviet Academy of Sciences was published by the publisher house "Mysl'." Conceived as an attempt to cover "all fundamental stages of the development of philosophical thought," this ambitious series was supposed to include 500 volumes. However, by the late 1990s the series was suspended and only 138 volumes came out. German idealism is represented in this series through works by Kant, Schelling, and Hegel. The series did not include Fichte's writings, which was negatively received by reviewers. Kant's writings appeared in the series as early as 1963 and included six volumes (1963–1966) of Kant's main texts on metaphysics and ethics. The first Schelling volume was published in 1966, and it contained only *Philosophy of Art*. In the early 1970s, Hegel's works came out and were organized into ten volumes. These volumes consisted of such works as *Science of Logic* (in 3 vols., 1970–1972), *Encyclopedia of the Philosophical Sciences* (in 3 vols.; 1974–1975, 1977), *Philosophy of Religion* (in 2 vols.; 1975, 1977), as well as a collection of short works written in different periods of the philosopher's career (1970–1971). In 1987 and 1989, the two volumes of Schelling's works appeared, followed by Hegel's *Philosophy of Right* published in this series in 1990.

    It is worth recalling that a model of classical German philosophy that dominated in the Soviet (Marxist) Russia, also included Feuerbach who along with the German idealists considered part of that philosophical movement. Interestingly, Feuerbach's works (in 3 vols; 1967) were released shortly after the series had been launched and several years before the appearance of Hegel's writings, which undoubtedly bore a certain ideological significance. It seemed to be a clear message that when answering the fundamental question of philosophy, a preference had to be given to materialism. Furthermore, in the introductory article to Feuerbach's writings, the main significance of Feuerbach was associated with his materialistic critique of Hegel and other German idealists.

16. In this context, works by Gaidenko are of a particular interest. Gaidenko was one of the first Soviet scholars to turn to a serious textological study of different versions of Fichte's *Wissenschaftslehre*. The project of *Wissenschaftslehre* also became a focus of research undertaken later by Gulyga and Dlugach. However, in this period, the topic that attracted the most attention of Russian scholars was Fichte's contribution to the development of dialectics. See, for example, works by Bakradze, Oizerman, and Narsky included in the *Selected Bibliography*.

17. See already mentioned publication of Hegel's works in the series "Philosophical Heritage." Particularly noteworthy here is the two-volume edition of Hegel's writings from various years (published in 1970–1971), which included newly translated essays and letters from Hegel's Jena and Berlin periods. Prepared by a highly engaged team of translators and commentators, able to masterfully navigate the intricacies of Hegel's thought, it was one of the best Hegel editions produced during the Soviet period that is still in use today. The volume opens with an extensive introductory article authored by one of the most brilliant classical German philosophy scholars of the Soviet era, Arsenij Gulyga. Among translators are such thinkers as Evald Ilyenkov,

Igor' Narsky, Anatoly Mikhailov, Tsolak Arzakanyan, Arsenij Gulyga, and others, who produced informed and lucid works on Hegel.

18. For details about the significance of the Congress for the development of the Soviet history of philosophy, as well as about Congress participants, see Motroshilova 2012, 84–92.
19. См. http://www.situation-rus.narod.ru/dialectic.htm
20. In this context, I would like to mention an impressive body of work by Gulyga that became accessible to Western readers. By that time, Gulyga had already established himself as one of the most original Russian scholars studying classical German philosophy. In addition to publishing special philosophical works (Gulyga 1986), he also produced the celebrated biographies of Hegel, Schelling, and Kant (Gulyga 1970; 1982; 1987), making complex ideas of German philosophers accessible to the broader audience. Gulyga's philosophical and literary talents and provocative writings earned him international recognition and fame. His biography of Hegel was translated into German as early as in 1975. This followed by translation of Gulyga's renowned *Immanuel Kant: His Life and Thought*, which was later published in both Germany and the US (Gulyga 1987). A few years earlier, Gulyga's article on Kant's aesthetics appeared in English translation in the journal *Soviet Studies in Philosophy* (Gulyga 1984). Other Russian scholars also began to enter the international scene. For example, Oizerman, Narsky, Bogomolov, Motroshilova, Lektorsky, Pogosyan and Nersesyants published their Hegel papers in a special volume of proceedings of the International Hegel Symposium (Henrich 1986). Around the same time, the Frankfurt publishing house Suhrkamp published a collection of eleven articles by Russian authors (Motroshilova 1986). Among the authors of the collection are outstanding Russian Kant, Fichte, and Hegel scholars—Gaidenko, E. Solovyov, Motroshilova, and others.
21. This period produced a great pleiad of Russian history of philosophy scholars working on German idealism, whose publications contributed to a better understanding of a number of ideas and notions put forward by German thinkers. They accomplished this by introducing Russian readers to a real complexity of German idealists' projects. These scholars did not only comment on classical texts, but also offered their own original readings of central concepts discussed in classical German philosophy, thus demonstrating its contemporary significance. Among those who shaped Russian reception of German idealist thought during this period were Gaidenko, Gulyga, Davydov, Dlugach, Karimsky, Motroshilova, Nersesyants, Oizerman, and Solovyev, along with Dzhangir Kerimov, Mikhail Kissel, Elena Mamut, Vladimir Shinkaruk, Alexander Volodin, and Vladimir Zhuchkov. In the second part of the 1980s, they were also joined by younger generation scholars, such as Marina Bykova, Andrei Krichevsky, and Andrei Sudakov. These scholars produced an impressive body of work on German idealism, which retains its scholarly value and continues to influence contemporary Russian scholarship in this field.
22. One of such examples is a theological interpretation of Hegel's project by Krichensky. Originally offered in his doctoral dissertation successfully defended in 1992, this position is developed in a more concise form in a book. See Bykova, Krichevsky 1993.
23. This view is similar to an interpretation of Hegel proposed by Ernst Cassirer and Karl Popper decades ago. While these inaccurate interpretations of Hegel had been since criticized and rejected in the West, they suddenly became popular among some Russian intellectuals after the collapse of the communist regime in Russia.

## BIBLIOGRAPHY


Bykova, Marina F. 2014. "On the Philosophical Relevance of Marx's Views Today," *Frontiers of Philosophy in China*, 9(3): 370–380.

Bykova, Marina F., Krichevsky, Andrei V. 1993. *Absoliutnaja ideja i absoliutnyi spirit v filosofii Gegelia*. [Absolute Idea and Absolute Spirit in the Philosophy of Hegel]. Moscow: Nauka.

Engels, Frederick. 2016. *Ludwig Feuerbach and the End of Classical German Philosophy*, 1–69. Create Space: LeoPard Books.

Gaidenko, Piama P. 1979. *Filosofiya Fichte i sovremennost'* [Fichte's Philosophy and the Contemporary Time]. Moscow: Mysl'.

Gaidenko, Piama P. 1990. *Paradoksy svobody v uchenii Fichte* [Paradoxes of Freedom in Fichte]. Moscow: Nauka.

Gulyga, Arsenij V. 1970. *Gegel'* [Hegel]. Moscow: Molodaja gvardija.

Gulyga, Arsenij V. 1982. *Shelling* [Schelling]. Moscow: Molodaja gvardija.

Gulyga, Arsenij V. 1984. "The Beautiful: Its Principles," *Soviet Studies in Philosophy*, 22 (3): 49–67.

Gulyga, Arsenij V. 1987. *Immanuel Kant: His Life and Thought*, translated by Marijan Despalatovic. Boston: Birkhäuser Boston Inc. [2nd ed.—2012]—This is a translation of A.V. Gulyga, A.V. 1977. *Kant*. Moscow: Molodaja gvardija. [2nd ed.—1981; 3rd ed.—1994]

Gulyga, Arsenij V. 1990. *Die klassische deutsche Philosophie: Ein Abriss*. Leipzig: Reclam-Verlag.—This is a translation of the original Russian book: Gullyga, Arsenij V. 1986. *Nemetskaja klassicheskaja filosfija*. Moscow.

Hegel, G.W.F. 1929–1959. *Sobranie sochinenii* [Collected Works], in 14 vols. Moscow: Sotsekgiz.

Hegel, G.W.F. 1985. *Introduction to the Lectures on History of Philosophy*, translated by T.M. Knox and A.V. Miller. Oxford: The Clarendon Press.

Henrich, Dieter. 1986. *Hegels Wissenschaft der Logik, Formation unde Rekonstruktion*. Stuttgart: Klett-Kotta.

Kalinnikov, Leonid A. 2005. *Kant v russkoj filosfii i kul'ture* [Kant in Russian Philosophy and Culture]. Kaliningrad: Izd-vo RG University.

Kliger, Ilya and Bakhurst, David (eds.). 2013. "Hegel in Russia" (Special Issue), *Studies in East European Thought*, 65(3/4):155–286.

Krouglov, Alexei N. 2006. "Russkie svidetel'stva ob Immanuile Kante" [Russian Testimonies About Immanuel Kant]. In *The Historico-Philosophical Yearbook 2006*, 204–227. Moscow: Nauka.

Krouglov, Alexei N. 2009. "Zametki o sovremennom rossijskom kantovedenii" [Notes on the Contemporary Russian Kant Scholarship]. In *Rossi'skaja postsovetskaja filosofija: Opyt samoanaliza* [Russian Post-Soviet Philosophy: The Experience of Self-Analysis], edited by M. Soboleva, 91–104. Műnchen: Kubon & Sagner Buchexport-Import GmbH.

Lapin, Nikolai I. 1976. *Young Marx*. Moscow: Politizdat.

Lenin, Vladimir I. 1977. *Materialism and Empiriocriticism. Critical Comments on a Reactionary Philosophy*. In Lenin, V. I. *Collected Works* in 45 volumes English, 4th ed., vol. 14, 17–362. Moscow: Progress Publishers. [1st ed.—1962]

Lubkin, Alexander S. 1805. "Pis'ma o kriticheskoy filosofii" [Letters on the Critical Philosophy], *Severny Vestnik* [North Herald], 7(8), 184–197; 7(9), 304–306.

Motroshilova, Nelli V. (ed.). 1986. *Studien zur Geschichte der Westlichen Philosophie. Elf Arbeiten Jüngerer Sowjetisher Autoren*. Frankfurt am Main: Suhrkamp.

Motroshilova, Nelli V. 2010. *"Fenomenologiia dukkha" Gegelia v kontekste sovremennogo gegelevedeniia* [Hegel's *Phenomenology of the Spirit* in the Context of Contemporary Hegelian Studies]. Moscow: Kanon+ ROOI "Reabilitatsiia."

Motroshilova, Nelli V. 2012. *Otechestvennaja filosofija 50–80-kh godov XX veka i zapadnaja mysl'* [Russian Philosophy in the 1950–1980s and Western Thought]. Moscow: Akademicheskii Proekt.

Motroshilova, Nelli V. and Tuschling, Burkhard (eds.). 1994–2014. Immanuel Kant, *Sochinenija na nemetskom i russkom yazykakh* [Works in German and Russian]/ Immanuel Kant. *Werke*. Zweisprachige deutsch—russische Ausgabe, in 5 vols. Moscow: Kami; Nauka; Kanon+ ROOI "Reabilitatsia."

Theunissen, Michael. 1978. *Sein und Schein*. Frankfurt am Main: Suhrkamp.

Van der Zweerde, Evert. 1989. "Rezension," *Zeitschrift für philosophische Forschung*, 43(4), 705–708.

Vazyulin, Victor A. 1968. *Logika "Kapitala" Marksa* [The Logic of Marx's Capital]. Moscow: Moscow State University Press.

Zinoviev, Alexander A. 2002. *The Ascent from the Abstract to the Concrete (On the Basis of K. Marx's "Capital")*. Moscow: IF RAS.

CHAPTER TWELVE

# Ilyenkov's Hegelian Marxism and Marxian Constructivism

TOM ROCKMORE

Since Socrates, philosophy has always had an uneasy relationship to politics. During the dark days of Soviet philosophy, when the tendency to reduce philosophy to politics was very strong, Ilyenkov resisted by calling attention to Marx's relation to Hegel, in focusing Marx's method in *Capital*, and in examining dialectical logic. It is appropriate now, after the wheel of history has turned, to examine Ilyenkov's reading of the crucial relation of Marx to Hegel.

Though I appreciate Ilyenkov's philosophical contributions, I disagree with his depiction of Marx's theories. He follows many other Marxists in reading Marx's position as a strongly scientific form of empiricism that supposedly presupposes a transition from idealism to materialism. My remarks on Ilyenkov's interpretation of Marx and Marxism have two aims: to evaluate Ilyenkov's philosophical contribution on strictly philosophical grounds, and to call attention to Marx's constructivism.

## ILYENKOV ON DIALECTICAL LOGIC

Writing in the third quarter of the last century, Ilyenkov represented a new and very interesting development in Russian philosophy during, though no one knew it at the time, the waning days of the Soviet period. But now, after a further turning of the historical wheel, Ilyenkov's approach appears less positive if it is measured on purely philosophical grounds. It should now be clear that Ilyenkov does not break with, but rather continues, the Marxist fiction of the flawless continuity between Marx, Engels and Lenin. Yet after the collapse of the Soviet Union, to save Marx, an extraordinarily important and influential thinker, from oblivion, we must relinquish special pleading in applying to Marx and Marxism the same scholarly standards used elsewhere in the discussion.

Ilyenkov's relation to Soviet Marxism is similar to Lukács' relation to Engels' Marxism. In both cases it is a question of finding arguments for claims that are more often asserted than demonstrated. Ilyenkov's contribution to the debate is framed by the nearly simultaneous publication of the *Paris Manuscripts* and the *Grundrisse*. It is an understatement to say that their publication changed the course of both Marx and Marxism.

Ilyenkov is especially influenced by the *Grundrisse*. He concentrates on the problem of dialectic within the broader framework of "dialectical materialism" that was so important in Soviet Marxism. We recall, in case it has been forgotten, that Stalin, who intervened in the debate between the dialecticians and the mechanists, decided that dialectical materialism conforms to the so-called proletarian conception of the world.

The term "dialectical materialism," which does not appear in Marx, was supposedly coined in 1887 after his death by Joseph Dietzgen. Marx mentions a "materialist conception of history," which Engels later refers to as "historical materialism." Engels further invokes "materialist dialectic" but not "dialectical materialism" in *Anti-Dühring* and in his unfinished *Dialectics of Nature*. Plekhanov, the father of Russian Marxism, apparently introduced "dialectical materialism" to the Marxist debate, where it later became a central doctrine of Marxism-Leninism. Dialectical materialism is distantly based on Engels' conception of the dialectics of nature. In the preface to the second edition of *Anti-Dühring*, Engels claims that the extension of dialectic exhibits the same dialectical laws as history.

Engels' treatment of dialectic reflects his inadequate grasp of even basic philosophical concepts. Ilyenkov, who was enormously more sophisticated, focuses on working out a materialist alternative to idealist dialectic. Marxism since Engels traditionally features materialism as distinguishing Marx and Marxism from idealism in particular and philosophy in general. Engels and subsequent Marxists understand "materialism" as the negation of idealism, which is in turn understood in different ways. It is then not surprising that Ilyenkov is constantly concerned with the meaning of this term in texts from this period.

In retrospect, Ilyenkov's main contribution lies in loosening the bonds of a dogmatic Marxism-Leninism, in which, in agreement with the Marxist theory of reflection, Marxist philosophy takes the form of a more or less faithful reflection of Soviet politics. Ilyenkov's aim was to go beyond mere dogma to create a "genuine" Marxist philosophy or a philosophical approach to Marx and Marxism. He was interested in recovering and/or formulating genuine philosophical positions based on the original texts.

## ILYENKOV AND THE PROBLEM OF MARX'S METHOD

Ilyenkov studies Marx's method in two main ways: initially in the progression from the abstract to the concrete, and later in the materialist variant of dialectical logic. His approach to Marxism-Leninism grew out of his early book, *Dialectics of the Abstract and the Concrete in Marx's "Capital"* (1960), which immediately attracted sustained attention. The title is taken from an important passage on method in the Introduction to the *Grundrisse*. Marx writes that

> Hegel fell into the illusion of conceiving the real as the product of thought concentrating itself . . . whereas the method of rising from the abstract to the concrete is the way in which thought appropriates the concrete, reproduces it as the concrete in the mind. (Marx 1973, 101)

This passage suggests Hegel incorrectly substitutes thought for the external world. On the contrary, he correctly understands we can only grasp the external world through reconstructing it in thought in a conceptual process running from the abstract to the concrete.

Ilyenkov's book provides detailed commentary on materialist dialectic in a series of five chapters running from general remarks on the problem of the abstract and the concrete through various stages. These include a chapter on logical development and concrete historicism. The fifth and final chapter offers an analysis of the method of the abstract and concrete in *Capital*.

As a study of Marx's *Capital*, Ilyenkov's book deserves comparison with other works due to Klaus Hartmann, Louis Althusser, Jindřich Zelený, and more recently Roman Rosdolsky, Tony Smith and many others. These and other writers stress Marx's reliance on Hegelian logic in his analysis of capitalism.[1] Ilyenkov's examination of the difference between the abstract and the concrete presupposes the crucial Marxist distinction between idealism and materialism. The problem can be stated as a question: if Hegel is concerned with the progression from the abstract to the concrete, and if Marx follows Hegel's approach, where does the difference between idealism and materialism lie?

Ilyenkov's examination of dialectical logic is never less than subtle, informed, and interesting. He is well informed not only about Marx but also about Hegel, whose writings he interprets knowledgeably and sympathetically. There has always been broad agreement among Marxists, non-Marxists and anti-Marxists alike that Marx needs to be understood in terms of his reaction to Hegel's theories. Yet neither Engels, nor Lenin, nor the other early Marxists know philosophy well enough to grasp Hegel or to grasp Marx through Hegel.

Hegelian Marxism, which was invented nearly simultaneously by Lukács and Korsch (Lukács more than Korsch) for the first time reached an adequate grasp of Hegel in Lukács' writings. Lukács later became interested in Hegelian logic that he believed was incompatible with Hegelian phenomenology (see Lukács 1984).

Ilyenkov's work developed in a different context, with different political constraints. For political reasons Lenin, though not a philosopher in any ordinary sense of the term, acquired authoritative philosophical status in the Soviet Union. According to Lenin, "We must organize a systematic study of the Hegelian dialectic from a materialist standpoint" (Lenin 1972, 227–236). Ilyenkov loosely follows Lenin's concern with Hegelian dialectic in formulating a so-called materialist dialectic. He goes beyond Lukács and Korsch, who knew Hegel and Marx well, and Lenin, who was not very familiar with either Hegel or Marx, but mainly relied on Engels, in examining the relations between Marx's and Hegel's understanding of dialectical logic in detail.

Ilyenkov's study of Marx's method culminates in Chapter 5 in an account of what is called universal logical elements in Marx's treatment of empirical elements.

Ilyenkov, who claims to follow Marx, considers the category of labor as an economic universal. Other Marxists, for instance Karl Korsch, believe that the Marxian categories are specific to modern industrial society (Korsch 1972, 29). Korsch is arguably correct against Ilyenkov. We can imagine a day in which the category of labor will no longer apply in a form of society situated beyond capitalism.

Ilyenkov is especially attracted to the theme of contradiction. He considers contradiction as central both to metaphysics (in which it is subjective) and to dialectic (in which it is objective) and where it takes what he considers to be the necessary logical form of thought. According to Ilyenkov, dialectical theory presupposes that reality unfolds through internal contradictions, which are resolved within the process itself.

Thus far, Ilyenkov mainly restates Hegel's view. He diverges from Hegel in his version of the familiar Marxist claim for the superiority of the dialectical materialist version of Hegelian idealism. Ilyenkov, who is unclear about how to understand contradiction, argues that only the dialectical materialism of Marx and Engels can solve the contradiction between matter and spirit. Though he does not say what this amounts to, the answer seems to lie in the study of concrete facts. Others, of course, concentrate on the supposed priority of the concrete over the abstract. This is, for instance, one of the central themes of Hegel's dialectical logic. Ilyenkov, who is aware of Hegel, can be understood as suggesting that, in studying the empirical world, Marxism succeeds where what Marxists call bourgeois thought fails. In Ilyenkov's view, Marx's treatment of contradiction is doubly central: it allows for the ascension from the abstract to the concrete, and it concerns the distinctive difference from idealism. According to Ilyenkov, there is a given that we access immediately on a pre-conceptual level, which is precisely captured through Marx's theory of value. In an important passage, Ilyenkov writes:

> Only this conception, assuming a concrete historical approach to things, makes possible special analysis of the form of value, special inquiry into the concrete content of the universal category-analysis of value as a *concrete sensually given reality, as an elementary economic concreteness,* and not as a concept. Value is not analyzed as a mental abstraction of the general but rather as a fully specific economic reality actually unfolding before the observer and therefore capable of being specially studied, as reality possessing its own concrete historical content, the theoretical description of which is identical with elaboration of definitions of the *concept* of value. (Ilyenkov, 1982)

In claiming that reality is directly given, Ilyenkov follows the traditional Marxist interpretation of Marx. I take Ilyenkov to be suggesting that Marx's method in *Capital* is grounded in so-called pre-conceptual experience. This suggestion has analogies with Husserlian and post-Husserlian phenomenology as well as with positivist empiricism, for instance with Carnap's early so-called protocol theory. In avoiding what they called metaphysics, the early logical positivists favored protocol sentences intended to support the inference from immediate experience to science as a continuous chain of reasoning. In relying on a demonstrably faulty reading of Wittgenstein's *Tractatus*, Carnap and others committed to the so-called empirical criterion of meaning hold that a proposition is meaningful if and only if it is grounded in observable facts. This effort was later abandoned in the face of Neurath's objection that there were and could not be any protocols in Carnap's sense of the term.

The early logical positivists feature what can be called scientific empiricism. Ilyenkov relies on a form of this approach in interpreting Marx. Yet scientific empiricism is arguably inconsistent with Marx's practice. Marx is not an empiricist as this approach is normally understood. Though there is a strong empirical component in Marx's position, he is not and must not be interpreted as an empiricist in any ordinary sense of the term. He rather follows Kant and Hegel in claiming that we require a categorial framework to appropriate what is not and cannot be directly given.

Ilyenkov regards Marx's theory of value as the solution to a concrete contradiction ultimately traceable to the distinction between use-value and exchange value. This distinction is central to what Ilyenkov calls the "mystery" of *Capital.* He claims dialectical materialism solves (or resolves) the contradiction in what amounts to a concrete description, in following the movement of reality itself. It turns out that for Marx as for Hegel, though Ilyenkov does not say this, external contradiction, in this case a contradiction between two main forms of value, is lodged internally within the object itself. From this perspective, "dialectic" refers to the inner contradictions of social reality and Marx's method is materialist in that it is concerned with objective contradiction. Yet since Hegel is clearly making a similar claim, the difference between Marx and Hegel needs to be explained and neither merely asserted nor simply presupposed.

Ilyenkov is interested in demonstrating the superiority of materialism, a familiar philosophical conception, which originates in ancient Greek philosophy. He argues for the difference between idealism and materialism in distinguishing the views of Marx and Hegel. According to Ilyenkov, for Hegel reality is not a substance, but rather a subject that develops. Ilyenkov similarly suggests Marx demonstrates internal contradiction through a materialist dialectic that in *Capital* takes an economic form.

This claim assumes the point, which Ilyenkov asserts but neither demonstrates nor even seeks to demonstrate, that there is immediate access to reality, in this case to economic reality, which is situated beyond, or rather prior to, concepts. One could argue, following Lukács, that only Marxism allows us to pierce the veil of ideological illusion to grasp social truth. Ilyenkov makes a different argument. His view, which seems unclear, apparently relies either on direct intuition of what is, a view current in the debate as early as Plato (philosophers are supposedly capable of "seeing" reality), or perhaps on the notorious reflection theory. Ilyenkov appeals to the latter approach in claiming the economic categories of *Capital* "reflect" mind-independent economic reality objectively and independently of their theoretical interpretation. Yet no argument has ever been devised to show that we in fact directly intuit or otherwise grasp reality as it is. It has also never been shown how to "reflect" the mind-independent world on the level of mind. And, finally, following Hegel, Marx denies immediate empirical claims in relying on categorial reconstruction. I come back to this point below.

## IDEALISM, MATERIALISM AND DIALECTICAL LOGIC

Ilyenkov develops his approach in an important collection of essays titled *Dialektitcheskaya logika. Otcheerki istorii i teorii* [Dialectical Logic. Historical and Theoretical Sketches] published in 1974 (Ilyenkov 1977). Here he makes the case for Marx's approach in terms of Hegel's view of logic. His account is broad, detailed and interesting, far surpassing the familiar Marxist efforts simply to discredit non-Marxist thought.

Ilyenkov follows Lenin's view that understanding Marx's *Capital* requires understanding Hegel's *Logic*.[2] He accepts Lenin's conviction that Marx brought together logic, scientific dialectic, and materialist theory of knowledge as well as the further view that the only way beyond Hegel's absolute idealism lies in materialism.

Ilyenkov, who presupposes the notorious theory of reflection, thinks logic is scientific if it reflects and thus reproduces in the form of concepts a mind-independent external object. He clearly states: "In other words, Logic must show how thought develops if is scientific, if it reflects, i.e. reproduces in concepts, an object existing outside our consciousness" (Ilyenkov 1977, 1–2).

Ilyenkov's approach to the difference between materialism and idealism is influenced by his view of the role of Spinoza. The latter is important for such Soviet Marxists as Akselrod (Akselrod (Ortodoks) 1952) and Deborin (Deborin 1952) as well as for the French Marxist Althusser. Althusser claims that Hegel historicized Spinoza.[3] Ilyenkov makes a different argument in two points. First, Spinoza saw that the familiar Cartesian dualism could be overcome through a deeper monism. Second, Marx and Engels rely on this idea, which they were the first to fully understand in their conception of dialectical materialism.

Ilyenkov follows Engels and other Marxists in claiming that Hegel fails to grasp the external world, which is correctly grasped through dialectical materialism. Hegel showed idealism fails since concepts disclose the real nature of things. According to Ilyenkov, Hegel, who is especially concerned with the identity of the subject and the objective, cannot go from concepts to the world through the theory of identity, which in Schelling and Hegel left reality outside it.

Ilyenkov contrasts his view of Hegel, who is supposedly dominated by a false god since he never leaves the realm of thought, with his view of Marx as grasping reality outside the mind. Hegel, who is uncritical, begins with thought rather than nature. Marx surpasses Hegel in grasping real contradictions of modern society. According to Ilyenkov, the contradictions of the labor theory of value are not contradictions in thought but real contradictions in the object.

This argument is a variation on the theme of metaphysical realism. It depends on the crucial assumption, which has never been demonstrated, that it is in fact possible to grasp the mind-independent world as it is. On the contrary, Marx, like Hegel, relies on concepts intended to cognize what is given in perception, but not as it is in itself. We do not and cannot know that concepts tell us the way the world really is. At most we only know that our theories about the world are not refuted by experience. We also do not know that any theory, such as the labor theory of value, reflects the way the world is. That would only be possible if we could somehow gain access to reality in independence of the theory about it in order to compare the theory and its object.

## DIALECTICAL MATERIALISM AND MARXIAN CONSTRUCTIVISM

I come now very briefly to epistemic constructivism, which is important as an alternative to familiar approaches to knowledge based on intuition, causal theories of perception, and so on. Dialectical materialism, which claims through the theory of reflection to know reality, belongs to the long series of modern philosophical efforts (none of which is successful) to demonstrate that we know the mind-independent world as it is. Beginning in Kant's so-called Copernican revolution, a term he never uses to describe his own position, German idealism, on the contrary, makes a very different, weaker claim. It abandons metaphysical realism for empirical realism in limiting claims to know what we in some sense "construct."

Kant and later German idealists are broadly speaking constructivists.[4] Constructivism is a modern alternative to empiricism of all kinds as it is usually understood. Marxism since Engels typically presents Marx as a special kind of empiricist that is incompatible with, in fact the refutation of, idealism. This approach to Marx is based on Engels' reading of the relation of Marx and Hegel. According to Engels, Marx leaves idealism, ideology and philosophy for materialism, truth and science. In its most general form, this approach precludes understanding Marx's own contribution to constructivism on the grounds that constructivism is an idealist doctrine. From this perspective, Marx does not belong to idealism, and perhaps also does not even belong to the philosophical tradition.

Kant, Fichte and Hegel generally follow a constructivist approach to knowledge. The situation is more complicated with respect to Schelling, who is a special case. Marxian constructivism is strongly influenced by the Hegelian approach. Marx and Hegel share a deeply historical constructivist approach to social phenomena and history. Hegel restricts knowledge claims to what is given in conscious experience through an interaction between the subject that knows and the object that is known. According to Hegel, knowledge unfolds in an experimental process in which through trial and error the subject formulates concepts adequate to grasp the contents of experience. Concepts, which amount to a theory of the object, are tested against and refined in relation to further experience in an ongoing process of knowledge.

What I am calling Marxian constructivism features an "anthropological" approach to knowledge. Marxian constructivism is based on a conception of the human subject as active, literally as activity, which Marx takes over from Fichte, and which he develops into an analysis of modern industrial society. According to Marx, in and through their actions, human beings produce commodities, social relations, and capitalism as well as the transition to communism, or human history in which the full development of human beings as individuals will in principle become possible.

Marx's constructivism is linked to a theory of cognition. He suggests that we can know the social world since we in effect construct it. Constructivism comes into modern philosophy through Hobbes and Vico, and, as noted above, into German idealism through Kant's Copernican revolution. In the critical philosophy, the Copernican revolution is intended as an alternative to the familiar representational approach to cognition. In different ways, the entire German idealist tradition turns on reading, criticizing and reformulating the constructivist approach to knowledge. In the process, Kant's approach to constructivism is turned inside out.

Marx's approach to constructivism draws on the entire German idealist tradition, and especially on Fichte's and Hegel's positions, as well as on Vico. Marxian constructivism, which relies on a quasi-Hegelian, categorial approach to capitalism, is basically different from the notorious reflection theory of knowledge.[5] It is also very different from, and in fact incompatible with, the reductionist thesis of consciousness to material relations underlying the conception of ideology expounded in the *German Ideology,* which was probably invented by Engels.

In *Capital*, Marx refers in passing to Vico's conviction that human history differs from nature in that we have made the former but not the latter. Marx, like Vico, thinks that human beings literally "make" history. He further thinks, again like Vico, that we can only know what we make, according to Marx by reconstructing it as a categorial framework on the level of mind. If there is no prior mind-independent object to be known, then it cannot be reconstructed. Unlike Kant, for Marx construction is not a priori. Rather construction takes place on the a posteriori and social planes, in the context of an interaction between human beings and between human beings and nature.

Marx, who notes that what one seeks to reconstruct exists autonomously outside the mind as a presupposition, does not grasp and does not claim to grasp the mind-independent world, or even social reality, as it is. Marxism, on the contrary, often makes that claim on his behalf. Yet this claim, which is like a claim to know the thing in itself, is indemonstrable as well as impossible. If the social context were in fact wholly "transparent" to mind, then we could indeed reliably claim not only to construct it through the actions of men and women in the social context, but also to reconstruct it reliably within the cognitive process on the level of mind, hence in fact to know it as it is.

Yet on even a charitable interpretation, Marx cannot reliably claim to grasp the social world as it is for at least two reasons. First, neither Marx nor anyone else can never cognize more than what at any given time appears in experience. Any claim about the world is always subject to later modification. Second, Marx proposes one among a series of possible conceptual "reconstructions" of the social world. At least implicitly, there is always a distinction, which cannot be measured or otherwise evaluated, between what we experience and the social world as it is outside the mind. Since we cannot reliably claim to encounter the social world as it is in itself, we also cannot reliably claim to reconstruct it as it is in itself, but only as it is given in experience. To think otherwise would be to conflate the subjective and the objective, what we seek to know with what in fact is. At the limit it may sometimes appear as if the subject matter we seek to know were ideally reflected as in a mirror, as if it were only a mere a priori construction. But, since we cannot claim to know the world as it is, we also cannot know this is the case.

## CONCLUSION: ILYENKOV'S HEGELIAN MARXISM AND MARX'S CONSTRUCTIVISM

In retrospect, Ilyenkov's Hegelian Marxism is interesting for three reasons. First, in the difficult context of Soviet Marxism Ilyenkov innovates in formulating a Marxist theory based on knowledge of texts according to the best standards of philosophical argument. Second, he extends Hegelian Marxism, which Lukács influentially formulates, in redescribing Marx's relation to the German idealist tradition, especially to Hegelian logic. Third, he adds to our understanding of the way that Marx relies on Hegelian logic in formulating his analysis of modern industrial society.

Marx's relation to Hegel passes through a series of different stages as a function of his interests at the time. At a minimum, there are at least four different phases:

(i) A strongly Hegelian approach to ancient philosophy of nature in Marx's dissertation,

(ii) Marx's very early critique of Hegel's supposed acceptance of the contemporary political situation in the *Philosophy of Right*,

(iii) Marx's critique of Hegel mainly centering on the *Phenomenology* from a Feuerbachian perspective in the *Paris Manuscripts*,

(iv) Marx's later critical appropriation of a Hegelian approach to logic in working out his reconstruction and critique of capitalism in the *Grundrisse* and then later in *Capital*.

Marx suggests that Hegel substitutes the movement of thought for the movement of the real, a suggestion which Ilyenkov and generations of other Marxists take as pointing to a basic distinction between idealism and materialism. What is "idealism"? What is "materialism"? If "materialism" means that nature precedes mind, then, since no idealist, none at all, ever denies this point, all idealists are materialists and this supposed distinction no longer seems meaningful. And, since Marx relies on a Hegelian approach in reconstructing the contents of experience, there is finally no clear difference, other than the difference between two important philosophers, between their positions. Certainly Marx is not Hegel and it would be incorrect to argue that they hold exactly the same position. The crucial point is whether the difference between them is other than the difference between any two important thinkers. Since Marxian materialism and Hegelian idealism both depend on a constructivist approach, I conclude that, at least from this perspective, both belong to the overall philosophical tendency known as German idealism.

## NOTES

1. It has been argued that he already did that in the *Grundrisse*, which served as an early version of the project formulated in *Capital*. See Meaney 2002. Meaney's basic claim is that in formulating the critique of political economy in the *Grundrisse*, Marx critically appropriated Hegel's *Science of Logic*. See ibid., x. See also Uchida 1998.
2. The numbers in parentheses in the text are references to Ilyenkov 1977.

3. See "Marx and His Discoveries" in Althusser 2009, 86–90.
4. For this reading of German idealism, see Rockmore 2016.
5. The reflection theory of knowledge introduced into Marxism by Engels, goes back at least to Greek philosophy. It is already mentioned by Plato in *Republic* (Book X, 597D), where Socrates talks about carrying around a mirror to make things appear. See Plato 1992, 267–268.

## BIBLIOGRAPHY

Akselrod (Ortodoks), L. I. 1952. "Spinoza and Materialism." In *Spinoza in Soviet Philosophy*, selected and translated by George L. Kline, New York: Humanities Press, 61–89. [A translation of "Spinoza i materializm," *Krasnaya nov'* [Red Virgin Soil], 1925 (7): 144–168.]

Althusser, Louis. 2009. *Reading Capital*, London: Verso.

Deborin, Alexander M. 1952. "Spinoza's Worldview." In *Spinoza in Soviet Philosophy: A Series of Essays*, selected and translated, and with an introduction by George L. Kline, 90–119. London: Routledge; Kegan and Paul.

Ilyenkov, Evald V. 1982. *Dialectic of Abstractness and Concreteness in K. Marx's* Capital, translated by Serguei Kuzyakov, Moscow: Progress Publishers.

Ilyenkov, Evald V. 1977. *Dialectical Logic: Essays on Its History and Theory*, translated by H. Campbell Creighton. Moscow: Progress Publishers.

Korsch, Karl. 1972. *Marxism and Philosophy*, London: NLB.

Lenin, Vladimir I. 1972. "On the Significance of Militant Materialism," in *Pod Znamenem Marksizma*, No. 3, 12 March 1922. [Reprinted in Lenin's *Collected Works*, vol. 33, 227–236, translated by David Skvirsky and George Hanna. Moscow: Progress Publishers.]

Lukács, György. 1984. "Hegels Dialektik "mitten im Dünger der Widersprüche." Zur Ontologie des Gesellschaftlichen Seins." Erster Halbband, *Georg Lukács-Werke*, Band 13.

Marx, Karl. 1973. *Grundrisse: Foundations of the Critique of Political Economy (Rough Draft)*. Harmondsworth: Penguin.

Meaney, Mark E. 2002. *Capital as Organic Unity: The Role of Hegel's Science of Logic in Marx's Grundrisse*. Dordrecht: Kluwer.

Plato. 1992. *Republic*, translated by G. M. A. Grube, revised by C. D. C. Reeve. Indianapolis/Cambridge: Hackett.

Rockmore, Tom. 2016. *German Idealism as Constructivism*. Chicago: University of Chicago Press.

Uchida, Hiroshi. 1988. *Marx's* Grundrisse *and Hegel's Logic*. London: Routledge.

CHAPTER THIRTEEN

# The Western Reception of Alexei Losev's Philosophical Thought

MARYSE DENNES

This chapter will go beyond a purely historical-philosophical investigation into the broader area of the philosophical inquiry, finding the intersection of both philosophy and history of philosophy.

As an introduction, I will refer to a highly informative article by Elena Takho-Godi about Losev's heritage and its reception in the West (Takho-Godi 2008). This work provides a retrospective analysis of the reception of Losev's thought in the contemporary Western Slavistics. Since the publication of this piece, however, there has been occurred the important development in scholarly work on Losev and thus it is essential to take into consideration also a more recent publication that highlights certain changes in the current Losev scholarship in the West (see A. Takho-Godi, E. Takho-Godi 2013). I will attempt to draw philosophical conclusions from these changes. To do this, I will first look into the current situation in France, the country where I work. I will discuss the impact of Losev's works on the development of the human sciences in France, and how they are received in Western Europe and in the USA.

I agree with Elena Takho-Godi when she writes about a difficult situation with the translation of Losev's texts. Only a very few number of these texts have been translated, and most of them focus on some specific issues in the areas of philology, literature, art, and the history of art and culture. Losev's works on science and philosophy remain largely untranslated. Although the Western view of Losev still remains rather incomplete, it is worth noticing that Losev became known to the Western reader as early as the 1930s, and the English press reported Losev's arrest when it occurred. Takho-Godi also points out that more recently Western Slavic scholars have become interested in Losev's philosophy of music (Michał Bristiger in Italy, Andreas Wehrmeyer in Germany, Milan Uzelac in Serbia) and that many Russian emigration waves promoted some of Losev's theological and philosophical ideas, and not only in Russian. In this chapter, I will not rely on Russian émigré press, specifically Russian language periodicals, such as *Vestnik RHD* and *Simvol* published in France, *Novy zhurnal* that appeared in the USA, etc., which were certainly important for introduction and dissemination of Losev's ideas in the West. Instead, I will be focusing on foreign language Losev publications that were available to Western scholars. I will discuss how the Western intellectual milieu developed an interest in Losev and how the engagement with Losev's work has influenced the development of the human sciences in the West. We shall look at all Losev's translations, as well as publications about him, and the material that had an influence on Western Losev scholarship. The data presented by Takho-Godi provides a great foundation for our analysis.

The German translation of Losev's *Dialektika mifa* [The Dialectics of Myth] was already published in 1994 (see Losev 1994).[1] In 1998, the work was translated into Spanish, and the Hungarian and Serbian translations appeared in 2000; the Bulgarian translation followed in 2003, and that same year the English translation was published by Routledge; and, finally, the Japanese version came out in 2006 (see Losev 1998, 2000a, 200b, 2003a, 2003b, 2006). These facts prove that in different countries and on different continents, Slavicists have responded to certain demands and expectations of the intellectual milieu with such translations. *The Dialectics of Myth* was the chief subject of Annett Jubara's study on the philosophy of the myth (Jubara 2000), that drew the attention of the Paris Solovyov Society (led by the French Solovyov scholar, Bernard Marchadier), where a whole series of presentations focused on the topic in 2007–2008. We can also recall a book by Paweł Rojek recently published in Poland (Rojek 2006).

Such publications and events concern not only Slavicists, but a broader circle of specialists who do not necessarily speak Russian. They, however, always view Russian culture with curiosity and scholarly interest. While the main group of scholars consists of professional philosophers, those with a genuine interest include theologians, fine art experts, political analysts, and even mathematicians and physicists. On the one hand, this is favorable for promoting certain elements of Russian culture and Russian philosophy that have remained, until now, the exclusive property of those who speak Russian. But on the other hand, it is the scholarly interest of these different specialists that defines the choice of topics and objects of research. In this regard Slavicists are only intermediaries, transmitters of culture: it is not the fact of translation that is important, but what is translated and what becomes this very object of scholarship. It is noteworthy that in recent decades the situation among Western Slavicists has changed, especially in the academic milieu: the defects of translations are being recognized in the human sciences, and the translation of philosophical texts began to develop parallel to the process of the rehabilitation of some important figures of Russian culture. The translations of Losev's texts and the interest in certain aspects of his work fall precisely within the scope of such changes in the overall situation. The attention of Western specialists is attracted by the new and the surprising—that which uncovers unknown facets of the Russian culture and opens new insights for the Western scholarship in the human sciences. The interest in *The Dialectics of Myth* is also included in this pattern: as the ideas presented in the book open new perspectives and play a greater role in the development of the human sciences, the book itself becomes more and more a focus of a thorough study.

The special interest that *The Dialectics of Myth* arouses among scientific communities is mainly due to the fact that Losev's understanding of myth differs from the traditional Western interpretation of this concept. I will emphasize two points that attract scholarly attention not only in the area of the history of philosophy, but also in the area of epistemology and logic as the foundation for a new type of interdisciplinary work.[2]

The first point that I would like to emphasize concerns the notion of myth and the specific meaning that Losev attributes to it. The second deals with the distinction between "absolute mythology" and "relative mythology" and the definition of these different mythological types. It is noteworthy that Losev, through his definition of myth, and in direct contrast to Ernst Cassirer, puts forward a notion that is completely alien to the Western consciousness. Yet by setting apart "absolute mythology" from "relative mythology," he offers to contemporary Western scholars a valuable tool for discovering a foundation for a new attitude to reality that the human sciences currently need. Losev offers an opportunity to understand how different approaches to reality can coexist in their distinction and contradiction, while a higher principle that continues to apply embraces and transcends them, reconciling their differences. This is what makes it possible for different types of logic and epistemology to coexist (classical type claiming universality, and generic type being local).

The contemporary relevance of Losev's interpretation of myth resides in the fact that along with culturally conditioned definitions of myth, there exists yet one more definition, which is what Losev describes as a "living mutual subject-object communication"—and this is what opens a communicative horizon of a higher level. The idea that the so-called "communicative version of hesychasm" (Gogotishvili) is not only a horizon of socio-cultural-religious communication but can become a horizon of "mutual scientific communication" seems to result from transposition of influences—that is to say, the influence that Losev's ideas can have in the West and the influence that contemporary Western scholars can have on the interpretation of Losev's ideas. In this context and from this standpoint, a foundation is laid for the corresponding type of "mutual scientific communication," which some Western scholars, such as Anne-Françoise Schmid, term the "collective intimacy of sciences." New prospects open simultaneously, not only for comparison of different worldviews, but also for conceptualizing a new type of attitude to sciences—not only to the human sciences, but to sciences in general, including physics, mathematics, biology, bioethics, art studies, and finally the interdisciplinarity itself, thus leading to a new general methodology of sciences.

Here is a proof in the interest of some mathematicians (S. Diner, J.-M. Kantor) and, also, such historians of mathematics and sciences as the well-known specialist in the history of Russian sciences, Loren Graham. The circle of such specialists also includes, for example in France, the above-mentioned Schmid and the research group that pursues François Laruelle's project of non-philosophy and non-standard philosophy (or quantum philosophy). These developments in France are also echoed in publications and scholarly events that took place in other Western European and North American countries. It is worth recalling in this regard Jubara's aforementioned monograph.

A special place in this development belongs to the 2002 Losev conference in Columbus (Ohio, USA) attended by many Russian experts and Western Losev scholars.[3] Undoubtedly, it was a significant philosophical event. Interestingly, however, that the conference speakers said nothing or very little about the influence of Losev's ideas on the development of the human sciences in the West. The discussion exclusively concerned Losev's rehabilitation in the context of Russian culture and his place in the development of philosophy and the human sciences in Russia. It seems that today the situation is different. Nowadays, thanks to growing interest to some aspects of Losev's work, we can speak about the influence of Losev's thought in the West, where his ideas introduce new concepts and bring specific features to Western philosophy and Western methodology of sciences, features that are based on Russian cultural tradition, yet also reflecting its Eastern Christian and Byzantine origins.

Phenomenology happens to be yet one more theme of Losev's work that has attracted the attention of Western philosophers and scholars. The interest in Losev's insights into phenomenology is growing because it helps better understand the new conception of phenomenology that Losev, Shpet and some other thinkers developed in Russia in the 1910s–1920s. Additionally, the original way of Losev's interpretation and prospects for the development of the human sciences in the West feed this interest. Alexander Haardt can be considered a pioneer in every respect here. In his book, he emphasizes the connections between music and phenomenology in Losev's work, Losev's transition to the phenomenology of the name and his interest in onomatodoxy (Haardt 1993). Haardt's work provided a good foundation for continuing research in this field.

Some years later, Annett Jubara in her book on Losev's philosophy of the world built upon some of Haardt's findings, putting a special emphasis on the role of phenomenology in the development of Losev's so-called absolute mythology. The fact is that the phenomenological approach opens the way to understanding the place that the name, and, more importantly, the name of God, occupies in the hierarchy of different forms of manifestations of being (which include the number, the myth and the artistic form). While A. Haardt himself took interest primarily in Losev's theory of art, other Losev scholars focused rather on questions of language and the Byzantine and medieval origins of Losev's philosophy (see, for example, work by Holder Kusse). In France, Losev's philosophy has been studied as a part of the broader topic of the reception of Husserl and Heidegger in Russia (see Dennes 1998). Losev's unique approach is viewed as an important example of the development of Husserl's phenomenology in Russia. In this context, Losev's focus on the topic of the constitution of the external world gains a special philosophical significance. Further elaborating upon this topic, the contemporary French scholarship demonstrates the possibility to define a variety of forms of "being-in-the-world" (*Dasein*) in terms of different "modes" of historicity, and, consequently, highlight the relativization of classic parallelism between Western history and the history of Being. Thus, an effort has been made to look into the difference or complementarity of Russian and Western cultural horizons as part of a broader history of Being.

In this sense, an approach to Losev's work through the prism of phenomenology leads to a similar result as does the thematization of the concept of myth, which involves an introduction of the differentiation of absolute and relative mythologies. This result in question is a possible co-existence of differing modes of Being (knowledge) within a common cultural and intellectual horizon. In this connection, we are now approaching the current issues in the human sciences: the problem of new (generic and not universal) epistemological forms, the problem of possible coexistence of universal and of generic epistemology, and the problem of "collective intimacy of sciences" (Schmid 2011).

Phenomenology's impact on Russia is returning to the West through the works firmly based in phenomenology. In this context, the effort of Western Losev scholars is not limited to opening new, unknown Russian cultural aspects. In fact, Russian philosophy studies have gained their well-deserved position in the current development of the human sciences in the Western world, and this process is mutually beneficial for both Russia and the West. For it allows to broaden a cultural horizon while growing an awareness of distinction and complementarity of both.

The US scholar George Kline was a pioneer in this regard when at the abovementioned conference in Columbus, Ohio, he presented Losev not only within the boundaries of Russian philosophy, but indeed as an autonomous thinker, and emphasized the complexity, paradoxicality and novelty of his thought, giving it a more comprehensive meaning which better suited expectations of Western experts who desired to renew and advance the human sciences (Kline 2005). At a conference in Bordeaux in 2008, which focused on Losev's work in the context of European culture, this tendency was even more prominent. Among the Western speakers I can mention several scholars who in their presentations had enthusiastically insisted on the current relevance of Losev's thought. They pointed to his original contributions to the contemporary human sciences, especially to the theory of semantics (Kusse, Germany), theory of language (Famikazu Osuka, Japan and Maria C. Ghidini, Italy), theory of symbols (Irina Danilova, Sweden), and music theory (Milan Uzelac, Serbia). For my part, based on latest publications by Liudmila Gogotishvili, Viktor Troitskiy, and Elena Takho-Godi, I highlighted some phenomena in Losev's work that have the potential to become a point of research in philosophy and such fields as philosophy of mathematics, and fiction.

The recognition of the contemporary significance of Losev's philosophical, humanitarian and methodological ideas in the West has seen a confirmation in including the entry on Losev in such publications as the *Biographical Dictionary of Twentieth-Century Philosophers* (1996) and the 10-volume *Encyclopedia of Philosophy* (2006). There is also a series of French translations of a variety of Russian and English publications, which among other figures so include Losev (Lossky 1954; Kline 1990; Maslin and Lesourd 2010).

Elena Takho-Godi, in her retrospective on the studies of Losev's heritage, points out that certain aspects of Losev's work—such as the study of antiquity and classical philology works—have been overlooked by Western scholars. Perhaps this provides another evidence for my claim that Western Slavicists, especially when it comes to Losev's thought, function more as transmitters, intermediaries and translators for specialists in other areas of intellectual inquiry. However, the present essay is devoted to Losev's philosophical legacy as well as his legacy in such areas as the human sciences and general methodology of the sciences. Thus the discussion of philology remains beyond the scope of this chapter.

## NOTES

1. It is necessary to mention Alexander Haardt's work on Russian phenomenology, which is devoted in part to Losev's perception of the ideas of German phenomenology (Haardt 1993), Cf. also: (Dennes 1998). Concerning the German translation of *The Dialectics of Myth*, see Haardt's "Afterword" to the volume, where the German translation of the work is described as "the greatest failure in the history of the publishing house" (Losev 1994, 206). Despite a serious defect of the publication, a poor quality of translation stimulated the scholarly activity eventually leading to realization that Losev's texts are stylistically multilayered and thus they should not be read literally.
2. For more details about the significance of Losev's concept of myth and the reception of this concept by scholars from different disciplines see my papers presented at the 1999 conference in Lyon (Dennes 2000) and at a Losev seminar I organized in Bordeaux in 2001 (Dennes 2002). It is worth mentioning that in addition to these two works, together with my colleagues, for three years, I collaborated with researchers from multiple fields (philosophy, art studies, epistemology, cognitive sciences, psycholinguistics, biology, bioethics) within the framework of a French-Russian philosophy seminar (organized in Paris, Moscow and Bordeaux). We were brought together by our common interest in Russian philosophy, where Losev holds an important place.
3. For conference proceedings see: Bird 2004a and Zakudalsky 2005.

## BIBLIOGRAPHY


Bird, Robert (ed.). 2004a. *Studies in East European Thought*, 56 (2/3). (A Special Issue: Aleksej Fedorovich Losev: Philosophy and the Human Sciences.)

Bird, Robert. 2004b. "Minding the Gap: Detachment and Understanding in Aleksej Losev's *Dialektika mifa*." *Studies in East European Thought*, 56 (2/3): 143–160.

Bristiger, Michał. 1996. "La questione principale della filosofia della musica secondo Aleksej F. Losev (1898–1988)" [The Main Question of the Philosophy of Music According to Alexei F. Losev]. In *Il pensiero musicale degli anni venti e trenta* [The Musical Thought of the Twenties and Thirties], edited by Bristiger Michał, Capogreco Nadia, Reda Giorgio, 259–272. Calabria: Centro Editoriale F. Librario, Università degli Studi della Calabria.

Bristiger, Michał. 2001. "O filozofii muzyki Aleksieja F. Łosiewa (1893–1988)" [About Aleksej Losev's Philosophy of Muzik]. *Res Facta Nova* 4 (13): 103–114.—[Reprint of Bristiger 2001.]

Danilova, Irina. 2010. "La signification de la théorie du symbole d'A.F. Losev pour la méthodologie des recherches actuelles sur le théâtre" [The Significance of A.F. Losev's Theory of Symbol for the Methodology of Current Theater Research]. In *L'Œuvre d'Alekseï Losev dans le contexte de la culture européenne* [Aleksej Losev's Work in the Context of European Culture] edited by Maryse Dennes, 69–76. [*Slavica occitania*. 31.] Toulouse: Toulouse University.

Dennes, Maryse. 1998. *Husserl-Heidegger. Influence de leur œuvre en Russie* [*Husserl-Heidegger. The Influence of their Work in Russia*]. Paris: L'Harmattan.

Dennes, Maryse. 2000. "Vitesse de la parole et déploiement du discours : de la *Glorification du Nom* à un fondement de temporalité" [The Velocity of the Word and Deployment of the Discourse: From the "Glorification of the Name" to Foundation of Temporality], *Modernités* 2 (3), 223–242.

Dennes, Maryse. 2002. "La "Mythologie absolue" chez Alexis Losev: Recherche du mythe fondateur et justificateur de la spécificité culturelle et historique de la Russie" [The "Absolute Mythology" of Aleksei Losev : Research to Found and Justify Myth of Cultural and Historical Specificity of Russia], *Eidôlon* (61): 203–221.

Dennes, Maryse. 2005. "The Place and Role of Husserlian Phenomenology in Aleksei Losev's Philosophy." *Russian Studies in Philosophy* 44 (1): 33–43.

Dennes, Maryse (ed.). 2010. *L'Œuvre d'Alekseï Losev dans le contexte de la culture européenne* [Aleksej Losev's Work in the Context of European Culture]. [*Slavica occitania*. 31.] Toulouse: Toulouse University.

Dennes, Maryse. 2013. "'Absoljutnaja mifologija' A.F. Loseva i aktual'nost' ego trudov v gumanitarnyh nauk" [The "Absolute Mythology" of A.F. Losev and the Topicality of His Works in the Human Sciences]. In *Tvorčestvo A.F. Losev v kontekste otečestvennoj i evropejskoj kul'turnoj tradicii* [A.F. Losev's Work in the Context of National and European Cultural Tradition], vol. 2, edited by A. A. Taho-Godi, 237–250. Moscow: Dom A.F. Loseva.

Emerson, Caryl. 2004. "On the Generation that Squandered its Philosophers (Losev, Bakhtin, and Classical Thought as Equipment for Living)." *Studies in East European Thought* 56 (2/3): 95–117.

Ghidini, Maria C. 2010. "A. Losev et P. Florenski." In *L'Œuvre d'Alekseï Losev dans le contexte de la culture européenne* [Aleksej Losev's Work in the Context of European Culture], edited by Maryse Dennes, 117–130. [*Slavica occitania*. 31]. Toulouse: Toulouse University.

Gogotishvili, Liudmila A. 2010. "'Polytropie positionnelle', le principe clé de la théorie losévienne de l'expression" ['Positional Politropie' as a Key Principle of the Losev's Theory of Expression]. In *L'Œuvre d'Alekseï Losev dans le contexte de la culture européenne* [Aleksei Losev's Work in the Context of European Culture], edited by Maryse Dennes 27–44. *Slavica occitania*. 31. Toulouse: Toulouse University.

Gogotishvili, Liudmila A. 2014. "Le Noyau radical de la 'philosophie du nom' d'A.F. Losev" [Radical Novelty of the Losev's Philosophy of Name]. Problèmes actuels de la philosophie russe [Current Problems of Russian Philosophy]. *Revue Philosophique de la France et de l'étranger*, (3): 315–332.

Haardt, Alexander. 1993. *Husserl in Russland, Phänomenologie der Sprache und Kunst bei Gustav Špet und Aleksej Losev*. München: Wilhelm Fink Verlag.

Helleman Wendy E. 1999. "Mirovaya dusha i Sofiya v rannej rabote Solovyeva" [World Soul in Solovyev's Early Work]. "Obraz mira—struktura i celoe" [Image of the World: The Structure and the Whole]. *Logos* (3): 465–472.

Helleman Wendy E. 2007. "A.F. Losev—Khristyanskaya filosofiya v Rossii XX veka" [A. F. Losev—Christian Philosophy in Russia]. In *Sovremenniki o myslitele* [Contemporaries About The Thinker], edited by A.A. Takho-Godi, V.P. Troitskiy. Moscow : Russkiy mir.

Jubara, Annett. 2000. *Die Philosophie des Mythos von Aleksej Losev im kontext "Russischer Philosophie."* Wiesbaden: Harrassowitz Verlag.

Kiejzik, Lilianna (ed.). 2010. *Palamas. Bułgakov. Łosiew. Rozważania o religii, imieniu Bożym, tragedii filozofii, wojnie i prawach człowieka [Palamas, Bulgakov, Losev.* Considerations About Religion, In the Name of God, Tragedy of Philosophy, War and Human Rights], *Filozofia Rosyjska,* vol. 2. Warszawa: Scholar.

Kline, George L. 1990. "La Philosophie en Union soviétique autour de 1930" [The Philosophy in the Soviet Union Around 1930]. In *Histoire de la littérature russe*, edited by Ilya Serman, Georges Nivat, Efim Etkind and Vittorio Strada 256–266. Paris: Fayard..

Kline, George L. 2005. "Five Paradoxes in Losev's Life and Work." *Russian Studies in Philosophy* 44 (1): 13–32.

Kusse, Holger. 2010. "La sémantique de l'interprétation d'A.F. Losev et les théories de la sémantique au XXe siècle" [The Semantics of the Interpretation of A.F. Losev and the Theories of Semantics in the Twentieth Century]. In *L'Œuvre d'Alekseï Losev dans le contexte de la culture européenne* [Aleksej Losev's Work in the Context of European Culture] edited by Maryse Dennes, 281–300. [*Slavica occitania.* 31.] Toulouse: Toulouse University.

Losev, Alexei F. 1994. *Die Dialektik des Mythos.* Translated by by Elke Kirsten. Edited by A. Haardt. Hamburg: Felix Meiner Verlag.

Losev, Alexei F. 1998. *Dialectica del mito.* Trans. M. Kuzmina. Bogota: Univ. Nac. de Colombia.

Losev, Alexei F. 2000a. *A mítosz dialektikája Myth.* Trans. József Goretity. Budapest: Európa.

Losev, Alexei F. 2000b. *Дијалектика мита.* Translated by И. Марић. Belgrad: Zepter Book World.

Losev, Alexei F. 2003a. *The Dialectics of Myth.* Translated by Vladimir Marchenkov. New York: Routledge.

Losev, Alexei F. 2003b. *Диалектика на мита.* Translated by E. Dimitrov. Sofia: Slavistika.

Losev, Alexei F. 2006. *Shinwagaku josetsu: Hyōgen sonzai seikatsu o meguru tetsugaku.* Translated by Fumikazu Oosuka.Yokohama: Seibunsha.

Lossky, Nikolai O. 1954. *Histoire de la Philosophie russe des origines à 1950* [History of Russian Philosophy From the Origins to 1950]. Translated from Russian. Paris: Payot.

Maslin, Mikhaïl and Lesourd, Françoise (ed.). 2010. *Dictionnaire de la philosophie russe* [Dictionary of Russian Philosophy]. Translated from Russian. Lausanne: L'Age d'Homme.

Marchenkov, Vladimir L. 2004. "Mythos and Logos in Losev's Absolute Mythology," *Studies in East European Thought* 56 (2/3): 173–186.

Obolevitch, Teresa. 2011. *Od onomatodoksji do estetyki. Aleksego Losewa koncepcja symbol.* [From Onomatodoxie to Aesthetics. Aleksej Losev's symbol concept]. Studium hystoryczno-filozoficzne. Krakow: Wydawnictwo WAM.

Osuka, Famikazu. 2010. "Actualité de la Philosophie du langage d'A.F. Losev" in *L'Œuvre d'Alekseï Losev dans le contexte de la culture européenne* [Aleksej Losev's Work in the context of European Culture] edited by Maryse Dennes 45–56. [*Slavica occitania.* 31.] Toulouse: Toulouse University.

Rojek. Paweł. 2006. "Rozwinięte imię magiczne. *Dialektyka mitu* Aleksego Fiedorowicza Łosiewa." *Rocznik Mitoznawczy* (1): 25–41.

Shmid, Anne-Françoise. 2011. "Rodovaya epistemologiya: ot Ego k 'kollektivnoj intimnosti' nauki" [Generic Epistemology: from *Ego* to the "Intimate Community" of

Sciences]. *Filosofiya i Kul'tura* 5 (41): 105–116.

Takho-Godi, Elena A. 2008. "Naslediye A.F. Loseva i sovremennaya zarubezhnaya slavistika" [Losev's heritage and the modern foreign Slavistics]. In *Al'manakh Russkiy mir i Latviya: Fenomen vospriyatiya russkogo* [Almanac Russian World and Latvia: The Phenomenon of Perception of the Russianness]. XVI, 47–57.

Takho-Godi, Aza A., Takho-Godi, Elena A., Troitskiy, Viktor P. (eds.). 2013. *Alekseï Fedorovich Losev: Bibliograficheskiy ukazatel'. K 120-letiju so dnya rozhdeniya* [Alexei Losev: Bibliographical Guide. On the Occasion of the 120th Anniversary of his Birthday]. (Spetsvypusk Byulletenya Biblioteki "Dom A.F. Loseva," vypusk 17) [A Special Issue of the Library Bulletin. "Alexei Losev House," Issue 17]. Moscow: Disayn i poligrafiya.

Troitskiy, Viktor P. 2010. "La Philosophie des mathématiques d'A.F. Losev et le problème du fondement de la glorification du Nom" [The Philosophy of Mathematics of A.F. Losev and the Problem of the Foundation of the Glorification of the Name] in *L'Œuvre d'Alekseï Losev dans le contexte de la culture européenne* [Aleksej Losev's Work in the Context of European Culture] edited by Maryse Dennes 147–156. [*Slavica occitania*. 31] Toulouse: Toulouse University.

Uzelac, Milan. 2010. "La philosophie de la musique d'A.F. Losev" [The Philosophy of Music by A.F. Losev] in *L'Œuvre d'Alekseï Losev dans le contexte de la culture européenne* [Aleksej Losev's Work in the Context of European Culture], edited by Maryse Dennes, 231–248. [*Slavica occitania*. 31.] Toulouse: Toulouse University.

Wehrmeyer Andreas. 1991. *Studien zum russischen Muzikdenken um 1920*. Frankfurt an Main: Peter Lang.

Zakudalsky, Taras (ed.). 2005. *Russian Studies in Philosophy* 56 (2/3). [A Special Issue: Alexei F. Losev].

Zenkin, Konstantin. 2004. "On the Religious Foundations of A.F. Losev's Philosophy of Music." *Studies in East European Thought* 56 (2/3): 161–172.

Zenkin, Konstantin. 2010. "La philosophie et la mythologie de la musique d'A.F. Losev" [The Philosophy and Mythology of Music of A.F. Losev]. In *L'Œuvre d'Alekseï Losev dans le contexte de la culture européenne* [Aleksej Losev's Work in the Context of European Culture], edited by Maryse Dennes, 157–176. [*Slavica occitania*. 31.] Toulouse: Toulouse University.

Zenkovsky, Basile. 1955. *Histoire de la Philosophie russe* [History of Russian Philosophy]. T. I-II. Paris: Gallimard.

[illegible] (2011) [illegible]
[illegible] (2009) [illegible]
[illegible]
[illegible]
[illegible]
[illegible] 2011 [illegible]
[illegible]
[illegible]
[illegible]
[illegible]
[illegible]
[illegible] (1950) [illegible]
[illegible]
[illegible]
[illegible]
[illegible]
[illegible]
[illegible] 2008 [illegible]
[illegible]
[illegible]
[illegible]
[illegible] 2001 [illegible]
[illegible]
[illegible]
[illegible]
[illegible] 2011 [illegible]
[illegible]
[illegible]
[illegible]
[illegible]
[illegible]
[illegible]
[illegible]

PART IV

# The Problem of Activity in Philosophy, Methodology and Human Sciences

CHAPTER FOURTEEN

# The Activity Approach in Soviet Philosophy and Contemporary Cognitive Studies[1]

VLADISLAV A. LEKTORSKY

The activity approach was a popular part of Soviet philosophy and psychology between the 1960s and the 1980s, after which it was somewhat forgotten and criticized, even by some of its former followers. Nowadays, there is reason to attempt to understand some specific features of examination of the activity approach.

First, concepts such as "embodied cognition" and "enacted cognition," which stress the close relations between activity, cognition and cultural objectifications, are very popular in contemporary cognitive science and are subject to intense discussion. There are two variants of these concepts. The first, which is connected with the works of Francisco Varela, uses some ideas of the French phenomenologist Maurice Merleau-Ponty (Varela, Thomson and Rosch, 1992). The second, represented primarily by the American philosopher Andy Clark, refers to the ecological theory of visual perception of James Gibson (Gibson, 1979) and to the ideas of Lev Vygotsky, as well as of the Soviet school of cultural-historical and activity-psychology (Clark, 1997, 45). In connection with an analysis of the current situation in cognitive science, the famous Russian psychologist and specialist in cognitive science Boris Velichkovsky wrote about the need to return to the activity approach (Velichkovsky 2006, vol. 2, 370).

Second, a number of Russian philosophers, psychologists and specialists in human sciences now share different constructivist conceptions (radical epistemological constructivism, social constructionism, and so on). From their point of view, constructivism is a more adequate interpretation of those phenomena that the activity approach dealt with previously. It is of interest to analyze the relations of the activity approach in Soviet philosophy in the 1960s–1980s and contemporary constructivism in epistemology and the human sciences. Third, there are nowadays several interesting examples of the fruitful application of a cultural-historical activity approach in psychology and other human sciences. Particularly relevant is the conception of the renowned Finnish psychologist Yrjo Engestrum, who elaborated an original theory using ideas from the Soviet psychologist Alexei Leontiev and the Soviet philosopher Evald Ilyenkov (Engeström 2005). Every three years, the International Society for Cultural and Activity Research organizes an international congress that includes psychologists, specialists in education, and philosophers from different countries who share ideas about the current of cultural-historical psychology in the Vygotskian tradition and the activity approach. This chapter attempts to analyze the main ideas of Soviet philosophers on the problems of activity and the activity approach between the 1960s and the 1980s in the context of their contemporary meaning and of the current discussions in epistemology and cognitive sciences.

## AN EARLY VARIANT OF THE ACTIVITY APPROACH IN SOVIET PHILOSOPHY AND PSYCHOLOGY: SERGEI RUBINSHTEIN

In 1934, the well-known philosopher and psychologist Sergei Rubinshtein, referring to early works by Marx, formulated a conception of the unity of consciousness and activity. Rubinshtein stressed that, contrary to the ideas of introspective psychology about the immediacy of psychic life (claiming a direct access to subjectivity), consciousness is in reality mediated by activity: "a new possibility is arising: to examine consciousness through human activity, in which consciousness is formed and developed" (Rubinshtein 1934, 8). Rubinshtein drew special attention to one of the principal ideas in Marx's early works regarding the role of human made things. Specifically, the human being does not simply double himself in things he makes and create a peculiar mirror in which he can see himself, but creates himself for the first time by this activity. This is the meaning of Marx's famous assertion, in the third thesis on Feuerbach, that practice must be understood as "the coincidence of the changing of circumstances and of human activity or self-change [*Selbstveränderung*]" (Marx 1975, 422). Proceeding from these philosophical principles, Rubinshtein elaborated a psychological conception according to which the psychological subject is formed in the process of his activity, and psychic processes are mediated by cultural objectivations. This conception became a basis for psychological (including experimental) investigations.

In 1969, an article appeared that Rubinshtein had written in Odessa in 1922, which had subsequently been forgotten; it was titled "Printsip tvorcheskoy samodeyatel'nosti" [The Principle of the Creative Activity]. There were no references to Marx or Marxism. The article criticized philosophical realism in general and materialism in particular (as well as subjective idealism). At the same time, the main idea of the future activity-conception of the author was already present in the article. In this version, Rubinshtein formulated some ideas that he did not develop at a later stage when he already had absorbed Marx's philosophy.

Rubinshtein criticized the viewpoint (which he ascribed to Kant's doctrine of the intelligible character) that viewed a subject as the subject of its actions (*deyaniya*) in which it expresses and manifests itself. Rubinshtein wrote: "If a subject is only expressed in its actions, but is not also created by them, then it is presupposed that the subject is something ready-made, given before and outside of its actions, thus independent from them" (Rubinshtein 1991, 23). According to Rubinshtein, if one accepts this position, it is not possible to understand a person as a coherent whole. "It breaks down into two heterogenic constituting parts. The subject that in the personality constitutes its 'selfhood,' remains behind the actions which are its manifestations: the subject is transcendent to its actions" (ibid., 94). From this Kantian and transcendentalist point of view, "actions are conceived of as belonging to a certain subject: they are its actions. But as actions are not included in the constitution of the subject, do not build up its structure, they do not determine the subject in question" (ibid.). Rubinshtein believed that there are certainly such actions that do not determine the character of a subject or a personality. But there are also those which constitute a subject itself; otherwise, the latter could not exist.

Rubinshtein formulated his main position as follows: "Thus, the subject not only becomes visible and manifests itself in the acts of its creative activity; it is also created and determined in them. Therefore, it is possible to determine what the subject is by that what it does" (ibid.). In creating a work of art, an artist produces his individuality. Only in organizing the world of thoughts is a thinker formed. "The creator himself is produced in the creative process" (ibid.). "There is only one way to create a grand personality: creating a grand work" (Rubinshtein 1991, 95).

There is a striking similarity between the main idea of the 1922 article and the 1934 formulation of the principle of the unity of consciousness and activity. Criticism of Kant and subjective idealism in the 1922 article stimulated some authors to interpret that article as a break with Neo-Kantianism. Rubinshtein was known to be a pupil of Hermann Cohen, one of the leading figures of German Neo-Kantianism at the beginning of the twentieth century and the article was seen as an elaboration of ideas that were very close to those of Marx. In reality, however, Rubinshtein was in this article completely under the influence of the Marburg school of German Neo-Kantianism, which actually was not so much Kantianism as neo-Fichteanism, and even neo-Hegelianism. Marx was formed in the traditions of German idealism, which influenced not only many problems of Marx's philosophy, but even some of his solutions. I believe that this fact explains the easy transition of Rubinshtein from Neo-Kantianism to a reception of Marx's philosophical ideas and the formulation of the principles of psychological activity theory.

The principle of the unity of consciousness and activity exerted considerable influence on Soviet psychology. In the 1960s, however, another well-known Soviet psychologist, Alexei Leontiev, formulated his own psychological theory of activity (Leontiev 1978), which in many respects was opposed to Rubinshtein's conception (there were, in addition, other conceptions of activity in the Soviet psychology of that time, such as those of Petr Galperin and Vasily Davydov). Here I am not seeking to analyze the conceptions of activity in Soviet psychology, as I am currently interested in philosophical ideas about the activity approach and the principle of activity. I would simply note that Rubinshtein did not formulate the philosophical principle of the unity of consciousness and activity very clearly, and in his later years he started to criticize the activity approach, stressing that not only activity but also pure contemplation would provide contact with the "Being" (Rubinshtein 1973, 339–340)—some Russian scholars even believe that Rubinshtein later rejected the activity approach.

## GENERAL FEATURES OF THE ACTIVITY APPROACH IN SOVIET PHILOSOPHY

I would like to formulate my own understanding of the role of the idea of activity, not only in Soviet philosophy and psychology, but also in other philosophical conceptions in the twentieth century. I believe that this role was connected with attempts to eliminate the sharp opposition between the subjective and the objective, between the "inner" and the "outer" worlds that philosophy and human science had presupposed since Descartes. This opposition determined the way of understanding the inner and the outer worlds and, in so doing, influenced research programs in the human sciences. Different philosophical conceptions attempted to eliminate the opposition, including pragmatism, the phenomenology of Merleau-Ponty and Sartre, and the philosophy of later Wittgenstein. Despite their differences, all of these conceptions understood activity as a specific mediator between the "inner world" of man and the world of outer objects, as well as of other persons and cultural artefacts. I believe it is possible to consider these as activity-conceptions, despite the fact that their interpretations of activity were very different.

In the Soviet Union, the understanding of the human being and activity was elaborated in the framework of tradition of Marx, but some ideas of German idealism from the early nineteenth century, primarily those of Hegel and Fichte, were also used. A specific feature of the activity approach in the Soviet philosophical literature consists in the important role given to the notion of object-oriented activity. This notion was understood not only as a means of eliminating the sharp opposition of the "inner" and "outer" worlds, but usually also as an openness toward the outer reality. In any case, it is important that a number of Western and Soviet philosophers who elaborated the activity approach dealt with the same problem, so that their conceptions are comparable. As noted earlier, the conceptions of activity in Soviet psychology have already been included in the development of world-psychology.

The activity approach was criticized by the official Soviet philosophy for several reasons. It was suspected of deviating from the theory of reflection and materialism. Moreover, the stress on creativity and freedom in the activity approach was understood as an attempt to doubt the leading role of the Communist Party and Marxist-Leninist ideology. The Soviet followers of the activity approach were suspected of closeness to the "Praxis" group, which arose among Yugoslavian philosophers in the 1960s and claimed to express the authentic views of Marx and a humanistic interpretation of Marxism. Official Soviet ideologists considered this group to be revisionist. Yet ironically, the two sides had several similarities. Both the Soviet adherents of the activity approach and the Yugoslav Praxis philosophers proceeded from the ideas of Marx (especially early Marx), and there were also some personal connections. For example, one of the leaders of the Praxis group, Mihailo Marković, visited the Soviet Union several times and had personal relations with some Soviet philosophers (Evald Ilyenkov, Genrikh Batishchev and myself). But there was also a difference. Philosophers from the Praxis group were mainly engaged in social criticism: their targets were bureaucratic socialism in the Soviet Union, authoritarian phenomena in Yugoslavia, the consumption-society in Western countries, and alienation all over the world. The Soviet followers of the activity approach had no such opportunities for social criticism, although they were, as a rule, very critical of the existing social reality in the Soviet Union. They too analyzed the problem of alienation (see Ilyenkov 1967) and of humanism (see Batishchev 1969). But the interest of Soviet philosophers primarily focused on investigating the very structure of activity, and toward the methodological problems of science, particularly human sciences. Thus, the Soviet representatives of the activity approach were connected with psychology (Ilyenkov, Georgy Shchedrovitsky), with pedagogy (Batishchev) and with the history of natural sciences (Stepin, Alekseev). An important final difference was that the philosophers of the Praxis group felt that interpreting praxis as the main feature of the human being eliminated the opposition between materialism and idealism. None of the Soviet followers of the activity approach rejected materialism, although official philosophers suspected them of doing so. (It is true that their interpretation of materialism differed from the primitive official understanding of it).

## MAIN VARIANTS OF THE ACTIVITY APPROACH IN THE SOVIET PHILOSOPHY IN THE 1960s–1980s

From the 1960s onward, the activity approach became one of the central subjects of a new movement in Soviet philosophy. I believe that this is connected primarily with publications by Ilyenkov, particularly with his famous article on "The Ideal" published in *Filosofskaya Entsiklopediya* [Encyclopedia of Philosophy] in 1962 and the article "Problema ideal'nogo" [The Problem of The Ideal], which was published in two subsequent issues of the journal *Voprosy filosofii* [Questions of Philosophy] in 1979, after Ilyenkov's death. These articles were interpreted by the official Soviet philosophy as a major heresy. According to Ilyenkov, the ideal (Ilyenkov 1967) exists in collective human activity and as a form of it; in other words, outside the individual head, as a form of a thing outside a thing. Objective reality, independent from a human being, is given to him through activity and in forms of activity. The subjective world, and such features of it as freedom, is determined by the inclusion of a human being in activity. The ideal form is a form of a thing, but it is outside this thing, namely in man, as a form of his dynamic life-activity, as goals and needs. Or conversely, it is a form of man's dynamic life-activity, but outside man, namely in the form of the thing he creates, which represents and reflects another thing, including that which exists independently of man and humanity. "Ideality" as such exists only in the constant transformation of these two forms of its "external incarnation" and does not coincide with either of them taken separately. It exists only through the unceasing process of the transformation of the form of activity into the form of a thing and back—the form of a thing into the form of activity, the activity of social man, of course (Ilyenkov 2014).

A human being, Ilyenkov continues, looks upon nature (matter) as the material in which his aims are "embodied," as the "means" of their realization. This is why he sees in nature primarily what is "adequate" for this role, what plays or may play the part of a means toward his ends, that is to say, what he has already drawn, in one way or another, into the process of his purposeful activity. For example, he first directs his attention upon the stars exclusively as a natural clock, calendar and compass, as means and instruments of his life-activity, and observes their "natural" properties and regularities only insofar as they are natural properties and regularities of the material in which his activity is being performed, and with which he must, therefore, reckon as completely objective (in no way dependent on his will and consciousness) components of his activity (ibid., 191).

Ilyenkov's insights were accepted by many Soviet psychologists, primarily by those who continued to elaborate Vygotsky's ideas and were followers of the cultural-historical theory (including Leontiev and Davydov). Moreover, I believe that Ilyenkov's interpretation of activity influenced the elaboration of the psychological theory of activity by Leontiev in the early 1970s. Mikhail Lifshitz, a Soviet philosopher who was close to Ilyenkov in many respects but did not accept the activity approach, wrote that the Soviet psychologists had exerted a bad influence on Ilyenkov with regard to his ideas on activity. Lifshitz was incorrect. In fact, the reverse was the case: it was Ilyenkov's philosophical ideas about activity that stimulated the further development of conceptions of activity in the Soviet psychology of that time.

In this connection, I would especially like to draw attention to the fact that Ilyenkov's philosophical ideas influenced not only the theoretical development of conceptions of activity in Soviet psychology, but also psychological experimental practices. Consider the famous results of the Soviet psychologists connected with educating deaf-blind children, managing to awake them into a genuine psychic life.

Ilyenkov was engaged in this practice: for him that meant an experimental testing of his philosophical ideas. Psychological experiments showed that apprehension of language-meanings by such a child is successful only if the child is involved in a collective activity. Attempts to teach language to such a child by simply referring language-signs to things were unsuccessful. It became successful when things were included in a collective activity (in this case, in a joint and distributed activity of a child and an adult). Activity is object-oriented, but it selects those features of objects that are important for activity. It is just the appropriation of the objective world in forms of activity, of which Ilyenkov wrote in his philosophical texts. It is evident in that case that communication is included in activity and is its essential component: without relation to another person(s), activity is impossible. In this process man-made things, such as spoons, cups, shoes and clothes, play a specific role. These are not simply things, but a means of inter-human communication. For Ilyenkov, the case of blind and deaf children was not something peculiar and specific (although there are a lot of specific features in it), but a distinctive "hard experiment" of Nature itself, which made it possible to observe the role of human activity in forming psyche, consciousness and personality as if in "a pure appearance" (Ilyenkov 1975, 82).

The works of Genrikh Batishchev played an important role in elaborating a philosophical-anthropological interpretation of the activity approach. Many Soviet authors in the 1970s considered Batishchev to be the protagonist of the concept of activity. In the seminal article "Deyatel'nostnaya sushchnost' cheloveka kak filosofskiy printsip" [The Activity Essence of Man as a Philosophical Principle],

Batishchev investigated the structure of activity: interrelations between objectification and de-objectification[2] (their unity is the essence of activity, as he wrote at that time), objectification and alienation, the mode of existence of cultural objectifications, and the connections between the transformation of outer reality (subject-object relations) and inter-human communication (subject–subject relations).

Batishchev especially analyzed the creative nature of activity, its openness, the overcoming of existing stereotypes in activity, and the connection of activity with critical social attitudes and with human freedom.[3] Human reality, which is also the reality of the human being as the subject, arises only as existing beyond the Nature—human reality is a specific domain, where in principle new possibilities are created, which are impossible for the Nature as itself, in other words where creativity takes place. The human object-oriented activity is a process in which the substantiality of the nature is "completed" with the appearance of that which is impossible for the nature itself and the same time is appropriated as natural (Batishchev 1969, 89).

Batishchev wrote much about the object-oriented nature of activity. Activity is an ability of a human being to act not according to the organization of his body, not as a slave of specific features of his organism, but in accordance with a specific logic of every specific object. In other words, it is an ability to be "faithful" not to "himself," but to the world of objects, as they exist by themselves. A human being becomes himself in this faith fullness to the immanent logic of objects. He is not a body or thing besides other bodies, not a finite thing besides other finite things, but a "being" with an object-oriented activity, an actor. Object-oriented activity proceeds and develops not from the peculiar specificity of an organism as a finite thing, but from the assimilation of objects as they are in themselves, in their measures and essences (Batishchev 1969, 82). I would like to draw special attention to a certain problem that was central to Batishchev's understanding of activity. It was the problem of relations between transformation of the outer reality (subject–object relations) and inter-human relations (subject–subject relations). At first, Batishchev considered these kinds of relations as two necessary components of activity: "The essence of the human being is activity as the identity of transformation and communication" (Batishchev 1969, 96). Then he began to give priority to subject–subject relations (he interpreted subject–object relations at this stage of the evolution of his ideas as only a supplement to subject–subject relations). At the last stage (in the 1980s), he sharply distinguished these two kinds of relations and reached the idea that subject–subject relations and communication connected with them are a genuine mode of understanding the objective nature of the Universe. He began to write about the limitations of the activity approach and the existence of such levels in consciousness that in principle cannot be understood in the framework of activity: communication, intuition, and so on. He began to consider deep communication as the most adequate mode of conceiving the Universe: "Activity is not only and not universal mode of being of a human, of culture and social life, is not only and universal mode of relations between a human being and the world" (Batishchev 1990d, 24–25; see also Lektorsky 1990). These ideas are connected with Batishchev's repudiation of Marxism at that time. He even wrote a text, as yet unpublished, criticizing Marx's "Theses on Feuerbach" (Khamidov 2009, 27, 75–76).

* * *

Soviet philosophy specifically interpreted the activity approach at that time in some works in the sphere of philosophy of science. Philosophers who investigated these problems mainly analyzed activity in respect of subject–object relations. In the 1970s, Vyacheslav Stepin developed a philosophical conception of scientific theory based on the results of analyzing the structure and dynamics of a theory in physics. He specially investigated the relations of experimental actions and of both formal and material operations in the process of constructing and developing of a scientific theory, relations between scientific ontologies and scientific "world-pictures" and these operations. The originality of Stepin's conception was the idea that theories in natural sciences are built not by a hypothetic deductive mode, as many specialists both in the USSR and the West believed, but by a genetic-constructive method that presupposes thought-experiments with ideal objects. Stepin suggested an idea of operational character and constructive substantiation of theoretical schemes (Stepin 2005). Stepin wrote about the possibility of understanding, in the framework of the activity approach, those objects that science deals with, but which a human being cannot influence. These include such objects of astronomy as the Sun, other stars, the planets of those solar systems, and so on. Stepin gave the following interpretation of this fact. First of all, he argued that there is a certain analogy between astronomical observations and a laboratory-situation when an interaction of a certain object with others is used as a kind of natural experiment (Stepin 1998, 662). The second part of his interpretation is connected with his general understanding of activity. He stressed that activity selects a limited class of features of objects from an indefinite set of actual and potential features. This applies to both practical and theoretical activity (Stepin 1998, 663). Stepin discussed this problem with another Soviet specialist in the philosophy of science, Igor' Alekseeev, who said that any observable object does not exist outside the activity. Alekseeev defended an idea that the world does not consist of constant objects with actual properties, but is a set of possibilities, only some of which can be realized. Human activity is a way of realizing what Nature by itself does not produce. Therefore, one could say that, in this sense, activity creates its objects; activity can even be understood as the primary substance (ibid.).

Alekseeev called his philosophical position "subjective materialism." Stepin opposed Alekseev and defended the position of object-oriented activity. I think that Alekseev's conception can now be interpreted as constructivist.

A special role in the development of activity-ideas in Soviet philosophy and human sciences (psychology, pedagogy and others) was played by Georgy Shchedrovitsky. He wrote about the theme of activity throughout his career. At first (in the 1960s), he attempted to elaborate an original activity theory of thinking, which was understood as activity on several levels, with definite relations between different operations: generating the content and transformations of sign-forms. Operations of practical comparison of objects produce the content, after which the operating of the form begins. All thinking operations were decomposed into their constituent parts; the number of operations was presupposed to be finite (Shchedrovitsky 1995, 34–49, 590–630). Shchedrovitsky and his followers studied definite empirical cases of thinking and interacted with psychologists and specialists in pedagogy, giving concrete recommendations. In the 1970s, Shchedrovitsky developed a "General Theory of Activity." He argued that activity is a collective system that includes goals of activity, means of their realization, norms, and division of positions of those who participate in it. The task of methodologists was understood as projecting different organized systems as systems of activity in several spheres of life, such as science, education and society. Shchedrovitsky and his followers established close relations with different spheres of practical life. This development of the activity approach led to the concept of the so-called organization-activity-games (*organisatsionno-deyatel'nostnye igry*) that have developed successfully to the present day. The problems of consciousness and personality is that they do not fall within the scope of interest for such forms of the activity approach. Shchedrovitsky was influenced by Marx, Hegel and the organizational theory ("tektology") of Aleksander Bogdanov. Bogdanov created a specific technocratic variant of the Activity approach that was in principle distinct from those of Ilyenkov and Batishchev. From Shchedrovitsky's point of view, Activity can be understood as a certain substance that only uses human beings for its own goals and which has an autonomous logic of its development. Shchedrovitsky made some provocative statements about human beings. For example:

> Does creativity belong to an individual or to a functional place in a human organization, to a structure? I will answer this question very strictly: certainly, not to an individual, but to a functional place. (Shchedrovitsky 1997, 570)

And, "the main fraud is the idea of a human being with mind, and the second fraud is the idea of a subject" (ibid.). Shchedrovitsky used the Activity approach to oppose the "natural attitude," which he criticized for supposing the existence of objects that are independent from activity. Therefore, I believe it could be said that some elements of constructivism can also be found in Shchedrovitsky's ideas.

In the Soviet philosophy of the 1960s–1980s, there were other influential conceptions of activity, produced by such philosophers as Yudin, Shvyrev, Lektorsky, and Rozov among others (see Yudin 1978; Shvyrev 2001; Lektorsky 1984; 1990; 1999; 2009a; 2009b; Rosov 2006). There was something common between them, but they were very different and criticized each other and other positions as discussed in this article.

I think that these differences had not been accidental, as they concerned real problems. My opinion is that these very problems are central to contemporary cognitive science and, in a broader sense, the human sciences.

## THE ACTIVITY APPROACH IN CONTEMPORARY EPISTEMOLOGY AND COGNITIVE SCIENCES

First, let us consider the interpretation of the main thesis of the activity approach: that the world is given to a human being in the forms of his activity. Does this mean that objective reality is something like the Kantian thing-in-itself (*Ding-an-sich*) and that a human being can deal only with those objects he has created (constructed) himself, as the philosophical-constructivism thesis claims?

I think that followers of Alekseev and Shchedrovitsky answer this question in the affirmative. Another answer was offered by Ilyenkov and early Batishchev with reference to Marx. They argued that human activity is always object-oriented and is fulfilled not according to the specific features of a human body, but according to the specific logic of each object—it is connected with the "universal nature" of a human being who is in principle distinct in this respect from all other living creatures.

The so-called "embodiment" approach, which is now popular in cognitive science, opposes philosophical constructivism, as the former proceeds from the presupposition that each cognizing and acting creature deals with the real world. According to the embodiment-approach, however, activity selects those features of the world that are essential for a certain kind of cognizing creature, and this selection depends on the demands of the creature, its bodily size, affordances for its movements, and so on. Thus, it is important from this point of view to distinguish the physical world and the surrounding world and, further, within the latter different "sub-worlds" or kinds and levels of reality—according to James Gibson, whose ideas essentially influenced the formation of the embodiment-approach (Gibson 1979).

For example, as Thomas Nagel famously noted, the reality perceived by a human being is not the same as that perceived by a bat (Nagel 1982). It seems that the embodiment-approach as a contemporary form of the activity approach and the thesis about the "universal nature" of human activity contradict each other. However, this is only a seeming contradiction.

The human relation to the world is not limited to the specific nature of a body and its demands: a human being as it leaves the confines of his body and creates a world of artificial things (beginning with simple tools and instruments and finishing with such "tools" as language and theories). Man uses these artificial things in trying to understand the relations between these different worlds.

This is the idea of the so-called "extended" interpretation of cognition (Andy Clark, Robert Wilson and others), which is popular today (Wilson 2004). But there is yet another problem: what about the relations between contemplation and activity? I have stated in this article that such founders of the activity approach in Soviet philosophy as Rubinshtein and Batishchev in their later years contrasted contemplation and activity and stressed that the former cannot be reduced to the latter. It is true that there is a certain difficulty in understanding the relations between contemplation (particularly perception) and activity. Activity means a transforming of reality, while cognition is conceiving reality. Therefore, it is not possible to identify activity and cognition, as some theoreticians of cognitive science have tried to do, particularly Francisco Varela. However, it is important to consider that cognition is intertwined with activity from the beginning, as the latter connects a cognizing subject and a cognized object and selects the essential features of the latter. If perception is understood as a simple result of the brain processing information received as an impact of the outer world, then ideas similar to the conception of "methodological solipsism" by Jerry Fodor (who suggested it as the methodology of cognitive science) are inevitable (Fodor 1980). In the framework of the activity approach, the new conception of perception has arisen. The activity approach refuses many ideas of classical interpretation of perception in philosophy and psychology. Perception is understood not as a result, not as a certain entity, but as a continuing process of extracting information from the world.

In such interpretation introduced by James Gibson, Ulrich Neisser and others, perception is not "given" and not "constructed," but is "taken" by means of physical actions (Neisser 1976).

A final problem is the relations between activity and communication. Such opponents of the activity approach as Boris Lomov in psychology (Lomov 1984) and Rubinshtein as well as Genrikh Batishchev at his later evolutionary stage in philosophy wrote that it is impossible to reduce subject–subject relations (communication) to subject–object relations (activity). It is true that the relation between a subject and another subject is not the same as its relation to an object. If I perceive another person as a real being, at that time I am aware that he perceives me in the same manner. This means that my perception of another includes my awareness of perception of me by another person. But why should activity be understood as the transformation of non-human reality only? Activity is transformation of different kinds of reality, including the reality of inter-human relations. Because the latter can be achieved by means of communication, it follows that communication is also activity, albeit of a very specific kind. In addition, it is important to stress that cognition and activity always presuppose communication, as a human being mediates his relations to the world by specific things made by other people.

The use of such things necessarily includes communication with others (I have written about it in this text in connection with the problem of psychic development of deaf and blind children). Finally, every act of communication has a meaning in the broad system of activity. Conceptions of "extended cognition" and "extended mind" are connected with these problems (Clark and Chalmers 1998, 7–19).

As noted at the start of this chapter, various constructivist conceptions are popular among philosophers, psychologists and other specialists in human sciences in present-day Russia. Especially popular are social constructionism (see Gergen 1994 and others) and the narrative approach in philosophy and psychology (Sarbin 1986), connected with it. I believe that this is a result of the fact that the followers of a constructionist approach claim to preserve some ideas of the activity approach, while at the same time going a step further and discovering new fields of research and suggesting new ideas. The followers of social constructionism stress the active, constructive nature of inter-human relations and the active role of an investigator of human beings. They write about the cultural and historical nature of psychic processes and personality and refer to works by Vygotsky and other Soviet psychologists. I think that, despite all that, social constructionism in reality is opposed to the activity approach and that the former cannot be a fruitful methodology of human sciences.

The point is that, in social constructionism, objects with which an investigator of human beings deals are not real, but constructions only. In this conception, communication has supplanted all other kinds of activity and become the main and independent force. From this point of view, research into human beings deals with two kinds of constructions. The first are results of different communications between humans having historical and cultural nature. The second are results of communicative interactions between a researcher and those whom he investigates. From this point of view, a researcher is not an investigator in the proper sense, but a participant in creating a certain ephemeral reality, about which one can speak only conventionally, as it exists only in the framework of these constructions. If we assume this viewpoint, experiment in human sciences becomes impossible, as an investigator and another person who is an object of research interact with each other through communication, which leads to an object of investigation being in principle transformed.

According to social constructionism, it is impossible to speak about a theory in the strict sense of this word in human studies. I think that the problems with which the activity approach deals in reality cannot be understood within the framework of social constructionism. On the contrary, the facts to which the followers of social constructionism refer can be better explained in the framework of the activity approach. There is something in social constructionism that is similar to the cultural-historical and activity approaches: the idea that mind, consciousness and personality are products of social interactions and communications and have a cultural-historical nature. Followers of social constructionism refer to the ideas of Lev Vygotsky and Mikhail Bakhtin, claiming that these ideas have been developed in constructionism. However, the assertion that a researcher cognizes something that is not real, that he creates an object of investigation, differs in principle from the activity approach in Soviet philosophy and psychology. In fact, each construction presupposes a certain reality that forms the basis of the constructing and which the construction tries to transform. On the other hand, a subject selects some features of real objects through his constructive activity.

If something is a product of construction, this does not mean that it is something unreal or real only in an ephemeral sense. For example, if the "ego" and the identity are social constructions, they are not unreal. The table I am sitting at is also a result of constructive activity, but it is real beyond any doubt.

It is possible to say that all social institutions are results of human activity—in other words, constructions in some sense—but they are real. A human being creates such things (material and ideal), which escape his control and begin to live by themselves. As these are social institutions, it is possible and necessary to study their structures and make theories about them. It is also a subjective world—an object of both theoretical and experimental psychological research. It is a world of ideal products of human creativity, which develops according to their specific laws, although within human activity, as shown by Ilyenkov.

This ideal world becomes separated from its human creators to such a degree that some philosophers think it is meaningless to speak about an individual author of a certain ideal construction (Lektorsky 2009a). In conclusion, the development of contemporary philosophy, psychology and cognitive science shows that further elaboration of the activity approach is urgently needed. The progress that was made in Soviet philosophy from the 1960s to the 1980s can be of interest in this respect. This does not mean that the Soviet philosophy of that time found answers to problems that are currently being discussed. It means only that the fruitfulness of some ideas formulated and elaborated in that philosophy can be understood in the present context.

## NOTES

1. The original version of this article was published in: Maidansky, Andrey and Oittinen, Vesa (eds.). 2016. *The Practical Essence of Man. The "Activity Approach" in Late Soviet Philosophy*. Leiden: Boston Brill, 137–153.
2. In Russian, "opredmechivanie" and "raspredmechivanie," which correspond to the German terms "Vergegenständlichung" and "Entgegenständlichung," found in the young Marx's *Economic and Philosophic Manuscripts* of 1844.
3. Batishchev's analysis of "revolutionary and critical activity" caused great displeasure among official ideologists, particularly Mikhail A. Suslov.

## BIBLIOGRAPHY

Batischev. Genrikh. 1969. "Deyatel'nostnaya suchchnost' cheloveka kak filosofskiy printsip" [The Activity Essence of the Human Being as a Philosophical Principle]. In *Problema cheloveka v sovremennoi filosofii* [Problem of the Human Being in Contemporary Philosophy], 73–144. Moscow: Nauka.

Batischev, Genrikh. 1990. "The category of Activity; Inexhaustible Possibilities and Limits of Applicability." In *The Activity: Theories, Methodology, and Problems*, edited by Vladislav A. Lektorsky, 7–14. Orlando, Helsinki, Moscow: Paul M. Deutsch Press Inc.

Clark, Andy. 1997. *Being There: Putting Brain, Body and World Together Again*. Cambridge: Cambridge University Press.

Clark, Andy and Chalmers, David. 1998. "The Extended Mind," *Analysis* (58): 7–19.

Engeström, Yrjö. 2005. *Developmental Work Research: Expanding Activity Theory in Practice*. Berlin: Lehmanns Media.

Fodor, Jerry 1980. "Methodological Solipsism Considered as a Research Strategy in Cognitive Science." *Behavioral and Brain Sciences* (3): 63–73.

Gergen, Keneth. 1994. *Realities and Relationships: Soundings in Social Construction*. Cambridge MA: Harvard University Press.

Gibson, James. 1979. *The Ecological Approach to Visual Perception*. Boston, MA: Houghton Mifflin.

Ilyenkov, Evald V. 1967. "From the Marxist Point of View." In *Marx and the Western World*, edited by N. Lobkovich, 391–407. Notre Dame: University of Notre Dame Press.

Ilyenkov, Evald V. 1975. "A.I. Mesherjakov i ego pedagogika" [A.I. Mesherjakov and His Pedagogy]. *Molodoi communist* [Young Communist] (2): 212–230.

Ilyenkov, Evald V. 2014. "Dialectics of the Ideal." In *Dialectics of the Ideal: Evald Ilyenkov and Creative Soviet Marxism*, edited by Felex Levant and Vesa Oittinen, 25–78. Leiden: Brill.

Khamidov, Alexander. 2009. "Put' otkrytii kak otkrytie puti: filosofskie iskanija G.S. Batishcheva" [The Way of Discoveries as the Discovery of the Way: G.S. Batishchev's Philosophical Search of G.S.Batisahev]. In *Genrikh Stepanovich Batishchev*, edited by Vladislav A. Lektorsky, 381–413. Moscow: ROSSPEN.

Lektorsky, Vladislav A. 1984. *Subject, Object, Cognition*. Moscow: Progress publishers.

Lektorsky, Vladislav A. (ed.). 1990. *Activity: Theories, Methodology, and Problems*. Orlando: Paul Deutsch Press.

Lektorsky, Vladislav A. 1999. "Historical Change in the Notion of Activity: Philosophical Presuppositions." In *Activity Theory and Social Practice: Cultural-Historical Approaches*, edited by Seth Chaiklin, Mariane Hedegaard, Uffe Juul Jensen, 111–113. Aarhus: Aarhus University Press.

Lektorsky, Vladislav A. 2009a. "Mediation as a Means of Collective Activity." In *Learning and Expanding with Activity Theory*, edited by Annalisa Sannino, Harry Daniels, Kris D. Gutiérrez, 156–170. Cambridge: Cambridge University Press.

Lektorsky, Vladislav A. 2009b. "Realism, anti-realism, konstruktivizm, i konstructivny realism v epistemologii i nauke" [Realism, Anti-realism, Constructivism and Constructive Realism in Epistemology and Science]. In *Konstructivny podhod v epistemologgii I naukhah o cheloveke*, [Constructive Approach in Epistemology and Human Sciences], 5–40. Moscow: Kanon publisher.

Leontiev, Alexei N. 1978. *Activity, Consciousness and Personality*. New York: Politizdat.

Lomov, Boris. 1979. *Metodologicheskie i teoreticheskie problemy psikhologii* [Methodological and Heretical Problems of Psychology].

Marx, Karl. 1975. *Early Writings*. Harmondsworth: Penguin Books.

Nagel, Thomas. 1974. "What is it like to be a bat?" In *The Mind's I*, edited by D. Dennett and D. Hofstadter, 391–402. New York: Basic Books.

Neisser, Ulric. 1976. *Cognition and Reality: Principles and implications of Cognitive Psychology*. New York: W.H. Freeman.

Rozov, Mikhail A. 2006. *Teorija socialnikh estafet i problema epistemilogii* [Theory of Social Relay Race and the Problems of Epistemology]. Moscow: Novyi Khronograph publishers.

Rubinshtein, Sergei L. 1934. "Problemy psikhologii v trudakh Karla Marksa" [Problems of Psychology in Karl Marx's Works]. *Sovetskaja psichotekhnika* [Soviet Psycho-Technics], (1): 8–15.

Rubinshtein, Sergei L. 1973. *Problemy Obschey Psikhologii*. [The Problems of General Psychology]. Moscow: Pedagogika publishers.

Rubinshtein, Sergei L. 1986. "Printsip tvorcheskoy samodejadel'nosti. K filosofskim osnovam sovremennoy pedagogiki" [The Principle of Creative Self- Activity. Toward Philosophical Foundations of Contemporary Pedagogics]. *Voprosy psikhologii*. (4): 101–107.

Sarbin, Theodor R. (ed.) 1986. *Narrative Psychology: The Storied Nature of Human Conduct*. New York: Prager.

Shchedrovitsky, Georgy P. 1995. *Izbrannye trudy*. [Selected Works]. Moscow: Shkola kul'turnoi politiki.

Shchedrovitsky, Georgy P. 1997. *Filosofiya, nauka, metodologiya* [Philosophy, Science, Methodology]. Moscow: Shkola kul'turnoi politiki.

Shvyrev, Vladimir S. 2001. "O deyatelnostnom podhode k istiolkovaniju fenomena chelobeka" (About Activity Approach in Interpretation of a Human Being). *Voprosy filosofii*. (2):108–110.

Stepin, Vyacheslav S. 1998. "V mire teoreticheskih idei" [In the World of Theoretical Ideas]. *Filosofiya ne konchaetsja* [Philosophy Never Ends], vol. 2, edited by Vladislav Lektorsky, 653–669. Moscow: ROSSPEN.

Stepin, Vyacheslav S. 2005. *Theoretical Knowledge*. Dordrecht: Springer.

Varela, Francisco, Thomson, Evan and Rosch, Eleanor. 1992. *The Embodied Mind: Cognitive Science and Human Experience*. Cambridge, MA: MIT Press.

Velichkovsky, Boris M. 2006. *Kognitivnaja nauka. Osnovy psikhologii poznanja* [Cognitive Science. Foundations of Psychology of Cognition], in 2 vols. Moscow: Academia publisher.

Wilson, Robert A. 2004. *Boundaries of Mind: The Individual in the Fragile Sciences: Cognition*. Cambridge: Cambridge University Press.

Yudin, Erik G. 1978. *Sistemny podhod i printsip deajatelnosti: methodologicheskie problem sovremennoi nauki* [System Approach and Activity Principle: Methodological Problems of Contemporary Science]. Moscow: Nauka.

CHAPTER FIFTEEN

# The Activity Theory in Soviet Philosophy and Psychology in the 1960s–1980s

PETR G. SHCHEDROVITSKY

It is not at all accidental that the analysis of a variety of activity theories in philosophy and psychology in the 1960s–1980s becomes a focus of contemporary philosophical discussions. Similarly, it should not come as a surprise that Sergei Rubinshtein, who was one of the founders of the so-called psychological "activity theory," has been put on the list of the top twenty Russian philosophers of the second half of the twentieth century. There is also a specialized volume devoted to philosophical psychology as part of a series of the volumes on the philosophy of the first half of the century, currently being published by ROSSPEN. In his recent publication, Karen Swassjan talked about a "psychologization of Marx's works" in the 1960s (Swassjan 2014, 65). I do not quite agree with this judgment. I would rather point to the process of the "philosophization of psychology" (and, in general, of all psychological issues) as the most important feature and characteristic of the legacy of the thinkers of that period as well as of the Soviet and Russian philosophy throughout the second half of the twentieth century.

Even if we take the extremes, such as the psychological theory of Alexei Leontiev or Vasiliy Davydov's use of the theoretical "activity theory" framework in the sphere of education, the philosophical underpinnings of their legacy are quite apparent.

This philosophic background of Russian psychological works could be clearly explained by some purely internal reasons. To begin with, both the 1930s and the 1960s did not leave much room for the philosophically-minded intellectuals reluctant to compromise their conscience and comply with the official dogmatic doctrine. As Mezhuiev once remarked with the reference to an anonymous contemporary intellectual, "A 'decent man' should devote himself to epistemology" (Mezhuev 2014, 52). Similarly, some other Soviet and Russian intellectuals, such as Pavel Blonsky, Lev Vygotsky, Sergei Rubinshtein, Petr Galperin and Vasily

Davydov—possibly, Vladimir Bibler and Georgy Shchedrovitsky, too—would probably put it this way: "A 'decent man' should devote himself to pedagogy and psychology." Pedagogy, despite its continuous persecutions and prosecutions, often remained a relatively free sphere of practice available to creative research of both an applied and a theoretical nature.

We could extend this situational interpretation addressing a larger philosophic tradition, whose different branches, in a way, regard pedagogy as a philosophy put into practice or even as a practice of philosophic idealism. These are the words of Paul Natorp, one of Rubinshtein's mentors (Natorp 2006, 297). This is what John Dewey believed was one of the missions of philosophy. No doubt, the upbringing and education of future generations is the crucial point in philosophic comprehension, the point where the practical educational functions are intertwined with pedagogical hermeneutics and pedagogical epistemology, and also with fundamental questions of philosophical anthropology.

The significance of this subject was always somehow exaggerated in Russia. The sphere of pedagogics as a sphere of education of a "full-fledged," or "proper" person remained one of the major themes of the public discourse, absorbing all the questions, impossible to ask and moreover impossible to solve in any other field during the eighteenth and nineteenth, let alone the twentieth centuries. By that, I mean the questions of societal development in general, which—according to the Russian mind more often than the western one—properly belonged in the realm of education.

The fact that it is into this sphere that the idea of activity approach, in its different forms, infiltrates seems less coincidental. The conception of human beings' actions and activity in European tradition has been developing for ages. In his article named "The Heritage of Activity Approach and the Present Day," Vladislav Lektorsky emphasizes that, "actually, Marx had only suggested one of the great number of the activity approaches, which in our country, due to specific historical conditions, was taken as the only one in existence. . . . [Before him,] Fichte had already started developing the idea that a subject defines itself solely through the activity of objectification, through creation of an object that is at once counterposed to the subject externally and functions as the only conceivable way of constituting it. The creation of "Nicht-Ich" is, according to Fichte, more than a mere objectification of "Ich," more than its mere duplication—it is its transformation from an indefinite [entity] into a definite one, its actual emergence. For it is through objectification alone that "Ich" is able to perceive itself reflexively, which is a necessary condition of its existence" (Lektorsky 2001, 77).

In this article, Lektorsky, as I see it, indicates convincingly that activity approach and the concept of activity are the keynote of European philosophic thinking from Hegel to Fichte, through all the neo-Kantians and neo-Fichteans of the late nineteenth century and the early twentieth century to the latest Wittgenstein, the Frankfurt School, Sartre, Bridgman and Piaget's operationalization.

Continuing this way, I would highlight the extension of activity approach and the concept of activity in the twentieth century into such scientific fields as sociology and economics. Let me name but a few—Max Weber, Émile Durkheim, and Talcott Parsons in sociology, works of the members of the Austrian political economy school and those of Ludwig von Mises, in particular, who insisted in his treatise devoted to the human action (1940) that economics are based on praxeology and general activity theory (Mises 1998, 3). This connection can of course be justified by Hegel and Marx's influence, which is doubtless present. But, in my point of view, it would be far more productive to approach this expansion of activity theory into philosophy and into a number of social humanitarian theories as a universal Pan-European—or even global—tendency related to the formation of a new ontology based on the general theory of action and thought.

Discussing the Russian philosophers and psychologists' contribution to this formation of an ontology of activity we should never ignore the works of Rubinshtein and Vygotsky written in the 1920s and 1930s. Roughly speaking, these works had already contained, in an incipient form, many of the problems and ideas that were developed in leaps and bounds in the second half of the century, in particular during the debates among the members of various Russian activity schools (communities) I was able to witness personally in the mid-1980s. Even some works written in the early 1920s by Rubinshtein—such as "About Cohen's Philosophical System" (1916–1918) (Rubinshtein 2003, 428) and, later, "The Principle of Creativity" (1922)—give us several fundamental principles which are but an extension of the Marburg School's ideas. According to this idea, "a subject isn't behind his actions, neither does he express himself via them; . . . a subject exists only in them, defined and self-defined by these actions of him" (Rubinshtein 1986, 106).

In his better-known later work, "Psychological Issues in Karl Marx's Works" (1933)[1]—I would say, one of the first interpretations of the *Economic and Philosophical Manuscripts of 1844*—using early texts of Marx to justify the new approach to organizing psychology and psychotechnics, Rubinshtein evidently "raises the bar." He states:

> Thus, man is not the Hegelian self-creating subject: if my consciousness is formed as a result of my activity through the products of that activity, then, objectively, it is formed through the results of social activity. In its inner core, my consciousness is mediated by objective relationships which become established in social practices and of which I become part, entering them with each and every instance of my activity—practical and theoretical alike. Every instance of my activity and I myself—within it and through it—are enmeshed by thousands of threads of diverse connections into the objective structures of a historically formed culture, and my consciousness is mediated by those ties through and through. (Rubinshtein 1973, 27)

And then:

> Language serves as a plane on which I imprint the existence that I reflect and on which I project my operations. Thus, an ideal plane is activated between the immediate actual situation cognized by me and the operation or action I am changing the world with. Therefore, the very structure of action inevitably proves different. The emergence of the mediating ideal plane rids action of its total dependence on the immediate actual situation. . . . Man ceases to be a slave to the immediate actual situation; having become mediated, his actions may be determined not only by stimuli caused by the immediate actual situation, but also by goals and tasks lying beyond it: they become selective and goal-oriented,

> acquiring will; it is these traits that characterize man's activity, plainly distinguishing his behavior from that of an animal. (Ibid., 28)

Almost the same ideas occurred at that time to Vygotsky. In his *Development of the Higher Psychological Functions* (1931) and, ever more clearly, in *Thinking and Speech* (1934), Vygotsky highlights that the transition from primal cognitive functions to the higher ones, the conscious self-regulation of human behavior, is due to the fact that the higher functions are mediated. On the way between the immediate "incentive" that starts action and the specifically human reaction to it, there is a "sign" or, more exactly, a set of sign systems of cultural and historical character.

The mediated action is equally defined by history and culture and by interactions of a person with other individuals, for instance between an adult and a child, which is vital in the educational process. The forms of these interactions create the specifically human way of existence quite different from that of animals. Vygotsky states: "Every function in the child's cultural development appears twice: first, on the social level, and later, on the individual level; first, between people (interpsychological) and then inside the child (intrapsychological). This applies equally to voluntary attention, to logical memory, and to the formation of concepts. All the higher functions originate as actual relationships between individuals" (Vygotsky 1978, 34).

These quotes are not only important for comparison to the works of the 1960s and 1970s, but also to the concepts developed in the same period, i.e., in the 1920s–1930s. We should keep in mind that the Institute of Psychology was headed by K. Kornilov, whose approach to the Marxian psychology was based on rather primitive reflexological ideas. Many talented psychologists—G. Chelpanov's adherents—were forced to leave the Institute and look for a new job. Trivial ideas many of you have never heard of prevailed as the principles for the creation of the psychological science of that time. The Institute's old-timers told me that the first department to be closed was that of introspection. Kornilov invited two graduates from the "worker's faculty"—*rabfak*—to inspect what the departments had been doing. They discussed the introspectionists thus: "Vasya, have you got that introspection?" "No." "Neither have I, so let's put an end to it."

Not of a lesser importance was another fact we should take into account. It is the equation of action with labor, typical of the Soviet humanitarian sciences in the 1920s. For instance, reading Blonsky's works on labor education (Blonsky 1978, 86) we immediately notice passages literally identical to Sergei Rubinshtein and Lev Vygotsky's quotes, the only difference being the term "labor" instead of "action." It can be also found in other works published then by Rubinshtein and Vygotsky themselves.

"Labor" has, in this case, the same attributes as "action": the focus, the culturally determined tools or means and ways of their use, collectivity, historicity, etc. The well-known fact is that the Scientific Management movement in the USSR of that time was extraordinarily powerful; following the European tradition, they developed a set of requirements for the social sciences, first of all psychology. This is why, as I said, Rubinshtein's article was published in the journal *Soviet Psychotechnics*—the voice of the Soviet Taylorists.

However, in the mid-1930s, the Central Institute of Labor began to be criticized, the applied sciences dealing with labor were accused of idealism. All the laboratories of industrial psychotechnics and psychophysiology of labor were closed, the work of the Institute itself and of its dozen or so branches was stopped. In 1939, the founder and the permanent head of the Institute K. Gastev was executed.

After the first post-revolutionary decade, the Russian term *trud* (labor) gradually loses its sacral meaning, although some of its important connotations become somehow expressed in the new concept of *deyatel'nost'* (usually translated into English as "activity"). The term "*deyatel'nost'*" absorbs two different groups of meanings: one associated with the term "labor" and another one with the "individual action." It involves the idea of action of an individual or a group of people (including cooperation and communication) and the idea of the social, historical practice of man, which merge together. This complex meaning is one of the reasons why translating works discussing *deyatel'nost'* into English is a difficult task. Vasily Davydov came across this difficulty involving the use of the English word "activity," which expresses only one aspect of the Russian original term that could be best rendered by two German terms: *Tätigkeit* (activity as a process or a set of goals and the tools to achieve them) and *Handlung* (more of a single act).

It needs to be mentioned that Rubinshtein and Vygotsky's works, along with the works of Blonsky unfairly disregarded in the 1920s–1930s, raised the bar in psychological and then in pedagogical research to an inaccessible height. Neither the struggle against "pedagogical perversions" nor the defamation of Vygotsky starting from the mid-1930s, after he—thank God—had already died, could be prevented. We should be grateful that this challenge was overcome by means of interpreting Marx's conception, including his "psychologization." Moreover, as I have mentioned, the basic lines of development of the ideas we observed forming in the 1960s–1980s were set down in the course of that work. Let us name but a few of them.

First, there is a number of works on the interaction between thinking and activity. Here I would name the works of Petr Galperin, in which he declared the necessity of restoring the objective, operational content of activity, which later drove him to another issue—to form the ideal image of the future action, the concept of orientation and the developed idea of orientational activity. In this context, another work should be named: the articles of L. Obukhova in which she analyzes Piaget's concept of preschool children's mental development and criticizes it, backing her criticism by experiment. Using an immense amount of empirical material, Galperin and his apprentices developed the idea of cogitative control of activity. These works, committed to the third type of orientation, showed, in particular, that the ability to create an independent action is based on the constructive comprehension of its object (this line of work was experimentally started by N. Pantina (Pantina 1957, 117). Another group of works, e.g., by Bibler, Davydov and Georgy Shchedrovitsky about the role of human self-reflection and thinking in planning and performing activity, belong in this sphere.

Second, there are studies on collective activity, cooperation and communication, including comprehension. Here I would name the works of Davydov, in which he developed the theory of collective activity, guided by D. Elkonin's rethinking of the concept of interiorization. Elkonin asserted he had been restoring the concept advanced by Vygotsky. Elkonin opposed reconsidering interiorization as appropriation of some collective activity forms by an individual and the social interaction to another idea (of Galperin) where interiorization was seen as a transfer of externally proceeded orientation of a future action into the internal plane.

"The main point is," his notes read, "[that] an objective action [should be regarded] as a social interaction unit. It contains an internal contradiction: 1) it is [performed] by a human, so the individual's attitude to society and the human nature manifest themselves, 2) it is material, so the attitude to the nature of things also manifests itself" (Elkonin 1989, 488). This idea was refined in the periodization of children's mental development and in the ideas of collectively distributed activity. In his later years, Davydov insisted that, while communicating, interlocutors constantly discuss various issues and tasks, learn to change their point of view and see themselves through one another's eyes, thereby perfecting their skills of self-reflection. Bibler and Shchedrovitsky also emphasized the role of communication, which they studied expansively, in their works.

Third, there are works related to the problem of involvement of the individual into the activity of creation of personal meanings and personality itself. Alexei Leontiev redefined "motive" and "goal" to describe "meaning" as a relation of these two, so as to be able to measure meaning by the degree of their accordance to each other. Based on these new terms, additional distinctions were specified between "activity," "action" and "operation." Another important feature of this research was the analysis of the processes of motive formation and of acquisition and loss of personal meaning seen in tasks and activity in general.

Fourth, there are works addressing the problems of the subject, his acts and his ethical choice. Here we need to mention the work of Sergei Rubinshtein and his apprentice K. Abulkhanova-Slavskaya. Here, I believe, some ideas of Bibler belong as well. From his point of view, any individual activity, while directed toward the exterior world, should always be seen as "self-commitment" and, as such, a divergence of the subject from itself. Due to this initial divergence of the objective activity from the acting individual, and due to its initial self-commitment, the individual becomes free from his own activity. In this space, according to Bibler, the mind and free will do exist.

And, finally, I would like to point out the development of activity conception by Georgy Shchedrovitsky, in whose works, one way or another, the questions of self-reflection and thinking, and perspective of communication are reflected. In the latest stages of his work, Shchedrovitsky introduced the concept of collective thinking-activity (*mysledejatel'nost'*) as the unity of all the processes: thinking, self-reflection and comprehension, communication and action.

Once again, I would like to emphasize the main conclusions. In the late nineteenth and early twentieth century, the activity approach and the activity conceptions based on it increasingly influence philosophy and special disciplines such as psychology, sociology and economics. Gradually, there appears the new ontology, which is based on a deeper and more detailed understanding of thought and action.

The development of Russian philosophy and psychology in the twentieth century moves in the same direction. The emphasis on psychological and pedagogical research typical of this period is caused by the specific social and cultural situation in the country, though it could also be interpreted as a peculiar Russian "specialty" in the more extended field of work conducted all over the world.

The works of the second half of the twentieth century are based on those of the authors who developed the activity theory in the 1920s and 1930s—first of all, Rubinshtein, Vygotsky and Blonsky. They gave us a sketch of a non-reductionist approach to the understanding of man and the means of his development. They wanted to interpret Marx's works, instead of the writings of adherents of "Marx's psychology," so they have built a foundation for further research. The researchers of the 1960s–1970s worked along several basic lines explaining and specifying concrete issues. The most important of them, I believe, are the studies of the interrelation of activity, thinking and self-reflection, activity and communication, the involvement of an individual into activity and development perspective.

## NOTES

1. The article was published in the *Soviet Psychotechnics* in 1934.

## BIBLIOGRAPHY

Blonsky, Pavel P. 1978. "Izbrannye pedagogicheskie i psihologicheskie sochineniya" [Selected Pedagogical and Psychological Works] in 2 volumes, vol. 1. Moscow: Pedagogika.

Elkonin, Daniil B. 1989. *Izbrannye psihologicheskie trudy* [Selected Psychological Works]. Moscow: Pedagogika.

Lektorsky, Vladislav A. 2001. "Nasledie deyatelnostnogo podhoda i sovremennost'" [The Heritage of Activity Approach and the Present Day]. In *Epistemologiya klassicheskaya i neklassicheskaya* [Classical and Non-Classical Epistemology]. Moscow: URSS.

Mezhuev, Vadim M. 2014. "Ot philosophii perioda 'ottepeli' k philosophii perioda 'zastoya'" [From the Philosophy of the Thaw Era to the Philosophy of the Stagnation Era]. In *Problemy i diskussii v filosophii Rossii vtoroi poloviny XX v.: sovremennyi vzglyad* [Problems and Discussions in Russian Philosophy of the Second Half of the 20th Century: A Contemporary Perspective], edited by Vladislav Lektorsky, 42–58. Moscow: ROSSPEN.

Mises, Ludwig von. 1998. *Human Action: A Treatise on Economics*. Auburn, Alabama: Ludvig von Mises Institute.

Natorp, Paul. 2006. *Izbrannye raboty* [Selected Works]. Moscow: Territoriya budushchego.

Pantina, Nelli S. 1957. "Formirovanie dvigatelnogo navyka pis'ma v zavisimosti ot tipa orientirovki v zadanii" [The Formation of Writing Skills According to the Kind of Orientation Used in the Assignment]. *Voprosy psihologii* [*Psychology Issues*] (4): 117–132.

Rubinshtein, Sergei L. 1973. *Problemy obshchey psikhologii* [The Issues of General Psychology]. Moscow: Pedagogika.

Rubinshtein, Sergei L. 1986. "Printsip tvorcheskoy samodeyatelnosti" [The Principle of Independent Creative Activity]. *Voprosy psihologii* [Psychology Issues] (4): 101–109.

Rubinshtein, Sergei L. 2003. *Bytie i soznanie. Chelovek i mir* [Being and Consciousness. Man and the World]. St. Petersburg: Piter.

Swassjan, Karen A. 2014. "O Sovetskoi philosophii" [On Philosophy in the USSR]. In: *Problemy i diskussii v filosophii Rossii vtoroi poloviny XX v.: sovremennyi vzglyad* [Problems and Discussions in Russian Philosophy of the Second Half of the Twentieth Century: A Contemporary Perspective], edited by Vladislav Lektorsky, 59–72. Moscow: ROSSPEN.

Vygotsky, Lev S. 1978. *Mind in Society: The Development of Higher Psychological Processes*. Cambridge, MA: Harvard University Press.

CHAPTER SIXTEEN

# Activity and the Formation of Reason

DAVID BAKHURST

Some thirty-five years ago, I arrived in Russia as a visiting student. My purpose was to spend a year conducting research on the philosophical culture of the USSR. I had been assigned to Moscow State University, but I was fortunate to have a mentor at another institution, the philosopher Felix Trofimovich Mikhailov, who at that time had a position at Moscow's Institute of General and Pedagogical Psychology. I had met Mikhailov on an earlier visit to Moscow and he had promised to help me find my way into the strange world of Soviet philosophy. In the course of that year I spent many happy hours discussing philosophy with Felix and other thinkers to whom he introduced me, including Vladimir Bibler, Anatoli Arsenyev, Vasily Davydov, and one of the editors of this volume, Vladislav Lektorsky. When I returned to my native England, I resolved to focus my studies on a particular philosopher, Evald Ilyenkov, who had died in 1979 and whose name seemed constantly on the lips of my Russian interlocutors.[1]

I chose Ilyenkov for a number of reasons. First among them was the intellectual calibre of his legacy. I came to Soviet philosophy as a philosopher, not a Sovietologist, and I wanted to focus my work on thinkers who had something philosophically profound to say. At the same time, I realized that I could not appreciate Ilyenkov's thought without understanding the whole history of the Soviet tradition in philosophy. Although Ilyenkov's finest creative achievements were products of Khrushchev's "thaw," their significance could not be understood without appreciating what had become of philosophy under Stalin. In addition, I felt that themes in Ilyenkov's work recalled important developments in Soviet thought in the post-revolutionary period of the 1920s, particularly the sociocultural psychology of Lev Vygotsky, on the one hand, and the impassioned debates between dialectical and mechanistic forms of Marxism, on the other. Moreover, the course of Ilyenkov's career after his remarkable early writings is in some ways indicative of the disappointments of the Brezhnev era. So Ilyenkov's life and work seemed to encapsulate the whole drama of the history of Soviet philosophy from its beginnings almost to its end.

Another important reason for my interest in Ilyenkov was that the concept of activity lay at the center of his thought, and my discussions with Mikhailov had convinced me that this concept was the key to understanding the distinctive character of Soviet Marxism.[2] So I came to focus on Ilyenkov and my research eventually culminated in a book, *Consciousness and Revolution in Soviet Philosophy* (Bakhurst 1991). (Unfortunately, the book was never published in Russian. I remember Lektorsky joking in the mid-1990s: "David, your book was too anti-Soviet to publish before the collapse of the USSR, and now unfortunately it's too pro-Soviet.")

One feature of Ilyenkov's philosophy that immediately fascinated me was his understanding of the social nature and origin of the human mind. It is a recurring theme in his work that "The subject of thought is the individual in the fabric of social relations, the socially-defined individual whose every form of life-activity is given not by nature but by history, by the process of the formation of human culture" (Ilyenkov 1974, 207–208 [2009, 165]).[3] On this view, our mindedness is not a gift of our biological nature, but emerges in us in the course of our upbringing and education. At birth the human child has a merely animal mode of existence and her mind is an animal mind. She becomes a person, a conscious thinking subject, as she enters human culture. A human life is therefore marked by a crucial transition whereby "the individual for the first time becomes a person, becomes a representative of the 'human race,' while before this she was merely a representative of a biological species" (Ilyenkov 1984, 68 [2014, 71]). I shall call this the "transformational view" of the development of the human individual. The idea is that the human child is born a mere animal and *becomes* human, *becomes* a person, *acquires* consciousness and will, and *attains* the status of a thinking subject capable of rational thought and free agency, as she is initiated into human culture.[4] In this paper, I propose to examine this idea and consider whether it is defensible and if so, in what form.

In Ilyenkov's philosophy, the transformational view follows from his approach to what he calls "the problem of the ideal." Ilyenkov argues that the ideal—by which he means the realm of concepts, meanings, values, norms—can be understood only in relation to human activity. We must look for the ideal, not in the natural world as it is in itself, nor in a platonic realm set apart from the nature. Rather, the ideal exists in the form nature acquires through human activity. Ideality is human activity "objectified" or "reified" in the natural world. As Ilyenkov puts it, expressing a view he finds in Marx: "'Ideality'—is a distinctive stamp impressed upon the substance of nature by social human life-activity; it is the form of the functioning of physical things in the process of social-human life activity. Therefore, all things incorporated into the social process acquire a new 'form of existence,' quite distinct from, and in no way contained in, their physical nature: an ideal form" (Ilyenkov 1984, 51 [2014, 58]). The environment into which the human child is born is thus not simply a physical environment. She enters a world of meanings, norms, rules, traditions, practices, reasons, values, and so on—the ideal realm of culture. And unlike other animals, which are equipped to orientate themselves in their natural environments by the forms of life-activity encoded in their genes, nature does not provide the human child with the means to orientate herself in such an ideal space. This facility she can acquire only through upbringing and education, for as Ilyenkov puts it, "Here the issue is not one of adjusting ready-made patterns of behavior, but of the child's assimilation of forms of life-activity that bear no relation to the biologically necessary ways in which the child's organism reacts to things and situations" (1984, 66 [2014, 70]). The realm of the ideal is the world of freedom and creativity. It has its own laws of evolution—cultural-historical evolution—and the child can inhabit this world only insofar as she acquires the means to orientate herself within it, only insofar, that is, as she becomes a person, a thinking subject with powers of consciousness and will. With this, the child herself attains a new form of existence or way of being: her mode of life is no longer confined by the demands of her immediate environment, but is open to the world, to the universal, the infinite, the ideal.

Ilyenkov's way of articulating this position was original—perhaps unique—but the transformational view was endorsed by a large number of thinkers, notably Alexei Leontiev and other philosophers and psychologists advocating the so-called "activity approach," many of whom were inspired by Vygotsky. Indeed, it might be said that the idea of the child's acquiring rational powers through initiation into culture is a distinctive theme of Soviet Marxism. It is important to be aware, however, that similar ideas are found in the writings of significant Western thinkers, whose ideas engage in a variety of interesting ways with Ilyenkov's.

Let me give three examples of parallel views in Western philosophy.

First, arguments that present the human mind as essentially social in nature are found in the works of a number of prominent twentieth century philosophers. Such arguments typically rest on the idea that human thought and action take place within what Wilfrid Sellars called "the space of reasons." When we exercise our powers of reason, the movement of our thought is, or at least aspires to be, governed by reasons. We form beliefs about our environment in light of what our perceptual experience gives us reason to believe, and when we engage in reasoning and deliberation, we proceed from one thought to the next in light of what the evidence, our prior beliefs, the testimony of others, and so on, give us reason to think. Similarly, when we act, we aspire to do what we have reason, indeed most reason, to do. Now any such rational activity is governed by norms. Indeed, the influence reasons have over us is essentially normative in character. Thought and action are not just causally initiated. They follow from the subject's self-conscious appreciation of what it is appropriate to think or do. But what determines these normative standards of appropriateness? Such norms are very different in kind from causal laws. They are, in Ilyenkov's terminology, ideal phenomena. As such, they surely cannot just exist. There must be some story to tell about their source. What brings them into existence and sustains them there? It is tempting to think that this question cannot be answered without essential reference to a community of agents, who by their practices institute and administer the norms in question. It must be a *community* because no individual in isolation could impose normative standards upon herself. Such standards presuppose a distinction between correct and incorrect practice, and, as Wittgenstein argued (2009, §258), an essentially solitary agent cannot distinguish between what strikes her as right and what really is right. That distinction requires the authority of more than merely individual judgment, and hence the reality of rational thought and action requires a plurality of agents.

Such an argument is advanced by, among others, Donald Davidson (2001) and Robert Brandom (1994), and figures in some readings of Wittgenstein (see Bakhurst 1995b). Here there are, I believe, important parallels with Ilyenkov. The latter's writings on the ideal can also be read as an account of the sources of normativity in human activity, notwithstanding the fact that Brandom and Davidson concern themselves not with the objectification of activity, as Ilyenkov does, but with the place of social practice in the constitution of normative standards of correctness. Of course, the exact role such thinkers as Wittgenstein, Brandom and Davidson attribute to the community is a subtle matter of some controversy. Nevertheless, their positions, like Ilyenkov's, are naturally wedded to a transformational view of human development. For if self-conscious rational activity essentially involves responsiveness to norms, then the very possibility of such activity depends upon initiation into the practices that constitute and sustain the realm of the normative, the space of reasons.

Another advocate of the transformational view is the philosopher John McDowell, the hero of my book *The Formation of Reason* (Bakhurst 2011b). Although McDowell distances himself from the kind of anthropocentric theory of normativity just described, he nevertheless endorses a strongly social account of the preconditions of our mindedness. McDowell expresses his position in a way reminiscent of Ilyenkov himself: "It is not even clearly intelligible," he writes, "to suppose a creature might be born at home in the space of reasons. Human beings are not: they are born mere animals, and are transformed into thinkers and intentional agents in the course of coming to maturity" (McDowell 1996, 125). McDowell's route to this conclusion is the following. Like Davidson and Brandom, he holds that responsiveness to reasons is the distinctive characteristic of human minds. But responsiveness to reasons is something acquired by human beings in the course of their upbringing and education, particularly with the acquisition of language which equips the individual with conceptual capacities that opens her to the world (McDowell cannot find a suitable English word to capture this process, so he invokes the German "*Bildung*," which has a similar etymology to the Russian "*obrazovanie*"). It is important that McDowell works with a far richer idea of language than many philosophers coming out of the analytic tradition. For him, language is not just the means to articulate thought and communicate it to others. Language embodies conceptions of the world and styles of thinking and reasoning, and its acquisition enables the child, not just to engage with the world as a totality and to entertain thoughts that are universal in character, but to respond immediately to the minds of others by discerning what they think in what they say. Thus, the child's entrance into language begins a radical transformation, one in which she acquires a "second nature" and becomes a being of a "metaphysically new kind" (McDowell 2009, 172). McDowell thus describes the process of entering the space of reasons as "the same thing as acquiring a mind, the capacity to think and act intentionally" (McDowell 1996, 126).

My third example comes from British philosophers of education, who were contemporaries of Ilyenkov. The political philosopher and intellectual historian Michael Oakeshott, for example, argues that human beings "inhabit a world of intelligibles," a world "composed not of 'things,' but of meanings" (Oakeshott 2001, 63, 65). Human beings are not born at home in this world, for "meanings have to be learnt." We must appropriate an "intellectual and moral inheritance" through initiation into what "Dilthey called a *geistige Welt*" (ibid., 37) (and what Ilyenkov called "humanity's spiritual culture"). This we can acquire only through upbringing and education, but acquire it we must for to "be initiated into this world is learning to become human; and to move within it freely is being human, which is an 'historic,' not a 'natural' condition" (ibid., 103).

Oakeshott therefore gives tremendous significance to education in his writings, as did Ilyenkov, for the reward of education is "emancipation from the mere 'fact of living,' from the immediate contingencies of place and time of birth, from the tyranny of the moment and from the servitude of a merely current condition; it is the reward of a human identity and of a character capable in some measure of the moral and intellectual adventure which constitutes a specifically human life" (Oakeshott 2001, 104). While Oakeshott stops short of the idea that initiation into culture is "the same thing as acquiring a mind," such a view seems to have been entertained by some of his followers, including the prominent philosopher of education R.S. Peters (2003).[5]

It might seem remarkable to find parallels between Ilyenkov and Oakeshott, since Ilyenkov was a communist and Oakeshott a political conservative. But perhaps this is not so strange, since both voiced hostility to forms of political authoritarianism, both affirmed high cultural educational ideals in opposition to scientism, managerialism and petty bureaucracy, and both saw education as the cultivation of well-rounded individuals who can think and act autonomously.

Of course, there are important differences of emphasis between Ilyenkov and the likes of Oakeshott and McDowell. The latter two are both preoccupied with language. Oakeshott's favourite metaphor for culture is *conversation* (see Oakeshott 1990). Accordingly, to be initiated into a culture is a matter of joining the conversation, of learning to discriminate the different "voices" that comprise it, gaining facility with the "languages" they speak and the texts they produce, and participating in the conversation, if only as an informed listener. As we saw, McDowell gives pride of place to first-language acquisition in his account of the development of mind. Inspired by Hans-Georg Gadamer, he argues that "a natural language, the sort of language into which human beings are first initiated, serves as a repository of tradition, a store of historically accumulated wisdom about what is a reason for what." Acquiring language emancipates the "human individual from a merely animal mode of living into being a full-fledged subject, open to the world" (McDowell 1996, 125).

Ilyenkov, of course, is much less concerned with language. His primary emphasis is on the way meaning is embodied in artifacts and non-linguistic practices. For him, the genesis of the individual mind resides not in the child's learning her first words, but in such basic activities as learning to eat with a spoon (one of his favourite examples).[6] For here the child must learn to subordinate her activity to the ideal form embodied in the artifact and in so doing she starts to move in a world of meanings. Only if we understand such pre-linguistic engagements with meaning will we comprehend how language itself is possible. Moreover, Ilyenkov's contribution is especially notable for his attention to the specific character of the world in which human beings live, to the way in which ideality is embodied in the very form of our "humanized" environment and how the core of human mentality resides in the child's ability to orientate herself in such a space (see Bakhurst 1991, Ch. 6). This is a novel and engaging theme, and one that has gone virtually unconsidered in Anglo-American philosophy.

I now want to consider an objection to the transformational view. As we have seen, the view represents the child born as a "mere animal," as something less than a person. She is not yet a thinking subject and not yet possessed of consciousness and will. Then, in virtue of her initiation into social practices, the child is said to *become* a human being, a person, a thinking subject. In this process, the child is said to acquire "a second nature" and thereby undergo a fundamental change, a *metaphysical*, change (this is McDowell's terminology, but there is reason to think Ilyenkov would concur.) One might wonder, however, whether this is really coherent. How can a creature acquire a new "nature" or become a being of a new "kind"? What could possibly initiate this kind of transformation? Ilyenkov and Leontiev sometimes speak as if the cause is *external* to the child. That is, the child becomes a thinking subject in virtue of the agency of others who bring the child into culture, initiate her into social activities, and thereby make her into a person, as if the child were one of the "things incorporated into the social process" that acquire a new ideal form. But it is by no means clear how one could turn something that was less than a thinking thing into a thinking subject, for a thinking subject is a *self*-determining being—an autonomous being—and there is something more than a little paradoxical about the idea that powers of autonomy and self-determination can be created in, or gifted to, a creature that previously lacked them.

Objections of this kind have been raised by Sebastian Rödl against my sympathetic treatment of the transformational view in *The Formation of Reason* (see Rödl 2016, and for discussion Bakhurst 2015b and 2016b). But similar objections can be found in the Soviet literature, most notably by Sergei L. Rubinshtein in his critique of Leontiev (see Rubinshtein 1976). They urge us to represent the child's development from the outset as a process of self-determination, a process in which she strives to become what she is, to put the matter somewhat dialectically. But if her development issues from self-determination, then she is the cause of her becoming, and we cannot represent the changes she undergoes, however great they may be, as anything other than an expression of her own nature. So, it is misleading to say that the child acquires a "second nature" or becomes a being of a new kind. Better to say that the child is born a person: that is, the human child is a creature of a kind, in whom powers of reason develop and find expression as she enters the human world of culture, acquires language, engages in norm-governed activities, and so on. But these powers are not given to her or produced in her.

Someone might argue that, although this looks like a substantive dispute, it is in fact a merely verbal one. Does it really make a difference whether we say that the child is born a person, a rational being, but acquires the capacity to exercise her powers of reason, or that the child is not a person at birth but only becomes so once she is able to think and act rationally? Well, there *are* important issues at stake. First, the term "person" has moral resonance. It is common in moral contexts to argue that it is in virtue of our status of persons that we are owed respect and concern, and that we possess rights and have duties. So it matters whether we think of young children as persons or not (remember that sometimes Ilyenkov goes so far as to say that young children are not even members of the human race). Second, the idea that consciousness is a social *product* paints a highly instrumental picture of the relation between parents, caregivers, educators and children, as if people had to be *produced*. This distorts the character of the natural relation between adults and children. Maybe a bureaucrat can ask the question "What kind of people should the education system manufacture?" But parents do not relate to their children as things to be engineered, as objects upon which they must act in order to turn them into something (let alone changed from one kind of thing (animal) into some other kind (human being, person)). Rather, we seek to create the conditions in which our children can become themselves, conditions that will facilitate their self-determination. This suggests that however remarkable may be the change between infant and adult, the metaphor with which we should be working is growth rather than metamorphosis.

One reason the transformational view looks attractive is because it seems to be the only alternative to thinking of personhood, consciousness and will as innate, as fundamentally biological phenomena that develop in the child under their own immanent logic. Ilyenkov was a famously harsh critic of such views (see e.g. Ilyenkov 2002, 72–77 [2007c]; cf. Bakhurst 2008). He thought they led to forms of narrow-minded naturalism that reduce the mind to the functioning of the brain. He also thought such reductive naturalism was allied to irresponsible conceptions of education that acquiesce in the idea that human development is limited by children's genetic endowment and therefore fail to take responsibility for creating social conditions that would facilitate the all-round development of every child (Ilyenkov 2002, 76 [2007c, 67–68]). Nonetheless, however much we might sympathize with Ilyenkov's distrust of reductive naturalism, we might feel that he rejects one unattractive position only to endorse another, one that too enthusiastically embraces the idea of the social "engineering of human souls" (to adapt Stalin's metaphor) and results in portraying human beings as set apart from the rest of nature.

I believe, however, that although Ilyenkov sometimes embraces the transformational view in its boldest, most radical form,[7] there are places in his writings that support a subtler reading. For example, in a little-known paper, Ilyenkov addresses Rubinshtein's critique of Leontiev (Ilyenkov 2002, 62–71 [2007b]). Here he makes it clear that the child's mental powers cannot develop unless she has the requisite potential instantiated in her biological nature (2002, 62 [2007b, 56]). So the emergence of those powers is an actualization of a potentiality that is all her own. Moreover, becoming a person does not transform something animal into something somehow no longer animal. A person is a human being, and a human being is an animal. Persons are animals of a certain kind; namely, the kind of animals that are endowed with rational self-consciousness.

Ilyenkov also need not deny that the child is a participant in the construction of the very sociality that calls forth her rationality. This is so not because she comes ready-made with concepts and thoughts pre-installed, but because of the way in which she is oriented toward other people from the moment of her birth. First, there is a fundamental intersubjectivity between mother and child from the first moment their eyes meet. The relation of mother and child immediately includes a communicative dimension, and this primitive intersubjectivity is surely the foundation for the later emergence of the ability to see oneself through the eyes of another, which Ilyenkov treats as central to rational self-consciousness (Ilyenkov 1984, 68 [2014, 71]). Second, as Rödl argues, the infant's development is driven by a profound desire to *be one of us*. She wants to walk and talk in order to be *one of a kind*. In this she expresses her standing a "species being," to use Marx's famous term. She is a being that wants not just to be but to *know herself* as one of a kind. At the same time, of course, she realizes her membership of the kind *human being* precisely by expressing herself as an autonomous individual in thought and deed. This is an important theme in Ilyenkov's writings on education, which consistently advance an ideal of teaching as creating the conditions in which the child must think and act autonomously, independently and self-critically. He writes: "The trick is not to stamp the individual with the ability to act in accord with some schema learned by rote, the ability to use it according to antecedently-determined criteria of application, but to put the child into situations in which she is forced to act as a 'self' as a 'subject'" (Ilyenkov 2002, 69 [2007b, 61]). And Ilyenkov emphasizes that one cannot cultivate in the child the ability to think independently "without the closest attention to her *individuality*," an attitude which we can think of as one of *love* (Ilyenkov 2002, 14 [2007a, 16]). With this, he acknowledges the child as a participant in her own formation, and hints at the developmental significance of affect and intersubjectivity between child and adult.

The significance of such phenomena is also a theme in the work of Ilyenkov's follower, and my mentor, Felix Mikhailov, who as far back as his renowned early work, *The Riddle of the Self* (Mikhailov 2010 [1980]), always portrayed the child's status as a self-determining being as intimately linked with her potential to express her subjectivity in and through her relations to others. This became a theme in our discussions (see Bakhurst 1995a) and I should surely have made more of it in my own writings. I am sure that critics of the transformational view would argue that once we introduce this problematic, and portray the child as a participant in her own development, whose rational powers come to be manifest in part through her own agency, rather than produced in her by initiation into culture and community, then talk of transformation is no longer apposite. But I do not think this is right. For even if we distance ourselves from cruder articulations of the transformational view, it remains that the difference affected by the actualization of the potential to exercise rational powers in self-conscious agency is an enormous one. Moreover, we are beings whose form of life is marked by transformation in another, related sense, for self-conscious, self-determining beings can pose for themselves questions of what to think and do, and for such beings the question "How should we live?" is always a live one. We are beings who, for better or for worse, can transform ourselves through the transformation of our culture and environment. Rational life is life lived in history, and we can express our individuality only through the mediation of a cultural inheritance, which is not merely a contingent vehicle of reason, but forms the fabric of our very souls. Consider Marx's remarks about human powers of perception:

> the senses of social man *differ* from those of non-social man. Only through the objectively unfolded richness of man's essential being is the richness of subjective *human* sensibility (a musical ear, an eye for beauty of form—in short, *senses* capable of human gratification, senses affirming themselves as essential powers of *man*) either cultivated or brought into being. For not only the five senses but also the so-called mental senses, the practical senses (will, love, etc.), in a word, *human* sense, the human nature of the senses, comes to be by virtue of *its* object, by virtue of *humanised* nature. The *forming* of the five senses is a labour of the entire history of the world down to the present. (Marx 1977, 103)

Ilyenkov's point is that, just as the development of the human senses proceeds by cultural evolution, so what Marx calls the human sense emerges in each individual only through her entrance into culture. I must leave it to the reader to decide whether this is a fact of sufficient weight to license talk of the "transformational" character of culture in human development.

My principal purpose in this paper has been to affirm that the issues addressed in Ilyenkov's writings on activity and the ideal, and the attendant conception of individual development, seem to me to be as alive today as they were when I first encountered them. The context is very different but the questions over the sources of normativity and the formation of reason are just as topical today as they were then. Indeed, there is now a far greater prospect of fruitful dialogue between Russian and Anglo-American philosophy. The Russian tradition is no longer bogged down in questions of Marxist exegesis and the Anglo-American tradition is far more intellectually open, as the boundaries between so-called analytic and continental approaches are breaking down and there is renewed interest in the German philosophers (especially Hegel) who inspired so much Russian thought. It is only a pity that the likes of Ilyenkov and Mikhailov are no longer with us to join in the conversation.[8]

## NOTES

1. I tell the story of my friendship with Mikhailov in Bakhurst 2011a. Bakhurst 1995a presents a transcription of seminar conducted with contributions from Mikhailov, Davydov, Bibler and Lektorsky.
2. Lektorsky 1990 and Maidansky and Oittinen 2016 provide detailed discussions of the significance of the concept of activity in Soviet thought. See also Bakhurst 1991, Ch. 6; 2009; and 2015.
3. In this chapter, I cite Russian editions of Ilyenkov's work, usually in my own translation, together with references to English editions. A number of Ilyenkov's works are available in English at the Marxist Internet Archive: www.marxists.org.
4. It is important, for Ilyenkov, that to have "consciousness" is to be in self-conscious possession of a conception of the world. The term implies more than mere awareness. And by "will" he means the power to formulate ends in accord with an appreciation of norms and to act that light. Understood in this way, consciousness and will are powers of self-conscious, rational agents.
5. Oakeshott's educational thought is explored in Bakhurst and Fairfield 2016.
6. He writes, "A spoon is a ticket into the realm of the human—social—culture, into the sphere of human life activity and human mindedness" (Ilyenkov 2002, 99 [2007d, 89]). Here he is describing the development of blind-deaf children, but he intends the point to be generalizable.
7. This is especially the case where he is discussing Meshcheryakov's work on the education of blind-deaf children. There is no doubt, I think, that Ilyenkov overstates the philosophical significance of Meshcheryakov's famous "experiment," though the context of his writings on this topic were complex. They are mainly short polemical pieces that do not, I think, adequately reflect his most considered views (see Bakhurst 1991: ch.7; Bakhurst and Padden 1990).
8. Some of the material presented in this chapter appeared in modified form in an interview I gave to *3:AM Magazine*, "Soviet Philosophy and Then Some" (June 14, 2013, https://www.3ammagazine.com/3am/soviet-philosophy-education-and-thinking-about-reasons/).

# BIBLIOGRAPHY


Bakhurst, David. 1991. *Consciousness and Revolution in Soviet Philosophy: From the Bolsheviks to Evald Ilyenkov*. Cambridge: Cambridge University Press.

Bakhurst, David. 1995a. "Social Being and The Human Essence" (A discussion with V. S. Bibler, V. V. Davydov, V. A. Lektorsky, and F. T. Mikhailov). *Studies in East European Thought* 47 (1–2): 3–60.

Bakhurst, David. 1995b. "Wittgenstein and Social Being." In *The Social Self*, edited by D. Bakhurst and C. Sypnowich, 30–46. London: Sage.

Bakhurst, David. 2008. "Minds, Brains and Education." *Journal of Philosophy of Education* 42 (3–4): 415–432.

Bakhurst, David. 2009. "Reflections on Activity Theory." *Educational Review* 61 (2): 197–210.

Bakhurst, David. 2011a. "*The Riddle of the Self* Revisited." *Studies in East European Thought* 63 (1): 63–73.

Bakhurst, David. 2011b. *The Formation of Reason*. Oxford: Wiley-Blackwell.

Bakhurst, David. 2015. "Training, Transformation and Education." In *Mind, Self and Person*, edited by A. O'Hear, 301–327. Royal Institute of Philosophy Supplement, 76. Cambridge: Cambridge University Press.

Bakhurst, David. 2016a. "Activity and the Search for True Materialism." In *The Practical Essence of Man: The "Activity Approach" in Late Soviet Philosophy*, edited by Vesa Oittenen and Andrey Maidansky, 17–28. Leiden: Brill.

Bakhurst, David. 2016b. "Response to Rödl, Standish and Derry." *Journal of Philosophy of Education*, 50 (1): 123–129.

Bakhurst, David and Fairfield, Paul. (eds). 2016. *Education and Conversation: Exploring Oakeshott's Legacy*. London: Bloomsbury Academic.

Bakhurst, David and Padden, Carol. 1991. "The Meshcheryakov Experiment: Soviet Work on the Education of Blind-Deaf Children." *Learning and Instruction*, 1 (3): 201–215.

Brandom, Robert. 1994. *Making It Explicit*. Cambridge, MA: Harvard University Press.

Davidson, Donald. 2001. "The Second Person." In *Subjective, Intersubjective, Objective*, 107–121. Oxford: Oxford University Press.

Ilyenkov, Evald V. 1974. *Dialekticheskaya logika* [Dialectical Logic]. Moscow: Politizdat.

Ilyenkov, Evald V. 1984. "Dialektika ideal'nogo" [The Dialectic of the Ideal]. In *Iskusstvo i kommunisticheskii ideal* [Art and the Communist Ideal]. Moscow: Iskusstvo.

Ilyenkov, Evald V. 2002. *Shkola dolzhna uchit' myslit'* [School Must Teach How to Think]. Moscow-Voronezh: MODEK. (A collection of papers translated in its entirety in *Journal of Russian and East European Psychology* 45 (4), 2007.)

Ilyenkov, Evald V. 2007a. "Our Schools Must Teach How to Think!" *Journal of Russian and East European Psychology*, 45 (4): 9–49.

Ilyenkov, Evald V. 2007b. "On the Nature of Ability." *Journal of Russian and East European Psychology*, 45 (4): 56–63.

Ilyenkov, Evald V. 2007c. "The Biological and the Social in Man." *Journal of Russian and East European Psychology*, 45 (4): 64–68.

Ilyenkov, Evald V. 2007d. "A Contribution to a Conversation about Meshcheryakov." *Journal of Russian and East European Psychology*, 45 (4): 85–94.

Ilyenkov, Evald V. 2009. *The Ideal in Human Activity*. Pacifica, CA: Marxist Internet Archive.

Ilyenkov, Evald V. 2014. "Dialectics of the Ideal." Translated by A. Levant. In *Dialectics of the Ideal: Evald Ilyenkov and Creative Soviet Marxism*, edited by A. Levant and V. Oittinen, 25–78. Leiden: Brill.

Lektorsky, Vladislav A. (ed.). 1990. *Activity: Theories, Methodology, and Problems*. Orlando, FL, Helsinki, Moscow: Paul Deutsch.

Maidansky, Andrey and Oittinen, Vesa (eds). 2014. *The Practical Essence of Man: The "Activity-Approach" in Late Soviet Philosophy*. Leiden: Brill.

Marx, Karl 1977. *Economic and Philosophical Manuscripts of 1844*. Moscow: Progress.

McDowell, John. 1996. *Mind and World*. 2nd edition. Cambridge, MA: Harvard University Press.

McDowell, John. 2009. *Having the World in View: Essays on Kant, Hegel, and Sellars*. Cambridge, MA: Harvard University Press.

Mikhailov, Felix T. 1980. *The Riddle of the Self*. Translated by R. Daglish. Moscow: Progress.

Mikhailov, Felix T. 2010. *Zagadka chelovecheskogo ya* [The Riddle of the Self]. 3rd edition (1st Russian edition 1964; 2nd edition 1976). Moscow: Ritm.

Oakeshott, Michael. 1991. "The Voice of Poetry in the Conversation of Mankind." In his *Rationalism in Politics and Other Essays*, new and expanded edition, 488–541. Indianapolis: Liberty Fund.

Oakeshott, Michael. 2001. *The Voice of Liberal Learning*. Indianapolis: Liberty Press.

Peters, R.S. 2003. "Education as Initiation." In *Philosophy of Education: An Anthology*. Edited by R. Curren, 55–67. Oxford: Blackwell.

Rödl, Sebastian. 2016. "Education as Autonomy." *Journal of Philosophy of Education*, 50 (1): 84–97.

Rubinshtein, Sergei L. 1976. "Problema sposobnostei i voprosy psikhologicheskoi teorii" [The Problem of Abilities and Questions of Psychological Theory]. In *Problemy obshchei psikhologii* [Problems of General Psychology], 2nd edition, 219–234. Moscow: Pedagogika.

CHAPTER SEVENTEEN

# Georgy Shchedrovitsky's Concept of Activity and Thought-Activity

VADIM M. ROZIN

As one of the founding fathers of Moscow Methodological Circle, Georgy Shchedrovitsky laid foundation for a new philosophical school. Together with his colleagues, he established methodology as a discipline. Thinking, agency and mental activity became cornerstones of his innovative approach. About twenty works authored by Shchedrovitsky have been translated into European languages, including English.[1] Nowadays, his followers invest much effort into widening the scope of his writings' availability across the globe (see, for instance, Dubrovsky 2004; Maracha 2014; Rozin 2017).[2] This contribution focuses on mental activity—the third pillar in Shchedrovitsky's conceptual ternary. Starting from the classical standpoint, I discuss systems studies, communication theory, theory of thought, agency theory, Kant's and Plato's scheme studies. Let me first provide a step by step definition of my explanatory framework.

The *Systemic Studies* yearbook for 1987 published an important article by Georgy Shchedrovitsky titled "Scheme of Thought-Activity: Systemic Structure, Meaning and Content." This text is thought today to belong to the later period in the work of the scholar who founded the Moscow Methodological Circle (MMC). The article was, on the one hand, a summation of MMC work and, on the other hand, heralded a transition from the study and analysis of thought and activity (the building, respectively, of "the theory of thought" and "the theory of activity") to the identification and analysis of a new reality he called *thought-activity*.

At the end of the article Shchedrovitsky writes:

> In my opinion, the TA [thought-activity] scheme carries a body of principles that determine the right approach to the study of all the phenomena connected with thought and activity. First of all, it asserts the organic link of any action and any activity with the thought and communicative-meaning processes that prepare it. From that viewpoint the expressions "activity" and "action," leaving aside their definition through reproduction schemes, are expressions of extremely powerful idealizations, excessive reductions and simplifications which, in reality, can be

> matched only by extremely rare artificially created and exotic cases. In the real world of social life, activity and action can and must exist only together with thought and communication. Hence the expression "thought-activity" which is more in keeping with reality and must therefore replace and oust "activity" both in research and in practical organization. (Shchedrovitsky 1995, 297–298)

But why, one may ask, a *scheme* of thought-activity and not simply, say, a new concept or model? And what prompted the need to create such a centaur by linking thought with activity (one cannot help recalling the Marxist concept of "life activity") which seem to have always been considered separately in philosophical and psychological tradition? Shchedrovitsky refers to the fact that the first MMC program "declared—and emphasized—that thought would be considered not in terms of the content of the knowledge moving in it, but as activity," but that in reality "the scientific theory of thought and knowledge and the scientific theory of activity began developing in totally different directions, each on the basis of its own schemes and practically not interacting with each other" (Shchedrovitsky 1995, 282).

Explaining the role of schemes, he writes at the very beginning of his article that even the first program:

> set as the main goal and task of methodological studies in these areas the creation of schemes depicting whole and complete *theoretical units of thought, knowledge and activity*. The shift of consciously fixed goals and tasks (building a theory of thought represented as activity—V.R.) can easily be understood if one recalls that scientific research (which differs above all from other types of analysis) requires as a necessary condition and prerequisite an identification of a general "meaning cloud" of understanding and thinking work of ideal objects of thought and fixation thereof in the material of sign systems. (Shchedrovitsky 1995, 281)

To understand these propositions today, a brief look at the history of the study of thought and activity of the MMC is in order. The fact that Shchedrovitsky's first degree was in natural sciences and the overall spirit of the times (the late 1950s and early 1960s) must have predetermined his attitude to thought. The Marxist idea of historicity is preserved, but the study of thought is seen largely as research similar to what natural sciences do. The thesis is formulated that logic is an empirical science and that thought is a process and cerebral activity that need to be modeled and theoretically described. Logic was mentioned, but it was interpreted more broadly than simply the rules of true reasoning and conclusions.

Shchedrovitsky recalled in 1962:

> Essentially, at the time the concepts of logic and methodology were not distinguished, these were practically synonyms. This is natural because Alexander Zinoviev and all the others proceeded from the Hegelian and Leninist thesis of the identity of logic, the theory of cognition and dialectic, or methodology. Therefore, it was quite natural that at the time methodology to us was logic and logic was methodology and the three above-mentioned points: 1) activity, 2) genetism and 3) identity of activity and aspects of content initially yielded an

entirely new concept of logic, that is, substantive-genetic logic. (Shchedrovitsky 2004, 257)

This explains the drift toward the study of the laws of the development of thought and its interpretation as activity. This was above all the result of the influence of Marxism and the related social-engineering approach. However, a natural question may arise: why was it necessary to study thought, and what is more, to study its development, in order to build a substantive logic? But then there was the Bacon-Descartes program that claimed that the main science was the science of thought and that the latter would make it possible to build methods. There was Marxism with its requirement to ground social action in the study of the laws of historical development; in the case of thought reform this develops into the task of studying the laws of historical development of thought and the building, on their basis, of a new logic. It was Lev Vygotsky who in his work *The Historical Meaning of the Psychological Crisis (Methodological Studies)* argued that psychology should be reformed on the basis of the natural science approach.

True, Vygotsky wrote about psychology and not logic, however, would Shchedrovitsky have the same thoughts as the father of Soviet psychology? He, too, argues that logic must be an empirical science, is convinced that the natural science is the ideal of science, also has a pragmatic approach (giving pride of place to the requirements of pedagogy and applied methodology), and as a Marxist is convinced that reform of thought implies revealing the laws of its historical development. In effect, substantive logic in Shchedrovitsky's project is a Marxist version of applied engineering in the field of thought. Influenced by the works of Vygotsky, as well as Saussure, Shchedrovitsky during that period interprets thought also in *semiotic terms*: he maintains that thought is replacement of objects with signs and actions with signs that make it possible to reveal and create the content of thought and to solve problems.

A methodological program is one thing and real work is another. As I have tried to demonstrate in the first Shchedrovitsky readings, although in creating their schemes and concepts of substantive-genetic logic the members of the MMC subjectively sought to get at the truth and understand the nature of thought, objectively (as we see it in retrospect today) the decisive factors were, on the one hand, the way collective work was organized—tough criticism, reflection discussions, joint tackling of certain tasks, etc. and on the other hand the opportunity to implement the value and methodological principles of the main members of the circle (natural scientific approach, activity-based approach, semiotic, historical approach, etc.). This method of organizing work and thought today can be likened to the ideas of *dialogue, communication and collective thought-activity*. But at the time it was not perceived as such.

Why then, did Shchedrovitsky and his colleagues (such as B. Sazonov, V. Kostelovsky, A. Moskayeva, N. Alekseev, I. Ladenko, V. Rozin, O. Genisaretsky and others) in the mid-1960s move to the study of activity and to building not "a theory of thought" which had engaged their minds in the previous years, but "a theory of activity?" This can be attributed to several circumstances. The first can be described as *epistemological*. This is epitomized by the failure to represent thought categorically as a process. But this setback turned out to be an important gain, on the one hand because it clarified some determinants of thought, namely the role of *means, task, procedures and object*, and on the other hand because the study made it possible to change the category (not a process but a structure). Analysis of the mechanisms of thought and development of knowledge also tended to push activity into the foreground.

The third circumstance that substantially influenced the change of ideas about reality can be described as situational-worldview-related. The members of MMC upheld an active Marxist normative position with regard to themselves and other experts. This was the background against which they changed the character of their activities. They practically ceased the study of thought as declared in the first program as Shchedrovitsky embarked on Vygotsky-style methodological expansion into several areas: linguistics, pedagogy, the science of science, design and psychology. Those who observed that work probably remember Shchedrovitsky's brilliant speeches and reports in the second half of the 1960s and 1970s. The typical scenario of his performances was as follows. First he made an analysis of a cognitive situation in a corresponding discipline. The approaches and methods of thinking characteristic of this discipline were undermined and the discipline was declared to be in deep crisis. Then a new picture of the discipline was proposed and a program of its restructuring and further development was advanced.

Invariably a methodological twist was performed as Shchedrovitsky moved from an object-oriented position to the analysis of thought, activity, concepts, situations, etc. For example, from the study of the psyche, which is the business of the psychologist, to the analysis of how the psychologist thinks and works, what concepts he uses, what science ideals he preaches, what tasks the psychological science grapples with, etc. Shchedrovitsky did not only make his listeners discuss disparate realities that were outside their area (procedures of thought, concepts, ideals, values, the situation within the discipline and the like, call it "reflexive content"), but proposed a new synthesis of these contents, a new interpretation. In analyzing the situation in the discipline and synthesizing the reflexive contents he implemented the aforementioned values and approaches, the historical and activity-base approach, the ideas of development, the natural science ideal, socio-technical attitude to reality, etc. In other words, the scientific object was restated with emphasis on these values and approaches.

But why, one may ask, did the representatives of "disciplines" (scientists, engineers, economic managers) have to follow Shchedrovitsky and switch from their objects of study to things they were not familiar with? Obviously, Georgy Shchedrovitsky's charismatic personality alone was not enough. It was necessary to substantiate the expansion by referring to reality itself. Let us see, however, what requirements were set to reality. First, the new reality had to switch the consciousness of the scientist from his subject to reflection on his own thought (work). Second, the new reality had to allow for the implementation of the values and approaches of content-genetic logic. Third, the scientists had to switch to disparate reflexive contents. Fourth, it nudged them to a new understanding and synthesis of these contents.

Thought in content-genetic logic had already been linked with activity. That activity was interpreted since the times of Vygotsky and Rubenstein simultaneously as reality being studied and the researcher's activity and as practice transforming reality, which already receives epistemological connotations. In this sense, Shchedrovitsky's positing of new reality as activity is hardly surprising. Gradually, activity came to be understood as a special reality which, first, made it possible to develop thought in science, engineering, design, and second, to transfer the knowledge obtained in the study of one type of thinking to other types of thinking.

And what was one to make of the work of Shchedrovitsky and members of his seminar after they passed on from the study of thought to projects of developing scientific disciplines? The idea of methodology as *a program for the research and restructuring of activity,* including thought as a particular case of activity, was born. It is at that stage, beginning from the second half of the 1960s that Shchedrovitsky identifies himself as a "methodologist" and calls his discipline "methodology."

With regard to thought, what was new was not only identification of thought with activity. Equally important was the fact that by thought the members of the MMC came to understand *not so much the study of thought*, as much as *their own work of thinking,* as Boris Sazonov very aptly wrote in his book devoted to Shchedrovitsky (Sazonov 2010, 227).

Thinking understood in this new way is now known as "methodological thinking," with Shchedrovitsky considering it to be the initial and basic form of thinking preceding even scientific thinking. Explaining methodology in his 1971 lectures Shchedrovitsky writes:

> Methodology arises precisely because we pay attention to the possibilities of acting and begin to form them. . . . The claim is that *there exists a special kind of thinking, methodological thinking,* which moves not only *in the pictures of objects* and the processes going on within them, but simultaneously in another space, *the space of activity itself, correlating these spaces with one another and establishing special relationships between them.* (Shchedrovitsky 2005, 58[3])

Analysis reveals that initially methodological thinking, influenced by activity-based interpretation was conceptualized as *a kind of projecting*. The project approach exerted a strong influence on Shchedrovitsky, especially since his Marxist perception of the world presupposed some kind of technology that made it possible to conceive and create the future. Projecting looked to be such a technology; methodologically-oriented scientists thought that on its basis they would be able to reform the existing scientific disciplines and other social practices. In the early 1980s, discussing the features of methodological work Shchedrovitsky writes that "the products and results of methodological work for the most part are not knowledge tested for its truth, but projects, project schemes and prescriptions." This is the inevitable conclusion, Shchedrovitsky explains, as soon as "we renounce the overly narrow, clearly cognitive attitude and adopt the thesis of Karl Marx on the revolutionary-critical, transformative character of human activity" (Shchedrovitsky 1995a, 96).

It is the project approach that gives prominence to methodological schemes. With its help methodologists schematized the subjects to be restructured, constructed new subjects called upon to produce new objects, transformed activity and thought to remove the problems and meet the requirements for the subject area being reformed.

Schemes are used to unfold and constitute *methodological thinking*. Indeed, inasmuch as schemes are to be turned into a kind of model (made to correspond to reality) methodologists proceed to formulate the rules and principles of work with schemes building an ontology of activity and systemic-structural logic (Shchedrovitsky 1995b, 376–377).

Thus, the study of thought was retained, but it was understood in a totally different way than he saw it at the first stage of his scholarly development. For example, what Shchedrovitsky has to say about methodological schemes in a 1966 article "Notes on Thinking According to Double Knowledge Schemes." We build schemes constructing them on the basis of other schemes that we have as well as various methodological considerations. To achieve a holistic picture of the empirical reality being studied we establish certain links between the elementary schemes we use for construction. But one cannot limit oneself only to positing the existence in the object of the dependencies, relations and links represented in the picture. It is necessary to build a structure and thus indicate and prove that the "dependencies, relations and links represented in the scheme are matched by corresponding dependencies, relations and links in the object itself" (Shchedrovitsky 1995c, 475). In turn, carrying out *research*, Shchedrovitsky concedes, is a necessary condition for building such structures.

The question arises: research into what, and what kind of research? Thought that has become established in a culture? But it raised objections from methodologists on various grounds. That leaves the thought of methodologists themselves, i.e. *methodological thought*. But what is the meaning of "study" if the methodologist himself generates the thinking in the process of his work? Could it be that everything hinges on the personality of the methodologist who, like a god creates reality and "cognizes himself"? Sometimes Shchedrovitsky says as much. "Total refusal to describe the external object. Priority is given to reflection, and the gist of the idea is to energetically create a new thought-activity world and fix it in a timely manner—this in order to create again and reflect again, only to create more precisely. Thus, in fact what is happening is not the study of an external object, but a continuous analysis and insight into the experience of one's work" (Shchedrovitsky 1997, 124).

Thus, the source of building methodological schemes on the basis of which ontological ideas are generated, Shchedrovitsky asserts, is not so much external reality as filiation of his own ideas. However, Shchedrovitsky realizes that the claim to knowledge implies special procedures that give grounds for claiming that the methodological schemes proposed are not just the play of the methodologist's mind, but *models* and *knowledge* of reality. We want, Shchedrovitsky says, methodological schemes to "correspond to the object studied, but in a mediated way, through the *scientific subject*" (Shchedrovitsky 1995d, 245).

How does one interpret the phrase "but in a mediated way, through the scientific subject?" I think thus. Yes, activity is above all Shchedrovitsky's own methods of work, but they have to correspond to the object being studied. The way out was pointed by Marx who maintained that his forecast of replacement of the capitalist system with a socialist one is scientifically based on the law of historical development of society. Shchedrovitsky thinks along similar lines: if our methods of analysis and description of the object studied are to be true, he says, these methods must be subordinate to the norm of scientific activity (which Shchedrovitsky calls "scientific object," containing such epistemological units as "problems," "tasks," "ontology," "models," "facts," "knowledge," "methods," and "expressive means" (Shchedrovitsky 1995d, 246)). Shchedrovitsky is sure that an investigation according with that norm makes it possible to capture the essence of the object studied, and the laws of its formation.

Shchedrovitsky shows that methodological thinking unfolds under the impact of a number of factors: reflection, the methodologist's "luggage" (his capabilities and perceptions), collective methodological work and communication with others, actual constructive activity in which schemes and projects play a big part and finally, the challenges of the time (and research problems) the methodologist seeks to answer (Rozin 2011, 175–266). These ideas combine to form what may be considered to be *the second conceptualization of thought.* It also includes a special principle that permits considering the constitution of methodological thinking to be one of the methods of its study and the study of thinking in general. In one of his works he writes: "*methodology came first and science appeared and took shape within it* basically as a specific organization of certain parts of methodology" (Shchedrovitsky 1995e, 151).

If one follows Shchedrovitsky, scientific thought (and indeed all other types of thought) is born of methodological thinking and is in a certain sense akin to it. This proposition lends itself to two interpretations: as real involvement of methodology in constituting other forms of thinking, but also as *grounds for identifying methodological thinking with other types of thinking.* In the latter case the study of methodological thinking can indeed be understood as the study of thought as such, including thought that existed in history. What then, is the meaning of the study (research) of methodological thinking if methodologists constitute it themselves? As we have seen, the answer was: the study of methodological thinking partly coincides with its reflection.

Let us go back to the scheme of thought-activity. As I argue in my works following Shchedrovitsky, schemes, on the one hand, help to resolve a problem situation (problems) by constituting a new reality (in our case oriented toward building ideal objects of science[4]), and on the other hand provide a new vision and methods of work (Rozin 2011a). What problems have been solved by applying the thought-activity scheme? Shchedrovitsky, as I have mentioned in the beginning of this article, points to the "obvious gap between the schemes of thought and knowledge, on the one hand, and the schemes of activity on the other" (Shchedrovitsky 1995, 282). This is the first problem. The second problem was the need to understand how to work with methodological schemes and how they are interconnected. It was in fact to do with the "logic" of work with schemes and configuring the schemes into a single methodological theory.

But there were at least two more problems. Shchedrovitsky felt that interpreting the development of activity only through reflection and immanent mechanisms of reproduction of activity were unsatisfactory, and he was looking for external sources of development. This search led him to the idea of communication.

Indeed, the practice of organized activity games revealed that methodological thinking is constituted and unfolds under the influence of *communication* (problemitization and critique, dialogue and reflection of various approaches and positions, non-understanding—understanding, collective thinking, etc.) In essence, this has always been the case at MMC, but an awareness of such determination emerged only in organized activity games, when different game groups clashed. Although methodologists staged games and tried to control the run of the game (by imposing methodological schemes, thought logic and general organization on its participants) nevertheless the organizers themselves had to change the original scripted behavior, enter into dialogue with the game participants and often abandon their own principles.

Besides, some methodologists refused to follow the general methodological norms and game scenarios initially set or approved by Shchedrovitsky himself. They began creating and proposing their own methodological norms and game scenarios, that had been no less effective and grounded. At that point a fourth problem arose: What was to be done in this situation, which ran counter to the important methodological principle of following the norm set by Shchedrovitsky? Interestingly, this time the conflict was solved in a non-traditional way: not by sending the offender into "another room," that is, negating any other form of thinking different from that confirmed and protected by the head of the MMC. The participants in the games and seminars were allowed to have their own point of view which would subsequently, however, *have to be introduced in the common communication field and then worked on jointly.* It was in this context that the concept of "thought-communication" arose, prompting the need for another revision of methodological reality. Simultaneously, that concept held the promise of a new solution to the problem of development: not only through reflection but also through communication which would make it possible to disconnect the ontology of activity and go beyond its limits.

It was to answer these four problems that Shchedrovitsky introduced the concept of thought-activity into his scheme. Being aware of the three determinations and components of methodological thinking (project, thought and communication) Shchedrovitsky, first, had to distinguish activity, thought and communication. Second, he realized that the concept of "activity" could not be the basis of methodology because it did not cover the second and third components. And thirdly, he introduced (posited) a new foundation of methodology, thought-activity containing three components (thought-activity "belts").

The first belt, "thought-activity" was a generalization and objectification of the project component of methodological thinking, the second, "pure thinking," i.e. objectification of the thought component and the third, "thought-communication," i.e. the communication component of methodological thinking. Thinking was interpreted as a subsystem in the scheme of thought-activity. Why was the new reality was called thought-activity? Probably because in organized activity games on the one hand they were tackling cognitive tasks, i.e. were engaged in thinking, and on the other hand, the thought of all the participants of the game was programmed and organized, which traditionally was understood as activity. Thus, an important step was made as a new framework for the study of thought was created and its context was indicated.

However, the setting of three layers of thought-activity and their graphic representation was only the first step in building a scheme and reality of thought activity. The second step was systemic categorization. Believing that activity in a categorical sense was a system Shchedrovitsky writes:

> Analysis of pure and autonomous processes of thought-communication, understanding, reflection, thinking and thought-activity, as it has usually been done up until now, cannot deliver success. Only a specific systemic analysis of the whole when all the above processes are seen as partial and forming subsystems of thought-activity can be effective. (Shchedrovitsky 1995, 298)

However, if the theory of activity and the systemic approach provide the paradigmatic system for thought activity, it turns out that thought-activity is again reduced as it were to activity and yet Shchedrovitsky himself denies the legitimacy of such reduction saying that interpreting reality as activity is "excessive reduction and simplification." Besides, Shchedrovitsky stresses, the main function of thought-activity is not ontological (i.e. portraying the object) but *methodological* (Shchedrovitsky 1995, 298).

However, there has to be yet another interpretation that is not categorical, but is based on the content of the objects of thought, thought-communication and thought-activity. In building schemes, writes Shchedrovitsky, we must bear in mind:

> first, general methodological and logical principles of analysis of systemic hierarchic objects [see first and fourth answers], second, the picture of the vision of the object established in accordance with the practical and engineering work chosen [in the event it was work aimed at resolving the four above mentioned problems] and third, the relations between the objective content of the models we are combining [this is precisely what I say is still absent]. (Shchedrovitsky 1995, 387)

How are communication, thought and thought-activity connected in terms of their object content? We do not find a direct answer in the article on the scheme of thought-activity, but an indirect answer can be gleaned from another work of Shchedrovitsky. "Activity," he writes, "exists only within the boundaries set for it by thinking consciousness" (OAG 2006, 683). Shchedrovitsky stresses that the methodologist does not merely describe activity and thinking, but determines his position with regard to them (Shchedrovitsky 2005a, 15, 18).

How can this be understood? It means that in fact this is not about thinking in general and not about concrete types of thinking (scientific, engineering, project, artistic, etc.). This is rather only about *methodological thinking* which is characterized, first, by *identity of activity and thought* (in the methodological project future activity is determined by the methodologist's thought), second, *reflection and control of one's own thinking* (as a consequence, "inserting understanding and interpretations into schemes"), and third, *immanent mechanisms of development* (that is why a reflective procedure of applying the following thought-activity to the previous thought activity is needed) to distinguish what the methodologist does and what appears in the process in the object (as an object) as a result of his activity and thought a distinction is introduced between two plans of methodological analysis—*organizing activity* (describing and organizing the methodologist's activity) and *object ontological* analysis (characterizing what appears in the object as a result of methodological activity) (Shchedrovitsky 2005a, 19).

It is possible that other schemes of thought activity ("development step," "control," etc.) follow the same logic: on the one hand, they describe the organized thought and the activity of methodologists and on the other hand, they are schemes of the reality (activity, thought, their objects) given by the methodologists and related not to itself but to others, and yet again contains to varying degrees the procedures of understanding and interpretation.

However, as I have said, Shchedrovitsky wanted to attain the analysis of other types of thinking and not only methodological thinking. And not only that: he had an intention, though not very well articulated, to disconnect the theory of activity and look for other external sources of development of activity and thought. Why then does Shchedrovitsky again turn to the systems approach which, as he claims, is built in the framework of methodology and the theory of activity? Because in this way Shchedrovitsky gets an opportunity, using schemes, to construct new types of activity and assume that he has the rules for such constructing. They are set by the systemic-structural categories coordinated with theoretical-activity based concepts (Shchedrovitsky, 1995e; 1995f; 2002). For example, in the course of reflecting on new activities the category of "organization" is introduced as such to explain both the reflection and the unfolding (cooperation) of activity on its basis (Shchedrovitsky 1995d, 273, 276).

What does this approach imply? Because Shchedrovitsky interprets the main units and links of thought-activity within the same logic of the theory of activity we have to conclude that the scheme of thought-activity provides not a new ontology but the self-same activity ontology, but oriented toward solving the above-mentioned problems. However, in the framework activity ontology, they, as I try to show in my works, cannot be solved in principle.

In conclusion, I would like to make several remarks.

- Methodological thinking does not exhaust all types of thinking. Yes, the methodologist seems to lift methodological culture by turning representatives of "disciplines" into methodologists in their own right (it is another question how this works out; it is seldom what it is conceived to be). But that work does not cancel out other types of thinking which need to be analyzed and methodologically supported.
- Shchedrovitsky's "pan-methodology," the principles of activity and thought-activity (socio-technical attitude, natural-science approach, development, reflection, etc.) are associated with a certain type of *sociality*, the position which I accept only partially. My "methodology with limited liability" oriented toward humanitarian and culture-centered approaches presupposes a different type of sociality.
- The thought-activity scheme reveals two intentions that give rise to contradictions. One is geared to the principles of pan-methodology, the

theory of activity and the systemic approach as preached by MMC. The other is aimed at disconnecting the theory of activity, two-vector communication and modern sociality.

- The concept of thought-activity is best understood as a methodological program oriented toward methodological thinking rather than as a new ontology.

## NOTES

1. For a list of Shchedrovitsky's works published in English see Khristenko, Reus, Zinchenko, et. al 2014, xxxi–xxxii.
2. I would also like to mention a volume, *Methodological School of Management* with contributions by Shchedrovitsky's followers (see Khristenko, Reus, Zinchenko, et. al 2014, xxvi). In the Foreword to the book, Lord Bell writes: "*The Methodological School of Management* will be met with interest by a wide range of specialists—historians, political commentators, industrialists—but most of all, it would be invaluable for those who are learning how to manage people and issues alike. So, read it, enjoy it, use it!" (Ibid., xxvi)
3. If methodology is interpreted in this way, it turned out that the development and study of activity simultaneously had to tackle the task of developing thought, for realization of methodological thinking implies, according to Shchedrovitsky, also analysis and control of the procedures of methodological thinking.
4. Shchedrovitsky thus envisages the logic of the emergence of the new scheme. First the problems ("problem situation") take shape and are formulated. The new scheme, says Shchedrovitsky, "should sublate and express in itself 'the meaning cloud' or real work in order to become a means of resolving the problem situation." The next stage if referring the scheme, with the meanings it seals, to a paradigmatic system of activity, which implies the isolation in the theory of activity of new meanings, knowledge and concepts. And then, if the scheme is awarded the status of reality in its own right, we speak about "the emergence of *an ideal object*, which may become *an object of research* and accordingly the focus and nucleus of a scientific discipline and object of scientific research proper" (Shchedrovitsky 1995, 285–286).

## BIBLIOGRAPHY

2006. OAG-1 *Organizatsionno- deyatel'nostnye igry ODI-1.* [Organizational Activity Games OAG–1]. Moscow. Nasledie MMK publisher.

Dubrovsky, Vitaly. 2004. "Toward System Principles: General System Theory and the Alternative Approach." In: *Systems Research and Behavioral Science*, 21(2):109–122.

Khristenko, Victor, Reus, Andrei, Zinchenko, Alexander, et al (ed). 2014. *Methodological School of Management*. London: Bloomsbury Publishing House.

Maracha, Vyacheslav. 2014. "Systems-Thinking-Activity Approach: Thinking Response to Global Challenges." In *Civilization at the Crossroads. Response and Responsibility of the Systems Sciences / European Meetings on Cybernetics and Systems Research.* Book of Abstracts, edited by Jennifer Wilby, Stefan Blachfellner, Wolfgang Hofkirchner, 743–747. Vienna: Bertalanffy Center for the Study of Systems Science.

Rozin, Vadim M. 2011. *Nauchnye issledovaniya i skhemy v Moskovskom metodologicheskom kruzhke* [Scientific Research and Schemes at the Moscow Methodological Circle]. Moscow: Development Institute.

Rozin, Vadim M. 2011a. *Vvedenie v skhematologiiu: skhemy v filosofii, kul'ture, nauke, proektirovanii* [Introduction to Schematology: Schemes in Philosophy, Culture, and Projecting]. Moscow: Izdatel'stvo "Librokom."

Rozin, Vadim M. 2017. "The Moscow Methodological Circle: Its Main Ideas and Evolution," *Social Epistemology*, 31(1):78–92.

Sazonov, Boris V. 2010. "Ponimanie 'problem' i protsessa proektirovaniia v MMK kak kliuchevye dlya ponimaniya metodologicheskogo myshleniia" [The Concepts of "Problem" and Processes of Problematization at MMC as the Key to Understanding Methodological Thinking]. In *Georgii Petrovich Shchedrovitsky (Filosofiia v Rossii vtoroy poloviny 20-go veka)* [Georgy Petrovich Shchedrovitsky (Philosophy in Russian in the Second Half of the Twentieth Century)], 193–234. Moscow: Rosspen.

Shchedrovitsky, Georgy P. 1995. "Skhemy myskedeiatel'nosti: sistemno-strukturnoe stroenie, smysl i soderzhanie" [Scheme of Thought-Activity: Systemic Structure, Meaning and Content]. In *Izbrannye Trudy* [Selected Works]. Moscow: Shkola kul'turnoi politiki.

Shchedrovitsky, Georgy P. 1995a. "Printsipy i obshchaia schema metodologicheskoi organizatsii sistemno-strukturnykh issledovanii i razrabotok" [Principles and General Scheme of Methodological Organization of Systemic-Structural Research and Development]. In *G. P. Shchedrovitsky*. *Izbrannye Trudy* [Selected Works], 88–115. Moscow: Shkola kul'turnoi politiki.

Shchedrovitsky, Georgy P. 1995b. "Chelovek kak predmet issledovaniia" [Man as the Object of Study]. In *G. P. Shchedrovitsky. Izbrannye Trudy* [Selected Works], 367–399. Moscow: Shkola kul'turnoi politiki.

Shchedrovitsky Georgy P. 1995c. "Zametki o myshlenii po skhemam dvoinogo dejstviia" [Notes on Thinking According to Double Knowledge Schemes]. In: *G.P. Shchedrovitsky. Izbrannye Trudy* [Selected Works], 474–477. Moscow: Shkola kul'turnoi politiki.

Shchedrovitsky, Georgy P. 1995d. "Iskhodnye predstavleniia i kategorial'nye sredstva teorii deiatel'nosti" [Primary Ideas and Categorical Means of the Theory of Activity]. In *G. P. Shchedrovitsky. Izbrannye Trudy* [Selected Works], 233–281. Moscow: Shkola kul'turnoi politiki.

Shchedrovitsky, Georgy P. 1995e. "Metodologicheskii smysl oppozitsii naturalisticheskogo i sistemodeiatel'nostnogo podkhoda" [Methodological Meaning of Opposition of the Naturalistic Approach and the System-Activity Approach]. In *G. P. Shchedrovitsky. Izbrannye Trudy* [Selected Works], 143–155. Moscow: Shkola kul'turnoi politiki.

Shchedrovitsky, Georgy P. 1995f. "Sintez znanij: problemy i metody" [Synthesis of Knowledge: Problems and Methods]. In *G.P. Shchedrovitsky*. *Izbrannye Trudy* [Selected Works], 634–666. Moscow: Shkola kul'turnoi politiki.

Shchedrovitsky, Georgy P. 1997. "Metodologicheskaia organizatsiia sfery psikhologii" [Methodological Organization of the Sphere of Psychology]. *Voprosy metodologii*. (1–2): 108–127.

Shchedrovitsky, Georgy P. 2002. "Two Concepts of System." In Proceedings of the 46th Annual Conference of the International Society for the Systems Sciences, edited by J. M. Wilby, Asilomar, CA.

Shchedrovitsky, Georgy P. 2004. "Iz istorii MMK (1952–1961)" [From the History of the MMC]. In *Moskovskii metodologicheskii kruzhok: razvitie idei i podkhodov (Iz arkhiva G. P. Shchedrovitskogo)* [The Moscow Methodological Circle: Development of Ideas and Approaches. (From G.P. Shchedrovitsky's archive)]. 8(1). Moscow: Put'.

Shchedrovitsky, Georgy P. 2005. *Znak i deiatel'nost'* [Sign and Activity]. Moscow: Vostochnaia literatura.

Shchedrovitsky, Georgy P. 2005a. "Ponimanie i interpretatsiia skhemy znaniia" [Understanding and Interpretation of the Scheme of Knowledge]. In Metodologiia: vchera, segodnia, zavtra [Methodology: Yesterday, Today and Tomorrow], in 3 vols. Vol. 1, 3–34. Moscow: Shkola kul'turnoi politiki.

Shchedrovitsky, Pyotr G. 2010. *Vvedenie v sintaksis i semantiku graficheskogo iazaka sistemno-myskedeiatel'nogo* [Introduction to the Syntax and Semantics of the Graphic Language of the STA Approach]. Semester 6; lecture 33. Moscow: Izdatel'stvo Akademii narodnogo khoziajstva. [Available online at: http://rudocs.exdat.com/docs/index-218080.html]

Tabatchnikova, Svetlana. 2007. *Le cercle de méthodologie de Moscou (1954–1989)*. Une *pensée, une pratique*. Paris: Ecole des Hautes en Sciences, Sociales.

PART V

# Dialogue and Communication

CHAPTER EIGHTEEN

# Between "Voice" and "Code": Encounters and Clashes in the Communication Space

NATALIA S. AVTONOMOVA

## CHARACTERS BEHIND CONCEPTS

I would like to begin by pointing to a specific function of the terms in quotation marks in the title of this chapter: the "voice" and the "code" should allude to the figures of Mikhail Bakhtin (1895–1975) and Yuri Lotman (1922–1993), respectively. In a way, these figures are different from those discussed earlier in this book. Today there is no need to prove the significance of these thinkers to anyone outside the Russian discourse, to elevate them to the "world level" and thus award them a "quality certificate," as it were. I do not know of a single Russian intellectual—be it a historian, philosopher or psychologist—whose world fame matches that of Bakhtin, about whom thousands of works have been written in many languages. In recent decades, Lotman has been catching up in popularity with Bakhtin among the Western readers. Lotman's works—especially those produced in his late period—have been translated, studied, and discussed in various thematic contexts across the humanities. Even a basic survey of scholarly publications focusing on these thinkers' ideas and works worldwide would fill many thick volumes. Just recently there appeared numerous influential studies in English and other European languages that systematically discuss various concepts and thoughts developed by Bakhtin or Lotman.[1] However, neither of the recent scholarly works attempts to put Bakhtin and Lotman in "dialogue" with each other and clarify a question of a relationship between their philosophical positions. This issue is seldom tackled in scholarly literature. To the best of my knowledge, there is only a few relevant publications, and I will comment on them below. Yet, in my opinion, it is very important to closely explore the question of this relationship, in order to avoid falling into extremes: either bringing the two authors' views too close to each other or position them as absolutely different and having nothing in common. Both tendencies would be inaccurate. While there are important conceptual similarities between philosophical positions of the two thinkers, too much seems to indicate their radical differences, which should not escape our attention. A serious consideration should be given to the paradoxical mechanisms of "attraction in spite of disagreement," which, in many ways, describe Lotman's complex relation to Bakhtin. My goal with this essay is to compare Lotman's and Bakhtin's key ideas and identify important conceptual affinities and disparities between them. By comparing the two thinkers' approaches, I seek to contribute to the topical discussion about the prospects of the humanities as the general study of human experiences and specific modes of expression of such experiences. Let me now turn to certain peculiarities in the reception of Bakhtin and Lotman in Russia and abroad.

The main feature of Bakhtin's intellectual career and his reception in Russia, as I see it, is the gap between the first and main period of his work (1920s) and the period of rediscovery (1960s): in the period of the thaw his concept of dialogue became a symbol of humanism and his concept of carnival proved that protest was possible under any circumstances. In the post-Soviet period (in the late 1980s and 1990s) Bakhtin came to be perceived as a symbol of spiritual Renaissance, the exit from the era of dogmatism and simultaneously as a methodological tool for promoting new thinking in the human sciences. Anthropologists, culture scholars and even epistemologists came to use widely—too widely in my opinion—some of his theses (such as "subject-subject" thinking, greater "time" and "the feast of revival") reveling in turning these theses against any theoretical thought which has a subject-object structure. But there was a danger in this tendency. Gradually Bakhtin's figure, both in Russia and other countries, experienced incredible interpretative broadening and at the same time became an object of ever closer critical examination. As for the French reception of Bakhtin, which was the first and the most dramatic in Europe, it was brought to Europe and later to the whole world by Julia Kristeva. That young and clever Bulgarian, endowed with an extraordinary flair for new ideas, put the phenomenon previously unknown in France in the context of trends that engaged her mind and those of French intellectuals at the time, i.e. Althusser's Marxism, Lacan's psychoanalysis and Bachelard's history of science. Though Kristeva did not always cite these names, they could easily be divined behind the key notions and terms in which she described Bakhtin in her better-known publications (Kristeva, 2004a, 2004b). I deal with all this in my book (see Avtonomova 2009, 2014).

Reception, of course, cannot be studied without analyzing translations. So, I compared the existing French translations of Bakhtin. Among my students in Switzerland was one Delphine Huser (a descendant of Herzen) who was writing a graduation paper under the tutorship of Professor Patrick Sériot. In her work, she analyzed the numerous textual and conceptual distortions that occurred in the process of translating Bakhtin into French (Huser 2001).

For example, in the 1970s the Russian word *slovo* ("word"), *mot* in French, was often translated as *discours* (discourse). This caused excitement at the thought of how much Bakhtin was in tune with the trendy "discourse analysis." Many ideological and conceptual shifts in the French reception of Bakhtin occurred as a result of that single inaccuracy.[2]

Here is another example from my personal experience. One of the colleagues who considered himself a specialist on Bakhtin, despite his inability to read Russian (it happens sometimes), was stunned when I told him that Bakhtin never uses the term "translinguistics" (which is the French translation of "metalinguistics") while the words and concepts of "meta-language" and "meta-linguistics" apparently caught Bakhtin's eye in a newly-published Russian translation of Carnap. There is no need to say that associations connected with the prefixes "trans" and "meta" generate serious semantic differences in understanding Bakhtin's theory. These are just some examples among dozens of others.

One begins to wonder whether it is worthwhile having international fame as the herald of discourse analysis or the pioneer of trans-linguistics. Or as the author of the concept of "carnival" which was widely used in the West and elsewhere, especially in the 1980s, with regard to any "deviant" and "subversive" social, gender and racial groups be they trans-sexuals, feminists or students in revolt. All this is added proof of the well-known thesis: the less clearly a concept is defined the broader its potential sphere of usage. Perhaps it would have been better to bide one's time rather than promoting such risky receptions? However, Bakhtin had no choice. His, again, is a different situation from the case when an individual is well-known inside a country and much less well-known abroad. Besides, many would disagree with me: no matter that the translations are inaccurate or false, no matter that the interpretations are biased, but still they lead us somewhere, away from what is palled and dogmatic.

It is worth recalling that the first serious biography of Bakhtin was written by the Americans Katerina Clark and Michael Holquist while it took some time for Russian scholars to join international discussions of Bakhtin. Initially these meetings and clashes of national, linguistic and communicative traditions gave rise to mutual misunderstandings and grudges, but gradually a new balance of forces emerged in the international research space. The period when Bakhtin was cannibalized and invoked in the most absurd contexts receded into the past giving way to painstaking work with texts; that task was undertaken by a group of Russian scholars to whom we owe the now completed publication of the *Collected Works of Bakhtin* (Bakhtin 2000–2012). It was made clear that one could only competently write about Bakhtin if one reads him in Russian and, among other things, studies newly-published archive materials and corresponding research results.

Compared to the enthusiastic reception of Bakhtin, the history of the reception of Lotman appears to be less impressive, although he too was quite widely known outside Russia. In any case no one abroad came forward to tell about Lotman at the time when he was not allowed to travel abroad himself and to show how he differed from the formalists, who were already known in France, for example, and when he was first allowed to travel abroad where Post-Structuralism was already gaining ground in Europe. In the Soviet times Lotman and his colleagues representing structuralism and semiotics, were accused of mechanicism, formalism and dehumanization. In his later years, when Lotman was able to travel abroad freely, structuralism did not seem to interest anyone anymore, having been replaced with "more advanced" theories of literature and culture. In the 1990s Lotman attracted the interest of scholars—in the West and in Russia—chiefly on account of how and why "he shifted away from structuralism." That was how the booklet "Culture and Explosion" (1992) dictated by an ailing Lotman was interpreted (Lotman 2001, 121–148). In the early 1990s when post-structuralist ideas flooded Russia (these were largely French concepts), the idea of structure, which was oriented toward science had been consigned to archives. I have little sympathy for such interpretations. I prefer to recall that Lotman's early articles showed "post-structuralist" attention to dynamics and that "structuralist" orientation toward science and objectivity is to be found in his later works; I appreciate him for both.

## PUBLIC EXCHANGE COURTESIES

Let me go back to the real or potential interaction between our protagonists. As I have mentioned above, in spite of the fact that the world Bakhtiniana is enormous and the number of works about Lotman is also considerable, little attention has been paid so far to comparing the theories of Bakhtin and Lotman. Some works exist that show the influence of Bakhtin/Voloshinov ideas on the Moscow-Tartu semiotics (Ivanov 1973; Titunik 1976; Torop 1995; Grzibek 1995) and some other aspects of Bakhtin's influence on Lotman's thought (Yegorov 1999; Reid 1990; Mandelker 1994; Bethea 1997). As a rule, their authors are literary scholars and historians of culture; there are practically no philosophers among them, which is a lamentable omission because a comparative analysis of the approaches of Bakhtin and Lotman to human sciences cuts to the core of contemporary discussions about the methodology and epistemology of science.

Bakhtin and Lotman, if they are mentioned at all, are bracketed together as representatives of a single line which one of them initiates and the other elaborates[3]. While they dealt with similar themes, their positions differed dramatically. To bring this out let us take a closer look at some elements (fragments) of their heritage. Whether that legacy remains as ballast or becomes part of modern discussions depends on us. This focus enables us to discern behind the concrete relations between my two protagonists some conceptual tension connected with the fate of structural-semiotic research in Russia: they are echoed in present-day arguments about the prospects of human sciences. I think that the thought traditions represented by these two characters, which sometimes look black-and-white, are in a far more complex and intricate relationship that scholars have yet to fully understand and appreciate.

Typologically speaking, the relations between these figures are in some ways similar to those between existentialism and structuralism, humanism and the so-called theoretical anti-humanism, and the "man" versus "science" in French debates of the 1960s and 1970s. In the intellectual history of France in the twentieth century it was a celebrated episode, a battle of titans, Sartre and Lévi-Strauss, which started off with a bang, but ended with a whimper without leaving a major conceptual elaboration in culture. This happened because the discussion of pivotal questions of epistemology and social philosophy which were seeking to grab center stage had been turned—in line with the traditions of French intellectual life—into an ideological carnival, into personification of the positions represented by the two protagonists. History and European consciousness were embodied by Sartre while structure and "the savage mind" by Lévi-Strauss, with this hasty ideological labeling muting the scientific, theoretical problems that the proposed terms could not accommodate. These shortcomings are noticeable to this day in our current discussions of science and humanism, discussions between the advocates of humanism, trans-humanism, etc. I would like to think that Lotman and Bakhtin would not have succumbed to such ideologization if only because Lotman felt at home discussing the issues of history (judging from his education and several publications) and structure, while Bakhtin seemed to be at home in any field. Besides, they both were exposed to their share of ideological brainwashing in and outside their native land.

Although in the title I refer to the positions of my protagonists as "voice" and "code" these are not part of my meta-language. These are the words and concepts Bakhtin himself used, and not in general, but to describe his own and Lotman's positions. So, to us these are identification signs of the approaches that were once fiercely opposed to each other, but today are often interpreted as demonstration of common trends in the communicative sphere. As I said earlier, I would be more interested in sensing the magnetic lines crossing the entire problem field, discerning the finer traces of interaction that permit us to see unity in what appears to be incommensurate and to observe differences in that which all but merges in a single blot. In short, I would like to build a differentiated image and a concept that would pinpoint not only the natural interaction of attraction, but also the paradoxical interaction of repulsion, with the latter sometimes playing the key role in the history of culture.

Let us examine more closely the conceptual positions of my two heroes. To begin with, the exchange of opinions between Bakhtin and Lotman in the Soviet era looked rather like a public exchange of courtesies. Thus, when the editorial board of the journal *Novy Mir* (1970) asked Bakhtin to speak about the most interesting trends in contemporary literary scholarship, Bakhtin mentioned Lotman along with other major literary scholars, both of the past (Potebnya, Veselovsky) and of the modern time (Tynyanov, Tomashevsky, Eichenbaum, Gukovsky). Lotman (and the issue of Proceedings on Semiotic Systems) was named as "a major phenomenon" in the same breath with Konrad and Likhachev.

In turn, Lotman answering a questionnaire from *Vorposy literatury* (1967) (Lotman 2003, 91–92) gave a list of names that almost coincided with that given by Bakhtin (Tynyanov, Gukovsky, Eichenbaum, Tomashevsky) and named Bakhtin's book *Rabelais and His World* (along with V.V. Ivanov and V.N. Toporov's *Slavic Language Modeling Semiotic Systems)* among the phenomena that merited wide publication and inclusion in anthologies.

However, the polite gestures failed to obscure the underlying conflict between these concepts. It is worth mentioning that among Soviet philosophers decent people avoided criticizing each other for fear of overly sharp ears and possible victimization. So, one could find more candid assessments in fragments from Bakhtin's notes and in Lotman's letters not intended for print (Lotman 1997). I have to say from the start that I do not claim to provide a systematic comparison of the programs of Bakhtin and Lotman in their entirety: I am trying to give an outline and compare fragments of the communicative fabric involving two characters—directly or indirectly, expressly or implicitly. An analysis of the textual fabric ("text" is etymologically related to "texture") is sometimes more revealing than full-scale declarations.

## NON-PUBLIC OPINIONS (BAKHTIN ON LOTMAN)

Let us now turn to Bakhtin's pronouncements on "voice" and "code." In his lifetime they were published under the rubrics "From Notes Made in 1970–1971" and "On the Methodology of Human Sciences" (as it has now transpired, they were printed from manuscripts unedited by Bakhtin himself) and in the latest *Collection* of his works were included in the section "Working Notes of the 1960s and early 1970s" (Notebooks 1, 2, 4 and "Miscellaneous Sheets.") All these fragments consist of nominative sentences and represent ideas to be further elaborated.

Here is the key quotation from Bakhtin's "working notebooks" that sums up his remarks concerning Lotman and structuralists:

> My attitude to structuralism. I am against concentrating solely on the text. Mechanistic categories: "opposition," "change of codes" . . . Consistent formalization and depersonalization: all the relationships have a logical character (in the broad sense). By contrast I hear *voices* (author's italics) everywhere and dialogic relations between them. (Bakhtin 2005d, 434; cf. similar ideas in Bakhtin 2005b, 394)

And elsewhere:

> Semiotics is primarily concerned with transmitting a ready message with the help of a ready code. In living speech, a message, strictly speaking, is created in the process of transmission and there is essentially no code. (Bakhtin 2005a, 380)

And finally:

> Context and code. Context is potentially incompletable. The code must lend itself to being completed. The code is merely a technical means of information, it has no cognitive creative meaning. The code is a deliberately established, devitalized context. (Bakhtin 2005c, 431)

These three remarks establish antinomies on three levels: code and voice, code and a living message, code and context. According to Bakhtin, the code epitomizes all that is negative: code is "a technical means" for conveying ready-made content, it has no "cognitive or creative meaning." "Cognition" and "creativity" are only possible on the side of the voice, utterance, and living speech.

Critics have more than once noted the one-sidedness of this interpretation of Lotman's work in which non-code situations and the creative role of codes loom large, as I will show later. True, B.F. Yegorov, Lotman's friend and colleague and a noted student of his work, in his later work studiously ignores Bakhtin's critique and prefers to call Bakhtin's remarks "very delicate," though simplistic (Yegorov 1999, 244). But while Yegorov glosses over the differences, S.G. Bocharov on the contrary stresses everything that distinguishes Lotman, i.e. to use our terminology, the gap between "code" and "voice." In Bocharov's opinion, for Bakhtin there is no terminology that can encompass all the human sciences (Bocharov 1999, 503–520). Thus, an attempt to represent all the humanities as "sign systems" is untenable. Bocharov contrasts this unifying trend with the language of Bakhtin as a unique voice, a special "personal language, which has nothing to do with the language of a trend or a school." (Bocharov 1999, 516). In general, Bocharov believes that the key to Bakhtin is not even his ideas, but the fact that he posits himself as a problem: his "nucleus" eludes our "interpretative nets." "Bakhtin is a problem in the distinctly Bakhtin sense: he has established himself (what he has left us is Bakhtin himself rather than any concept)." (Bocharov 1999, 519). Interpreted in this way, Bakhtin turns out to be the most existential of existentialists taking existentialism to its limits.

## FROM THE NON-PUBLIC TO THE PUBLIC (LOTMAN ON BAKHTIN)

Let us now change focus and look at Bakhtin from Lotman's side. Lotman undoubtedly had profound respect for Bakhtin. Arguably, he shared with him some pet creative ideas, for example, his abiding interest in acts and in general responsible human behavior. From Lotman's letters one can learn how he exerted efforts to organize Bakhtin's moving to Tartu (Lotman 1997, 512–513), raised money to be sent to Bakhtin (Lotman 1997, 235), helped in publishing both Bakhtin's works and articles on him, although he admits that not all his efforts were crowned with success (Lotman 1997, 255, 522, 682). I repeat, publicly, he never argued with Bakhtin though he was sometimes more candid in private.

I would like to quote Lotman's remark about Bakhtin from published correspondence (I have to note that the letter was about Tynyanov, while Bakhtin was mentioned merely as an analogy, but a weighty analogy):

> Scientifically, Tynyanov was in a certain sense similar to Bakhtin, [Lotman writes]: concrete ideas are often false and concepts are biased (Pushkin—Tyutchev[4] is a fiction shoehorned "into an idea," "Unnamed Love"[5] is the ultimate in unprovedness and invention, etc.) But [the author underlines the word] the general thrust is *extremely fruitful and fertile.* (Lotman 1997, 331; my italics)

Apparently, through a comparison with Tynyanov—and in a letter to a close friend, Lotman is saying something about Bakhtin he would never have permitted himself to say aloud and publicly. However, I would like to emphasize that one has to be Lotman in order to pass on in the same breath from criticism ("unprovedness," "false inventions") to ultimate praise: "he was in any case a genius," gave an "immense" creative impulse, the general thrust of his thought is "extremely fruitful and fertile" (ibid.).

In hindsight one gets a feeling that much in Lotman's conceptual attitude to Bakhtin tallies with this characteristic of Tynyanov/alias Bakhtin: he perceived creative impulse, the creative dynamics while leaving aside what he considered to be contrived, unproven and prejudiced. This can be seen from Lotman's report on Bakhtin delivered at Friedrich Schiller University in Jena in 1983 (Lotman 2002, 147–156). This is the picture presented by Lotman: Bakhtin enunciates inspired hunches, formulates them in vague and uncertain language, further development of science clarifies these hunches and grateful successors remember who gave the first push to their thought. To recap, the main theme of Lotman's report was the role of Bakhtin's ideas in the development of modern semiotics. Lotman points to three impulses emanating from Bakhtin and inspiring modern science: the impulse to develop a dynamic idea of the character of the linguistic sign[6]; the idea of dialogism (Lotman notes the diffuse and uncertain character of this concept just like he notes in his other works the diffuseness of the concepts of "carnival" and "folk fun culture"); and finally, Bakhtin's "stroke of genius" in declaring artistic communication to be the central problem of modern science.

Indeed, Lotman constantly tries to translate Bakhtin's ideas into his own language, to formulate it in terms he feels comfortable with. Thus, Lotman replaces Bakhtin's "polyphony" with "multi-lingualism" or a complicated interplay of subsystems in a structure; in place of dialogues (for example, in Dostoevsky's novels and Bakhtin's research into them) Lotman introduces "conflicting systems" or even "dialogic structures" (Lotman 2001, 289). In short, this is a far cry from Bakhtin's dialogue. Let us try to trace how Lotman clarifies Bakhtin's notion of dialogue from the viewpoint of what he calls a new stage of science development in the preamble to his report. Here one can see precisely what reveals "clashes that turn out to be meetings of minds" and vice versa. Thus, Lotman links the scientific content of the "dialogue" concept, with

1. the discovery that it takes more than one (two or several) communication channels to create information
2. the analysis of asymmetry between cerebral hemispheres as a dialogic mechanism and
3. the study of the functioning of semiotic systems oriented toward other's speech (he considers the relations between mother and baby to be an example of such a system).

If one continues this list, one should be able to see, for example, that Bakhtin's "carnival" becomes in Lotman's conceptual language an invasion of dynamic structures into the sacral world (Lotman 2001, 660), whereas Bakhtin's "ambivalences" are interpreted as a cultural-semiotic phenomenon which attests to the softening of the former oppositions and a readiness of the system to move into a "dynamic state" (Lotman 2001, 552). Lotman permits himself to openly challenge only Bakhtin's epigones (for example, for unpardonably broad interpretation of the carnival tradition (Lotman 2001, 324). Lotman resolutely objects to inaccuracies in understanding the folk fun culture: laughter does not always exclude fear, as Bakhtin believed, but sometimes, on the contrary, implies fear (Lotman 2001, 684), he noted that pagan elements in the West European carnival and similar Russian rites often differ essentially, something that is unfortunately ignored even by specialists (Lotman 2001, 692), and so on. But the most important thing for Lotman is that Bakhtin blazed the trail to the study of a system that is capable of generating new texts. One gets a feeling that for Lotman Bakhtin was the driving force that caused him to move along his own path even if that movement was prompted by the logic of repulsion. Incidentally, an ability to admire something of which there is no proof (as in the above-cited extract about Tynyanov/Bakhtin) is almost an artistic emotion, but then it was not for nothing that Lotman spoke about the role of artistic communication in modern science as Bakhtin's inspired discovery.

All this adds up to a special pattern of relationships. There is a sense that Bakhtin always tries to keep a low profile while Lotman includes and writes Bakhtin into all significant relationships; he feels drawn to Bakhtin. To be sure, Bakhtin differs from formalists: they proceed from atoms in order to attain wholeness whereas for Bakhtin an indivisible whole is a given from which he proceeds. However, in all the other basic relations Bakhtin, according to Lotman, goes hand-in-hand with other significant figures. Thus, together with Propp, Tynyanov and Jakobson he challenges the semiotic ideas of the Geneva (Saussurian) school while at the same time following them; together with L. P. Yakubinsky, Ye.D. Polivanov or Ya. Mukarzhovsky he creates the tradition of dialogic thinking, etc.

Lotman broadens the concept of dialogue: initially he interprets it in what may be called a banal way as alternate "transmission" and "reception" of a message, and one has to bear in mind that dialogue is impossible if there is no difference between the communicating parties. Lotman also sees dialogue in the relations between languages with different structures (verbal and non-verbal languages, the languages of film[7], theatre, literature, music) and even in exchange of signs between animals (the conceptual connotations of these propositions have nothing to do with Bakhtin).

However, Lotman's broadening of dialogue is not infinite, it bumps into its own limit: thus, Lotman never writes about a dialogue of individuals of equal stature. And of course, he has no use for Bakhtin's "voices," just like Bakhtin never mentions "codes" except in the negative critical sense. In interpreting dialogue Lotman never emphasizes the unique and incomplete as a value in its own right; still less what Bakhtin shares with Averintsev and his concept of symbol, the reveling in "the warmth of a unifying mystery" and new hopes for symbology as "alternative science." The term, apparently borrowed by Bakhtin from Averintsev's article about the symbol in the Shorter Literary Encyclopedia (a detailed summary of that article has been discovered in Bakhtin's archives) was destined for a big future in philosophy, at any rate among those who believed that "science" as such was irretrievably discredited. By contrast, Lotman does not seem to have ever mentioned "alternative science" but he spoke about "alternative culture": for him the difference of languages and cultures is the starting point for any cognition of a human being.

Lotman's system of ideas is in many ways remote from that of Bakhtin. However, this does not prevent him, as shown above, from giving Bakhtin his due, valuing and respecting him. Lotman says that much (and not rhetorically, but with apparent sincerity) at the end of his Jena report: "we should speak not only about how we perceive Bakhtin, but about how we ourselves are seen by him. I hope that in studying Bakhtin we prove to be worthy of what he has written."[8]

## MEETING / CLASHES?

Bakhtin's assessment of Lotman and his School did not quite correspond to its prototype. Even if one agrees that the picture which polarized codes on the one hand and incompleteness and open-endedness on the other existed at the early period of Tartu structuralism, it did not remain unchanged over time. What is known about Lotman shows the dynamics of his creative path, constantly probing for new methods and engaging with ever more complex objects. Thus, in a preface to the Polish translation of Pushkin's biography (published in Russian in 1980) Lotman writes that his main ambition is to "show the human, personal (i.e. individual) element in semiotics as a science" (Bethea 1997, 6). This, in my opinion, marks a new departure in the career he was following.

An important aspect of study is the analysis of the processes taking place on the boundaries of cultural space, the study of semiosis as sign activity. According to Lotman, the boundary separating semiosis from extra-semiotic reality is porous. The exchange with the extra-semiotic sphere is a constant source of dynamics of the semiotic space; owing to the "unfinalized nature of the system" (Lotman 2001, 102) there is a kind of "perpetual motion," invasion of some elements and ouster of other elements. The open-endedness does not lead to chaos because of the inner dynamics of the system. The idea of open-endedness, as I see it, is in keeping with some of Bakhtin's insights albeit it is embodied in a different material.

The high point of Lotman's advance along this path, in my terminology, is the idea of "an open structure," though Lotman speaks not about "a structure" but about "an open model" of describing the cultural world represented by many languages and many cultures:

> While traditionally the semiotic process addressed the space of one language and represented a closed model, the time is apparently coming for a basically *open model*. The window of the cultural world is never shut. (Koshelev 1994, 416; my italics)

This fragment introduces a separate vast theme which I cannot discuss here in detail. With Lotman, one sees essentially a kind of unity of the thought of *an open structure* and simultaneously an idea of *translation* as a mechanism of its dynamics (which implies the presence of more than one language and their interaction in the process of cultural communication). The theses of an open structure and translation are coextensive, being the conditions and justification of each other so that every result marks a new beginning. And one can discern a change in Lotman's understanding of code. In fact it is not the code, but "code plus its history" that becomes the operational unit (Lotman 2001, 15). Structure without history, "structure without memory" could well ensure total identity of what is transmitted and what is received, but that would not be a meaningful conversation, but an exchange of commands. The idea of unfinalizability in one way or another is part of the conceptual register of Lotman's thought.

But what of Bakhtin? Has he changed in any way as a result of this interaction at a distance? Has he become more articulate where the incompleteness of his thought is not of a fundamental nature, but is due to insufficient explication of certain theses? As it is well known, Bakhtin distinguished these two types of incompleteness in his own work. Some scholars (including David Bethea for whom I have high regard) are likely to answer this question in the negative: Bakhtin remained standing where he was, reveling in the situation of incompleteness and unfinalizability. However, an analysis of the evolution of Bakhtin's interpretation of the relationship between language and speech, stabilization and dynamic processes suggests a somewhat different picture. One can argue that Bakhtin too covered his own, if small, "part of the way" toward structural conceptualization that he previously shied away from. One can see this, for example, in the change of his interpretation of language and speech between his works of the 1920s and the works and notes in the 1960s and 1970s. While in the 1920s, for example, in *Marxism and the Philosophy of Language* he does not recognize the "real existence" of language or the theoretical "language"-"speech" dichotomy concentrating entirely on the single dynamic of an utterance as a kind of melted-down element, in the 1960s and 1970s not only "language" and "speech," but also "thing" and "personality," "reification" and "personification" become meaningful and even pivotal in Bakhtin's conceptualization system. Bakhtin stresses (!) the cultural significance of the processes of "monologization," that is, natural obliteration of "the other's speech" in the process of dialogue (Bakhtin 2005c, 425). Bakhtin calls the above-mentioned categories "limits," i.e. limits of thought and practice or, to put it another way, "types of relationships" which are in fact relations of complementarity.

For Lotman—and I think most scholars, for all the differences of their views, would agree with this—the main purpose was to build science, to make humanities scientific. This thesis sounds somewhat old hat today, reminding us of the distant past, but in reality it is anything but old hat. While some thirty years ago it might have seemed, both in the West and in Russia, that structural-semiotic studies had spent themselves and scholars had turned their attention to Post-Structuralism and Post-Modernism that were on the way to replacing them now that the sunset of Post-Modernism is at hand, a new need arises that stresses not a reveling in chaos, but reviving structures with all the transformations they may undergo in the modern epoch. That is why it is so important for us today to take stock of the content of our cultural archives and choose those resources that may sustain us at this turning point.

But it has to be noted that Bakhtin—even in the limited aspect represented here, Bakhtin as an antagonist of structuralism—is paradoxically present in this productive dynamic. He was clearly averse to being regarded a prophet of structuralism and semiotics as he was often seen in the West. But he could not help being what he was: a man with a rare feel for the new. Reflecting again on the impact of Bakhtin, Lotman in his later years came to the conclusion that his influence is everlasting, but not through any specific concept and recipes, but owing to his overall impact on culture and on philosophical consciousness. Thus, speaking about Bakhtin's influence on modern art (drama and cinema, not to speak of stage productions of Dostoevsky's novels) Lotman stressed that this impact is exerted "through restructuring the philosophical consciousness of our contemporary." (Lotman 1998, 604). In other words, by his very presence—provided one has learnt to protect any form of his presence from yet another attempt at canonization—Bakhtin could give an impetus to the broader movement of culture, including its elements that he himself might well have regarded as being alien to him.

It is probably too soon to clarify all the points in the overall conceptual picture. Perhaps this is not that important. What is significant is that our two protagonists—whether due to attraction or repulsion—have made their contributions to the dynamics of thinking processes in which, luckily, there are no fixed dogmatic determinations.

## NOTES

1. Among the most notable recent Western publications on Bakhtin are the following: Polyuha, Thomson, Wall 2012; Bagshaw 2013; Haynes 2013; Steinby, Klapuri 2013; Erdinast-Vulcan 2014; Bialostosky 2016; and Bandlamudi 2016. The Western Lotman scholarship is not less impressive. It is presented by a cluster of important recent publications that among others include volumes by Schönle 2006; Frank, Ruhe, Schmitz 2012; Semenenko 2012; Costantini 2013; Velmezova 2015; and Makarychev, Yatsyk 2017. These works are different in their main focuses and genres. Some aim at budding scholars, others target more advanced academic audience. A few are individual monographs, the rest is edited collections of essays. Along with the volumes, which are mainly interested in gaining valuable insights into the working of Bakhtin's and Lotman's thoughts, there are those whose authors attempt to apply the thinkers' concepts and techniques to new areas of research including literary criticism, cultural studies, art, psychology, indeed, the entire social and political sphere in its modern, expanded sense.
2. However, in the history of culture, errors are sometimes rectified. Thus, the new bilingual publication of *Marxism and the Philosophy of Language* which was full of such mistakes had been translated by Patrick Sériot and Inna Tylkowski-Ageeva (Vološinov 2010). The text in this publication is attributed solely to Voloshinov, however, because it seems impossible to scientifically resolve the question of authorship of this work, I list it under two names as Bakhtin/Voloshinov.
3. This position is presented, for example, in Kasavin 2008.
4. In this connection, Boris F. Yegorov states: "The reference is to Tynyanov's article "Pushkin and Tyutchev" (1923) in which the author seeks to prove that Tyutchev was remote from and alien to Pushkin" (Lotman 1997, 333).
5. Boris Yegorov's comment: "Lotman uses the title of Tynyanov's article, "Unnamed Love" to refer to the hypothesis of Pushkin's secret love for Karamzin's wife" (Lotman 1997, 333).
6. It is worth noting that the idea was by no means characteristic of early reception of Saussure in Russia but was very manifest in the Bakhtin/Voloshinov book *Marxism and the Philosophy of Language*. This position is shared by Vladimir Alpatov (Alpatov 2005). Bakhtin, according to Alpatov, was saying about Saussure things that were not thought to be relevant at the time they were being said, i.e. in the 1920s, however, several decades later the Bakhtin/Voloshinov critique reached its peak of relevance in such areas of language studies as speech linguistics, linguistics of utterance, various areas of communicative linguistics, etc.
7. Lotman cites interesting examples of the use of Bakhtin's notion of other's speech and the concept of "polyphonic structures" in film study, notably the films of Andrzej Wajda (Lotman 1998, 660).
8. This is the translation from the German transcript of the report (Lotman 2002, 156). Makhlin quotes this fragment in his own translation: in the face of Bakhtin's legacy (*Erbe*) it is not about "how *we* see Bakhtin, but how *he* sees us" (Lotman 2002b, 40).

## BIBLIOGRAPHY

Alpatov, Vladimir M. 2005. *Voloshnov, Bakhtin i lingvistika* [Voloshinov, Bakhtin and Linguistics]. Moscow: Yazyki slavyanskikh kul'tur.

Avtonomova, Natalia S. 2009. *Otkrytaya struktura: Yakobson—Bakhtin—Lotman—Gasparov* [Open Structure: Jakobson—Bakhtin—Lotman—Gasparov]. Moscow: ROSSPEN. (2nd revised and enlarged ed., 2014—Moscow, St Petersburg: Tsentr gumanimarnykh initsiativ.)

Bagshaw, Hilary B.P. 2013. *Religion in the Thought of Mikhail Bakhtin: Reason and Faith*. Farnham, Surrey: Ashgate Publishing.

Bakhtin, Mikhail M. 1965. *Tvorchestvo Fransua Rable i narodnaya kul'tura srednevekov'ya i Renessanca* [François Rabelais and Folk Culture of the Middle Ages and Renaissance]. Moscow: Khudozhestvennaya literatura.

Bakhtin, Mikhail M. 2000–2012. *Sobranie Sochinenij v 7 tomakh* [Collected Works in 7 vols.]. Moscow: Russkie slovari. Yazyki slavyanskikh kul'tur.

Bakhtin, Mikhail M. 2005a. "Rabochie zapisi 60—nachala 70 godov. Tetrad' 1" [Working Notes of the 1960s—Early 1970s. Notebook 1]. In *Sobranie Sochinenij v 7 tomakh*. Vol. 6. Moscow: Russkie slovari.

Bakhtin, Mikhail M. 2005b. "Rabochie zapisi 60—nachala 70 godov. Tetrad' 2" [Working Notes of the 1960s—early 1970s. Notebook 2] In *Sobranie Sochinenij v 7 tomakh*. Vol. 6. Moscow: Russkie slovari.

Bakhtin, Mikhail M. 2005c "Rabochie zapisi 60—nachala 70 godov. Tetrad' 4" [Working Notes of the 1960s—Early 1970s. Notebook 4]. In *Sobranie Sochinenij v 7 tomakh*, Vol. 6. Moscow: Russkie slovari.

Bakhtin, Mikhail M. 2005d. "Rabochie zapisi 60—nachala 70 godov. Razroznennye listy" [Working Notes of the 1960s—Early 1970s. Miscellaneous Sheets]. In *Sobranie Sochinenij v 7 tomakh*. Vol. 6. Moscow: Russkie slovari.

Bandlamudi, Lakshmi. 2016. *Difference, Dialogue, and Development*. New York, NY: Routledge.

Bethea, David M. 1997. "Bakhtinian Prosaics Versus Lotmanian 'Poetic Thinking': The Code and its Relation to Literary Biography." *Slavic and East European Journal* 41 (1): 1–15.

Bialostosky, Don H. 2016. *Mikhail Bakhtin: Rhetoric, Poetics, Dialogics, Rhetoricality*. Anderson, South Carolina: Parlor Press.

Bocharov, Sergey G. 1999. "Sobytie bytiya. M.M.Bakhtin i my v dni ego stoletiya"» [The Event of Being. M. M. Bakhtin and Us on the Day of His Centenary]. In Idem. *Syuzhety russkoj literatury* [Episodes from Russian Literature], 503–520. Moscow: Languages of Russian Culture.

Costantini, Michel (ed.). 2013. *Glissements, décentrements, déplacement. Pour un dialogue sémiotique franco-russe*. Saint-Denis: Université Paris 8.

Erdinast-Vulcan, Daphna. 2014. *Between Philosophy and Literature: Bakhtin and the Question of the Subject*. Stanford, CA: Stanford University Press.

Frank, Susi K., Ruhe, Cornelia, Schmitz, Alexander (eds.). 2012. *Explosion und Peripherie. Jurij Lotmans Semiotik der kulturellen Dynamik revisited*. Bielefeld: Transcript Verlag.

Grzibek, Peter. 1995. "Bakhtinskaya semiotika i moskovsko-tartuskaya shkola" [Bakhtin's Semiotics and the Moscow-Tartu School]. In *Lotmanovskij Sbornik. Vyp. 1* [Lotman Collection. Issue 1], 240–259. Moscow: Garant.

Haynes, Deborah J. 2013. *Bakhtin Reframed: Interpreting Key Thinkers for the Arts*. London: I.B. Tauris.

Huser, Delphine. 2001. *(Mémoire). Réception en France de l'œuvre de Bakhtine-Volochinov "Marxisme et théorie du language." Le décalage spatio-temporel des contexts scientifiques se reflète-t-il dans la traduction française?* Lausanne.

Ivanov, Vyacheslav V. 1973. "Znachenie idej M. M. Bakhtina o znake, vyskazyvanii i dialoge dlya sovremennoj semiotiki" [The Relevance of M. M. Bakhtin's Ideas on the Sign, Utterance and Dialogue to Contemporary Semiotics]. *Uchenye zapiski Tart. Gos. Un-ta, 1973. Vyp. 308. Trudy po znakovym sistemam* [Proceedings of Tartue State University, 1973. Issue 308. Works on Sign Systems VI], 5–44 [reprinted in *Dialog, Karnaval, Khronotop* [Dialogue, Carnival, Chronotope] 1996 (3): 5–58 with a new afterword (59–67)].

Kasavin, Ilya T. 2008. *Tekst. Diskurs. Kontekt* [Text, Discourse, Context]. Moscow: Kanon+.

Koshelev A. D. (ed.). 1994. *Yu.M. Lotman i tartusko-moskovskaya semioticheskaya shkola* [Yuri M. Lotman and the Tartu-Moscow Semiotic School]. Moscow: Gnozis.

Kristeva, Julia. 2004a. "Razrushenie poetiki" [Destruction of Poetics]. In *Izbrannye trudy* [Selected Works ]. Translated by Georgij Kosikov. Moscow: ROSSPEN, 5–30.

Kristeva, Julia. 2004b. "Slovo, dialog i roman" [Word, Dialogue and Novel]. In *Izbrannye trudy* [ Selected Works], 165–193. Translated by Georgij Kosikov. Moscow: ROSSPEN.

Lotman, Yuri M. 1994. "Tezisy k semiotike pusskoj kul'tury" [Theses for Semiotics of Russian Culture], Programme of Russian Culture Department, Institute of World Culture, Moscow State University. In Koshelev A.D. (ed.) *Yu. M. Lotman i tartusko-moskovskaya semioticheskaya shkola* [Yuri M. Lotman and the Tartu-Moscow Semiotic School]. Moscow: Gnozis.

Lotman, Yuri M. 1997. *Pis'ma* [Letters]. *1940–1993*. Moscow: Languages of Russian Culture.

Lotman, Yuri M. 1998. "Yazyk teatra" [The Language of Theater]. In Idem. *Ob iskusstve* [On Art], 603–608. St.Petersburg: Iskusstvo—SPb.

Lotman, Yuri M. 2001. *Semiosfera* [Semiosphere]. St.Petersburg: Iskusstvo—SPb.

Lotman, Yuri M. 2002a. *Istoriya I tipologiya russkoj kul'tury* [History and Typology of Russian Culture]. St. Petersburg: Iskusstvo—SPb.

Lotman, Yuri M. 2002b. *"Bachtin—sein Erbe und aktuelle Probleme der Semiotik," Roman und Gesellschaft. Internationales Michail Bachtin-Colloquium. Friedrich-Schiller-Universität* (Jena, 1984); Russ. Transl.: "Nasledie Bakhtina i aktual'nye problemy semiotiki" [The Legacy of Bakhtin and Current Problems of Semiotics]. In *Istoriya i tipologiya russkoj kul'tury* [History and Typology of Russian Culture]. St. Petersburg: Iskusstvo—SPb.

Lotman, Yuri M. 2003. "Otvety na anketu Voprosov literatury" [Answers to *Voprosy literatury* questions]. In Idem. *Vospitanie dushi* [Education of the Soul], 91–92. St.Petersburg: Iskusstvo—SPb.

Makarychev, Andrey, Yatsyk, Alexandra. 2017. *Lotman's Cultural Semiotics and the Political*. London: Rowman & Littlefield International.

Mandelker, Amy 1994. "Semiotizing the Sphere: Organicist Theory in Lotman, Bakhtin and Vernadsky," *PMLA* (109): 385–396.

Polyuha, Mykola, Thomson, Clive, Wall Anthony (eds.). 2012. *Dialogues with Bakhtinian Theory. Proceedings of the Thirteenth Mikhaïl Bakhtin International Conference.* London (ON): Mestengo Press.

Reid, Alan. 1990. "Who is Lotman and Why is Bakhtin Saying Those Nasty Things About Him?" *Discours social / Social Discourse* 3 (1–2): 325–338.

Schönle Andreas (ed.). 2006. *Lotman and Cultural Studies. Encounters and Extensions*. Madison: Wisconsin University Press.

Semenenko, Aleksei. 2012. *The Texture of Culture: An Introduction to Yuri Lotman's Semiotic Theory*. N.Y.: Palgrave Macmillan.

Steinby, Liisa, Klapuri, Tintti (eds.). 2013. *Bakhtin and his Others: (Inter)subjectivity, Chronotope, Dialogism*. London: Anthem Press.

Titunik, Irvin R. 1976. "M. M. Baxtin (The Baxtin School) and Soviet Semiotics." *Dispositio* (1): 327–338.

Torop, Peeter. 1995. "Tartuskaya shkola kak shkola" [Tartu School as School]. In *Lotmanovskij Sbornik. Vyp. 1* [Lotman Collection. Issue 1], 223–235. Moscow: Garant.

Velmezova, Ekaterina (ed.). 2015. *L'école sémiotique de Moscou-Tartu. Tartu-Moscou: histoire, épistémologie, actualité*. Toulouse: Université de *Toulouse*-Le Mirail. [*Slavica Occitania* (40).]

Vološinov, Valentin N. 2010. *Marxisme et philosophie du langage. Les problèmes fondamentaux de la méthode sociologique dans la science du langage*. Translated by Patrick Sériot and Tylkowski-Ageeva. Limoges: Lambert-Lucas.

Yegorov, Boris F. 1999. "Bakhtin and Lotman." In Idem. *Zhizn' i tvorchestvo Yu. M. Lotmana* [The Life and Work of Yu. M. Lotman], 243–258. Moscow: Novoe literaturnoe obozrenie.

CHAPTER NINETEEN

# A Belated Conversation

VITALY L. MAKHLIN

This chapter focuses on ideas of the Russian thinker *Mikhail M. Bakhtin* (1895–1975). I argue that a proper discussion of his ideas, including his "dialogism" (Holquist 1990), has not yet taken place. Furthermore, such a discussion and productive conversation with the thinker could not have taken place either during the Soviet epoch or even after. Bakhtin's fame must not mislead us. I would suggest that the situation we encounter in Bakhtin scholarship can be rather described as a sad misinterpretation of the thinker's ideas, which is present worldwide, but particularly in Bakhtin's fatherland.

Today the initial enthusiasm about Bakhtin, apparent in the 1960s and beyond, has reached its lowest level, if it has not ceased completely. In a sense, the end of the "boom," which came around 2000, was not a surprise. It revealed and essentially reflected—along with other reasons and factors—a certain historical *breach of communication* between Bakhtin's intellectual and cultural epoch with its specific context, on the one hand, and the postmodern, post-revolutionary period, both in the Soviet Russia and the West, on the other. The internal and yet objective failures of understanding and contact have come into view at the historical moment when the external limitations were gone and the "freedom" of interpretations revealed something that was not so evident under the Soviet regime, namely, *a substantial lack of freedom* on the part of those who provided those interpretations and comments, i.e., their own dependence on the presumptions and prejudices of the philosophical and scholarly thinking that Bakhtin himself had criticized *decades before* he was "discovered" in the USSR and abroad.

How did it all come about and how was it possible? And why, at the same time, does Bakhtin's work remain important for the humanities and philosophy, at least in post-Soviet Russia (but, presumably, not only there), despite what might be called a recent anti-Bakhtinian wave of *resentment* even in some seemingly scholarly publications? (Makhlin, Dolgorukhova 2013).[1]

In order to approach these questions, it is necessary to clarify what might be called the *conditions of impossibility* of a dialogue with the non-Soviet thinker in the Soviet century. I am not going to dwell into individual works and interpretations here—there exists enormous critical literature on Bakhtin. As he once remarked: "For the qualified reader they [individual works] are unnecessary, and for the unqualified, useless" (Bakhtin 1990, 257). I will rather focus on historically systematic and methodological questions, which are central here. I am mainly interested in the reception history "without names" (to use Heinrich Wölflin's famous phrase from the sphere of art history). In the history of Bakhtin's reception during the "first hundred years" (Emerson 1997), the Russian philosopher seems to have been discovered and then almost immediately "lost," which was caused by the "conditions of impossibility" to establish the mutual, bilateral communication, or dialogue between the thinker and his reader. It would be worthwhile to examine this phenomenon in the light of the major issue central to hermeneutics, from Schleiermacher and Kierkegaard to Gadamer and Bakhtin. The issue in question is this: Under what conditions one could *share* creative experience of the "other" and to become a co-participant of the other's thinking within the confines of one's own historicity—and under what conditions it turns out to be impossible?

## THE DIALOGIC IMPERATIVE

The initial formulation of the Bakhtinian dialogism (in which the world "dialogue" is still absent, but the fundamental idea or, rather, *imperative* is already present) runs as follows:

> Even if I know a given person thoroughly, and I also know myself, I still have to grasp the truth of our interrelationship, the truth of the unitary and unique *event* which links us and in which we are participants. (Bakhtin 1993, 17)

In the context of Bakhtin's philosophical project of the early 1920s, this existentially and ontologically substantiated imperative seems to imply something like this: I and another ("a given person") are connected or linked to each other by an "event" that seems to exceed both myself and this other person, an event in which we are participants (and, possibly, interlocutors) insofar as we are mutually different and "outside" one another in our "interrelationship." Even before each of us takes the other into account in his/her consciousness/self-consciousness, we *already* participate, one way or another, in the common "being-as-event"; that is, in the "truth" of our interrelationship, this truth being already given before any cognitive objectification and before any direct contact. Bakhtin speaks in this connection of a "profound *ontological difference in significance* within the event of Being" (ibid., 75). It is this objective, not an objectifiable "ontological difference in significance," that I "have to grasp" *more than merely theoretically*; this is the task of my "answerability." The "eventful" truth of my relation to another or others is something more than merely cognitive, and an "event of Being" is more than Being "in itself." The truth of our interrelationship, as Bakhtin would write half a century later, is a "supra-existence" (Bakhtin 1986, 137), because a "relationship is wider than thinking" (Bakhtin 2002, 435).

To be answerable or responsible, according to Bakhtin, means to enrich some cognitive sense that I have grasped or understood, with the "truth of our interrelationship"—whether the "other" is "another person" or another epoch, or culture, or a scientific discipline in its relation to other disciplines. Thus, from his 1919 printed "manifest" about the interrelationship between "art" and "life" (Bakhtin 1990, 1–3), up to his latest notes and unfulfilled projects of the early 1970s, Bakhtin seems to have developed one and the same (yet changing from decade to decade) epistemological and ethical imperative which is widely known today as his "dialogism."[2]

All this seems to be more or less known today, at least to the "qualified reader." And yet, this cognitive side of the matter, I would argue, appears to be inadequately discussed even today, not to mention the Soviet past and, to some extent, the Western "postmodernity."

## MUTUAL EXTERNALITY

A "seriocomic" (to use his own term) element in the reception history of Bakhtin's work during the Soviet period (both in Russia and abroad) was the fact that the ontological precondition of any "dialogue" as Bakhtin had himself formulated it (the latest formulation being "*mutual externality*" (Bakhtin 2002, 432) was either completely ignored or was not taken seriously.

Although the impression that Bakhtin had not been "our game" was clear from the very beginning, that is, from the 1960s on, a "gap" between his thinking and historical and cultural background, on one hand, and the social atmosphere and background of the 1960s and beyond, on the other, was so wide that this gap, or "mutual externality," has become a real issue only recently, *after* the end of the "official" Soviet era and *after* the Bakhtinian "boom" in Russia and the West was largely over. In other words, this became apparent *after* "the entire ideological culture of recent times" had exhausted its "*event potential*" (Bakhtin 1984, 80–81; see also: Makhlin 2010).

This, I believe, resulted in Bakhtin's "present moment" after "the first hundred years." This is his "unofficial" presence in the new century, almost as unofficial or "silent" as it was for the most of the twentieth century.

This paradoxical silent presence was correctly perceived, though not quite completely understood, by the prominent Soviet scholar Yuri M. Lotman, who declared in his 1984 talk at the Bakhtin conference in East Germany that it is not so much as *we* and *we alone* who see and discuss Bakhtin; rather, it is *he* who sees us all (Lotman 1984, 40). This is "mutual externality," or the historically concrete "ontological difference in significance" *turned upside down* or "carnivalized," quite in the Bakhtinian sense of the term, but in reference to the reception history of his ideas, primarily in the Soviet Union.

Thus, the question remains: What are those conditions of impossibility that prevented even Bakhtin's most enthusiastic readers and interpreters from the direct yet "belated" engagement with his ideas and from perceiving him *on his own terms*?

## THE IMAGE AND THE DOUBLE

In the Soviet Union of the 1960s–1970s, Bakhtin was a kind of an exotic rarity, an unexpected phenomenon within the confines of strictly established concepts, traditions and discourse. (Interestingly, in the same way, though with the different result for himself and his ideas, the "Soviet scholar" was viewed and received in the West.) Why so?

In his books and essays on literature, language and culture, Bakhtin discussed "unofficial culture" and non-classicist genres, discourses, and worldviews of the previous epochs so vividly or, to be more exact, so hermeneutically that his ideas and terms were absorbed and almost immediately applied by some influential critics (including the humanists). For example, what Jaspers had called an *abgebrochene Kommunikation* (communication, which broke off) were not a historical fact, the reality "behind-the-text" that had to be taken seriously (i.e., hermeneutically or dialogically) *prior to* any judgment and "appropriation." In other words, Bakhtin's notions and concepts were identified, in the last Soviet decades, with some imaginary but urgent "event potential" of his readers' *future*—an aberration that was, as a matter of fact, not quite an aberration. Bakhtin and his "dialogic imagination" were perceived, more often than not, as an "unofficial" *promise of political and cultural emancipation*—emancipation from the "iron cage" of the official ideology (in the Soviet Russia) or from the "bourgeois culture" (in the West).

Thus, the image was not only a misapprehension; on the other hand, this image was, in a sense, a "double," a projection of the unrealized event potential of "postmodernity" with its "horizon of expectations," that is, to a certain extent, *the wrong side of the true other*. No wonder that *after* the collapse of the Soviet Union, from the 1990s on, Bakhtin's sympathetic image has lost its currency and came to be often deconstructed the "double," the wrong side of the previous image, has persisted and almost replaced the image proper.

The difference between an "image" and a "double" concerns the very essence of any modern dialogics or hermeneutics (see Bialostosky). This essence or core is actually the phenomenon and problem of the "other," more precisely, is the way one could approach and treat another human being, or another epoch or worldview, as another meaningful or "subjective" activity, a "thou art" of the other.[3] Thus, an ethical, aesthetic and methodological alternative seems to emerge. Either I understand the other by establishing a space "in-between" us, i.e., a space of "mutual externality" as a common ground for our "interrelationship" and its possible "truth" (in this respect, Gadamer, as is well known, speaks of a "fusion of horizons" between the text and its interpreter). Or we see in another, or in a text, not so much his/her subjective "thou art" as a projection of my own existential, or "monologic" drive and historical presuppositions.

## THE LAUGHTER INVISIBLE TO THE WORLD

One more aspect, and a very important one, of the "double" should also be taken into account here—a "linguistic" aspect of Bakhtin's writing and, inevitably, of the history of its reception. I mean the language or, rather, "languages" or discourses that Bakhtin—a non-Soviet and non-Marxist thinker and scholar who had been formed in the pre-revolutionary decade and during the decisive "paradigm shift" in European philosophy and the humanities (approximately, between 1914 and 1923)—appropriated (and constantly changed) from the mid-1920s up to the mid-1970s, in order to "inscribe" himself into the "official" and overwhelming discourse(s) of his day.

In any case, with the exception of his fundamental programmatic texts from the early 1920s (actually manuscripts without a beginning or end), Bakhtin could not help expressing his thoughts and ideas under the mask(s) of the dominant ideological discourse(s) of power. A distinctive irony of that inevitable strategy also had (and, to a certain extent, still has) its dark side. For, Bakhtin, while hiding himself behind the official mask(s) of a Marxist he never was, had actually used the "languages" of his time, which partially contributed to misunderstanding of Bakhtin and often identifying him with those "official" (not necessarily "political") discourses that were more or less common in that period. As a result, it was more or less "natural" and convenient for Bakhtin's belated readers to see in the "Soviet scholar" an "event potential" of that thinking or scholarly trend which a critic or interpreter identified himself/herself with, proceeding from the "natural" assumption that "we know better." Consequently, one way or another, one could not help creating some "double," even if he/she made an honest attempt to understand. But even the most interesting and productive efforts to clarify and absorb Bakhtin's thinking did not survive the "boom" of the 1980s and 1990s.

That is why, I believe, it would not be an exaggeration to say that Bakhtin's own words (paraphrasing Gogol) about "laughter invisible to the world" (Bakhtin 1984, 178) could be used as a motto of the reception history of his work. For it is much easier to see the other as an object of laughter excluding oneself from that object. This exclusion marks out a "profound ontological difference in significance" between the "carnival" laughter of the Middle Ages and the modern or postmodern laughter of the "modern times" stressed in Bakhtin's "well-known" interpretation of Rabelais and his novel.

* * *

This short history of reception we have tried to outline here seems to be instructive at least in one respect—that of "event potential." It helps one identify a historical watershed, the "end without an end" if you like. The Soviet—and, even more so, Western—reception of Bakhtin's work was a history "without an address." We are conscious (or half-conscious) of it for at least two reasons. On the one hand, the addressee seems to come out of his previous images, masks or doubles: now Bakhtin turns out to be, to a large degree, a very different author than he was thought to have been in the Soviet era; in any case, we are free to analyze and discuss a lot of new data provided by the Collected Works in six volumes published between 1996 and 2012 by a team of specialists headed by Sergei G. Bocharov. On the other hand, paradoxically enough, the longer the historical distance between Bakhtin's world and our own, the shorter it appears to be in the new century. In this context, the "conditions of impossibility" I have discussed are being more and more *seen as our own* projections and thus "carnivalized" in the strict Bakhtinian (not in the "postmodern"!) sense of the term. To paraphrase his own remark on Dostoevsky, one could say: Bakhtin has not yet become Bakhtin, he is becoming him.

This slow process of becoming or identifying Bakhtin the author—outside the mirror images of his postmodern interpreters—one could easily see at least *three* comparatively new recent shifts of interest and tendencies of research in the field of Bakhtin studies, both in Russia and the West. The first and perhaps the most important one is associated with the appearance of Bakhtin's Collected Works that I have mentioned earlier. This edition provides, in fact, new, and for many unexpected, possibilities of research. It allows to approach Bakhtin's authorship and view his ideas not only from the perspective of a single text, but put them into a more broader context of the development of his own thoughts masterfully reconstructed and analyzed in the extensive commentaries of the well-known Bakhtin scholars. In this connection, I believe, very rare memoires are especially indispensable (Bocharov, Blackwell, Liapunov 1994). The second major recent trend seems to be a palpable "shift" of interest from Bakhtin's most famous works on the novelistic genre, most notably on Dostoevsky and Rabelais, to his early philosophical essays written around 1920 (Bakhtin 1990; Bakhtin 1993). The focus in Bakhtin studies on the thinker's philosophical and religious origins and background (see Haardt 2009; Steiby 2011; Guseynov 2017) might help us, in the future, reconstruct a complete picture of Bakhtin's own intellectual development through better understanding of the vicissitudes and dynamic of his time. Finally, there seems to be a tendency to apply Bakhtinian categories to a variety of fields in the humanities thus trying to overcome strict borderlines between the disciplines (Batt 2003; Webb 2008; Weiss 2010; Erdinast-Vulcan 2013). All these interrelated tendencies are determined by an attempt to truly comprehend and appreciate Bakhtin's *own* program and contents in a comparatively new socio-historical situation of the twenty-first century, and, in this way, to "carnivalize" aberrations and "doubles" of his "postmodern" reception since the 1960s.

## NOTES

1. The emotional and intellectual background behind these reactions seems to consist globally in an unofficial and all-encompassing social atmosphere of "silence" *after* the end of the "new times" in the last century. This silence might strangely remind us of the "taciturn philosopher" (*filosof-molchun*), an impression Bakhtin often produced on his younger interlocutors and colleagues. One of them wrote later: "Bakhtin's silence in the last years of his life is one more riddle, perhaps the most profound" (Broitman 1990, 114).
2. In an unfinished preface to the 1975 collection of his essays, Bakhtin stressed that the collection "is unified by one single theme in various stages of its development" (Bakhtin 1986, 155).
3. This is, clearly, the point of departure in Bakhtin's famous interpretation of Dostoevsky's poetics and "authorial position." As is well known (much less understood, though), Vyacheslav Ivanov, a great Russian critic and poet, was the first to have "groped" the "task" of Dostoevsky's protagonists which was to "overcome their ethical solipsism, their disunited "idealistic" consciousness, and transform the *other person* from a shadow into an authentic reality"—the task that, according to Bakhtin, was accomplished not by Dostoevsky's characters, but—in contrast to Ivanov's metaphysical approach—by Dostoevsky's "vision" of the truth of their interrelations (see: Bakhtin 1984, 10).

## BIBLIOGRAPHY

Bakhtin, Mikhail M. 1984. *Problems of Dostoevsky's Poetics*. Translated by Caryl Emerson. Minneapolis: Minnesota University Press.

Bakhtin, Mikhail M. 1986. *Speech Genres and Other Late Essays*. Translated by Vern W. McGee. Edited by Caryl Emerson and Michael Holquist. Austin: University of Texas Press.

Bakhtin, Mikhail M. 1990. *Art and Answerability: Early Philosophical Essays*, edited by Michael Holquist and Vadim Liapunov (trans.). Austin: University of Texas Press.

Bakhtin, Mikhail M. 1993. *Toward a Philosophy of the Act*, edited by Vadim Liapunov (trans.) and Michael Holquist. Austin: University of Texas Press.

Bakhtin, Mikhail M. 2002. *Sobranie sochineniy* [Collected Works]. Vol. 6. Edited by Sergei G. Bocharov and Ludmila Gogotishvili. Moscow: Yazyki slavjanskihk kul'tur.

Batt, Noëlle. 2003. "Pour un dialogisme des disciplines: avec Bakhtine," *Théorie. Littérature. Enseignement* 21: 5–20.

Bagshow, Hilary B. 2013. *Religion in the Thought of Mikhail Bakhtin. Reason and Faith*. Burlington, VT: Ashgate Publishing.

Bialostotsky, Don H. 1989. "Dialogic, Pragmatic and Hermeneutic Conversation: Bakhtin, Rorty, Gadamer." In *The Bakhtin Circle Today*, edited by Myriam Diaz-Diacaretz. *Critical Studies: A Journal of Critical Theory, Literature and Culture* 1, (2): 107–119.

Bocharov, Serge, Blackwell, Stephen, and Liapunov, Vadim. 1994. "Conversations with Bakhtin," *PMLA*, 109 (5): 1009–1024.

Braham, R. Bracht (ed.). 2002. *Bakhtin and the Classics*. Evanston, Ill.: Northwestern University Press.

Broitman, Samson N. 1990. "Dve besedy s M.M. Bakhtinym ["Two Conversations with M. M. Bakhtin.]." In *Khronotop: Mezhvuzovskiy sbornik* [Chronotop: An Inter-University Collection], edited by Samson N. Broitman, 110–114. Makhachkala: Dagestan University Publishers.

Emerson, Caryl. 1999. *The First Hundred Years of Mikhail Bakhtin*. Princeton and New Jersey: Princeton University Press.

Erdinast-Vulcan, Daphna. 2013. *Between Philosophy and Literature: Bakhtin and the Question of the Subject*. Stanford: Stanford University Press.

Guseynov, Abdusalam A. 2017. "Filosofiya postupka kak pervaya filosofiya (popytka interpretatsii nravstvennoj philosophii Bakhtina" [The Philosophy of the Act as the First Philosophy (an attempt at interpretation of Bakhtin's moral philosophy)].—First article: "Byt' znachit postupat'" [To Be is to Act], *Voprosy filosofii,* (6): 5–15; Second article: "Pervaya filosofiya kak nravstvennaya filosofiya" [The First Philosophy as the Moral Philosophy], *Voprosy filosofii,* (7): 65–74.

Haardt, Alexander. 2009. "Ethische und ästhetische Persönlichkeit. Zum Verhältnis des Ethischen und Ästhetischen bei Sören Kierkegaard und Michail Bachtin," *Studies in East European Thought*, 61 (2/3): 326–342.

Lotman, Yuri M. 1984. "Bachtin—Sein Erbe und aktuelle Probleme der Semiotik." In *Roman und Gesellschaft: Internationales Michail-Bachtin-Colloquium*, Edited by Hans Günter, 32–40. Jena: Friedrich Schlegel Universität.

Makhlin, Vitaly L. 2010. "Beyond the Text." In *Critical Theory in Russia and the West*. Edited by Alastair Renfrew and Galin Tihanov, 195–214. London and New York: Manchester University Press.

Makhlin, Vitaly and Dolgorukhova Natalya. 2013. "Ressentiment odurachennykh" [The Resentment of the Fooled]. *Voprosy literatury* [Questions of Literature], (6): 444–450.

Spektor, Alexander, Denischenko, Irina M., et al. 2017. "Bakhtin Forum: The Dark and Radiant Bakhtin. Wartime Notes," *Slavic and East European Journal*, 21 (2): 233–298.

Steiby, Lisa. 2011. "Herman Cohen and Bakhtin's Early Aesthetics," *Studies in East European Thought*, 63 (3): 227–249.

Webb, Geoff R. 2008. *Mark at the Threshold. Applying Bakhtinian Categories to Markan Characterization*. Leiden/Boston: Brill.

Weiss, Daniel H. 2010. "A Dialogue between Philosophy and Scripture: Rereading Herman Cohen through Bakhtin," *The Journal of Religion*, 90 (1): 15–32.

CHAPTER TWENTY

# From Historical Materialism to the Theory of Culture: The Philosophy of Mikhail Bakhtin as a Cultural Phenomenon

MAJA E. SOBOLEVA

Soviet philosophy has now become a part of the history of modern Russian philosophy. At the same time, as a dynamic phenomenon, it had its own unique history worthy of consideration. The topic of my chapter is Soviet philosophy of the 1970s. I argue that the reception of Mikhail Bakhtin's philosophy in the 1970s promoted the transformation of Soviet philosophy and the overcoming of Marxist-Leninist dialectical and historical materialism, which at that moment had been the Russian official philosophical doctrine over fifty years.

It would be hard to speak about the reception of Bakhtin in the Soviet Union since during the Soviet period Russians had little acquaintance with Bakhtin's ideas, and even the present limited exposure to them was sporadic and mostly latent.[1] The well-known exceptions are Vyacheslav Ivanov's notes "The value of ideas about the sign, sentence and dialogue for modern semiotics" (Ivanov 1973) and the collection of papers dedicated to Bakhtin's 75th anniversary and 50th anniversary of his scholarly and pedagogical activity (Konkin 1973). However, starting in the 1960s, Bakhtin's works began gradually entering into Russian intellectual life and drawing attention of professional Soviet philosophers. His study *Problems of Dostoevsky's Poetics* was reprinted three times: in 1963, 1974, and 1979 (see Bakhtin 1963). The book *Francois Rabelais's Work and Folk Culture of the Middle Ages and Renaissance* (known in English as *Rabelais and His World*) came out in 1965 (Bakhtin 1965). After that followed three collections of articles: *Questions of Literature and Aesthetics*

(Bakhtin 1975), *The Aesthetics of Verbal Art* (Bakhtin 1979)—with the commentaries by Sergei Averintsev and Sergei Bocharov—and *Essays on the Literary Critiques* (Bakhtin 1986).[2]

Today we can speak about the Bakhtin studies "industry" (Morson 1986, 86).[3] As a result of the breadth of topics with which Bakhtin dealt, he has influenced such disciplines as literary studies, philosophy, cultural studies, anthropology, political science, semiotics and even theory of communication. The reception of his ideas took place in a variety of forms, such as exegesis of the texts or their close reading accompanied by explanation and interpretation. Some authors used Bakhtin's approach and his conceptual tools for developing their own theoretical constructions. After all, the reception of Bakhtin also involved the simple invocation of particular concepts rather than the development of a coherent theory. This type of reception was the most common way of disseminating Bakhtin's intellectual legacy. Many of Bakhtin's terms, such as *dialogism*, *polyphony*, *multilingualism*, *heteroglossia*, *chronotope*, *outsidedness*, *carnivalesque* and *the big time* entered the lexicon of modern literary criticism, literary theory, philosophy and theory of culture. As a rule, these concepts changed their semantics and retained only the form. Sometimes, they had the sole function of indicating their initial belonging to Bakhtin (in order to give more weight to the scholars by referring to his authority). The cases when Bakhtin's terms turned into familiar quotations and were used in arbitrary and alien contexts can be considered, in general, as their instrumentalization. This sort of usage contradicts sometimes both the letter and the spirit of Bakhtin's works, so that one experiences a need to "return to the original Bakhtin." For instance, Ken Hirschkop writes that "we need a more 'historical' Bakhtin. A Bakhtin who does not deliver philosophical verities about dialogue, or a new ontology of language, but, something more modest and more pointed" (Hirschkop 1999, VII).

The most productive type of reception consisted of attempts to develop the potential inherent in his concepts, which served as a basis for the establishment of a new theory. Among those who became inspired by Bakhtin's ideas and who incorporated them into their own theories are such Russian/Soviet philosophers as Vladimir Bibler, Genrikh Batishchev, and Yuri Lotman. Through this kind of reception, the application of Bakhtin's ideas contributed to the modernization of Soviet Marxist philosophy.

## THE CASE OF BIBLER

The central concept of Bibler's theory is the concept of dialogue. On this basis he sought to develop a theoretical frame for a new logic in comparison with Marxist materialist dialectics. The aspired "dialogic" had to become not just a logic of scientific thinking, but a logic of the socio-historical being of humanity. Bibler presented his deliberations in the books *Myshlenie Kak Tvorchestvo* [Thinking as Creativity] (1975) and *Ot Naukouchenija k Logike Kul'tury* [From a Doctrine of Science to the Logic of Culture] (1991). It is becoming clear that one of the crucial sources of Bibler's theory in these works was ideas formulated in Bakhtin's works. Moreover, he found in them the foundation on which to build his own conception. Bibler's reading of Bakhtin can be summarized in the following statement: "Bakhtin's poetics of dialogue (or—in other words—the poetics of culture) is, as a matter of fact,—an *introduction to the logic* of dialogue, to the dialogical reason, to the *logic* of culture." (Bibler 1991, 163)[4]

Bakhtin's concept of dialogue provided Bibler with an opportunity for a new way of thinking about the world in comparison with norms and strategies developed by dialectical and historical materialism. Against the background of Soviet philosophy, Bibler's originality consists in offering a *new object* of philosophical reflection, namely being as culture, as well as a *new methodology* for philosophical reflection about this object, namely the dialogical logic of culture in the form of the "dialogue of different logics."

Three ontological dimensions can be differentiated in Bibler's conception of culture. Culture is, firstly, "a form of simultaneous existence and communication between people of different—past, present and future—cultures, a form of dialogue and mutual generation of these cultures" (Bibler 1991, 289). Culture is, secondly, "a form of self-determination of the individual within the horizon of personality, the form of self-determination of our life, consciousness, and thinking" (Bibler 1991, 289). Finally, culture is "the invention of the world for the first time" (Bibler 1991, 290). Three logical levels are connected with these ontological levels of culture in his theory. There is

1. "the dialogue of logics,"
2. "the transduction" as a mutual transition and mutual foundation of the logics, and
3. "the logic of the beginning of logic" (Bibler 1991, 291).

The relationship between the logical and ontological levels in Bibler's conception can be reconstructed as follows: "the dialogue of logics" is the way in which culture exists, and culture is a result of this dialogue. "The transduction" is a way of interaction between cultures, and each culture is only "able to live and to develop itself on the periphery of cultures" (Bibler 1991, 286). "The beginning of logic" is the moment of the formation a culture as a "work of art" (Bibler 1991, 10), which reflects our understanding of the world.

It follows from this scheme that logic in Bibler's theory is not only a tool of reflection, not only an organ of philosophical cognition, but rather it is related to Hegelian onto-logic in the sense that culture appears at the same time both as a form and as a result of activity of the concept (i.e., of human thought). In general, Bibler's theory can be understood as a modernization of the Marxist version of Hegel's onto-logic by means of Bakhtin's concept of dialogue which is interpreted in it as dialogic. In Bibler's project, dialogue becomes an element of dialectics. In this sense one can interpret Tamara Dlugach's metaphor that "if Hegel was an eternal opponent of V.S. [Bibler], Bakhtin was, in contrast, his vital conversational partner" (Dlugach 2012, 158).

It must be stressed that this re-thinking of dialogue as a unitary and monistic dialogic is an essential point which demonstrates the contrast between Bakhtin's and Bibler's theories. In Bakhtin's conception, monologism and dialogism are opposed to each other as the mutually exclusive paradigms of the cognitive attitude to the world.

The first—monologism—is a real phenomenon which is represented by Western European philosophy in general and by the theory of knowledge in particular; the second—dialogism—is Bakhtin's *ideal* which is not yet realized in philosophy, but rather expressed in literature and, above all, in the works of Dostoevsky. While monologism arises from and focuses on philosophy of mind, dialogism emerges due to the switching of attention from the concept of consciousness to the concept of language. Language is seen by Bakhtin as a productive semantic and communicative activity and not as a formal system of signs and sentences. In this case, not an abstract and solipsistic subject, but the speaking and acting empirical human being in the plural becomes the main producer of knowledge, and, hence, of all symbolic being. "Idea,—Bakhtin states,—is a living event which is unfolding in a point of a dialogical meeting of two or several consciousnesses" (Bakhtin 2002, 99). Hegel's idea of identity of being and concept is completely abandoned by Bakhtin. The place of contact of humanity with being is a place where every form of identity is destroyed. The world appears to be not a logical, but a hermeneutical phenomenon, while the subject gives place to inter-subjectivity.

Unlike Bakhtin, Bibler interprets being and human reason in their immanence. He tries to construe the idea of dialogue in its "generality" and sees an "ultimate" idea of a modern logic of culture in "communication": "It is the logic of communication that is the form of a modern logical answer to the Hegelian question: 'What is the most general?'" (Bibler 1991, 14). According to him, the term "communication" expresses the identity of being and human being. Besides, philosophical logic of culture is not only capable of going into the general "theory of culture" by means of the concept of "dialogue," but can also provide a foundation for the "culture of logic" as a normative "logic of creation of logic" through the dialog. This pan-logical strategy can be interpreted as a residual fundamentalism, but, nevertheless, thanks to the symbiosis of the philosophy of Bakhtin and the philosophy of Hegel, Bibler drafted a new form of social interaction with respect to Marxist historical dialectics which was carried not by conflict, but by dialogical—even if still formal-logical—communication.

## THE CASE OF BATISHCHEV

Genrikh S. Batishchev was another active recipient of Bakhtin's philosophy. Batishchev saw his major task in the "development of a whole conception of dialectics in general" (Batishchev 1997, 29). He called his concept of dialectics the "dialectics of creativity" (dialektika tvorchestva). The latter was for him identical with the "creativity of dialectics" and with the process of "its unconditional self-critical development" (ibid.). Unlike the Soviet Marxists, Batishchev understood dialectics not as a power of the anonymous objective laws of development of nature and society, independent of the human being. On the contrary, he understood a real historical human being as the only creator of dialectics. Thanks to this step, he returned a freedom to a subject whom Marxism regarded as a casual product of necessary structures.

The idea of the "development of the form of development itself," which was offered by Batishchev, consists in the transformation of Marxist objective dialectics into the dialectics of intersubjective communication (Batishchev 1997, 31). In his conception, three directions of reconstruction of dialectics can be differentiated: the first involves (a) the intersubjective relations, (b) the second—the concept of subject, and (c) the third—the relationships between subject and object. Here is a brief elaboration of these points.

### *(a)*

The core issue of the proposed dialectics consists of the "inter-paradigmatic," "harmonious" and "polyphonic" relations between the agents of historical processes (it should be stressed that these terms belong to the lexicon of Batishchev, not Bakhtin). This dialectics is interpreted as a relationship between the part and the whole. Here, the part is a concrete subject which possesses her own essence, norm and "her own infinite prospect of development" (Batishchev 1997, 48). The whole is the "continuously becoming, living synthesis of many paradigms which are being established repeatedly" (ibid.). The structure of such a dialectical system is built by the "logic of polyphony"; the way in which this system functions is by means of dialogical interactions (Batishchev 1997, 45).

Batishchev is not coy about borrowing the idea of dialectics as constructive communication (dialog) from Bakhtin. However, he is very critical of Bakhtin. According to Batishchev, "M. M. Bakhtin not only does not consider the polyphonic idea as a necessary and intrinsically valuable development of the *dialectics of becoming* (*dialektika stanovlenija*), i.e., as something that should be 'inscribed' into it (freed from Hegel's 'monologism'), but even decisively excludes all this" (Batishchev 1997, 50). On this point, Batishchev is right. In fact, the concept of polyphony is *deeply anti-dialectical* in Bakhtin's works, and therefore his theory is more consistent from the point of view of its inner dialogical logic. After all, Hegel's dialectics in Marxist interpretation is established through the unity and conflict of opposites and through the resolution of conflict due to the removal of the opposition between thesis and antithesis at a higher level of synthesis. In such a case, there is no place for real polyphony and real diversity of worldviews. That is why Bakhtin's theory gives an account of development as co-existence and as *dialogical*, but *not* dialectic interaction. It is not the unity of one consciousness that underlies reality, but rather reality results from the multiple dialogical relations between social agents.

### *(b)*

One can say that Batishchev thinks together with Bakhtin and at the same time against him. This can be shown by analysis of all his concepts including the concept of subject. Batishchev refused both the Marxist understanding of the subject as a product and projection of social relations and the sociological reduction of the subject to the role she plays in society. The subject appears in his theory as an entity, which has substantial depth and her own inexhaustible potential for development. According to Batishchev, the essence of the subject consists of "intersubjectivity," which is understood *hermeneutically*, in the manner of Bakhtin. That means that the subject is a product of the process of education; she is the heir of "all the multi-layered and multi-dimensional cultural history, of all or many of its formations, ways of life and paradigms" (Batishchev 1997, 52). Thus, the external intersubjective relations enter the inner life of the human being to make up her essence. According to Batishchev, other persons enter and determine the very ontology of individual human life (Batishchev 1997, 129). The dialectics and ontology of creativity are inextricably and holistically connected with each other in his conception whereby, from the ontological point of view, the essence of creativity consists in the forming of ingenious personality that will be able to become a subject of the dialectic of creativity, i.e., become its producer.

Batishchev's account of creativity as a "construction of man" (Batishchev 1997, 131) explains his criticism of the so-called "activity approach." According to him, the creative process cannot be reduced to its material results; on the contrary, its value lies primarily in the actualization of the specific nature of humanity as a being created by the world of culture and creating the world of culture. Therefore, the representational side of the "objective dialectics" of creativity expresses the inner freedom of humanity, her creative potential (Batishchev 1997, 171).

The foundations of Batishchev's intersubjective ontology of human existence are provided by Sergey Rubenstein's psychological ideas and by Bakhtin's dialogical philosophy. Giving preference to Rubenstein's views, Batishchev is critical of Bakhtin:

> Unfortunately, M. M. Bakhtin does not elevate *the whole being of humanity* onto the level of such "inter-subjectivity," the weave constituted by the living meeting, the event; he does not illuminate it as a mutual interpenetration of the entire human "I" with his others. (Batishchev 1997, 129–130)

However, this criticism appears to be irrelevant, since the word in Bakhtin's theory has intrinsically dialogical structure; it results of and represents intersubjective relations. It is able to function only in the context of question and answer. Since human consciousness, according to Bakhtin, has a linguistic nature, dialogism can account for the very essence of human existence. That is why we can claim that Bakhtin's theory can be interpreted as a *theory of dialogical reason* par excellence.

### *(c)*

In developing his dialectics of subject-object relations, Batishchev again addresses Bakhtin's works. And again we hear the critical tone which now concerns the theory of carnival. According to Batishchev, "carnival and Rabelaisian trends" are aimed at "depriving the human being of the objectively dialectic, universal perspective of meaning in which "the absolute movement of becoming [dvizhenie stanovlenija] could unfold" (Batishchev 1997, 50–51). Batishchev considers the Carnivalesque as an attempt by humanity to overthrow the "hierarchy of the universe for achieving a place in its center" (Batishchev 1997, 51).

However, Batishchev's interpretation above does not correspond to the context of Bakhtin's deliberations, since carnival is considered by Bakhtin, in the first instance, as *lexical carnival*, as a mechanism of generating new meanings and as an instrument of the fight against semantic monologism (see Soboleva 2010, 117–138). On the one hand the Carnivalesque constitutes a counter-place and a resistant practice, on the other it is a resource of a new ideology and new senses. Nevertheless, the concept of carnival plays an important, although negative, role for the development of the theory of Batishchev himself. Negating a carnival as a parade of human aggressive ambitions, he tries to stress the responsibility of humanity for the whole planet and culture in particular. For him, creativity does not imply the conquest and assignment of nature; it is not the "pantagruelism" of nature, but the establishment by the human being of a trustful and nearly intimate relationship with it. Creative activity must change its character from the anthropocentric to "polycentric" (Batishchev 1997, 433). The human being must relinquish her position as a master of nature and become the "heir of the entire Universe" (Batishchev 1997, 431). She should take her proper place in cosmic evolution, taking into account the "criteria of value" (Batishchev 1997, 29) of her presence in the world and recognizing the dignity of the Universe, its own canon and autonomy. The creative dialectics "means not the anthropologization of the Universe, not an imposition of the limited human parameters, but an expansion and enrichment of an open human essence, its unity with ever-increasing universal contents, the historical process of its cosmization" (Batishchev 1997, 289). In this regard, Batishchev takes up a position which is close to the position of Russian cosmism (Konstantin Tsiolkovsky, Vladimir Vernadsky, etc.) with its ecological ethics, which recognizes the absolute value of nature and the relative value of humanity as only its element.

This reconstruction of Batishchev's theory shows that he interprets the philosophical sense of creativity as "relation" (Batishchev 1997, 29) based on reciprocity and on establishing a mutual participation at all possible levels—at the level of the subject, at the intersubjective level and at the level of subject-object interactions. The essence of his dialectics of creativity, understood as a universal form of inter-relations, is expressed by the category of "communication" borrowed from Bakhtin and re-thought in that "deep sense" (Batishchev 1995, 103) in which the commonality in form of togetherness (*soobshchnost'*), i.e., as recognition of the polyphony of semantic centers, builds a necessary ontological prerequisite of dialogical communication. The goal of communication as an absolute movement of formation consists in the acquisition of selfness and, at the same time, of togetherness both with other human beings and with nature. Thanks to Bakhtin, Batishchev's dialectics of creativity is impossible without a constitutive dialogue with other members of society. Due to this aspect his theory reveals itself as a humanistic project, challenging traditional Marxism with its monological, rigorous logic and rhetoric.

## THE CASE OF LOTMAN

The case studies of Bibler's and Batishchev's theories demonstrate that the reference to Bakhtin's works promoted the transformation of Marxist-Leninist historical materialism toward a general theory of culture. With reference to Yuri Lotman's works, it is possible to show that Bakhtin's ideas promoted also the development of structural semiotics in the USSR. In his programmatic article "Literaturovedenie Dolzhno Byt' Naukoj" ["Literary Theory Has to Become a Science"], Lotman postulated in the sense of Marxism that "dialectics is the methodological fundament of structuralism" (Lotman 1967, 93). Under dialectics he understands the principles of combining elements in a system and the study of such systems, both in a synchronous and a diachronic perspective. Lotman writes: "A scholar does not list 'characteristics', but constructs a model of relations. Each structure—the elements of the organic unity, built according to this type of system,—is, in turn, only an element of a more complex structural unity, and its own elements—individually—can be considered as further independent structures" (ibid.). He extends the systematic approach to the understanding of semiotic phenomena of different levels of complexity, such as work of art, culture and history, and combines structural analysis with the temporal analysis of systems. According to Lotman, "the knowledge of the previous state is an inevitable condition for successful modeling" (ibid.). Therefore, structuralism is not an opponent of historicism, but is complementary to it.

For Lotman, the dialectic approach symbolizes the scientific approach, i.e., the orientation of human sciences to the ideals of strict scientism such as mathematical precision, verifiability and absolute truth.[5] Thereby his structuralism enshrines the principle of materialism and the principle of development, which are characteristic for "scientific" Marxist dialectics, as methodological foundations allowing for objective knowledge to be attained. Materialism in structuralism means that the sign appears to be an initial empirical element of analysis, allowing penetration into the ideal structure of its meaning. Therefore, Lotman argues, materialistic structuralism can exist only in the form of semiotics. Since the sign is not only a fixed form, but is able to generate different meanings, depending on the context, structuralism adheres, Lotman continues, to the principle of historical development. From this he draws a conclusion that semiotics can be realized only in the form of dynamic functional analysis, allowing for the passage from empirical reality to ideal structures, to meaning.

Lotman sees the benefits of his interpretation of materialist dialectics in the fact that it delivers a methodology, which is immune to both a mechanistic, static materialism and idealism. He names this methodology "functional analysis." For him, the main goal of semiotics consists in giving an account of a system of signs as a complex of significant elements. Lotman begins with formal elements and determines their content under the premise that the elements which are pulled out of the system cannot have any meaning. He considers only such elements of the system significant which are included in a structure of oppositions. He relates the term "opposition" to Hegel's principle of "unity of opposites" and sees "a deep dialectism of the principle of opposites" in the fact that "the antithetic is here understood as a special form of unity" (Lotman 1967, 97). Lotman's dialectic method aspires to disclose the essence of the element by means of analysis of the oppositions in which this element is included. This is a kind of contextual analysis. He reveals the meaning of the sign system thanks to the complex hierarchy of significant elements, constructed according to the structural laws of this system.

Lotman's semiotic method of materialistic dialectics contradicts Soviet Marxist dialectics at least on three points. First, it no longer includes the principle of the "struggle of opposites," by preserving the harmonizing principle of the "unity of opposites." According to Lotman, the oppositions which are neutralized within a sign system guarantee its stability. The conflict of oppositions would finally lead to destruction of the whole system. Arguing in this way, he challenges the main system principle of Marxist theory of development. Second, the principle of historicism in Marxism assumes that culture results from social and economic issues of a particular time. It is only a secondary appearance related to the material base. In contrast to it, Lotman understands a sign system analogically to an organic cell as a "complex, functioning, self-adjusting" system (Lotman 1967, 96). Thus, he revisits the fundamental Marxist assumption about the strong dependence of cultural phenomena on material factors. Third, Lotman's methodology is not monistic, but dialogical. He is convinced that "some sides of the structure reveal themselves only when we look at it with the "eyes" of the structure of a different type and translate its concepts into languages of other systems" (Lotman 1967, 98). This principle resembles a hermeneutical key rule of "outsideness" in Bakhtin's theory which is a condition for adequate understanding of semantic structures. By the way, Bakhtin's name is mentioned in this methodological article as one of the representatives of structuralism. As we know, later on Lotman will use a number of concepts introduced by Bakhtin, such as *memory of the text*, *existence on the border*, *polyphony of culture*, *dialogical consciousness*, etc. These concepts are not marginal for Lotman, but underlie his semiotic theory.

Thanks to Lotman and Vyacheslav Ivanov, Bakhtin is often held to be one of the representatives of semiotics, while Bakhtin, in effect, did not accept this discipline. For example, Bakhtin claims that "a statement (verbal work) as a whole is part of completely new realm of verbal communication . . ., which cannot be described and defined in terms and methods of linguistics, and—more general—of semiotics" (Bakhtin 1979, 359). Bakhtin is convinced that "semiotics deals mostly with transferring of ready messages by means of a ready code. In the living speech, a message, strictly speaking, is for the first time created during the process of transmission and there is, in principle, no code" (Bakhtin 1979, 371).

It is undoubtedly true that philosophy of language is the major subject of Bakhtin's works. However, he conceived a science of language not as a semiotics, but as "meta-linguistics," as a philosophical theory of living dialogue (see also Soboleva 2010, 83–95). This theory not only focuses on the functioning of the active, spoken word in the process of social intersubjective interactions, but also examines all philosophical problems through the prism of dialogical language and dialogical consciousness. However, even if not being adequately construed, Bakhtin's philosophy of dialogue did play an important role in Russian culture. Thanks to his works (along with the works of Lev Vygotsky, Sergei Rubenshtein, Alexei Leontiev and Valentin Voloshinov), a kind of *linguistic turn* took place in Soviet philosophy in the second half of the twentieth century. A swathe of theories, such as structural semiotics, linguistic pragmatism, theory of speech acts, communicative linguistics, theory of linguistic personality and communicative theory of society, were developed, in which language as a form of social activity built a basis for reflexion.

## CONCLUSION

In conclusion it can be said that the case studies of the theories of Bibler, Batishchev and Lotman help to explain the cultural phenomenon of Bakhtin in late Soviet philosophy. It is obvious that the transformation of Soviet Marxist discourse was promoted in many respects by the application of Bakhtin's works to new theories. The popularity of Bakhtin's works can be explained, first of all, by their extraordinariness, since they were sharply dissonant in relation to the dominant way of thought in the USSR. Everything was different, starting with the *methodology* of Bakhtin's works, which imposed a logical and ethical ban on monological thought and on the possibility of only one, absolute truth. The other major contrast to official Soviet philosophy was Bakhtin's understanding of the place of the subject in history, which emerged from his account of human life as a sphere of action. His *anthropology of action* exempted the subject from Marxist assumption of the fatalism of objective historical laws and emphasized the creative role of the individual. Bakhtin's scientific ethics and his social ontology based on dialogical communication and recognition of a plurality of worldviews and ways of life differed from the Soviet monological ethics of the class struggle and from the Marxist ontology of the uniform, determined social being. Finally, the *spirit of freedom* inherent in Bakhtin's philosophy affected everyone who encountered it and stimulated the development of independent thinking.

From the socio-political and ethical points of view, Bakhtin's popularity can be to some extent explained by the fact that he was mostly perceived not as a Soviet, but as a Russian philosopher. Thus, Merab Mamardashvili drew attention to Bakhtin's "extraterritorial" position of the outsider, "obtained by conquest and suffering" ("*zavoevannuju i vystradannuju*") (Mamardashvili 1988, 23). Michail Gasparov believed that although Bakhtin was born due to the Revolution, he was not attracted by it, but moved back from it in a "solipsistic gap" (solipsicheskuju shchel') (Gasparov 2004, 9). Bakhtin had, paraphrasing his own expression, an "alibi" in the Soviet social and political reality; he occupied a strict position of "outsideness" in relation to it. Bakhtin's case can be interpreted as an example, demonstrating that the reformation of Soviet philosophy occurred, to some extent, thanks to the return to Russian philosophy, which has been only fragmentarily received in the Soviet Union.

Finally, Bakhtin's philosophy itself was polycentric, fragmental and not finalized. Therefore it had potential for multiple developments. These and other similar properties made it convertible, pliable and self-actualizing. Corresponding in time and in spirit to a new awakening of the 1970s, it could be successfully used for modernization of Soviet philosophical models.

## NOTES

1. For example, Batishchev's book *Vvedenie v Dialektiku Tvorchestva* [Introduction to Dialectics of Creativity] which was inspired by Bakhtin's ideas, was completed in 1981, and deposited in the Institute of Scientific Information on Social Sciences of the Academy of Sciences of the USSR in 1984 (see Batishchev 1997).
2. All Bakhtin's works listed in this section had been written and originally published in the Russian language. For complete details about these works see Selected Bibliography given at the end of this volume.
3. There are some examples for this: Isupov 1991; Gogotishvili, Gurevich 1992; Norenkov 1992; Vakhrushev 1997; Vasil'ev 1998; Isupov 2001, 2002. Since 1992 the journal "Dialogue. Carnival. Chronotope" which is committed to studies of Bakhtin's works has been published.

4. All translations into English are my own.
5. Compare with Gasparovs's view in Gasparov 1996; Gasparov, Lotman 1996.

# BIBLIOGRAPHY

Bakhtin, Mikhail M. 1979. "Iz Zapisok 1970–1971 g.g." [From the Notes of the 1970–1971]. In *Estetika slovesnogo tvorchestva* [Aesthetics of the Verbal Art]. Moscow: Iskusstvo.

Bakhtin, Mikhail M. 2002. *Problemy poetiki Dostoevskogo* [Problems of Dostoevsky's Poetics]. In *Sobranie sochinenij* [Collected Works], Vol. 6. Moscow: Russkie slovari. Yazyki slavjanskoj kul'tury.

Batishchev, Genrikh S. 1995. "Osobennosti kul'tury glubinnogo obshchenija." [The Specifics of the Culture of the Deep Communication]. *Voprosy filosofii* [Problems of Philosophy]. (3): 95–129.

Batishchev, Genrikh S. 1997. *Vvededenie v dialektiku tvorchestva.* [Introduction to the Dialectics of Creativity], Sankt Petersburg: Russkij Gumanitarny Khristianskij Institut.

Bibler, Vladimir S. 1991. *M.M. Bakhtin ili poetika kul'tury.* [M.M. Bakhtin or the Poetics of Culture]. Moscow: Progress.

Dlugach, Tamara B. 2012. "V. S. Bibler kak fenomen filosofskoj kul'tury 20 veka." [V. S. Bibler as a Phenomenon of the Philosophical Culture of the Twentieth Century]. *Voprosy filosofii* [Problems of Philosophy], (9): 154–166.

Hirschkop, Ken. 1999. *Mikhail Bakhtin: An Aesthetic for Democracy*. Oxford: Oxford University Press.

Gasparov, Michail L.1996. "Lotman i marksizm." [Lotman and Marxism]. *Novoe literaturnoe obozrenie.* [New Literary Review]. (19): 7–13.

Gasparov, Michail L., Lotman, Yu. M. 1996. "Nauka i ideologija." [Science and Ideology]. In *O poetakh i poezii.* [On Poets and Poetry], edited by Ju. M. Lotman, 9–16. Sankt Petersburg: Iskusstvo SPb.

Gasparov, Michail L. 2004. "Istorija literatury kak tvorchestvo i issledovanie: sluchaj Bakhtina." [History of Literature as Creativity and Study: Bakhtin's Case] *Russkaja literatura XX-XXI vekov: problemy teorii i metodologii izuchenija. Materialy mezhdunaodnoj konferencii.* [Russian Literature of the Twentieth—Twenty-first Centuries Proceedings of the International Conference], edited by I. Kormilov, 8–10. Moscow: MGU.

Gogotishvili, Ljudmila A., Gurevich, Pavel S. (ed.). 1992. *M.M. Bakhtin kak filosof.* [M. M. Bakhtin as a Philosopher]. Moscow: Nauka.

Isupov, Konstantin G. (ed.). 1991. *Problemy Bakhtinologii* [Problems of Bakhtin Study]. Sankt Petersburg: RGPU.

Isupov, Konstantin G. (ed.). 2001, 2002. *M. M. Bakhtin: pro et contra. Tvorchestvo i nasledie M. M. Bakhtina v kontekste mirovoj kul'tury.* [M. M. Bakhtin: pro et contra. Bakhtin's Work and Legacy in the Context of the World Culture]. Sankt Petersburg: Russkij Gumanitarnyj Khristianskij Institut.

Ivanov, Vyacheslav V. 1973. "Znachenie idej o znake, vyskazyvanii i dialoge dlja sovremennoj semiotiki." [The Value of Ideas about the Sign, Utterance and Dialogue for Contemporary Semiotics]. In *Trudy po znakovym sistemam. Uchenye zapiski*

*Tartusskogo universiteta.* [Works on Signs and Semiotic Systems. Journal of the University of Tartu], Vol. VI, 5–44. Tartu: Tartusskij Universitet.

Konkin, Semen S. (ed.). 1973. *Problemy poetiki v istorii literatury. K 75-letiju so dnja rozhdenija i 50-letiju nauchno-pedagogicheskoj deyatel'nosti M.M. Bakhtina.* [The Problems of Poetics in the History of Literature. On the 75th birthday anniversary and 50th anniversary of scholarly-pedagogical activity of M. M. Bakhtin]. Saransk: Mordovskij Gosudarstvennyj Universitet.

Lotman, Yuri M. 1967. "Literaturovedenie dolzhno byt 'naukoj'." [Literature Theory Should be a Science]. *Voprosy literatury.* [Problems of Literature] (1): 90–100.

Mamardashvili, Merab K. 1988. Esli osmelit'sj i byt' [If One Dares To Be]. *Nashe nasledie.* [Our Heritage] (3): 22–27.

Morson, Gary S.1986. "The Bakhtin Industry." *Slavic and East European Journal.* 30 (1): 81–90.

Norenkov, Sergei V. 1992. "Bakhtinovedenie kak osobyj tip gumanitarnogo myshlenija." [Bakhtin Studies as a Special Type of the Humanities Thinking]. In *M. M. Bakhtin. Esteticheskoe nasledie i sovremennost'.* [M. M. Bakhtin. Aesthetic Legacy and the Contemporary Time], edited by Arkadij F. Eremeev. Vol. 2, 133–145. Saransk: Mordovskij Gosudarstvennyj Universitet.

Soboleva, Maja. 2010. *Die Philosophie Michail Bachtins. Von der existenziellen Ontologie zur dialogischen Vernunft.* Hildesheim: Georg Olms Verlag.

Vakhrushev, Vladimir. 1997. "Bakhtinovedenie—osoby tip gumanitarnogo znanija?" [Are Bakhtin Studies a Special Type of the Humanities Knowledge?]. *Voprosy literatury.* [Problems of Literature] (1): 239–301.

Vasily'v, Nikolai L. 1998. "Baktinizm kak istoriko-kul'turnyj fenomen." [Bakhtinism as a Historico-Cultural Phenomenon]. In *M. M. Bakhtin i vremja: IV-ye Bakhtinskie nauchnye chtenija (20–21 nojabrja 1997 gorod Saransk).* [M. M. Bakhtin and Time: The Fourth Bakhtin Conference]. Saransk: Mordovskij Gosudarstvennyj Universitet.

CHAPTER TWENTY-ONE

# On the Role of the Communication Topic in the Discussions of the 1980s–1990s

## *A Philosophical Reflection*

VIKTOR A. MALAKHOV

Studying the history of philosophy of the late Soviet period, which attracts more and more attention now, we encounter a noticeable paradox: on the one hand, the epochal shift, which has happened since that time, makes this period appear much more remote than it could have hypothetically been after several decades of a more peaceful, inwardly consecutive development. On the other hand, key circumstances of that time are still fresh in people's minds, and most actors are alive and well now; sometimes they even present updated interpretations of their activities in those times.

In spite of general expectations, the degree of mysteriousness inherent in the described historical phenomenon of the "close remoteness" only increases with the course of time. There appear more and more to be causes to ask ourselves a puzzling question: what did they really think about, what did all these so familiar people argue about? Then something begins which I would call the process of *disacquaintance*: the obliterated unique features of a person and their ideas, which remain misunderstood, are gradually replaced by certain standard characteristics which make no sense. Needless to say, there is nothing simpler than to define Evald Ilyenkov as a late Soviet Hegelian or to say that Alexei Losev was a brilliant religious thinker. However, perhaps it is something that remains beyond such definitions that deserves attention and comprehension.

In any case, people who took their career path during that period still remember that philosophy was then treated seriously; the necessity to overcome numerous complications and temptations connected with the choice of such an uncommon profession only strengthened the adherence to this vocation in those who really had it. In spite of mostly alternative-free conditions of the then intellectual situation (the exclusively Marxist indoctrination received via education, the poor knowledge of languages, the virtual absence of contacts with foreign colleagues, etc.), representatives of the Soviet philosophical community maintained close professional contacts, read attentively and thought over not only Marx's works but all accessible classics of world philosophy. Most independent thinkers tried—still in the true Marxist spirit—to make their way through the trackless "inter-paradigmality" in the growing conceptual chaos. It is noteworthy that such attempts were not mostly fruitless: their real thinking experience was often appreciable. A treacherous role was played by the language of the then philosophic discourse: the territory of unfounded, untold or deliberately inadequate words. Thus the content of this discourse obviously needs—and will need in the future—a careful translation, the translation not only into the world languages but also into an understandable professional philosophic language. So what was the subject of philosophers' conversations and debates in those years over which they were ready to fight so frantically?

A specific question in which I am interested is how the topic of communication entered the circle of meditations of philosophers of the late Soviet time. To my knowledge, it is one of the most principal questions for the philosophy of the last century all over the world. Of course, I can touch only on a few aspects of this big topic which still needs a rounded and detailed investigation. It is wonderful (and the philosophy is genetically related to the phenomenon of "wonder") that, living in a world of their own and moving along the thought pathways predetermined by the crisis of the Soviet ideology and the living conditions in the USSR, the Russian philosophers of those years (I mean such diverse figures as Genrikh Batishchev, Vladimir Bibler, Moisey Kagan) have come to the comprehension of the problems which arose then before their Western colleagues who dealt with an entirely different sphere of discourse. I have already talked and written about the amazing facts of "message exchange" between Batishchev and Emmanuel Levinas (Malakhov 2009, 305–309)—especially vivid against the background of polemics between Batishchev and Mikhail Bakhtin (Batishchev 1992b, 123–141); observations of this kind could be continued.

Entering the space of words about the Other, which always arose afresh and were realized in the home culture, I cannot help but admire the works of such scholars as Victor Vizgin (Vizgin 2004), Vitaly Makhlin (Makhlin 1997), and others, who worked on the understanding of this theme more and better than it may be expected from me and my modest efforts. I could justify my claims saying that, for the generation of philosophers and philosophic milieu which to which I have the honor to belong, "the shift to the Other" had a special formative meaning. Correspondingly, the sense landscape of the above problems appeared before us as a certain special perspective, which I would like to present here.

I am especially interested in exploring what I would call the "worldview meaning" of the theme of communication. The use of this somewhat antiquated (by modern standards) terminology is not a tribute to nostalgia; for me and my colleagues, whose intellectual and philosophic formation took place during the 1960s–1970s, and, I would think, for all intellectual community of those years the foci of arising interest in communication and of renewed comprehension of its vital importance proved to be "built-in" in our perception of the world of that time, which had opened its horizons of spring that came after Khrushchev's "thaw"; I must say that this was the last spring in the history of the great country that has passed into oblivion.

A wider outlook is a typical "optical effect" of any spring. In sharp contrast to the previous winter constraints, you suddenly find yourself in a space where many roads are open, so you can choose any way leading over the horizon, and this prospect makes you dizzy. I can testify that the prevailing spirits in my youth were as follows: we lived in a world of wide-open distances, in a world of prospects which suddenly became accessible; we looked forward to books we had not read, music we had not heard, and "impossible," unimaginable ideas and thoughts. It is no coincidence that most people of our generation, and those who were close to it, were keen on tourism—tourism in the old Soviet sense of the word; we always liked travels, physical and intellectual, including those to various philosophic worlds. Having pined in the Soviet "nature preserve" for quite a while, we were enticed then by freedom as a possibility of the Other, and the sheer novelty of the forthcoming turn to the Other was still blocking its actual features from our view, also obscuring our obligations and responsibilities to it.[1] I would add that this sense of the novelty of a free world and openness of the Other, as I did observe, was something more than mere superficial enthusiasm. The *Zeitgeist* made the sense of permanent tragedy of existence a necessary element of the then romanticism. Romeo and Juliet—and darkness; we understood that it was beautiful—and also that it was the truth. The very striving to reach for the Other, for all its wonderful quality, was felt as a joyful self-waste; besides, the Other as such, in those days, could be described primarily as elusive and ontologically fragile, compared to the iron power of "mundanity" breathing down our neck. Few of us had read Max Scheler, Nikolai Hartmann, let alone Emmanuel Levinas—the authors whose books could elucidate certain points in this regard. But everybody knew Saint-Exupéry and his *Le Petit Prince* (*The Little Prince*), knew that ravishing flowers attaching meaning to life are ephemeral. And reading about "the luxury of human communication" by the same author, we, I dare say, comprehended well the risk and the beauty and the inevitable failure of such a venture as staying with each other in this world.

It is easy to understand that those who became philosophers in our country looked for a philosophic substantiation of the moral and generally vital role of communication first of all in the works of young Marx. And we could find it there. Nevertheless, the official Marxist doctrine of the late Soviet period was as such exemplarily monological and propagated an exemplary monologism. It can be said without exaggeration that the word "human" did not imply any plurality in the main philosophical texts of that time. Leaving aside the ideological supports of this monologism and considering only the philosophical ones, the famous principle of activity is to be acknowledged as nearly the most reliable and efficient of them—heated discussions about it did not cease for decades.

These discussions did not bypass the Kiev philosophic community which included such experts in the problems of human activity—I am glad to call these names—as Mikhail Bulatov, Vadim Ivanov, Sergei Krymsky. As I have personally taken, to a certain extent, part in the discussion of a number of relevant problems, I have a reason to maintain that every serious philosophic discussion of communication, every attempt to view it as a fundamental human reality implied for us (this was not necessarily the case with those who proceeded directly from Bakhtin, though) the necessity to take into account the powerful methodological inertia of the above-mentioned activity principle, which was not so easy to overcome. The matter lay not so much in the "normal" difficulties of transition from one terminal theoretical basis to another as in the fact that the activity-based picture of the world (as can be ascertained through its consistent analysis) *per se* has a potential of self-substantiation that is too well-developed and too deeply implanted in European tradition of thought to fail to resist most effectively any infringement of its monopoly in those spheres where it was once accepted as a basis of philosophic thought. The literature of the time demonstrates hundreds of examples illustrative of how a peculiar activity-oriented rubrication of being had been originally laid at a deeper level in a discussion of the problems of communication, as well as of the problems of culture or morals independently of conscious methodological coordination of such discussion with the activity principle. It is natural that such a line led to the presentation of communication—as well as of other essential aspects of human reality—as another province of "the world of activity" where, one way or another, the ubiquitous principles of "objectification" and "dis-objectification" are in command, where the dialectics of "the mediate" and "the immediate," "the end," "the means" and "result" reigns, where a human subject "actively transforms" one or another objective environment, embodies certain ideals, develops his essential powers, overcoming any predetermined limits—and eventually remains alone.

Naturally, it should be taken into account that something like a constructionist guideline (Kasavin 1990, 177; Shvyrev 1990c, 259) often prevailed in the discussions about the idea of activity. Certain conceptual blocks were introduced into the above notion: on the one hand, they legitimated it in the context of the materialist understanding of history, on the other hand, they made the potentialities of its use as an explanatory principle in different concrete spheres more versatile and substantial. Thus, the inclusion of such ideas as "available forms of culture" (Shvyrev 1990b, 12),"subject-subjective relationships" (Sagatovsky 1990, 78–80; Shvyrev 1990a, 162; Batishchev 1969, 93–103; Kagan 1974, 45–47, 80–90), etc., into the *construct* of activity looked quite cogent to most adherents of the activity principle—a good example of the functioning of sensible philosophic rationality in the border land between methodologism and ideology, isn't it? But, as a result of such "enrichment," the notion of activity became blurred and lost its inner resilience. Meanwhile, such theoretical "blurring" of the problem cannot replace its authentic solution—especially taking into account *the real ontological sense of the idea of activity itself*, as it is presented in the history of European and, subsequently, world philosophy, intellectual culture and civilization.

I repeat: such subjects ought to be discussed seriously at greater length, and in more detail. There is no room for this right here, although the author of these lines had the opportunity to express his views on the subject more thoroughly (Malakhov 2005, 109–117; Malakhov 2009, 265–276).

As is known, the problems of *ideas* and of the nature of their reality are, since time immemorial, discussed in philosophy in different contexts in addition to—and also above and beyond—empirical subjects and theoretical constructs. Be it as it may, the idea of activity reflects the extremely solid structure of human self-actualization which finds a versatile, "protean," but easily recognizable embodiment in historical reality. This structure is strong enough to enable us to call the lawfulness of "constructivist" deviations from it into question. At the same time, this structure, as historical experience implies, is sometimes capable of combining, and even of fusing, with other formations of the same rank condensed by human thought and embodied in specific sociocultural phenomena.

The essential *monologism* of the idea of activity is the main thing that can be averred in the context of this discourse if we take into consideration the semantic and actual reality of human self-actualization behind this idea. The activity-centered rubrication of existence, which have been developing on the basis of the impulse of self-assertion—which is a key impulse for European Modernity—through self-mediation, reduces the reality surrounding the subject to the level of a mere "environment" supplying "objects" for his purposeful activity, or even to a set of handy tools for the latter, which leaves no room for the Other. On the other hand, it imposes the imperative of endless self-assertion on the subject, as the only possible and worthy way of existence: to be means to lay claim to existence, to strive for existence, to evince the *conatus essendi*! On closer examination, the above self-assertion as such proves to be a fairly depersonalized process which reproduces the "anonymous pressure of being on itself" (Levinas 1999, 2)—the pressure for which the subject himself is no more than a transmitting link in his fixed self-centeredness. The notorious "feedback" (Shvyryov 1990a, 164) received by active subjectivity from reality which is transformed by this activity appears from this perspective as a merciless ontological trap: the more active the human subject is while asserting his powers in the world of objects-means, the more he depends on the elements of the "all-embracing . . . being," to which he is "open" (Shvyrev 1990a, 161–163) only ontologically, without any moral choice. What moral choice could there be, when morals as such are absent? If the Other does not exist, then there is no ethics nor love, and freedom is reduced not even to a necessity, but to a fate of permanent self-assertion.

I have to say that the pressure of this activity-based *perpetuum mobile*, which excludes otherness, love and freedom from the human world, has been for some time noticeably oppressing us, who live with feelings and hopes of our times. It is clear that, in these conditions, the "discovery" of a communicative paradigm in the fullness of its vital and spiritual sense would become a stirring philosophic event. Resorting to this paradigm necessarily assumed an explosive and radical character. "A rupture in the order of being": if we had heard then this formula of Levinas concerning the way ethics exist, we would have surely accepted it with enthusiasm.

As for the well-known book by Mikhail Bakhtin, *The Problems of Dostoevsky's Poetics* (Bakhtin 1984), it had initially failed to elicit any spiritual response from us (I mean primarily the young Kiev philosophers of that time). I, for example, was somewhat disappointed by its accentuated methodologism (I am sorry to say that I was able to properly appreciate Bakhtin only after the collection of his works and notes *The Aesthetics of Verbal Art* (Bakhtin 1979, 424) was published in 1979). Nevertheless, there were texts which really sparked our interest and stimulated me and other people from my philosophic generation to turn to the topic and issues of communication. Among those, as I remember, were Alexei Ukhtomsky's letters (Ukhtomsky 1973, 251–266) published in the early 1970s, Vladimir Bibler's book *Thinking as Creative Work* (Bibler 1975), Sergei Rubinshtein's unfinished work *Man and the World* (Rubinshtein 1976, 253–381), as well as publications by Batishchev that appeared in most unlikely editions and in most unlikely places, which I and my friends tried not to miss (of course, we also closely followed publications by such thinkers as Alexei Losev, Sergei Averintsev, Merab Mamardashvili, and many others).

Recently, I looked again at the materials concerning the discussion about activity published back in the 1990s, and I was surprised to see that in my reaction to the debate I still keep the same preferences: I cannot help it but, even today, the thoughts of Genrikh Batishchev (who defended then, and later, the absolute irreducibility of communication to activity) seem to me the most profound and grounded. However, as it is well known, the most profound and grounded viewpoints do not often win in the notorious "ideas struggle." This struggle is usually won by the ideas that better fit into the "spirit of the time." This gives us all the more reason to remember Batishchev's reflections (that are contrary to the dominant vectors of today's life) on the crucial role of human communication on its "beyond-the-threshold" levels, on generosity and self-denial, on the human-formative meaning of aspiring to the highest values of existence. It seems to me that the memory of such "outmoded" reflections and sentiments is of special importance to the present, if only to prevent the notorious superficiality of our time from becoming too superficial. Batishchev's texts (which are much more polemical with respect to today's key intentions, than to the time when they appeared) give our young contemporaries at least a wonderful opportunity for self-examination: have we chosen the path we are following now consciously enough?

In the course of his philosophic career, Batishchev often engaged in heated debates with people who largely shared his ideas, such as Bakhtin, Ilyenkov, Bibler. Batishchev was also engaged in a dialogue with his own early works, criticizing his accounts of several concepts, including the activity-oriented concept of human existence (Batishchev 1990, 24–25). As to Batishchev's critical analysis of Bakhtin's "dialogism" (Batishchev 1992b, 123–141), it could be said that, regardless of the degree to which Batishchev's criticism was substantiated, the divergence between the two scholars was inwardly necessary for Batishchev as a theorist of "profound communication." In essence, this rift revealed and actualized in the post-Soviet cultural context the fundamental watershed in the dialogic thought of the latest century: the one between the "symmetry" and "asymmetry" in communication, between mutuality and preference of the Other, between the relativity (or "dilution") of values and the assertion of a "vertical values [hierarchy]" transforming a dialogue into communion. This watershed, as can be easily seen, touches the fundamentals of the so-called communicative philosophy and ethics, which has been successfully developed for decades by Karl-Otto Apel, Jürgen Habermas and their followers.

The difference of possible trends of thought, which is rather significant for all the European philosophy of dialogue, is expressed, in my opinion, in a marked divergence between Batishchev's and Bibler's positions. As I remember, Batishchev once said in the mid-1980s that Bibler's topics are too far from him, since they have no relation to real intersubjectivity. And indeed, if we take the work, which has brought Bibler a fame, i.e., his monograph *Thinking as Creative Work*, we can see that the developed "*dialogue pattern* of creative . . . thinking" (Bibler 1975, 44) is in essence an outstanding example of the *dialogue without communication*: a purely "mental" dialogue in the "mind chamber" implying no existential difference between the subjects taking part in it. In this connection, I would like to refer to Levinas' categorical statement: "'I' in the capacity of the Other is not the Other . . . the Otherness of 'I' mistaking itself for the Other . . . is just a game of the Self-identical; it is the repudiation of 'I' by itself that is one of the modi of self-identification of 'I'" (Levinas 2000, 76). Is it a coincidence that in the tradition of the European philosophy of dialogue (supported in this case by Levinas) the images of *alter ego* and the true Other are also radically different?

In conclusion, I would like to mention a characteristic feature bridging the gap between Batishchev and Bibler: the interest in novelty, in the *instant of beginning*, peculiar to both of them. The point is that no new beginning whatsoever can be found in the framework of the above activity-centered "generative model" of human existence, with its interminable spiral motion of self-transformation through self-reproduction; we can only talk here about the unstoppable absorption of new contents by the same actuality (which is equal to itself) of self-reproducing activity. But the world outlook of that time, as I said, have necessarily made us susceptible to the novelty of the world—and to its future. The spring openness of the then "intra-world being" sharpened the premonition of its tragic fate—and this premonition crawled all over us from everywhere. Besides, among other things (or perhaps at their head?), the expression "global problems" was step by step becoming very real for us. By the time of our acquaintance with the earliest samples of the philosophy of communication of the 1970s–1980s, our (that is, mine and my colleagues') attitude to the world had already developed deep-rooted beginnings of a certain final-stage concern that, rather than prompting us to await the day to come, urged us to care for something that existed or was emerging before our very eyes—and to protect it. In this context, that original striving for the future which proved to be peculiar to the philosophy of communication (in the broad sense) could not go unnoticed and could not fail to be felt most deeply. A true meeting with the Other always endows a person with something that is characterized by essential novelty, something that cannot be extracted from the depths of his own *ego* or from immanent tendencies of his activity. In other words, it endows him with the prospect of a "pure future" (Levinas)—the future which is free from the activity-based expectations of human selfness that has its roots in the past (Rosenstock-Huessi 2000, 39, 60–70).

It is significant that already Bibler's monograph of 1975 had such a "futurological" aspect which was not only declared (such things abounded in the society that had not, at least openly, relinquished the idea of communism building), but also constitutive. The then readers of philosophical literature can remember how uncommon it was: an allegedly "serious" monograph dedicated to historical and scholarly problems is ending in a suspicious "*beginning* of the future controversy" (Bibler 1975, 397). However, the point is that, to be able to reason within the context of the self-asserting "dialogics," it was necessary for the author to grant his interlocutors a right to an uncompleted, not predetermined future. Later—when Bibler will express his beautiful thoughts about a "work of culture" as "the world for the first time" and "the eve of existence" (Bibler 1990, 290, 402), about the idea of beginning as "the pivotal idea of all the culture of our time" (Bibler 1990, 375)—the dialogical presumption of urgency of the future will also appear "built-in" (not without some affectation, I think) into his philosophic pathos of understanding of "the eve" (when "thought is comprehended on the eve of thought, existence on the eve of existence . . . culture on the eve of culture" (Bibler 1990, 10)).

The above-mentioned tendency to face the future and be receptive to novelty and freshness of the world can be recognized in a more persuasive—and, at any rate, more humanly comprehensible—form in Batishchev's works. Aside from his general style of thinking and his respect for life[2] (Batishchev 1992a, 143), we would also speak in this connection of his deep interest in the values of the "secret childhood" (Batishchev 1997, 38–44),[3] which he closely examined with truly philosophical amazement and curiosity as a "barely explored land" (Batishchev 1997, 38),[4] and of his keen interest in pedagogics, his permanent inclination to dialogue with thinking young men, in which he acted rather as a careful interlocutor than a mentor.

As is clear, one could feel a certain challenge in all Batishchev's behavior in his communication with the youth of his time. To be more precise, it was a call or, maybe, exhortation not to lose their good spirits, their faith in the bright and high ideals of being. Once, during a conversation, he said with ardor (in response to the standard complaints of his young friends concerning the end and the general decay): "There you go again! And what if everything in the world is only a beginning?" I have retained these words in my memory forever.

And indeed—what if this is the case? Does not this idea make life harder, attaching to it more responsibility, but also endowing it with more depth and happiness?

Paul Ricoeur once said about the necessity "to elicit the future of our past into the world" (Bianchi 2010, 97). The point is not to understand the past itself better, though it is important. It does not also mean preserving wisely for "tomorrow" something which had not been realized "yesterday." Maybe it is important to comprehend and keep in memory those hopes that became things of the past—first of all, for the sake of our human nature, for a live human pulse beats in these hopes and anxieties connected with them. So, as we can see, the spectrum of attitudes to the future developed in the late Soviet period as well as of the variants of their philosophical interpretation was largely connected with the actualization of the theme of communication. It is with pointing out the worldview aspect of this connection that I would like to conclude this reflection of mine.

## NOTES

1. In philosophy (most notable in phenomenology, as well as in M. Bakhtin, J-P. Sartre, and E. Levinas) the Other is considered as the other human being, different from the self and connected with the self-image.—Ed.
2. As is known, he always reflected on it. I shall cite a fragment from the *Dialectical Lines*, which is significant in this respect:

> Progress-minded is not that person . . .
> Who endeavors to shut himself and others out
> In the inert extension of past events,
> But the one who gladly expects the unexpected
> And lives in a continuous meeting
> With the untried, enigmatic Future. (Batishchev 1992a, 143)

3. It must be added that Vitaliy Tabachkovsky, among Kiev philosophers of the recent past, showed a deep interest in childhood anthropology (see: Tabachkovsky 2005, 282–300). He wanted to dedicate a special book to this subject shortly before his death.
4. It is noteworthy that Batishchev was ready to find references to the "country of childhood" with its "richest potential" even in the social theory of Karl Marx (see: Batishchev 1997, 369).

## BIBLIOGRAPHY


Bakhtin, Mikhail M. 1979. *Estetika slovesnogo tvorchestva* [The Aesthetics of Verbal Art]. Moscow: Iskusstvo.

Bakhtin, Mikhail M. 1984. *The Problems of Dostoevsky's Poetics*, edited and translated by Caryl Emerson. (Theory and History of Literature. Volume 8). Minneapolis, London: University of Minnesota Press.

Batishchev, Genrikh S. 1969. "Deyatel'nostnaya sushchnost' cheloveka kak filosofskiy printsip" ["The Activity Essence of Man as a Philosophical Principle"]. In *Problema cheloveka v sovremennoy filosofii* [The Problem of Man in Modern Philosophy], 73–144. Moscow: Nauka.

Batishchev, Genrikh S. 1990. "Neischerpannye vozmozhnosti i granitsy primenimosti kategorii deyatel'nosti" ["The Unexhausted Possibilities and the Limits of Applicability of the Category of Activity"]. In *Deyatel'nost': teorii, metodologiya, problemy* [Activity: Theories, Methodology, Problems], edited and arranged by Ilya Kasavin, 21–34. Moscow: Politizdat.

Batishchev, Genrikh S. 1992a. "Dialekticheskie stroki (Seriya A)" ["Dialectical Lines (Series A)"]. *Filosofskaya i sotsiologicheskaya mysl'* (10): 140–150.

Batishchev, Genrikh S. 1992b. "Dialogizm ili polifonizm? (Antitetika v ideynom nasledii M.M. Bakhtina)" ["Dialogism or Polyphonism? (Antithetics in M. M. Bakhtin's Ideological Heritage)"]. In *M. M. Bakhtin kak filosof* [M. M. Bakhtin as a Philosopher], 123–141. Moscow: Nauka.

Batishchev, Genrikh S. 1997. *Vvedenie v dialektiku tvorchestva* [An Introduction to the Dialectics of Creativity]. St. Petersburg: RHGI.

Bibler, Vladimir S. 1975. *Myshlenie kak tvorchestvo (Vvedenie v logiku myslennogo dialoga)* [Thinking as Creative Activity (An Introduction to the Logic of Inner Dialogue)]. Moscow: Politizdat.

Bibler, Vladimir S. 1990. *Ot naukoucheniya—k logike kul'tury: Dva filosofskih vvedeniya v dvadtsat' pervyi vek* [From the Science of Knowledge to the Logic of Culture: Two Philosophical Introductions into the Twenty-First Century]. Moscow: Politizdat.

Bianchi, Enzo. 2010. *Leksikon vnutrenney zhizni* [The Lexicon of Inner Life]. Translated by Irina Varzhanskaya. Kyiv: Duh i litera.

Kagan, Moisey S. 1974. *Chelovecheskaya deyatel'nost' (Opyt sistemnogo analiza)* [Human Activity (An Attempt at System Analysis)]. Moscow: Politizdat.

Kasavin, Ilya T. 1990. "Opredelyat' deyatel'nost' v kontekste issledovatel'skoy zadachi" ["Defining Activity in the Context of Research Problem"]. In *Deyatel'nost': teorii, metodologiya, problemy* [Activity: Theories, Methodology, Problems], edited and arranged by Ilya Kasavin, 177–186. Moscow: Politizdat.

Levinas, Emmanuel. 1999. *Mizh namy: Doslidzhennya Dumky-pro-Inshogo* [Between Ourselves: A Study of the Thought-about-the-Other].Translated by Valeriy Kurinskiy. Kyiv: Duh i litera; Zadruga.

Levinas, Emmanuel. 2000. *Izbrannoe: Total'nost' i Beskonechnoe* [Selected Works: Totality and the Infinite]. Translated by Irena Vdovina a. o. Moscow, St. Petersburg: Universitetskaya kniga.

Makhlin, Vitaly L. 1997. *Ya i Drugoy: K istorii dialogicheskogo printsipa v filosofii XXv.* [I and the Other: On the History of the Dialogical Principle in the Philosophy of the Twentieth Century]. Moscow: Labirint.

Malakhov, Viktor A. 2005. *Uyazvimost' lyubvi* [The Vulnerability of Love]. Kyiv: Duh i litera.

Malakhov, Viktor A. 2009. "Paradigma obshcheniya v filosofskom tvorchestve G.S. Batishcheva" ["The Paradigm of Communication in Philosophical Works of G. S. Batishchev"]. In *Genrih Stepanovich Batishchev*, edited by Vladislav Lektorskiy, 243–312. Moscow: ROSSPEN.

Rosenstock-Huessi, Eugen. 2000. *Izbrannoye: Yazyk roda chelovecheskogo* [Selected Works: The Language of the Human Race]. Translated by Aleksandr Pigalyov. Moscow, St. Petersburg: Universitetskaya kniga.

Rubinshtein, Sergei L. 1976. "Chelovek i mir" ["Man and the World"]. In Rubinshtein, Sergei L. *Problemy obshchey psihologii*. Second edition. [The Problems of General Psychology], 253–381. Moscow: Pedagogika.

Sagatovsky, Valery N. 1990. "Kategorial'nyi kontekst deyatel'nostnogo podhoda" ["The Categorical Context of the Activity-Oriented Approach"]. In *Deyatel'nost': teorii, metodologiya, problemy* [Activity: Theories, Methodology, Problems], edited and arranged by Ilya Kasavin, 70–82. Moscow: Politizdat.

Shvyrev, Vladimir S. 1990a. "Deyatel'nost'—otkrytaya sistema" ["Activity as an Open System"]. In *Deyatel'nost' teorii, metodologiya, problemy* [Activity: Theories, Methodology, Problems], edited and arranged by Ilya Kasavin, 159–168. Moscow: Politizdat,

Shvyrev, Vladimir S. 1990b. "Problemy razrabotki ponyatiya deyatel'nost' kak filosofskoy kategorii" ["The Problems of Elaborating the Concept of Activity as a Philosophical Category"]. In *Deyatelnost': teorii, metodologiya, problemy* [Activity: Theories, Methodology, Problems], edited and arranged by Ilya Kasavin, 9–20. Moscow: Politizdat.

Shvyrev, Vladimir S. 1990c. "Seryoznaya kontseptual'naya problema, a ne sholasticheskoye teoretizirovanie" ["A Serious Conceptual Problem,not Scholastic Theorizing"]. In *Deyatel'nost': teorii, metodologiya, problemy* [Activity: Theories, Methodology, Problems], edited and arranged by Ilya Kasavin. Moscow: Politizdat.

Tabachkovsky, Vitaly G. 2005. *Polisutnisne homo: filosofs'ko-mystets'ka dumka v poshukah "neevklidovoyi reflektyvnosti"* [*Homo* Polyessential: Philosophical and Artistic Thought in Search of "Non-Euclidean reflexivity"]. Kyiv: Parapan.
Ukhtomsky, Alexei A. 1973. "Letters," *Novyi mir* (1): 251–266.
Vizgin, Viktor P. 2004. *Na Puti k Drugomu. Ot shkoly podozreniya k filosofii doveriya* [On the Way to the Other. From the School of Suspicion to the Philosophy of Trust]. Moscow: Yazyki slavyanskoy kul'tury.

PART VI

# Philosophical Anthropology

CHAPTER TWENTY-TWO

# Human Ontology: On Discussion in Soviet Philosophy in the Late Twentieth Century

ALEXANDER A. KHAMIDOV

The second half of the twentieth century was much more favorable for Soviet philosophy than the first one. In fact, all spheres of spiritual life, including philosophy, started to flourish only after the Twentieth Party Congress (1956), when the so-called cult of Stalin's personality was denounced. However, the so-called period of "thaw" was short-lived. It soon gave way to a long period of cold "stagnation." After the Warsaw Pact's invasion of Czechoslovakia in August 1968, the authorities began to "tighten the screws." But a complete return to the past was impossible. It was impossible to forcibly lower the bar raised by the philosophers of the sixties. However, the freedom of philosophical work was limited within officially specified bounds. These restrictions defined a new version of state ideology: "Marxist-Leninist philosophy." In accordance with these restrictions, Soviet philosophy had to be necessarily *materialistic*, and the authority of Marx, Engels and Lenin were to be *indisputable*. Undoubtedly, this version of state philosophy was much less stringent than the Stalinist dogma, but, nevertheless, it also fettered the freedom of philosophical reflection. In this situation, thinking philosophers found salvation in the fact that philosophy of Marx was not limited to the doctrine of the basis and superstructure, or of the dictatorship of the proletariat. It is to direct reference to the legacy of Marx that Soviet philosophy owes its many achievements in the sphere of the theory of dialectics, human philosophy and philosophy of history. I will discuss human philosophy, as represented mainly in the works of such prominent Russian philosophers as Mikhail Bakhtin, Sergei Rubinshtein and Genrikh Batishchev.

As mentioned above, the philosophic reference frame in the Soviet Union was constructed according to Marxism-Leninism. Issues concerning human nature were basically retrieved from the texts of Marx. Its most famous definition was given in the text which the Institute of Marx–Engels–Lenin–Stalin of the Central Committee Party of the Soviet Union titled "Theses on Feuerbach."[1]

Before citing this definition, it is necessary to say a few words about the above text. It was compiled from eleven abstracts from a notebook of Marx written between 1844 and 1847. These abstracts are known to have been sketched by Marx in April 1845 under the general heading "1) Ad Feuerbach," which means "To Feuerbach." These abstracts were to be explicated in the first chapter of *The German Ideology*, a book planned by Marx and Engels. This chapter was titled as follows: "Feuerbach: Opposition of the Materialist and Idealist Outlook." The title "To Feuerbach" was borrowed from this text. Consequently, none of the titles—like the "Theses on Feuerbach," given by the Institute of Marx and Engels (apparently referring to the following words of Engels: "in an old notebook of Marx's I have found the 11 Theses on Feuerbach" (Engels 1961, 371)), "Marx on Feuerbach" offered by the Institute of Marx–Engels–Lenin–Stalin, and the title given by Engels in publishing them as an appendix to his "Ludwig Feuerbach and the End of Classical German Philosophy"—matches either the content or the meaning of the Marxian "Theses." These famous eleven theses have *nothing* whatever to do with the philosopher Ludwig Andreas Feuerbach.

There is one more point about these "Theses." There are *two* versions of them: the one that is contained in the notebook of Marx (Marx 1974b, 261–263) and the one published by Engels. A friend and collaborator of Karl Marx, Engels found it necessary to *edit* them before publishing. He explained his actions as follows: "These are notes hurriedly scribbled down for later elaboration, absolutely not intended for publication" (Engels 1961, 371). The publisher of the "Theses," D. B. Ryazanov compared both versions and noticed all changes made by Engels (Archive 1924).[2] In the foreword to the publication, he wrote: "As Engels did not accurately reproduced these theses, and Plekhanov's translations were not always accurate, I am giving below the translation of these abstracts taken directly from the authentic text, which I found in the notebook of Marx" (Ryazanov 1924, 199). In fact, Engels did not just reproduce the notes incorrectly—he edited them consciously and deliberately. I can mention at least one significant correction made by Engels.

In Marx's version of the third thesis it is written: "Das Zusammenfallen des Änderns der Umstände und der menschlichen Tätigkeit oder Selbstveränderung kann nur als *revolutionäre Praxis* gefasst und rationell verstanden werden" (Marx 1933, 534). That is: "The coincidence of the changes in circumstances and in human activity, or self-transformation, can be conceived and rationally understood only as *revolutionary practice*." Ryazanov underlines: "Engels omitted 'or self-transformation,' and for some reason used, instead of *revolutionäre*, the word *umwälzende* [i.e., transforming]. Probably it was done as a proofreader's amendment" (Ryazanov 1924, 200).[3] In this regard, there has occurred a case of a misunderstanding. Batishchev wrote in 1967: "In the third of the 'Theses on Feuerbach' by Marx, the main concept '*self-transformation*,' which reflects the *essence* of the problem (see MEGA, Abt. I, Bd. 5, S. 534), is simply omitted in Russian translation (see Marx, Engels. Works, V. 3, p. 2)" (Batishchev 1967, 28). In fact, it is not the translation but the friend and collaborator of Karl Marx that is at fault.

I can give, finally, the definition of human nature, which is presented in the second edition of the *Selected Works of Marx and Engels* (Vol. 3; reprinted in Vol. 42). Objecting to Feuerbach, who, in Marx's words, "resolves the religious essence into the *human* essence," Marx remarked: "But the human essence is no abstraction inherent in each single individual. In its reality, it is the ensemble of all social relations" (Marx 1955, 3). And here is the authentic text of Marx in the original language: "Aber das menschliche Wesen ist kein dem einzelnen Individuum innewohnendes Abstraktum. In seiner Wirklichkeit ist es das *ensemble* der gesellschaftlichen Verhältnisse" (Marx 1933, 535; italics mine).[4] It should be noted that, in this case, Marx uses the French word "ensemble," which was replaced with the German word "das Ensemble" by Engels. Hence, the human essence is "the ensemble of social relations." An ensemble is a kind of *architectonics*, certain orderliness, harmony—at best, a *structure*, but not the totality of *all*. I must say that Ryazanov translated "ensemble" simply as "the totality" into Russian without adding the word "all" (Ryazanov 1924, 201).

This translation (due to the word "all") has created a number of pseudo-reflections. Thus, a well-known sociologist, and later sexologist, I. S. Kon stated: "May I call myself the totality of all social relations, when the scope of my (and yours, and any specific individual's) activities obviously includes only a small part of these relations?" (Kon 1967, 9). But, along with lack of critical attitude to the translation, the author reveals a misunderstanding of the category of essence. Essence is not an abstraction inherent in *any* entity, it belongs only in man.

However, there is another important provision concerning human essence in the Marxian "Theses." In the first of the theses, Marx criticized both philosophical idealism and philosophical materialism that preceded it. He notes that human activity should be taken "as the *objective* [*gegeständliche*] activity" (Marx 1955 c, 1). This side of his work was left without attention in Soviet philosophy from the early 1930s to the late 1950s. Prior to that, P. L. Kucherov (1930) worked on objective activity (including its attributes, such as objectification [*die Vergegenständlichung*] and disobjectification [*die Entgegenständlichung*]). In the early 1960s, the category of objective activity [*gegenständliche Tätigkeit*] revived and began to be applied by Evald Ilyenkov (Ilyenkov 1962) and Genrikh Batishchev (Batishchev 1963, 12–18). Then it became an object of study for other philosophers, psychologists, theorists of pedagogy and others.

But for a long time Soviet philosophers did not notice the connection between the thesis about objective activity and the thesis about human essence as the ensemble of social relations. The pioneers who drew attention to this issue were Ilyenkov, Batishchev and a few others. In 1966, Batishchev unambiguously stated: "The public nature of man is nothing but his active essence" (Batishchev 1966, 247). Meanwhile Marx, as early as in the first half of 1844, wrote: "Since *human* nature is the *true community* of men, by manifesting their *nature* men *create*, produce the *human community*, the social entity, which is no abstract universal power opposed to the single individual, but is the essential nature of each individual, his own activity, his own life, his own spirit, his own wealth" (Marx 1974 c, 23). It should be noted that the word "community" (Russian *obshchestvennaya svyaz'*) translates here, and in all other translations of the quoted work, Marx's *Gemeinwesen*—the term that cannot be rendered satisfactorily into Russian (Marx 1932, 536).[5] Finally, I will quote another Marxian statement on human nature. In his *Critique of Hegel's Philosophy of Right*, he writes that Hegel is wrong in

> conceiving the activities and agencies of the state in the abstract, and particular individuality in opposition to it. He forgets that particular individuality is a human individual, and that the activities and agencies of the state are human activities. He forgets that the nature of the "particular personality" is not his beard, his blood, his abstract *Physis*, but rather his *social quality*, and that the activities of the state, etc., are nothing but the modes of existence and operation of the *social qualities* of men. It is evident, therefore, that individuals, insofar as they are the bearers of the state's activities and functions, are to be considered according to their social and not their private quality. (Marx 1955b, 242)

Marx's definition of human nature has a significant limitation: it *exhausts* this essence restricting it to social reality without extending it to the level of general ontology, it does not link man with the extra-human world, with the Universe. Marx himself deliberately avoided dealing with problems of ontology. The subject of his attention is the socio-historical reality. However, it is impossible to create a holistic philosophy without solving ontological problems. This side of his work was compensated somewhat crudely by such Engels's works as the *Anti-Dühring* and the *Dialectics of Nature*. The followers of Marx and Engels "patched together" the official philosophy from the works of Marx and Engels, titling the latter "dialectical materialism" and the former "historical materialism." Herewith the latter was interpreted as application of the former to human society and history.[6] Marx's definition of human essence as the ensemble of social relations in the light of the holistic State Philosophy has features of "sociological" reductionism. Hence it is implicitly perceived as formulated only in terms of "historical materialism." As a reaction to this type of reductionism, a new stream emerged in Soviet philosophy, which formed the concept of *bio-social* nature of man. But it was also a kind of reductionism and even *dualism*, which was noted by Ilyenkov.

According to Ilyenkov, the essence of each particular individual who is part of society is "in that *entirely concrete system of individuals who interact among themselves* which alone makes each of them what he is." (Ilyenkov 1979, 188)

> Biological relationship expressed in the identity of morpho-physiological organization of the *homo sapiens* species is a *prerequisite* (albeit an absolutely necessary, even the *most vital* one) of a generic human condition in a human, but by no means the "essence," or an internal condition, or a *concrete community*, or a social and human community, or a union of *a personality with* [*other*] *personalities*. (Ilyenkov 1979, 188–189)

As Ilyenkov states, the failure to understand this creates the chimera of a "bio-social" nature of man. He adds:

> Socio-biological dualism in the understanding of the nature of human individuality (personality) is only the beginning of a pluralistic end. This is the grave of thinking guided by the logic of reduction—leading further and further away from that particular "essence," which they attempted to understand—the logic of decomposition of concreteness into components that are not specific to it.

> Ultimately, this logic will inevitably lead to a "socio-biological-chemical-electrophysical-microphysical-quantum-mechanical" understanding of the nature of man. (Ilyenkov 1979, 189)

It turns out, therefore, that all advocates of the concept of bio-social nature of man are *methodologically inconsistent*: they stop at the level of biology and do not go further, into the "*bad*" or "*spurious*" *infinity* (*die Schlecht-Unendliche* of Hegel).

But, of course, reducing and even reductionism is not always a great evil. Batishchev wrote that, in a special scientific research,

> it is impossible to take any step without temporary, transient and limited reductions! There can be no justification for the sweeping condemnation of all reductionism and negation of its positive significance within strictly local objective boundaries. But as for a philosophical, generally methodological and evaluative reductionism, which claims universality and, most importantly, irreversibility, it poses a very serious threat. (Batishchev 1986, 178)

If, trying to solve the problem of man's essence, representatives of the natural sciences come to the conclusion that it is of a bio-sociological or socio-biological nature, it is to some extent excusable for them, but not for the philosophers! Marx warned that

> it is absolutely wrong to *apply* a lower sphere as a *measure* for a higher sphere; in this case, the laws that are reasonable within specific limits become distorted and transformed into a caricature since they arbitrarily receive the status of laws not in their proper sphere, but in another, higher one. It's as if I compelled a giant to live in the house of a pygmy. (Marx 1955a, 74)

And this is what was pursued by philosophers who saw in man two entities (biological and social) or just a bio-social essence. Batishchev drew attention to the worldview and methodological basis of bio-social reductionism. According to him, this basis is an absolutization of the role and status of the *needs* and *interests* in the life of man and society, or the replacement of those levels of human existence that involve *values* and *meanings* with the concept of needs, which, accordingly, transforms human attitude to life. He wrote: "The 'consumer' point of view . . . is the ground for many kinds of naturalization and biologization of man" (Batishchev 1977a, 92). As for Ilyenkov's own stance on human nature, he remained within Marxian scope, reducing human essence to its social dimension.

However, the problem of human ontology existed and was developed in the depths of Soviet philosophy. It was originally developed by two outstanding people, Mikhail Bakhtin and Sergei Rubinshtein. They were almost of the same age (the former is six years the latter's junior) and began to publish their works almost simultaneously. Most likely, they neither met nor knew one another. Both positioned themselves as philosophers, but were mainly involved in the problems of other disciplines. "I am a philosopher. I am a thinker" (Bakhtin 2002, 47) said Bakhtin in an interview with V. D. Duvakin, although most of his attention was paid to literary criticism. Rubinshtein wrote: "By vocation and by the way of thinking, I am a philosopher and, moreover, a philosopher to whose heart the theory of knowledge and, especially, ethics are close. But officially I am a psychologist. Hence I have a humorous attitude to my profession ('I am an accidental man in psychology')" (Rubinshtein 1989, 421). In fact, he was mainly engaged in psychology and even known as the head of one of the two basic Soviet state psychological schools (the other was headed by Lev Vygotsky). In some ways, the fates of these two scholars concerned with the problems related to ontology are similar. They became widely known as philosophers posthumously. Let us turn to their ideas.

Bakhtin was concerned with human ontological problems in his concept of an act (in the 1920s) and in his concept of dialogue, developed mainly in the 1960s. The concept of action is expounded in a text that survived without a beginning and without an end. It had been written in the early 1920s, but was first published only in 1986, under the title "K Filosofii Postupka" ["On the Philosophy of Action"] provided by the publishers (Bakhtin 1986). Since this work was introduced into academic sphere only then, I may regard it, to some extent, as belonging to the second half of the twentieth century.

From the standpoint of ethics as a philosophic discipline, it might seem at first glance that Bakhtin treats human acts too broadly. "My each thought with its content is my individual responsible act, one of the acts which my whole, one and only life as a continuous action is made of, since life as a whole can be considered a certain complex act: I have been acting all my life, every single act and experience is a moment of my [continuous] life-action" (Bakhtin 2003, 8). According to Bakhtin, each human manifestation of life, both internal and external, is a human act. He writes: "And, [when I commit] such an act, everything ought to be in me, my each movement, gesture, worry, thought, feeling—all this solely in me, in the only participant of life-event. Only under this condition, I do live, without tearing myself off the ontological roots of real life. I am in a world of desperate reality, not of random opportunity" (Bakhtin 2003, 41–42). When Bakhtin writes, "I am thinking—I am acting with [my] thought," he to some extent blurs the distinction between the Western and Eastern esoteric world outlook. However, in accordance with the latter, thinking and its consequences are more powerful than practical actions or behavior.

Bakhtin writes: "Action in its entirety is more than rational, it has responsibility. Rationality is an only a point of responsibility" (Bakhtin 2003, 30). A man, this one particular person, says Bakhtin, occupies here-and-now only a very specific location in reality that surrounds him on all sides, and his whole life is involved in the event of Being. He lives *out of himself*, out of his own single location and is, with all his modality, *part* of Being. At the same time, Bakhtin emphasizes, "we must remember that to live *out of yourself*, out of your single location, does not mean to live by yourself alone"; "Living out of yourself is not living for yourself, but it means being a responsible participant out of yourself, arguing persistently your actual non-alibi in being" (Bakhtin 2003, 45–46).

According to M. M. Bakhtin, a really responsible act, which every time asserts its non-alibi in being, has its own architectonics. Its main features are as follows:

> I-for-myself, the-other-for-me and I-for-the-other; all the values of real life and culture are located around these basic architectonic points of the real world of actions, including scientific, aesthetic, political (including ethical and social), and finally, religious values. All spatial, temporal, content- and sense-oriented values and attitudes gravitate to these focal points that have to do with emotions and will: myself, the other and I-for-the-other. (Bakhtin 2003, 49–50)

The subject of action interpreted in the above terms forms a different, *non*-object-centered attitude to the objective world: "Since I have thought an object, I have entered an event relationship with it. The object is inseparable from its function in that event in its relation to me" (Bakhtin 2003, 32). Such a subject also has a special kind of consciousness and thinking. This is a *participating* consciousness and thinking. According to Bakhtin, to think in the "participating mode" means "not to separate your action from its product, but correlate them and strive to define them as inseparable [things] in the one and only context of life" (Bakhtin 2003, 21).

Bakhtin came to the issue of dialogue mainly working on the study of Dostoevsky's work, which later was published as *Problemy Tvorchestva Dostoevskogo* [*Problems of Dostoevsky's Creativity*"] (1929). But his most intensive work on this issue took place in the 1960s. However, all Bakhtin's thoughts on the subject have been scattered in various sketches, notes in workbooks and even in the second edition of the book on Dostoevsky, *Problemy Poetiki Dostoevskogo* [*Problems of Dostoevsky's Poetics*] (1963).

Unlike other literary scholars and some philosophers who studied Fyodor Dostoevsky's creative work, Bakhtin came to the conclusion that "Dostoevsky is the creator of the *polyphonic novel*. He has created an essentially new novel genre" (Bakhtin 2000, 12).[7] As states Bakhtin, this genre is opposed to the *monologue* novel genre. Borrowed from the world of music, the concept of polyphony is a *metaphor* for Bakhtin. He writes: "But we are turning this metaphor into the term 'polyphonic novel,' as we cannot find a more fitting designation" (Bakhtin 2000, 29–30).[8] Bakhtin repeated the same idea in a revised edition of his book on Dostoevsky. He writes: "We regard Dostoevsky as one of the greatest innovators in the field of artistic form. In our view, he has created a completely new type of artistic thinking, which we have conventionally called *polyphonic*" (Bakhtin 2002, 7). He explains why he chose the concept of polyphony rather than that of dialogue in relation to the poetics of Dostoevsky's novels. "The essence of polyphony is in the fact that the voices here remain independent and, as such, are combined in a unity of a higher order than in homophony" (Bakhtin 2000, 29).

Polyphony is a special composition of a novel, in which its heroes have the right to their own voice, which is not absorbed by the voice of the author "on high," which is typical of novels of the monologue type. The heroes' polyphony is inherent in Dostoevsky's novels: "Worlds of heroes are built on the usual ideological-monological principle, as if constructed by themselves" (Bakhtin 2000, 33). Each character has his own attitude in life, his own truth, his own values, and so on. Bakhtin claims: "The world of Dostoevsky is deeply *pluralistic*" (Bakhtin 2000, 35). So where is the dialogue, then? It is *within* the polyphonic architectonics. "The basic pattern of dialogue in Dostoevsky is simple: the confrontation of a person with a person as a confrontation between 'self' and 'the other'" (Bakhtin 2000, 157). Such was Bakhtin's understanding of dialogue during his work on the first version of the book on Dostoevsky. The second phase began in the 1960s. Since 1961, Bakhtin began redrafting the book on Dostoevsky. Before that, in 1959–1960, he worked on the essay "The Problem of Text," which demonstrated the author's interest in the problems of linguistics. It was at this intersection of interests in literature and linguistics that a new concept of dialogue was born. As a result, the concept of dialogue became *basic* for Bakhtin, while the notion of polyphony almost faded into insignificance. However, the concept of "polyphonic dialogue" was coined, which will be discussed below.

In terms of linguistics, Bakhtin distinguishes dialogue as a speech or text composition from dialogical relationships. He suggests: "These relationship are deeply specific and cannot be reduced to any logical, or linguistic, or psychological, or mechanical, or any other natural ratios. This is a special type of *semantic* relations, the members of which may be only *integral expressions*" (Bakhtin 1996a, 335).[9] According to Bakhtin dialogic relationships may exist both between different texts and within the same text.

However, working on linguistic issues and on the redrafting of his book on Dostoevsky, Bakhtin, on the basis of linguistic and literary data, formulates such ideas as go far beyond the scope of these disciplines. He turns to philosophical anthropology and human ontology. Here are some examples:

> Any utterance always has an addressee (of a different character, different degrees of affinity, specificity, awareness, and so on) whose reciprocal understanding the author of the statement seeks and anticipates. This [addressee] is the "second" (again, not in the arithmetic sense). But, in addition to this addressee (the "second"), the author assumes, more or less consciously, the existence of a higher "*super-addressee*" (the "third") whose perfectly unbiased reciprocal understanding is visualized as existing either in a metaphysical distance or in the remote past. ([This is] the loophole addressee.) At different times and under different worldviews, this super-addressee and his flawlessly correct reciprocal understanding assumes various specific ideological guises (God, the absolute truth, the court of impartial human conscience, the people, the judgment of history, science, and so on). (Bakhtin 1996a, 337)

But, objectively, the matter never boils down to utterances. A man, whenever he commits an act or deed which can be misunderstood by others or even by the majority—though he is sure that he is right—appeals, directly or indirectly, to such a *super*-addressee. The famous phrase, "Father, forgive them; for they know not what they do," belongs in this category.

Here is, for example, a scholarly thesis concerning a works of the polyphonic type:

> The author is profoundly *active*, but his activeness has a specific, *dialogical* character. Activity in relation to inanimate things, voiceless matter that can be molded and shaped in any way, is one thing, while activity *toward another living*

> *and full-fledged consciousness* is something else entirely. This activity is questioning, provoking, responding, agreeing, objecting, and so on. It means that the dialogical activity is no less vigorous than the activity which concludes, objectifies, causally explains and deadens, choking the voice of the other with arguments unrelated to sense. (Bakhtin 1996b, 341–342)

But such activity is extended not only to the hero of a composition and not only to his mind. A whole man is not reducible to his consciousness. Bakhtin formulates the philosophical and anthropological thesis that "a person is not an object, but another subject" (Bakhtin 1996b, 360). And more: "To assert another's 'Self' not as an object but as another subject [means] . . . to transform another person from a shadow into a true reality" (Bakhtin 2002, 15).

The phenomenon of dialogical attitude is also reconsidered. It now extends to a whole man. It is now understood "as the only form of treating a man-person that preserves his freedom and inability to become complete" (Bakhtin 1996b, 349). Now monologue is interpreted more broadly as well: "In its extremity, *Monologism* denies the existence, outside of itself, of another equal consciousness enjoying the same rights to response, of another equal 'Self.' In a monologic approach (in its extreme or pure form), 'the other' wholly remains a mere *object* of consciousness, not another consciousness" (Bakhtin 1996b, 350). Dialogic attitude is developed by Bakhtin into the concept of *communication*. He writes (his most frequently quoted words):

> The very existence of man (both external and internal) is *the deepest [kind of] communication. To be* means to *communicate*. . . . To be means to be for the other, and to be for yourself through that other. Man has no internal sovereign territory, he is, wholly and always, on the verge; looking inside himself, he looks *into the eyes of the other*, or *through the eyes of the other.* (Bakhtin 1996b, 344)[10]

In such perceived type of communication a person is *directly* raised to the universal ontological plane of existence by transcending all individual final definitions and forms. This idea is attested as early as in the first version of his manuscript of the work on Dostoevsky. Bakhtin writes:

> The exceptionally acute sense of another person as "the other" and as your own "Self" suggests that all those definitions which enveloped "Self" and "the other" in concrete social structures like family, caste, class—as well as all other kinds of definitions—have lost their credibility and their power to create forms. Man feels himself and the world as a whole, without any intermediate instances, in addition to the entire social community he belongs to. (Bakhtin 2000, 173–174)

Such communication is an act of *creativity*, and, as noted by Anatoly Arsenyev, "in any field during the process of creation, a man in the moment of creation goes beyond his profession, his specialty, and acts like man *in general*, as an individual acts for the Universe" (Arsenyev 1981a, 66).

Bakhtin begins to understand that "a personality is always greater than itself" (Bakhtin 2002, 436). He writes:

> A man never coincides with himself. The equation *A* = *A* cannot be applied to him. . . . The actual life of a person occurs at the point of this non-coincidence of a man with himself. It happens at the point of his exit from everything that identifies him as an objective being that can be spied on, defined and predicted against his will, "in absentia." The real life of a person is only accessible *dialogically*, [when] *he* responsively and freely reveals himself. (Bakhtin 2002, 70)

In this context, the concepts of polyphony and *polyphonic* dialogue assume a new meaning. Among Bakhtin's working drafts, we read the following: "Features of 'polyphony'. The [impossibility of] completing a polyphonic dialogue (a dialogue on the latest issues). This type of dialogue is carried on by infinite (lit. 'impossible to complete') individuals, not by psychological subjects. The well-known disembodiment of these individuals (selfless excess)" (Bakhtin 2002, 415).

In his works of the 1960s and the first half of the 1970s (having died 1975, he was not able to see his book, *Voprosy Literatury i Estetiki. Issledovanie Raznykh Let* [Questions of Literature and Aesthetics. Studies of Different Years], in print—it was published later the same year), Bakhtin starts dealing, among other things, with ontological problems. According to him, the emergence of man led to the formation of a new ontological reality and to a certain transformation of other realities. He writes:

> With the emergence of consciousness in the world (being)—and perhaps with the emergence of biological life (maybe not only animals, but also trees and grass witness and judge)—the world (being) changes radically. A stone remains stony, the sun solar, but the event of being in its whole (impossible to complete) [state] becomes completely different, because there emerges an absolutely new, and main, actor of the event—the witness and judge. And the sun, staying physically the same, became different because it started to be perceived by that witness and judge. It ceased just to be, but started to be in and for itself (these categories emerged there for the first time), and for the other, because it started to be reflected in the consciousness of the other (the witness and judge). Thereby, the sun has fundamentally changed, having become enriched and transfigured. (Bakhtin 2002, 395)[11]

From the standpoint of vulgar materialism, all this is idle speculation, but in terms of actual ontology it is a fact.

In this period of his creative work, both man and the world are taken by Bakhtin as unconditionally infinite, as being, in the words of Marx, "in the absolute movement of becoming" (Marx 1968, 476). Bakhtin writes that "nothing definitive in the world has yet happened, the last word of the world and on the world has not yet been uttered, the world is open and free, everything is still ahead and will always be ahead" (Bakhtin 2002, 187). The same applies to man: "As long as a man is alive, he lives because he is yet incomplete, and has not yet said his last word" (Bakhtin 2002, 69). At the same time, there is some inconsistency between Bakhtin's anthropology and ontology. In his *Philosophy of Action*, he described the architectonics of action as a unity of "I-for-myself, the-other-for-me and I-for-the-other." He repeated the same formula in the 1970s: "I am for myself and I am for the other, the other is for me" (Bakhtin 2002, 379). This formula *leaves out* the attitude to the World and the World itself, though, as we can see, Bakhtin writes about the World as well.

This omission was rectified in the last work of his contemporary, Sergei Rubinshtein. This work is called *Chelovek i Mir* [Man and the World]. It was written after the publication of Rubinshtein's famous monograph *Bytie i Soznanie. O Meste Psihicheskogo vo Vseobshchey Vzaimosvyazi Yavleniy Material'nogo Mira* [Being and Consciousness. On the Significance of the Mental Sphere in the Universal Relationship between the Phenomena of the Material World] (Rubinshtein 1957). These were the last years of his life (Rubinshtein died in early 1960), and this work was first published in 1973, with certain passages entirely removed. In the preface, the author wrote:

> I hope that our book *Bytie i Soznanie* [Being and Consciousness] has posed and, touching *en passant* on a large number of questions, partly solved a very major problem (or advanced its solution)—the one of the nature of the mental sphere and its significance in the universal relationship between the phenomena of the material world. The problem of being and consciousness announced in the book's title has not, on the whole, been covered there.
>
> Moreover, the main result of our study into the metal sphere in *Bytie i Soznanie* [Being and Consciousness] has shown that the very formulation of the problem declared in the book's title cannot be final. . . . When posed correctly, the problem of being and consciousness will necessarily be transformed into another one that lurks behind it. Consciousness itself exists only as a process and the result of man's awareness of it. Beyond the problem of being and consciousness, the problem of being, existence and man—who cognizes them and is aware of them—is revealed. Thus, the central problem that arises before us is a problem of being, existence and man's place in it. (Rubinshtein 1997, 4)

While Bakhtin managed to stay away from the dogmas of dialectical and historical materialism, positioning himself as an outsider with regard to them, S. L. Rubinshtein, due to the fact that his works were mainly related to the problems of psychology, could not adopt a similar attitude. However, he could not explore the "man–the universe" problem from the materialistic standpoint whose principal theses had been set out in *Materializm i Empiriokrititsizm* [Materialism and Empirio-Criticism] by Lein and in *O Dialekticheskom i Istoricheskom Materializme* [On Dialectical and Historical Materialism] by Stalin. Even though the Twentieth Congress of the Communist Party of the Soviet Union had delivered the latter Soviet philosophers and psychologists from worshipping the leaders, no one relieved them from the Leninist dogma.

However, in his new book, Rubinshtein criticized the foundations of dialectical materialism. He writes:

> The point of view introduced by Descartes . . . regards being merely as things, as objects of cognition, as an "objective reality." The category of being is limited to

> materiality. In addition, the "subjects," i.e., humans, become excluded from being—and, along with them, go all those functional properties of things, such as tools and products of practice that are inherent in "human objects." In the "constitutive" world, which defines the system of categories, only things exist, and there are no people whose relations are realized through things; even as "tools," they allegedly function independently of people. Man is omitted from the doctrine of categories, including even the doctrine of reality and being. He is obviously "listed" solely in the "book" of historical materialism as a source of social relations; he features nowhere as a human being, except perhaps as a subject to whom everything is an object and nothing but an object. With regard to himself, he seemingly cannot become the object of thought and philosophic study. It is only nature that turns out to be "being" in the fullest sense of the word. The superior kinds of being (existence)—man's existence, his social life style, history—become deontologized, excluded from existence by virtue of the equation: *being = nature = matter.* (Rubinshtein 1997, 6)

In order to overcome this reductionist tenet of the official Soviet philosophy, Rubinshtein suggests the following:

> Man as a subject is to be put inside, included into the composition of existence and, correspondingly, the range of philosophical categories is to be defined. In this case, man acts as a conscious being and the subject of action, first of all, as a real, material, practical creature. However, the general thesis (viz., that, with the emergence of new [higher] levels of being, its inferior levels start functioning in a new capacity) we have advanced as early as in our *Being and Consciousness* remains valid. In other words, human existence is more than an insignificant detail subject only to anthropological and psychological examination and having no bearing on the philosophic plane of the universal, categorical properties of being. As long as with the appearance of human existence the whole ontological plan becomes radically transformed, [relevant] categories ought to be modified to include human presence. Therefore the question that arises is not only that of man in relation to the universe, but also of the universe in its correlation with man as an *objective* relationship. (Rubinshtein 1997, 6–7)

In fact, the above fragment sets the agenda for a holistic philosophy, which is not artificially divided into "dialectical materialism" and "historical materialism." I must admit that, despite the advances in Soviet philosophy, which it owes to people like Ilyenkov, Batishchev, Arsenyev, but also Vladimir Bibler, Pavel Kopnin, Vladislav Lektorsky, Lev Naumenko and others, this set agenda was *not fully implemented.*

Rubinshtein asserts that "man, along with being in a definite relation to the universe and being determined by it, also is part of the universe and defines his attitude to it himself. It is in this that man's conscious self-determination lies" (Rubinshtein 1997, 83). But man, whose being is to be introduced into ontology and into the content of categories, is not some kind of singularity. In accordance with the thesis of Marx about human nature, Rubinshtein notes that "man can be a man only in his relation to another person: man is people in their relations to each other" (Rubinshtein 1997, 4).[12] However, he expands the Marxian definition of human nature as the ensemble of social relations. "In addition to being the ensemble of social relations (according to Marx), man is characterized by the basic human relations through which his specific ontology may be revealed" (Rubinshtein 1997, 65). He also accepts the well-known thesis of Marx, "Man is *the world of man*, the state, the society" (Marx 1955 b, 414), giving it a general ontological character: "The problem . . . of man's relation to existence as a whole includes, along with things and inanimate nature, subjects, personalities, people; [human] attitude to nature is mediated by relations between people" (Rubinshtein 1997, 7).[13] However, he also has a thesis that goes beyond the Marxian understanding of man. He writes:

> The attitude of man to man, to other people cannot be understood without determining the source of man's relation to the universe as a conscious and active creature. Eventually, everything boils down to relations between humans, but to consider only that, beginning and ending with that, is a narrow anthropologism, ethics that does not take into account man's the objective place in the universe . . .[14] Hence, along with the problem of man in correlation with the universe, the problem of the universe in correlation with man as an *objective* relationship is to be posed. (Rubinshtein 1997, 7)

Above, I have quoted Bakhtin's idea that the emergence of man is an act of an *ontological* significance. The same idea is expressed by Rubinshtein. He writes that:

> with the emergence of a new level of existence, new properties reveal themselves in all inferior levels. . . . With the appearance of man, the universe becomes a conscious and meaningful universe, which is transformed with man's actions in it. The universe lives not only [as a cosmos existing] regardless of the subject, i.e., man who is aware of it, [not only as] a pure objective reality plus the subject of cognition. The very conscious and meaningful universe, modified or modifiable by man's actions, is an objective fact. (Rubinshtein 1997, 63)

Rubinshtein's interpretation of *contemplation* is also noteworthy. The official Soviet philosophy regarded contemplation as a *derivative* of objective activity. Rubinshtein distinguishes between contemplation and activity as two [different] ways of man's interaction with the universe. He claims:

> *This contemplation should not be understood as a synonym of passive inaction of man*. It is (in correlation with action, production) the other way of man's attitude to the universe, to being, to existence, a way of sensual aesthetic relation and of a cognitive attitude. The greatness of man and his activity are revealed not only in his actions, but also in contemplation, in the ability to comprehend and to correctly approach the universe, the world and being. Nature is neither a mere object of contemplation nor a mere product of human history; neither a mere material nor a mere prefabricated article of human industrial activity. (Rubinshtein 1997, 72–73)

The quoted passage clearly shows that Rubinshtein understands contemplation, first of all, as something different from man's practical approach to the world, and secondly, he believes that it is inherent not only in man's cognitive approach to the world, but also in the aesthetic one.

In the second half of the twentieth century, Batishchev was one of the first in Soviet philosophy who understood that interpretation of human essence should not be limited only to its social dimension, but ought to ascend to the ontological level. He understood this necessity as early as in the mid-1960s without being familiar with Rubinshtein's *Chelovek i Mir* [Man and World]. Here it is worth giving a brief description of the evolution of his philosophical views. He himself believed that his philosophical evolution went from *substantialism* through *anti-substantialism* to the "the logic of deep communication, inter-subjective involvement, polyphony" (Batishchev 1990c, 329). The actual picture of this evolution is slightly different, though (see Khamidov 2009). I would like to point out here that he did pass through a period of substantialism period, while anti-substantialism never happened. But, more importantly, there can be distinguished an *anthropocentric* (before 1970) and a non-anthropocentric periods (until his death in 1990) in this evolution. At each stage of this evolution, Batishchev waged polemics—mostly against the philosophical standpoints [of other scholars] and his own views he no longer upheld, not against specific philosophers. His most fierce polemics against specific authors is to be found in his *Vvedenie v Dialektiku Tvorchestva* [Introduction to the Dialectics of Creativity],[15] and in his original books in the form of debate: *Dialekticheskoye Protivorechie* [Dialectical Contradiction] (Dialectical 1979) and *Deyatel'nost': Teorii, Metodologiya, Problemy* [Activity: Theories, Methodology, Problems] (Deyatel'nost' 1990). Now I will turn to the evolution of Batishchev's views on the problem of man's essence.

Until the early 1970s, Batishchev remained entirely within the sphere of Marx's philosophy, but even then he ascended to the ontological level of interpretation of human nature. The essence of man and the way of his existence were regarded by him as profoundly *ontological* phenomena. His concept of that period is presented most comprehensively in his fundamental article on the Activity Essence of Man (Batishchev 1969). There he primarily protests against the naturalistic interpretation of man as *part of nature*. According to him, "*man*, as a cognizing, ethical and aesthetic subject *is not part of nature*, i.e., [he is] neither a part among parts, nor a thing among things, nor an object among objects" (ibid., 77). According to him, the essence of man is in his objective activity. But this activity is not isolated from human relationships, from social relations. Batishchev writes: "The essence of man is activity as oneness of doing and communication" (ibid., 96). It should be noted that the concept of oneness is not used in the formal-logic sense ($A = A$), but in the sense of dialectical logic ($A + not - A$). In other words, objective activity is a unity of two vectors: "subject–object" and "subject–subject."

He notes that "the 'presence' of nature in a man as a living body produces a strong impression on a researcher who has naturalistic views . . ." But "man is by no means a kind of a living *natural body* as 'part of nature.' Even his body is truly and tangibly comprehensible only in the context of such characteristics of human existence as cannot be attributed to him as his own—he only functions as their carrier. For, in fact, it is not the body that possesses a person but the person that owns the body as one—though by no means the only—'vessel' of his real being" (Batishchev 1969, 87). Man as a person is unthinkable without that world of culture which is being created by him in the process of mastering and transforming nature. The way of existence of biological entities is *adaptation*; whereas man in the process of development of his objective activity overcomes adaptive existence; "in anthropogenesis, man loses the inherited behavioral determinants that restrict his attitude to the universe to a preset 'algorithm' and that impose [on him] a strictly defined way of interaction with the world as a [natural] environment" (ibid., 86). Major Soviet philosophers were inclined to consider the sociocultural reality to be man's *habitat*, but Batishchev criticized this position as early as in 1967 in the above-cited article (Batishchev 1967).

At that stage of his work, Batishchev regarded activity as a mode of man's existence and reality. He highlights the *objectification* (*die Vergegenständlichung*) and *disobjectification* (*die Entgegenständlichung*) as the main attributes of objective activity [*gegenständliche Tätigkeit*]. By the former, he means the process of transformation of content of activity from its potential existence in the form of activity's capacity into the form of actualized objectivity. The subject, performing any activity, effects objectification. By disobjectification, he means the opposite process—namely the transformational process of the object's definitions, both natural and cultural, into the form of the subject's capacity for acting. Objectification and disobjectification are opposite to each other, but they are such opposites as are not separated from each other in space and time. "Objectification and disobjectification create a true dialectical *unity* of interpenetrating opposites. This unity of opposites *is activity* in its specific definition" (Batishchev 1963, 14).

The concepts objectification and disobjectification were not invented by Batishchev. Marx wrote about them as well. Objectification, as interpreted by both Marx and Batishchev, is an essential attribute of activity and work corresponding to its concept (i.e., *non-alienated* labor). For example: "Labor's realization is its objectification [*Vergegenständlichung*]" (Marx 1974a, 88). But disobjectification is interpreted by Marx differently from Batishchev. The term "disobjectification" (*die Entgegenständlichung*) is found in Marx's *Economic Philosophical Manuscripts of 1844* in chapter titled "Critique of Hegel's Dialectics and Philosophy in General." The German original reads: "Hegel die Selbsterzeugung d[es] Menschen als einen Prozeß faßt die Vergegenständlichung als Entgegenständlichung, und als Entäusserung, und Aufhebung dieser Entäusserung" (Marx 1982, 37–40). In Russian we have: "Gegel' rassmatrivayet samoporozhdenie cheloveka kak protsess, rassmatrivayet opredmechivanie kak raspredmechivanie, kak otchuzhdenie i snyatie etogo otchuzhdeniya . . ." ["Hegel regards the self-generation of man as a process, regards objectification as disobjectification, as alienation and the removal of that alienation . . ."] (Marx 1974, 158–189). The fact that the term *Entäusserung* is rendered in Russian translation as "alienation" (actually, the German word for "alienation" is *Entfremdung*) should not confuse us, since Marx in this period has not yet developed in detail his concept of alienation; therefore both *Entäusserung* and *Entfremdung* are synonyms to him.

Thus, disobjectification [*Entgegenständlichung*] is for Marx in *opposition* to objectification [*Vergegenständlichung*]. A similar opposition is found in Marx's quoted essay "Die Verwirklichung—die Entwirklichung" (Marx 1982, 365) (translated into Russian respectively as "pretvorenie v deystvitel'nost'" ["realization," "actualization"] and "vyklyuchenie iz deystvitel'nosti" ["exclusion from reality"]). The term *Entmenschlichung* (Marx 1982, 396) is translated into Russian as "beschelovechenie" ("dehumanization"). Consequently, disobjectification is for Marx a form of manifestation of *alienation*.

Thus, Batishchev considers the term "disobjectification" (*Entgegenständlichung*) in the *opposite* sense to Marxian one. He endows it with a *deeply positive* meaning, not *negative* one. However, he is not the author of this interpretation. The author of this interpretation is the aforementioned P. L. Kucherov. In 1930, he wrote:

> Revealing the essence of the subject, practical activities also reveal the essence of the object. The transformation of activity into an object reveals an objective existence for activity. The object loses its opposite appearance of a subject revealed in the subject's action, finds its real essential nature, "disobjectifies" (Marx's expression) its nature.
>
> The disclosure of the object for the subject, "disobjectification," is found in practice in the penetration of subjective activity into an object, i.e., in "objectification." The penetration into the object, the transformation from the form of activity into the form of being is at the same time the revelation of the object. The transformation of subjective activity into being (objectification) and the revelation of the object to the subject (disobjectification) represent a single process, the process of practice, objective activity. "Objectification" should be understood as "disobjectification," both processes being in unity with each other. It is in the unity of the both processes at work that the existence of the subject is demonstrated; the subject is a form of practice, objective activity. (Kucherov 1930, 76)

The quoted passage indicates that, although P. L. Kucherov repeats Marx's expression that "objectification is disobjectification," he, unlike Marx, views the concept disobjectification (*Entgegenständlichung*) in a *positive* sense. However, he encloses the term in quotation marks. Another scholar who used the term "disobjectification" in a positive sense was Evald V. Ilyenkov. In his article "Ideal'noye" ["The Ideal"], he writes: "The ideal, as a form of subjective activity, is perceived only through active co-operation with the object and with the product of this activity, i.e., through the form of its product, through the objective form of a thing, through its acting '*disobjectification*'" (Ilyenkov 1962, 226). The word "disobjectification," as in Kucherov, is also given in quotation marks here. But Ilyenkov used quotation marks to show the term is employed as a *metaphor*, not strictly in its *conceptual* sense. And that is where his position differs from that of Kucherov who, while enclosing the word in quotation marks, gave it a *conceptual* sense, making it a special *term*. In this regard, Batishchev sides with Kucherov and develops his point of view on disobjectification. And then he uses the term *without* quotation marks. Of course, it remains unclear how the adherents of "Marxism-Leninism" and the "watchdogs" of the state ideology managed that. It is most likely because they had not studied the texts of Marx thoroughly. Otherwise, certainly, he would have been accused of "revisionism" and the necessary "tough decisions" would have been made.

However, it must be noted that, thanks to the introduction of the *concept* of disobjectification [*Entgegenständlichung*], Batishchev, following Kucherov, goes *far beyond* Marx in understanding the essence of human activity. After all, it was with intent that Marx himself did not develop the attribute or aspect of the objective human activity currently defined as disobjectification (*Vergegenständlichung*) *conceptually*. In his studies, he limited himself to the attribute or aspect of objectification. This is primarily due to the fact that, in his *Economic Philosophical Manuscripts of 1844* (which properly should be called "Philosophical-economical"), Marx comes to the nature of activity through the work of politicians and economists, whereas in *Das Kapital* he explores economic reality. A. Smith, D. Ricardo and Marx examined the capitalist method of organization of material production. In this production, firstly, activity appears in the form of *labor* and, secondly, the scope of the exchange *prevails* over the sphere of production. In other words, in this case the products of labor (goods) and their processing have in this case social and economic values. In this context, labor is taken into account only as the *production* of goods, only from the angle of *objectification* (*Vergegenständlichung*).

According to Batishchev, human activity, along with mastering special (*Besondere*) formations, also masters the attributes of substance through them. That is why man approaches any special morphogenesis from the position of universality, which is developed and perfected in the course of anthropo-sociocultural genesis. Therefore, man's real origins are traced not only to the higher anthropoids, not only to nature in its external manifestations, but also to the universal substance. However, mastering the latter's attributes, man develops them further. Thereby he creates a special world—the world of sociocultural reality. Man is a *transcending* being: the way of his being in the world is *creativity*. Proceeding from this, Batishchev poses the question of human essence. He formulates the following antinomy:

> Man has the essence which makes his activity possible within the system of capabilities, limited by all the inherited wealth of *objects* of his culture and by his level of development as a subject realized in this wealth, i.e., [he has] the *essence that is historically defined and limited*. But, at the same time, man does *not* possess *any* essence that is preset once and for all and has a limited, rigid, finite system of possibilities within which he would have developed; on the contrary, as the *subject* of culture he progresses, acquiring essentially new, previously unavailable possibilities. . . . In order to own an essence, he must reject it, and to reject it, he should own it. (Batishchev 1969, 96–97)[16]

Such is this antinomy, i.e., a *dialectical* contradiction expressed verbally. It cannot be solved by eliminating the thesis and leaving the antithesis, and vice versa. After all, both the thesis and the antithesis are equally objective meaning-wise. Therefore, it is necessary to find such an understanding of human essence in which the thesis and the antithesis would combine organically to create a *synthesis*. Batishchev finds this synthesis. He writes that, to solve this antinomy,

> means to develop a completely different and unique concept of essence: man's essence ought to consist in the fact that he *has no single*, *particular*, once and for all preset and limited nature. In other words, it is necessary to come to such an understanding in accordance with which man's nature is that he *has no finite nature "of his own"* which could have been a predefined blueprint of his development, a preset measure of his life. (Batishchev 1969, 97)

In the light of this thesis, we see that not only "human nature . . . becomes modified with each historical epoch," which is mentioned by Marx in *Capital I* (Chicago: Charles H. Kerr & Co. 1906, c. 668), but human essence is also subject to the same modification.

Mastering and developing specific and universal substantial definitions, man, as the subject, creates a special *supra*-natural world—a world of culture as its objective reality. In the formative structures of culture, not only man's consciousness and thinking, but also his entire objective activity in all its essential characteristics becomes objectified. Batishchev wrote in this regard:

> When M. K. Mamardashvili finds in Marx ['s works] the analysis of consciousness *by [instances of] its objectiveness* rather than by its presence in the acts of a concrete "mental" individuality, this [situation] can be viewed as a sort of a *particular case* or an aspect of man's analysis according to his objective world. However, M. K. Mamardashvili interprets it not as man's study, but as an "impersonal analysis" according to which people are not the authors, but the *readers* of the "text" of their consciousness, whose author is "society." . . . The real person, who acts as an author outside of his consciousness and independently of it, is not recognized in the so-called "society." "Impersonal" analysis corresponds to Mamardashvili's view of personal independence as a *mere illusion* of philosophical classics (defined, in addition, by entirely transitory conditions) rather than as human potential, no matter how illusory it appears and how far from triumph it might be. . . . No matter how "impersonal" such interpretations might appear, they still help one to prepare to analyze man in accordance with his objective world, with his *ecumene*, they help one to develop an *ecumenic* approach. (Batishchev 1977b, 152)[17]

The principle of objective activity was initially perceived with distrust by Soviet philosophers and psychologists (they were afraid that the "demon" of *idealism* was lurking inside it), but later it was accepted and even absolutized. It must be noted that Batishchev was nearly the only Soviet philosopher who, having reached a certain level in his solution of philosophic problems, ascended to a new, higher one, and transferred his achievements there. His acquaintance with A. A. Ukhtomsky's letters (Ukhtomsky 1973, 371–434) and with the teachings of Agni Yoga ("The Living Ethics") led Batishchev to the conclusion that the categories of activity—and, accordingly, of the principle of objective activity—are limited. In late 1980, he wrote: "As so, now I have to protect at the same time both the non-acting layers of the subject's existence (from being placed in the super-category of activity) and the semantic content of the category of activity (from certain fashionable versions of 'activity approach' with their persistent claims to universalism)" (Batishchev 1990a, 23). Batishchev believed that some of thinkers made the category of activities into an absolute. He pointed to Vasily V. Davydov as to one of those examples. In his works, says Batishchev, "the activity approach is transformed . . . into activity reductionism" (Batishchev 1990b, 171). Agreeing with V. S. Shvyrev that the category of activity ought to be preserved he adds: "But the main problem is: can the *most extreme* human openness be effected only *from inside* activity as a self-contained sphere, or could it be the case that it is at its most extreme and profound instances that this [openness] is inaccessible from inside such a sphere, so that something [that lies] above activity is required here?" (Batishchev 1990c, 319). In this period, Batishchev identifies three levels in the being of man as the subject: *pre*-activity, activity, and *supra*-activity. According to him, "activity is not the only possible, universal *way of being* of man, culture, social life; it is not the only and all-embracing way of man's interaction with the world" (Batishchev 1990a, 24–25).

Beginning with his doctoral thesis, Batishchev studied the phenomenon of *alienation*. This concept is beyond the scope of this chapter. However, I would like to mention here a few relevant points. The most complete interpretation of alienation is presented in Batishchev's article on the activity essence of man (Batishchev 1969).[18] Subsequently, when an unspoken taboo was imposed from above on the development of problems of alienation, Batishchev started studying individual aspects of alienation, especially *reification* (*Versachlichung*, *Verdinglichung*) (see, e.g. Batishchev 1983). He even criticized his like-minded colleagues for their insufficiently consistent and deep understanding of various aspects and consequences of reification. He writes: "A. S. Arsenyev who, on the face of it, so persistently criticizes 'objective relations,' suddenly shows the 'subject-creator' as extraordinarily similar to the naturalistic *thing*-winner" (Batishchev 1997, 214).[19]

In the 1970s–1980s, Batishchev criticizes *substantialism* (a philosophic worldview proceeding from exaggerating the philosophical status of matter as a basic principle of objective reality to the detriment of the subject), *anti-substantialism* (a philosophic worldview proceeding from exaggerating the ontological status of the subject to the detriment of matter) and *anthropocentrism* (a philosophic and—as evidenced by the current ecological crisis—often practical worldview that places man at the center of the Universe, or at the top of creation). Batishchev finds substantialism not only in the works of Spinoza, Hegel and in the official "dialectical materialism," but also in the ideas of Evald Ilyenkov, Mikhail Lifshitz and others. Anti-substantialism is discovered by him not only in the works of Fichte, Kierkegaard and others, but also in his own works. It is for the latter view that he criticized, first of all, his own ideas developed in his earlier article on the activity essence of man (Batishchev 1969). Under the influence of Agni Yoga he also comes to criticize anthropocentrism. He finds anthropocentrism both in his own works written prior to the first half of the 1970s and in Marx's early works. He therefore dissociates himself from Marx and expounds his objections to him in his so-called "Tezisy ne k Feyerbakhu" [Theses not to Feuerbach] (Batishchev 2015, 400–425). The above work was written during the period of 1974–1980 and was not intended for publication. After all, given the conditions of that time, its publication was inconceivable. While the situation has changed, the text still remains unpublished.

Now I would like to briefly summarize certain important ideas formulated by Batishchev after his rejection of Marx and overcoming substantialism and anti-substantialism, activity-centered reductionism and anthropocentrism.

Firstly, he put the subject-subject relation above the subject-object one, interpreting the latter as an instance of the former. This, by and large, still fits into Marx's concept. However, Batishchev expands the *Subject–Object–Subject* formula by adding *product* to it. He writes: "the result is a synthetic, uniting formula: 'the subject–the product–the object–the product–the subject'" (Batishchev 1989, 24).

Secondly, having construed man as a multi-level being, Batishchev reconsiders the phenomenon of communication. He states: "Communication is a meeting-process unfolding simultaneously on *different levels* that are fundamentally not reducible to each other and are radically different as to their degree of explicitness" (Batishchev 1990a, 30). Therefore communication does not coincide with social relations that are created and reproduced through activity, which means that they have an activity-based nature. Meanwhile, in the Soviet philosophy communication continued to be interpreted as "the highest form of matter in motion," or as "a special type of social activity," or as "an individualized form of social relations." Some traced communication to *interaction*—something that reigns supreme in nature. But the phenomenon of interaction is inherent in a *finite*, i.e., purely natural structures. This was stressed by Batishchev, who wrote: "In spite of the universally prevailing interaction, human activity is by no means in a similar relation of 'reciprocity' with its object. In other words, where only the 'reciprocity' of interaction between 'man' and things triumphs, no true man and his activity exist yet (or any longer)" (Batishchev 1969, 84).

Thirdly, based on the principle of multi-levelness, Batishchev assigns activity and *creativity*—the latter being, more or less, the principal subject of his philosophic attention—to different levels. He asserts:

> Creativity is different from activity in that it *can* do exactly that which activity *cannot* do inherently, for [creativity] is a progressive shifting of the very thresholds of disobjectification that restrict activity and enclose it in its own sphere—at any [degree] of its relatively external (paradigmatically, still the same) expansion. Of course, creativity *is also an act*, a creative act. But, before becoming an act and in order to become an act, creativity has first to be a special kind of supra-active *attitude* of the subject to the world and to himself—such an attitude as [considers] everything in existence to be able to become *different*. Creative attitude is an attitude of the subject to the world as to a world of puzzling problems and, most importantly, such a relationship that he enters carrying his [entire] contents, both subliminal *and supraliminal*. (Batishchev 1990a, 29)

By publicizing his ideas, Batishchev *entered into polemics* with views different from his own and, particularly, with his own ideas he no longer upheld. In 1977, he converted to Orthodoxy, which had inevitably affected his philosophical creativity. For a long time, the change remained largely unnoticeable, which was the case almost until 1992, when in his article "Nayti i Obresti Sebya" [Searching and Finding Oneself] (Batishchev 1992b), published posthumously, he freely discussed his new outlook, uncompromisingly permeated with the spirit of Orthodoxy. Everything that he wrote about man throughout the preceding period of his philosophical work is entirely absent from that paper—and, therefore, ***rejected***. I will not analyze it, but rather refer the reader to this work (Batishchev 1992b, 18–27; Batishchev 1995, 103–109).

Since around the mid-1980s, Bakhtin's idea of dialogue becomes popular. The vast majority of philosophers accepted it quite uncritically. Batishchev was the only scholar to have seen an intrinsic antithesis in Bakhtin's ideological heritage. Batishchev wrote that the later revealed:

> in his heritage two ideologically different positions or trends. They are both "dialogical," both are alien and opposed to monologism, to authoritarian thinking and to panlogism . . . And yet, not a mere difference, but an axiological abyss lies between them. Firstly, this is a cold, non-involved dialogism typical of self-asserting "atomized" individuals who acknowledge no vertical value systems, no hierarchies of meanings, no levels of existence; this is relativism, a carnival. Secondly, this is a polyphonic dialogue, a multi-level, profound encounter, which includes supraliminal tiers; dominance of the other, willingness to prefer others to yourself, fullness of fateful involvement, loyalty to the absolute values, striving for unobtrusive Harmony. (Batishchev 1992a, 123)

Batishchev valued above all the concept of Rubinshtein outlined in his latter's work *Chelovek i mir* (Rubinshtein 1997). This was quite well-founded. For that philosopher, better known as a psychologist, expressed in that book many of those ideas and theses which Soviet philosophers, even such major ones as Ilyenkov, Batishchev and some others, managed to arrive at much later. Batishchev dedicated several works to the study of philosophical doctrines of Rubinshtein (see Batishchev 1989b; 1989c; 1989d). However, giving him precedence as regards the formulation of a fair number of productive ideas, he highlights some errors in his formulations. For example, he notes Rubinshtein's uncritical approach to some ideas in Marx's early works that were imbued with the spirit of anthropocentrism, which had a negative impact on the interpretation of some problems by Rubinshtein (Batishchev 1989d, 251).

* * *

In conclusion, it should be noted that the very name of Batishchev was often suppressed during his lifetime. Scholars who worked on similar problems hardly referred to his works, including his colleagues from the Institute where he worked. The situation did not improve even after his departure. For instance, in 1992, the journal *Filosofskie Nauki* [Philosophic Sciences] published an article of Dr. Vera Samokhvalova, a research fellow of the Institute of Philosophy of the Academy of Sciences of the USSR (Samokhvalova 1992). The article discussed the problem on which Batishchev worked for nearly 30 years until his death. It was sent in for publication on December 10, 1991, which is less than a year and two months after his death on October 31, 1990. However, Batishchev, who was almost the only scholar criticizing anthropocentrism throughout the 1980s, was *not even mentioned* in this article. On the other hand, it mentioned a certain Academician N. G. Kholodny who, in his certain book of 1944, "called anthropocentrism the original sin of mankind" (Samokhvalova 1992, 161). What can I add?

There was a special volume on Batishchev, though, published in 2009 in the series "Filosofiya Rossii Vtoroy Poloviny XX Veka" [Russian Philosophy of the Second Half of the Twentieth Century]. But this is clearly not enough. Besides, most of the philosopher's works are still not readily available to the general reader. It is time to return his works.

## NOTES

1. Let me note that the volumes 1–4 of the second edition of *Works of Marx and Engels*, published in 1955, were prepared by the Institute of Marx–Engels–Lenin–Stalin of the Central Committee of the Communist Party of the Soviet Union. Beginning with the fifth volume (published in 1956), the edition had been published by the Institute of Marxism-Leninism of the CCCPSU.
2. They are presented in the original (Archive 1924, 200–202) and in Russian (ibid., 208–210). For the facsimile of all eleven theses, see ibid., 203–207.
3. In the Russian translation of Engels's variant of the "Theses" the phrase "*revolutionary practice*" was used (see Marx, Karl. 1955 c, 2).
4. There is a misprint in the text. Instead of the word *innewohnendes*, the word *inwohnendes* is used.
5. Yuri Davydov discussed this term in a special article (see Davydov 1983), but still failed to clarify its meaning.
6. We should pay special attention to *how* Marx and Engels treated *matter*. Marx's understanding went back to Plato, Aristotle and other philosophers who correlated matter with *form*. Engels's understanding of matter derived from Hobbes and French materialists who distinguished matter from form, and preserved only its attribute of movement, thereby giving it the ontological status of the universal Substance. Therefore, we may conclude that the *materialistic concept of history* is *different* in Marx and subsequent Marxists, whom, as we know, he tended to disown.
7. Bakhtin asserts that, "due to this, his creativity is outside any framework, it does not conform to any of those historico-literary patterns that we normally apply to the phenomena of the European novel" (Bakhtin 2000, 12–13).
8. Bakhtin warned: "It should not be forgotten that our term has a metaphorical origin" (Bakhtin 2000, 30).
9. "Thus dialogical relations are much broader than dialogical speech in the narrow sense of the word" (Bakhtin 1996 a, 336). Cf. Bakhtin 2000, 51.
10. "Life itself is dialogical by nature. To live means to participate in a dialogue—ask questions, listen, answer, agree and so on. In this dialogue, man participates wholly and with his whole life: with his eyes, lips, hands, soul, spirit, whole body, actions. . . . He takes part in it not only with his thoughts, but also with his whole fate and his whole individuality" (Bakhtin 1996b, 351).
11. "The emergence of life and consciousness as the emergence of a *witness* of the event of existence radically changes the entire meaning of the event" (Bakhtin 2002, 395).
12. In his book *Bytie i Soznanie*, S. L. Rubinshtein wrote: "One's attitude to another person, to people constitutes the main fabric of human life, its core. Man's 'heart' is totally woven of his human relationships with other people" (Rubinshtein 1957, 263).

13. "Man's attitude to the universe, to being, and man's attitude to man are considered in their interdependence and mutual causality" (Rubinshtein 1997, 8).
14. Rubinshtein notes: "There is no right attitude to man without the right attitude to the universe. Only a full-fledged person—which means one having the right attitude to the universe, to nature and to life—can enter full-fledged relations with other people and can become a condition of human existence for another person" (Rubinshtein 1997, 110).
15. This manuscript was deposited at the Institute of Scientific Information on Social Sciences of the Academy of Sciences of USSR in 1984.
16. Batishchev clarifies: "In other words, man has at each point historically conditioned *limits* of the possible and the impossible. But he gets to *this* fixed border only because he always overcomes or *transcends* his own borders constantly removing them" (Batishchev 1969, 96–97).
17. In the former case, Batishchev refers to an article by Mamardashvili, "Analiz Soznaniya v Rabotah Marksa" [Analysis of Consciousness in the Works of Marx], in the latter, he refers to an article "Klassicheskaya i Sovremennaya Burzhuaznaya Filosofiya. Opyt Epistemologicheskogo Sopostavleniya" [Classical and Modern Bourgeois Philosophy. An Experience of Epistemological Comparison] written by Mamardashvili in co-authorship with E. Yu. Solovyev and V. S. Shvyrev.
18. Here one will find a special paragraph that discusses this notion: "Chelovek i Ego Otchuzhdenie" [Man and His Alienation]. See 110–135.
19. Here Batishchev quoted Arsenyev 1981b.

## BIBLIOGRAPHY


Archive 1924. *Arkhiv K. Marksa i F. Engelsa, Kniga 1* [Archive of Marx and Engels, vol. 1], Moscow: Gosudarstvennoe Izdatelstvo.

Arsenyev, Anatoly S. 1981a. "Problema Tseli v Vospitanii i Obrazovanii. Tsel' v Vospitanii Lichnosti" [The Problem of Purpose in Upbringing and Education. Purpose in the Upbringing of an Individual]. In *Filosofsko-psihologicheskie Problemy Razvitiya Obrazovaniya* [Philosophical and Psychological Problems in the Development of Education]. Moscow: Pedagogica.

Arsenyev, Anatoly S. 1981b. "Problema Tseli v Vospitanii i Obrazovanii. Vzaimootnoshenie Yestestvennonauchnogo i Gumanitarnogo Znaniya" [The Problem of Purpose in Education. The Correlation of Sciences and the Humanities]. In *Filosofsko-psikhologicheskie Problemy Razvitiya Obrazovaniya* [Philosophical and Psychological Problems in the Development of Education]. Moscow: Pedagogica.

Bakhtin, Mikhail M. 1986. "K Filosofii Postupka" [On the Philosophy of Action]. In *Filosofia i Sotsiologia Nauki i Tehniki. Ezhegodnik 1984–1985.* [Philosophy and Sociology of Science and Engineering. Yearbook. 1984–1985], 80–160. Moscow: Nauka,

Bakhtin, Mikhail M. 1996. *Sobranie Sochineniy v 7 Tomakh, t. 5.* [Collected Works in 7 Volumes, vol. 5]. Moscow: Russkie slovari, Yazyki slavianckoy kul'tury.

Bakhtin, Mikhail M. 2000. *Sobranie Sochineniy v 7 Tomah, t. 2* [Collected Works in 7 Volumes, vol. 2]. Moscow: Russkie slovari, Yazyki slavianckoy kul'tury.

Bakhtin, Mikhail M. 2002. *Sobranie Sochineniy v 7 Tomach, t. 6* [Collected Works in 7 Volumes, vol. 6]. Moscow: Russkie slovari, Yazyki slavianckoy kul'tury.

Bakhtin, Mikhail M. 2003. *Sobranie Sochinenii v 7 Tomach, t. 1* [Collected Works in 7 Volumes, vol. 1]. Moscow: Russkie slovari, Yazyki slavianckoy kul'tury.

Bakhtin, Mikhail M. 2002. *M. M. Bakhtin: Besedy s V. D. Duvakinym* [M. M. Bakhtin: Conversations with V. D. Duvakin]. Moscow: Soglasie.

Batishchev, Genrikh S. 1963. *Protivorechie kak Kategoria Dialekticheskoy Logiki* [Contradiction as a Category of Dialectical Logic]. Moscow: Vysshaya shkola.

Batishchev, Genrikh S. 1966. "Deyatel'nostnaya Sushchnost' Cheloveka kak Filosofskiy Printsip" [The Activity Essence of Man as a Philosophical Principle]. In *Chelovek v Sotsialisticheskom i Burzhuaznom Obshchestve. Simposium (Doklady i Soobshenia)* [Man in the Socialist and Bourgeois Society. Symposium (Papers and Reports)], 245–286. Moscow: IF AN SSSR.

Batishchev, Genrikh S. 1967. "Obshchestvenno-Istoricheskaya, Deyatel'naya Sushchnost' Cheloveka" [Socio-Historical, Active Essence of Man], *Voprosy filosofii* (3): 20–29, Moscow: Nauka.

Batishchev, Genrikh S. 1969. "Deyatel'naya Sushchnost' Cheloveka kak Filosofskiy Printsip" [The Activity Essence of Man as a Philosophical Principle]. In *Problema Cheloveka v Sovremennoy Filosofii* [The Problem of Man in Modern Philosophy], 73–144. Moscow: Nauka.

Batishchev, Genrikh S. 1977a. "Kul'tura, Priroda i Psevdoprirodnye Fenomeny v Istoricheskom Protsesse" [Culture, Nature and Pseudo-Natural Phenomena in Historical Process]. In *Trudy NII Kultury MK RSFSR. Problemy Teorii Kul'turi. t. 55* [The Works of Scientific Research Institute of Culture of the Ministry of Committee of RSFSR. Problems of Theory of Culture, v. 55], 78–100. Moscow: NII Kultury MK RSFSR.

Batishchev, Genrikh S. 1977b. "Ponyatie Tselostno Razvitogo Cheloveka i Perspektivy Kommunisticheskogo Vospitaniya" [The Concept of Full-Fledged Man and the Prospects of Communist Education]. In *Problema Cheloveka v "Ekonomicheskih Rukopisyah 1857–1859 Godov" K. Marksa* [The Problem of Man in Marx's "Economic Manuscripts of 1857–1859"], 147–170. Rostov-na-Donu: Rostovskiy universitet.

Batishchev, Genrikh S. 1979. "Kategoriya Protivorechiya i Yego Mirovozzrencheskaya Funktsiya" [The Category of Contradictions and Its Worldview Function]. In *Dialekticheskoye Protivorechie* [Dialectical Contradiction], 39–58. Moscow: Politizdat.

Batishchev, Genrikh S. 1983. "Problema Oveshchneniya i Yego Gnoseologicheskoye Znachenie (v Svete Marksovoy Kontseptsii Oveshchneniya)" [The Problem of Reification and Its Epistemological Significance (in the Light of Marxian Conception of Reification)]. In *Gnoseologiya v Sisteme Filosofskogo Mirovozzreniya* [Epistemology in the System of Philosophical World Outlook], 250–272. Moscow: Nauka.

Batishchev, Genrikh S. 1986. "Dialektika Pered Litsom Global'no-Ekologicheskoy Situatsii" [Dialectics Faced with the Global Ecological Situation]. In *Vzaimodeystvie Obshchestva i Prirody. Filosofsko-Metodologicheskie Aspekty Ekologicheskoy Problemy* [Interaction of Society and Nature. Philosophical-Methodological Aspects of the Ecological Problem], 175–197. Moscow: Nauka.

Batishchev, Genrikh S. 1989a. *Dialekticheskiy Kharakter Tvorcheskogo Otnosheniya Cheloveka k Miru. Dissertatiya v Forme nauchnogo Doklada na Soiskanie Uchenoy Stepeni Doktora filosofskih Nauk* [The Dialectical Character of Creative Attitude to the World. Dissertation in the Form of Scientific Report for the Degree of Doctor of Philosophy]. Moscow: IF AN SSSR.

Batishchev, Genrikh S. 1989b. "Filosofskaia Kontseptsiya Cheloveka i Kreativnosti v Nasledii S. L. Rubinshteyna" [The Philosophical Concept of Man and Creativity in the Heritage of S. L. Rubinshtein]. *Voprosy filosofii* (4): 96–109.

Batishchev, Genrikh S. 1989c. "Filosofsko-aksiologicheskie Idei v Kontseptsii Cheloveka S. L. Rubinshteyna [Philosophic and Axiological Ideas in the Concept of Man by S. L. Rubinshtein]. *Filosofskie nauki* [Philosophic Sciences] (7): 26–36.

Batishchev, Genrikh S. 1989d. "Filosofskoe Nasledie S. L. Rubinshteyna i Problematika Kreativnosti" [The Philosophic Heritage of S. L. Rubinshtein and the Problem of Creativity]. In *Sergey Leonidovich Rubinshteyn. Ocherki, Vospominaniya, Materialy. K 100-letiyu so Dnya Rozhdenia* [Sergei Leonidovich Rubinshtein. Essays, Memories, Materials. On the 100th Anniversary], 245–277. Moscow: Nauka.

Batishchev, Genrikh S. 1990a. "Neischerpannye Vozmozhnosti i Granitsy Primenimosti Kategorii Deyatel'nosti" [The Endless Possibilities and Limits of Applicability of the Category of Activity]. In *Deiatelnost': Teoriya, Metodologiya, Problemy* [Activity: Theory, Methodology, Problems], 21–34. Moscow: Politizdat.

Batishchev, Genrikh S. 1990b. "Deyatel'nostnyi Podhod v Plenu Substantsializma" [Activity-Centered Approach in the Clutches of Substantialism]. In *Deiatelnost': Teoriya, Metodologiya, Problemy* [Activity: Theory, Methodology, Problems], 169–176. Moscow: Politizdat.

Batishchev, Genrikh S. 1990c. "Ne Deyaniem Odnim Zhiv Chelovek" [It is not by Action Alone that a Man Lives]. In *Deiatelnost': Teoriya, Metodologiya, Problemy* [Activity: Theory, Methodology, Problems], 317–329. Moscow: Politizdat.

Batishchev, Genrikh S. 1992a. "Dialogism ili Polifonism? (Antitetika v Ideynom Nasledii M. M. Bakhtina" [Dialogism or Polyphonism? (Antithetics in the Ideological Heritage of Bakhtin)]. In *M. M. Bakhtin kak Filosof* [M. M. Bakhtin as a Philosopher], 123–141. Moscow: Nauka.

Batishchev, Genrikh S. 1992b. "Nayti i Obresti Sebya" [Searching and Finding Oneself]. In *Stupeni Samoobreteniya (Problemy Obrazovaniya i Kul'tury v Malom Gorode)* [Stages of Finding Oneself (Problems of Education in Towns)], 18–27. Moscow: Nauka.

Batishchev, Genrikh S. 1995. "Nayti i Obresti Sebya" [Searching and to Finding Oneself], *Voprosy filosofii* (3): 103–109.

Batishchev, Genrikh S. 1997. *Vvedenie v Dialektiku Tvorchestva* [Introduction to the Dialectics of Creativity]. St. Petersburg: RHGI.

Batishchev, Genrikh S. *Izbrannye Proizvedeniya* [Selected Works]. Almaty: IFPR KN MON RK.

Davydov, Yuri N. 1983. "Sotsiologicheskoye Soderzhanie Kategorii 'Gemein-wesen' v Rabotah K. Marksa" [The Sociological Content of the Category "Gemeinwesen" in the Works of K. Marx], *Sotsiologicheskie Issledovaniya* [Sociological Studies] (4): 36–49.

Deyatel'nost' 1990. *Deyatel'nost': Teorii, Metodologiya, Problemy* [Activity: Theory, Methodology, Problems]. Moscow: Politizdat.

Dialekticheskoe 1979. *Dialekticheskoye Protivorechie* [Dialectical Contradiction]. Moscow: Politizdat.

Engels, Friedrich 1961. "Predislovie k Knige Ludvig Feyerbah i Konets Klassicheskoy Nemetskoy Filosofii" [Foreword to *Ludwig Feuerbach and the End of Classical German Philosophy*]. In *Marks K., Engels F. Sochineniya, Izd. 2, t. 21* [Marx K., Engels F. Works, second edition, vol. 21], 370–371. Moscow: Politizdat.

Ilyenkov, Evald V. 1962. "Ideal'noe" [The Ideal]. In *Filosofskaya Entsiklopediya, t. 2* [Philosophical Encyclopedia, vol. 2], 219–227. Moscow: Sovetskaya Entsiklopediya.

Ilyenkov, Evald V. 1979. "Chto zhe takoye Lichnost'?" [What is an Individuality?]. In *S chego nachinayetsia Lichnost'?* [What is the Beginning of Individuality?]. Moscow: Politizdat.

Khamidov, Alexander A. 2009. "Put' Otkrytiy kak Otkrytie Puti: Filosofskie Iskania G. S. Batishcheva" [The Road of Discoveries as the Discovery of the Road: Batishchev's Philosophical Quest]. In *Genrih Stepanovich Batishchev* [Genrikh Stepanovich Batishchev], 211–242. Moscow: ROSSPEN.

Khamidov, Alexander A. 2011. "Neobychnoye Proizvedenie G. S. Batishcheva" [An Unusual Work by G. S. Batishchev], *Voprosy filosofii.* (8): 144–156.

Kon, Igor S. 1967. *Sotsiologiya Lichnosti* [Sociology of Personality]. Moscow: Politizdat.

Kucherov, P. L. 1930. "Praktika i Dialekticheskaya Logika" [Practice and Dialectic Logic] *Pod Znamenem Marksizma* [Under the Banner of Marxism] (7–8).

Marx, Karl. 1932. "[Excerptum]. James Mill, Éléments d'économie politique. Traduits par J. T. Parisot. Paris, 1823" [[Excerptum.] James Mill, Elements of Political Economy. Translated by J. T. Parisot. Paris, 1823]. In *Marx K. und Engels F. Historisch-kritische Gesamtausgabe. (MEGA). I. Abt. Bd. 3* [Marx K., Engels F. Full Historical-Critical Edition, pt. I, vol. 3]. Berlin: Dietz Verlag.

Marx, Karl. 1933 "1) ad Feuerbach" [1) ad Feuerbach]. In *Marx K., Engels F. Historisch-kritische Gesamtausgabe. (MEGA). I. Abt. Bd. 5* [Marx K., Engels, F. Full Historical-Critical Edition, pt. I, vol. 3]. Moscow: Leningrad.

Marx, Karl. 1955a. "Debaty Shestogo Reynskogo Landtaga. (Statya pervaya). Debaty o Svobode Pechati i ob Opublikovanii Protokolov Soslovnogo Sobraniya" [Debates of the Sixth Rhine Landtag. (Article One). Debates on the Freedom of the Press and Publication of the Proceedings of the Assembly of the Estates]. In *Marks K., Engels F. Sochineniya, Izdanie 2, t. 1* [Marx K., Engels F. Works, second edition, vol. 1], 30–84. Moscow: Politizdat.

Marx, Karl. 1955b. "K Kritike Gegelevskoy Filosofii Prava [On Critique of Hegel's Philosophy of Right]. In *Marks K., Engels F. Sochinenia, Izdanie 2, t. 1* [Marx K., Engels F. Works, second edition, vol. 1], 219–368. Moscow: Politizdat.

Marx, Karl. 1955c. "Tezisy o Feyerbahe" [Theses on Feuerbach]. In *Marks K., Engels F. Sochineniya, Izdanie 2, t. 3* [Marx K., Engels F. Works, second edition, vol. 3], 1–4. Moscow: Politizdat.

Marx, Karl. 1968. "Ekonomicheskie Rukopisi 1857–1859 Godov. (Pervonachal'nyi Variant 'Kapitala')" [Economic Manuscripts of 1857–1859. (The First Version of *Das Kapital*)]. In *Marks K., Engels F. Sochinenya, Izdanie 2, t. 46, part 1.* [Marx K., Engels F. Works, second edition, vol. 46, part 1]. Moscow: Politizdat.

Marx, Karl. 1974a. "Ekonomichesko-filosofskie Rukopisi 1844 Goda" [Economico-Philosophical Manuscripts of 1844]. In *Marks K., Engels F. Sochineniya, Izdanie 2, t. 42* [Marx K., Engels F. Works, second edition, vol. 42], 41–174. Moscow: Politizdat.

Marx, Karl. 1974b. "Tezisy o Feierbahe (Tekst 1845 Goda)" [Theses on Feuerbach (Text of 1845]. In *Marks K., Engels F. Sochineniya Izdanie 2, t. 42* [Marx K., Engels F. Works, second edition, vol. 42], 261–263. Moscow: Politizdat.

Marx, Karl. 1974c. "Konspekt Knigi Dzhemsa Milla 'Osnovy Politicheskoy Ekonomii'" [Economic Manuscripts: Comments on James Mill by Karl Marx]. In *Marks K., Engels F. Sochineniya Izdanie 2, t. 42* [Marx K., Engels F. Works, second edition, vol. 42], 5–40. Moscow: Politizdat.

Marx, Karl. 1982. "Ökonomisch-philosophische Manuskripte (Zweite Wiedergabe)" [Economical-Philosophical Manuscripts (Second Reproduction)]. In *Marx K., Engels F. Gesamtausgabe (MEGA). I. Abt. Bd. 2. Text* [Marx K., Engels F. Complete Historical-Critical Edition, pt. I, vol. 2]. Berlin: Dietz Verlag.

Rubinshtein, Sergei L. 1957. *Bytie i Soznanie. O Meste Psihicheskogo vo Vseobshchey Vzaimosvyazi Yavleniy Material'nogo Mira* [Being and Consciousness. On the Significance of the Mental Sphere in the Universal Relationship between the Phenomena of the Material World]. Moscow.

Rubinshtein, Sergei L. 1989. "Istoriya Sozdaniya Knigi 'Chelovek i Mir'" [The History of Creation of the Book "Man and the Universe"]. In *Sergey Leonidovich Rubinshteyn. Ocherki, Vospominaniya, Materialy. K 100-letiyu so Dnya Rozhdenia* [Sergei Leonidovich Rubinshtein. Essays, Memories, Materials. On to the 100th Anniversary]. Moscow: Nauka.

Rubinshtein, Sergei L. 1997. *Chelovek i Mir* [Man and the Universe]. Moscow: Nauka.

Ryazanov, David B. 1924. "Predislovie Redaktora" [Editor's Preface]. In *Arhiv K. Marksa i F. Engel'sa, Kniga 1* [The Archive of K. Marx and F. Engels, vol. 1], 191–199. Moscow: Gosudarstvennoye Izdatel'stvo.

Samokhvalova, Vera I. 1992. "Chelovek i Mir: Problema Antropotsentrizma" [Man and the Universe: The Problem of Anthropocentrism]. *Filosofskie Nauki* [Philosophic Sciences] (3): 121–135.

Ukhtomsky, Aleksei A. 1973. "Pis'ma" [Letters]. In *Puti v Neznayemoye. Pisateli Rasskazivayut o Nauke, Sbornik 10* [Roads to the Unknown. Writers Speak on Science, Collection 10]. Moscow: Sovetskiy Pisatel'.

CHAPTER TWENTY-THREE

# On the Problem of Morality in Soviet-Era Philosophy

YURI V. PUSHCHAEV

Morality as a distinct phenomenon and subject matter of a philosophical discipline—ethics—began to be actively studied in Soviet philosophy in the late 1950s to early 1960s. On the crest of the "thaw" and the Twentieth Congress of the CPSU that caused a degree of humanization of the post-Stalin system, chairs of ethics and aesthetics were opened at philosophical faculties at Moscow State University (MGU) and Leningrad State University (LGU). These authorities themselves were aware of the need to renew the nation's moral foundations. It is not by chance that the Twenty-second CPSU Congress in 1961 adopted the famous Moral Code of the Builders of Communism. The charges against Stalin and the pre–thaw period were essentially of a moral character: violation of the principles of socialist legality. It is indeed very important that cult of Stalin and mass repressions were declared to be unacceptable on moral grounds.

However, this criticism of Stalinism appears to be superficial and not deep enough to reveal any essential ideas. Stalin is a historical figure on a Shakespearian scale or even larger, but who today seriously reads Stalin? To condemn Stalinism and not to read Stalin is like talking about Islam without even having read the Quran.

The Stalin years are generally contrasted with the years of the "thaw" and the period of change in the 1960s. However, the Stalin era (the 1930s to 1940s), is actually linked with the subsequent mildly anti-Stalinist period, including the emergence of a new philosophical tradition in Russia represented by Ilyenkov, Mamardashvili, Zinoviev and others. The very fact that these historical periods are distinguished and even juxtaposed shows a certain unity in the framework of a broader whole. Indeed, the Stalin years provide many subjects for study that have to do with the history of philosophy and culture in Russia. For instance, Stalin's *Economic Problems of Socialism* and *Marxism and the Issues of Linguistics* are veritable ideological masterpieces. They do not contain any deep thoughts and it would not occur to anyone to interpret or "decode" them, like the early works of Marx were interpreted by the 1960s philosophers. Yet the balanced, unsophisticated clarity and pragmatic common sense are outstanding examples of ideological thinking. They represent the triumph of ideological logic. In general, Stalin is one of the most logical leaders the world has ever seen. Interestingly, of the early major works of young Stalin, *Anarchism and Socialism* speaks about what the state would be like under socialism and *Marxism and the Nationalities Question* analyzes the Marxist approach to the nationalities issue. That is anything but accidental. This would be his brief as People's Commissar for Nationalities under Lenin and his main concern when he would become the ruler of the Soviet state.

But let us go back to our discussion of Soviet philosophers. Talented and dedicated Marxists were bound to inherit from the founders of Marxism-Leninism their ambivalent attitude to the issues of morality. The latter categorically denied that morality and ethics were problems in their own right. Lenin in his early (1894) book *The Economic Essence of Narodnichestvo and Its Critique in Mr. Struve's Book* writes:

> One cannot but agree with Zombart's assertion that "Marxism from beginning to end does not contain a grain of ethics": in theoretical terms he makes the "ethical point of view" subordinate to "the principle of causality"; in practical terms he reduces it to "class struggle." (Lenin 1958, 440–441)

However, later when he became the leader of the state and had to deal not with a comparatively narrow circle of revolutionaries, but with the population of the whole country, Lenin recognized morality. Yet this morality was of a very special kind. In his famous speech at the Congress of the Komsomol (Young Communist League) in 1920, Lenin said that communist morality existed (and bourgeois accusations of communist immorality were therefore false), but at the same time Communists rejected morality in a certain sense:

> In what sense do we reject morality, reject ethics? In the sense it was preached by the bourgeoisie which derived morality from God's bidding. To this we say, of course, that we do not believe in God and know very well that the clergy, the landowners and the bourgeoisie spoke on behalf of God in order to further their exploitative interests. We reject any morality that is not derived from human and class concepts. We say that this is cheating, deception and befuddling of the minds of the workers and peasants in the interests of the landowners and capitalists. We say that our morality is entirely subordinate to the interests of the proletarian class struggle. Our morality is derived from the interests of the class struggle of the proletariat . . .
>
> For a communist morality is all about cohesive solidarity in discipline and conscious mass struggle against the exploiters. We do not believe in eternal morality and we expose the falsehood of all kinds of tales about morality. (Lenin 1963, 309–313)

Thus, the distinctive feature of communist morality is that the overarching goal to which it is geared is the interests of the proletarian class struggle. In denying the significance of moral problems, Lenin follows Marx and Engels who said that the commonly understood morality was impotence translated into illusory action.

On the other hand, Marxism is a very moralizing doctrine in its intent. It is permeated with moral pathos, the pathos of rejecting exploitation and coercion of other people. It denies morality, so to speak, on moral grounds. Morality interpreted as distinction between good and evil as an end in itself is impotence in the eyes of Communists because such distinction, they believed, precluded active struggle against oppression and exploitation.

* * *

In the approach to morality and moral problems of Soviet-era philosophy one can (roughly) identify two lines. The first is Hegelian and it was much closer to Marxism. It is represented by such original philosophers as György Lukács and Evald Ilyenkov. The other line gravitates more toward Kant than to Hegel (to varying degrees, from moderate sympathy in the case of Oleg Drobnitsky to almost total acceptance by mature and later Merab Mamardashvili). The second line arose and gained momentum against the background of growing disenchantment with orthodox Marxism.

For the adherents of the Hegelian line, morality is not an end in itself. It is the object of "sublation" within a wider whole on which it depends, namely, social practice. For example, Ilyenkov in his book *On Idols and Ideals* distinguishes real relations among people from subjective morality and calls them after Hegel, "*nravstvennost*" (which is usually rendered in English as "ethical order"). According to Ilyenkov, it is the sphere of practical, real human activities. The only way to make Man truly moral is to make life circumstances, and the entire order of human society, genuinely moral.

Ilyenkov believes that morality is part of the ultimate general category of the ideal, which is also marked by a duality which he ascribes to all ideal phenomena. On the one hand, the ideal is the main problem for Ilyenkov, the central meaning of all his philosophical quests. On the other hand, he is forced by the logic of Marxism to deal with the problem of the ideal in such a way as to put it in a subordinate position and to speak only about its "relative independence." Morality, being "abstract," is subject to "sublation" in concrete social practice. Under Communism, Ilyenkov argues, after the gap between "what should be" and "what is" is removed, to be moral would be as natural as to wash oneself in the morning (Ilyenkov 2006, 275). It is a version of earthly bliss, the Kingdom of God on Earth when Good at last becomes real.

These ideas were shared by Lukács who believed that morality would become the true "regulator of reality" only in Communist society. There are many interesting episodes involving Lukács in connection with this theme. His path to Marxism and Marxist interpretation of morality was tortuous and difficult. Suffice it to say that shortly before he joined the Communist Party of Hungary, just days before it, Lukács wrote an article "Bolshevism as a Moral Problem" in which he explained why he cannot and does not want to be a Bolshevik. He seems to be trying to persuade himself. The article gives a strong impression that he wants to be a Communist, but at this point in time considers such a path to be a temptation. Lukács writes that Bolsheviks believe that it is possible through evil and violence, at one mighty stroke, to pass on to Good, "to break through to the Truth," as one of Dostoevsky's characters in the *Brothers Karamazov* puts it. Lukács considers this to be ethically unacceptable. He argues that the right way is that of the so-called "prolonged labor." This is the path of real and incremental improvements, and not a leap into the bright future inevitably involving bloodshed and violence. Nonetheless, he decided to write the article, and several days later joined the Hungarian Communist Party to become one of its leaders.

Although Lukács cannot be strictly regarded as a Soviet philosopher, he was a Soviet-era philosopher only in the broadest sense. He had lived in the Soviet Union for 15 years. His philosophy has much in common with that of Ilyenkov. They think along the same lines in many ways in that they understand dialectics to be the essence of philosophical Marxism, both adhere to Hegelianism, and criticize Stalinism from the humanistic perspective.

The key feature of Lukács' Marxism, its hidden core, is its inherently moral quality. It manifests itself, among other things, in his conviction, articulated in his article "The Role of Morality in Communist Production," that Communism will be a kingdom of genuine morality and genuine freedom. So strong is his belief in the natural rationality of the world and Man, in the possibility of building a just society here on Earth that he believes humanity will inevitably end up being totally moral:

> The ultimate goal of Communism is to build a society in which, in regulating human activity, freedom-based morality would supplant coercion-based law. As any Marxist knows, a necessary prerequisite of such society is final elimination of division into social classes. For if we ask ourselves whether human nature allows of a morality-based society (an incorrect formulation of the question, in my opinion) then even if the answer is strictly positive one has to bear in mind that the power of morality cannot be established as long as society is divided into classes. (Lukács 2008, 106–107)

Thus, Communists put morality on hold during the period of revolutionary transformation to assure its triumph in the future society. As Vladimir Mayakovsky put it, revolution is the last and main war in which it is allowable to resort to amoral means if the need arises. Of course, Communists and Communist philosophers were particularly sensitive to the issues of good and evil and to moral issues. The question is what metamorphoses moral principles were undergoing under the pressure of revolutionary logic. In his unpublished notes about Dostoevsky, Ilyenkov says that it is hard to think about the principles of humanism during a bayonet charge, and that Dostoevsky would be relevant as long as socialism is associated with blood-spilling and violence (Novokhat'ko 1997, 7). Incidentally, unlike Ilyenkov, Lukács himself practically took part in bayonet charges. During the several months in 1919 when the Soviet Hungarian Republic existed, he was Deputy People's Commissar of Education (and de facto head of the People's Commissariat, or ministry). On one occasion, when he was sent to the front as a commissar, he ordered every tenth soldier from the unit that had succumbed to fear and fled from the battlefield to be shot.

Revolutionary philosophers and poets were sensitive to the beauty of the old world, the beauty of pristine human feelings. Sometimes this sense came to them in the intervals between bayonet charges. Here is what a Young Communist poet Jack Altausen wrote about Karamzin's *Poor Lisa* in his 1929 poem "Ballad of Vetluga."

Yesterday there was a battle,
All around were grey swords.
Brigade commander with a disfigured face
Waved his sleeve.
I hacked to death
An officer in a ditch.
In his side pocket
I found a book
In a yellow binding,
Written by a Karamzin.
Two swallows alight on
A machine-gun barrel,
And my carbine lies in the bushes.
Zhurbenko, stop clinking
With your spoon.
Gooseberry is flowering,
Elder trees are in bloom.
Let us read,
Let us read and weep
Over this book of Karamzin's.
My friends,
Tomorrow we'll gallop into battle,
The bayonet is sharp,
The gun is loaded.
But now
We weep over a girl
Deceived a hundred years back.

The hero of the poem, a Red cavalry man, found Nikolai Karamzin's story *Poor Lisa* in the pocket of a White officer he had killed with his sword, started reading it . . . and wept over the fate of a girl deceived a hundred years ago. A powerful move, a stark contrast between the description of a fierce battle and a sudden pang of pity for a girl deceived a so long ago. Incidentally, Altausen was the poet who wrote almost Herostratus-like words about Minin and Pozharsky:[1] "They saved Russia/So what?/ Perhaps it would have been better if they hadn't." He died for Russia at the front in 1942. Is it not one of the paradoxes of history?

Nevertheless, for revolutionary philosophers, morality as a phenomenon which makes it possible to tell good from evil is an abstraction that is worthless because it has no practical force. It cannot change the world for the better, nor can it put an end to suffering in the world. Is it moral to be reconciled to the suffering of other people? This was the question asked by the revolutionaries who were smitten by compassion for other people. However, their compassion when translated into politics paradoxically engendered its opposite: indifference to concrete suffering.

On the one hand, for all the brutality and ruthlessness of their deeds, revolutionaries are extremely compassionate, even sentimental. It was not by chance that Pushkin described Robespierre as "a sentimental tiger." On the other hand, the need for "blood and violence" engendered indifference in the name of lofty goals. In the end it becomes second nature.

Lukács *consciously* considered evil to be permissible in the name of higher goals several years before he joined the Communist party when reflecting on Boris Savinkov's famous novels about terrorists. In his notes for his Dostoevsky book he says that a revolutionary also makes a sacrifice, he sacrifices his soul in order to save the world. According to Lukács, the new revolutionary ethics holds sacred someone who must become a sinner. We are looking at a paradoxical case of a religious atheist. Characteristically, both he and Ilyenkov had started writing a book about Dostoevsky but never finished it. This bespeaks their deep concern about moral issues and a sense that some logical inability to follow their argument through constrains them from being totally upfront about this issue.

The Hungarian Communist Jozsef Lengyel recalled what he had heard from the members of the "ethical" circle that Lukács's admirers had formed. He was startled when they advised him to read extracts about Father Zosima from Dostoevsky's *Brothers Karamzov*. He duly read them, as directed. Then he looked up and said: "All this is very well, and even excellent, but what has all that to do with me?" He also cites other ideas that were mooted in the Lukács circle: "We Communists are like Jews. Our bloody mission is to crucify Christ. But this sinful work is at the same time our mission: Christ becomes God only through his death on the cross, and this is necessary in order to save the world. Hence we Communists take upon ourselves the sins of the world in order to save the world" (Lukács 2008, 48–49).

Closely linked with this ethical vision was a certain ontology and methodology of viewing Being. Lukács understood morality through the prism of dialectics. He said that orthodox Marxism was a method. In the dialectical view, no phenomenon can be deemed to be immutable, it is fraught with its opposite. Its meaning depends on the surrounding context, on the Whole of which it is a part. That attitude was bound to be transferred by Marxists to ethics. There are no eternal values, everything is determined by the interests of class struggle because that struggle in turn underlies all pre-Communist history (with the exception of the primitive forms of society) and constitutes its main law.

Here is a German Communist recounting her conversation with Lukács:

> A distinguished theoretician, probably the brightest brain in Hungarian Communism, at a crucial moment thus answered my question as to whether deception of party members by its leaders was admissible: 'The Communist ethics regards it as the highest duty to adopt the necessity of evil acts. This, he said, was the greatest sacrifice demanded from us: the conviction that evil transmutes itself into good through the dialectic of historical development . . . This Communist sermon is being spread like a secret doctrine by word of mouth until it is semi-officially recognized as the essence of a true Communist, as the sole hallmark of a genuine Communist.' (Dmitriev 2001, 96–97)

Lukács believed that in keeping with the dialectics of history, what is ethically evil could transform itself into ethical good, and that the former is necessary if the latter is to become reality. So, it is not accidental that the problems of dialectics as the main philosophical essence of Marxism, became central to the philosophy of Lukács. Dialectics as the logic of Marxism "admitted" revolutionary evil to the world and justified it because it provided philosophical grounding for this turnaround. This is what helped to unshackle the demons of violence. However, no one dared articulate it aloud and the doctrine remains "oral" and "tacit" without attaining the status of an official doctrine.

Another stunning pronouncement by Lukács is worth quoting. Asked what the secret of his longevity was and how he had managed to live through so much, he replied: "Ich habe keine Seele" ["I had no soul"] (Lifshitz 2002).

What, then, did he have? In Marxism, personality is "an ensemble of social relations." Of course, Lukács had a soul, but he reflected it in the following way: you have to live and act as if you had no soul. His task is to sacrifice it for the sake of new "social relations" and a new society. (Recall that Lukács was also an anti-Stalinist.)

Yuri Pyatakov, a prominent revolutionary and Soviet public figure, said in a moment of frankness that faith in Communism calls for uncompromising violence primarily toward oneself: you have to cast aside your own convictions that may contradict the party line. The Bolshevik must do it although, Pyatakov added, it is a more difficult thing to do than shooting oneself.

* * *

The 1960s and 1970s saw some Soviet authors gradually drifting away from Marxism. They came to believe that moral problems (in many ways) were not reducible to social practice and social interests. They no longer diluted morality entirely in "social practice." They groped for ethics, a discipline that sought to release itself from the grip of class and social pragmatism. Abdusalam Guseinov described it as the definitive period in the history of Soviet ethics.

Drobnitsky with his book *The Concept of Morality* (1974) must take the center stage here. This vast and thoroughly researched work grapples with the definition of morality and ethics in general and attempts to identify its distinctive features. It provides a detailed and perceptive analysis containing many new things compared with the revolutionary-philosophical approach to ethics of Lukács and Pyatakov.

On the whole Drobnitsky finds himself at a crossroads between recognizing the irreducible importance of moral issues of good and evil and their reduction to social structures and historical practice. Following the Marxist tradition, he concedes that morality has a social-historical nature, but at the same time he interprets it in a way that takes it beyond the notion of morality as something derivative that can be violated and ignored. Vladimir V. Bibikhin described the ethics of Drobnitsky, who died an untimely death in an air crash, as Marxist, but sincere and questioning.

Drobnitsky's main interest lay in trying to reconcile or combine the abiding moral distinctions with social being or social interest as well as the Marxist determination of consciousness as general method. "Apparently, man's interests and his moral motives are by no means always opposed to and challenging each other. One morphs into the other and in turn is determined by the other" (Drobnitsky 2002, 15). One way in which he formulates the question is: what is morality and what are its features that make it impossible to reduce it to the rest of human Being? (Drobnitsky 2002, 65). Drobnitsky looks at "the structure and functions of morality in social life" (Drobnitsky 2002, 121), but at the same time sees them as something that is unique and cannot be replaced by anything else. Drobnitsky's book is informed, so to speak, with a yearning or inclination toward irreducible morality. He argues extensively, for example, that morality is ubiquitous, that it is not limited to any specific subject area, but is present in all the spheres of social life, in all types of human relations and all types of behavior (Drobnitsky 2002, 212). He considers it to be a "multi-plane structure," a complex and "multi-dimensional entity that does not lend itself to reduction to any one plane of phenomena" (Drobnitsky 2002, 214). Therefore the question of morality cannot be eliminated or diluted in general sociological problems. Not surprisingly, he writes at length and approvingly about Kant and his moral teaching, while giving much less space and being more critical in his comments on Hegel.

At the same time Drobnitsky in his reasoning resorts to the time-tested Soviet dialectical method of presenting paradoxes or antinomies and subsequently reconciling them. He treats moral commands as simultaneously local and particular and at the same time totally universal. He opposes inner moral phenomena and their sociological determinants only to choose to reconcile the two. Being still a Marxist, he stresses that it is necessary to go beyond morality in order to define it and pinpoint its meaning or definition. He makes a point of stressing that he seeks to steer clear in his definition of the so-called logical circle when morality is defined through moral concepts of good and evil, justice, duty, etc. because these are "precisely the concepts of morality that need to be defined" (Drobnitsky 2002, 220). For him, to talk about morality theoretically is not the same thing as "reasoning from the viewpoint of moral consciousness." Therefore the moral theory should culminate in what he calls hidden moralizing:

> Defining morality presupposes a high degree of abstraction, *theoretical* reflection on the phenomena we face "in life." It should consist in *deriving* disparate phenomena of moral experience (however "evident" and "obvious" they may appear to be in the framework of this experience) from scientific concepts obtained as a result of a very different (extra-moral and extra-mundane) method of cognition of social reality. (Drobnitsky 2002, 215)

In other words, ethics is a theoretical science or discipline like other sciences. Therefore, objective and proof-based knowledge of morality is possible.

Interestingly, however, Drobnitsky chooses as the methodological basis not the Hegelian-Marxist method, of ascending from the abstract to the concrete (hence derivation of morality from social practice) that was advocated by Ilyenkov. He chooses as the methodological basis M. Mamardashvili's work *Analysis of Consciousness in the Works of Marx* in which Marxism is in many ways reinterpreted in the phenomenological vein. On the whole, in my opinion, in his book *The Concept of Morality* Drobnitsky still stops just short of departing from Marxism. Who knows what direction his thought would have taken but for his tragic death in an air crash at the age of 36? However, beginning from around the mid-1970s, many philosophers inexorably move away from Marxism. For example, Mamardashvili. It can be said by a bit of a stretch that the latter marks the next stage in moral-philosophical reflection in Soviet-era philosophy following the revolutionary-dialectical (Lukács, Ilyenkov) stage and the stage of transition from revolutionary-Marxist (Drobnitsky) to an attempt to build autonomous ethics. Mamardashvili takes the next step, as it were, on the way "back to Kant." So I would like to discuss some aspects of Mamardashvili's moral philosophy.

In ethics, Mamardashvili in many ways adheres to Kant's position. For him, morality and moral categories (good, conscience, etc.) are, first, autonomous and not derived from anything: neither from social practice nor from religion. Second, they are formal in the sense that they cannot be interpreted in any positive or meaningful way. That is why he refers to the main moral phenomena as fruitful tautologies. Good is good, it generates good and good deeds, but it is in principle impossible to determine its content, it is captured only by inner intuition that cannot be verbalized.

His interpretation of moral problems is part and parcel of his philosophy of consciousness. He links his ontological concept of consciousness and its structure on the day-to-day level with a certain notion of morality. Incidentally, Mamardashvili is often criticized for not having an ideological core and for, being a Georgian Socrates, improvizing without generating any ideas of his own. That is untrue. He had at least two pivotal ideas which, it has to be said, he varied by using different terms to denote them. In any case, he interpreted consciousness and morality and socio-political problems on the basis of, first, the idea that nothing could replace personal existence and personal effort. He often spoke about non-verbal evidences, a philosophical paraphrase of Luther's "Here I stand, I can do no other," which provides the foundation of human knowledge and morality. However, effort or personal existence are not enough by themselves, they must rest on something. Emphasizing personal or inner effort would appear to be anarchism and voluntarism. Therefore, he adds to it the assertion of the existence of certain intelligible objects, material bodies of culture which generate, form, and support individual human efforts. Mamardashvili used different words to denote these bodies of culture: works, symbols, noogenic machines. However, the lack of terminological uniformity does not change the essence of the notion.

Mamardashvili believed that moral states and acts are only possible on the basis of these two elements. A good deed must arise from a person's inner state (this is, its content) and at the same time doing good requires skill, which is guaranteed by form. Good, Mamardashvili said, is an art (i.e., what he called the form of an act).

It is a feature of Mamardashvili's philosophical views that he linked the possibility of moral behavior with a certain social-political order, a kind of "ideal Europe." For thought and moral states to materialize there needs to be public space (*agora*). Thus, states of consciousness would be discussed and grow as it were, through communication and form "thought muscles." Clearly, *agora* is the civil society, a combination of subjects acting in the legal field. In other words, he considered "ideal Europe" to be a more favorable moral state due to its civil, socio-political order. In that sense he counterposed it to Russia. It is no accident that his work is highly valued by many of our avowed Westernizers and liberals, and he is typically detested by many representatives of, for want of a better word, what I would call the patriotic camp. So, the attitude to Mamardashvili marks a socio-political cleavage: many patriots often consider him to be almost a Russophobe and take a fairly negative view of him, by contrast he commands great respect among the philosophically-minded advocates of the "strictly European vectors of Russia's development."

He also believed that Russian spiritual and socio-political space was afflicted by a certain "infantilism" by which he meant undeveloped personal elements and autonomous social institutions independent from power and the state. He described it as "avoidance of form" allegedly inherent in Russian culture and Orthodoxy in general. Mamardashvili's critique of Russian and Soviet history and Russian mentality was fueled by a powerful "modernizing charge." He said, for example, that the nation should "meet the image and task of civilization" (Mamardashvili 1992, 325), it should be up to modern challenges, etc. But to speak and think along these lines one has to believe in progress and be Euro-centric. For all his critical acuity, Mamardashvili had excessive trust, bordering on utopianism, in modernity as represented by the West, if only as a symbol and an ideal in the head.

In contrast to this ideal world Mamardashvili considered the Soviet world to be an anti-world, a world of ghosts, an anti-life: "When Sovietism dominates, life loses its function. Soviet life is anti-life. I do not recognize myself as being alive, I do not feel life in a single word, sentence, pose or action characteristic of Sovietism. Where there is Sovietism there is no life" (Mamardashvili web). His extremely critical attitude to "Sovietism" covered Russia in general, the entire Russian civilizational and cultural space: "The Russians, wherever they moved—as Cossacks to Baikal area or Kamchatka, they even reached Alaska but, thank God, sold it off in time and it avoided becoming the abomination we would most likely have turned into—wherever they moved, they brought slavery on their backs" (Mamardashvili 1992, 331).

Mamardashvili says: "There has never been a grain of spirituality in the ordinary Soviet man" (Mamardashvili 2000, 321). One feels like asking, really, not a grain? And elsewhere he writes: "The ability of the population of that country to accomplish anything at all can evoke contempt and disgust" (Mamardashvili 2000, 334). That, pardon me, reeks of misanthropy. For all that, Mamardashvili consciously decided against emigrating from the USSR. I have a hunch that if he had left for the West, his judgments would have ceased to be so extreme.

Thus, for Mamardashvili, understanding ethics as an autonomous area (absolute morality not derivable from anything) went hand-in-hand with a fiercely pro-Western attitude. I think that vindicates the statement by another Russian philosopher (belonging to a different trend of thought)—K.N. Leontiev: "This general moral attitude, pure ethics free of any orthodoxy, any mystical influences—is it not the ethics of the selfsame average bourgeois type?" (Leontiev 1993, 128). Indeed, the project of autonomous philosophy that could realize itself in various philosophical schools and trends (phenomenology, the philosophy of science, etc.) became widespread mainly in the Western countries. So phenomenologists or philosophers of science outside Europe often became to varying degrees *Kulturtragers* of Euro-centrism.

The starting point of the project of autonomous philosophy is the individual, Cartesian *cogito*, who tries to derive the ultimate reasons in himself and from himself, from his reason (self-legislating reason in Kantian ethics). In the socio-political realm it is matched by an ideal picture of the civil society where governing one's own life and social reality means self-ordering which must also draw on reasonable and autonomous activity of individuals. However, the utopian character of these ideals and intentions has today become obvious. The onslaught on the individual in the society of abundance and consumerism, which created a gigantic and hard-to-regulate "second nature" is too powerful for the individual to seriously count on his autonomous space which he could reasonably order.

As a result, we see that Mamardashvili's ethical ideal is self-contradictory because while asserting autonomy and lack of prerequisites in the field of morality it is far from being without premises itself. Its requirement of being without pre-existing premises is itself based on its own premises, including social ones.

## NOTES

1. Kuzma Minin and Dmitry Pozharsky were the leaders of the movement against the Polish intervention to Russia in 1612.—Ed.

## BIBLIOGRAPHY


Dmitriev, Alexander N. 2001. *Marxism bez proletariata (György Lukács i rannyia frankfurtskaya shkola 1920s–1930s)* [Marxism without a Proletariat: (György Lukács and the Early Frankfurt School 1920s–1930s)]. St. Petersburg: Letniy sad. Izdatel'stvo evropeiskogo universiteta.

Drobnitsky, Oleg G. 2002. "Ponyatie morali" [The Concept of Morality]. In *Moral'naya filosofiya* [Moral Philosophy], Moscow: Gardariki.

Ilyenkov, Evald V. 2006. *Ob idolah i idealah* [On Idols and Ideals], Kiev: Chas-krok.

Lenin, Vladimir I. 1958. *Polnoe sobranie sochineniy.* Tom 1. [Complete Works, Vol. 1.], Moscow: Politizdat.

Lenin, Vladimir I. 1963. *Polnoe sobranie sochineniy.* Tom 41. [Complete Works, Vol. 41.]. Moscow: Politizdat.

Leontiev, Konstantin N. 1993. "Srednyi evropeets kak ideal i orudie vsemirnogo razrusheniya" [The Average European as an Ideal and Weapon of Worldwide Destruction]. In Leontiev K. N. *Selected Works.* Moscow: Moskovsky rabochiy.

Lifshitz, Mikhail A. 2002. "Lukács." *Voprosy filosofii* [Questions of Philosophy], (12): 232–241.

Lukács, György. 2008. "Kommentirovannye fragmenty rukopisi knigi 'Dostoevsky'" [Commented Fragments of the Book "Dostoevsky"]. In *Lenin i klassovaya bor'ba* [Lenin and Class Struggle]. Moscow: Algoritm.

Lukács, György. 2008. "Rol' morali v kommunisticheskom proizvodstve" [The Role of Morality in Communist Production]. In *Lenin i klassovaya bor'ba* [Lenin and Class Struggle]. Moscow: Algoritm.

Mamardashvili, Merab. K. 1992. *Kak ya ponimayu filosofiyu* [How I Understand Philosophy]. Moscow: Progress.

Mamardashvili, Merab. K. 1995. "Gruzia vblizi i na rasstoyanii" [Georgia Up Close and from a Distance], *Novoe Russkoe Slovo* [A New Russian Word], November 25–26, 8.
Mamardashvili, Merab K. 2000. "Zapisi v ezhednevnike (1968–1970s)" [Diary Notes (1968–1970s)]. In Mamardashvili, M. *Moi opyt ne tepichen* [My Experience is Not Typical]. St. Petersburg: Azbuka.
Novokhat'ko, Alexei G. 1997. "O E.V. Ilyenkove" [About E. V. Ilyenkov]. In Ilyenkov E. V. *Dialektika abstraktnogo i konkretnogo v nauchno-teoreticheskom myshlenii* [Dialectics of the Abstract and the Concrete in Scientific-Theoretical Thinking]. Moscow: ROSSPEN.

CHAPTER TWENTY-FOUR

# The Individual and the Problem of Responsibility: Merab Mamardashvili and Alexander Zinoviev

DANIELA STEILA

During the last few years, the study of Soviet philosophy (or Russian philosophy during the Soviet time, as it is sometimes called) has turned out to be particularly interesting. The opinion that philosophy was completely repressed in Russia during the Soviet era had prevailed in the Western world for decades, but for a few sporadic specialists. Today, however, the consideration of Russian philosophy during the second half of the twentieth century, in its richness and variety, imposes itself on the international scientific community[1]. For a scholar that observes the question from the outside, as a foreign researcher, it is not easy to work on recent authors, since they took part in the life, both public and private, of many contributors to the ongoing discussion. Moreover, it is particularly difficult to deal with authors like Merab Mamardashvili and Alexander Zinoviev, whose works are constantly republished in different editions, and to whom "theory" was always closely related to their lives.

As for the subject of my paper, one might add that probably the moral issue of responsibility is not a crucial theme of Soviet philosophy. Nonetheless, it seems to me that it can provide us with an interesting point of view from which to consider the ethical content that, more or less openly, has been discussed in the Soviet ideological milieu. In November 2011, during an international conference about "Philosophy during the Soviet period," held in Kues, Professor Holger Kuße of the University of Dresden presented a paper on the concepts of "responsibility," "duty" and "righteousness" and their role in the conceptual elaboration of the Soviet time. This paper offered an enlightened account of the subject matter from the linguistic point of view, but, unfortunately, the conference proceedings have yet to be published. By limiting myself to some general observations, I would like to make only a few remarks. It is worth noticing that, in the "official" Soviet language, the word "responsibility" acquired a different meaning from the one common in the

European philosophic tradition, from the theological debate on free will during classical antiquity up to Scholasticism and the Reformation, to the contemporary discussion about the freedom of will in the analytic philosophy of mind. Responsibility is a constitutive dimension of the human personality in the traditional philosophic language, because only she, who is responsible of her deeds, who deliberately takes on herself the weight of her choices[2], can truly be called a "person." On the other hand, in the "Soviet" language, the word becomes a *socio-philosophic concept*, as says the classic *Encyclopedic Dictionary of Philosophy* published in 1983, "that reflects the objective, historically tangible character of mutual relationships between person, collective, and society *under the point of view* of the aware realization of mutual needs." And again:

> In the individual, Responsibility forms as a result of *external* needs, which are presented to him by society, class, a certain collective. . . . In the socialist society, where the principle of "all for one and one for all" is asserted, where the free development of each becomes a condition for the free development of all, the relations of responsible dependence become relations that are indeed mutual. The completeness of the responsible individual is realized on the base of his practical participation in the communist construction, and the responsible behavior of the individual toward the society corresponds more and more to his personal efforts. (Ilyichev et al. 1983)[3]

The fourth edition of the *Philosophical Dictionary* published in 1981 openly declares:

> In the communist morality, personal Responsibility includes questions that relate not only to the deeds, but also to the becoming conscious by the individual of the interests of the society as a whole, which is to say, ultimately, the understanding of the laws that regulate the development of history toward the future. (Frolov 1981)

In the "official" vocabulary of the Soviet time, "responsibility" articulates the relationship to the collective: one is responsible before the collective, not before oneself.

But this repositioning of the meaning of the concept of "responsibility" can actually drift into the progressive weakening of that meaning, ending in its systematic denial. With Michael Kirkwood's words: "'Collective' responsibility encourages personal irresponsibility" (Kirkwood 1988, 52). If responsibility is a personal matter, the individual will be committed without needing external judges or sanctions; if it depends ultimately on the collective, *seeming* responsible will be more important than *being* responsible. Discharging responsibility on others will be more important than accepting it for oneself[4]. The word "responsible" ceases to designate a moral quality, and begins to indicate the social acknowledgment of hierarchical relevance. The expressions "responsible official" of the party, "responsible agency," or "responsible post" come into use. But, as Zinoviev writes in *The Yawning Heights*: "The expression 'responsible post' is stupid since all posts are irresponsible"

(Zinoviev 1978, 41). As Mamardashvili has pointed out in more than one occasion: "Systematically declining any responsibility was a typical trait of the *homo sovieticus*" (Mamardashvili 1991, 62). According to Mamardashvili, two elements could be recognized in the conscience of the *homo sovieticus*: "First of all, never *on one's own* (which is to say, at one's own risk—and responsibility), but always *together*. And secondly, never today, but always *tomorrow*" (Mamardashvili 1992b, 137).

Both our philosophers bestowed, however, a great value upon the possibility of the individual to establish herself as the master of her own deeds and choices, which is why my personal dignity and my integrity depends completely and exclusively on me, regardless of the context.

This theme is certainly present in Mamardashvili, although it probably isn't his most typical and original trait from the theoretical point of view (as the theme of conscience is, for instance). Many of those who have written about him in the last few decades have underlined that the themes of "freedom, responsibility, honor and dishonor" had a particular role in Marmardashvili's philosophical constructions (Ryklin 2009, 153; Motroshilova 2007, 6; Guseynov 2011, 15). These are exactly the themes that exert a relevant influence on the Soviet and Russian public. A witness to the first class that Mamardashvili held in Tbilisi remembers: "he talked exactly of what tormented me: of the human person, of its responsibility and freedom" (Kruglikov 1994, 235).

At first sight, attributing to Zinoviev a reflection upon this theme could seem problematic. In his writings, the word "responsible" mostly applies to "power": "responsible comrades of the Agencies" and "responsible officials of the apparatus" (Zinoviev 1991a, 15, 125). But, beyond this fundamental meaning of the word, the structure itself of personal responsibility, as an undertaking upon oneself of one's deeds and therefore a claim of autonomy, finds an almost paradigmatic expression in Zinoviev's "theory of life."

Furthermore, both Zinoviev and Mamardashvili, although in different ways and measures, confronted the question of responsibility not only in their philosophical meditations, but also in the orientation of their lives. What Mamardashvili wrote of philosophers in general can actually be applied to both these philosophers. We are interested in philosophers' living and concrete thought, in their *personal experiments*, and not only in their abstract formulas. We are interested in the real experience of the philosophers, "where a real personal experiment, which remains as the invention of a life form, has been realized in one's own flesh and blood, in one's own body, putting one's life at stake" (Mamardashvili 1994). Also Zinoviev often emphasized that his *theory of life* is valid for everyone, singularly, beginning with one's personal experience, with the *experiment*—this is the formula that he often uses—that one had a mind to carry out on one's own life. In the preface to his novel *Go to Golgotha*, the author explains that, once the inescapability of life's conditions is accepted, "I decided that how the given society is not so important as it is how I must become in this society's conditions, according to my representations of the ideal man" (Zinoviev 2006a). On the subject of himself, Zinoviev often declared that, starting from 1939 (the year of his first substantial anti-Stalin gesture that cost him the expulsion from the institute, the psychiatric clinic and Lubjanka), he had understood that "an ideal society as the one I dreamed of does not exist and is never going to." And he made the decision: "I accept the Soviet society as it is, and I bestow upon myself as a task to make an ideal society of myself only. I decided to become that person who corresponds to my ideal. I began my experiment. And my whole life has been that experiment" (Zinoviev 2007, 25). The experiment, as Guseynov has synthesized in many occasions, consists of "being a person, in spite of everything; being a person in the middle of the abomination of reality."[5] Furthermore, it cannot but be an individual experiment: "The moral programs have to become unique, as every human person is unique" (Guseynov 2008b, 69).

I have no intention of urging any possible similarity between the positions of these two philosophers (although almost anything could be demonstrated by matching some quotes of theirs). Much more modestly and, I hope, with better reason, I would like to outline briefly Mamardashvili's and Zinoviev's positions, in order to show that for both that, although in a different manner, within the Soviet context (and not only) personal salvation is possible only if the individual consciously accepts his constitutive role in the world, if he becomes the legislator of his own sovereign state.

I will not insist here on the entwining of biographies, on the fact that Zinoviev has been considered to be Mamardashvili's "master"[6] to some extent, or that this latter has been the model for "The Thinker" in *The Yawning Heights*.[7] I will consider what results from their works, as they have expressed their ideas and talked about themselves. But, starting from here, two moments can be extracted from their lives and activities that clearly show an essential difference between the two. Firstly, although there is a difference of only eight years between them (Zinoviev was born in 1922, Mamardashvili in 1930), they belonged to two different generations. It was the different experience of the war that divided them: Zinoviev fought in the war serving in the Soviet Army, while Mamardashvili attended school in Tbilisi. Speaking of that time, Erikh Solovyov said that in the universities during the 1950s "'fathers' and 'sons' winded up at the same desk; as for their age, they differed from each other only as elder and younger brothers. The father-brothers were those who had gone through the experience of the war" (Solovyov 2010, 308).

Secondly, just during those years, Mamardashvili, who had been brought up in a family of no humble origin (his father was in the military, his mother was a noblewoman), found himself in a "peripheral" environment, not only geographically. In Tbilisi, in the local library, he could read the French classics (Montaigne, La Boetie, Montesquieu, and Rousseau) that had accidentally escaped the censorship, and he began his education of "citizen of the world." He had rather somber memories of the school. There he had not learned anything, it was only necessary to learn by heart a textbook of Marxist-Leninist philosophy and "repeat [it] word by word during the test" (Mamardashvili 1992a, 72–73).

On the contrary, Zinoviev, who had been born in a rather poor family in the Muscovite region, was built as a person in the Soviet school of the Stalin time, and he judged this experience positively through his whole life. He never renounced to the ideals that were explained during the lessons, even though they sound grandiloquent now. According to Zinoviev, the education received in the Soviet school of the 1930s was excellent. There, knowledge and love for the great literature were relayed and "the best that had been produced by the pre-revolutionary Russian pedagogy" (Zinoviev 2007, 140) was preserved. About his experience and his family, Zinoviev wrote: "I received an excellent education thanks to the Soviet power. We left a boring life in the country and we moved to the city. I became a professor, my brother a colonel, another brother a bank executive. This is not so easy" (Zinoviev 2007, 49). Zinoviev stated with pride: "I think of myself as a product of the Soviet system. I am a Soviet man!" (Zinoviev 2007, 142). And in another place:

> I was born after the revolution and I grew up in Soviet Russia. We have been brought up to the best communist and revolutionary ideals. . . . I grew up as an ideal communist. Or, as we used to say, "a real communist," which is not just a "member of the party who makes a career," but a Communist with a capital C. (Zinoviev 2007, 20; 24)

But, because of this, he soon understood that reality did not correspond to the ideals in the least:

> When I was still a boy of fifteen or sixteen . . . I came to the conclusion that, if everyone would have been a real communist, life would have been right, pure, honest. But in reality there was nothing of the sort. In reality people stole, mugged, reported each other. In other words, the absolute opposite was happening. This is where the problem lay. (Zinoviev 2007, 25)

In the name of these same ideals, Zinoviev became an anti-Stalinist as a boy, and then a merciless analyst of communist reality, but also, later, a fierce critic of the *perestroika*, of post-Soviet Russia and of the Occidental world as well[8].

Although they were deeply different from one another, both Zinoviev and Mamardashvili were much more than eminent philosophers. They represented two complex cultural "phenomena." Without a doubt Mamardashvili represented an interesting "phenomenon" of Soviet culture during the 1960s, 1970s and 1980s. Although, during the 1970s, he was denied the possibility of holding any regular classes, and he began to wander from one non-philosophic institution to another (Motroshilova 2011a, 28), Mamardashvili had an audience of his own and the public that was loyal to him began to move with him from place to place. The director Alexander Sokurov witnesses that Mamardashvili's lectures were an event not only for the institution that hosted them, but for the whole city (Sokhurov 1991). His thought was never easy to take in, his statements seemed often obscure. Nonetheless, his lectures turned into social events that were attended by "the whole of Moscow" (Volkova 2011, 282); this occurred in every city where he happened to hold a seminar. Zinoviev too intervened successfully by holding lectures "that turned into *sui generis* concerts" (Zinoviev 2007, 208), and he achieved a huge international accomplishment as a writer (his novel *The Yawning Heights* is translated into thousands of languages). In Russia, during the *"katastrojka"* years (as Zinoviev called the end of the 1980s and the early 1990s), he became, mostly because of his copious interviews[9], "the only commendable author for many people, for he provided an analysis of the situation in Russia in a mercilessly harsh and extremely ferocious and brave manner" (Barashev 2008, 132). Probably, it was his uncompromising critical severity and his reputation of "natural contrarian" (*principial'nyj voprekist*), according to A. A. Guseynov's words (Guseynov 2008b, 68), that prevented him from really turning into a mass leader.

Both Zinoviev and Mamardashvili were strikingly original thinkers. Since the university years, his colleagues jokingly called Mamardashvili's *Weltanschauung* (in Russian *mirovozrenie*) *"merabozrenie,"* Merab's own *Weltanschauung*. In his turn, Zinoviev's theory was often defined *"zinovyoga"*: such an original thought to deserve an eponym (Geller 2008, 213; Guseynov 2008c, 338, 347). Both these philosophers expressed their theories with originality of forms, of language, and of style too. Zinoviev's literary forms and linguistic mixture have been the subject of many a writing.[10] It will be sufficient here to underline the "unveiling" to which Zinoviev systematically subdues the "official" language in his novels, his short stories, his sociological writings, his poetry, his interviews, thus always showing the swerve between the literal meaning of the words and their actual meaning. So, for example, in the novel *Go to Golgotha*, regarding the party and the government, which "teach men to live for society, for the people's good," he adds caustically: "How can the people live for the people's good?!" (Zinoviev 2011, 18). Or, in *Notes of the Nightwatchman* he analyzes the expression "superior considerations": "'Superior considerations' is the formula of the agencies' arbitrary will and of superior individuals upon the inferior."[11]

Mamardashvili's language, which evokes associations and emotions, is apparently the opposite of the rigor and dryness that characterize Zinoviev's language. Nonetheless, also Mamardashvili emphasized systematically his distance from the dead language of the authority. Ju. A. Shrejder has pointed out in regard of this matter that "he once said that it is very important, in the act of philosophizing, to free oneself from the current linguistic meaning, in order to generate philosophic meaning" (Shrejder 2010, 560). Mamardashvili believed that, in the time of a few decades, language as a creative storage of forms and structures of knowledge and experience (as he conceived language itself) had been systematically destroyed in the Soviet Union, and a dead, deformed, and dry pseudo-language had taken its place. A "dead" language generates "dead" individuals, unreal ghosts, "zombies," who live in the space of an overturned world, the world "beyond the mirror."[12] According to Mamardashvili, in order for the mortal strength of ideology to work, it was not necessary that people believe in it. The destruction of the linguistic space was enough: "People now may disbelieve in every word of any ideology, but if they are made to exist only in a space that is given by certain material symbols, then they cannot think on the basis of these symbols, not because it is forbidden, but because the fundamentals of the language have been destroyed."[13]

When Mamardashvili suggested to his audience a live example of authentic language, independent of official rhetoric, this was for him not only a theoretical gesture, but also an ethical one. He wanted to guarantee the action of language as a "form of life"; he wanted language to produce authentic human experiences, problems and discussions.

Such have been two eminent thinkers, two very interesting cultural "phenomena" in the difficult context of Soviet experience. What then are their considerations on the theme of personal responsibility as a constitutive element of human personality?

In Mamardashvili, as has been said above, the theme is treated openly. Erikh Solovyov has even defined his late thought "soteriology," which is to say doctrine of salvation: "The traditional existential problem of how a human being can stay himself, or find himself, reaches in Merab an extreme tension; it turns into the question of how not to die here, during life" (Solovyov 2010, 311).

In Mamardashvili's philosophy this is a really important problem. We become persons (which is not at all natural, because a person is a cultural phenomenon, not a natural one) when we are capable of referring to cultural forms, which are the foundation and the horizon of our existence as persons in the world (Mamardashvili 1992b, 193–194). But the forms of culture are a human realization, and thus need, in order to continue to exist, an uninterrupted effort from the human being: they are alive only when the human being who produces them is present (Mamardashvili 2012, 21–22). Therefore, every person, by consciously entering a cultural tradition, takes upon herself the responsibility both of herself and of that tradition. Mamardashvili clarifies that he means here "responsibility in the metaphysical sense of the word" (Mamardashvili 2010, 52).

Thinking is possible only in the context of a traditional culture. Without it, a human being is "naked." "But being naked—adds Mamardashvili—is useful to the utopists-experimenters" (Mamardashvili 1992b, 194). According to Merab Kostantinovich, Soviet power has been maintained for decades thanks to the destruction of culture, and therefore to the destruction of persons. As I have said before, this was already noticeable in language. Its impoverishment, according to Mamardashvili, acted contagiously in the whole country:

> In human beings who find themselves face to face with reality, this is cause for a dulling of the senses and of perceptions. Human beings are formed who can look at an object without seeing it, who can look at human sorrow without feeling it. (Mamardashvili 1992b, 203)

Kafka has described very well the conditions of the overturned world: they "are in every way similar to the human conditions, but they are actually beyond the human being; they only imitate that, which is, in fact, dead" (Mamardashvili 2011, 14). People have found themselves in such a situation during the Soviet time, when everything was dead, twisted, and false. In this "world of dead ghosts" everything was inexistent and unreal (Mamardashvili 1991, 50). Dead is that which "cannot be different" But, if human beings are made to live their whole life in a dead world, a real "anthropological catastrophe" is bound to happen, because, for men, full of "passion for their consciences," "the most terrible punishment is to suddenly feel and gain a conscience of themselves as an imitation of life, or as puppets that someone else is steering by their wires, leaving them to feel like zombies" (Mamardashvili 2012, 546). The whole of Soviet culture was established on this.

During the last few years of his life, Mamardshvili observed with suspicion and severely criticized the nationalistic exaltation that was developing in Georgia and that seemed to him a new victory of the "dead" language over the alive one. As Mikhail Ryklin has pointed out, in present Russia, "the place of Soviet culture has been intentionally taken . . . by nationalism and religious fundamentalism. As a result, the enlightened project, on which the philosopher was insisting so passionately, was once again threatened" (Ryklin 2009, 158). Or, as a supporter of the first Georgian president Z. Gamsakhurdija said, "we do not need any enlightenment, we need patriotism" (Mamardashvili 2012, 552). In Tbilisi, where Mamardashvili had moved, he was accused many times of betraying the Georgian cause, but he still continued to go against the tide. Although he was under the strong pressure of the nationalists, he persisted in saying two weeks before he died, "I do not fight against the Georgian language, but against what is now being said in this language. I do not want a faith; I want liberty of conscience" (Mamardashvili 1991, 8).

In the Soviet Union, the transition to the post-totalitarian era would lead only to the "free manifestation of interior impediments and malformations" (Mamardashvili 2011, 252). Instead, "moral, ethics, philosophy, culture are physics, muscles, ability" (Mamardashvili 2012, 273), that must be practiced daily for the civil society to appear and to be preserved. In order to become a real citizen, a human being must take upon herself the responsibility of her deeds. She must become a person.

Although Mamardashvili realized the heavy consequences of the dominion of Soviet ideology that influenced the citizens' capacity to think in an autonomous and critical manner, he believed that this could not be invoked in any way as a defense. The moment of personal responsibility is necessary in order to become an authentic human being, a person. Mamardashvili talks about it with extreme clarity:

> This elusive moment of the human being, which I have called the final point of responsibility, that nobody can get involved with (no education, no influence, no training), also is, on one side, the most repressed moment of twentieth century society, and, on the other side, it is the one we most feel deprived of, but it is necessary to us; we cannot live without it. (Mamardashvili 2012, 144)

Existentialism has rightly maintained that human beings are responsible for everything they are and do *here and now*, without leaning on their nation, their society, their class or education as an excuse (Mamardashvili 2012, 236–238). According to Mamardashvili, everyone must act immediately *here* and *now*, bearing responsibility for every deed, without hiding behind a divine will or behind history's inexorable laws. In 1988 he declared: "First of all, we must turn our irresponsible world into the world of responsibility, where good and bad can be *given a name*, and where the concepts of 'punishment' and 'atonement', 'sin' and 'repentance', 'honor' and 'dishonor' make sense and exist" (Mamardashvili 1992b, 196).

In Zinoviev's works, the theme of personal moral responsibility is less explicit, but equally relevant. As it is already known, according to Zinoviev, the starting point of any disenchanted consideration of reality is the analysis of what is there, carried out with the attitude of a zoologist who studies an anthill. The laws for living together, which Zinoviev sometimes calls "social," sometimes "communalist" (Zinoviev 1978, 52–56; Zinoviev 1981), have the same naturalness and unavoidability of natural laws; they represent the foundation of communal life, without any indication of value. Here are some examples from Zinoviev himself: "less give and more take; less risk, more profit; less responsibility, more kudos; less dependence on others, greater dependence of others on myself" (Zinoviev 1978, 53). It would be wrong to value these rules according to the criteria of morality and immorality. They are neither moral nor immoral, because they belong to the "natural" sphere, so to speak, of communal life. Humans cannot but accept them as a fact of their existence in society "as a natural social environment" (Zinoviev 2011, 28).

Civilization, according to Zinoviev, is built to escape these fundamental laws. Human beings develop "institutions that counter these laws and limit them" (Zinoviev 1981). "In the end, the whole history of civilization has been the history of the limitation of the spontaneity of the communitarian principle" (Zinoviev 2007, 18). And again: "Human progress has mostly happened as a process of invention of the means that limit and rule the action of these laws: morality, right, religion, the press, the public opinion, the ideas of humanism etc." (Zinoviev 1981).

Zinoviev believes that human beings are not just a "natural" phenomenon, that they are not just animals among other animals. They become actually human by turning the world of given things and relations into a world of their own, specifically "human" (Skvorcov 2008, 268; Guseynov 2004, 10). Human freedom, ethics, responsibility are not at all "natural" neither in nature nor in society. On the contrary, they are born, in Guseynov's words, "firstly, as a manner of personal-individual existence and, secondly, beyond the limits of sociality, as a deviation from its laws" (Guseynov 2008a, 17). In Zinoviev's last monumental work, *The Factor of Cognizance*, which was published after his death, he insists heavily on the transition of human beings from nature to culture and their specific existence only at this second level, starting from the elaboration of an apparatus of signs, which is not "biologically innate in humans" and "does not pass from one generation to the next one as biological heritage," although it is rooted in the biological structure of humans, in the brain and in the sensory apparatus. The element that represents the transition to the truly human level of evolution can be summarized, according to Zinoviev, with the word "consciousness": "Human beings detached themselves from the animal world and they formed a qualitatively new level of the evolution of living matter thanks to consciousness and conscious behavior" (Zinoviev 2006b, 187). As Guseynov has summarized:

> Human beings do not only live by doing this or that deed; they are also capable of answering for why they do them. They are capable of comprehending. Comprehension is the factor that allows human beings to have an influence on their life, to bestow upon it the dignity of a responsible existence.
>
> — Guseynov 2008b, 66

As humanity has learned to escape gravity by building airplanes, without canceling gravity itself, but acting within its limits, so human beings "create the ideal society within themselves to escape the yoke of society, and they can do it by staying in the society and by using it" (Guseynov 2008c, 355–356). Though for Zinoviev, this is never a stable acquisition of humanity. This seems to me to be very important: the overcoming of the laws of "communitarianism" can only be accomplished by the single individual, *here* and *now*.

This has two important implications. On the one hand, it means that aiming for supreme social ideals does not imply at all that it is possible to achieve them on a large scale. A clear example of this, according to Zinoviev, is Soviet society:

> Soviet ideology has tried to build an ideal, highly moral man on a large scale. . . . The experiment has failed. The natural qualities of human beings and the qualities that developed in them in the experience of practical life and by any kind of negative influence resulted stronger than those that were inserted artificially. (Zinoviev 2003, 174)

The meticulous analysis of the *homo sovieticus* shows how a system where a person is "only a partial function of the collective" (Zinoviev 1991a, 198) "ends up relentlessly and unavoidably crushing people" (Geller 2008, 213) instead of achieving its high ideals.

On the other hand, though, the fact that the overcoming of the laws of "communitarianism" can only happen in the single individual means that the system can bend the individual as much as it wants, but the individual will always have the possibility of acting according to one's own ideals, of being autonomous, of becoming legislator of one's own sovereign state. There always is, in any circumstance, the possibility of living in a worthy manner. In the novel *The Yawning Heights*, one of the characters, the Visitor, declares:

> It is by his own desire . . . that man becomes what he is in the moral sense. . . . One cannot become an evildoer by force of circumstance or by ignorance. One cannot be paid to become a decent man. If a man is a rogue it is because he wanted to become one and has striven toward that end. Man himself bears the full responsibility for his morality. Anyone who takes this responsibility away from man is immoral. (Zinoviev 1978, 407)

It is evident that, through this character, Zinoviev ascribes to everyone the full and total responsibility for what one is, for what one chooses to be. In the short story *Temptation*, he writes:

> Everything was clear to us since school. Maturation is only the choice of the path. And we choose it in full awareness. The responsibility of their deeds cannot be taken away from human beings by unburdening the guilt on the environment, on the education, on the situations. Education is not only constriction but voluntary choice too. The most part chooses the path of the adaptation to circumstances. Only exceptional individuals suffer the torment of comprehending the way things are and the sense of the injustice of what happens. They too choose this trail voluntarily. (Zinoviev 1991b)

Everyone is presented with the choice between living by adapting to the requests of the environment, thus getting some practical advantages and some recognitions, and living according to the laws of one's own sovereign state, coherently with one's own principles. Zinoviev believes that the choice is always each one's responsibility.

Zinoviev has written of himself:

> Generally, I have followed my principle during my whole life: do not pursue a career, do not renounce your principles for material advantages. I have kept to this road. But when I am asked whether this road is good for others, I answer: no, it is not good for many. (Kozhemjako 2009, 79)

Zinoviev's "theory of life" is not for everyone. The choice of life is necessarily personal, and this not only in the commonplace sense that each person chooses singularly, but also because, in a deeper sense, it is this choice that constitutes one as a person. I once again take the liberty of referring to Guseynov's words in this respect:

> The theory of life is the theory of how to become a person. How to be a person not when you hold a privileged position in the society, you have a servant, you live in your own house, you are guarded by the police etc., but when you have nothing of all this. (Guseynov 2008c, 358)

The problem of "how to live" is first of all psychological and ethical, not political:

> It is a personal problem. To a human being, the world is first of all constituted by himself. Here, in your head, is your world. How you evaluate your behavior: this is what matters. When I say that I am a state, I see a state in every human being. Each man is a universe; he is an entire cosmos. . . . To take responsibility before your own world! This is the main thing. (Kozhemjako 2009, 78–79)

The individual is a sovereign state because she is the autonomous legislator of herself, and consequently she is responsible for what she is and what she does. It is not surprising that Zinoviev's ethics has been compared to Kant's (Skvorcov 2008, 269–270). Unlike Mamardashvili, Zinoviev does not discuss Kant directly, and he generally does not often explicitly mention his relation with the philosophical tradition. But, during one of his last interviews, he acknowledged that his ideal of human being, "the civil man, the idealist man, the utopian man, the naive man, the unpractical man, the not selfish man, the disinterested man," is the same of which "dreamt and wrote Rousseau and Locke, Hobbes and Descartes" (Zinoviev 2007, 229–230). Kant's name does not appear, but it is really difficult not to think of Kant when Zinoviev insists on the absoluteness of ethics and on the autonomous "sovereignty" of the I that legislates herself. In the novel *The Yawning Heights*, for example, is written:

> The assessment of acts as good or bad is absolute. . . . Anyone who insists on the relativity of good and evil, i.e. on some relationship between the morality of actions and the circumstances in which they are performed, is *a priori* negating morality. (Zinoviev 1979, 407)

So, for Zinoviev, responsibility is essentially responsibility before oneself, but also before what is human in us (which sometimes Zinoviev defines divine, in the sense in which Ivan Laptev, the protagonist of the novel *Go to Golgotha*, believes to be God). Therefore, I think that some rather emphatic expressions of Zinoviev's regarding the responsibility that one can and must take on "for the destiny of the country and of the people" (and, conversely, the critics to the "irresponsible chitchat" of the politicians during the *perestroika*, for example) take on a much more radical and anti-rhetoric meaning. Lastly, the Supreme Court is always that of one's own conscience. In the short story *Temptation*, the protagonist is engaged in this conversation:

> We are responsible before the future generations.
> – Posterity will never appreciate the sacrifices of their ancestors.
> – How they will consider us is their business. We have a duty before our conscience. (Zinoviev 1991b)

The problem of many of his characters and of Zinoviev himself, according to the memories of Ol'ga Mironovna Zinoviev, was "how to live . . . if you want to remain a moral individual" (Zinoviev 2008, 206). This was a problem for Mamardashvili too. Zinoviev chose an extreme coherence of ideas even at the cost of being expelled and of living for a long time as an émigré. Mamardashvili claimed for himself a role not of "martyr," but of critic. In a conversation with Bernard Murchland, he admitted:

> Some of us ended up in a laager, . . . some teaching in the countryside, some have gone into internal exile, and some have taken my path: they have hidden in the shadows, trying to avoid trouble. (Murchland 1994, 194)

He acted as a "spy"—philosopher, and not as a captain on the barricades (Mamardashvili 2011, 210–211). Nonetheless, although they were very different from each other as persons, and therefore as philosophers, they both chose their ways honestly: to act, in spite of everything, in an autonomous, worthy, and free manner in unfree conditions. They reflected on Soviet Russia, but the problem of how to "remain a moral individual" has been important not only during that period and not only in Soviet Russia. The problem of the role of intellectuals and of their relation to authority, be it of any kind, is crucial nowadays as well.

## NOTES

1. See Malakhov 2011, 64.
2. Eshleman 2016, accessed December 28, 2016. https://plato.stanford.edu/archives/win2016/entries/moral-responsibility/.
3. See http://dic.academic.ru/dic.nsf/enc_philosophy/886/ОТВЕТСТВЕННОСТЬ (Accessed July 10, 2018.) On the same web page, the entry of the more recent Ivin 2004 presents a definition that is compliant with the European philosophic tradition: "responsibility is the dependence of a human being from something that is perceived by him as a decisive foundation to make decisions and carry out deeds."
4. According to Zinoviev, one of the principles that regulate cooperative relations is: "Every individual seeks to shuffle off his responsibility on to other people's shoulders" (Zinoviev 1978, 148).

5. Guseynov 2004, 24. See also Mironov 2008, 20; Fursov 2008, 317.
6. In the essay *The Russian Fate*, Zinoviev defines Mamardashvili with these words: "a dear friend . . ., who has been once considered my pupil and follower. Then our paths went two different ways" (Zinoviev 1999, 417).
7. See Zinoviev 1999, 418; Kantor 2008, 230; Mitrokhin 2008, 41–42.
8. See Zinovieva 2008, 172; Kirkwood 1988, 44–46.
9. Zinoviev said of his interviews: "In the West there have been so many that once I answered to a reporter's question on my profession by saying: 'interviewable'" (Zinoviev 2007, 208).
10. For an overlook, see Kirkwood 1993, especially the chapter 2: *Zinoviev's Style and Language*.
11. "This formula means: 1. upstairs they have pondered everything and they made the absolutely rational decision to act exactly this way; 2. this decision is not liable to undergo discussion, and your task is to do, not to think; 3. those who made the decision are responsible for it, but you will suffer punishment if you do not fulfill it" (Zinoviev 1979, 112).
12. See Mamardashvili 2011, 13–15, 23–26, 110–111; Andronikashvili 2011, 186–187; Motroshilova 2011b, 209–210; Motroshilova 1994, 28–29.
13. Mamardashvili 2010, 236–237. According to Zinoviev too, "belief is not a requirement of ideology. As long as people apparently accept it, that is sufficient" (Kirkwood 1988, 55).

## BIBLIOGRAPHY

Andronikashvili, Zaal. 2011. "'Svoja strana', 'Evropa' i 'provincija'—topograficheskie figury svobodnogo i nesvobodnogo prostranstva" ["One's Own Country," "Europe" and "Province": Topographical Figures of Free and Not-Free Space]. In *Merab K. Mamardashvili: Byt' filosofom—eto sud'ba* [Merab K. Mamardashvili: Being a Philosopher is a Fate], edited by Nelli V. Motroshilova, 179–190. Moscow: Progress-Tradicija.

Barashev, Petr P. 2008. "Sverknul kak meteor (Kak Zinoviev prepodaval filosofiju v MFTI)" [He Flashed like a Meteor (How Zinoviev Taught Philosophy in MFTI)]. In *Aleksander Aleksandrovich* Zinoviev, edited by Abdusalam A. Guseynov, 115–132. Moscow: ROSSPEN.

Eshleman, Andrew. 2016. "Moral Responsibility." In *The Stanford Encyclopedia of Philosophy*, edited by Edward N. Zalta (Winter 2016 Edition). Accessed July 10, 2018 at: https://plato.stanford.edu/archives/win2016/entries/moral-responsibility/.

Frolov, Ivan T. (ed.). 1981. *Filosofskij slovar'* [Philosophical Dictionary], fourth edition. Moscow: Politizdat.

Fursov, Andrei I. 2008. "Alexander Zinoviev: Russkaja sud'ba—eksperiment v russkoj istorii" [Alexander Zinoviev: Russian Fate as an Experiment in Russian History]. In *Aleksander Aleksandrovich Zinoviev*, edited by Abdusalam A. Guseynov, 308–336. Moscow: ROSSPEN.

Geller, Mikhail Ya. 2008. "Toska po zone" [Longing for Prison]. In *Aleksander Aleksandrovich Zinoviev*, edited by Abdusalam A. Guseynov, 212–223. Moscow:

ROSSPEN. [Originally published in *Obozrenie. Analiticheskij zhurnal "Russkoj mysli."* 12 (1982).]

Guseynov, Abdusalam A. 2004. "Uchenie o zhitii Alexandra Zinovieva" [Alexander Zinoviev's Teaching on Life]. In Alexander A. Zinoviev. *Idi na Golgofu. Ispoved' verujushchego bezboznika.* [Go to Golgotha. Confession of a Believing Atheist], 4–24. St. Peterburg: Neva.

Guseynov, Abdusalam A. 2008a. "Alexander Zinoviev. Enciklopedicheskaja spravka" [Alexander Zinoviev. Encyclopedical Information]. In *Aleksander Aleksandrovich* Zinoviev, edited by Abdusalam A. Guseynov, 7–18. Moscow: ROSSPEN.

Guseynov, Abdusalam A. (ed.). 2008b. "Myslitel' i chelovek (Materialy "kruglogo stola" zhurnala "Voprosy filosofii")" [A Thinker and a Man (Materials of the "Round Table" at the Journal "Questions of Philosophy")]. In *Aleksander Aleksandrovich Zinoviev*, edited by Abdusalam A. Guseynov, 60–97. Moscow: ROSSPEN. [Originally published in *Voprosy filosofii*. 4 (2007).]

Guseynov, Abdusalam A. 2008c. "Uchenie o zhitii Alexandra Zinovieva" [Alexander Zinoviev's Theory of Life]. In *Aleksander Aleksandrovich Zinoviev*, edited by Abdusalam A. Guseynov, 337–358. Moscow: ROSSPEN.

Guseynov, Abdusalam A. 2011. "Slovo o Mamardashvili" [Some Words about Mamardashvili]. In *Merab K. Mamardashvili: Byt' filosofom—eto sud'ba* [Merab K. Mamardashvili: Being a Philosopher is a Fate], edited by Nelli V. Motroshilova, 12–16. Moscow: Progress-Tradicija.

Ilyichev, Leonid F., Fedoseev, Petr N., Kovalev, Sergej M., Panov, Viktor G. (eds.). 1983. *Filosofskij enciklopedicheskij slovar'* [Encyclopedic Dictionary of Philosophy]. Moscow: Sovetskaja enciklopedija.

Ivin, Alexander A. (ed.). 2004. *Filosofia. Enciklopedicheskij slovar'* [Philosophy. Encyclopedic Dictionary]. Moscow: Gardariki.

Kantor, Karl M. 2008. "Logicheskaja sociologija Alexandra Zinovieva kak social'naya filosofiya" [Alexander Zinoviev's Logic Sociology as Social Philosophy]. In *Aleksander Aleksandrovich Zinoviev*, edited by Abdusalam A. Guseynov, 224–245. Moscow: ROSSPEN.

Kirkwood, Michael. 1988. "Ideology in the Works of A. A. Zinoviev." In *Alexander Zinoviev as Writer and Thinker,* edited by Philip Hanson, Michael Kirkwood, 44–60. London: Macmillan.

Kirkwood, Michael. 1993. *Alexander Zinoviev: An Introduction to His Work.* Basingstoke: Macmillan.

Kozhemjako, Viktor, ed. 2009. *Alexander Zinoviev o russkoj katastrofe. Iz besed s Viktorom Kozhemjako* [Alexander Zinoviev on the Russian Catastrophe. From his Conversations with Viktor Kozhemjako]. Moscow: Algoritm, Eksmo.

Kruglikov, Vitim A. (ed.). 1994. *Kongenial'nost' mysli. O filosofe Merabe Mamardashvili* [Congeniality of Thought. About Philosopher Merab Mamardashvili]. Moscow: Progress-Kul'tura.

Malakhov, Viktor A. 2011. "Opyt soprotivljajushchejsja mysli." [An Experience Resisting Thought] In *Merab K. Mamardashvili: Byt' filosofom—eto sud'ba* [Merab K. Mamardashvili: Being a Philosopher is a Fate], edited by Nelli V. Motroshilova, 64–72. Moscow: Progress-Tradicija.

Mamardashvili, Merab K. 1991. *La pensée empêchée. Entretiens avec Annie Epelboin.* La Tour d'Aigues: Éditions de l'Aube.

Mamardashvili, Merab K. 1992a. "Mysl' pod zapretom. Besedy s A. E. Epel'buen" [The Banned Thinking. Conversations with A. E. Epelboin]. Translated by Tat'jana Ju. Borodaj. *Voprosy filosofii* (4): 70–78; (5): 100–115.

Mamardashvili, Merab K. 1992b. *Kak ja ponimaju filosofiju.* [The Way I Understood Philosophy] 2-oe izd. Edited by Yuri P. Senokosova. Moscow: Progress-Kul'tura.

Mamardashvili, Merab K. 1994. "Filosofiya i lichnost'" [Philosophy and the Person], *Chelovek* (5): 5–19. Available online at: http://www.psychology.ru/library/00044.shtml Accessed July 10, 2018.

Mamardashvili, Merab K. 2010. *Vil'njusskie lekcii po social'noj filosofii* [Lectures on Social Philosophy in Vilnius]. St. Peterburg: Azbuka.

Mamardashvili, Merab K. 2011. *Soznanie i civilizacija* [Consciousness and Civilization]. St. Peterburg: Azbuka.

Mamardashvili, Merab K. 2012. *Ocherk sovremennoj evropejskoj filosofii* [An Essay on Modern European Philosophy]. St. Peterburg: Azbuka.

Mironov, Vladimir V. 2008. "Zhizn' kak postupok" [Life as Action]. In *Aleksander Aleksandrovich Zinoviev*, edited by Abdusalam A. Guseynov, 19–24. Moscow: ROSSPEN.

Mitrokhin, Lev N. 2008. "O fenomene A. A. Zinovieva" [On the Phenomenon A. A. Zinoviev]. In *Aleksander Aleksandrovich Zinoviev*, edited by Abdusalam A. Guseynov, 25–59. Moscow: ROSSPEN. [Originally published in *Voprosy filosofii.* 4 (2007).]

Motroshilova, Nelli V. 1994. "Civilizacija i fenomenologija kak central'nye temy filosofii M. K. Mamardashvili" [Civilization and Phenomenology as Central Themes in M. K. Mamardashvili's Philosophy]. In *Kongenial'nost' mysli. O filosofe Merabe Mamardashvili* [Congeniality of Thought. About Philosopher Merab Mamardashvili], edited by Vitim A. Kruglikov, 17–47. Moscow: Progress-Kul'tura.

Motroshilova, Nelli V. 2007. *Merab Mamardashvili. Filosofskie razmyshlenija i lichnostnyj opyt* [Merab Mamardashvili. Philosophical Reflections and Personal Experience]. Moscow: Kanon+.

Motroshilova, Nelli V. 2011a. "Sociokul'turnyj kontekst 50–80-kh godov XX veka i fenomen Mamardashvili" [Sociocultural Context of the 1950–1980s and the Phenomenon Mamardashvili]. In *Merab K. Mamardashvili: Byt' filosofom—eto sud'ba* [Merab K. Mamardashvili: Being a Philosopher is a Fate], edited by Nelli V. Motroshilova, 19–43. Moscow: Progress-Tradicija.

Motroshilova, Nelli V. 2011b. "Simvolika trekh 'K' (Kartezij, Kant, Kafka) v filosofii Meraba Mamardashvili" [The Symbolism of the Three Ks (Descartes, Kant, Kafka) in Merab Mamardashvili's Philosophy]. In *Merab K. Mamardashvili: Byt' filosofom—eto sud'ba* [Merab K. Mamardashvili: Being a Philosopher is a Fate], edited by Nelli V. Motroshilova, 201–210. Moscow: Progress-Tradicija.

Murchland, Bernard. 1994. "V krugu idej Mamardashvili" [In the Circle of Mamardashvili's Thoughts]. In *Kongenial'nost' mysli. O filosofe Merabe Mamardashvili* [Congeniality of Thought. About Philosopher Merab Mamardashvili], edited by Vitim A. Kruglikov, 177–197. Moscow: Progress-Kul'tura. [Originally published in *The Mind of Mamardashvili. Interview by Bernard Murchland.* Ohio: Kattering Foundation.]

Ryklin Mikhail. 2009. "Soznanie kak prostranstvo svobody. Metafizicheskaja tema u Meraba Mamardashvili" [Consciousness as the Space of Freedom. The Metaphysical Theme in Merab Mamardashvili]. In *Merab Konstantinovich Mamardashvili*, edited by Nelli V. Motroshilova, 153–173. Moscow: ROSSPEN.

Shrejder, Julij A. 2010. "Zagadochnaja pritjagatel'nost' filosofii (sub"ektivnye zametki)" [The Enigmatic Attractiveness of Philosophy (Subjective Remarks)]. In *Kak eto bylo. Vospominanija i razmyshlenija* [The Way it Was. Memories and Reflexions], edited by Vladislav V. Lektorsky, 547–578. Moscow: ROSSPEN. [Originally published in *Filosofiya ne konchaetsja . . . Iz istorii otechestvennoj filosofii. XX vek* [Philosophy Does Not End . . . From the History of National Philosophy. Twentieth Century], edited by Vladislav A. Lektorsky. Vol. II. 171–206. Moscow: Rossijskaja politicheskaja enciklopedija, 1998.]

Skvorcov, Alexander A. 2008. "Sociologija Alexandra Zinovieva: mezhdu logikoj i etikoj" [Alexander Zinoviev's Sociology: Between Logic and Ethics]. In *Aleksander Aleksandrovich Zinoviev*, edited by Abdusalam A. Guseynov, 246–270. Moscow: ROSSPEN.

Sokhurov, Alexander. 1991. "Pamjati Meraba Mamardashvili" [In Memory of Merab Mamardashvili]. *Seans* 3 (1991), http://seance.ru/n/3/mamard_sokurov/ (Accessed July 10, 2018.)

Solovyev, Erikh Yu. 2010. "'Prostornoe slovo avtoritetov'. Beseda T. A. Umanskoj s E. Yu. Solovyevym" ["The Extensive Discourse of Authorities." Conversation of T. A. Umanskaja with E. Yu. Solovyev]. In *Kak eto bylo. Vospominanija i razmyshlenija* [The Way it Was. Memories and Reflexions], edited by Vladislav V. Lektorsky, 307–324. Moscow: ROSSPEN. [Originally published in *Voprosy filosofii*. 4 (2004): 81–91.]

Volkova, Paola D. 2011. "Merab na 'Vysshikh kursakh'" [Merab in the "High Courses"]. In *Merab K. Mamardashvili: Byt' filosofom—eto sud'ba* [Merab K. Mamardashvili: Being a Philosopher is a Fate], edited by Nelli V. Motroshilova, 278–291. Moscow: Progress-Tradicija.

Zinoviev, Alexander A. 1978. *The Yawning Heights*. Translated by Gordon Clough. London: Bodley Head.

Zinoviev, Alexander A. 1979. *Zapiski nochnogo storozha* [Notes of the Night-Watchman]. Lausanne: L'age d'Homme.

Zinoviev, Alexander A. 1981. *Kommunizm kak real'nost'* [Communism as a Reality]. Lausanne: L'age d'Homme. http://www.zinoviev.org/files/zinoviev-kommunism.pdf Accessed December 28, 2016.

Zinoviev, Alexander A. 1991a. *Gomo sovieticus. Para bellum* [Homo sovieticus. Para bellum]. Moscow: Moskovskij rabochij.

Zinoviev, Alexander A. 1991b. *Iskushenie* [Temptation] http://royallib.com/book/zinovev_aleksandr/iskushenie.html Accessed December 28, 2016.

Zinoviev, Alexander A. 1999. *Russkaja sud'ba, ispoved' otshchepenca* [The Russian Fate. The Confession of a Dissident]. Moscow: Centrpoligraf.

Zinoviev, Alexander A. 2003. *Russkaja tragedija* [The Russian Tragedy]. Moscow: Eksmo.

Zinoviev, Alexander A. 2006a. *Idi na Golgofu* [Go to Golgotha]. Moscow: Eksmo. [Available online at: http://royallib.com/book/zinovev_aleksandr/idi_na_golgofu.html]

Zinoviev, Alexander A. 2006b. *Faktor ponimanija* [The Factor of Cognizance]. Moscow: Algoritm; Eksmo.

Zinoviev, Alexander A. 2007. *Ja mechtaju o novom cheloveke* [I Dream of a New Man]. Moscow: Algoritm.

Zinoviev, Alexander A. 2011. *Idi na Gol'gofu. Gomo sovietikus. Rasput'e. Russkaja tragedija.* [Go to Golgotha. Homo Sovieticus. The Crossroads. The Russian Tragedy] Moscow: AST: Astrel'.

Zinovieva, Ol'ga M. 2008. "Alexander Zinoviev: tvorcheskij ekstaz" [Alexander Zinoviev: A Creative Ecstasy]. In *Aleksander Aleksandrovich Zinoviev*, edited by Abdusalam A. Guseynov, 160–211. Moscow: ROSSPEN.

CHAPTER TWENTY-FIVE

# Alexander Zinoviev's Teaching on Life

ABDUSALAM A. GUSEYNOV

Alexander Zinoviev (1922–2006), a key figure in Russian philosophy in the second half of the twentieth century, gained prominence and recognition above all as a logician, social thinker and writer. However, he is also known as a poet and artist[1]. Zinoviev's ethics has received less than its fair share of attention, although in my opinion, and indeed in his own opinion, it is the driving force of his personality development and an important element of his literary and sociological works from *The Yawning Heights* (Zinoviev 1976) to *The Factor of Cognizance* (Zinoviev 2006b). It is distilled in his poems "My Home My Exile" (1983), "A Gospel for Ivan" (1984), the stories "Go to Golgotha" (1985), "Live" (1988) and in his autobiographical work "The Confession of a Dissident" (1989).

Zinoviev's ethical teaching, to which he referred as the "teaching on life" or *Zinovyoga*, does not share the shape of the systematically structured text more typical of the European intellectual tradition. Indeed, one wonders whether it lends itself to such a generalization because its aim is not "to pluck a person out of his habitual way of life, but to improve his life in the framework of the path that fell to his lot." (Zinoviev 2006, 158). The starting point of his reasoning is not an abstract statement assumed as an axiom, but a concrete, living individual. The heroes of the stories "Live" and "Go to Golgotha" have names, which is not normally a feature of Zinoviev's style. In *The Yawning Heights, The Yellow House* and his other sociological novels and stories, the characters as a rule have no names and represent personified functions and social roles: Thinker, Pretender, Brother, Bonehead, Schizophrenic, Chatterbox, etc. In ethically oriented stories the proponents of the author's idea at least have proper names and individual lives. This is not only due to the fact that the subject of morality is a person as distinct from a social subject defined through his belonging to a group. Zinoviev does not claim to have created a universally relevant moral doctrine, believing that ethical programs are always individualized and are within the competence and responsibility of the individual.

Among many of Zinoviev's unorthodox statements, the most unusual one is that he is a sovereign state. This is not a figurative expression, but the principle to which, Zinoviev maintains, he adhered all his life. Those who are baffled by this statement are in for an even tougher mental and moral test because it turns out that Zinoviev is not only an independent state, but also God. Regarding the latter thesis a clarification is in order: it is correct only to the extent that the author can be identified with a literary character which is the mouthpiece for the author's idea. It is a feature of Zinoviev the thinker that he is at his most literal and serious precisely in statements that look at first glance to be incredible, paradoxical, and tongue-in-cheek. The hero's identification of himself with God is an example in point. The thesis merits a close analysis because it brings out the true meaning of Zinoviev's own life formula. In general, the hero of Zinoviev's teaching on life is particularly close to the author, because, as we learn, for example, from autobiographical testimony in *The Confession of a Dissident* (Zinoviev 2008), it was developed by Zinoviev for himself and has guided his life so completely that it can be considered to be an experiment conducted on the teaching.

Thus, the hero of "Go to Golgotha," who is the author surrogate as well as the exponent and preacher of the teaching on life, considers himself to be God. He is God while being a consistent and complete atheist. To him, atheism does not mean the absence of God. It merely means the negation of God. Thereby God is present in some form. "If there is no God, there are no godless people" (Zinoviev 2006, 149). Just like faith in God, understood as separate from the believer, implies doubt about His existence and needs to be bolstered by knowledge (proof of the existence of God), so atheism, being a denial of God, is premised on the existence of God and allows for faith in Him. In only one case is a believer an atheist or, to put it another way, an atheist a believer, and that is if he himself is God. "God cannot believe in His own being because he cannot regard Himself as being something outside Himself" (Zinoviev 2006, 47). At the same time He cannot but believe in His own existence because He exists. There is no solution to the question, how to be a believer without obscurity, as a person living in the era of science, an atheist, or, being an atheist and remaining one, become a believer except the only solution, when man faced with this question is himself God. This is the discovery the hero of the story describes as fundamental: "He is needed precisely because He does not exist and there is no life after death. If He existed, there would have been no need for Him—this is the main paradox of being" (Zinoviev 2006, 72). Truly: Zinoviev is not for the lazy mind.

The hero, as we learn in the early pages of the story, is God owing to infinite loneliness and absolute hopelessness, being doomed to suffering. When a person is unhappy, abandoned by everyone and has nothing to hope for, he may turn to God. This means that he is still not totally abandoned and has not lost all hope. To whom, then, can God turn? He has no one to whom he can turn. When a person is in despair he can hope that his suffering may be relieved by God. But who will give solace to God himself? No-one. This means that when a person is totally alone, without any hopes, when no one and nothing can relieve his suffering, then he is in a position in which only God can find Himself. "To be God means to go to Golgotha" (Zinoviev 2006, 16). Zinoviev approaches the idea of God from a strictly psychological and ethical angle.

Psychologically, a person's considering himself to be God is the supreme degree of personal self-assertion. This self-assertion occurs in two ways. First, in the sense that he lives for himself. This is not to be confused with an individual's selfish concentration on his own interests and benefits. This means total acceptance of life in all its concrete manifestations that are presented to him, an attitude to life as if he were the only living thing. Kant compared the moral law within us to the starry skies above us in which the former is infinitely superior to the latter. Zinoviev's hero says something similar, only in less refined language: "I don't give a damn about Galaxies, stars and societies. For me my life is more important and more interesting than, for example, the evolution of a stellar system worlds away" (Zinoviev 2006, 118). Secondly, in the sense that he himself is the basis of his life. "It's all in you yourselves," says Zinoviev's character paraphrasing Jesus Christ.[2] In an unusual reflection titled "Form of Addressing God" he wonders why it is at all necessary to turn to someone outside ourselves. This, he thinks, is because we are the products of the European-Christian civilization which assumes that man contains substance, the Self. Each of us is a Self from birth and through a number of generations. Unlike, for example, Oriental people, we have no need to concentrate on ourselves to generate and shape a Self within us. "We have it anyway. It is willing outside. We need external props to provide our internal Self with reason" (Zinoviev 2006, 161). A modern, educated, scientifically-thinking European who understands that God does not exist outside him, must engender God within him as an instance that holds back the Self that wills outside and ignores all the odds. Man's faith in God is connected with resolving only such problems whose solution depends entirely on himself. God is the crowning of the human Self. The kind of crowning that reconciles the Self with the world and simultaneously considers himself to be its reformer.

According to Zinoviev, the main function of God is moral. To be God is not a piece of luck, still less a reward. Rather, it is suffering and torment. The individual does not end with God. He only begins with God. God is the beginning. When it is said that somebody is God it only means that he himself determines the program of his existence and lives in the world he himself has created. "Your Self is the way you live . . . the teaching about Self is the teaching about life" (Zinoviev 2006, 164), Zinoviev says through the mouth of his hero. In fact, man can be considered to be God only to the extent that he has his own teaching about life, his own religion. Listen to the reasoning of the hero of the story who lives according to his own system and has the reputation in his city of an all-powerful healer of human bodies and souls: "If God is, by definition, the creature that creates religion, I, according to the definition of the concept of God, am God. What a primitive logical operation, and what a grandiose conclusion" (Zinoviev 2006, 15).

Zinoviev's teaching about life proceeds from the fundamental premise that the world, including human society, is objective. It exists according to its own laws. One can worsen it by improving it, and improve it by worsening it. The world, including oneself as part of it, is to be accepted as a fact, a hard fact no one, not even God, can do anything about. Man may change the attitude to the world and create his own world in or above the real world. Zinoviev's itinerant God from "Go to Golgotha" compares himself and his mission with who Christ was and what He did and thinks of himself as equal to God. Christ, he says, "invented a new world for men . . . I too want to turn people's minds in a different direction" (Zinoviev 2006, 104). In what direction?

First of all, one has to discover one's soul as a kind of sixth sense. It does not lend itself and does not require an explanation in terms of natural science. He who has discovered it in himself knows what it is. He who has not discovered it is deaf to any explanations, just like it is impossible to explain light to a blind man. The soul reveals itself through behavior. It is the ability to tell good from evil, to do good and rejoice in it, to oppose evil and be distressed by it. The soul is the source and space of man's value world. The notions of death and immortality are not applicable to the soul, they are only applicable to the body, but only an animate body. The soul is oriented toward eternity, it provides an umbilical cord that links man to eternity, a link civilization seeks to cut.

The soul must not only be man's central concern, but the only concern. This manifests itself in his attitude to everything that is not the soul. "If we cannot change the circumstances, we can change ourselves in a way that robs circumstances of their meaning" (Zinoviev 2006, 164). The right attitude to the soul is revealed through active recognition of the fact that everything is transitory and vain. "My claim to be God, we read in the story, is the greatest of all possible human claims. It is immeasurably higher than the wish to become a millionaire, to win fame or be a dictator. It implies omnipotence and possession of everything . . . Therefore, no amount of suffering or loss can stop me because they are nothing compared to what I potentially possess as God" (Zinoviev 2006, 41).

Two paths are open to a person, Zinoviev says: "Either to become immersed in the struggle for life's benefits according to the laws of society or to evade this struggle" (Zinoviev 2006, 173). His answer is unequivocal: to evade. But to evade does not mean to become isolated, withdraw into an artificially created environment, and limit one's communication to a narrow circle of those you consider to be "us," and so on. It does not even mean to withdraw into one's shell. It is a very different kind of evasion when a person is deeply rooted in social life, immersed in the quagmire of life while spiritually being in a special world and being guided by one's own criteria of values and assessments. Zinovyoga answers the question, "how to be a saint without withdrawing from sinful production" (Zinoviev 2006, 157). Unlike those who sought to move from earthly hell to heavenly paradise and those who wanted to transform earthly life from an inferno into paradise, here hell and paradise are intertwined. Zinoviev's position is as follows: man cannot escape the earthly world with its ordeal of mundane existence because no other world exists. He cannot do anything about the earthly world full of torment and suffering because the world is what it is; it is not that it cannot be improved, but it cannot be improved without worsening it, improved in a way that would rid it of suffering, disease, death, poverty, meanness, envy and other evils and abominations. Therefore, if man does not want to abandon the dream of paradise, his ideals, he must learn to live a blissful life while remaining in hell. How does one go about achieving it? Before turning to the details of the teaching about life let us consider one more of its features.

The central ethical problem—how to be a saint in the environment of sinful production—is brought into high relief in the story "Live (Confessions of an Invalid)" whose hero finds himself not just in an inferno of social life, but in its very center. "For never was a story of more woe than this of Juliet and her Romeo." These are the final words of Shakespeare's famous tragedy. After reading Zinoviev's story "Live" one may well say that there was such a story. Truly, a story of more woe could not be invented. With Shakespeare the romantic love of a young man and a maiden is crushed by sociality as manifested in the feud between two families. Zinoviev deals with a more developed, sophisticated and powerful sociality which could not simply destroy love, but prevent it from being born. It blocks the path of love, and in general everything that is moral and lofty in man, on the distant approaches, at its natural beginnings. I am talking about sociality that has entered the finishing stretch leading to a condition when communal laws are entirely embodied in the mechanical coercive force of technical devices. It is moving toward its ideal state while "the ideal social organization is only that whose elements are mathematical points without dimension, i.e. are nothing in the socio-biological sense" (Zinoviev 2004, 191–192). The stage of sociality described in the story witnesses a proliferation of socially and technologically determined physical monstrosities.

The main character by the name of Andrey Ivanovich Gorev, nicknamed "Robot," was born without both legs, a victim of a city that sprang up around a nuclear plant where one of his two closest friends ("Theoretician") is without arms and the other is a "Blind Man." He, a born loser haunted by his failure because he failed to avoid being born, describes himself as "a failure on an epochal scale" (Zinoviev 2004, 21) and he cannot hope to ever enjoy full-blooded mutual love. The only thing that is still within his reach is the yearning for love. A yearning for love is of course dwarfed by real love, but Gorev clings to this trifle, lives by it and turns it into a feeling that makes him tick. He lives by a dream about the Only and Peerless woman who would be his and with him forever. He would not settle for anything less than that. The object of his feelings is a woman by the name of Anastasia, diminutive Nastya or Nastyenka whom everybody calls "Bride." She got that nickname because she had many suitors who promised to marry her but ended up marrying other women. At the time of the narrative she lives in the same capacity with Gorev's neighbor nicknamed "Soldier." Soldier, incidentally, once offered to rent her out to Gorev for a night for five rubles only to get an earful of real man's talk from Gorev. When Gorev told Bride about the incident, she reacted by saying "Bloody fool" (Zinoviev 2004, 163). She didn't mean the Soldier who made the cynical offer, but Gorev, who had turned it down. One episode tells all about Bride. Gorev was constantly proposing to her. Bride refused on the grounds that "I am looking for someone special, someone brilliant." However, when Soldier jilted her she proposed a deal: She would marry Gorev but without promising to be faithful. Gorev answered with a firm: "No. I need the whole of you, fully. I'll give you all of myself" (Zinoviev 2004, 206). Bride embarked on another dead-end affair.

Unlike Ivan Laptev, the character of "Go to Golgotha," Gorev is smitten not only by the ugly social order, but by being a cripple. These two circumstances conspire to produce a synergy effect. His physical defect is compounded by the knowledge that it is the product of the activity of healthy people and even more by the sense that individuals doomed to living with these defects have to emulate the achievements and capacities of healthy people. Social defectiveness seen as sociality that destroys the individual is at its ugliest and most relentless in the case of invalids. Society, on the one hand, does a great deal using technical devices, social benefits to elevate invalids to a level where they can live and work like normal people and become part of the social structure (Gorev, for example, works as an inventor and test expert at an advanced prosthetics enterprise). On the other hand, society does it so that they, like all the others, could immerse themselves and live in degraded society (Gorev's neighbors envy him because being an invalid he has a room to himself; an old woman with aching legs tells him: you are fine, you have your artificial limbs; his bosses elbow him out of a trip abroad although his profession makes him the only eligible candidate for the trip; etc). Society behaves like a hoodlum who knocks his victim down, then lifts him from the ground only to hit him on the jaw and knock him down again. In short, the environment in which Gorev has to live is appalling.

Worms are a symbolic background to the story. The worms who emerge on the pavements in damp weather are inevitably crushed by pedestrians even though they try to avoid stepping on them. "Worms and People," "the Worm Experiment," "A Worm's Thoughts" are all titles of short chapters. Gorev describes his ideology as the "ideology of a worm." If only a worm could have an ideology it would consist in the faith that he would be able to crawl through life without being crushed midway. Man-worm, what could be more lowly? If he manages to keep his human dignity and show himself to be a personality, then any individual can do it. In this story, like in other stories, perhaps even more so than in other stories, Zinoviev takes the experiment to its limit, which is simultaneously the limit of clarity.

The main character of "Go to Golgotha" is Ivan Laptev. His ideology is, accordingly, called "Ivanism" or, better still, "Laptism." The names Zinoviev chooses for his characters (both proper names or symbolic ones like Dumbhead, Pretender, Schizophrenic, Chatterbox and so on) always carry an extra message indicating the main idea (role, function, social attitude) the character embodies. In this case the thoroughly Russian name Ivan Laptev means that he is a Russian God and speaks on behalf of and for Russians. Zinoviev writes that he developed the teaching not as a replacement for previous such concepts and not as a true system for all people in general, but as a set of rules for himself and people in the same social position as himself. It was a set of ready-to-use rules. Here is what he has to say about it:

> It is not enough to think up one's own life system. One has to learn to live according to the rules of the system, one needs training. In the Soviet Union I had such training every day in abundance . . . In addition to the above-mentioned training, seeking to be a citizen of my type there needed to be conditions for maintaining my civic standard. Chief of them were: 1) guaranteed social status; 2) the chance to demonstrate my civic virtues to the people around me and to be recognized as possessing them; 3) be reassured that I am preserving these virtues and there are people around me who appreciate them. (Zinoviev 2008, 493)

The position expressed in the formula "I am a sovereign state" was not a position of isolation from people, but a position of a certain type of social behavior among people. Moreover, it implied even more intensive, diverse and broad communication than the usual position of "a man in society" (Zinoviev 2008, 490–491). This teaching proved to be useless in the West. Zinovyoga is a tree that can only bring fruit on Russian soil. What is there in this soil that makes it so special?

Right off: Zinoviev is anything but a Russian *pochvennik* "native soiler," still less is he a Russian nationalist in any sense. He categorically rejects these notions. In terms of the usual Westernizer-Slavophil opposition Zinoviev is undoubtedly a Westernizer and thinks of himself as such. Speaking about the special features of the human material that created Russia and Russian history, he means above all and solely the way of life, sociologically conditioned behavioral stereotypes. Russians, in his opinion, have exaggerated forms of collective being, the communal aspect invariably prevails over the business and formal legal aspect in their social system. This was true of pre-Soviet Russia and this is characteristic of modern—post-Soviet—Russia. However, these forms were most developed and classically ordered in Soviet Russia. The Soviet collective as the primary social cell and organization of the whole society, representing a complex, internally structured and hierarchic system of relations in the shape of collectives—this is what best suits the Russian people (call it Orthodox, Soviet or Russian) and offers the best chances for its development. This is not Russia's advantage. Nor is it its shortcoming. It is its specificity. Such is the position of Zinoviev as a scholar and as a person.

"Communality," *Sobornost',"* collectivism"—these are the concepts that inspire most thinkers trying to express the spiritual composition of the Russian people, its national idea. These words describe the moral rectitude of the people and its lofty mission in history. Zinoviev's relentless and sober view is a far cry from this perception. For him the prevalence of the collective element in the entire order of life means the sway of sociality whose essence is existential egoism. It is not so much a good to be nurtured, but rather a social Darwinist free-for-all to be protected against. A person in this environment is a constant victim of hypocrisy, cheating, envy, back-stabbing, pity, concern, intrigues, demagogy and so forth. An individual, being part of the social entity, acts according to the same laws just as, being a natural creature, he lives according to biological laws. Zinovyoga protects man from himself, from other people, social groups and organizations. It does not work in societies with an atomized structure, but in societies of the Russian type where sociality in various forms of collectivity imposes itself on individuals never releasing them from its warm, caring embrace.

There is one other feature of Russian life linked with the teaching about life, in particular its method of opposing sociality (evading the struggle for social good) and that is drunkenness ("One remarkable thing about life is // you can shake up the world a hundred times, like in October, // but all the same Russia's delight // will forever be unbridled drunkenness" (Zinoviev 2006a, 241).) Ivan Laptev, who first appears in the story sleeping in a children's playing sandpit after another night of heavy drinking and calls himself "initiator and inspiration of drinking bashes," "theoretician and poet of drunkenness" is a great specialist on booze. Drunkenness as a Russian phenomenon is a kind of symbolic behavior:

> Only we Russians have it in this capacity. This is not alcoholism (like with Americans, Finns, Swedes) and not part of a meal (like with the French and Italians) this is to all intents and purposes our national religion which matches our spirit and way of life. Of course, drunkenness here leads to people behaving

> like pigs. But behaving like pigs is also our national trait. Drunkenness without behaving like a pig is not drunkenness, but drinking in the Western style, or in the Georgian style. A Russian drinks with the express purpose of behaving and acting like a pig. Having a drink implies choosing a company, a certain state of mind, etc. Drunkenness does not imply anything. One drinks anything, in any place with anyone with any kind of snack. This is the basis of all the rest: company, a mating of souls, love and friendship. (Zinoviev 2006, 24)

Such words are not supposed to apply to a great people. But on the other hand, one has to belong to a great people and be at the appropriate level in order to be able and daring enough to say such things.

So, what does drunkenness symbolize? We learn about it from a poem titled "A Gospel for Ivan," a work of genius. In it we find such a full description and profound analysis of the phenomenon that psychology and sociology with their traditional methods could hardly add anything to it. It needs a special philosophical and aesthetic investigation. I will confine myself to general remarks on how it is reflected in the teaching about life. From that point of view three issues are of interest. Their fanciful combination forms the inner message of the poem:

1. what and who causes it,
2. with whom, and
3. why people escape into drunkenness.

The first issue is key. The author takes his time answering the question with epic sweep and love of detail. We learn the main cause of "Ivan's teaching" from the start. It consists in the fact that "The age of poetry is behind us, // and ahead, alas, looms the age of prose" (Zinoviev 2006a, 241). People escape into drunkenness out of hell and because of hell. They drink because "not people but only epochs form the essence of being" (Zinoviev 2006a, 243), because they had to kill and to burn themselves. "People drink to escape the memories of a lieutenant bleeding to death. The wholesale cheating by historians and pseudo-wisdom of philosophers. The windbags at the Party Central Committee. A wicked wife. A boring job. The bosses. Stale shchi and stinking hamburgers. Despair, the unbearable boredom of life?" (Zinoviev 2006a, 262). Because "they stub out cigarettes on your soul" (Zinoviev 2006a, 262). The work shifts and productivity drives. Having to kowtow "to every petty bureaucrat." Women's infidelity. Fallen women. Unbearable neighbors. Snitchers. The authorities representing God. The mugs of fellow workers. Lecturing. Lack of recognition. Slander. Having to be a sycophant. Constant bad luck. Unrealized dreams. Fear of death. Triumphant progress. Vexation of the spirit. Expecting a new Stepan Razin. Tortuous road of life. To avoid "having your healthy collective trying to get you to mend your ways" (Zinoviev 2006a, 298). The greyness of workaday life. Having to glorify idiots "and give pledges to fulfill a Five-Year Plan in four years" (Zinoviev 2006a, 299). Betrayal by friends. In short, "the abomination of being." The kind of abomination even God would not have tolerated: "I would tell him, my Lord, in my place // you would drink yourself silly like me" (Zinoviev 2006a, 265). The kind of abomination that when you find yourself in Heaven facing the Supreme Judge you have only one thing to ask him about and that is to allow you to remain dead.

The answer to the second question is linked to the first one. People drink with whoever comes along. Often it turns out to be the very same people they want to forget. In the poem there are former airmen, a colonel, a historian, a sociologist, a poet, an intellectual, an invalid, an old man, young liberals, an ageing writer, an atheist, a womanizer, a virtuous man, a neighbor, a police informer, a work mate, an unrecognized genius, a rebel, a suicide case, a loser. In short, drink:

> with bookkeepers, turners,
> drink with Komsomol and Party secretaries
> drink with a Muslim, a Buddhist,
> with a purser, a cleric, an actor,
> drink alone, drink in company,
> drink from the bottle, a tin, a cup
> drink more rather than less,
> drink wherever, whenever and with whoever. (Zinoviev 2006a, 264)

The individuals with whom they drink are the very same individuals whom they would like to forget through drinking. That is understandable, because there are no other. This is a very tell-tale circumstance. "Ivan's teaching" is not an escape from the world (you cannot escape from it because no other world exists) but a special position in the world. It affirms the world through negating it in a different capacity. This brings us to the question: "What for?" The answer is simple: to damn everyone and everything and enter a different, higher space, to become like gods ("people, live like gods // drink yourself to inebriation" (Zinoviev 2006a, 293)). This space is a special "fraternity of people"; a pub in the poem is referred to as a temple where you can sense a "kinship of soul with people like yourself." Another thing about it is that people live not by tomorrow, but by today. Here they achieve a fullness of the experience of life "here" and "now," of time standing still: "While you are alive remember one thing: // Live now while you are alive" (Zinoviev 2006a, 291). Yet another—and probably the most important—feature of the drunken world behind the looking glass consists in a sense of freedom which may take on an ugly physical form when the people who drink together may start stabbing one another and then, without any pause, start hugging one another, but above all it is about talking, about pouring out one's soul. "Let me talk into the wee hours // with my drinking companion" (Zinoviev 2006a, 287), says one of the prayers in the "A Gospel for Ivan." It does not matter that the interlocutor may turn out to be a snitcher: "He who is in a solitary cell would be glad to share it with a hangman" (Zinoviev 2006a, 287). Drunkenness is an escape from loneliness, from the most terrible and hopeless kind of loneliness in the midst of people, in the midst of the collective that "loves you." This is the paradox. Drunkenness which obviously destroys the personality is at the same time a form of asserting human dignity, an attempt to break out of a cage from which there is no escaping, to smile in a situation in which one only wants to moan.

Ethics is a look at reality through the prism of opposition between good and evil. From that point of view the teaching about life is so unusual that one may well begin to wonder whether it is moral at all. As far as I know, Zinoviev did not make any extended statements on the issue. Very sketchily his position is articulated by Ivan Laptev in the following way: evil for evil—this is the actual principle of our life. God is powerless to oppose it . . . I teach neither good nor evil. I teach how to live in a dimension of being when the notions of good and evil become meaningless" (Zinoviev 2006, 60–61). In an attempt to understand how this is possible and what it means three points need to be made.

First, Zinoviev (through his literary alter ego Ivan Laptev) developed the teaching about life not to make humanity happy but for his own sake. The above quotation was from the short chapter "Good and Evil" and the chapter cheek by jowl with it called "More about Good and Evil" puts it precisely: "What a person does for himself is neither good nor evil" (Zinoviev 2006, 64). God, if by God one understands the instance that demands that people be good, is one of the "selfs" within the individual. Along with this self he has other selfs, dozens, hundreds, maybe thousands of other "selfs." The individual, deep down, is not one of his "selfs," even though it be the highest of his selfs, but their totality which wakes up his individual "self." The individual "self" of man as a soul that is contradictory, all-embracing, should be distinguished from abstract and flat role-playing selfs.

Second, the teaching about life is not intended to make a bad world good or to rely on what is good in the world in order to avoid what is bad, it is intended to evade the world while remaining in it with all its filth (negative attitude to reality and its rejection is a prerequisite of any ethics, otherwise the ethical view of the world would not make any sense). If, for example, evading the world in its ethically negative capacity, the method of evading is to be considered good and active being inside the world is to be considered evil then man, even when he attains the level of God ("a sovereign state") would remain the same tangle of good and evil in which no ends can be found. The starting point of the teaching about life is that good is done through evil, and in that sense transcends that juxtaposition, at least in its traditional interpretation when one thing is separated from the other like in the formula: "yes, yes," "no, no," and what is beyond that is from the devil. So, logical contradiction becomes the norm of the teaching: "Be tolerant and resist any violence. If you see that struggle is futile fight with redoubled force. Go to people, and therefore be alone . . . Have everything and therefore give everything away. Resign in rebelling. Rebel in resigning. In short for every principle there is an opposite principle through which it is implemented" (Zinoviev 2006, 116).

Thirdly, " 'Laptism' in strictly determining life strategy, offers every man total freedom in choosing life tactics, within the limits circumscribed by the general principles, of course" (Zinoviev 2006, 191). It is impossible to determine in general what is good and what is evil. Each time there needs to be concrete decisions for concrete individuals in concrete situations, which leaves no option but to become oneself the criterion of good and evil. This is not to say that the models and commandments have no meaning. They do have meaning, only there have to be very many of them. Besides, they should be so precise as to make "advice for specific cases their consequences," i.e., they have to be created anew independently by every acting individual.

The teaching about life comprises a huge number (probably hundreds) of rules applying to various spheres of life and circumstances and the analysis of almost as many typical cases. All this combines to form the whole human world which is remarkable not for its logical rigor, aesthetic beauty, certain expressed moral principles but for the fact that it exists as a real and humanly understood world created by this particular person—Alexander Zinoviev, Ivan Laptev. Ivan Laptev is no God who creates the world in his own likeness, but God who happens to live in the world that has no likeness. He creates not the world, but himself.

Among the total body of the rules of "Laptism" of the greatest interest in terms of interpretation as an ethical teaching are the rules brought together under the rubric "I and Others" (Zinoviev also reproduces them literally in "The Confessions of a Dissident" as his own credo) (See: Zinoviev 2008, 351–359). I would name just some of them: Keep people at arm's length. Treat everyone with respect. Do not attract attention to yourself. Do not force your help on others. Do not try to get into other's souls, and do not allow anyone into your soul. Do not lecture. In a struggle give the opponent all the chances. Do not force others. Blame only yourself.

At first glance these rules apparently can be reduced, in a general way, to the moral behest of "love thy neighbor." But actually it is about something else. One may encounter all sorts of propositions in Zinoviev's numerous texts, but one thing they do not have and cannot have in principle is the ethical maxim of love of one's neighbor ("Man's enemies are his close ones" (Zinoviev 2006, 74)). The above quoted set of rules of relating to others begins with the rule "Preserve your personal dignity" and ends with the rule "Never count on people assessing your acts objectively . . . Remember: You are the sole and supreme 'objective' judge of your behavior because it is your behavior and you are at liberty to judge it as you see fit" (Zinoviev 2006, 178, 179–180).

The body of rules of dealing with others, according to Zinoviev, is intended to ward off the dangers emanating from them. The paradoxical realism of his idea consists in the assertion that by treating others with respect we are protecting ourselves from them. Every living creature protects itself in its own way: by emitting certain smells, by becoming invisible, demonstrating aggression, by running away, etc. Man does it through conscious, coordinated and generally recognized norms of behavior, norms which in fact create a zone in which people can coexist safely. Zinoviev's ideas on this score are similar to the concept of sociogenesis of Thomas Hobbes. There is one difference though. Hobbes believed that the natural state of everyone fighting everyone else is overcome by the creation of the state. From Zinoviev's point of view social life organized by the state has an abiding capacity to generate conflicts and if it is at all different from the natural state the difference is that the struggle is even more ferocious and dangerous. The way out is for everyone to become a kind of sovereign state in his own right. However strange Zinoviev's position may seem, one has to admit that it is one of the few rationally argued answers in the history of philosophy to the question of why the individual concerned only with becoming perfect, and following the right path in an absolute perspective should in addition think and care about other people.

The story "Live" has an episode that is typical of the "Human Comedy" Zinoviev depicts in work after work. Gorev was tipped to be promoted to the position of chief of department, which promised some obvious benefits (higher salary, an apartment, etc.). The people around him ("his very own collective") envied his luck. Someone wrote a denunciation to the party bureau and rumors were sent flying about the factory that he was a drug addict, a lecher, etc. In short, the usual and highly effective mechanism was set in motion. Gorev did not get his promotion although he was certainly entitled to it. The reason he did not get it was precisely because he deserved it. His personal character filled the bill, but he was not the right candidate according to the laws of communal life. Discussing the libelous anonymous denunciation of Gorev, the armless Theoretician says that libel is the will of the collective, the ideal image of man in the consciousness of the people around him. To live according to the laws of the collective does not mean that slander has to be ubiquitous. But it means that you have to know how to slander because slander is part of the arsenal of possible weapons. That applies to all the other qualities that are usually considered to be moral faults. The conditions of collective life only relate to morals in that they subjugate morality to the goals of existential egoism forming in individuals an ability both to violate justice and to protect it. Gorev is clearly aware of this. "In our conditions the moral position is a false position" (Zinoviev 2004, 180), he says.

The first and key choice an individual makes on the way to becoming a personality is to shift the center of gravity of one's decisions and actions from outside to inside. To follow not the will of the collective (in whatever form it manifests itself) but one's own will. Having discovered that the people around him are kind to him only as long as he does not seek to rise above the average level and does not reveal his individuality, Gorev draws the only correct conclusion: he can become and remain a personality if he himself is his own support and criterion. He realized that "it makes no sense to count on just judgment of the surrounding people—such a judgment does not exist and cannot exist in principle . . . You are yourself the highest and fairest judge of yourself" (Zinoviev 2004, 199).

Is it possible for man to be self-reliant, to be totally alone inside? A man cannot but live among other people and cannot disregard them. And one more thing. To exist in the moral sense means not to have but to be. Not to take, but to give. Gorev turns his life into an experiment in looking for a way out of what seems a dead-end situation. Two things are in my opinion essential for that experiment.

First, he disciplines his life in such a way as to put it in line with certain principles. These are not the principles of abstract morality although, as we shall see, they are correlated to them. They all represent taboos (with the exception of morning exercises and other procedures that keep one physically in shape). They are taboos because it is only in this form that man can manifest his autonomy. When he does something he always depends on external circumstances. When he does not do something he may refrain from doing it out of principle and he does not depend on anyone. Gorev's taboos are concrete and are aimed at blocking actions in which and through which the surrounding people (the collective, sociality in the broad sense) exert a largely corrupting influence on the personality. There are three such main taboos. Not to drink, which is particularly important in view of the special role of drunkenness in the Russian/Soviet environment and especially in the case of Gorev who has no legs. Not to have sex with women unless it reflects love. The third principle can be formulated as renunciation of the struggle for occupying a more comfortable perch in life. It refers not to ascetic denial of pleasures or something of the kind, but merely a readiness to be content with the amount of benefits to which the collective agrees, which means that they become available without visible rivalry and are thought by the collective (public opinion, established norms, the position of the superiors, etc.) to be acceptable for a person of his station. Gorev calls these principles his props. Just like he needs artificial limbs physically in order to stand, so he needs principles in order to straighten up morally. To be sure, they do not rescue him from the surrounding quagmire; that is impossible and indeed unnecessary (for example, Gorev, although he does not drink himself, readily takes part in booze parties because they allow of uninhibited free communication which is at once the Russian underground and the Russian Symposium). Nevertheless they create a certain inner space that enables a person to be himself.

The second important aspect of Gorev's experiment is his programmatic, strategic life principle expressed in the one word in the title of story: "Live." Not to love life because, as Zinoviev the logician rightly notes, love of life is a position (protective reaction) of those who live badly, but simply to live. Gorev wakes up and goes to sleep with the word "Live," it is his prayer: "Live." "Since you exist you must live. Live in spite of anything. If you were born a cockroach, live like a cockroach. If you were born a rat live like a rat. If you were born an eagle, live like an eagle. The time will come and you will vanish forever. But while you live, live and enjoy the fact of living" (Zinoviev 2004, 97). In Gorev's case such a moral program means living in spite of being an ugly legless creature. One might think that it has meaning only for cripples. It is and is not so. It is so because the injunction to "live" may only arise when life contains negative impulses that put into question its practicability and reason, i.e., contains a certain deformity. Yet it is not so because everyone is in some sense a cripple. The norm is always an average value from which individual cases are deviations. The story has a pianist who had an invisible defect of the hand that prevented him from using his little finger fully. This applies even more to the moral norm. Here, deviation is the norm. Painting the moral portrait of man as a social creature Zinoviev uses only dark colors. His misanthropy is well known. In this story it is expressed with particular gusto, here man is simply "a worm who thinks he is somebody important" (Zinoviev 2004, 107, 37). Cripples such as Gorev and his friends, according to the story, are second-level cripples, they differ from the cripples that all other individuals are only in that they need moral principles more than the others and it is far more difficult for them to follow these principles. Without them they cannot keep straight. The commandment "Live" is their Gospel.

Just like a song hinges on the refrain, so this story is sustained by the incantation: "Live." A very important detail: "Live without any explanations, grounding or justification, just live" (Zinoviev 2004, 163). Philosophers have expended a lot of effort on the grounding of morality although one of the most incisive of them has aptly noted that in justifying it they undermine it. Thus, he puts into question the role of morality as the underlying personal principle that organizes life. Life does not need to be justified. Its existence is its own justification. It is a fact. Moreover, it is a fact preceding all other facts. Gorev begins his confession (the whole story "Live" is his confession) in order to cleanse himself and continue "to live without claiming anything more than the fact of living). Perhaps nowhere has Zinoviev's characteristic scientific cool-headedness and logical rigor manifested themselves in such a concentrated and complete way as in the fact that he has reduced the fundamental ethical formula to a single word, “Live.” It did not occur to any of the numerous philosophers who formulated moral laws.

In *The Yawning Heights* there were the words over the entrance to a crematorium: “Before you leave, take the urn with your ashes with you” (Zinoviev 1976). This is more than stunning satire. This is a considered life position. According to Zinoviev, one should leave this world without leaving any cares about oneself. Truly, let the dead bury their dead. Zinoviev’s novels and stories have nothing remotely resembling a happy end. Life does not end like a musical or a Hollywood film. It does not have a final chord. Good does not conquer evil. This, among other things, means that the personality ends in the same place where it begins. Life and the moral acts in which it is embodied are their own rewards and have no other value beyond that. The hero of the story, Gorev, has been abandoned by his parents, he has no roots. He has no relatives and no commitments to them. The fact is symbolic in the sense that if in the biological sense life is a thread that can be pulled at least from one end into infinity, in the moral sense there is always a new beginning. Man as a personality does not, in the moral sense, continue what others have been doing, but begins doing anew what all the other personalities were doing: building his own state, his own one-man world.

Zinoviev’s ethics is connected with sociology and can only be understood in relation to it. Social laws (the laws of sociality) which represent the laws of organization, functioning and development and large masses of people (“Human hills”) are just as objectively rigid in their objectivity as the laws of nature. On the basis of the laws of the sociality and in the space where they apply there is no room for human freedom or morality. Both arose, first, as an individual mode of existence and second, outside sociality as evasion of its laws. These are the underlying premises of the teaching about life. Just like a person builds planes in order to escape the iron vice of the laws of gravitation (Zinoviev’s simile) while doing it staying within the same limits, so he creates an ideal society within himself in order to escape the oppression of society and he can do it remaining in society and through society. One can put it like this: the laws of sociality allow of negative morality, in the sense that the latter is possible only as their negation.

The contradictory character of sociality in man’s moral experience is highlighted in the poem “My Home My Exile.” Its main message is contained in its title. True, the title can be read with varying accents. One variant is: a person finds himself in a situation when exile becomes his home. But this interpretation is trumped by another one. Home and exile, although interconnected, are clearly differentiated and the hero does not confuse his native Russian home with exile in the West. But the tragedy of his predicament is that his own home is his exile. Not in the sense that he finds himself away from home and he wants to come back: home is always a better choice. The home itself is an exile, this is the whole point. The hero is eager to return home from detested exile, but his fear of the prospect is even greater because he knows that his home is just as much of an exile, perhaps even worse than exile. This is his brooding over the fate of the soldiers buried in the European soil as if hearing their voices yearning for the Russian snowstorms. He shudders at the prospect of sharing their fate. But the prospect of not sharing it is even worse. The following quatrain conveys the author's and the hero's position:

> Believe me, there is no rabble
> More wicked than my people.
> But I will never exchange them for others
> As long as I am alive. (Zinoviev 2004a, 262)

The situation Zinoviev describes is ambivalent and contradictory. By describing it in this way we do not explain it but rather own up to our inability to explain it. It is not by chance that psychological motives, introspection, generally alien to Zinoviev's work, crop up in the poem. It speaks of nostalgia, of the land inhabited by the forefathers. In the story "Live" we read that in the West people spit into spittoons and in this country into souls. Spitting into souls is thought to be better because, if only in this way, through spitting into each other's souls, people become linked to one another. This seems to be vaguely the message of the poem. In exile, for example, there are no drunken parties. The contradictory feelings of the hero that defy reason arise from the fact that he does not just see the shortcomings of his own home and is drawn toward it in spite of the shortcomings. Following the tradition of Russian revolutionaries of loving the Motherland with open eyes, he sees the shortcomings of his Motherland and loves it on account of them. This is a Lermontov situation ("I love my Fatherland, but with a strange love").

The poem in which the hero leaves his home for exile while being afraid to be there, and once in exile, is yearning for home, though being afraid to come back home, graphically describes the relationship between individual and society as Zinoviev understands it. The individual can be likened to a grain and society to a grindstone that ruthlessly and relentlessly crushes it. The grain finds itself between the grindstones, is doomed to be crushed, and dreams of somehow escaping.

In Zinoviev's worldview no two notions are more remote from each other than morality and sociality. And no two notions are more tightly linked with each other. They are like two wrestlers who are locked together and only manage to stay on their feet because they lean on each other. Morality exists as the negation of sociality. It has no other substance than this negation. Sociality relativizes morality to make it easier to pass on from good to evil and back using these value judgments out of existential egoism. Without it, it would never be considered to be a form and result of human activity.

The teaching about life is a teaching about how individuals can preserve their moral dignity in the midst of the hideousness of being, contrary to the laws of sociality which are laws of existential egoism. It is a teaching about the individually responsible existence of man.

## NOTES

1. For more details on his versatility see: Guseinov, Zinovieva, and Kantor 2002.
2. See Gospel from Luke, Chapter 12: "The Kingdom of God is in you yourself."

## BIBLIOGRAPHY

Guseinov, Abdusalam A., Zinovieva, Olga M., and Kantor, Karl M. (eds.) 2002. *Fenomen Zinov'eva.* [The Zinoviev Phenomenon]. Moscow: Contemporary Notebooks.

Zinoviev, Alexander A. 1976. *Ziyayushchie vysoty* [The Yawning Heights]. Lausanne: L'Age d'Homme.

Zinoviev, Alexander A. 1980. *Zheltyi dom: Romanticheskaya povest' v chetyrekh chastyakh, s predosterezheniem i nazidaniem.* [The Yellow House, The Madhouse]. Lausanne: L'Age d'Homme.

Zinoviev, Alexander A. 2004. *Zhivi* [Live]. St. Petersburg: Neva Publishing House.

Zinoviev, Alexander A. 2004a. "My Home My Exile." In *Zhivi* [Live], 215–307. St. Petersburg: Neva Publishing House.

Zinoviev, Alexander A. 2006. *Idi na Golgofu* [Go to Golgotha]. Moscow: Eksmo.

Zinoviev, Alexander A. 2006a. "Evangelie dlya Ivana" [A Gospel for Ivan]. In *Idi na Golgofu* [Go to Golgotha], 241–318. Moscow: Eksmo.

Zinoviev, Alexander A. 2006b. *Faktor ponimaniya* [The Factor of Comprehension?]. Moscow: Algorithm, Eksmo.

Zinoviev, Alexander A. 2008. *Ispoved'* Zinoviev, Alexander A. 1976 [The Confession of an Outcast]. Moscow: Astrel.

# A CHRONOLOGY OF KEY EVENTS IN THE RUSSIAN PHILOSOPHY (1953–1991)*

## 1953

March 5. Joseph Stalin dies.

September. Evald Ilyenkov defends a doctoral dissertation "Some Issues of Materialist Dialectics in the Work of Karl Marx *Critique of Political Economy*" at the Philosophical Faculty of the Lomonosov Moscow State University (MGU). The dissertation makes a case for a perception of cognition and thought (in particular the interpretation of the inter-relationship between scientific theory and empirical reality) as fundamentally different from the sensualist approach derived from the works of Lenin. There emerges a group of disciples of Ilyenkov. Many of those who belonged to this group grew into prominent Russian philosophers. Among them are Vladislav Lektorsky, Vadim Mezhuev, Lev Naumenko, Genrikh Batishchev, and Nelli Motroshilova.

## 1954

April. Alexander Zinoviev defends a doctoral dissertation "The Method of Ascending from the Abstract to the Concrete" at the Philosophical Faculty of MSU. Zinoviev offers an interpretation of the method that is different from that of Ilyenkov. A group of students forms around Zinoviev. Among those students are future prominent philosophers Merab Mamardashvili, Georgy Shchedrovitsky, and Boris Grushin.

Fall and winter. The Academic Council of the Philosophical Faculty of MSU holds a discussion of the *Theses* on the subject of philosophy written by Evald Ilyenkov and Valentin Korovikov, promoting the idea that the subject of philosophy is thinking as it exists in its basic forms and laws. The theses are condemned as anti-Marxist.

## 1955

Ilyenkov and Zinoviev quit their professor positions at the Philosophical Faculty of MSU and assume positions of research associates at the Institute of Philosophy, the USSR Academy of Sciences (SAS).

An upsurge of interest in issues relevant to the theory of knowledge (epistemology), methodology and logic of science occurs among young philosophers.

* In this Chronology, all titles of Russian publications are given in English translation. For the transliterated Russian titles, see the Bibliography.

## 1956

February. The 20th Congress of the Communist Party of the Soviet Union (CPSU) takes place where First Secretary of the CPSU Central Committee Nikita Khrushchev delivers a "Secret Speech" denouncing the personality cult, dictatorship, and policy of mass repressions of Joseph Stalin. A period of de-Stalinization known as the "thaw" is enacted.

## 1956–1958

Shchedrovitsky establishes the Moscow Methodological Circle and develops a content-genetic concept of thought (operational-genetic logic). The adherents of this program study thinking in close cooperation with psychologists, education theorists, and history of science specialists.

## 1957

Sergei Rubinshtein publishes his book *Bytie i Soznanie* (Rubinshtein 1957). In this book, problems of the philosophy of psychology come in for a serious discussion for the first time. [Translation: *Sein und Bewußtsein* (Berlin, 1962).]

## 1958

Ilyenkov contacts the Italian publishing house Feltrinelli with a request for translation and publication of his book that discusses the dialectic of ascending from the abstract to the concrete. The book was to be published in Russian later that year. The publisher approves the book proposal, but Ilyenkov has to withdraw his manuscript after learning that this very company had published Boris Pasternak's novel *Doctor Zhivago*, the novel for which the author was awarded the Nobel Prize, considered a political scandal by the Soviet officials. Reports about contacts with Feltrinelli trigger a wave of baiting of Ilyenkov at the Institute of Philosophy, SAS. The typeset of his book prepared for publication in the USSR is destroyed.

Zinoviev embarks on the study of symbolic logic and creates an original concept. He establishes a research school in the field.

## 1960

A censored version of Ilyenkov's *The Dialectics of the Abstract and the Concrete . . .* (see Ilyenkov 1960) is published. The circle of Ilyenkov's followers broadens; his ideas become applicable to the problems of the methodology of scientific thought. [The book has been translated into numerous languages. See: *La dialettica dell astrato e del concreto nel Capital di Marx*. Milano, Feltrinelli 1961 (the same publisher whose attempt to publish this book in 1958 caused the typeset of the book in the USSR to be shattered); *Die Dialektik des Abstrakten und Konkreten im*

*"Kapital" von Karl Marx*. West Berlin, 1979; *La dialectica de lo abstracto y lo concreto en El Capital di Marx*. Madrid, 1971; *The Dialectics of the Abstract and the Concrete in Marx's "Capital."* Moscow, 1982.] On Ilyenkov's ideas see *Evald Ilyenkov's Philosophy Revisited*. Ed. by Vesa Oittinen. Helsinki, 2000.

The journal *Voprosy filosofii*, publishes an article by Lektorsky and Sadovsky "On the Principles of Studying Systems" (Lektorsky and Sadovsky 1960) which furthers the development of philosophical analysis of the systems approach in the Soviet Union. [Translation: "On the principles of studying systems," *General Systems*, vol. 10, 1961.]

## 1960–1970

Publication of a five-volume *Philosophical Encyclopedia* which, for the first time, addresses many issues that were previously illicit in Soviet philosophy. A series of important articles is published on the history of Russian religious philosophy (Vladimir Solovyov, Nikolai Berdyayev, Sergei Bulgakov, and others) a subject previously ignored in the USSR. Among the contributors to the *Encyclopedia* are such noted philosophers as Ilyenkov, Zinoviev, Alexei Losev, Batishchev, and Sergei Averintsev.

## 1962

Ilyenkov's entry "The Ideal" in the second volume of the *Philosophical Encyclopedia* offers an original (albeit heretical from the perspective of the official philosophy of the USSR) interpretation of the ideal as something not reducible to individual consciousness and associated with collective human activity.

## 1962–1972

Bonifaty Kedrov is the head of the Institute for the History of Natural Sciences and Technology, the USSR Academy of Sciences. A distinguished historian of science (of the history of chemistry, notably the history of Dmitry Mendeleev's discovery of the periodic law of elements) and an eminent philosopher, Kedrov assembles in his Institute a group of philosophers who are in bad standing with Russian officials due to their unorthodox views. Among them are Vladimir Bibler, Anatoly Arsenyev, Piama Gaidenko, Alexander Ogurtsov, Nikolai Ovchinnikov, and later also Mamardashvili.

## 1962–1968

Pavel Kopnin, a noted specialist in the field of logic and methodology of science, becomes the head of the Institute of Philosophy at the Ukrainian National Academy of Sciences. Under him, the Institute emerges as a center for the study of the philosophy of science in the Soviet Union.

## 1963

An expanded edition of Mikhail Bakhtin's book on Dostoevsky (Bakhtin 1963) appears. (The first edition came out in 1929; translated into English: *Problems of Dostoevsky's Poetics*. Minneapolis, 1984.) Bakhtin moves from internal exile in Saransk to Moscow, where he acquires a large following among philosophers and other intellectuals. In the following years, Bakhtin's books had been published in the West creating an "international boom" in the popularity of his work. In addition, hundreds of articles and dozens of books about Bakhtin's philosophical ideas were published, among which are: Emerson, K. *The First Hundred Years of Mikhail Bakhtin*. Princeton: Princeton University Press, 1997; *Dialogism: An International Journal of Bakhtin Studies*, edited by D. Shepherd. [University of] Sheffield, UK (1998–).

## 1963–1988

Alexei Losev publishes a seven-volume *History of Antique Aesthetics* in which he develops an original concept not only of antique aesthetics, but also of antique philosophy in general.

## 1964

Felix Mikhailov's book *The Riddle of the Self* (published in English translation under this title (New York, 1978)) offers an original view on the problem of the Self, considering it from the cultural-historical perspective.

## 1966

Publication of Ovchinnikov's book, *The Principles of Conservation*. The work is a study of various principles of conservation in modern physics. It develops original ideas on the structure of scientific theory.

Publication of Vladimir Shvyrev's book, *Neopositivism and the Problem of Empirical Grounding of Science*, that contains a thorough critical analysis of logical positivism and an original view of the relationship between theoretical and empirical levels of scientific knowledge.

## 1966–1967

Two articles on Existentialism authored by Erikh Solovyov appear in the journal *Voprosy filosofii*. The articles offer, for the first time in the Soviet Union, a thorough and objective analysis of the philosophy of Existentialism, revealing its strengths and weaknesses. This mind-opening publication became a cultural milestone.

## 1968

May. The appointment of a new editorial board of the journal *Voprosy filosofii* headed by Ivan Frolov that includes well-known philosophers, such as Merab Mamardashvilii (deputy chief editor), Alexander Zinoviev Bonifaty Kedrov, Pavel Kopnin, Boris Grushin, Yury Zamoshkin, Vladislav Kelle, Vladislav Lektorsky, and others. The journal begins publishing articles with groundbreaking ideas, organizing round tables with eminent philosophers and scientists. The journal's role in Soviet Russia's philosophy increases in prominence dramatically.

August. Soviet troops invade Czechoslovakia to block the "socialism with a human face" experiment organized by Czechoslovak reformers. This begins an ideological suppression in the Soviet Union that extends to the field of philosophy.

Kopnin publishes the book *The Logical Foundations of Science* (Kiev) that contains a program for the study of science through the analysis of its logical structure. The book greatly influences such studies carried out by Ukrainian and Russian philosophers.

## 1968–1971

Kopnin is appointed Director of the Institute of Philosophy at the USSR Academy of Sciences. He attempts to reform the Federal Institute of Philosophy in a way similar to one he had earlier used to reform the Ukrainian Institute of Philosophy and seeks to weaken the Communist Party's ideological dictates. This, unfortunately, leads to his victimization and early death at the age of 49.

## 1969

Mikhail Petrov's article "The Subject and Purpose of Studying the History of Philosophy" published in the journal *Voprosy filosofii* calls into question the official view of Soviet philosophy (formulated by Lenin) that the whole history of philosophy can be understood as a history of the struggle between materialism and idealism. The article as well as the journal draws criticism from the Communist Party press.

Batishchev publishes an article "The Activity Essence of Man as a Philosophical Principle," which provides one of the most detailed expositions of the activity approach popular in Soviet philosophy and psychology. A circle of like-minded scholars is formed around Batishchev.

Kedrov's book *Classification of Sciences* (in 2 vols.) comes out. The book offers an analysis of different versions of the classification of sciences undertaken in the history of thought. This work plays an important role in the development of the theory and history of science in the Soviet Union. [Translation: *Le classification des sciences*. Moscow, 1980.]

Lektorsky is appointed the Head of the Sector of the Theory of Knowledge at the Institute of Philosophy, SAS. The Sector becomes a center for the study of epistemology and the philosophy of science.

Publication of the book *Systems Approach: Prerequisites, Problems, Difficulties* authored by Blauberg, Sadovsky and Yudin. The work develops the philosophical foundation of the systems approach going back to Alexander Bogdanov and popular in the Soviet Union in various sciences (biology, sociology, etc.). [Translation: *Systems Theory. Philosophical and Methodological Problems*. Moscow, 1977.]

## 1970

Zinoviev publishes his book *Complex Logic* in which he presents his original concept of logic. A Zinoviev's logic school is formed. [Translations: *Komplexe Logik. Grundlagen einem Theorie des Wissens*. Berlin, 1970; *Foundations of the Logical Theory of Scientific Knowledge (Complex Logic)*. Dordrecht, 1973.]

Publication of Lotman's book *The Structure of Poetic Text*. [Translations: *Analysis of Poetic Texts*. Ann Arbor: Ardis.1976; *Universe of the Mind. A Semiotic Theory of Culture*. London, New York: I.B.Tauris and Co Ltd. 1990.] The book substantiates a semiotic approach demonstrating its applications to the analysis not only of literary works, but also of all other cultural texts. This and others of Lotman's works gave rise to the Tartu-Moscow Semiotic School at Tartu University (Estonia) where Lotman held a professor position. The School included philologists, linguists, philosophers, and specialists in cultural studies. The works of Lotman and his school have gained recognition abroad.

## 1972

Publication of the book *Philosophy, Methodology, Science* edited by Lektorsky. Several essays (by Stepin, Lektorsky, Shvyrev, Nikitin, and others) included in the collection propose new approaches to understanding the structure and dynamics of the development of science.

## 1973

Boris Gryaznov, Boris Dynin and Evgenii Nikitin author the book, *Theory and Its Object*, that provides an original concept of the relationship between theory, empirical studies, and ontology of scientific knowledge.

Valentin Asmus publishes *Immanuel Kant*, a book that offers the most thorough analysis of Kant's philosophy that ever came out in the Soviet Union.

## 1973–1974

Kedrov is appointed Director of the Institute of Philosophy, SAS. His attempts to reform the Institute were met with resistance on the part of Party authorities which forced Kedrov to eventually resign from the Director's post and leave the Institute of Philosophy.

## 1974

Ilyenkov's *Dialectical Logic* is published. The book offers an extended presentation of the author's original views of the problems of thought, man and activity. [Translations: *Dialectical Logic. Essays on its History and Theory*. Moscow, 1977: *Logica dialectica: essyos sobre historia y teoria*. La Habana, 1984.]

Publication of Oleg Drobnitsky's book, *The Concept of Morality: Historical and Critical Essay*. The book is the first systematic study of all the main questions of moral philosophy undertaken in Soviet philosophy.

## 1975

Vladimir Bibler's book *Thought as Creativity (An Introduction to the Logic of Mental Dialogue)* presents the concept of creative activity using the history of science and drawing from Mikhail Bakhtin's ideas on dialogue. A circle of like-minded scholars is formed around Bibler.

Frolov publishes *Progress of Science and the Future of Man* that discusses the challenges humans face as a result of the development of science.

Ivan Kuznetsov's collection of essays published as a book titled *Selected Works on the Methodology of Physics* summarizes the author's original study of the principles of physical science, such as the principle of correspondence, the principle of causality, etc.

Shchedrovitsky writes "Initial Representations and Categorical Tools of the Theory of Activity," which is published in a narrowly specialized volume titled *The Development and Introduction of Automated Systems in Design*. In this essay, he outlines his concept of activity which is taken up by many who shared his ideas and then used in the design of different organizational systems, including the so-called organizational and activity games, and in the study of the problems of thinking. The author is banned from official philosophy, but has a large group of followers and regularly presides over the meetings of his methodological circle. Shchedrovitsky's works had been suppressed and not published in official philosophical venues, thus were known only within his inner circle. Only in the 1990s–2000s, when his works were collected and published in several volumes, did his ideas become known to the broader public. Shchedrovitsky's followers continue to be active in both theory and practice.

## 1975–1980

Mamardashvili delivers hugely popular philosophical lectures to audiences consisting of philosophers, psychologists, art scholars, and movie-makers.

## 1976

After publishing in the West a book critical of life in the Soviet Union, Zinoviev is evicted from the Institute of Philosophy, SAS.

Stepin's book *Building a Scientific Theory* (Minsk) expounds the author's original concept of scientific theory, one of the most interesting in the world literature on the philosophy of science. The book and the work it inspires have a great impact on the philosophy of science in the Soviet Union and in post-Soviet Russia. [Partial translations of the book's chapters: "Genetically-Constructive Ways of Theory Building," *Philosophical Logic and Logical Philosophy*, edited by P.I. Bystrov and V. Sadovsky. Kluver Academic Publishers: Dordrecht, 1986; "Ideals and Reasons as Aspects of Scientific Traditions," *World Futures*, vol. 34, 1992.] Stepin becomes the leader of a center for the study of philosophy of science problems that emerges in Minsk.

## 1977

Mamardashvili, Solovyov, and Shvyrev write an essay, "Classics and Modernity: Two Epochs in the Development of Bourgeois Philosophy" published in the collection, *Philosophy in Modern Culture*. The essay presents a new unorthodox view of contemporary Western philosophy.

Natalia Avtonomova publishes a monograph, *Philosophical Problems of Structural Analysis in Human Sciences,* which offers an in-depth study of French structuralism and attempts to define the role of structural analysis in linguistics, literary studies, and psychology.

Vadim Mezhuev's book *Culture and History* offers an original interpretation of historical consciousness in the context of culture.

The essay "From Unpublished Legacy of S. Rubinshtein 'Man and the World'" is published, posthumously, in the journal *Voprosy filosofii*. In this text (which was not published in full in book form until 1973), Rubinshtein develops a new concept of philosophical anthropology and advances unconventional ideas on Being, consciousness, and man's inclusion in the world, criticizing some officially accepted philosophical views.

## 1978

After the publication in Switzerland of the second anti-Soviet novel *Bright Future*, Zinoviev is deprived of his nationality as a Soviet citizen and forced to leave the country. He moves to the West.

## 1979

Publication of Bakhtin's book *The Aesthetic of Verbal Creativity* that further elaborates the author's original dialogic concept of Man and culture. [Translation: *Art and Answerability*. Austin, University of Texas Press. 1993.]

Sergey Averintsev's article "Classical Greek Philosophy as a Historical-Literary Phenomenon" in the book *New Developments in Classical Philology* presents an original view of ancient Greek philosophy, putting it in a broader cultural context. In the late 1970s to early 1980s, Averintsev regularly gives highly popular lectures on philosophy and culture to philosophers, philologists, cultural studies scholars, and the broad circles of intellectuals. Guseynov's book *The Golden Rule of Morality* is the first detailed and original analysis in the Soviet Union of this central problem of ethics.

Ilyenkov's essay "The Problem of the Ideal" is published in two issues of *Voprosy filosofii*. This is a further elaboration of the ideas discussed in the author's entry "The Ideal" published in *The Philosophical Encyclopedia* (1962). The essay was published posthumously because during the author's lifetime, in 1976, the highly dogmatic and orthodox leadership of the Institute of Philosophy, SAS, banned the publication of the essay in a volume prepared by the Epistemology Sector, on accusations of the author's revisionism. Ilyenkov's article had an enormous impact on the study of the problems of consciousness, the ideal, and investigations into the human being undertaken by philosophers and psychologists. [Translations: "Dialektik des Ideellen," *Dialektik des Ideellen*. Ausgewählte Ausätze, translated and edited by Gudrun Richter. Münster/ Hamburg: LIT Verlag. 1991; "Dialectics of the Ideal,"/*Dialectics of the Ideal: Evald Ilyenkov and Creative Soviet Marxism*. Leiden, Brill. 2013.]

## 1980

Lektorsky's book *Subject, Object, Cognition* introduces an original cultural-historical and activity-based concept of cognition based on the history of science, history of philosophy, and modern psychology. A detailed analysis is given of the concepts of Thomas Kuhn, Karl Popper, Imre Lakatos, and other influential philosophers of science. The book made a large impact on the study of epistemology and philosophy of science in the cultural-historical context. [Translations: *Subject, Object, Cognition*. Moscow: Progress, 1984; *Subjekt-Objekt- Erkenntnis. Grundlagen einer Theorie des Wissens*. Frankfurt am Main, Bern, New York: Peter Lang Verlag, 1985.]

*Evolution of the Concept of Science. The Emergence and Development of Early Scientific Programs* by Piama Gaidenko offers a philosophical analysis of the emergence and development of science in connection with antique and medieval philosophy. The book heavily influenced research in the fields of the philosophy and history of science.

## 1981–1987

Stepin is appointed Head of the Philosophy Department at Belorussian State University (Minsk). The department emerges as a major Soviet center for the study of the philosophy of science.

## 1981

A Swiss publishing house in Lausanne brings out Zinoviev's book *Communism as Reality,* in which the author offers an analysis and critical interpretation of the phenomenon of Soviet socialism. Although the book was banned in the Soviet Union, its copies were secretly circulating among Russia's intellectuals and had a major impact on their mindsets. [For details about Zinoviev see: Philip Hanson and Michail Kirkwood (eds). *Alexander Zinoviev as Writer and Thinker: An Assessment.* Houndmills, Basingstoke, Hampshire and New York: Palgrave Macmillan, 1988.]

Stepin edits the book *Ideals and Norms of Scientific Cognition* (published in Minsk) with contributions by Stepin, Lektorsky, Shvyrev, Motroshilova, and others. The book offers a new approach and serves as an important step in the promotion of research in the field of the philosophy of science in the Soviet Union.

## 1983

*Voprosy filosofii* publishes two articles by Ivan Frolov under the common title "On Life, Death and Immortality, Essays on New (Real) Humanism." For the first time in Soviet philosophy, the author addresses the philosophical problems of death in the context of new ideas in human biology and genetics. Prior to this, the philosophical study of the phenomenon of death was unofficially banished. [Translation: "La vie et la conaissance," *Philosophes d'eux memes.* Bern, Frankfurt am Main, New York: Peter Lang Verlag, 1984.]

Publication of *Epistemology in the System of Philosophy.* The collection edited by Lektorsky includes contributions by Batishchev, Lektorsky, Shvyrev, Nikitin, Trubnikov, Pruzhinin and others. It offers a detailed analysis of the cultural-historical context of the development of cognition, notably of scientific cognition.

The book by Teodor Oizerman and Aleksei Bogomolov *Foundations of the Theory of the Historical-Philosophical Process in Philosophy* presents an original concept of the history of philosophy, which had an impact on the meta-philosophical studies of Soviet and Russian philosophers. [Translation: *Principles of the Theory of the Historical Process in Philosophy*. Moscow: Progress.1986.]

Publication of Losev's book *Vladimir Solovyov* is banned.

## 1984

Nelli Motroshilova's monograph *Hegel's Path toward "The Science of Logic"* is the first in-depth study of the early Hegel in Soviet philosophy.

Mamardashvili's book *Classical and Non-Classical Ideals of Rationality* is released in Tbilisi. After being expelled from the journal *Voprosy filosofii* and later also from the Institute of the History of Natural Science and Technology at the Academy of Sciences of the USSR, in 1980 Mamardashvili moves to Georgia accepting a professor position at the Tbilisi Institute of Philosophy. His book about the ideals of rationality was ground-breaking and influenced the study of the problem of rationality in Soviet philosophy. [For details about Mamardashvili, see: *Le pensée empêchée. Entretiens avec An. Epelboin.* Paris, 1991.]

Publication of an article by Mikhail Lifshitz "On the Ideal and the Real" published in *Voprosy filosofii*, an important contribution to the discussion on the nature of the ideal. The author agrees with Ilyenkov that the ideal cannot be reduced to the individual consciousness, but unlike the latter believes that the ideal exists in nature itself.

Batishchev's manuscript *Dialectics of Creativity* has been copyrighted. The work presents an original concept of philosophical anthropology and an insight into the mutual relationship of activity and communication developed by the author. A copy of the manuscript could be ordered for scholarly purposes, but it was not available at libraries or for sale in bookstores. Only in 1997 was the manuscript published, posthumously, under the title *An Introduction to the Dialectics of Creativity.*

## 1985

Publication of Guseynov's book *An Introduction to Ethics* that addresses the main problems of moral philosophy and reflects on the history of ethical teachings.

## 1986

Bakhtin's essay "Toward a Philosophy of Act" is published in the yearbook *Philosophical and Social Problems of Science and Technology* edited by Frolov. The essay was written in the early 1920s, but had not been previously published. It presents a new approach to central ontological and ethical issues. This publication had a big impact on the study of philosophical anthropology by Soviet and post-Soviet Russian philosophers. [Translation: *Toward a Philosophy of Act.* Austin: University of Texas Press, 1993.]

Ivan Frolov and Boris Yudin release the book *Ethics of Science. Problems and discussions.* For the first time in Soviet philosophy the ethical problems of science are discussed in a book-length format.

## 1987

Stepin edits the collection *Scientific Revolutions in the Dynamics of Culture* (published in Minsk) that includes contributions by Stepin (who proposes a concept of scientific revolutions different from that of Thomas Kuhn), as well as by Lektorsky, Shvyrev, Mezhuyev, and other scholars. It is a milestone in Soviet research into the philosophy of science.

Publication of Nikolai Trubnikov's book *The Time of Human Being* that remained unpublished for seven years, released four years after the author's death. It offers a unique concept of time and how it is related to the phenomenon of the human being.

Gaidenko publishes *Evolution of the Concept of Science. 17th–18th Centuries* that advances research into the development of science in conjunction with philosophy.

Vladimir Smirnov's book *Logical Methods of Analyzing Scientific Knowledge* marks a new stage in the development of logic and the methodology of science. A logical and philosophical school is formed around Smirnov.

In December, Lektorsky becomes the editor-in-chief of the country's principal philosophical journal *Voprosy filosofii* (he held this position until the end of 2009). This marks a new period in the journal's development. The journal organizes discussions of new topics central to philosophy but largely ignored in the past, such as issues of political philosophy, philosophy of religion, questions of nonviolence ethics, new approach to the history of Russian religious philosophy, etc. The journal launches the publication of a series of books by Russian pre-revolutionary religious philosophers, including such authors as Vladimir Solovyov, Nikolai Berdyayev, Sergei Bulgakov, Pavel Florensky, and others. The number of copies of the journal printed increases dramatically as sales soar. *Voprosy filosofii* is widely read by broad circles of intellectuals inside and outside of Russia.

## 1988

Posthumous publication of Ilyenkov's treatise "Cosmology of the Spirit" in the journal *Nauka i religiya* [Science and Religion]. The author elaborates the heretical concept of the role of Man in the evolution of the Cosmos.

Posthumous publication of Losev's book *Vladimir Solovyov and His Time.*

Stepin is appointed the Director of the Institute of Philosophy, SAS; his tenure continued until 1998. New research units and centers are formed at the Institute and new problems are studied. The Institute remains the country's principal philosophical research center, also emerging as a center of Russian culture.

## 1990

The release of the collection of articles *Activity: Theories, Methodologies, Problems* edited by Lektorsky. The book presents differing and often conflicting points of view on the activity approach popular among Soviet philosophers and psychologists. Among contributors to the volume are Lektorsky, Batishchev, Shvyrev, Nikitin, and other eminent scholars. In the same year, the volume is translated into English and published under the same title in the USA. [On the development of the activity approach in Soviet philosophy see: *The Practical Essence of Man. The "Activity Approach" in Late Soviet Philosophy*, edited by Andrey Maidansky and Vesa Oittinen. Leiden, Boston: Brill, 2016.]

## 1991

December. The Soviet Union collapses and officially ceases to exist.

# SELECTED BIBLIOGRAPHY[1] (1953–1991)

1. Akchurin, Igor A. 1974. *Edinstvo estestvennonauchnogo znaniya* [The Unity of Natural Sciences]. Moscow: Nauka.
2. Akchurin, Igor A. 1975. *Metodologicheskie printsipy fiziki* [Methodological Principles of Physics]. Moscow: Nauka.
3. Akchurin, Igor A. 1984. *Teorija poznanija i sovremennaja fizika* [Theory of Knowledge and Contemporary Physics]. Moscow. Nauka.
4. Akchurin, Igor A. 1990. *Estestvoznanie, sistemnost' i dinamika* [Natural Sciences, Systematicity and Dynamics]. Moscow: Nauka.
5. Akhutin, Anatoly V., Bibler, Vladimir S., and Kurganov, Sergei Yu. 1995. *Antichnaja kul'tura: Voobrazhaemye uroki v 3–4 klassakh Shkoly dialoga kul'tur.* [Ancient Culture: The Imagined Lessons in the Third and Fourth Grades at the School of the Dialogue of Cultures]. Moscow: Interpraks.
6. Asmus, Valentin F. 1954. *Uchenie logiki o dokazatel'stve i oproverzhenii* [The Doctrine of Logic About the Proof and Rebuttal]. Moscow: Gospolitizdat.
7. Asmus, Valentin F. 1956. *Dekart* [Descartes]. Moscow: Gospolitizdat.
8. Asmus, Valentin F. 1957. *Filosofiya Immanuila Kanta* [Immanuel Kant's Philosophy]. Moscow: Znanie.
9. Asmus, Valentin F. 1962. *Nemetskaja estetika XVIII veka* [German Aesthetics of the Eighteenth Century]. Moscow: Iskusstvo.
10. Asmus, Valentin F. 1963. *Problema intuitsii v filosofii i matematike: (Ocherk istorii: XVII—nachalo XX veka).* [The problem of Intuition in Philosophy and Mathematics: (The Historical Sketch: Seventeenth to the Beginning of the Twentieth Century)]. Moscow: Socegiz.
11. Asmus, Valentin F. 1973. *Imannuil Kant* [Immanuel Kant]. Moscow: Mysl'.
12. Averintsev, Sergei S. 1973. *Plutarkh i antichnaja biografija: K voprosu o meste klassiki zhanra v istorii zhanra.* [Plutarch and Ancient Biography: To a Question of the Place of the Classic of a Genre in the History of a Genre]. Moscow: Nauka.
13. Averintsev, Sergei S. 1977. *Pojetika rannevizantijskoj literatury.* [Poetics of the Early Byzantine Literature]. Moscow: Nauka.
14. Averintsev, Sergei S. 1988. *Popytki objasnit'sja: Besedy kul'ture.* [Attempts to Explain Oneself: Conversations About the Culture]. Moscow: Pravda.
15. Avtonomova, Natalia S. 1977. *Filosofskie problemy structurnogo analiza v gumanitarnykh naukakh (Kriticheskii otcherk kontseptsii frantsuskogo structuralizma)* [Philosophical Problems of the Structural Analysis in Human Sciences (A Critical Essay on the Concept of French Structuralism)]. Moscow: Nauka.

[1] The books listed that are published after 1991 contain only the texts written between 1953 and 1991.

16. Avtonomova, Natalia S. 1988. *Rassudok. Razum. Ratsional'nost'*. [Reason. Understanding. Rationality]. Moscow: Nauka.
17. Bakhtin, Mikhail M. 1963. *Problemy pojetiki Dostoevskogo*. [Problems of Dostoevsky's Poetics]. Moscow: Sovetskij pisatel'.
18. Bakhtin, Mikhail M. 1965. *Tvorchestvo Fransua Rable i narodnaja kul'tura srednevekov'ja i Renessansa*. [Francois Rabelais's Work and Folk Culture of the Middle Ages and Renaissance]. Moscow: Hudozhestvennaja Literature.
19. Bakhtin, Mikhail M. 1975. *Voprosy Literatury i Estetiki* [Questions of Literature and Aesthetics]. Moscow: Hudozhestvennaja Literature.
20. Bakhtin, Mikhail M. 1979. *Estetika slovesnogo tvorchestva*. [Aesthetics of Ceative Discourse]. Moscow: Iskusstvo. [Six short works from this volume translated into English as *Speech Genres and Other Late Essays*, edited by Caryl Emerson and Michael Holquist; translated by Vern W. McGee. (Austin: University of Texas Press, 1986).]
21. Bakhtin, Mikhail M. 1984. *Problems of Dostoevsky's Poetics*, edited and translated by Caryl Emerson. London, Minneapolis: University of Minnesota Press.
22. Bakhtin, Mikhail M. 1986. *Literaturno-kriticheskie stat'i*. [Essays on the Literary Critiques]. Moscow: Sovetskij pisatel'.
23. Bakhtin, Mikhail M. 1993. *Toward a Philosophy of Act*. Austin: University of Texas Press.
24. Bakhtin, Mikhail M. 1996. *Sobranie sochinenij. T.5: Raboty 1940-h—nachala 1960-h godov*. [Collected Works. T.5: Works of the 1940s–1960s]. Moscow: Russkie slovari.
25. Bakhtin, Mikhail M. 2002. *Sobranie sochinenij. T. 2: "Problemy tvorchestva Dostoevskogo," 1929; Stat'i o L. Tolstom, 1929; Zapisi kursov lektsii po istorii russkoi literatury, 1922–1927* [Collected Works. Vol. 2: Problems of Dostoevsky's Creativity (1929); Articles on Leo Tolstoy (1929); Lecture Notes on the History of Russian Literature (1922–1927)]. Moscow: Russkie slovari.
26. Bakhtin, Mikhail M. 2002. *Sobranie sochinenij. T. 6: "Problemy pojetiki Dostoevskogo"* [Collected Works. Vol. 6: Problems of Dostoevsky's Poetics]. Moscow: Russkie slovari. Jazyki slavjanskoj kul'tury.
27. Bakhtin, Mikhail M. 2003. *Sobranie sochinenij. T. 1: Filosofskaya estetika 1920-ykh godov* [Collected Works. Vol. 1: Philosophical Aesthetics of the 1920s]. Moscow: Russkie slovari. Jazyki slavjanskoj kul'tury.
28. Batishchev, Genrikh S. 1963. *Protivorechie kak kategorija dialekticheskoj Logiki* [Contradiction as a Category of Dialectic Logic]. Moscow: Vysshaja shkola.
29. Batishchev, Genrikh S. 1969. "Deyatel'naya suchost' cheloveka kak filosofsky printsip" [Activity Essence of the Human Being as a Philosophical Principle], *Problema cheloveka v sovremennoy filosofii* [The Problem of the Human Being in Contemporary Philosophy]. Moscow: Mysl'.
30. Batishchev, Genrikh S. 1997. *Vvedenie v dialektiku tvorchestva*. [Introduction to the Dialectic of Creativity]. St. Peterburg: Russkij Gumanitarny Khristianskij Institut.
31. Bazhenov, Lev B. 1961. *Osnovnye voprosy teorii gypotezy*. [Main Problems of the Theory of a Hypothesis]. Moscow: Mysl'.
32. Bazhenov, Lev B. 1978. *Struktura i funktsii estestvennonauchoi teorii* [The Structure and the Function of a Theory in Natural Sciences]. Moscow: Nauka.
33. Bazhenov, Lev B. 1986. *Obschenauchnyi status reduktsii* [Reduction as a General Principle of Science]. Moscow: Nauka.

34. Bibler, Vladimir S. 1958. *O sisteme kategorij dialekticheskoj logiki.* [On a System of the Categories of Dialectical Logic]. Stalinabad.
35. Bibler, Vladimir S. 1975. *Myshlenie kak tvorchestvo (Vvedenie v logiku myslennogo dialoga).* [Thinking as Creativity (Introduction to the Logic of a Mental Dialogue)]. Moscow: Izdatel'stvo politicheskoi literatury.
36. Bibler, Vladimir S. 1988. *Nravstvennost'. Kul'tura. Sovremennost'.* [Morality. Culture. Contemporarity]. Moscow: Politizdat.
37. Bibler, Vladimir S. 1997. *Na granjakh logiki kul'tury: Kniga izbrannyh ocherkov.* [On the Edges of the Logic of Culture. A Book of Selected Essays]. Moscow: Russkoe fenomenologicheskoe obshchestvo.
38. Blauberg, Igor V., Sadovsky, Vadim N., Yudin, Erik G. 1969. Sistemnyi podhod: predposylki, problemy, trudnosti [Systems Approach: Prerequisites, Problems, Difficulties]. Moscow: Znanie.
39. Blauberg, Igor V., Sadovsky, Vadim N., Yudin, Erik G. 1977. *Systems Theory. Philosophical and Methodological Problems.* Moscow: Progress publishers.
40. Blauberg, Igor V., Mirsky, Eduard M. and Sadovsky, Vadim N. 1984. "Systems Approach to Systems Analysis." In *Rethinking the Process of Operational Research and Systems Analysis*, edited by Rolfe Tomlinson and Istvân Kiss, 19–32. Oxford, New York, Toronto: Pergamon Press.
41. Bogomolov, Aleksei S. 1962. *Filosofiya anglo-amerikanskogo neorealizma.* [Philosophy of Anglo-American Neo-Realism]. Moscow: Izdatel'stvo Moskovskogo universiteta.
42. Bogomolov, Aleksei S. 1962. *Ideja razvitija v burzhuaznoj filosofii XIX i XX vekov.* [The Idea of Development in Bourgeois Philosophy of the Nineteenth and Twentieth Centuries]. Moscow: Izdatel'stvo Moskovskogo universiteta.
43. Bogomolov, Aleksei S. 1973. *Anglijskaya burzhuaznaya filosofiya XX veka.* [The British Bourgeois Philosophy of the Twentieth Century]. Moscow: Mysl'.
44. Bogomolov, Aleksei S. 1974. *Burzhuaznaya filosofiya SShA XX veka.* [The Bourgeois Philosophy of the USA of the Twentieth Century]. Moscow: Mysl'.
45. Bogomolov, Aleksei S. 1982. *Dialekticheskij logos: Stanovlenie antichnoj dialektiki.* [Dialectical Logos: Formation of the Ancient Dialectics]. Moscow: Mysl'.
46. Bogomolov, Aleksei S., Oizerman, Teodor I. 1983. *Osnovy teorii istoriko-filosofskogo protsessa.* [Foundations of the Theory of the Historico-Philosophical Process]. Moscow: Nauka. [Translation: Bogomolov, Alexei S., Oizerman, Teodor I. 1986. *Principles of the Theory of the Historical Process in Philosophy.* Moscow: Progress publishers.]
47. Boroday, Yuri M. 1966. *Voobrazhenie i teorija poznanija: k kritike kantovskogo uchenija o produktivnoi sposobnosti voobrazhenija* [Imagination and the Theory of Knowledge: Toward the Critique of Kant's Theory of the Power of Imagination]. Moscow: Vyshaja shkola.
48. Bransky, Vladimir P. 1962. *Filosofskoe znachenie problemy nagljadnosti v sovremennoi fizike.* [Philosophical Significance of the Problem of Visuality in the Contemporary Physics]. Leningrad: Izdatel'stvo Leningradskogo universiteta.
49. Drobnitsky, Oleg G. 1967. *Kritika sovremennyh burzhuaznyh eticheskih koncepcij.* [The Critique of the Contemporary Bourgeois Ethical Concepts]. Moscow: Vysshaja shkola.
50. Drobnitsky, Oleg G. 1967. *Mir ozhivshih predmetov: Problema cennosti i marksistskaya filosofiya.* [The World of Objects Coming to Life: The Problem of the Value and the Marxist Philosophy]. Moscow: Politizdat.

51. Drobnitsky, Oleg G. 1974. *Ponjatie morali: Istoriko-kriticheskij ocherk.* [The Concept of Molarity: A Historical and Critical Essay]. Moscow: Nauka.
52. Drobnitsky, Oleg G. 1977. *Problemy nravstvennosti.* [The problems of Morality]. Moscow: Nauka.
53. Dynin, Boris S. Nikitin, Evgenii P., Glinsky, Boris A., Grjaznov, Boris S. 1965. *Modelirovanie kak metod nauchnogo issledovanija.* [Modeling as a Method of the Scientific Investigation]. Moscow: Mysl'.
54. Dynin, Boris S., Grjaznov, Boris S., Nikitin, Evgenii P. 1973. *Teorija i ee object* [Theory and its Object]. Moscow: Mysl'.
55. Dubrovsky, David I. 1980. *Informatsija, soznanie, mozg* [Information, Consciousness, Brain]. Moscow: Mysl'
56. Dubrovsky, David I. 1983. *Problema ideal'nogo* [The Problem of the Ideal]. Moscow: Nauka.
57. Frolov, Ivan T. 1965. *Ocherki metodologii biologicheskogo issledovanija. (Sistema metodov biologii).* [Sketches on Methodology of a Biological Research. (The System of the Biological Methods)]. Moscow: Mysl'.
58. Frolov, Ivan T. 1968. *Genetika i dialektika.* [Genetics and Dialectics]. Moscow: Nauka.
59. Frolov, Ivan T. 1972. *Mendel', mendelizm i dialektika.* [Mendel, Mendelizm and Dialectics]. Moscow: Mysl'.
60. Frolov, Ivan T. 1975. *Progress nauki i budushchee cheloveka. (Opyt postanovki problemy, diskussii, obobshhenija).* [Progress in Science and the Future of Man. (An Attempt at the Formulation of a Problem, Discussion, Generalizations)]. Moscow: Politizdat.
61. Frolov, Ivan T. 1976. *Mendelizm i filosofskie problemy sovremennoj genetiki.* [Mendelizm and Philosophical Problems of the Contemporary Genetics.]. Moscow: Mysl'.
62. Frolov, Ivan T. 1979. *Perspektivy cheloveka: opyt kompleksnoj postanovki problemy, diskussii, obobshhenija.* [The Perspectives of Man: An Attempt at a Complex Formulation of a Problem, Discussion, Generalizations.] Moscow: Politizdat.
63. [Fedoseev, Petr N.], Frolov, Ivan T., Lektorsky, Vladislav A., Shvyrev, Vladimir S., Yudin, Boris G. 1980. *Materialisticheskaja dialektika (kratkij ocherk teorii)* [Materialistic Dialectics (A Short Sketch of the Theory)]. Moscow: Politizdat.
64. Frolov, Ivan T. 1981a. *Global'nye problemy sovremennosti: nauchnyj i social'nyj aspekty.* [Todays Global Problems: Scientific and Social Aspects]. Moscow: Mezhdunarodnye otnoshenija.
65. Frolov, Ivan T. 1981b. *Zhizn' i poznanie: O dialektike v sovremennoj biologii.* [Life and Cognition: on Dialectics in Contemporary Biology]. Moscow: Mysl'.
66. Frolov, Ivan T. 1985. *O smysle zhizni, o smerti i bessmertii cheloveka: (Nauchnyj, real'nyj gumanizm i nravstvenno-filosofskie iskanija v istorii russkoj kul'tury).* [On Meaning of Life, Death and Immortality of Man (Scientific, Real Humanism and Moral and Philosophical Searches in the History of the Russian Culture)]. Moscow: Znanie.
67. Frolov, Ivan T., Yudin Boris G. 1986. *Etika nauki: Problemy i diskussii.* [Ethics of Science: Problems and Discussions]. Moscow: Nauka.
68. Frolov, Ivan T. 1988. *Filosofiya i istorija genetiki : Poiski i diskussii.* [Philosophy and the History of Genetics: Searches and Discussions]. Moscow: Nauka.

69. Frolov, Ivan T. 1990. *Man, Science, Humanism: A New Synthesis*. Buffalo, N-Y. Prometheus Books.
70. Gaidenko, Piama P. 1963. *Ekzistentsializm i problema kul'tury*. [Existentialism and the Problem of Culture]. Moscow: Vysshaja shkola.
71. Gaidenko, Piama P. 1970. *Tragedija estetizma*. [Tragedy of an Estheticism]. Moscow: Iskusstvo.
72. Gaidenko, Piama P. 1979. *Filosofiya Fikhte i sovremennost'*. [Fichte's Philosophy and the Contemporary Time]. Moscow: Mysl'.
73. Gaidenko, Piama P. 1980. *Evoljutsija ponjatija nauki. Stanovlenie i razvitie pervyh nauchnyh programm*. [The Evolution of a Concept of Science. The Formation and Development of the First Scientific Programs]. Moscow: Nauka.
74. Gaidenko, Piama P. 1987. *Evoljutsija ponjatija nauki (XVII—XVIII vv.). Razvitie fundamental'nykh nauchnykh program Novogo Vremeni*. [The Evolution of a Concept of Science (Seventeenth to Eighteenth centuries). The Development of the Fundamental Scientific Programs of the Modern Time]. Moscow: Nauka.
75. Gaidenko, Piama P. 1990. *Paradoksy svobody v uchenii Fikhte*. [The Paradoxes of Freedom in Fichte's Philosophy]. Moscow: Nauka.
76. Gaidenko, Piama P. 1991. *Istorija i racional'nost'*. [History and Rationality]. Moscow: Politizdat.
77. Gorsky, Dmitri P. *Filosofiya, logika, jazyk* [Philosophy, Logic, Language]. Moscow: Progress publishers.
78. Grjaznov, Boris S., 1982. *Logika, ratsional'nost, tvorchestvo*. [Logic, Rationality, Creativity]. Moscow. Mysl'.
79. Grushin, Boris A. 1961. *Otcherki logiki istoricheskogo issledovanija*. [Essays on Logic of the Historical Research]. Moscow. Mysl'.
80. Gulyga, Arsenij V. 1963. *Gerder*. [Herder]. Moscow: Socjekgiz.
81. Gulyga, Arsenij V. 1970. *Gegel'*. [Hegel]. Moscow: Molodaja gvardija.
82. Gulyga, Arsenij V. 1977. *Kant*. [Kant]. Moscow: Molodaja gvardija.
83. Gulyga, Arsenij V. 1978. *Iskusstvo v vek nauki*. [Art in a Century of Science]. Moscow: Sovremennik.
84. Gulyga, Arsenij V. 1982. *Shelling*. [Schelling]. Moscow: Molodaja gvardija.
85. Gulyga, Arsenij V. 1986. *Nemeckaja klassicheskaja filosofija*. [The Classical German Philosophy]. Moscow: Mysl'.
86. Gulyga, Arsenij V. 1987. *Principy estetiki*. [Principles of an Aaesthetics]. Moscow: Politizdat.
87. Gulyga, Arsenij V. 1987. *Putjami Fausta: Etjudy germanista*. [On the Ways of Faust: The Germanist's Studies]. Moscow: Sovetskij pisatel'.
88. Guseynov, Abdusalam A. 1974. *Social'naja priroda nravstvennosti*. [The Social Nature of Morality]. Moscow: Izd-vo MGU.
89. Guseynov, Abdusalam A. 1979. *Zolotoe pravilo nravstvennosti*. [The Golden Rule of Morality]. Moscow: Molodaja Gvardija.
90. Guseynov, Abdusalam A. 1984. *Etika Aristotelja*. [Aristotle's Ethics]. Moscow: Znanie.
91. Guseynov, Abdusalam A. 1985. *Vvedenie v etiku*. [Introduction to Ethics]. Moscow: Izd-vo MGU.

92. Ilyenkov, Evald V. 1960. *Dialektika abstraktnogo i konkretnogo v "Kapitale" K. Marksa.* [Dialectics of the Abstract and the Concrete in Marx's *Capital*]. Moscow, Nauka. [Translation: Ilyenkov Evald. 1982. *The Dialectics of the Absract and the Concrete in Marx's* Capital. Moscow: Progress publishers.]
93. Ilyenkov, Evald V. 1961. "Ideal'noe." In *Filosofkaja Entsiklopedija*. Tom 2. ["The Ideal," in Encyclopedia of Philosophy. Vol. 2], 219–227. Moscow. Mysl'.
94. Ilyenkov, Evald V. 1967. "From the Marxist Point of View." In *Marx and the Western World*, edited by N. Lobkovich. Notre Dame: University of Notre Dame Press.
95. Ilyenkov, Evald V. 1968. *Ob idolakh i idealakh*. [About Idols and Ideals]. Moscow: Politizdat.
96. Ilyenkov, Evald V. 1974. *Dialekticheskaja logika. Ocherki istorii i teorii.* [Dialectic Logic. Sketches of History and Theory]. Moscow: Mysl'.
97. Ilyenkov Evald V. 1979. "Problema ideal'nogo" [The Problem of the Ideal], *Voprosy filosofii* [Questions of Philosophy], (6):128–149; (7):145–158.
98. Ilyenkov, Evald V. 1980. *Leninskaya dialektika i metafizika pozitivizma.* [Lenin's Dialectics and Metaphysics of Positivism]. Moscow: Mysl'.
99. Ilyenkov, Evald V. 1984. *Iskusstvo i kommunisticheskij ideal.* [Art and Communistic Ideal]. Moscow. Mysl'.
100. Ilyenkov, Evald V. 1988. "Kosmologiya dukha" [Cosmology of the Spirit]. In *Nauka i religija* [Science and Religion]. No. 8–9.
101. Ilyenkov, Evald V. 1991. *Filosofija i kul'tura.* [Philosophy and Culture]. Moscow: Mysl'.
102. Ilyenkov, Evald V. 2009. *The Ideal in Human Activity*. Pacifica, CA. (Marxist Internet Archive.)
103. Ilyenkov, Evald V. 2014. "Dialectics of the Ideal." In *Dialectics of the Ideal: Evald Ilyenkov and Creative Soviet Marxism*, translated by A. Levant, edited by A. Levant and V. Oittinen, 25–78. Leiden: Brill.
104. Karmin, Anatoly S. 1981. *Poznanie beskonechnogo* [Knowledge of the Infinity]. Moscow. Mysl'.
105. Kasavin, Ilya T. 1990. *Poznanie v mire traditsii* [Cognition in the World of Traditions]. Moscow. Mysl'.
106. Kasavin, Ilya T. (ed.). 1990. *Zabluzhdajuschiisja razum?* [Mistaken reason?]. Moscow. Mysl'.
107. Kedrov, Bonifaty M. 1955. *Brauner—spodvizhnik Mendeleeva: K stoletiju so dnja rozhdenija Boguslava Braunera.* [Browner is Mendeleev's Associate: On the Occasion of the 100 Anniversary of the Birth of Boguseaw Browner]. Moscow: Izd-vo AN SSSR.
108. Kedrov, Bonifaty M. 1958a. *Den' odnogo velikogo otkrytija: (Ob otkrytii D. I. Mendeleevym periodicheskogo zakona).* [The Day of One Great Discovery: [About the Discovery of the Periodic Law by D. I. Mendeleev]. Moscow: Socegiz.
109. Kedrov, Bonifaty M. 1958b. *O sootnoshenii form dvizhenija materii v prirode.* [On the Correlation of Forms of Motion of Matter in the Nature.] Moscow: Izd-vo AN SSSR.
110. Kedrov, Bonifaty M. 1959. *Filosofskiy analiz pervyh trudov D. I. Mendeleeva o periodicheskom zakone (1869–1871).* [The Philosophical Analysis of the First Works by D. I. Mendeleev about the Periodic Law (1869–1871)]. Moscow: Izd-vo AN SSSR.

111. Kedrov, Bonifaty M. 1961. *Klassifikatsija nauk.*—[Kn.] 1: Engel's i ego predshestvenniki. [Classification of Sciences.—[Book] 1: Engels and his Predecessors]. Moscow: VPSh i AON pri CK KPSS.
112. Kedrov, Bonifaty M. 1963. *Edinstvo dialektiki, logiki i teorii poznanija.* [The Unity of Dialectics, Logic and Theory of Knowledge]. Moscow: Gospolitizdat.
113. Kedrov, Bonifaty M. 1969. *Tri aspekta atomistiki:* [Ch.] 1–3. [Three Aspects of Atomistics]. Moscow: Nauka.
114. Kedrov, Bonifaty M. 1969a. *Lenin i revoljutsiya v estestvoznanii XX veka: Filosofiya i estestvoznanie.* [Lenin and the Revolution in Natural Sciences of the Twentieth Century: Philosophy and Natural Science]. Moscow: Nauka.
115. Kedrov, Bonifaty M. 1970. *Mikroanatomija velikogo otkrytija: K 100-letiju zakona Mendeleeva.* [The Microanatomy of the Great Discovery: To the 100th Anniversary of the Mendeleev Law]. Moscow: Nauka.
116. Kedrov, Bonifaty M. 1974. *O sovremennyh problemah periodicheskoj sistemy.* [About the Contemporary Problems of the Periodic System]. Moscow: Atomizdat.
117. Kedrov, Bonifaty M. 1977. *Prognozy D. I. Mendeleeva v atomistike:* [Kn.] 1: Neizvestnye elementy. [D. I. Mendeleev's Forecast in Atomistics:—[Book] 1: Unknown Elements]. Moscow: Atomizdat.
118. Kedrov, Bonifaty M. 1978. *Prognozy D. I. Mendeleeva v atomistike.*—[Kn.] 2: Atomnye vesa i periodichnost'. [D. I. Mendeleev's Forecasts in Atomistics.—[Book] 2: Atomic Weight and Frequency]. Moscow: Atomizdat.
119. Kedrov, Bonifaty M. 1979. *Prognozy D. I. Mendeleeva v atomistike.*—[Kn.] 3: Za gran'ju sistemy elementov. [D. I. Mendeleev's Forecasts in Atomistics.—[Book] 3: Beyond the System of the Element] Moscow: Atomizdat.
120. Kedrov, Bonifaty M. 1983. *Besedy o dialektike: Shestidnevnye filosofskie dialogi vo vremja puteshestvija.* [Conversations About Dialectics: Six-Day Philosophical Dialogues During the Travel]. Moscow: Mol. gvardija.
121. Kelle, Vladislav Zh. 1969. *Kurs istoricheskogo materializma.* [The Course in Historical Materialism]. Moscow: Vysshaja shkola.
122. Kelle, Vladislav Zh. 1974. *Nasledie Karla Marksa i problemy teorii obshhestvenno-jekonomicheskoj formacii.* [Karl Marx's Legacy and Problems of the Theory of Socioeconomic Formation]. Moscow: Politizdat.
123. Kelle, Vladislav Zh. 1981. *Teorija i istorija (Problemy teorii istoricheskogo processa).* [Theory and History (Problems of the Theory of Historical Process)]. Moscow: Politizdat.
124. Kelle, Vladislav Zh. 1988. *Nauka kak komponent social'noy sistemy.* [Science as Component of Social System]. Moscow: Nauka.
125. Kopnin, Pavel V. 1962. *Gipoteza i poznanie dejstvitel'nosti.* [Hypothesis and Knowledge of Reality]. Kiev: Gospolitizdat USSR.
126. Kopnin, Pavel V. 1963. *Ideja kak forma myshlenija.* [Idea as Form of Thinking. Kiev]: Izd-vo Kievskogo universiteta.
127. Kopnin, Pavel V. 1966. *Vvedenie v marksistsuju gnoserologiju.* [Introduction to Marxist Epistemology]. Kiev: Naukova Dumka.
128. Kopnin, Pavel V. 1968. *Logicheskie osnovy nauki.* [Logical Foundations of Science]. Kiev: Naukova dumka.

129. Kopnin. Pavel V. 1969. *Filosofkie idei V.I. Lenina i logika* [Philosophical Ideas of V. I. Lenin and Logic]. Moscow: Nauka.
130. Kuznetsov, Ivan V. 1975. *Izbrannye terudy po metodologii fiziki* [Selected Works on Methodology of Physics]. Moscow: Mysl'.
131. Lektorsky, Vladislav A. Sadovsky, Vadim N. 1960. "O printsipakh issledovanija system," *Voprosy filosofii*. (8):77–89. [Translation: Lektorsky, Vladislav A. Sadovsky, Vadim N. 1960. "On Principles of Systems Research (Related to L. Bertalanffy's GST)." In *General Systems: Yearbook of the Society for General System Research*, (5):171–179.]
132. Lektorsky, Vladislav A. 1965. *Problema sub"ekta i ob"ekta v klassicheskoj i sovremennoj burzhuaznoj filosofii*. [A Problem of the Subject and an Object in Classical and Modern Bourgeois Philosophy]. Moscow: Vysshaja shkola.
133. Lektorsky, Vladislav A. (ed.) 1972. *Filosofiya, metodologija, nauka* [Philosophy, Methodology, Science]. Moscow: Nauka.
134. Lektorsky, Vladislav A. 1980a. *Sub"ekt, ob"ekt, poznanie*. [Subject, Object, Cognition]. Moscow: Nauka. [Translation: Lektorsky Vladislav A. 1984. *Subject, Object, Cognition*. Moscow: Progress publishers.]
135. Lektorsky, Vladislav A. (ed.). 1990. *Activity: Theories, Methodology, and Problems*. Orlando: Paul Deutsch.
136. Lektorsky, Vladislav A., Oizerman, Teodor I. (eds.). 1991. *Teorija poznjania*. 4 toma. [Theory of Cognition, 4 Volumes]. Moscow: Mysl'.
137. Lifshitz, Mikhail A. 1972. *Karl Marks. Iskusstvo i obshhestvennyj ideal*. [Karl Marx. Art and Public Ideal]. Moscow: Hudozhestvennaja literature.
138. Lifshitz, Mikhail A. 1973. *Iskusstvo i sovremennyj mir*. [Art and Modern World]. Moscow: Izobrazitel'noe iskusstvo.
139. Lifshitz, Mikhail A. 1974. *Nezamenimaja tradicija*. [Irreplaceable Tradition]. Moscow: Iskusstvo.
140. Lifshitz, Mikhail A. 1980. *Mifologija drevnjaja i sovremennaja*. [Mythology Ancient and Modern]. Moscow: Iskusstvo.
141. Lifshitz, Mikhail A. 1983. *G.V. Plehanov*. Moscow: Iskusstvo.
142. Lifshitz, Mikhail A. 1985. *V mire estetiki*. [In the World of an Esthetics]. Moscow: Izobrazitel'noe iskusstvo.
143. Lifshitz, Mikhail A. 1984–1988. *Sobranie sochinenij v treh tomah*. [Collected Works in Three Volumes]. Moscow: Izobrazitel'noe iskusstvo.
144. Lifshitz, Mikhail A. 2003. *Dialog s Eval'dom Ilyenkovym (problema ideal'nogo)*. [Dialogue with Evald Ilyenkov (Problem of the Ideal)]. Moscow: Progress-Tradicija.
145. Lifshitz, Mikhail A. 2004. *Chto takoe klassika? Ontognoseologija. Smysl mira. "Istinnaja seredina"* [What is Classics? Onto-Epistemology. The Meaning of the World. "The True Middle"]. Moscow: Iskusstvo—21 vek.
146. Lifshitz, Mikhail A. 2007. *Liberalizm i demokratija. Filosofskie pamflety*. [Liberalism and Democracy. Philosophical Lampoons]. Moscow: Iskusstvo—21 vek.
147. Losev, Alexei F. 1963. *Istorija antichnoy estetiki*. Tom 1: Rannija klassika. [The History of the Ancient Aesthetics. Vol. 1: The Early Classics]. Moscow: Vyschala shkola.
148. Losev, Alexei F., Shestakov, Vjacheslav P. 1965. *Istorija esteticheskikh kategorii*. [The istory of the Aesthetic Categories]. Moscow: Mysl'.

149. Losev, Alexei F., 1969. *Istorija antichnoy estetiki*. Tome 2: Sofisty, Sokrat, Platon [The History of the Ancient Aesthetics. Vol.2: Sophists, Socrates, Plato]. Moscow: Mysl'.
150. Losev, Alexei F., 1974. *Istorija antichnoy estetiki*. Tome 3: Vysokaja klassika. [The History of the Ancient Aesthetics. Vol. 3: The High Classics]. Moscow: Mysl'.
151. Losev, Alexei F. 1975. *Istorija antichnoy estetiki*. Tome 4: Aristotel' i pozdnja klassika. [The History of Ancient Aesthetics. Vol. 4: Aristotle and the Late Classics]. Moscow: Mysl'.
152. Losev, Alexei F. 1976. *Problema simvola i realisticheskoe iskusstvo*. [The Problem of Symbol and the Realistic Art]. Moscow: Mysl'
153. Losev, Alexei F. 1977a. *Antichnaja filosfija istorii*. [The Ancient Philosophy of History]. Moscow: Mysl'.
154. Losev, Alexei F. 1977b. *Estetica Vozrozhdenija*. [Aestetics of the Renaissance]. Moscow: Mysl'.
155. Losev, Alexei F. 1979. *Istorija antichnoy estetiki*. Tom 5: Rannyi ellinizm. [The History of the Ancient Aesthetics. Vol. 5: The Early Hellinism]. Moscow: Mysl'.
156. Losev, Alexei F. 1980. Istorija antichnoy estetiki. Tom 6. Pozdnii ellinizm. [The History of the Ancient Aesthetics. Vol. 6: The Late Hellenism]. Moscow, Mysl'.
157. Losev, Alexei F. 1982a. *Znak, simvol, mif.* [Sign, Symbol, Myth]. Moscow: Mysl'.
158. Losev, Alexei F. Taho-Godi Elena. 1982b. *Aristotel'. Zhizn' i smysl*. [Aristotle. Life and Meaning]. Moscow: Mysl'.
159. Losev, Alexei F. 1983. *Vladimir Solovyev*. [Vladimir Solovyov]. Moscow: Mysl'.
160. Losev, Alexei F. 1988a. *Istorija antichnoy estetiki*. Tom 7. Chast' 1. Poslednie veka [The History of the Ancient Aesthetics. Tom 7. Part 1. The Late Centuries]. Moscow: Mysl'.
161. Losev, Alexei F. 1988b. *Istorija antichnoy estetiki*. Tom 7. Chast' 2. Poslednie veka. [The History of the Ancient Aesthetics. Tom 7. Part 2. The Last Centuries]. Moscow: Mysl'
162. Lotman, Yuri M. 1970. *Struktura khudozestvennogo texta*. [The Structure of the Artistic Text]. Moscow: Nauka.
163. Lotman, Yuri M. 1972. *Analiz pojeticheskogo teksta: Struktura stiha*. [Analysis of the Poetic Text: The Structure of a Verse]. Tartu. Iz-stvo Tartusskogo universiteta.
164. Lotman, Yuri M. 1973. *Semiotika kino i problemy kinoestetiki*. [Semiotics of the Cinema and Problems of a Film Aesthetics]. Tallin.
165. Lotman, Yuri M. 1976. *Analysis of Poetic Texts*. Anna Arbor: University of Michigan Press.
166. Lotman, Yuri M. 1977. *Kul'tura kak kollektivnyj razum i problema iskusstvennogo razuma*. [Culture as Collective Intelligence and Problem of the Artificial Intelligence]. Moscow: Nauka.
167. Lotman, Yuri M. 1990. *Universe of the Mind. A Semiotic theory of Culture*, translated by Ann Shukman. Bloomingtoan, Indianapolis: Indiana University Press.
168. Mamardashvili, Merab K. 1968. *Formy i soderzhanie myshlenija* [Forms and Content of Thinking]. Moscow: Vyschaja Shkola.
169. Mamardashvili, Merab K. 1968. "Analiz soznanuja v rabotakh Marksa." [The Analysis of Consciousness in Marx's Writings]. *Voprosy filosofii*, (6):14–25.

170. Mamardashvili, Merab K. 1970. "Forma prevraschennaya." [Form of the Imagination]. In *Filosofskaja enciclopedija*. [Encyclopedia of Philosophy], vol. 5, 386–389. Moscow: Sovetskaja encikpopedja.
171. Mamardashvili, Merab K., Solovyov Erikh Yu., Shvyrev, Vladimir S. 1970. "Klassicheskaya i sovremennaya burzhuaznaya filosofiya: opyt epistemologicheskogo sopostovleniya. Chast' 1" [Classic and Contemporary Bourgeois Philosophy: An Attempt of Epistemological Comparison. Part 1]. *Voprosy filosofii*, (12): 23–28.
172. Mamardashvili, Merab K., Solovyoev Erikh Yu., Shvyrev, Vladimir S. 1971. "Klassicheskaya i sovremennaya burzhuaznaya filosofiya: opyt epistemologicheskogo sopostovleniya. Chast' 2" [Classic and Contemporary Bourgeois Philosophy: An Attempt of Epistemological Comparison. Part 2]. *Voprosy filosofii*, (4):58–73.
173. Mamchur, Elena A. 1975. Problema vybora teorii. K analizu perekhodhih situatsii v razvitii fizicheskogo znanija, [The Problem of Theoretical Choice. On Analysis of Transitional Situations in the Developmemt of Physics]. Moscow: Nauka.
174. Mamchur, Elena A. Ovchinnikov, Nikolai F., Uemov, Avenir I. 1989. *Printsip Prostoty i Mery Slozhnosti* [The Principle of Simplicity and Measures of Complexity]. Moscow: Nauka.
175. Mezhuev, Vadim M. 1967. *Kul'tura i istorija*. [Culture and History]. Moscow: Politizdat.
176. Mezhuev, Vadim M. 1968. *O ponjatii "kul'tura."* [About the Concept "Culture"]. Moscow: Znanie.
177. Mikhailov, Feliks T. 1961. *Za porogom soznanija*. [Behind a Consciousness Threshold]. Moscow: Gospolitizdat.
178. Mikhailov, Feliks T. 1964. *Zagadka chelovecheskogo ja*. [Riddle of the Human I.]. Moscow: Politizdat. [Translation: Mikhailov, Feliks T. 1981. *The Riddle of the Self.* New York: International Publishers.]
179. Mikhailov, Feliks T. 1990. *Obshhestvennoe soznanie i samosoznanie individa*. [Public Consciousness and Consciousness of the Individual]. Moscow: Nauka.
180. Mikeshina, Liudmila A. 1990. *Tsennosntnye predposylki v strukture nauchnogo znanija* [Value Presuppositions in the Structure of Scientific Knowledge]. Moscow: Mysl'.
181. Mitrokhin, Lev N. 1961. *Khristianskaja #oFnauka zhizni#cF.* [The Christian "Science of Life"]. Moscow: Gospolitizdat.
182. Mitrokhin, Lev N. 1990. *Religija i my. "Kvintjessencija. Filosofskij al'manah."* [Religion and We. "Quintessence. Philosophical Almanac"]. Moscow: Politizdat.
183. Mitrokhin, Lev N. 1966. *Baptizm*. [Baptism]. Moscow: Politizdat.
184. Molchanov, Yuri B. 1990. *Problema vremeni v sovremennoi nauke* [The Problem of Time in Contemporary Science]. Moscow: Nauka.
185. Motroshilova, Nelli V. 1968. *Principy i protivorechija fenomenologicheskoj filosofii*. [Principles and Controversies of the Phenomenological Philosophy]. Moscow: Vysshaja shkola.
186. Motroshilova, Nelli V. 1969. *Poznanie i obshhestvo: Iz istorii filosofii XVII-XVIII vekov.* [Cognition and Society: From History of Philosophy of the Seventeenth to Eighteenth centuries]. Moscow: Mysl'.
187. Motroshilova, Nelli V. 1976. *Nauka i uchenye v uslovijah sovremennogo kapitalizma: Filosofsko-sociologicheskoe issledovanie.* [Science and Scientists in the

Conditions of the Modern Capitalism: Philosophical-Sociological Study.] Moscow: Nauka.

188. Motroshilova, Nelli V. 1984. *Put' Gegelja k "Nauke logiki": Formirovanie principov sistemnosti i istorizma.* [Hegel's Path to the *Science of Logic*: Emerging of the Principles of Systematicy and Historicism.] Moscow: Nauka.
189. Motroshilova, Nelli V. 1990. *Social'no-istoricheskie korni nemeckoj klassicheskoj filosofii.* [Social-Historical Roots of the Classical German Philosophy.] Moscow: Nauka.
190. Motroshilova, Nelli V. 1991. *Rozhdenie i razvitie filosofskih idej.* [Birth and Development of the Philosophical Ideas]. Moscow: Politizdat.
191. Narski, Igor' S. 1961. *Sovremennyj pozitivizm.* [Modern Positivism]. Moscow: Izdatel'stvo Akademii nauk SSSR.
192. Narski, Igor' S. *Dialekticheskoe protivorechie i logika poznanija.* [The Dialectic Contradiction and the Logic of Cognition]. Moscow: Mysl'.
193. Narski, Igor' S. 1983. *Otchuzhdenie i trud: Po stranitsam proizvedenij K. Marksa.* [Alienation and Labor: According to Works of K. Marx]. Moscow: Mysl'.
194. Narski, Igor' S. 1983. *Sovremennaya burzhuaznaya filosofiya: dva vedushchikh techeniya nachala 80-h godov XX veka.* [Modern Bourgeois Philosophy: The Two Leading Currents in the Beginning of the 80th Years of the 20th Century]. Moscow: Mysl'.
195. Narski, Igor' S. 1991. *Teorija poznanija Kanta* [Kant's Theory of Knowledge.] Moscow: Nauka.
196. Nikiforov, Alexander L. 1983.*Ot formalnoi logiki k istorii nauki* [From Formal Logic to the History of Science]. Moscow: Mysl'.
197. Nikiforov, Alexander L. 1987. *Logika nauchnogo poznanija. Aktual'nye problemy* [Logic of Scientific Cognition. Contemporary Problems]. Moscow: Mysl'.
198. Nikiforov, Alexander L. 1991. "Rationality and freedom." In *The open curtain: A U.S.-Soviet. Philosophy Summit*, edited by Keith Lehrer, Ernest Sosa. Boulder: Westview Press.
199. Nikitin, Evgenii P. 1970. *Ob'jasnenie—funktsija nauki* [Explanation as a Function of Science]. Moscow: Nauka.
200. Nikitin, Evgenii P. 1981. *Priroda obosnovanija: substratny analiz* [The Nature of Justification: Substrate Analysis]. Moscow: Nauka.
201. Ogurtsov, Aleksander P. 1978. *Marksistskaja kontseptsija istorii estestvoznanija. XIX v.* [The Marxist Concept of History of Natural Sciences. The 19th Century]. Moscow: Nauka.
202. Ogurtsov, Aleksander P. 1985. *Marksistskaja kontseptsija istorii estestvoznanija. Pervaja chetvert' XX v.* [The Marxist Concept of History of Natural Sciences. First Quarter of the 20th Century]. Moscow: Nauka.
203. Ogurtsov, Aleksander P. 1988. *Disciplinarnaja struktura nauki: ee genezis i obosnovanie.* [Disciplinary Structure of Science: Its Genesis and Justification]. Moscow: Nauka.
204. Oizerman, Teodor I. 1969. *Problemy istoriko-filosofskoi nauki.* [Problems of the History of Philosophy]. Moscow: Mysl'.
205. Oizerman, Teodor I. 1971. *Glavnie filosofskie napravlenija: teoreticheskiy analiz istoriko-filosofskogo protsessa.* [The Main Trends in Philosophy: A Theoretical Analysis of the History of Philosophy]. Moscow: Mysl'.

206. Oizerman, Teodor I.. 1979. *Dialekticheskiy materialism i istorija filosofii: istoriko-filosofskie ocherki*. [Dialectical Materialism and the History of Philosophy: The Historical-Philosophical Essays]. Moscow: Mysl' [Translation: Oizerman, Teodor I. 1982. Dialectical Materialism and the History of Philosophy: Essays on the History of Philosophy. Moscow: Progress publishers.]
207. Oizerman, Teodor I. 1981. "Kant's Doctrine of the "Things in Themselves" and Noumena," *Philosophy and Phenomenological Research*, 41 (3): 333–350.
208. Oizerman, Teodor I. 1988. *The Main Trends in Philosophy: A Theoretical Analysis of the History of Philosophy*. Moscow. Progress publishers.
209. Omelyanovky, Mikhail E. 1956. *Filosofskie problemy kvantovoi mekhaniki* [Philosophical Problems of Quantum Mechanics]. Moscow: Nauka.
210. Omelyanovky, Mikhail E. 1973. *Dialectica v sovremennoi fizike* [Dialectics in Contemporary Physics]. Moscow: Nauka.
211. Ovchinnikov, Nikolai F. 1966. *Printsipy sokhranenija*. [The Principles of Conservation]. Moscow: Nauka.
212. Ovchinnikov, Nikolai F. 1988. Tendentsija k edinstvu nauki (poznanie i priroda) [Tendency of the Unity of Science (Cognition and the Nature)]. Moscow: Nauka.
213. Ovsjannikov, Mikhail F. 1959. *Filosofiya Gegelya*. [Hegel's Philosophy]. Moscow: Socjekgiz.
214. Ovsjannikov, Mikhail F. 1963. *Ocherki istorii esteticheskikh uchenij*. [Essays on the History of Aesthetic Doctrines.] Moscow: Izdatel'stvo Akademii hudozhestv SSSR.
215. Ovsjannikov, Mikhail F. 1971. *Gegel'*. [Hegel]. Moscow: Mysl'.
216. Ovsjannikov, Mikhail F. 1978. *Istorija esteticheskoj mysli*. [History of the Aesthetic Thought]. Moscow: Vysshaja shkola.
217. Ovsjannikov, Mikhail F. 1979. *Iskusstvo i kapitalizm*. [Art and Capitalism]. Moscow: Iskusstvo.
218. Ovsjannikov, Mikhail F. 1985. *Estetika v proshlom, nastojashchem i budushchem*. [Aesthetics in the Past, Present, and Future]. Moscow: Prosveshchenie.
219. Petrov, Mikhail K. 1969. "Predmet i tseli izuchenija istorii filosofii" [The Subject Matter and the Aims of the Study of the History of Philosophy], *Voprosy filosofii* (2).
220. Petrov, Mikhail K. 1991. *Jazyk, znak, kul'tura*. [Language, Sign, Culture]. Moscow. Nauka.
221. Petrov, Mikhail K. 1995. *Iskusstvo i nauka. Piraty Egejskogo morja i lichnost'*. [Art and Science. Pirates of the Aegean Sea and Personality]. Moscow: ROSSPEN.
222. Petrov, Mikhail K. 1997. *Antichnaja kul'tura*. [The Ancient Culture]. Moscow: ROSSPEN.
223. Petrov, Mikhail A. 1996. *Istoriko-filosofskie issledovanija*. [Historico-Philosophical Studies]. Moscow: ROSSPEN.
224. Popovich, Miroslav V. 1966. *O filosofskom analize jazyka nauki* [On the Philosophical Analysis of Languge of Science]. Kiev: Naukova dumka.
225. Porus, Vladimir N. 1983. *Aktual'nye problemy analiza nauchnykh revolutsii* [Contemporary Problems of the Analysis of Scientific Revolutions]. Moscow: Mysl'.
226. Pruzhinin, Boris I. 1986. *Ratsional'nost' i istoricheskoe edinstvo nauchnogo znanija; gnoseologicheskii aspect* [Rationality and the Historical Unity of Scientific Knowledge: An Epistemological Aspect]. Moscow. Nauka.

227. Pruzhinin Boris I., Korshunova L.S. *Voobrazhenije i ratsional'nost': opyt metodologicheskogo analiza poznavatel'noi funktsii voobrazhenija.* [Imagination and Rationality: An Attempt of the Methodological Analysis of the Cognitive Function of Imagination]. Moscow. Moscow University publishers.
228. Rozov, Mihail A. 1965. *Nauchnaja abstrakcija i ee vidy.* [Scientific Abstraction and its Types]. Novosibirsk: Nauka.
229. Rozov, Mihail A. 1977. *Problemy empiricheskogo analiza nauchnyh znanij.* [Problems of the Empirical Analysis of Scientific Knowledge]. Novosibirsk: Nauka. Sibirskoe otdelenie.
230. Rubinshtein, Sergei L. 1957. *Bytie i soznanie. O meste psikhichyeskogo vo vseobschey vzaimosvjazi javlenii material'nogo mira* [Being and Consciousness. On the Place of the Psychic in the Universal Interconnection of Material World Phenomena]. Moscow. Nauka.
231. Rubinshtein, Sergei L. 1958. *O myshlenii i putjah ego issledovanija.* [On Thinking and Ways of How to Study It]. Moscow: Nauka.
232. Rubinshtein, Sergei L. 1959. *Principy i puti razvitija psihologii.* [Principles and Ways of the Development of Psychology]. Moscow: Nauka.
233. Rubinshtein, Sergei L. 1977. "Iz neopublikovannogo nasledstva: chelobek i mir" [From the Unpublished Legacy: The Human Being and the World], *Voprosy filosofii* (7): 161–170.
234. Rubinshtein, Sergei L. 1997. *Izbranny filosofsko-psihologicheskie trudy. Osnovy ontologii, logiki i psikhologii.* [Selected Philosophical and Psychological Works. Fundamentals of Ontology, Logic and Psychology]. Moscow: Nauka.
235. Sachkov, Yuri V. 1971. *Vvedenie v verojatnostnyi mir* [Introduction to the World of Probability] Moscow. Mysl'.
236. Sadovsky, Vadim N., Blauberg, Igor V.,. Yudin, Erik G. 1969. *Sistemnyi podkhod: predposylki, problemy, trudnosti* [Systematic Approach: Presuppositions, Problems, Difficulties]. Moscow: Mysl'.
237. Sadovsky, Vadim N. 1974. *Osnovanija obschey teorii sistem. Logiko-metodologicheski analiz* [Foundations of the General Theory of the Systems. Logical and Methodological Analysis]. Moscow: Nauka.
238. Sadovsky, Vadim N. 1991. "Philosophical and Methodological Foundations of System Theory." In *A Science of Goal Formulation. American and Soviet Discussions of Cybernetics and System Theory*, edited by Stuart A. Umpleby and Vadim N. Sadovsky, 9–18. New York, London, Washington: Hemisphere Publishing Corporation.
239. Shchedrovitsky, Georgy P. 1975. "Izhodnye predstavlenija i kategorial'nye sredstva teorii deyatel'nosti." [Basic Ideas and Categories of the Theory of Activity], In *Razrabotka i vnedrenie avtomatizirovannyh system v proektirovanii (teorija i metodologija)* [Development and Introduction of Automatic Systems in Projecting (Theory and Methodology)], 233–280. Moscow.
240. Shchedrovitsky, Georgy P. 1995. *Izbrannye trudi.* [Selected Works]. Moscow: School of Cultural Policy.
241. Shchedrovitsky, Georgy P. 1996. *Filosofiya. Nauka. Metodologiya.* [Philosophy. Science. Methodology]. Moscow: School of Cultural Policy.
242. Shchedrovitsky, Georgy P. 2005. *Myshlenie. Ponimanie. Refleksija* [Thinking. Understanding. Reflection]. Moscow: School of Cultural Policy.

243. Shinkaruk, Vladimir I. 1964. *Logika, dialektika i teorija poznanija Gegelja.* [Hegel's Logic, Dialectics and the Theory of Knowledege]. Kiev: Naukova Dumka.
244. Shtoff, Viktor A. 1966. *Modelirovanie i Filosofiya* [Modeling and Philosophy]. Moscow: Mysl'.
245. Shvyrev, Vladimir S. 1966. *Neopozitivizm i problemy empiricheskogo obosnovanija nauki.* [Neopositivism and Problems of Empirical Justification of Science]. Moscow: Nauka.
246. Shvyrev, Vladimir S. 1970. Znak i deyatel'nost'. [Sign and Activity]. Moscow: Politizdat.
247. Shvyrev, Vladimir S. 1978. *Teoreticheskoe i empiricheskoe v nauchnom poznanie* [Theoretical and Empirical in Scientific Knowledge]. Moscow: Nauka.
248. Shvyrev, Vladimir S. 1988. *Analiz nauchnogo poznanija: osnovnye napravlenija, formy, problemy.* [Analysis of the Scientific Cognition: The Main Trends, Forms, and Issues.] Moscow: Nauka.
249. Smirnov, Vladimir A. 1972. Formal'nyj vyvod i logicheskie ischislenija. [Formal Conclusion and Logical Calculations]. Moscow: Nauka.
250. Smirnov, Vladimir A. 1986. "Modality 'de re' and Vasiliev's Imagery Logic," *Logique et Analyse.* Vol. 29 (114): 205–212.
251. Smirnov, Vladimir A. 1986. "Logical Relations Between Theories," *Synthese*, 66 (1): 71–87.
252. Smirnov, Vladimir A. 1987. *Logicheskie metody analiza nauchynogo znanija.* [Logical Methods of Analyzing Scientific Knowledge]. Moscow: Nauka.
253. Sokolov, Vasilii V. 1964. *Filosofiya Spinozy i sovremennost'.* [Spinoza's Philosophy and Contemporary Time]. Moscow: Mysl'
254. Sokolov, Vasilii V. 1979. *Srednevekovaya filosofiya.* [Philosophy in the Middle Ages]. Moscow: Mysl'.
255. Solovyov, Erikh Yu. 1966. *Ekzistentsializm i nauchnoe poznanie.* [Existentialism and the Scientific Cognition]. Moscow: Vysshaja shkola.
256. Solovyov, Erikh Yu. 1966. "Existentializm" [Existentialism], *Voprosy filosofii*, (12).
257. Solovyov, Erikh Yu. 1966 & 1967. "Existentializm" [Existentialism], *Voprosy filosofii*, (1).
258. Solovyov, Erikh Yu. 1984. *Nepobezhdennyj eretik: Martin Ljuter i ego vremja.* [The Undefeated Heretic: Martin Luther and His Time]. Moscow: Molodaja gvardija.
259. Solovyov, Erikh Yu. 1991. *Proshloe tolkuet nas: Ocherki po istorii filosofii i kul'tury.* [The Past Interprets Us: Essays on the History of Philosophy and Culture]. Moscow: Politizdat.
260. Stepin, Vyacheslav S. 1963. *Sovremennyj pozitivizm i chastnye nauki.* [Modern Positivism and Concrete Sciences]. Minsk: Izdatel'stvo Ministerstva vysshego i srednego special'nogo obrazovanija BSSR.
261. Stepin, Vyacheslav S. 1974. *Metody nauchnogo poznanija.* [The methods of Scientific Cognition]. Minsk: Izdatel'stvo "Vyshjejshaja shkola."
262. Stepin, Vyacheslav S. 1976. *Stanovlenie nauchnoj teorii.* [Formation of the Scientific Theory]. Minsk: Izdatel'stvo Belorusskogo gosudarstvennogo universiteta.
263. Stepin, Vyacheslav S. (ed.). 1979. *Priroda nauchnogo poznanija.* [The Nature of Scientific Cognition.] Minsk: Izdatel'stvo Belorusskogo gosudarstvennogo universiteta.

264. Stepin, Vyacheslav S. (ed.). 1981. *Idealy i normy nauchnogo issledovanija.* [Ideals and Norms of the Scientific Investigation.]. Minsk: Izdatel'stvo Belorusskogo gosudarstvennogo universiteta.
265. Stepin, Vyacheslav S. 1996. "Genetically-Constructive Ways of Theory Building." In *Philosophical Logic and Logical Philosophy. Essays in Honor of Vladimir A. Smirnov*, edited by Peter I. Bystrov and Vadim N. Sadovsky, 17–31. Dordrecht: Springer.
266. Tolstykh, Valentin I., Kozlova, Natalia N., Mezhuev, Vadim M, Sizemskaia Irina N. 1981. *Dukhovnoe proizvodstvo. Sotsial'no-filosofskij aspect problem dukhovnoij deyatel'nosti.* [Spiritual Production. Social-Philosophical Aspect of the Problem of The Spiritual Activity.] Moscow. Nauka.
267. Trubnikov, Nikolai N. 1987. *Vremja chelovecheskogo bytija* [The Time of Human Being]. Moscow: Nauka.
268. Uemov, Avenir I. 1963. *Veschi, svoistva i otnoshenija.* [Things, Properties and Relations]. Moscow: Mysl'.
269. Uemov, Avenir I. 1978. *Sistemnyi podhod i obschaja teorija system* [System Approach and the General Theory of Systems]. Moscow: Mysl'.
270. Yudin, Boris G. 1986. *Metodologicheskii analiz kak napravlenie izucvhenija nauki* [Methodological Analysis as a Way to Study Science]. Moscow: Nauka.
271. Yudin, Erik G. 1978. *Sistemnyj podhod i princip deyatel'nosti. Metodologicheskie problemy sovremennoj nauki.* [System Approach and Principle of Activity. Methodological Problems of Contemporary Science]. Moscow: Nauka.
272. Yudin, Erik G. 1997. *Metodologija nauki. Sistemnost'. Deyatel'nost'.* [Methodology of Science. Systematicity. Activity]. Moscow: URSS.
273. Zinoviev, Aleksander A. 1960. *Filosofskie problemy mnogoznachnoj logiki.* [Philosophical Problems of Multiple-Valued Logic]. Moscow: Nauka.
274. Zinoviev, Aleksander A. 1962. *Logika vyskazyvanij i teorija vyvoda.* [Logic of Utterances and the Theory of Conclusion]. Moscow: Nauka.
275. Zinoviev, Aleksander A. 1967. *Osnovy logicheskoj teorii nauchnyh znanij.* [The Foundations of the Logical Theory of Scientific Knowledge.] Moscow: Nauka. [Translation: Zinoviev Alexander. 1973. *Foundations of the Logical Theory of Scientific Knowledge (Complex Logic).* Dordrecht Holland: D. Reidel Publishing Company.]
276. Zinoviev, Aleksander A. 1970. *Kompleksnaja logika.* [The Complex Logic]. Moscow: Mysl'.
277. Zinoviev, Aleksander A. 1971. *Logika nauki.* [Logic of Science]. Moscow: Nauka.
278. Zinoviev, Aleksander A. 1974. *Logicheskaja fizika.* [Logical Physics]. Moscow: Nauka.
279. Zinoviev, Aleksander A. 1981. *Kommunizm kak real'nost'.* [Communism as Reality]. Lausanne. L'Age d'Homme.
280. Zinoviev Alexander A. 1983. "The Non-Traditional Theory of Quantifiers." In *Language, Logic and Method*, edited by R. Cohen and M. Wartofsky. Dordrecht-Boston- London: Reidel.
281. Zotov, Anatolii F. 1977. *Structura nauchnogo myshlenija* [The Structure of Scientific Thinking]. Moscow: Politizdat.

# SUBJECT INDEX

# NAMES INDEX